SMARTSTART series

How to Form a California Corporation or LCC from Any State

Additional Titles in the Entrepreneur Press Smart Start Series

How to Form a Nevada Corporation or LLC from Any State by Michael Spadaccini

How to Start a Business in ...

Alabama	Montana
Alaska	Nebraska
Arizona	Nevada
Arkansas	New Hampshire
California	New Jersey
Colorado	New Mexico
Connecticut	New York
Delaware	New York City
District of Columbia	North Carolina
Florida	North Dakota
Georgia	Ohio
Hawaii	Oklahoma
Idaho	Oregon
Illinois	Pennsylvania
Indiana	Rhode Island
Iowa	South Carolina
Kansas	South Dakota
Kentucky	Tennessee
Louisiana	Texas
Maine	Utah
Maryland	Vermont
Massachusetts	Virginia
Michigan	Washington
Minnesota	West Virginia
Mississippi	Wisconsin
Missouri	Wyoming

SMARTSTART series

How to Form a California Corporation or LCC from Any State

Kevin W. Finck

Entrepreneur Press

Editorial Director: Jere L. Calmes
Cover Design: Beth Hansen-Winter
Editiorial and Production Services: CWL Publishing Enterprises, Inc.,
Madison, WI, www.cwlpub.com

This publication is designed to provide accurate and authoritative information in regard to the subject matter covered. It is sold with the understanding
that the publisher is not engaged in rendering legal, accounting, or other professional services. If legal advice or other expert assistance is required, the
services of a competent professional person should be sought.

—From a Declaration of Principles jointly adopted by
a Committee of the American Bar Association and
a Committee of Publishers and Associations

ISBN 1-932531-38-6

Library of Congress Cataloging-in-Publication Data

Finck, Kevin W., 1954-
   How to form a California corporation or LLC from any state / by Kevin
Finck.
      p. cm.
   ISBN 1-932531-38-6 (alk. paper)
   1. Incorporation—California—Popular works. 2. Private companies—
California—Popular works. I. Title.
   KFC348.F56 2005
   346.794'06622--dc22

                                                            2005008975

10 09 08 07 06 05   10 9 8 7 6 5 4 3 2 1

Contents

Introduction		**xi**
Chapter 1	**Choosing Your Business Entity**	**1**
	Sole Proprietorships	1
	Partnerships	2
	Limited Partnerships	4
	Limited Liability Companies	5
	Corporations	7
Chapter 2	**Setting up Out of State**	**10**
	Qualifying the Business Entity	11
	Penalties for Failure to Qualify a Corporation	12
Chapter 3	**Steps to Incorporating**	**15**
	Selecting and Reserving a Corporate Name	15
	Fictitious Business Name Statement	18
	Filing Articles of Incorporation	19
	Preparing the Bylaws	22
	First Meeting of the Board of Directors	23
	Amending the Articles of Incorporation and Bylaws	23
	Statement of Information	24
	Post-Incorporation Matters	24

Chapter 4 Capitalizing the Corporation and Issuing Stock   27

Capitalizing the Corporation   27
Issuing Stock   28
Information to Include on the Stock Certificate   29
Federal Securities Law Requirements   29
California Securities Law Requirements   30
Securities Laws of Other States   36
Accredited Investors   36

**Chapter 5 Incorporating or Forming an LLC from an Ongoing
Business   39**

Offer to Transfer Business Assets   39
Additional Requirement for Certain Businesses—Bulk
    Transfers   40
Assignment of Real Property Interests   40
Bill of Sale Agreement   41
Wrap-Up of Old Business   41

Chapter 6 Maintaining the Corporation or LLC   42

Piercing the Corporate Veil   42
Keeping Minutes   44
Annual Meetings of Shareholders   45
Special Meetings of Shareholders   46
Necessity of a Record Date   47
Meetings of the Board of Directors   47
Action by the Shareholders or Board of Directors
    Without a Meeting   48
Suspension of Corporate or LLC Powers   48
Buy-Sell Agreements   50

Chapter 7 Corporate and LLC Variations   54

Statutory Close Corporations   54
Professional Corporations   57
Limited Liability Partnerships   59
Single-Member LLCs   60

Chapter 8 S Corporations   62

Advantages of an S Corporation Election   62
Disadvantages of an S Election   63
Election Requirements   63
How and When to File   64
Inadvertent Termination of S Corporation Eligibility   66
Requesting a Determination   66
Taxation of S Corporations   67

Chapter 9	**Limited Liability Companies**	**70**
	Forming a Limited Liability Company	71
	Taxation of an LLC	71
	Articles of Organization	72
	Naming Your LLC	72
	Management Structure	73
	Statement of Information	73
	Operating an LLC	74
	Securities Law Considerations	75
	Converting or Merging an Existing Business Entity into an LLC	75
Chapter 10	**Taxes**	**77**
	Corporations	77
	Limited Liability Companies	84
Chapter 11	**Nonprofit Corporations**	**87**
	Factors for Choosing the Nonprofit Corporate Form	88
	Nonprofit Corporations and for-Profit Corporations: Similarities and Differences	88
	Alternatives to Nonprofits	89
	Director and Officer Liability in the Nonprofit Context	89
	Formation	90
	Information to Include in the Articles of Incorporation	91
	Exemption from Taxation	92
Chapter 12	**Intellectual Property**	**97**
	Types of Intellectual Property	98
	Copyright	101
	Patents	104
	Trade Secrets	105
	Protect Your Rights	106
	Helpful Information	107
Chapter 13	**Legal Obligations of Employers**	**109**
	Employer's Reporting and Tax Obligations	109
	Overview of California Employment Laws	114
	At-Will Employment	115
	Employee vs. Independent Contractor	116
	Minimum Wage and Payroll Practices	118
	Vacation Leave and Pay	119
	Inspection and Retention of Employee Records	119
	Anti-Discrimination Laws	120

Immigration Law Requirements 121

Worker's Compensation Insurance 122

Protecting the Company's Trade Secrets and
    Confidential Information 122

Dispute Resolution Policies 125

Forms for Chapter 2 132

Forms for Chapter 3 147

Forms for Chapter 4 220

Forms for Chapter 5 247

Forms for Chapter 6 255

Forms for Chapter 7 338

Forms for Chapter 8 343

Forms for Chapter 9 347

Forms for Chapter 10 363

Forms for Chapter 11 398

Forms for Chapter 13 438

Index 473

Dedication

**This book is respectfully dedicated
to my mother, Esther "Bonnie" Finck,
and to the memory of my father,
William A. Finck**

Introduction

This book is designed to assist the small business owner in addressing many of the legal issues inherent in organizing and operating a business. It will aid the business owner in making a decision as to which business entity would be most appropriate and advantageous for his or her particular operations. Additionally, this book provides insight, information, and draft forms to allow a small business owner to set up a corporation or limited liability company, with the goal of keeping start-up costs to a minimum.

This book is not designed, however, to assist in the formation of a complex business structure with more than one class of ownership or more than a limited number of owners. If you plan to take your company public in the near future, or want to have more than 75 shareholders, you will need more extensive professional help than a book of this nature can provide.

There are many advantages to incorporating or setting up an LLC for a small business. Both legal structures provide limited liability protection to the owners, simplify the transfer of ownership of the business, entitle the owners to more liberal insurance and pension plans, and provide a format whereby income tax obligations may be reduced by splitting the owners' salaries from the corporation's net profits or by passing profits and losses directly to the corporation's shareholders.

There is no legal prohibition against an individual preparing and filing articles of incorporation and most other corporate documents or setting up a limited liability company, as long as it is done for his or her own business. There are instances in which the advice of an attorney or other professional is recommended. Additionally, there are many areas surrounding the management and operation of a corporation in which the assistance of an experienced professional is helpful to prevent the corporation and its shareholders from accidentally incurring unwanted liabilities. A good corporate counsel who can assist with contractual needs and identify and research potential issues before they become actual problems is invaluable. Even if the decision is made to not retain an attorney to set up a corporation or a limited liability company, I strongly recommend that one be retained to act as the corporation's general counsel and as agent for service of process. The ounce of prevention is far less expensive than the pound of cure.

How to Use This Book

Most of the forms and materials needed to form a California corporation or limited liability company are contained in this book, following the text. There is a separate forms index, which is organized alphabetically by form name as it is referenced in the text. In the case of forms issued by public entities, e.g., IRS or Franchise Tax Board forms, the index indicates the form name followed by its number. Most, if not all, of these forms may be downloaded from the particular agencies' web sites (a list of which is provided). Additionally, some of these forms may be filled in and submitted online. The forms provided in this book were current at the time of publication and may be photocopied and submitted in person or by mail. However, because state and federal forms are constantly updated and occasionally superseded by other forms, contact the appropriate governmental agency to ensure that you are utilizing the current version.

By using and submitting the forms, articles, bylaws, and minutes that apply to your specific type of corporation included in this book, you can easily set up and maintain the corporation's minute book.

Many forms may be used as they appear in this book, although some will require modifications or additions. You should modify the forms or substitute other provisions and language as dictated by your specific business needs. Italic type appears in some forms, either to provide you with important information or to indicate options from which you will need to make a selection.

Although a corporate seal is not required in California, you may wish to adopt and purchase one. If nothing else, a seal adds a certain authenticity and prestige to corporate documents. Some banks and other institutions often will demand that company authorizations and resolutions be embossed with the corporate seal.

Check Before Mailing

If the time you have to complete the incorporation process is limited, you are encouraged to check with the Secretary of State's office to verify state agency addresses and name availability. State agencies often relocate or consolidate offices with little or no advance notice and even a few days' delay can mean missing important filing deadlines. It is possible to expedite the issuance of the Articles of Incorporation or Articles of Organization by filing them over the counter at a Secretary of State's office near you.

About the Author

Kevin W. Finck is a San Francisco attorney specializing in business and commercial law. He acts as general counsel for many small and mid-sized companies involved in different types of domestic and international businesses. He has extensive experience in the formation of corporations and limited liability companies and in advising start-up businesses on how best to avoid trouble and litigation.

Mr. Finck is a graduate of Hastings College of the Law. He has authored many legal articles and has lectured for both the Learning Annex and the International Bar Association. Mr. Finck has received the highest "AV" (legal ability and ethics) rating from Martindale-Hubbell and is listed in *Who's Who in American Law*. He lives in the San Francisco Bay Area with his wife, Kathy, and his daughter, Callie.

Acknowledgments

I would like to express my sincere appreciation for the assistance of the following people in revising this new edition: my associates, Saideh

Dadras and David Horne; my staff, legal secretary Esther Kinyua, paralegal Barbara Booth, and attorney James Atencio; along with Phil Wenger, CPA.

CHAPTER 1

Choosing Your Business Entity

There are several forms of business entities from which a business owner may choose. The most common forms are sole proprietorships, partnerships, limited partnerships, limited liability companies, and corporations. Each of these forms has its advantages and disadvantages, many of which are discussed below.

Sole Proprietorships

A sole proprietorship is the simplest form of doing business. It is not a legal entity in itself; it refers to the individual who owns the business and who is personally responsible for its operations and debts.

Advantages of Sole Proprietorships

The advantages of a sole proprietorship include:

- **Complete control of the venture**—A sole proprietor has the advantage of total autonomy over the business. The business owner can run the business as he or she chooses.
- **Little or no organizational cost**—Sole proprietorships may be formed without any special legal formalities. The

only limitation is that the sole proprietor must file and publish a fictitious business name statement if the business is being operated under a name other than the personal name of the sole proprietor in any county in which the business is operating.

- **Tax and income advantages**—The profits and tax advantages of the business are passed directly to the sole proprietor. Indeed, the sole proprietor's personal tax return will list all of the business's income and expenses.

Disadvantages of Sole Proprietorships

The disadvantages of a sole proprietorship include:

- **Personal liability**—Sole proprietors, like partners of a partnership, are faced with personal liability if the assets of the business are insufficient to cover the claims of the business's creditors.
- **Community property subject to attachment**—When sole proprietors begin doing business, not only do they subject their own personal property to creditors' claims but also their spouse's half of any community property may be subject to the claims of the business's creditors as a means of satisfying a debt.
- **Credibility**—Potential clients are frequently wary of doing business with a sole proprietor as the failure to set up a corporation, LLC, or partnership suggests a lack of resources and business acumen.
- **Tax withholding**—Due to increased scrutiny by the taxing authorities, a number of businesses will not retain sole proprietors as independent contractors for fear that the Franchise Tax Board or IRS will reclassify the "independent contractor" as an employee and demand payroll tax withholding. Sole proprietor independent contractors have also sued large companies and demanded benefits, which is another reason why people prefer to do business with corporations or LLCs. Consequently, your failure to incorporate or set up an LLC could cost you business.

Sole proprietors, like partners of a partnership, are faced with personal liability if the assets of the business are insufficient to cover the claims of the business's creditors.

Partnerships

A general partnership is a form of entity in which two or more co-owners engage in operating a business.

Advantages of Partnerships

Advantages of a general partnership include:

- **Greater pool of resources**—Each of the partners may bring to the partnership his or her individual wealth with which to create a financial base for the business.
- **Little organizational cost**—There is little structural organization or formality required for a partnership. No filing is required with the state. There are no requirements to maintain paperwork, such as minutes and other corporate filings. The partnership may simply be created by a contract signed by all of the partners. No written partnership agreement is required, although one is strongly recommended.
- **No restriction on the number and nature of the partners.**
- **Profits passed directly to the partners**—Profits earned by the partnership are passed directly to the partners without the double taxation that occurs in most corporations.
- **Tax benefits of the partnership passed directly to the partners**—Any losses suffered by the partnership are passed directly to the partners as a possible tax write-off. Also, there are no taxes on accumulated earnings or personal holdings on partnerships.

Disadvantages of Partnerships

Disadvantages of a general partnership include:

- **Personal liability**—If the debts of the partnership exceed the assets, creditors of the partnership may pursue the individual partners to satisfy partnership debts.
- **Binding partnership**—One partner may act on behalf of the partnership simply by signing a contract. In other words, even when the partners do not agree on taking a particular action, one partner may still make agreements that can bind all partners.
- **Undistributed income taxed to partners**—Even if the partnership retains its earned profit, the profit will still be taxed proportionately to each partner, at his or her individual tax bracket.
- **Dissolution potentially difficult**—In the absence of a well-written partnership agreement, the dissolution of a partnership can be very litigious, time-consuming, and expensive.

There is little structural organization or formality required for a partnership. No filing is required with the state.

Limited Partnerships

A limited partnership consists of one or more *general* partners, who manage the business and who are personally liable for its debts, plus one or more *limited* partners, who contribute capital and share in profits, but take no part in the management or operation of the business. This entity is used to attract passive investors who are unwilling to risk more than their invested capital in a business.

Advantages of Limited Partnerships

In this business entity, general partners essentially have the same advantages and disadvantages as the partners in a regular partnership, including the advantage of passing profits and tax benefits directly to the partners (although there are some limitations relating to passive vs. nonpassive income or loss).

For limited partners, however, the main advantage is limited liability. Here, the limited partner may invest in the partnership and receive income from the operation, yet will not be held personally liable for the debts of the partnership.

Disadvantages of Limited Partnerships

The disadvantages of a limited partnership include:

- **Formalities required**—The state requires that a certificate of limited partnership be filed with the Secretary of State. Furthermore, a written limited partnership agreement must be prepared and signed by all of the general partners and the limited partners. Thus, a greater amount of formality must be observed in a limited partnership.
- **Loss of control**—In exchange for the benefit of limited liability, the limited partners relinquish control over the operations and policy-making decisions of the partnership to the general partners. To the extent that a limited partner actually controls the business operations of the partnership, that partner may become equally liable for the debts of the partnership as the general partners.
- **Limited tax advantages**—To the extent that the partnership experiences a loss that is then spread out to the limited partners, the loss can be deductible only against passive activity income. The tax code should be consulted in this regard, as it limits the deductibility of various types of losses.

For limited partners, however, the main advantage is limited liability.

Limited Liability Partnerships

Many states authorize the formation of limited liability partnerships (LLPs). In an LLP, unlike any general partnership, the liability of each partner for acts of his or her other partners may be limited. Indeed, in most states, the applicable laws provide that a partner in an LLP is immune from liability for the negligence, wrongful acts, and omissions of the other partners as well as of the employees and other agents of the LLP. In most circumstances, however, the LLP partners remain liable for the LLP's contractual obligations.

California law currently authorizes LLPs only for lawyers, accountants, and architects. It also authorizes foreign LLPs to do business in California. To be an owner of an LLP, one has to be a licensed professional. Please note that the inclusion of the practice of architecture as a professional LLC currently extends only until July 1, 2007.

> In an LLP, unlike any general partnership, the liability of each partner for acts of his or her other partners may be limited.

Limited Liability Companies

Effective September 30, 1994, California small business owners obtained access to another type of business—limited liability companies (LLCs).

LLCs are a *hybrid* form of business entity. They are similar to corporations in that they offer limited liability protection for active participants. They are dissimilar from corporations and more like partnerships in the following respects:

- They lack continuity of existence. They are subject to dissolution upon the death, retirement, resignation, bankruptcy, or dissolution of an LLC member.
- Transfer of an LLC equity may require the written consent of all or some of the members to interest. Unless the operating agreement expressly provides otherwise, membership interests may not be freely transferred without the consent of all other members.
- When properly structured, they enjoy pass-through (single level) tax treatment.

The provisions governing LLCs can be found commencing with Section 17000 of the California Corporations Code (www.leginfo.ca.gov/calaw.html). Until recently, an LLC needed to have more than one owner. Now California recognizes single-member LLCs. For federal and California tax purposes, a California LLC with one member is disregarded and the single-member LLC's tax information is reported on the single member's personal tax return. Like S corporations, LLCs pay no federal tax. California charges an $800 annual fee for the privilege of doing business in the state, plus a graduated gross income tax that starts into effect after $250,000 in annual gross revenue. (Note that the state taxes S corporations on profit, not on gross income, at a rate of 1.5 percent.)

Advantages of LLCs

Advantages of LLCs include:

An LLC, unless it makes an election to be taxed like a corporation, avoids the double taxation that is applied to C corporations.

- **Tax considerations**—An LLC, unless it makes an election to be taxed like a corporation, avoids the double taxation that is applied to C corporations and it may specially allocate income and losses to its members in percentages different from their ownership interests.
- **No restrictions on number or nature of members**—An LLC can have corporate members, foreign resident members, and other equity investors who could not act as owners of an S corporation.
- **Not subject to some of the ongoing formalities of a corporation**—For example, an LLC is not required to hold annual meetings of the board of directors and shareholders. The power of the managers to act without the knowledge and approval of the other members and the removal of managers can be customized based on the specific needs of the business, as set forth in the LLC's operating agreement.
- **Limited liability**.

In corporations, the receipt of an equity interest in return for services (besides raising securities law issues) is a taxable event, e.g., equal to the value of the stock one receives. This can also provide tax withholding issues for the employer company. In LLCs, if a member contributing services receives an interest in profits, rather than a capital interest, he or she will not recognize income, subject to limited exceptions.[1]

Disadvantages of Limited Liability Companies

Disadvantages of LLCs include the following:

- **All members should enter into an agreement,** which can add cost and complexity to the formation of an LLC.
- **The LLC entity is not available for licensed professionals** (i.e.,

businesses licensed or registered under the California Business and Professions Code, such as attorneys and accountants).

- **LLCs have not been around as long as corporations,** which can cause reservations in raising capital and confusion in operations.
- **LLCs are taxed by California based on gross revenue,** unlike corporations, which are taxed on profits.
- **An owner/manager of an LLC cannot be an employee of an LLC for employment tax purposes** and must instead file estimated tax payments every quarter of the year on his or her share of the LLC's income, regardless of whether he or she actually receives those funds.
- **An LLC cannot be utilized for a nonprofit business.**
- **If any members are nonresidents, it may lead to burdensome tax withholding obligations.**
- **It may be more expensive to set up an LLC** than most other entities, including corporations. A corporation, for example, is exempt from the minimum franchise tax fee during the first year of operations; LLCs are not exempt, which can result in an $800 minimum franchise tax fee in the first year of operations.

Corporations

A corporation is a totally separate legal entity that exists apart from its shareholder-owners. It has its own identity and power to act in any way permitted by law and not inconsistent with its charter.

Advantages of Corporations

Advantages of corporations include:

- **Limited liability**—The most valuable aspect of the corporate form of business is that it protects its shareholders from liability for corporate debts. The corporation must, however, observe certain corporate formalities in order to maintain this protection. The amount of effort required to maintain these formalities is usually greatly outweighed by the benefit of limited liability.
- **Control by shareholders**—Although the directors of the corporation are primarily responsible for making most decisions concerning the business, the shareholders have the ability to determine who the directors will be.
- **Easier to go public**—Once the corporate form is in place and

The most valuable aspect of the corporate form of business is that it protects its shareholders from liability for corporate debts.

stock has been issued, transferring shares in the corporation is relatively easy. This becomes especially helpful when additional capital is needed to expand the operations of the business.

- **Easier to obtain financing**—Based on historical practice, investors tend to prefer investing in corporations over financing other entities.
- **More suitable in certain regulated industries**—One example of an industry in which the corporation is the preferred form is banking.
- **Continuous**—Unlike partnerships, which dissolve with the death or withdrawal of a partner, corporations enjoy perpetual existence and continuity even when a major shareholder transfers all of his, her, or its stock to another party.
- **Tax advantages of a partnership may be gained**—By properly filing an S corporation election (discussed at greater length in Chapter 8), a corporation, while providing the benefit of limited liability, may avoid tax at the federal level and create federal tax benefits for its individual shareholders.
- **Easier to transfer equity**—Corporate equity is more easily transferred than other choices of entity.

Disadvantages of Corporations

Disadvantages of corporations include:

- **Greater start-up costs**—There are costs associated with incorporating a business that sole proprietorships don't have, such as corporate filing fees and other expenses, discussed in greater detail ahead.
- **Regular maintenance complications**—Unlike sole proprietorships and LLCs with only one owner, corporations prepare separate tax returns. Corporations also require regular meetings of both the board of directors and the shareholders, unlike partnerships and LLCs.
- **Possible restrictions on the number or nature of the shareholders,** based on whether the corporation makes an S election and other securities law issues.
- **Potential tax disadvantages**—It is difficult to take assets out of a corporation without creating a taxable event. Without proper structuring, corporate profits may be subject to double taxation. Therefore, careful tax planning is necessary to avoid the imposi-

> Unlike partnerships, which dissolve with the death or withdrawal of a partner, corporations enjoy perpetual existence.

tion of various forms of adverse taxes. While C corporations can deduct health insurance and other fringe benefits (such as group health, disability, and accident insurance) for their shareholder employees without generating taxable income to the shareholder employees, these fringe benefits are taxable to shareholder employees of S corporations who own a two percent or greater interest in the corporation.

- **Compliance issues**—The issuance of stock in a corporation is always subject to securities law compliance issues while the issuance of membership interests in an LLC to an owner actively involved in the business may not.

The remainder of this book focuses on the formation and maintenance of California corporations and California limited liability companies. You should think carefully about the nature of your business and its future before you decide whether to incorporate or set up an LLC. While incorporation may offer your business many advantages, it may also force you to give up others that you could enjoy as a sole proprietorship or partnership. Many legal practitioners prefer limited liability companies over corporations for flexibility and maintenance issues, at least for those businesses that can be LLCs. California's approach to taxing LLCs on gross revenue rather than profit, combined with a corporation's savings of the first year's $800 minimum franchise tax fee, however, may make a corporation a better option. Should you continue to be unsure as to what entity is best for your business, speak with your accountant and attorney.

Note

1. See Revenue Procedure 93-27, 1993-2 Cumulative Bulletin 343.

CHAPTER 2

Setting up Out of State

I t is possible to incorporate and to set up LLCs in states other than California. Indeed, several major corporations listed on the New York Stock Exchange are incorporated in Delaware even though they transact most of their business in California. Corporate giants often incorporate in Delaware because it has lower initial and ongoing corporate fees and fewer restrictive corporate regulations than most other states.

The corporate laws of each state vary greatly and, in some circumstances, these differences may justify the expense of incorporating out of state. There can also be advantages in setting up LLCs outside of California depending on the circumstances.

For example, in Delaware, an LLC's operating agreement may limit a manager's fiduciary duties to the members of the LLC to a greater degree than permitted in California.[1] Furthermore, Delaware permits an LLC to indemnify managers for breaches of fiduciary duties in ways that California does not. In general, Delaware law is more comprehensive and pro-management than California law. If a business intends to go public at some point, it may be wise to incorporate in Delaware because underwriters often insist that California corporations reincorporate in Delaware prior to being listed. The reincorporation process, taking a California corporation and turning it into a Delaware corporation, can be lengthy and expensive.

Although there are some advantages to setting up outside of California, if you choose that option you should be aware of some serious disadvantages. Corporations setting up out of state (known in California as *foreign* corporations) are subject to lawsuits in the state of incorporation. Consequently, if you set up in Delaware, you can be sued in Delaware, even if all of your operations are effectively in California. Defending a lawsuit in a distant state can prove to be a serious drain on a small business's resources.

Setting up in another state does not relieve a business of the duty to file certain documents with California or pay California taxes. By setting up outside of California, a business operating in California is subjecting itself to legal compliance requirements in more than one state.

A foreign corporation that does more than half of its business in California and has half of its shareholders in California is subject to many of the same provisions of the California Corporations Code that apply to domestic California corporations.[2] This "pseudo foreign" rule may outweigh many of the pro-management objectives of incorporating in out-of-state jurisdictions such as Delaware. Consequently, for most small corporations, the benefits of incorporating out of state are outweighed by the costs and burdens of qualifying to do business in California as a foreign corporation.

Setting up in another state does not relieve a business of the duty to file certain documents with California or pay California taxes.

Qualifying the Business Entity

All foreign entities transacting business within California must qualify with the California Secretary of State. Indeed, if a corporation that is incorporated in a state other than California maintains its principal office in California, it must register as a foreign corporation doing business in California even if all of its operations occur entirely outside of California. However, certain types of mail order, loan, and out-of-state sales companies are excluded from qualification.[3]

To become qualified in California, a foreign corporation must first apply for registration with the Secretary of State. This is accomplished by filing a Statement and Designation by Foreign Corporation (see Form 2-A), along with a Certificate of Good Standing executed by an authorized public official of the state or place in which the corporation is organized. The current fee for filing the Statement and Designation by Foreign Corporation is $100. A foreign corporation that qualifies to do business in California is not subject to the minimum franchise tax fee for its first and second taxable years. The minimum $800 annual California franchise tax must be paid for every year thereafter.[4] After qualification, the corporation must file an annual report with the Secretary of State just like a domestic corporation. (See Form 2-B.)[5]

A foreign LLC may register in California by submitting an application (Form 2-C) and paying the statutory fee (currently $70) to the California Secretary of State. A Certificate of Good Standing executed by an authorized public official of the state or place where the LLC is organized is also required. The form may be delivered by hand, mail, or facsimile. Experience has proven that, if you are in a hurry, the filing will be processed more quickly if it is done in person. Also note that all LLC filings must be done in the Sacramento office of the Secretary of State, while other corporate filings can be done in other offices of the Secretary of State throughout California. If the Secretary of State finds that the application conforms to law, the registration will be granted subject to any licensing requirements for the particular business in which the applicant intends to engage. As described in the prior chapter, this may be a major issue, as California law prohibits conducting certain businesses as LLCs (i.e., banks, trusts, insurance, and the practice of any profession requiring a license). Upon registration, the LLC will also be obligated to pay the Franchise Tax Board an annual fee of $800. (See Form 2-D.) If circumstances change and make the original application inaccurate (name, type of management), the LLC is required to amend its registration. (See Form 2-E.) A foreign LLC is required to file the same biennial statement of information that a domestic LLC is required to file. (See Form 2-F.) The first statement should be filed within 90 days of registration in California.

Penalties for Failure to Qualify a Corporation

If a foreign corporation fails to properly qualify itself, the exercise of its corporate powers, rights, and privileges in California may be forfeited. Revenue and Taxation Code Section 23304.1 provides that all contracts made by a non-qualified foreign corporation are voidable at the option of the other party. A foreign corporation can also forfeit its powers or rights by failing to file its annual statement.[4] Other penalties for a foreign corporation's failure to qualify or be in good standing to transact intrastate business in California include being unable to maintain or defend against any cause of action in a California court, per diem fines,

If a foreign corporation fails to properly qualify itself, the exercise of its corporate powers, rights, and privileges in California may be forfeited.

and the option for third parties to unilaterally void an otherwise enforceable contract with the company.[5] Directors of foreign corporations that fail to properly register in California may also be subject to personal liability for the corporation's actions.[6]

More specifically, a $250 fine for pursuing such a suit may also be imposed. A foreign corporation that transacts intrastate business without holding a valid Certificate of Registration may be subject to a $20 per day penalty. Such a corporation may also be charged with a misdemeanor, punishable by a fine of not less than $500 and not more than $1,000.[7] The forfeiture of exercise of corporate powers usually takes effect when the Franchise Tax Board notifies the Secretary of State that a corporation is delinquent in paying taxes or filing returns. The Secretary of State may also withdraw the privilege of a foreign corporation to transact intrastate business in California on its own volition.

The penalties for a foreign LLC that does not register in California are similar to those imposed on foreign corporations that do business in California without qualifying.[8] The failure to register does not by itself make a foreign LLC's members liable for the obligations of the LLC.[9] A foreign LLC may not be denied registration due to the difference between foreign law and California law.[10] Many of the "pseudo foreign" protection rights that apply to foreign LLCs doing business in California do not apply to foreign corporations doing business in California. Consequently, this may provide a reason to set up an LLC rather than a corporation.[11]

As outlined in this chapter, the procedures for qualifying a foreign entity to do business in California are lengthy and complicated. The consequences for failure to maintain good standing can be severe. Therefore, for most businesses, it often makes more sense to set up in California, unless the corporation will be doing most of its business outside of California.

Notes

1. See 6 Delaware Code §18-1101 (b), (c).
2. California Corporations Code §2115(a).
3. See California Corporations Code §2115.
4. Revenue and Taxation Code §23153(f)(1).
5. See California Corporations Code §191.
6. See California Corporations Code §2117.
7. See California Corporations Code §2206.

8. See California Corporations Code §2203(c).

9. See California Corporations Code §2116.

10. See California Corporations Code §2258.

11. See California Corporations Code §§17456, 2203.

CHAPTER 3

Steps to Incorporating

Selecting and Reserving a Corporate Name

The first step toward incorporating is selecting a corporate name. Though only a statutory close corporation must include in its name the word "corporation," "incorporated," or "limited," one of these words denoting a corporate form should be included to emphasize the limited liability nature of your business entity and ensure that you will not be perceived as merely a sole proprietorship. An abbreviation of one of these words will be sufficient. Special requirements often apply to the names chosen for professional corporations, as discussed in greater detail in Chapter 7.

Personal names may only be used as a corporate name when some other word or words are added to denote a corporate ending, such as "corporation," "incorporated," "limited," or one of their abbreviations. The corporate name should be selected on the basis of business and personal preference factors.

Careful thought should be given to selecting the corporation's name. The mere approval of a selected name by the Secretary of State does not grant a company immunity from potential third-party claims for trademark or trade name infringement. You should check telephone books, trade publications, and the internet (including the U.S. Patent and Trademark Office, www.uspto.gov) to ensure that the proposed name or a potentially confusing similar one is not already in use by a competitor.

It can be expensive and damaging to a business to begin operations under one name and then be forced to change to another name in response to a trademark infringement claim. This is especially problematic when substantial sums are utilized to promote the company and develop goodwill pursuant to an expensive initial marketing plan. If your company intends to expand its operations beyond California, you should also investigate potential future markets prior to selecting a name. The Secretary of State keeps a separate data bank for corporations and LLCs. Consequently, a name may be available for an LLC, but not available for a corporation, or vice versa.

The Secretary of State will not file articles of incorporation containing:

- A name that is prohibited by statute;
- A name that would tend to deceive the public;
- A name that would misleadingly resemble the name of another corporation doing business within the state; or
- A name that would otherwise fall within the provisions of California Corporations Code Section 201, which generally prohibits using the words "bank," "trust," "trustees," or related words.

For these reasons, it is best to suggest two or three alternatives when applying for a corporate name, to save time in getting official acceptance. You can also investigate a name's availability and reserve it prior to filing your articles. This requires the filing of a Name Reservation— Order Form with the Secretary of State listing alternate names in order of preference. (See Form 3-A.) Once the name is found to be available, it will be reserved using the same order form. A corporate name reservation is effective for 60 days and costs $10 per name.

If the request is made in person, allow approximately one hour to check three names. There is an additional in-person charge of $15 per name. If the request is submitted by mail, up to four names may be checked. To reserve a proposed name, submit the Order Form with a $10 reservation fee to:

Secretary of State
Corporate Filings

If your company intends to expand its operations beyond California, you should also investigate potential future markets prior to selecting a name.

Attn: Name Availability Unit
1500 11th Street, 3rd Floor
Sacramento, CA 95814

You can also call or visit any of the following regional offices of the Secretary of State:

Fresno Regional Office
1315 Van Ness Avenue, Suite 203
Fresno, CA 93721-1729
559 445-6900

Los Angeles Regional Office
300 South Spring Street, Room 12513
Los Angeles, CA 90013-1233
213 897-3062

San Diego Regional Office
1350 Front Street, Suite 2060
San Diego, CA 92101-3609
619 525-4113

San Francisco Regional Office
455 Golden Gate Avenue, Suite 14500
San Francisco, CA 94102-7007
415 557-8000

You can also obtain up-to-date information at the Secretary of State's web site: www.ss.ca.gov/business/business.htm.

Phone orders are not accepted unless the caller has a prepaid account, which many attorneys who represent small businesses have. Please note that the name of a suspended corporation may be reserved and adopted by another corporation. (This is another reason to avoid allowing your business to be suspended.) One should take care, however, when adopting the name of a suspended corporation, because customers and/or creditors may understandably confuse the new entity with the old.

Only a single incorporator is required to form a California corporation.[1] Any individual, partnership, or corporation may act as incorporator.[2] The incorporator may or may not have any ongoing relationship with the new corporation. Indeed, in many instances, the incorporator merely prepares, signs, and files the articles of incorporation, without any continuing relationship thereafter with the new corporation. In many instances, it is the attorney for the new corporation who acts as the incorporator.

If initial directors are not named in the articles of incorporation, the incorporator has pretty much the same powers and responsibilities as initial directors, until the directors are elected. These powers and responsibilities include adopting the corporate bylaws, amending the articles of incorporation, electing directors, and "whatever is necessary and proper to perfect the organization of the corporation."[3]

Fictitious Business Name Statement

Filing and Publication

If the corporation plans to do business under a name other than the one given in the articles of incorporation, it is necessary to file and publish a Fictitious Business Name Statement.

A business incorporated under one name can conduct business under another name as well. If the corporation plans to do business under a name other than the one given in the articles of incorporation, it is necessary to file and publish a Fictitious Business Name Statement. (See Form 3-B.) A Fictitious Business Name Statement must be filed with your county clerk within 40 days from the commencement of business. (A number of counties require use of their own forms, so contact your county clerk's office to find out what is required locally.) Typically a filing is made with the clerk of the county in which the company has its principal place of business. It is also recommended that you file in any other county in which the company will be transacting business. (Please note, however, that county filings are not required for a company's corporate or LLC name. Once on file with the Secretary of State, no further notice is required for the use of your official corporate or LLC name throughout the State of California.)

Within 30 days of the time of filing, the notice must be published in a newspaper of general circulation in the area where the business is conducted. The notice must be published at least once each week for three consecutive weeks. Three publications in a newspaper regularly published once a week or more, with at least five days intervening between the respective publication dates, not counting such publication dates, are sufficient.

The period of notice commences on the first day of publication and terminates at the end of the 21st day, including the first day. An affidavit showing the publication of the statement must be filed with the county clerk within 30 days after the completion of the publication.[4] The

Fictitious Business Name Statement should be completed and submitted to the newspaper, along with a check covering filing and publication fees. Once completed, the newspaper will return copies of the published statement and proof of filing.

Upon completion of the filing requirements, the Fictitious Business Name Statement is effective for five years; it may be renewed thereafter. To receive a Fictitious Business Name Statement form, contact the California Newspaper Service Bureau: 915 East 1st Street, Los Angeles, CA 90012, 213 229-5500, or 901 H Street Suite 312, Sacramento, CA 95814, 916 444-3950. If you abandon the use of a name, you should file a Statement of Abandonment of Use of Fictitious Business Name. (See Form 3-C.)

Some practitioners recommend that foreign LLCs file a Fictitious Business Name Statement at the county level in which business is conducted, in addition to registering with the Secretary of State.

Filing Articles of Incorporation

The articles of incorporation should be filed as quickly as possible following the reservation of the corporate name. The final deadline for filing the articles is 60 days after the name has been reserved, since this is the maximum length of time for which the name may be reserved. The Secretary of State cannot issue certificates reserving the same name for two or more consecutive 60-day periods.[5] If the 60-day period runs out before the articles get filed, you can wait one day and request a new reservation certificate.

Forms 3-D, 3-E, and 3-F are sample articles of incorporation to serve as guidelines for your corporation. These forms can be used as articles simply by filling in the blanks. However, do not modify the language set forth in those forms, as any additions or subtractions to the language may cause the Secretary of State to reject your articles of incorporation.

The number of directors will affect the usage of many of the forms in this book. If the initial directors are named in the articles of incorporation, review Form 3-E carefully. Each director named in the articles must sign and acknowledge the articles. If the initial directors are not named, use Form 3-F instead. If using Forms 3-D and 3-F, the articles must be signed by the incorporator(s) of the corporation. Please note that California law requires that there be at least one director for every shareholder, up to a minimum of three. If you are going to have three

The articles of incorporation should be filed as quickly as possible following the reservation of the corporate name.

or more shareholders, you must authorize at least three directors. If you have two shareholders, you are required to have a minimum of two directors. If you have only one shareholder, one director is sufficient. You can always have more than the minimum.

Indemnification

California permits corporations to eliminate or limit the personal liability of directors for monetary damages for breach of their duties to the corporation and its shareholders.

Beginning in 1987, California permits corporations to eliminate or limit the personal liability of directors for monetary damages for breach of their duties to the corporation and its shareholders.[6] This permits statutory indemnification, or corporate reimbursement, of negligent corporate agents; however, that liability cannot be eliminated or limited in matters involving a director's reckless or grossly negligent conduct.

In some instances, corporate indemnification is mandatory. For example, a corporation is required to reimburse a director or officer if he or she is sued for wrongdoing but ultimately wins a judgment in defense of that action. In such circumstances, as a matter of law, the corporation must reimburse the director or officer for all expenses actually and reasonably incurred.[7]

In situations other than shareholders' suits, indemnification is permissive. This issue often arises when an officer or director is personally sued for actions taken on behalf of the corporation in good faith and in a manner reasonably believed to be in the best interests of the corporation. Also, indemnification can be available in a civil case, where the director or officer had no reason to believe his or her conduct had been criminal.[8] In certain circumstances, a corporation may be obligated to indemnify a California employee regardless of Corporation Code §317.[9] These statutes are somewhat conflicting, but should be problematic only if the Company is considering adopting an indemnification policy more limiting than provided for in the Labor Code. Some foreign jurisdictions also permit and require greater indemnification rights for officers and directors than California. If this is of paramount importance, this may provide a reason for setting the business up in Delaware or some other jurisdiction.

The area of corporate indemnification is more complex than can be briefly covered here. Therefore, I strongly recommend discussing the issue with competent legal counsel. To the extent that you want to attract outside directors, it is highly recommended that you provide indemnification to the maximum extent provided by law. For an added measure of protection, a corporation can purchase and maintain *direc-*

tors' and officers' liability insurance—known as D&O insurance. When available, such insurance enables persons accepting corporate offices greater comfort about being sued and having to defend themselves out of their own pockets. It also discourages dissident shareholders from filing frivolous suits, since those sued will have their defense costs covered and consequently will be more likely to vigorously defend.

Under the 1987 statute, a corporation's articles and bylaws may include indemnification language. The forms included in this book for use as articles of incorporation (Forms 3-D, 3-E, and 3-F) include the statutory indemnification language. Because indemnification is discretionary, however, this language may be eliminated if the corporation does not wish to provide indemnification for its directors. If your corporation does not want to indemnify its directors, simply eliminate from Forms 3-E or 3-F the last sentence under "Article III. Directors" of the articles, as well as the entirety of "Article V. Indemnification." Likewise, the sample bylaws (Form 3-G) include indemnification language. Delete Article VI if indemnification is not desired.

Filing with the Secretary of State

Once the articles of incorporation are prepared, an original and three copies should be filed with the Secretary of State, Corporate Filing Division. The articles of incorporation must be accompanied by a check covering the applicable filing fees, as well as a cover letter to the Secretary of State (Form 3-H). The current fee for filing articles of incorporation is $100. Corporations formed on or after January 1, 2000 are not required to pay a minimum franchise tax fee of $800 for their first taxable year.[10] This tax will be due all subsequent years. The minimum franchise tax fee, as the term suggests, is a minimum tax. After the first year, a corporation must state its taxable income, if any, and pay the estimated tax fee for the next income tax year. If the estimated tax for any year after the initial year does not exceed the $800 minimum, then $800 is due and payable on the 15th day of the fourth month of the income tax year. If it is estimated that the tax will be over $800, the franchise tax is payable in equal installment on the 15th day of the fourth, sixth, ninth, and 12th months of the income tax year. The first payment, however, must be at least $800.[11]

If time is of the essence, you can hand-deliver the articles of incorporation to any one of the Secretary of State's regional offices. (See the list of locations at the beginning of this chapter.) There is a $15 handling

Once the articles of incorporation are prepared, an original and three copies should be filed with the Secretary of State.

fee (paid by separate check) for over-the-counter filings made in person. There are some advantages in filing over the counter and paying the extra fee. Sometimes, if the articles of incorporation are delivered before noon, a company can be incorporated on the same day. A sample letter to the Secretary of State to file articles of incorporation is included in Form 3-H and as Form 3-K. Please note that the articles of incorporation can always be amended later. (See Forms 3-I and 3-J.) Form 3-L is a sample letter for a certificate of amendment of the articles of incorporation.

Within a couple of weeks, the Secretary of State will return the articles of incorporation with the date of incorporation stamped in the upper right corner. Keep the stamped form in your corporation's minute book. The Secretary of State will certify two copies of the articles free of charge if they are submitted with the original at the time of filing. Certified copies can be obtained for $6. Be sure to then have the incorporator execute the Action of Incorporator (Form 3-M).

A delayed filing date can be requested for up to 90 days after physical filing. Otherwise, the filing date will be the date the articles are received and accepted. This delayed filing date is especially helpful if you are considering setting up a corporation near the end of any calendar year and you want the date of incorporation to be January 1, so as to avoid filing unnecessary corporate tax returns and paying annual franchise tax fees.

Preparing the Bylaws

Once the Secretary of State returns the certified copies of the articles of incorporation, you should prepare the corporation's bylaws. Form 3-G contains a complete set of bylaws that can be used for most businesses.

It is important to carefully read and understand these bylaws, since they establish specific procedural rules for organizing and conducting the internal affairs of the corporation. Note that there are several blanks in the bylaws that must be filled in to make them operational. The bylaws can always be amended at a later date (Form 3-N).

In general, bylaws serve two major functions:

1. They provide an easy reference for the company's officers and directors on how to comply with California law in conducting the corporation's business. This is especially important for purposes of establishing voting rights; procedures for the transferability of shares; setting the time, place, and notice of meetings; and dealing

> It is important to carefully read and understand these bylaws, since they establish specific procedural rules for organizing and conducting the internal affairs of the corporation.

with vacancies of officers and directors.

2. They may vary and modify some of the standard provisions of the California Corporations Code that would apply if there were no specific bylaws to the contrary. Please note, however, that a bylaw is invalid if it is contrary to the corporation's articles of incorporation or in violation of state or federal law.

First Meeting of the Board of Directors

Once the articles of incorporation have been filed and the bylaws prepared, it is time to hold the first meeting of the board of directors. At this meeting, the bylaws should be reviewed and adopted, the business and tax elections should be made, and the corporate officers should be elected and authorized to take whatever further action is necessary to fully organize the corporation. Be sure to have all of the directors execute a Waiver of Notice and Consent to Holding of the First Meeting of the Board of Directors (Forms 3-O and 3-P) at the start of the meeting and then file the executed waiver permanently in the minute book.

Once a corporation is established, it is imperative that minutes be taken at all meetings of the board of directors and stockholders. These minutes should then be filed in the Minutes section of the minute book.

Form 3-Q offers minutes for the first meeting of the board of directors and gives a guideline of matters that should be discussed and resolved during the first meeting.

Amending the Articles of Incorporation and Bylaws

The articles of incorporation may subsequently be amended for purposes such as changing the corporate name or authorizing additional shares of stock. By filing its Statement by Domestic Stock Corporation, discussed below, the corporation may change the name and address of its first directors or initial agent for service of process as set forth in the original articles without requiring a formal amendment of the articles of incorporation.

If the shares have not been issued, the articles of incorporation can be amended by the signature of a majority of the directors of the corporation (Form 3-I). After the shares have been issued, however, the procedure is more complicated and Form 3-J should be used instead. The approval of the board of directors and a majority of the shareholders is then required. Prepare the necessary minutes for the directors' and shareholders' meetings using Forms 3-R and 3-S.

After an amendment has passed, the corporation must file a Certificate of Amendment of Articles of Incorporation with the Secretary of State. The necessary forms, as previously mentioned, are Forms 3-I and 3-J, depending on whether the amendment occurs before or after the issuance of corporate shares. A proposed letter to the Secretary of State can be found in Form 3-L. A check for $30 must also accompany the Certificate of Amendment.

After the issuance of corporate shares, bylaws may be amended, adopted, or repealed by the approval of a majority of the board of directors or by a majority of the shareholders. Form 3-N sets out the appropriate board resolutions authorizing amendment of the corporate bylaws. Please note, however, that only the shareholders can approve a change of the number of directors in the bylaws.

> After the issuance of corporate shares, bylaws may be amended, adopted, or repealed by the approval of a majority of the board of directors or by a majority of the shareholders.

Statement of Information

Within 90 days after the filing of your articles of incorporation, the incorporator must file a Statement of Information (Domestic Stock Corporation) (Form 3-T). Thereafter, the corporation is required to file a similar form biannually at the end of the calendar month of the anniversary date of its incorporation. A $20 filing fee must accompany the Statement of Information, with the check or money order made payable to the California Secretary of State.

Every two years, within several months of the anniversary date of incorporation, the Secretary of State will forward a new Statement of Information to the corporation for completion. The corporation is responsible for timely filing the statement, even if it does not receive the form from the Secretary of State's office. Consequently, if the corporation has not received it within a month of its incorporation anniversary date, it can use Form 3-T or obtain a blank form from the local office of the Secretary of State and file it by the corporation's anniversary date. If a corporation fails to timely file the statement, the Secretary of State may impose a $250 fine and possibly even suspend the corporation.

Post-Incorporation Matters

After incorporation there remain several additional operational requirements that must be addressed prior to starting business.

California requires a variety of businesses to first obtain a state license before conducting business. *The California Professional and Business License Handbook* is available through the California Office of Small Business (commerce.ca.gov, under "Permits & Licenses" link to "License Handbook"). This handbook provides several forms for obtaining applicable licenses for doing business in California and provides guidelines for license requirements and regulatory agencies. It also lists several California taxes that apply to California licenses. Another good resource is *The California Permit Handbook*, published by the Office of Permit Assistance, which has recently been eliminated. The handbook provides a comprehensive list of permits required for manufacturing and development. You may obtain a copy of the handbook online (commerce.ca.gov, under "Permits & Licenses" link to "California Permit Handbook"). Additionally, you may apply for permits on line at www.calgold.ca.gov.

Local licenses are frequently required by cities, counties, and other governmental agencies. In an abundance of caution, you may want to investigate local zoning, environmental, and tax policies prior to deciding where to locate your company's business offices. This can especially be an issue if you plan to have a home office in your residence in an area not zoned for business.

Every corporation, whether it has employees or not, is required to obtain an Employer Identification Number (EIN) from the Internal Revenue Service. The application and instructions for obtaining an EIN are attached as Form 3-U. Application for an EIN should be made immediately after incorporation. The law requires that an EIN be obtained no later than seven days after the first payment of wages.

A decision on S corporation status must also be made before the 16th day of the third month after incorporation. It is easy to miss this deadline. By way of example, if you incorporate on July 30, you would have until September 15 to make an election. July would be considered the first month, August the second, and September the third. If the deadline is missed, the corporation will be taxed as a C corporation subject to corporate tax for its first year. A delinquent S election will become effective for the corporation's second tax year. Further discussion of S corporations and instructions on making the S election can be found in Chapter 8.

Any business that owns taxable personal property with an aggregate value of $100,000 or more in any assessment year must file a signed property statement with the county assessor in the county where the

California requires a variety of businesses to first obtain a state license before conducting business.

property is located, between March 1 and the last Friday in May, or face interest charges and penalties.

If your business engages in the sale of tangible personal property at a retail level, it will probably be subject to California Sales and Use Tax requirements. Instructions and the form to apply for a sales and use tax permit are attached as Form 3-V. In some circumstances, leases may also be subject to sales tax.[12]

Notes

1. California Corporations Code §200(a).
2. Ibid.
3. California Corporations Code §§210, 901, and 906.
4. Business and Professions Code §17917.
5. California Corporations Code §201(c).
6. California Corporations Code §204(a)(10).
7. California Corporations Code §317(d).
8. California Corporations Code §317(b).
9. See Labor Code §2802.
10. Revenue and Taxation Code §23153(f)(1).
11 See Revenue and Taxation Code §19025(a).
12. See Revenue and Taxation Code §§6006-6006.3 and 6010.

CHAPTER 4

Capitalizing the Corporation and Issuing Stock

Capitalizing the Corporation

The Importance of Adequate Capitalization

The money and assets obtained in exchange for the issuance of corporate stock provide a new corporation with operating capital. A new corporation must have sufficient operating capital to meet its expenses until it is in a position to pay all of its operating expenses through profits, loans, and/or the sale of additional shares.

It is the policy of California law that shareholders should, in good faith, put up unencumbered capital that is at risk and will be adequate for the corporation's prospective liabilities.[1] Otherwise, the corporate shield of limited liability protection may not be available to protect the corporation's shareholders.

Although it is true that California does not require a corporation to have any minimum amount of assets, it does recognize that if a corporation goes into business without adequate capitalization, the directors, corporate officers, and shareholders may be held personally liable for the corporation's debts (piercing the corporate veil—see Chapter 6).

The amount and form of capitalization will depend on the nature and needs of the business. You should make efforts to ensure that a significant portion of the initial capitalization consists of equity capital. It is also a good idea to prepare a business plan, cash flow statement, and other documentation prior to capitalization. This documentation can always be introduced later in court to support a shareholder's good-faith estimate of the corporation's prospective capital needs. As a rule of thumb, I often advise my clients to prepare a budget (without including projected revenue or payment of salaries to shareholders) showing the company's financial needs for its first six months of operation. This total amount provides a reasonable estimate for adequate initial capitalization.

Furthermore, as the saying goes, it takes money to make money. An undercapitalized business has little hope for success. I see more businesses fail due to undercapitalization than for any other reason. To protect yourself in court and to make sure that your business has a good chance of success, be sure to capitalize the corporation with enough money and other assets to pay for all start-up costs and foreseeable short-range expenses and liabilities.

> You should make efforts to ensure that a significant portion of the initial capitalization consists of equity capital.

Issuing Stock

It is crucial that the corporation issue stock to its owners in order to maintain limited liability protection. After the first meeting of the board of directors (Form 3-Q in Chapter 3), the corporation should issue a stock certificate to each shareholder in exchange for cash, cancellation of indebtedness, or assets of an ongoing business. You should also take care to adequately capitalize the corporation (in return for the shares) with a significant amount of working capital and/or other assets that provide the corporation with a legitimate starting point to allow it to succeed. If shares are issued for cash or cancellation of indebtedness, the chief financial officer of the corporation should prepare and execute a receipt acknowledging delivery to the corporation. A copy of the receipt should then be placed in the minute book along with the other corporate records. The shares should be issued on the same date as the corporation receives the consideration (money, cancellation of indebtedness, or assets of another business). This date of issuance is important in establishing the due date for mailing the Limited Offering Exemption Notice, discussed later in this chapter.

Included in the Forms section of this book are blank, ready-to-use stock certificates. Each certificate can represent more than one share of stock or unit of membership interest. Shares or units should be issued in the same proportion as the percentage of ownership of the corporation or limited liability company.

Information to Include on the Stock Certificate

Before beginning to fill out the actual certificates, first write out the exact information for each on scratch paper. Determine:

- The date of issuance,
- The number of certificates that will be issued,
- The correct legal name of each shareholder, and
- The exact number of shares to be allocated on each certificate.

Next, carefully type or print the information on the certificate and corresponding stub. Then, double-check each certificate and stub. Finally, have both the corporation's president and secretary sign. (If the same person holds both positions, he or she should sign twice.) You can give certificates to the shareholders and keep stubs in the corporate minute book. In the alternative, the original certificates (together with the stubs) may be stored in the corporate minute book for safekeeping. The latter approach may be preferable because shareholders frequently lose their stock certificates. You should also record the stock issuance information in the ledger in the minute book.

Federal Securities Law Requirements

In general, every issuance of securities by a corporation and every subsequent transfer must either be registered with the Securities and Exchange Commission (SEC) or be exempt from SEC registration requirements. SEC registration is a very time-consuming and expensive process and is required in order for shares to be eligible for trading on public securities markets (such as the NASDAQ Stock Market or the New York Stock Exchange). Even where SEC registration is not required by virtue of an exemption from such requirements, federal securities laws require extensive (and expensive to prepare) written disclosure to any purchaser *other than* persons who either exert substantial control over the corporation (such as founders and executive officers and directors) or meet the financial criteria of an "accredited investor" contained in Regulation D of the federal Securities Act of 1933. A copy of the definition of an "accredited investor" is included at the end of this chapter.

In order to avoid SEC registration requirements for public offerings or the requirements for extensive written disclosure for private offerings, you must carefully structure the issuance of shares to qualify for an exemption from such requirements. This compliance will generally require the review of an attorney with experience in securities compliance matters.

If you set up your corporation and issue shares following the guidelines set forth below regarding compliance with requirements under California law, you probably will not have to register your shares with the SEC. However, your corporation remains subject to SEC disclosure and anti-fraud requirements and may be required to file of a Notice of Sale of Securities on Form D with the SEC. (See Form 4-A.) To be certain, you should discuss securities law matters with your attorney before issuing any shares or accepting any investment by the corporation or its founders.

It is important to bear in mind that securities compliance requirements become much more stringent when a corporation proposes to issue shares to persons other than the original founders of a company, e.g., to employees or outside investors. Under federal and state securities law, the corporation is required to provide certain minimum written disclosure regarding the capitalization and financial and business status of the corporation before an employee or any outside investor decides to purchase securities. In addition, if the corporation intends to raise capital from outside investors who are not actively involved in the management of the business, the corporation will have to deliver very extensive written disclosure to such passive investors, unless the investor is "accredited." (See the definition at the end of this chapter.) Finally, under the federal anti-fraud provisions (including Rule 10b-5 of the Securities Exchange Act of 1934) and comparable state laws, it is always unlawful for any person to make any untrue statement of a material fact or to omit to state a material fact in connection with the sale of any security, regardless of compliance with registration and qualification requirements or exemptions.

> It is important to bear in mind that securities compliance requirements become much more stringent when a corporation proposes to issue shares to persons other than the original founders of a company.

California Securities Law Requirements

Section 25110 of the California Corporations Code makes it illegal for any person to offer or sell a security (including stock) for the direct or indirect benefit of an issuer in California, unless the sale has been qualified with the state or is otherwise exempt from qualification. These requirements apply *in addition* to the federal securities law requirements discussed above.

Exemption from California Qualification Requirements

Since the qualification of securities with the State of California is a lengthy, expensive, and complicated procedure, it is preferable for a small business to set up its capital structure under one of the exemptions to qualification, such as Section 25102(f) or (h), explained below. Because obtaining an exemption from qualification is a crucial element to a simple incorporation, it is very important that you review your organizational scheme to make sure you are able to take advantage of one of these exemptions. Conduct the review as early as possible, before filing the articles of incorporation. If you have questions, consult an attorney immediately.

Section 25102(f) Exemption

Section 25102(f) provides an exemption from qualification under California law for certain nonpublic offerings of securities and is the most commonly used California exemption. Section 25012(f) is designed to exempt the offer and sale of shares to 35 or fewer persons (including persons outside California) if the following conditions are met:

- Each purchaser must:
  - have a preexisting personal or business relationship with the corporation or any of its officers, directors, or controlling persons; or
  - have the capacity to protect his or her own interests in connection with the transaction, by reason of his or her business or financial experience, or the business or financial experience of his or her professional advisors (who have no relationship to the corporation); and
- Each purchaser must represent that he or she is purchasing only for his or her own account, or a trust account if the purchaser is a trustee, and not with a view to or for sale in connection with any distribution of the stock; and
- The offer and sale of the shares must not be accomplished by the publication of any advertisement. Under the California Corporations Code, "advertisement" is defined to include "writ-

ten or printed communication or any communication by means of recorded telephone messages or spoken on radio, television, or similar communications media, published in connection with the offer or sale of a security";[2] and

- The corporation must file a Limited Offering Exemption Notice (also known as a Notice of Transaction Pursuant to Corporation Code Section 25102(f)) (see Form 4-B) with the California Commissioner of Corporations within 15 calendar days after the first sale of securities in California, signed by an officer of the corporation and accompanied by the filing fee in the amount set forth below.

Note that that officers and directors of the corporation and "accredited investors" (see definition at the end of this chapter are excluded from the 35-person limitation. Section 25102(f) counts married couples as one person.

It is very common for corporations to use written questionnaires to determine if prospective investors meet the "sophistication" standards imposed by the 25102(f) exemption. The questionnaire should be presented to proposed investors to complete prior to the issuance of any shares. Then, the corporation and legal counsel should carefully review the questionnaires to determine whether or not the issuance can qualify under this exemption. Note, however, that the failure of even one investor to meet the 25102(f) requirements will disallow the use of that exemption by the corporation for the entire issuance for all investors. Two sample investor questionnaires are included, one for individuals (Form 4-C) and one for entities (Form 4-D).

Section 25608(c) provides that the fee for filing notices under Section 25102(f) and (h) is based on the value of the securities proposed to be sold in the transaction for which the notice is filed. As of October 1, 2004, the fee schedule is:

Value of Securities Proposed to Be Sold	Filing Fee
$25,000 or less	$25
$25,001 to $100,000	$35
$100,001 to $500,000	$50
$500,001 to $1,000,000	$150
Over $1,000,000	$300

Determining the Value of Securities

Value is determined by the price paid for the securities, by the actual value of any consideration other than money received for the securities, or by the value of the securities when issued, whichever is greatest.[3] You should provide the attorney with copies of the corporation's articles of incorporation, bylaws, minutes of the first meeting, stock certificate stubs, and documentation as to consideration paid for the transferred shares. Form 4-E is a suggested letter to be sent along with the Limited Offering Exemption Notice and the applicable filing fee.

Filing the Limited Offering Exemption Notice

It is important to have documentation of the fact that you sent the Limited Offering Exemption Notice to the Commissioner of Corporations within 15 days after receipt of the consideration for the shares. The notice should be sent by certified mail, return receipt requested. Keep a copy of the notice and the certified mail receipt in the corporate minute book.

The address for filing by mail is:
Department of Corporations
State of California
1515 K Street, Suite 200
Sacramento, CA 95814-4017

In addition, you may now file the Limited Offering Exemption Notice online at www.corp.ca.gov/loen/loen.htm. As of October 2004, the Commissioner of Corporations has proposed making online filing mandatory; this requirement may take effect in the near future. Accordingly, you should check the commissioner's web site at www.corp.ca.gov/loen/loen.htm before making any filing.

You may obtain further information regarding this exemption by visiting the following web site: www.corp.ca.gov/loen/rules.htm. In addition, the Department of Corporations has published an overview of the Section 25102(f) exemption, which can be obtained from its web site at www.corp.ca.gov/commiss/67c.pdf.

Section 25102(h) Exemption

Section 25102(h) provides an exemption from qualification under California law for certain small private issuances of stock. To be eligible for a Section 25102(h) exemption, the following requirements must be met:

■ The corporation may not have more than 35 shareholders. (A married couple counts as only one shareholder.)

■ The stock must be common voting stock without special preferences to certain shareholders in dividends, liquidation, or other rights. Note that unless the corporation's articles of incorporation or bylaws contain provisions to the contrary, all stock issued by a corporation is considered to be common voting stock.

■ There can only be one class of stock (voting, nonvoting, preferred, etc.) outstanding. If the corporation has previously issued stock, it must be of the same class and have the same provisions as the current stock issuance for which the exemption is being sought.

■ The offer and sale of stock must not be accompanied by the publication of any kind of advertising. (See definition above.)

■ Commissions, discounts, or other compensation must not be given, paid, or incurred in connection with the offer and sale of the stock.

■ No promotional consideration, including stock or money, can be given for services rendered in forming and organizing the corporation. Put simply, this means that no one (whether incorporator, officer, director, employee, promoter, or outsider) can receive money, property, stock, or any other form of compensation in return for founding or organizing the corporation. Generally speaking, the term "promoter" includes any person who, acting alone or in conjunction with one or more other persons, directly or indirectly takes the initiative in founding and organizing the corporation.[4]

■ Each purchaser must represent that he or she is purchasing only for his or her own account, or a trust account if the purchaser is a trustee, and not with a view to or for sale in connection with any distribution of the stock.

■ The stock can be issued for only one of the following types of consideration:

– Cash and/or cancellation of indebtedness for money borrowed, or both, upon the initial organization of the corporation, provided all of the stock is issued for the same price per share; or

– Assets of an existing business, which may include cash, provided all of the following conditions are met:

1. All of the assets of the prior business are transferred to the corporation;

No promotional consideration, including stock or money, can be given for services rendered in forming and organizing the corporation.

2. The business has been in operation for at least one year immediately preceding the proposed issuance;

3. The prior business was owned during the prior year by the same persons to whom the shares are now being issued; and

4. The prior owners of the business receive stock in the new corporation in the same proportion of ownership of the business immediately before the proposed issuance (that is, if A and B each owned 50 percent of the prior business, then each must receive 50 percent of the issued stock in the new corporation); or

- Cash only, provided the sale is approved in writing by each of the existing shareholders and each purchaser is an existing shareholder; or

- Any legal consideration if after the issuance there will be only one shareholder.

Note that the foregoing types of acceptable consideration are mutually exclusive and the exemption is not available if the consideration paid for all the shares is not the same. In other words, all stock must be sold for cash, or all stock must be sold for cancellation of indebtedness, or all stock must be sold for the assets of the going business. The consideration cannot be mixed or combined in the offering.

A Notice of Issuance of Shares (Form 4-F), must be signed by an officer of the corporation *and* by an active California attorney and filed with the office of the Commissioner of Corporations within ten business days after the corporation receives the consideration for the shares, accompanied by a check to cover the filing fee. (See above for amount.) Note that the "opinion of counsel" portion of the notice must be signed by an attorney who is an active member of the State Bar of California.

The small offering exemption contained in Section 25102(h) may be used as often as necessary. It is available on subsequent issuances of additional stock in the corporation, provided all of the requirements of a small offering exemption are satisfied. Note, that, after the initial issuance, the only kinds of consideration that are allowable for subsequent issuances of shares are:

- Cash only, provided the sale is approved in writing by each of the existing shareholders and each purchaser is an existing shareholder.

- Any legal consideration if after the issuance there will be only one shareholder.

Securities Laws of Other States

If the corporation proposes to issue shares to residents of states other than California, you should consult with an attorney who will review the compliance requirements under the laws of the applicable jurisdictions. Fortunately, compliance with other state securities laws is often simpler than compliance with California requirements (with a few notable exceptions, such as New York).

Penalties for Failure to Comply with Securities Laws

Compliance with federal and state securities laws is mandatory. Failure to comply invites severe penalties, including rescission (allowing investors to get their money back), private suits for damages, civil fines or injunctions, and potentially even criminal sanctions. In addition, the failure to comply (and document compliance) may negatively impact the ability of the company to raise further capital or sell the corporation at a future date, even if no shareholder or government agency has taken any action.

Accredited Investors

As noted under the Federal Securities Law Requirements discussion above, obtaining investments from "accredited investors" greatly reduces the amount of written disclosure materials that must be prepared for investors and simplifies the process of securing the necessary exemptions under both federal and state securities law.

Following is the definition of "accredited investor" under Section 501(a) of the Securities Act of 1933:

1. A person or entity who is a director or executive officer of the company;

2. Any bank as defined in section 3(a)(2) of the Act, or any savings and loan association or other institution as defined in section 3(a)(5)(A) of the Act whether acting in its individual or fiduciary capacity; any broker or dealer registered pursuant to section 15 of the Securities Exchange Act of 1934; any insurance company as defined in section 2(13) of the Act; any investment company registered under the Investment Company Act of 1940 or a business development company as defined in section 2(a)(48) of that Act; any Small Business Investment Company licensed by the U.S. Small Business Administration under section 301(c) or (d) of the Small Business

If the corporation proposes to issue shares to residents of states other than California, you should consult with an attorney who will review the compliance requirements.

Investment Act of 1958; any plan established and maintained by a state, its political subdivisions, or any agency or instrumentality of a state or its political subdivisions, for the benefit of its employees, if such plan has total assets in excess of $5,000,000; any employee benefit plan within the meaning of Title I of the Employee Retirement Income Security Act of 1974, if the investment decision is made by a plan fiduciary, as defined in section 3(21) of such Act, which is either a bank, savings and loan association, insurance company, or registered investment advisor, or if the employee benefit plan has total assets in excess of $5,000,000 or, if a self-directed plan, with investment decisions made solely by persons that are accredited investors;

3. Any private business development company as defined in section 202(a)(22) of the Investment Advisers Act of 1940;

4. Any organization described in section 501(c)(3) of the Internal Revenue Code, corporation, Massachusetts or similar business trust, or partnership, not formed for the specific purpose of acquiring the securities offered, with total assets in excess of $5,000,000;

5. Any natural person whose individual net worth, or joint net worth with that person's spouse, at the time of his or her purchase exceeds $1,000,000;

6. Any natural person who had an individual income in excess of $200,000 in each of the two (2) most recent years or joint income with that person's spouse in excess of $300,000 in each of those years and has a reasonable expectation of reaching the same income level in the current year;

7. Any trust, with total assets in excess of $5,000,000, not formed for the specific purpose of acquiring the securities offered, whose purchase is directed by a person who has such knowledge and experience in financial and business matters that he or she is capable of evaluating the merits and risks of the prospective investment; or

8. Any entity in which all of the equity owners are accredited investors.

As used in this Section (501), the term "net worth" means the excess of total assets over total liabilities. For the purpose of determining a person's net worth, the principal residence owned by the individual should be valued at fair market value, including the cost of improvements, net of current encumbrances. As used in this Section, "income" means actual economic income, which may differ from adjusted gross income for income tax purposes. Accordingly, an investor should consider whether he or she should add any or all of the following items to his or her adjusted gross income for income tax purposes in order to reflect more accurately his or her actual economic income: any amounts attributable to tax-exempt income received, losses claimed as a limited partner in any limited partnership, deductions claimed for depletion, contributions to an IRA or Keogh retirement plan, and alimony payments.

Notes

1. *Automotriz del Golfo de California v. Resnick* (1957) 47 Cal 2d 792, 797.
2. California Corporations Code §25002.
3. California Corporations Code §25608(g).
4. Rule 1-02(s) of SEC Regulation S-X.

CHAPTER 5

Incorporating or Forming an LLC from an Ongoing Business

You can face an ever-changing array of issues in incorporating or forming an LLC from an ongoing business, including some serious tax consequences. The contribution of property to a corporation or an LLC may result in a taxable event that results in a tax liability, as well as causing other problems.

For example, unless careful attention is paid to Internal Revenue Code Section 351, property in which liabilities exceed adjusted basis may be transferred into a corporation, thereby creating an immediate gain to the contributing taxpayer and possibly contribute to capital problems for the corporation. Thus, it is recommended that you consult with your accountant or a tax attorney to structure the transaction before taking a pre-existing business and incorporating or forming an LLC.

Offer to Transfer Business Assets

After you have filed the articles of incorporation or articles of organization with the Secretary of State, you should then prepare an offer to transfer ongoing business assets to the new corporation or LLC. Two forms have been provided in this book: use Form 5-A if the existing business is a partnership and Form 5-B if the existing business is a sole proprietorship. You should prepare a financial statement showing the assets and liabilities of the existing business as of the date of the offer. The financial statements should then be attached to the offer. If the new entity is a corporation, at the next meeting of the board of directors, the offer should be reviewed and accepted, signed by the president and secretary, and placed in the corporate minute book for safekeeping. If the new entity is an LLC, the offer should be reviewed, accepted, and signed by the managing member(s) or manager(s) and placed in the LLC minute book for safekeeping. Also, you must be aware of the prohibition described in Chapter 9 against certain types of business operating as an LLC.

Additional Requirement for Certain Businesses—Bulk Transfers

If the business being transferred is a bakery, cafe, restaurant, garage, cleaner, dyer, retail, or wholesale merchant or manufacturer, the corporation must prepare and publish a Notice to Creditors of Bulk Sale in the county in which the property to be transferred is located. Form 5-C contains a sample notice. This notice should be published 12 or more business days prior to the date of transfer of the property to the corporation or LLC in the closest legal newspaper for the judicial district in which the property is located.

> Often, there are distinct advantages to transferring real property to an LLC rather than to a corporation.

The original notice should also be filed with the county recorder's office in the county or counties in which the transferor's business is located 12 or more business days before the business assets are to be transferred to the corporation or LLC. A copy of the notice should also be sent by certified mail to the county tax collector's office for the county or counties in which the property is located 12 or more business days before the transfer.

Assignment of Real Property Interests

If the unincorporated business is transferring any real property interest to the corporation or LLC, it is necessary to execute transfers of leases, rental agreements, or ownership deeds. Often, there are distinct advantages to transferring real property to an LLC rather than to a corporation. Consult your attorney or accountant.

Bill of Sale Agreement

A Bill of Sale Agreement (Form 5-D) is necessary to legally transfer the assets of the previous business to the corporation in exchange for stock or to the LLC in exchange for membership interests or units. Be sure to list all of the tangible assets that are being transferred and attach a complete inventory to the Bill of Sale Agreement.

Any asset that is not going to be transferred to the corporation or LLC should be listed as an exception at the end of paragraph one of Form 5-D. The Bill of Sale Agreement should be executed on the date the shares are actually issued in return for the assets of the ongoing business.

Wrap-Up of Old Business

After taking the preceding steps, the old business should file final sales tax returns and cancel any permits or licenses issued to the unincorporated business or prior business owners. New licenses and permits should then be obtained in the name of the new corporation or LLC.

All of the old creditors of the unincorporated business and all other interested parties should be notified in writing of the termination and dissolution of the prior business entity and the continuation of the business under a corporate or LLC structure. A simple letter will do, unless the prior business was a partnership.

If the prior business was a partnership, it is necessary to publish a Notice of Dissolution of Partnership (Form 5-E) in a legal newspaper circulated in the county or counties in which the business was regularly conducted. An affidavit of publication must also be filed with the county clerk within 30 days of publication. The newspaper's staff should be able to help you on both of these counts. The partnership should also notify creditors of the dissolution of the partnership by way of letter. Attach a copy of the published notice to the letter. Copies of each letter and one copy of the published notice should then be retained in the corporate or LLC minute book.

CHAPTER 6

Maintaining the Corporation or LLC

One of the major benefits of using the corporate or LLC form of doing business is that shareholders or members have limited liability for the acts and obligations of the entity. Because a corporation or LLC is deemed by law to be a separate entity from their shareholders or members, claimants may generally look only to the assets of the corporation or LLC to satisfy their claims. Consequently, the liability of the shareholders or members is limited to their investment in the corporation or LLC.

Piercing the Corporate Veil

Even if you have incorporated or set up an LLC, it does not necessarily guarantee that your business will be treated as such by a court or the Internal Revenue Service.

If your business is not properly organized and maintained, a court can disregard the corporate or LLC entity and hold the owners of the business personally liable for the business's debts. This is known as "piercing the corporate veil." When the corporate veil is pierced for the reasons described below, the courts may also hold an owner personally liable for the physical, emotional, or monetary harm the corporation or LLC causes another party.

Courts can also pierce the corporate veil for other reasons. For example, a court may hold a stockholder, officer, director, member, or manager personally responsible for corporate contracts, which would otherwise be the sole responsibility of the business, because the business did not enter into a particular contract officially through formal action of its board of directors, such as when a shareholder of the corporation signs a contract without proper authorization. Likewise, the IRS can also disregard the business entity in order to tax the corporation's or LLC's income directly to the shareholders or members as part of their taxable income. Payroll taxes, if not paid by a business, are subject to a personal assessment by the IRS against any and all "responsible officers" who paid other creditors instead of the IRS.

The specific circumstances under which a court will pierce the corporate veil are not easily predicted. The courts emphasize that the facts of a particular case control the decision. The rule has been generally stated, however, that a corporation's or LLC's separate identity will be disregarded only when, and to the extent that, it is necessary to prevent fraud or injustice or an abuse of the limited liability privilege. So, it is extremely important that all shareholders or members consistently treat the corporation or LLC as a separate entity in order to minimize personal exposure for business liabilities.

When the courts have disregarded the corporate or LLC entity, they have based their decisions on factors such as the following:

- Co-mingling of corporate or LLC and personal funds or the unauthorized diversion of business assets for personal use;
- Treatment of the corporate assets by the shareholders as their own;
- Disregard of legal formalities, such as failing to hold directors' and shareholders' meetings and not conducting corporate affairs through proper board authorization;
- Failure of the shareholders or members to "present" themselves as doing business as a corporation or LLC by not having stationery or business cards in the name of the business that indicate "Inc." or "LLC."
- Failures to make sure that all contracts are in the name of the business and that all signatures are followed by title (e.g. President or Manager).
- Failure to issue stock;
- Failure to maintain minutes and adequate corporate records;

> The specific circumstances under which a court will pierce the corporate veil are not easily predicted.

- Failure to adequately capitalize the business; and
- The operation of the business, if a corporation, by corporate insiders or officers or, if an LLC, by LLC members or managers, while the business is in suspension.

Corporate formalities—such as properly serving notice of meetings of the board of directors and shareholders, holding these meetings regularly, and keeping a record of decisions via accurate minutes—may seem unnecessary or unimportant. However, shareholders are much more likely to have to personally pay for a corporation's liabilities if the prescribed procedures are not followed. One of the advantages of an LLC structure over that of a corporation is that there is no requirement that an LLC have annual meetings of managers or members. This does not mean, however, that an LLC can avoid personal liability exposure. Close attention must always be given to ensure that the members and managers of an LLC comply with the terms of its operating agreement.

Keeping Minutes

Another purpose of keeping regular and accurate minutes is to document the fact that the directors or shareholders have taken particular actions. The minutes memorialize the events of the board meeting and represent some proof that the directors' actions were considered, debated, and consistent with the corporate charter. Opposing viewpoints by directors, if any, should be reflected in the minutes.

To ensure that the IRS or a court recognizes the corporate status, it is crucial that the minutes of each corporate meeting be taken and kept, and that such meetings occur on a regular basis.

Decisions that should be documented in the minutes include, but are not limited to, the following:

- Appointment, approval, and removal of officers and directors; delineation of assigned duties to corporate personnel; loans or bonuses to officers; and justification of special compensation to officers or other corporate employees;
- Major acquisitions of corporate assets or other businesses;
- Authorization for the issuance of securities; approval of buy/sell agreements for shares of the corporation; financial arrangements; agreements with lenders; and declarations of dividends;
- Creation of special committees and the duties of each committee member; and

> Another purpose of keeping regular and accurate minutes is to document the fact that the directors or shareholders have taken particular actions.

- Revisions to the structure of the corporation, including changes in the bylaws or the articles of incorporation.

Copies of all contracts, committee reports, budgets, correspondence, and other relevant documents should be attached to the minutes because, in the event of a legal challenge regarding the corporation's actions, these attachments can help demonstrate the basis for the challenged action.

Annual Meetings of Shareholders

Neither the bylaws nor the articles may dispense with the legal requirement that a corporation conduct an annual shareholders' meeting.[1] Usually, the annual meeting is held three or four months after the end of each year (either fiscal or calendar) so that the financial status of the past year can be reviewed. Each succeeding stockholder meeting must take place no later than 15 months after the prior meeting and must be held within 60 days of the time specified in the bylaws. Any meeting not held within the required time frame can be ordered by a court of competent jurisdiction upon application of any shareholder.[2]

Section 3.03 of the corporate bylaws provides that the directors shall be elected at the annual shareholders' meeting. Prior to conducting the meeting, it is necessary to give the shareholders proper notice. (See Sections 2.04 and 2.05 of the bylaws and Form 6-I.) The minimum notice requirement is ten days and notice must be given by first class mail unless the corporation has in excess of 500 shareholders. You should conduct the annual meeting on the date selected in Section 2.02 of the bylaws.

Form 6-B contains all of the language necessary to document the valid election or re-election of the board of directors. The Minutes of the Annual Meeting of the Shareholders (Form 6-B) should be completed immediately after the meeting is conducted and then placed in the corporate minute book.

In order to have a valid meeting of the shareholders, a quorum is necessary. A quorum exists if a majority of the shares entitled to vote are represented at the meeting either in person or by proxy. A proxy is similar to a power of attorney whereby a shareholder gives a third party the right to vote his or her shares. Frequently, a corporation solicits proxies in advance of the meeting to ensure that there will be a quorum of shareholders present. Attached as Form 6-J is a proxy that may be uti-

Neither the bylaws nor the articles may dispense with the legal requirement that a corporation conduct an annual shareholders' meeting.

lized for this purpose. The requirement of a simple majority cannot be increased in the bylaws, but it can be decreased, although not to less than one-third of the shares entitled to vote.[3]

Once a quorum is present, even if shareholders then withdraw and leave less than a quorum, the remaining shareholders may vote to do business. However, there are limitations as to what action can be taken in the absence of a quorum. If the meeting is adjourned for lack of a quorum, it may be continued for a period of up to 55 days without the necessity of sending another formal notice.

Special Meetings of Shareholders

A special meeting of the shareholders may be called by any one of the following: the board, the chairman, the president, a vice president, or any shareholder with ten percent or more of the voting power of the corporation.[4] Also, the bylaws may expand the list of people permitted to call a special meeting, such as the secretary or the chief financial officer.

Form 6-D can be used to record the minutes of a special meeting of the shareholders. A special meeting may occasionally prove necessary when corporate action requires or allows shareholder approval. For example, shareholder approval is necessary where the articles of incorporation are amended after shares have been issued (Form 6-N). Proper notice of the special meeting must also be given. (See sections 2.03, 2.04, and 2.05 of the bylaws.) The bylaws may vary the manner of calling and giving notice of a special meeting of the shareholders as long as the variation is not in conflict with the law or the articles. If proper notice cannot be given, however, due to time constraints, all of the shareholders can waive the notice requirement by executing Form 6-F.

Cumulative Voting

Under California law, cumulative voting is required for director elections, if requested by a shareholder.[5] To initiate cumulative voting, one or more shareholders must give notice to the rest of the shareholders of their intent to cumulate their vote prior to the beginning of voting.[6] If any shareholders give notice of their desire to cumulate their vote, then all shareholders may do so, but only for candidates whose names have been placed in nomination. By way of example, if the bylaws provide for three directors and there are 1000 shares outstanding, a shareholder owning 200 shares would have 600 votes that he or she could cast for

Under California law, cumulative voting is required for director elections, if requested by a shareholder.

one director (1000 shares x 3 directors = 3000 shares x 20 percent = 600 cumulative votes).

Necessity of a Record Date

A *record date* is necessary to determine the identity of those shareholders entitled to vote, receive dividends, attend meetings, and obtain notices of information relating to the corporation's shareholders. The board is authorized to fix a record date for shareholders' meetings and other purposes within certain specified limitations.[7] Shareholders of record are those parties listed as owners on the corporate books at the close of business on the given record date, regardless of whether there are later transfers of shares on a corporation's books. If the directors do not fix a record date, there are detailed rules delineated in California Corporations Code §701(b) for determining shareholders of record for a given event.

Shareholders of record are those parties listed as owners on the corporate books at the close of business on the given record date.

Meetings of the Board of Directors

All business transacted by the board of directors at any and all meetings must be properly recorded in the corporate minutes. It is probably most convenient to hold the annual meeting immediately after the annual shareholders' meeting for the purpose of electing officers. (See Section 3.06 of the bylaws.) Form 6-C is suggested for the minutes of the annual meeting of the board of directors. Unless required by the bylaws, notice of the annual meeting is not required.

Regular meetings of the board of directors are held, and notice shall be given, pursuant to Sections 3.05, 3.06, and 3.07 of the bylaws.

Special meetings of the board of directors may be called at any time by the chairman of the board, the president, the vice president, the secretary, or a majority of the directors. Notice, however, must be given for a special meeting (see Section 3.08 of the bylaws) unless a waiver of notice is executed. (See Section 3.10 of the bylaws and Form 6-G.)

Special meetings of the directors are often necessary to document a resolution needed for specific business purposes, such as a resolution authorizing a bank loan. A guideline for special meeting minutes can be found in Form 6-E.

Action by the Shareholders or Board of Directors Without a Meeting

Any action required or permitted to be taken by the board of directors or shareholders may be taken without a meeting if all of the board members consent in writing to such action. Action by unanimous written consent has the same force and effect as a unanimous vote of the board of directors. (See Form 6-H for written consent form.) After execution, this document should also be filed with the other minutes of the board in the corporate minute book. A shareholder action by written consent without prior notice is permitted, but may be restricted by the articles of incorporation. Any shareholder action, except the election of directors, may be taken by written consents executed by shareholders holding the same number or more of the shares as would be required for any action taken at a meeting at which all shares entitled to vote were present. Unless all shareholders entitled to vote actually participate, however, the corporation must give all non-consenting shareholders entitled to vote prompt notice of any corporate action approved by a written consent of the majority of the shareholders without a meeting. An election of directors by written consent is not permitted unless all of the shareholders consent.

Any action required or permitted to be taken by the board of directors or shareholders may be taken without a meeting if all of the board members consent in writing to such action.

Suspension of Corporate or LLC Powers

A California corporation or a California LLC may be suspended from exercising its powers, rights, and privileges for any of the following reasons:

- Failure to file a franchise tax return, even if no tax is due.[8]
- Failure to timely pay franchise taxes.[9]
- Failure to timely file its biannual Statement by Domestic Stock Corporation (for a corporation) or its biannual Statement of Information (for an LLC).[10]

Among other things, during the period of suspension, the corporation or LLC may not:

- Sue or defend itself in court; or
- Engage in any real estate transaction.

Furthermore, any contracts entered into by a suspended corporation or LLC are voidable at the option of the other contracting party (but not by the suspended entity). The right to declare a contract void is, however, exercisable only if the other party files a lawsuit and obtains a judgment that rescinds the contract.[11] Unless there is a rescission order, the contract is still enforceable.[12]

Finally, any person who attempts to act on behalf of a suspended corporation or suspended LLC may be subject to fine and imprisonment.[13] He or she may also be personally liable for any obligation that he or she incurs on behalf of the suspended corporation or LLC.

If the corporation or LLC is suspended for failing to timely file the annual or biannual Statement of Information, the corporation or LLC can generally be reinstated with the Secretary of State by simply filing the delinquent statement. Unless it shows "reasonable cause or unusual circumstances" justifying the filing oversight, however, a statutory penalty of $250 may be assessed against the corporation and must be paid when the statement is finally filed.[14] Likewise, an LLC suspended for failing to file its Statement of Information may be reinstated by filing the form and paying any delinquencies.

If, on the other hand, the suspension is for failing to timely file a franchise tax return or for failure to timely pay franchise taxes, the corporation or LLC may be reinstated only by application to the Franchise Tax Board (see Form 6-A, Application for Certificate of Revivor), by filing the necessary returns, and by paying any delinquent taxes, interest, and penalties to the Franchise Tax Board.[15] Once this has been done, the Franchise Tax Board issues a certificate of revivor and forwards a copy of it to the Secretary of State to revive the entity's good standing. The certificate of revivor has the effect of restoring all of the entity's previously suspended powers, rights, and privileges and of validating all acts and transactions that occurred during the period of suspension that have not otherwise been rescinded by final court order.

Simultaneously with the filing of the application for certificate of revivor to the Franchise Tax Board, a corporation or LLC may now also seek formal relief from the voidability of contracts entered into during the period of suspension.[16] By doing so, the corporation or LLC can obtain the added benefit of formal "validation" of the enforceability of those contracts.

If a corporation or LLC fails to pay franchise taxes for more than five years, the California Attorney General has the authority to sue to dissolve the corporation or LLC and forfeit its corporate charter.

If your corporation or LLC has been suspended, you can probably get it reinstated by following the steps outlined in this chapter. In some

> Any person who attempts to act on behalf of a suspended corporation or suspended LLC may be subject to fine and imprisonment.

instances, however, the steps for reviving a suspended corporation or LLC are more complicated. If this is the case, you should consult qualified legal counsel.

Buy-Sell Agreements

Buy-sell agreements (also known as *buyouts* or *shareholder agreements*) are commonly used by shareholders or members of closely held corporations or LLCs. The purpose of such agreements is to restrict the transfer of shares or membership interests to unwanted outsiders or inactive heirs and to produce a mechanism for the purchase of shares or membership interests upon the death, retirement, or withdrawal of a shareholder or member from the corporation or LLC. Buy-sell agreements also enable corporation shareholders or LLC members to achieve the following objectives:

- To provide continuity of ownership and control among the remaining shareholders or members;
- To prevent shareholders or members from unilaterally selling to other parties and thereby upsetting the existing control of the corporation or LLC; and
- To provide a market for the shares or membership interests and to establish their value for federal estate tax and gift tax purposes.

These are the most common events triggering a buyout of a shareholder's shares or member's interests:

- Receipt by a shareholder or member of a bona fide offer from a third party to buy the shares or membership interests, provided the shareholder or member is interested in selling;
- Death;
- Divorce;
- Retirement from active participation in the business of the corporation or LLC;
- Disability; and
- Bankruptcy.

There are generally two methods of buying out a shareholder or member upon a triggering event. One is by a corporate repurchase, known as a *redemption*, and the other is purchase by the remaining shareholders or members, known as a *cross-purchase*. Many buy-sell agree-

> The purpose of buy-sell agreements is to restrict the transfer of shares or membership interests to unwanted outsiders or inactive heirs.

ments are drafted to include both forms: i.e., the corporation or LLC is given the first option to repurchase (redeem), but if unable or unwilling to do so, the remaining shareholders or members have the option to purchase the shares or membership interests. Both methods involve significant legal, tax, and practical considerations that are beyond the scope of this chapter. For example, under California Corporations Code §§500 and 501, a corporation may be prohibited from purchasing its shares depending on its final balance sheet. The basis behind this rule is that if the entity's assets are not significantly higher than its liabilities, any purchase of a shareholder's shares or membership interests could work as a preference when the corporation's shareholders or LLC's members are preferred over its creditors. I therefore recommend consulting with legal counsel to discuss the implications of any corporate stock repurchase before proceeding. Additionally, you may also wish to deal with any issues relating to divorce or dissolution of a domestic partnership in a buy-sell agreement if the shareholders or members are married or registered domestic partners.

To be enforceable, a buy-sell agreement should set forth a mechanism to establish the price at which the shares or membership interests are to be sold upon the triggering event. Any number of methods can be used in this regard. In some buy-sell agreements, the shareholders or members simply agree on a price at the time they enter into the agreement and periodically revise it to reflect changed values. Other agreements leave the price open, to be mutually negotiated by the parties upon the triggering event. Any impasse is then resolved by independent appraisal or third-party arbitration. Finally, some buy-sell agreements provide a formula (e.g., a multiple of annual net earnings over the past three years or a percentage of gross sales) for determining the purchase price for the shares or membership interests.

A sample buy-sell agreement for a corporation with three shareholders is included as Form 6-M. This form, while helpful, is only one way to structure a buy-sell shareholder's agreement. A sample buy-sell form for an LLC is provided in the long-form LLC Operating Agreement (Form 6-L). Before finalizing any buy-sell agreement, the shareholders or members should consider numerous variations concerning timing, valuation, requirement vs. option to exercise, and who controls the option. Your attorney can help you explore all of these variations.

The shareholders or members must consider several other details before drafting and executing a buy-sell agreement. For example, the

> To be enforceable, a buy-sell agreement should set forth a mechanism to establish the price at which the shares or membership interests are to be sold upon the triggering event.

corporation or LLC may wish to fund the purchase price of a shareholder's shares or member's interest through life insurance on each shareholder or member. Additional questions that should also be considered include the following:

- Should any transfers, such as to a shareholder's or member's living trust or beneficiaries, be exempt from the transfer restrictions of the buy-sell agreement?
- Must all of a shareholder's or member's shares be purchased upon the triggering event or may only some be purchased?
- What events will trigger a buyout?
- Should the buyout be mandatory or optional?
- Who controls the option, the shareholders or members or the company?
- Should both sides have the option?
- Will the agreement have a specified term?
- If the effect of the agreement is to create more than one class of stock, will any of the corporation's securities exemptions be jeopardized? What is the effect, if any, on an S corporation election?
- What are the tax objectives and consequences of a particular agreement?
- How will one shareholder's or member's dissolution of marriage or domestic partnership impact the other shareholders or members?
- What about a shareholder's or member's retirement or permanent disability?

The terms of a buy-sell agreement can vary dramatically to reflect the needs of the signatories. The complication is to get everyone to agree. It is recommended that once the terms of a buy-sell are agreed to it be made a condition that any and all new shareholders or members must sign the agreement as a precondition to a change of ownership. This may help avoid ongoing and unproductive debate and renegotiation.

Notes

1. See California Corporations Code §600.
2. See California Corporations Code §600(c).
3. California Corporations Code §602(a).
4. California Corporations Code §600(d).
5. California Corporations Code §708.

6. California Corporations Code §708(b).

7. California Corporations Code §701(a).

8. Revenue and Taxation Code §23301.5.

9. Revenue and Taxation Code §23301.

10. California Corporations Code §2205(a).

11. Revenue and Taxation Code §23304.5.

12. Ibid.

13. Revenue and Taxation Code §19719(a).

14. Revenue and Taxation Code §19141; California Corporations Code §2205(d).

15. Revenue and Taxation Code §23305.

16. Revenue and Taxation Code §23305.1

CHAPTER 7

Corporate and LLC Variations

Statutory Close Corporations

One way to avoid some of the formalities required in maintaining the corporate status is to form a California statutory close corporation. The legislature has recognized that small corporations sometimes operate more informally than large corporations. In providing the close corporation statutes, lawmakers have made it possible for small corporations to bypass many of the usual corporate procedures, yet still maintain corporate status.

Here are the qualifications a corporation must meet in order to benefit from being a statutory close corporation:

1. All shareholders must enter into a shareholders' agreement that must be filed with the secretary of the corporation. The agreement must be available for inspection by prospective buyers of corporate shares.

2. There must be no more than 35 shareholders. Married couples are treated as one shareholder, as are corporations, trusts, partnerships, and other business associations not created solely for the purpose of buying stock in the close corporation.

3. The articles must state that there must be no more than 35

shareholders and must contain the words, "This corporation is a close corporation."

4. The share certificates must feature this paragraph in conspicuous print:

This corporation is a close corporation. The number of holders of record of its shares of all classes cannot exceed 35. Any attempted voluntary inter vivos transfer which would violate this requirement is void. Refer to the articles, bylaws, and any agreements on file with the secretary of the corporation for further restrictions.[1]

By contrast, *closely held* corporations (not to be confused with statutory close corporations) need not have shareholder agreements or stock legends as set forth in the preceding paragraph.[2] In addition, closely held corporations are not subject to the advantages and disadvantages of statutory close corporations, as stated below.

Advantages of Close Corporations

Non-observance of corporate formalities cannot be a basis for piercing the corporate veil. A close corporation may dispense with annual election of directors, annual meetings of shareholders, and regular meetings of the board of directors.

By written unanimous agreement, the shareholders can bypass the board of directors in decision-making.

The shareholders can enter into a voting agreement without being subject to the formalities normally imposed by voting trust requirements.

Close corporation status may facilitate control by persons owning less than a majority of the shares.

A close corporation permits profit splits disproportionate to share ownership.

Disadvantages of Close Corporations

A written shareholders' agreement must be prepared, negotiated, and filed with the secretary of the corporation. This can add additional expense and delay the start-up process.

The shares of the corporation will be less marketable, due to the restrictions imposed on transferability by the statute and by the shareholders' agreement.

The limitation of 35 or fewer shareholders can be jeopardized by

A close corporation may dispense with annual election of directors, annual meetings of shareholders, and regular meetings of the board of directors.

involuntary acts, as well as by actions of third parties. For example, if a shareholder dies having willed his shares to several people, the number of shareholders may then exceed 35 and statutory close corporation status will be lost. Likewise, divorce can affect the shareholder count.

Corporate formalities are avoidable only insofar as specifically mandated in the bylaws and in the shareholders' agreement. Should you choose to use this entity, it is advisable that you consult an attorney, since there are legal limitations on what shareholders may accomplish through the shareholders' agreement. Additionally, lenders often require that resolutions by the board of directors be passed or that other formalities be observed by close corporations before a loan may be processed.

Even though lack of corporate formalities cannot be a basis for piercing the corporate veil, other grounds for a finding of personal liability, such as undercapitalization or failure to issue stock, can still apply.

Although shareholders' agreements may dispense with corporate formalities if the shareholders usurp the directors' powers, shareholders may nevertheless be exposed to personal liability for actions that would normally be attributable to the directors.

If the shareholders' agreement provides for profits to be distributed to some stockholders in disproportion to the amount of stock owned, the corporation may then be deemed to have more than one class of stock and may thereby lose its S corporation status or its exemption from securities law 25102(h). (Note that this does not apply to 25102(f) status.) Forms 7-A and 7-B provide guidelines for drafting articles of incorporation for a statutory close corporation.

In regular corporations, the shareholders must own at least one-third of the total outstanding shares to be able to initiate an involuntary dissolution of the corporation. In close corporations, any shareholder may seek such remedy, regardless of the number of shares he or she holds.

The shareholders of a statutory close corporation may alter or waive the statutory requirements of governance of the corporation and establish their own rules of conduct for managing the corporation. If the formalities of separate corporate existence, such as board authorization of corporate actions, prove too difficult to live by, they may be changed by shareholders' agreements. The shareholders may prefer, for example, that the corporation be governed more like a partnership, whose owners have equal management powers. Such an agreement is permitted as long as it is executed in writing, voted upon unanimously, and properly filed with the corporation's secretary.

> Corporate formalities are avoidable only insofar as specifically mandated in the bylaws and in the shareholders' agreement.

In addition, shareholders' agreements provide other advantages to dispensing with the formalities of directors' and shareholders' meetings in connection with corporate management. The shareholders may provide for a division of profits or distribution of assets upon liquidation in a manner other than in proportion to shareholdings. Shareholders' agreements are also frequently used to establish share transfer restrictions or buyout agreements. In so doing, the shareholders may control ownership of the corporation and the identities of their associates. Shareholders' agreements may also provide that either the shareholders or the corporation can purchase the shares of a retiring, withdrawing, or deceased shareholder.

A shareholders' agreement, however, is not necessarily a cure for all procedural corporate requirements. Some statutory requirements of corporate management may not be waived. Also, it is not always clear what impact variations from statutory corporate formalities may have upon a court's decision to pierce the corporate veil.

For example, when shareholders begin to assume management powers or take management action, they also assume the liability of the board of directors and officers for breaches of the duties of care and loyalty to the corporation. Because of these problems, and recognizing that a shareholders' agreement must be specially drafted to satisfy the needs of a particular situation, I recommend consulting an attorney before you decide to utilize a statutory close corporation vehicle. I rarely advise my clients to become a statutory close corporation.

Shareholders' agreements are also frequently used to establish share transfer restrictions or buyout agreements.

Professional Corporations

A "profession" for purposes of incorporation is generally defined as a licensed business activity, such as the practice of law or medicine. Traditionally, these professions were not allowed to incorporate because California did not want to distance the relationship between a professional and his or her client. Now, however, incorporation is permitted.

As a precautionary measure, however, these professions are often subject to additional and more rigid incorporation requirements. This book is concerned only with the legalities of general incorporation and is not intended for use in incorporating certain professional businesses. It does not address the additional requirements peculiar to incorporating particular professional businesses. Professions that are not subject to the additional requirements of professional corporations may incorporate as described in this book.

Specific Provisions of Corporate Law

As a general rule, professional corporations are subject to the same general corporation law as other corporations. In addition, however, there are special provisions of the law specifically applicable to professional corporations. For instance, all professional corporations are governed by the Moscone-Knox Professional Corporation Act.[3] Such corporations are also subject to those sections of the Business and Professions Code that specifically regulate the particular profession being practiced by the professional corporation.

Professional corporations are also subject to the regulations of the agency charged with licensing the particular profession. Such requirements make the incorporation of a "profession" much more complex and more difficult than the incorporation of other businesses. For example, the incorporation of a law practice is governed by the Moscone-Knox Act, by Sections 6160 through 6172 of the Business and Professions Code, and by the law corporation rules of the California State Bar. These laws and rules require, for example, that the articles of incorporation name the profession to be practiced in corporate form (such as the word "incorporated") and specify that the corporation is a "professional corporation."

Other requirements for incorporating a law practice include:

- A certificate of registration from the State Bar;
- The sale or transfer of shares in the event of death or disqualification of a shareholder;
- Special annual reporting requirements; and
- A shareholders' requirement to guarantee payment of claims against the corporation up to a specified amount.

In general, professionals may not limit their own malpractice liability by using a corporate structure. Individuals may, however, limit their personal liability for malpractice of their associates.[4] There are some exceptions:

- The assets of the corporation will remain liable for all corporate obligations.
- The personal assets of the employee performing and supervising the work remain subject to any malpractice obligations arising from it.

Apart from the malpractice obligations, stockholders may enjoy limited personal liability for the non-professional service obligations, e.g. rent, office supplies, and loans.

> Professional corporations are also subject to the regulations of the agency charged with licensing the particular profession.

Restrictions

In addition, professional corporations are subject to a myriad of significant restrictions, including the following:

- The name of the corporation must be restricted to the names of the shareholders and must identify the corporate existence through the use of the word "incorporated";
- The ownership of shares is restricted to only "licensed" persons;
- There are restrictions on who may be an officer or director of the corporation;
- There are restrictions on share transfers, which must appear on the share certificates; and
- The corporation may engage in other business only if permitted by that profession's governing board.

The requirements for incorporating a business as a professional corporation will vary according to the applicable rules and regulations. Over the years, the number of professions that may be incorporated as professional corporations has increased greatly. I recommend that you consult Corporations Code Section 13401.5 before making any assumptions that your profession may be incorporated as a regular corporation or as a professional corporation. The following is a partial list of professions that may be incorporated as professional corporations:

accounting	nursing
acupuncture	optometry
architecture	osteopathy
audiology	pharmacology
chiropractic	physician assistants
clinical social work	physical therapy
dentistry	podiatry
law	psychology
marriage, family, and child counseling	shorthand reporting
medicine	speech pathology

Since there are so many complexities involved, if you want to incorporate one of the professional businesses listed above, I recommend that you first consult with an attorney.

Limited Liability Partnerships

California recently allowed accountants, architects, and lawyers to set

Over the years, the number of professions that may be incorporated as professional corporations has increased greatly.

up a new limited liability form of business called a *limited liability partnership* (LLP). All owners of such entities must be licensed, registered, or authorized to practice the profession the company engages in either in California or in another jurisdiction. There are different rules for each permitted program to set up an LLP. Besides filing with the California Secretary of State, an LLP must comply with all applicable registration and filing requirements of the board, commission, or other agency regulating the particular profession.[5] An LLP must have a written agreement and the name of the LLP must contain the words "Registered Limited Liability Partnership" or "Limited Liability Partnership" or some abbreviation thereof, e.g., LLP, L.L.P., R.L.L.P, or RLLP. LLPs are not required to file fictitious business name statements in the county in which they do business. An $800 minimum franchise tax fee is due annually on the date the LLP's return is due.

The major advantage of using an LLP is that the owners can immunize themselves from personal liability for malpractice committed by the other owners, unless they are involved in a supervisory capacity. In return for this protection, an LLP must maintain one or more types of security to respond to malpractice claims.[6] The security may be in the form of malpractice insurance, cash, cash equivalent, or any combination of the foregoing. The required coverage amounts are as follows:

- $100,000 for each licensed person (including nonpartners) rendering professional services on behalf of the LLP.
- $500,000 in minimum collateral for an LLP with fewer than five licensed persons.

LLPs may also satisfy the security requirement by filing an annual statement with the Secretary of State showing assets of at least $15 million for attorneys and $10 million for accountants and architects.

Single-Member LLCs

When California initially authorized LLCs, there was a requirement that there must be at least two owners before a business could qualify as an LLC. It was not possible to have a single-member LLC. This requirement changed as of January 1, 2000.

The advantage of a single-member LLC is that a separate LLC tax return is not required. All of the income and expenses of the business may be reflected on the sole member's personal tax return on a Schedule C. If an entity has only one owner, it can elect to be taxed as a

The major advantage of using an LLP is that the owners can immunize themselves from personal liability for malpractice committed by the other owners.

corporation (in which case the owner may want to file an S election). If the choice is made not to be taxed as a corporation, the entity is ignored for federal income tax purposes and taxed as a sole proprietorship. This may at first appear an attractive option; however, in some instances it can become problematic. Personal tax returns are usually difficult to obtain in litigation discovery. Obtaining business tax returns when the business is sued is less difficult. When defending a lawsuit in which your business is a named defendant, you may not want the plaintiff and other parties to the lawsuit to have access to information regarding your assets, which may be reflected on your personal return showing the LLC's income and loss.

A married couple can elect to be a single-member or a dual-member LLC by issuing ownership to one or both spouses. If the business is created during the marriage using community property assets, the business will be considered community property (owned equally by both spouses) regardless of whether or not both spouses are listed as the owners.

Notes

1. California Corporations Code §418(c).
2. California Corporations Code §7.1(4).
3. California Corporations Code §§13400-13410.
4. See Business and Professions Code §6160.
5. California Corporations Code §16953(h).
6. California Corporations Code §16956(a)(1)-(3)).

CHAPTER 8

S Corporations

In general, a corporation will be a C corporation by default if an S election is not timely made. A corporation that elects to become an S corporation avoids federal corporate taxation and has all of its profits and losses passed through to the corporate shareholders in proportion to their respective stock ownership. For tax purposes, profits pass through to the shareholders on the last day of the corporation's tax year, whether or not such profits are actually distributed to them. The decision whether or not to make an S corporation election is often one of the most important financial decisions a corporation can make.

Advantages of an S Corporation Election

Shareholders can usually deduct corporate losses on their individual income tax returns subject to basis and passive activity loss limitations and can also claim corporate deduction credits. Consequently, for corporations that expect to incur losses in their initial years, an S corporation election is often advisable, as long as there is other income of an amount and nature sufficient to absorb the shareholders' allocable losses from the S corporation.

An S corporation pays no tax at the federal corporate level and a dramatically reduced tax at the state level. Consequently, shareholders avoid the burden of double taxation involved in the payment of dividends.

Subject to certain caveats, an election may allow corporate income to be spread among family members to minimize the total income tax for the family unit.

If the shareholders are in a lower tax bracket than the corporation, the total tax paid between the individual shareholders and the corporation can be reduced. It should be noted that nonresident shareholders of a California S corporation are taxed for their share of the corporation's income that is attributable to California sources.[1]

Unlike C corporations, S corporations can often use the cash method of accounting.

Disadvantages of an S Election

If the corporation plans to reinvest its profits for several years (e.g., the business has substantial capital needs or will need to reinvest for expansion), an S election may be undesirable, because the individual tax rate paid by S corporation shareholders may be higher than the corporate tax rate. There is no double taxation in an ordinary C corporation if earnings are reinvested rather than distributed.

If the expected losses during start-up will be higher than the shareholders' tax, it may be preferable to keep the losses at the corporate level rather than have them flow to a shareholder who cannot use them.

If an S corporation provides medical insurance for its employees, S corporation shareholder-employees receiving said benefits must include the amount of the premiums on their personal returns as taxable income. To the extent said premiums will be high, a C corporation may be preferable, especially if profits will normally be distributed out as reasonable compensation and bonuses to employees.

S corporations usually are required to use a calendar year rather than a fiscal year for tax purposes.[2]

Unlike LLCs and partnerships, S corporations cannot make special distributions of profit and loss between shareholders.

Unlike LLCs, S corporations are limited as to who may be a shareholder.

Election Requirements

There are certain requirements that must be met before a corporation can elect to be an S corporation:

> If the shareholders are in a lower tax bracket than the corporation, the total tax paid between the individual shareholders and the corporation can be reduced.

- The corporation must be a domestic (U.S.) corporation that is not an ineligible corporation, i.e., not an affiliated corporation as defined in Internal Revenue Code Section 1504(a), a financial institution that is allowed bad debt deductions under Section 585 or 593, an insurance company subject to tax under Subchapter T, or a corporation electing the Puerto Rico and possessions tax credit.
- The corporation must have no more than 75 shareholders. (Married couples are treated as one shareholder.)
- Each shareholder must be an individual, estate, or specified type of trust. No shareholder can be a nonresident alien, corporation, partnership, or limited liability company.
- The corporation can have only one class of stock; however, it can have differences in voting rights within that class if it follows certain rules carefully.
- A corporation filing for S status under federal law is deemed to have elected to be treated as an S corporation for California taxes unless the owners elect otherwise in their first California tax return.[3]
- All initial shareholders must agree to make the S election and sign the election form.

How and When to File

Once it has been determined that it is advantageous to make an S corporation election and that the corporation is eligible to make this election, the corporation must file Form 2553, Election by a Small Business Corporation (Form 8-A), with the IRS. The election can be made at any time prior to the election year or on or before the 15th day of the third month of the election year. If the election is not made within this period, it will be treated as made for the next tax year-end after the form is mailed to the IRS.

This "15th day of the third month" standard is often misunderstood. The month in which business was first conducted is month number one. For example, if a corporation started doing business on July 29, July would be the first month and August the second month, so an election would have to be filed on or before September 15, a little more than 45 days after the corporation started doing business! Do not miss this deadline.

Even if the election is made on or before the 15th day of the third month of the election year, it won't be effective until the following taxable year if, during the pre-election period of the election year, either the corporation did not meet one of the requirements for eligibility listed above or anyone holding stock in the corporation, even if they disposed of the stock during the period, failed to consent to the election.

For the purpose of an S corporation election, the corporation's first tax year begins when it issues stock to shareholders, acquires assets, or begins doing business, whichever comes first. Since the IRS is often quite strict about enforcing timely S corporation elections, be sure to pay close attention to the filing requirements and the date your first tax year begins if you want to be sure that the corporation receives S corporation status during its first year. As a precautionary measure, it is advisable that you treat the date on which the corporation's articles of incorporation are filed as the start of the corporation's first tax year.

Please also note that the spouse of the stockholder must also sign the consent, since in California he or she has a community property interest in the stock even if his or her name is not on the stock certificate, provided that the stock was acquired during the marriage with community property assets.

Under the S corporation rules passed at the end of 1982, once an S corporation election has been made, a new shareholder may not terminate it by refusing to consent to the election. An S corporation election can be terminated if the new shareholder owns more than 50 percent of the corporation's stock and elects to revoke the election.

A valid election is effective for the year for which it is made and continues in effect for all later years until it is terminated or voluntarily revoked. An election is terminated or revoked for any of the following reasons:

- Voluntary revocation of the election by consent of the majority of the shareholders;
- Failure of the corporation to continue to satisfy any of the qualification requirements; or
- Having more than 25 percent of the corporation's gross receipts for three successive tax years derived from certain forms of passive income as well as having accumulated earnings and profits from its days as a regular corporation at the end of each such year.

> For the purpose of an S corporation election, the corporation's first tax year begins when it issues stock to shareholders, acquires assets, or begins doing business, whichever comes first.

Inadvertent Termination of S Corporation Eligibility

When a corporation's S corporation eligibility has been terminated unintentionally, the corporation can file a request with the Internal Revenue Service for a reinstatement and determination that the termination was inadvertent.[4] The request must be made in the form of a "private letter ruling request" and must include all relevant facts and circumstances relating to the termination, as well as a detailed explanation supporting the corporation's contention that the termination was inadvertent.

Notwithstanding the terminating event, the corporation may nonetheless continue to be treated as an S corporation during the period of consideration by the Internal Revenue Service if the IRS ultimately finds that:

- The termination was truly inadvertent;
- Within a reasonable period of time after discovering the terminating event, the corporation took steps to correct the event so that the corporation again qualifies as an S corporation; and
- The corporation and all of the shareholders agree to make any adjustments requested by the Internal Revenue Service to resume treatment as an S corporation.

Requests for determination of inadvertent termination of S corporation status can be made to the associate chief counsel of the IRS:

Internal Revenue Service
Associate Chief Counsel (Technical)
Attn: CC:PS
1111 Constitution Avenue
Washington, DC 20224

Please note that, should there be a flaw in making the initial S election (for example, stock being issued to an ineligible shareholder), the S election is fatally flawed and cannot be remedied by an application for inadvertent termination. This is because an S election must be effective before it can be terminated. Be very careful, therefore, that everything is proper and in order before first making an S election. The adverse tax consequences can be devastating.

Requesting a Determination

The process for requesting determination for inadvertent termination as

> Be very careful that everything is proper and in order before first making an S election. The adverse tax consequences can be devastating.

well as obtaining a favorable IRS ruling can be very complex. I recommend, therefore, that the corporation retain competent legal counsel to assist it in this process.

Once an election has been revoked or terminated, the general rule is that a new election may not be made until the fifth tax year beginning after the revocation or termination. However, the IRS may consent to an earlier re-election upon application. It should be noted that an attempt to come within the S corporation provisions in favorable years and outside it in other years will not succeed.

Taxation of S Corporations

The 1986 Tax Reform Act repealed the General Utilities rule, which provided that a corporation does not recognize gain or loss on a sale or distribution of assets pursuant to a plan of complete liquidation. If a regular corporation (a C corporation) converts to an S corporation, a corporate-level tax will be imposed in the event of a sale of a corporation's assets on any gain arising before the conversion and will be recognized through sale or distribution within ten years of the conversion. Gains will be presumed to have occurred before the conversion, except to the extent that the corporation can demonstrate otherwise. Consequently, a reputable appraisal at the date of conversion is well advised. Corporations that made an S election prior to 1987 avoided this new ten-year rule on gains with respect to appreciation in the assets before conversion.

It should be considered, however, that no gain or loss will be recognized to the liquidating corporation on its distribution to an 80 percent distributee of any property in a complete liquidation to which IRC Section 332 applies.[5] The property received by the corporate shareholder will have the same basis as the liquidating corporation's basis in the property. Thus the gain, if any, will be recognized by the corporate shareholder if and when he, she, or it disposes of the distributed property.

There are several exceptions to this rule, which are not within the scope of this book. Needless to say, if the assets of a corporation will be subject to substantial appreciation, tax-planning advice is recommended before incorporation, the dissolution of corporate assets to shareholders, and liquidation.

The IRS requires S corporations to adopt a calendar year, unless the IRS gives express permission to adopt a fiscal year. Such permission

It should be noted that an attempt to come within the S corporation provisions in favorable years and outside it in other years will not succeed.

may be obtained by demonstrating to the IRS that a valid business reason exists for such fiscal year and that it is not being adopted for tax-deferral purposes.

The California Franchise Tax Law was amended in 1987 to allow a corporation to elect to be taxed as an S corporation. Once a corporation has made a federal S election, it will be considered to have made a California state S election unless it files a contrary notice with the Franchise Tax Board. (Even if the corporation is an S corporation for federal purposes, it can remain a regular corporation for California Franchise Tax purposes.) As indicated above, a corporation cannot go back and forth between S corporation status and C corporation status. Once a revocation of S status occurs, the corporation usually has to wait five years before it can make another election (subject to certain relief for unintentional terminations).

Further, California S corporations must:

- Provide a list of nonresident shareholders to the Franchise Tax Board on FTB Form 3830 (Form 8-B); and
- Require each nonresident shareholder to file a statement with the Franchise Tax Board consenting to the jurisdiction of California to tax his or her pro rata share of income attributable to California sources. Nonresident shareholders of an S corporation may elect to file as a single group.

The California rules for S corporations generally follow the federal rules. One significant difference, however, is that, unlike the federal rules, the California rules state that there is still a tax imposed on the corporation (in addition to the tax on the individual shareholders) at a rate of 1.5 percent of corporate net income. Oftentimes, the decision between being an S corporation and being an LLC will focus on the difference between the California tax rates for LLCs (which are based on gross revenue rather than net income) and the California tax rates for S corporations. Prior to making a final decision on your choice of entities, you should compare prospective calculations of state taxes.

This discussion of S corporations is intended to be very general in nature. The rules relative to S corporations are complicated. If you are considering making an S corporation election, you may want to consult with an accountant or attorney who is familiar with all of the intricacies.

Oftentimes, the decision between being an S corporation and being an LLC will focus on the difference between the California tax rates for LLCs and the California tax rates for S corporations.

Notes

1. See Revenue and Taxation Code §23801(b).
2. Internal Revenue Code §441.
3. Revenue and Taxation Code §23801(a).
4. Internal Revenue Code §1362.
5. Revised Internal Revenue Code §337.

CHAPTER 9

Limited Liability Companies

I n 1988, the Internal Revenue Service began to recognize limited liability companies (LLCs) as business entities that can be taxed as partnerships. California recognized the LLC as a business entity beginning on September 30, 1994. The potential benefit of the LLC is that it not only provides the taxation benefits of a partnership—no double taxation on profits—but also offers business owners the limited liability of a corporation.

The following discussion is intended to provide a general overview on the formation and operation of LLCs. In many instances, you are well advised to consult with competent legal counsel before attempting to form or operate an LLC. Although some LLC organizational forms prescribed by the Secretary of State's office have been provided in the Forms section of this book, these forms merely meet the statutory requirements under the California LLC law. Also provided are two sample forms for an LLC operating agreement, which may need to be altered or redrafted to satisfy federal and state income tax requirements to ensure partnership tax treatment for the new LLC and to satisfy other business or legal objectives.

One very important limitation on the use of an LLC: a business required to be licensed, certified, or registered under the California Business and Professions Code generally *cannot* be formed or operate as an LLC. Lawyers and accountants cannot operate as an LLC but may set up a form of entity called a *limited liability partnership* or LLP.[1]

Forming a Limited Liability Company

One or more persons—called *members* rather than *shareholders*—are required to form and operate an LLC. Unlike S corporations, members of LLCs can be foreign persons, nonresidents, or business entities like corporations, partnerships, or other limited liability companies. Furthermore, while S corporations have limitations on the maximum number of permissible shareholders, LLCs do not have comparable limitation on the maximum number of members.

Taxation of an LLC

As mentioned above, LLCs, if properly structured, enjoy pass-through (single-level) tax advantages similar to partnerships and S corporations for federal income tax purposes. One major difference between LLCs and S corporations is that S corporations pay a 1.5 percent state tax on California source net income (profits), subject to a minimum franchise tax of $800 (with the minimum tax waived during the first calendar year). In contrast, LLCs must pay a graduated state fee based upon California source gross revenue in excess of $250,000, plus an $800 minimum franchise tax (starting in the first calendar year). The LLC gross revenue fee structure is as follows:

Total Revenue	Fee Amount
$0 to $250,000	$800
$250,000 to $499,999	$1,700
$500,000 to $999,999	$3,300
$1,000,000 to $4,999,999	$6,800
$5,000,000 or more	$12,590

Consequently, from a California state tax perspective, if your business will have substantial gross income but only modest profit, an S corporation may be more attractive. If the gross revenue will be modest but the profit margin will be high, an LLC might provide a better mechanism for minimizing California taxes. Your accountant can best advise you as to the California tax consequences of forming as an LLC.

One or more persons, called members rather than shareholders, are required to form and operate an LLC.

Articles of Organization

As a general proposition, an LLC is formed by filing articles of organization with the California Secretary of State. (See Form 9-A or go to www.ss.ca.gov/business/llc/forms/llc-1.pdf.) This document is the LLC equivalent of a corporation's articles of incorporation. There is currently a $70 fee for filing the articles of organization, which can only be filed with the main Sacramento office of the Secretary of State, not at any of the regional offices:

> As a general proposition, an LLC is formed by filing articles of organization with the California Secretary of State.

Secretary of State
Document Filing Support Unit
1500 11th Street, 3rd Floor
P.O. Box 944228
Sacramento, CA 94244-2280
916 657-5448

Because of sometimes substantial backlogs in filings at the Secretary of State's office, particularly early in the calendar year, you may wish to arrange for faster handling via over-the-counter filing (for an additional fee of $15), either in person or using a private service company. Unfortunately, it is not unusual for the Secretary of State to be so backed up on LLC filings that it can take four to six weeks after submission before you receive confirmation of filing. The names of various private filing services may be found at www.ss.ca.gov/business/bpd_service_companies.htm. The service company will charge an additional fee.

Naming Your LLC

The name of any new LLC must contain the initials "LLC" or the phrase "Limited Liability Company." As with corporate names, the Secretary of State will not accept any new LLC name that is so similar to an already existing LLC that the public is likely to be misled or confused. In some instances, the Secretary of State may nonetheless accept a similar name upon proof of consent from the existing LLC if the Secretary determines that, under the circumstances, the public is not likely to be misled. Finally, as with corporations, LLC names can be reserved in advance with the Secretary of State's office for a fee of $10. The name reservation is good for a period of 60 days. To reserve a name, send a letter containing the proposed LLC name and a $10 check to the Document Filing Support Unit of the Secretary of State at the address indicated above. It has been my experience that some names are not available for incorporation but can be used for an LLC. This can, however, create problems in the area of trademark and/or service mark infringement. (See Chapter 12.)

Management Structure

When filing your articles of organization, you must designate whether your LLC will be managed by one manager, more than one manager, or all members.

If your LLC will have only one member or a small number of members who will all actively share in management responsibilities, it may be simplest to elect management by all members. This is the structure reflected in the sample short-form operating agreement described below and included as Form 9-B. Under this structure, each member has authority to enter into commitments that are binding on the LLC and the other members.

If there will be members who are not actively sharing in management, it may be preferable to designate management by one manager or more than one manager, rather than all members. In this case, a more elaborate form of operating agreement will be required. This form of operating agreement must describe how the manager is selected and the responsibilities and limitations on authority of a manager. An example of a form of operating agreement for a manager-managed LLC is included as Form 9-C. Managers may be members of the LLC, but are not required to be.

> When filing your articles of organization, you must designate whether your LLC will be managed by one manager, more than one manager, or all members.

Statement of Information

Once the articles of organization are filed, the new LLC has 90 days in which to file a Statement of Information with the Secretary of State. (See Form 9-D or go to www.ss.ca.gov/business/llc/forms/llc-12.pdf.) A copy of this form is initially provided with the certified copy of the articles of organization and is thereafter mailed by the Secretary of State to the LLC biannually for filing. There is a $20 filing fee for this form. Failure to file this form on a timely basis can lead to substantial penalties and to suspension by the Secretary of State.

Operating an LLC

Whereas the internal operations of corporations are governed by bylaws, the internal operations of LLCs are governed by operating agreements. Because LLCs are taxed as partnerships, operating agreements tend to be more similar to partnership agreements than to corporate bylaws. As with corporate bylaws, however, operating agreements are maintained internally and never filed with the Secretary of State's office.

Operating agreements can be oral or written. It is, however, recommended that they be written to avoid future disputes over interpretation and provide grater protection and specificity than statutory provision, which will be controlling in the absence of any other agreement.[2] When written, the operating agreement is signed by all of the initial members of the LLC, who thereafter hold an organizational meeting similar to the first meeting of the board of directors of a new corporation. Members may manage the LLC themselves or elect managers (who are not necessarily members) to be responsible for the day-to-day operations of the LLC.

Since LLCs are still relatively new in California, there is little legal authority as to operating agreements and the obligations of members and managers of the LLCs. A strong argument can be made that these obligations are similar to those of a partner in a partnership, at least with respect to managers of the LLC.[3] Although in time the courts and the legal profession will reach a consensus on acceptable forms and variations of LLC operating agreements, until then I strongly recommend retaining competent legal counsel for purposes of setting up an LLC and drafting the operating agreement. Sample forms of LLC operating agreements based on models published by the Business Law Section of the State Bar of California, and included by permission, are included as Forms 9-B and 9-C.

In addition to filing articles of organization and signing an operating agreement, you may need to file a fictitious business name statement (if conducting business under a different name) and a report of new employees (Form DE 34). These requirements are similar to those described for corporations in Chapter 3. You also need to capitalize the LLC and make the required securities law filings as described in Chapter 4. You should also review the following section regarding securities law issues specific to LLCs. Finally, it may be appropriate to enter into a buy-sell agreement among the members (see discussion in Chapter 6), unless these provisions are incorporated into the LLC oper-

> Since LLCs are still relatively new in California, there is little legal authority as to operating agreements and the obligations of members and managers of the LLCs.

ating agreement. Most of the post-incorporation steps set forth in Chapter 3 will also apply to LLCs (except the subchapter S election).

Securities Law Considerations

Under the California Limited Liability Company Act, there is a presumption that membership interests in an LLC are securities for state law purposes. There is a statutory exception, however, for a membership interest in an LLC if all members are actively engaged in the management of the LLC. Please note, however, that the right to vote or to participate in management, without more, is not sufficient to qualify for this exception. As a result, whether or not a membership interest in an LLC will be considered to be a security depends on the particular management characteristics of each LLC. In many situations, the offer, sale, issuance, or transfer of LLC membership interests is subject to California securities laws, requiring either the qualification of the transaction or perfection of an exemption applicable to the transaction.

Federal securities laws do not have the same presumption as California law that membership interests in an LLC are a security. However, just as with the state securities laws, the management characteristics of each LLC will determine whether or not the membership interest will be considered a security. If the federal authorities consider the membership interest to be a security, then a transaction involving that interest must either be registered or qualify for an exemption. The discussion of securities law issues contained in Chapter 4 (including the discussion of California Section 25102(f), but not the discussion of Section 25102(h)) is applicable to LLC membership interests that constitute securities.

The determination of whether an LLC membership interest is or is not a security is very fact-specific and should be reviewed on a case-specific basis. Consequently, you should consult competent legal counsel on this matter before issuing any membership interests. In the event of a close call, it is always preferable to assume that the securities laws apply and proceed accordingly.

Converting or Merging an Existing Business Entity into an LLC

Should the shareholders or partners of an existing business entity wish to convert their business entity into an LLC, they may perform either a conversion or a merger into an LLC formed for this purpose. Under the

California Limited Liability Company Act, corporations, limited partnerships, general partnerships, business trusts, real estate investment trusts, or unincorporated associations (other than nonprofit organizations) may merge or be converted into an LLC.

Generally, to merge a business entity into an LLC, the parties to the merger must approve an agreement of merger, file a certificate of merger with the California Secretary of State, and obtain a tax clearance certificate from the California Franchise Tax Board. The merger will be effective upon the filing of the certificate of merger, unless the certificate specifies another future date.

Just as with mergers, an existing business entity may be converted into an LLC. However, depending on the type of business entity, the conversion process may be rather involved and may result in certain adverse tax consequences. For example, the conversion of an existing C corporation into an LLC is treated by the IRS as liquidation of the corporation followed by a contribution to a partnership, which in most cases results in a taxable recognition of gain for the LLC members. Therefore, persons wishing to change the existing form of their business entity should carefully select the conversion method that minimizes gain and other adverse tax consequences. Speak with a competent tax consultant before undertaking a conversion or a merger of an existing business entity into an LLC. It should also be noted that it is often possible to convert an LLC to a corporation (but not the reverse) without generating a tax liability. Before attempting such a conversion, however, you should seek professional advice of a qualified attorney and/or accountant.

Notes

1. California Corporations Code §§15001-15046.
2. California Corporations Code §§17001 and 17050.
3. California Corporations Code §17153.

CHAPTER 10

Taxes

A lthough this book is not designed to be a treatise on corporate or LLC tax planning, here are a few general pointers regarding some of the applicable federal and state tax filing requirements and ramifications inherent in the operation of a corporation or an LLC. Remember: all federal and state employment taxes are computed on a calendar year basis, regardless of the business's fiscal year. Due to the complexity and ever-changing nature of state and federal taxation, I recommend that the business retain an accountant or a qualified tax attorney (or both) for more specific advice in this area.

Corporations

State Taxes

Payment of Estimated Taxes—Corporations. Shortly after filing your articles of incorporation, you should receive a Corporate Estimated Tax Form, Form 100-ES, from the California Franchise Tax Board (Form 10-A). Read the instructions enclosed with the form to determine when the form should be filed and how it should be completed. The minimum franchise tax fee is generally $800. A newly formed or "qualified newer corporation" is not subject to this minimum tax for the first year. Thereafter, it is subject to such minimum tax. Payment of the estimated tax with

Form 100-ES is a prepayment of the tax estimated to be due with the initial franchise tax return of the corporation. However, newly formed corporations are still required to make declarations of estimated tax for the first year of existence. Such declarations are based on the expected tax of the corporation, computed net of any applicable credits, for the first taxable year. Note that the corporation franchise tax reported on the initial franchise tax return is for the right to do business in the second tax year.

The estimated tax payments for the first year of the corporation are calculated using an anticipated corporate tax year-end. The actual year-end of the corporation is determined when the election of an annual accounting period is made by filing the initial tax return (Form 100 or 100S). The state tax year must coincide with the federal tax year. There are certain restrictions on the ability of certain corporations (primarily personal service corporations, as defined in the Internal Revenue Service) to adopt a non-calendar year-end. In California, any profits made by an S corporation are taxed at a rate of 1.5 percent. C corporations are taxed at the corporate franchise tax rate of 8.8 percent. Both S and C corporations receive credit for the paid minimum $800 franchise tax fee when paying any additional tax.

When to File. The return must be filed on or before the 15th day of the third month following the close of the tax year. Payment of any portion of tax due that was not paid during the tax year must accompany the filing of this return. The corporation may be subject to the imposition of penalties if the sum of the estimated tax payment made during the tax year is less than 90 percent of the tax shown on the annual return.

The state of California also has adopted rules that allow a corporation to elect S corporation status. These provisions are discussed in Chapter 8.

State Employment Taxes

Upon hiring its first employee(s), the corporation will be subject to all California tax withholding laws and the California unemployment insurance code. Income taxes and state disability insurance payments (SDI) must be withheld from all employees' paychecks. The corporation must register with the California Employment Development Department (EDD) within 15 days after becoming subject to the unemployment insurance code and the California personal income tax withholding law by filing Form DE 1 (Form 10-B). Upon registration, the corporation will be assigned an account number that must be used on

> The estimated tax payments for the first year of the corporation are calculated using an anticipated corporate tax year-end.

all subsequent withholding return forms.

For further information on withholding, contributing, paying, and reporting state employment taxes, including unemployment and disability insurance, you may want to obtain the *California Employer's Guide* (DE 44) from:

State of California
Employment Development Department
P.O. Box 826880
Sacramento, CA 94280-0001
It is also available online:
www.edd.ca.gov/taxrep/taxform.htm#Publications.

An accountant can be of great assistance in this area in addition to the *California Employer's Guide*, which may be obtained from the tax web site at www.ftb.ca.gov.

Sales and Use Tax

All California corporations that engage in retail sales or in transactions subject to the California Sales and Use Tax must obtain a seller's permit (see Form 10-C) from the State Board of Equalization (BOE). The BOE has field offices located throughout the state. (A list is provided in the information appearing on the back of Form 10-C.) It is the corporation's responsibility to collect all state, local, and district sales and use taxes. The state board has many pamphlets that describe the sales tax rules as they relate to various industries, as well as general filing requirements. It will send them to you upon request.

A wholesaler, just like a retailer, must obtain a sales and use tax permit. However, a wholesaler is not required to collect sales tax from a retailer in possession of a valid seller's permit, as long as a resale certificate is completed documenting the transaction on Form 10-D.

The corporation must file a state, local, and district Sales and Use Tax Return within 30 days after the end of the fiscal quarter. Sales taxes are generally required to be paid quarterly; however, the State Board of Equalization may require that they be paid monthly. The BOE will provide the forms that are used to calculate the tax prior to the dates they should be submitted. The return, which reports all sales taxes collected over the period, must be accompanied with a check in payment of the taxes owed.

It is important that your corporation keep accurate and detailed records of all business transactions, including sales receipts, purchases,

> All California corporations that engage in retail sales or in transactions subject to the California Sales and Use Tax must obtain a seller's permit.

and other expenditures. Any questions on the imposition of sales taxes can be addressed to the local office of the State Board of Equalization.

It must be noted, however, that state tax forms, just like the federal tax forms, change annually. Always make it a point to check to make certain that the forms your corporation uses are current. Further information can be found at www.boe.ca.gov.

Corporations using a non-calendar year-end must file corporation franchise tax and U.S. corporate income tax returns on the forms for the year that the fiscal year begins. The year of the form is usually in the upper right corner of the document.

Federal Taxes

Immediately after filing the articles of incorporation, the corporation should apply for a federal Employer Identification Number (EIN) by filling out IRS Form SS-4. (See Form 10-E.) The completed form should be sent to the IRS Service Center in the region specified in the instructions for Form SS-4 (www.irs.gov/pub/irs-pdf/iss4.pdf). You may also obtain an EIN by telephone (800 829-4933) or by fax. See the IRS web site at www.irs.gov for the fax number. The corporation must thereafter use its EIN on all of its federal tax forms.

Every corporation is responsible for withholding income taxes and Social Security—Federal Insurance Contributions Act (FICA)—and Medicare taxes from wages paid to its employees. A word to the wise: treat employees as employees. Many small corporations try to establish their workers as independent contractors instead of as employees in an effort to avoid the problem of withholding taxes and paying employment taxes. Corporations that are undercapitalized or having cash flow problems have also been known to pay other creditors in preference to paying withholding taxes to the IRS. These are very dangerous practices that can cause the IRS to impose substantial penalties on the corporation as well as on its principals equal to the full amount of the delinquent tax plus interest and penalties. Penalties can even be assessed on non-principal employees having the authority to direct the expenditure of cash. If it does not pay employee withholding taxes, the business can even be closed by the taxing authorities.

It is also recommended that you obtain from the IRS the *Employer's Tax Guide*, Publication 15 (Circular E), for an in-depth explanation of all federal withholding, paying, depositing, and reporting requirements. Further, a reading of Form SS-8, Determination of Worker Status for

Corporations using a non-calendar year-end must file corporation franchise tax and U.S. corporate income tax returns on the forms for the year that the fiscal year begins.

Purposes of Federal Employment Taxes and Income Tax Withholding, is helpful (Form 10-F).

Upon employment, each employee must fill out Form W-4, Employee's Withholding Allowance Certificate (Form 10-G). This form lists numbers of dependents and marital status, which affects the amount of individual income taxes the corporation is required to withhold from an employee's wages.

Social Security Tax

Social Security (FICA) tax is to be withheld from each employee's wages for the 2005 calendar year at a rate of 6.2 percent of the employee's wages, up to $90,000. Additionally, 1.45 percent of the employee's wages, without limitation, is withheld for Medicare (Old-Age, Survivors, and Disability Insurance—OASDI). The employer is also required to match the FICA and Medicare contributions for each employee. The corporation is also required to prepare quarterly payroll tax returns by filing IRS Form 941 (Form 10-H). This form sets forth all income, Social Security, and Medicare taxes withheld from employees' wages, as well as the corporation's Social Security and Medicare tax contributions. The form must be filed by the last day of the month following the close of each calendar quarter. The IRS should send the blank form to the corporation prior to each due date. However, if the IRS fails to send the form to the corporation, that is not an adequate reason for the corporation to fail to file the form on time.

The corporation is responsible for computing the total amount of compensation paid to each employee during the calendar year. The corporation must prepare forms W-2 (Form 10-I) showing total wages paid to and taxes withheld from each employee. A copy of the W-2 form must be distributed to each employee and to the Social Security Administration along with transmittal Form W-3 (Form 10-J).

Deposits of federal income taxes withheld and employee and employer Social Security and Medicare taxes are made to the Internal Revenue Service based on a schedule set forth in the *Employer's Tax Guide* (Circular E). All deposits must be accompanied by a Federal Tax Deposit Coupon, Form 8109-B (Form 10-K), which can be found in the Federal Tax Deposit Coupon Book supplied by the IRS after the corporation submits Form SS-4. For a more detailed explanation of the federal depository requirements, refer to the *Employer's Tax Guide* (Circular E). You should note that when deposit amounts (both corporate income tax and employment tax withholdings) exceed $200,000, the corporation is required to utilize electronic funds transfers to the Department of the Treasury.

Your corporation will also be responsible for paying Federal Unemployment Tax (FUTA) if, during a current or preceding year, the corporation:

- Paid wages of $1,500 or more in a calendar quarter; or
- Had one or more employees for some portion of at least one day during each of 20 different calendar weeks (not necessarily consecutive).

Unemployment insurance taxes are paid by the corporation, not withheld from employees' wages. Starting in 1998, the tax rate was 6.2 percent (before credits) on the first $7,000 of wages paid to a covered employee during the calendar year. A state credit of up to 5.4 percent is allowed. Thus, the FUTA liability may be as low as 0.8 percent. Similar to federal withholding taxes, there are periodic reports and deposits that must be filed. Refer to your *Employer's Tax Guide* and Form 940 instructions for specifics.

Federal Income Tax

A regular for-profit (Subchapter C) corporation is required to file an annual corporate income tax return (IRS Form 1120 or Form 1120A) on or before the 15th day of the third month following the close of its calendar or fiscal tax year. The tax year must be the same as the accounting year and is formally established upon the filing of the first corporate tax return.

If so desired, the first tax year can be shorter than 12 months. For example, a corporation established in June can select the calendar year instead of a fiscal year. Consequently, its first return would be for a short year, June through December. There are restrictions on the ability of certain corporations (primarily personal service corporations) to use a non-calendar year for income tax reporting. This is especially difficult for S corporations.

If the corporation's annual income tax liability is expected to be $500 or more, the corporation is required to make estimated tax payments. To determine the estimated tax liability, date of submission, and amount of deposit required, use Form 1120-W (Form 10-M). This form is used for computational purposes only. A completed Federal Tax Deposit Form (Form 8109-B), contained in the Federal Tax Deposit

If the corporation's annual income tax liability is expected to be $500 or more, the corporation is required to make estimated tax payments.

Coupon Book, must accompany any payment. You should note that if the deposit of these taxes with the Deposit Form is mailed to the IRS, it must be postmarked at least two days before its due date.

S corporations do not pay federal income tax. Their profits are distributed to the shareholders on a pro-rata basis consistent with ownership interests to be taxed at their respective personal rates pursuant to K-1's issued from the corporation.

The current federal corporate tax rates for C corporations are as follows:

Taxable Income	Tax Rate
$0 -$50,000	15%
$50,001-75,000	25%
$75,001-$100,000	34%
$100,001-$335,000	39%
$335,001-$10,000,000	34%
$10,000,001-$15,000,000	35%
$15,000,001-$18,333,333	38%
Above $18,333,334	35%

Section 1244 Stock. One of the advantages of closely held corporations is that shareholders can treat losses from the sale, exchange, or worthlessness of their stock as an ordinary loss up to a maximum of $50,000 ($100,000 in a joint return) provided that the stock qualifies under Section 1244 of the Internal Revenue Code. Any loss above these limits is treated as a capital loss.

For stock to qualify as Section 1244 stock, it must meet the following requirements:

- The stock must be common or preferred stock of a domestic corporation.
- The stock must be issued in exchange for money or other property (but not stock or securities).
- The issuing corporation must be a small business corporation. This means that the amount of money and other property received by the corporation as a contribution to capital and paid-in surplus must not exceed $1 million. This figure is to be determined at the time the stock is issued.
- During the corporation's five most recent tax years ending before the date the stock is sold by a taxpayer, more than 50 percent of the corporation's gross receipts must come from sources other

than rents, royalties, dividends, interest, annuities, or gains from the sale of securities.

Most of the corporations that are formed by using this book will meet the above qualifications. Consequently, in the Minutes of First Meeting of the Board of Directors (Form 10-N), you will find a resolution whereby the corporate securities are qualified as Section 1244 stock. If, at a later date, it turns out that the stock does not qualify under Section 1244, a shareholder will be allowed only a capital loss, instead of an ordinary loss. One way or another, you should keep this important tax benefit in mind, should a stock loss ever occur.

Limited Liability Companies

In 1994, the legislature of the State of California, by way of the Beverly-Killea Limited Liability Company Act of 1994, allowed taxpayers to form limited liability companies. These entities were designed to employ both traditional corporation and partnership characteristics. In 2000, the law was amended to allow single-member LLCs.

The reader should note that LLCs are not allowed to operate businesses that are registered under the California Business and Professions Code. These businesses are able, however to operate as a *limited liability partnerships* (LLPs). Such entities have specific insurance requirements as well as particular limited liability rules, which are beyond the scope of this volume.

Income Taxes

LLCs are taxed in much the same manner as partnerships and the members have limited liability similar to that of corporate shareholders. An LLC, if not classified as a corporation, is taxed much like a partnership for federal and California income taxation. As such, it generally calculates its income and deductions pursuant to the California personal income tax law. Accordingly, an LLC must file a federal Form 1065, Return of Partnership Income (Form 10-O), and a California Form 568, Limited Liability Company Return of Income (Form 10-P). Generally an LLC is required to have a calendar year that corresponds with the year-end of its members. As such, these returns are due to the taxing authorities on April 15 of the year following the year-end of the LLC.

LLCs filing as partnerships in California are taxed according to the following rates:

> LLCs are taxed in much the same manner as partnerships and the members have limited liability similar to that of corporate shareholders.

Total Income	Tax
$250,000-$499,999	$900
$500,000-$999,999	$2,500
$1,000,000-$4,999,999	$6,000
$5,000,000 or more	$11,790

As stated in Chapter 9, the LLC is taxed based upon its gross receipts. This contrasts greatly from the method used for taxing an S corporation. The S corporation is taxed on its net income after deducting all expenses, including the salaries paid to the owners/officers. Accordingly, you should choose the type of entity based upon the financial results anticipated from the business. For example, if high revenues and low profits are anticipated, an S corporation might be more appropriate than an LLC. If lower revenues but high profits are anticipated, the LLC may be the better choice.

Employment Taxes

The federal and California employment taxes for an LLC are very similar to those of a corporation, with one major exception. That exception is that an LLC, like a partnership, cannot pay wages to its members. Rather, the LLC pays draws and/or guaranteed payments. A draw is a distribution of earnings and capital. A guaranteed payment is a payment to a member that is not calculated based on the profits of the LLC. Neither is subject to the taxes on wages at the LLC level. However, they may be subject to self-employment taxes (with certain limitations) on the members' individual income tax returns. Further, these guaranteed payments, as well as the members' distributive share of the net profits of the LLC, are taxed to the members on their individual income tax returns.

An important element of LLC taxation is that an LLC can allocate the profits or losses of the LLC to its members in ratios that are not proportionally equal to the ownership of the capital of the LLC. The major constraint to this allocation is that the method used for the allocation must have "substantial economic effect" to the members and the LLC without taking tax consequences into effect. For example, an LLC cannot allocate all of the profits to member A and none to member B solely because A is in a lower tax bracket than B. There must be a rational economic reason for such allocation. This is a complex area where you would be well advised to seek the assistance of a qualified accountant.

When choosing the form of entity, you should also take into consideration the local taxing authorities and the manner of the members taking remuneration. Some jurisdictions (San Francisco, for example) have local payroll taxes, which may include guaranteed payments of LLCs.

You should always check with the jurisdiction in which the company is headquartered as well as that in which it may be doing business.

CHAPTER 11

Nonprofit Corporations

The organization and operation of California nonprofit corporations are governed by the California Nonprofit Corporation Act.[1] Other laws, regulations, and codes, such as the Internal Revenue Code, may also govern and control, depending on the type of nonprofit corporation involved. Furthermore, because the law on nonprofit corporations is very complex, the following discussion is intended only as a general description of how to start up, organize, and initially operate a nonprofit corporation. Additional research and reference may be necessary beyond the scope of this chapter. Since there are such complex rules regarding qualification, ongoing businesses, methods of operation, and maintaining tax-exempt status, I recommend that all nonprofit organizations retain competent counsel to assist in the corporation's formation and start-up and an accountant who is familiar with tax exemption applications and other tax-related documentation.

Although there are 27 tax-exemption categories under Internal Revenue Code §501(c) and somewhat fewer under California Revenue and Taxation Code §23701, there are three primary types of nonprofit corporations that are used in most circumstances:

- Public benefit corporation, formed for public or charitable purposes;[2]

- Religious corporation, formed primarily or exclusively for religious purposes;[3] and
- Mutual benefit corporation, formed for the mutual benefit of the corporation's members.[4]

Factors for Choosing the Nonprofit Corporate Form

The availability and choice of nonprofit corporate form will depend upon a number of factors, including:

- The nature and purpose of the corporation's proposed activity;
- The likelihood of obtaining funding through charitable and/or governmental contributions;
- Whether the corporation's members will receive dividends during the course of conduct of the corporation;
- Whether corporate assets will be distributed to members upon dissolution; and
- Whether the tax advantages of qualifying as a nonprofit corporation outweigh the numerous additional costs, restrictions, and regulations otherwise imposed on such corporations. Exempt organizations must prepare periodic filings and reports for various government agencies, which are subject to public inspection and audit. Nonprofit corporations face stringent restrictions on their activities, management, and sources and disposition of assets and income. Perhaps most importantly, a nonprofit cannot inure to the benefit of any private shareholder or individual.[5] Tax-exempt status will not be granted, or will be revoked, if the IRS believes that individuals involved in the organization are personally benefiting from the operation of the corporation through salaries, distributions of profits, or direct collateral benefit to related for-profit enterprises. The bottom line is that business owners should not look at non-profit organization as a tool to minimize their taxation and maximize their profits. It will not work.

> Nonprofit corporations face stringent restrictions on their activities, management, and sources and disposition of assets and income.

Nonprofit Corporations and for-Profit Corporations: Similarities and Differences

Nonprofit corporations have several similarities with regular for-profit corporations. For example, articles of incorporation must be filed with the California Secretary of State. (Note, however, that the articles must contain the requisite restrictive language to be acceptable for a non-profit corporation. See discussion on "Formation," below.) Bylaws must also be adopted. The corporation's officers and directors conduct the day-to-day operations of the corporation, much like regular corporations. Finally, as with shareholders of regular corporations, members of nonprofit corporations enjoy limited personal liability for the debts and liabilities of the corporation.

Nonprofit corporations are distinguished from regular for-profit corporations, however, in many ways. While they may or may not have members, they cannot have shareholders. If the corporation is to be without members, then the board of directors may unilaterally approve all corporate action. On the other hand, if the corporation is to have members, the transferability of memberships is greatly restricted. Also, unlike shares in a regular corporation, memberships in a nonprofit corporation can be issued for little or no financial consideration whatsoever.

It is also worth pointing out that nonprofit corporations are permitted to conduct business for profit. Unlike regular for-profit corporations, however, the profits of a nonprofit corporation cannot be distributed to members, as in the form of dividends, but must instead be reinvested into the corporation.

> Unlike regular for-profit corporations, however, the profits of a nonprofit corporation cannot be distributed to members, as in the form of dividends, but must instead be reinvested into the corporation.

Alternatives to Nonprofits

There are alternatives to nonprofit corporations that may fit your particular needs. Frequently, the costs and administrative burdens of setting up and maintaining a nonprofit outweigh the benefits. For example, for individual donors, it may be better to set up a donor-advanced fund than a stand-alone foundation. It can also be more efficient to establish a fiscal sponsorship relationship with a local community foundation or public charity than to set up a small operating stand-alone nonprofit charity. Some other options that may suit your needs are an unincorporated association or a charitable trust.

Director and Officer Liability in the Nonprofit Context

Because there is a strong public interest in encouraging qualified individuals to volunteer in the nonprofit business context, directors and officers of nonprofit corporations, who serve without compensation, are generally protected by statute against personal liability for actions taken in their corporate capacity.[6] Thus, any director or officer who performs his or her duties in good faith, in a manner believed to be in the best interests of the corporation, and with such care as an ordinarily prudent person would use under similar circumstances will not be subject to personal liability for decisions made and actions taken in his or her nonprofit corporate capacity. This is known as the *business judgment rule.*

The main exception to the business judgment rule is where a director's or officer's own tortious conduct causes harm to the plaintiff. (A tort is a wrongful act, other than a breach of contract, for which a plaintiff may obtain relief in the form of damages or an injunction.) In that context, the business judgment rule will not shield the director or officer from possible personal liability.

It should be pointed out that the law regarding personal liability for an unincorporated association is not as clear. Association members who expressly, or by implication, consent to or participate in association transactions may be held personally liable for any resulting obligation.[7] This issue by itself provides a strong argument not to operate as a nonprofit association.

Finally, whereas at one time directors' and officers' liability insurance—D&O insurance—was available to for-profit corporations only, now nonprofit corporations can often obtain it as well.

Formation

As with regular corporations, a nonprofit corporation may be formed by one or more persons executing articles of incorporation. (See Forms 11-A, 11-B, and 11-C.) An original and four copies of the proposed articles are filed with the Secretary of State. That office forwards one copy to the California Attorney General.

California no longer imposes a minimum franchise tax on the first year of a corporation's existence.[8] Consequently, nonprofits should be able to complete the exemption process without paying any franchise tax. Should the corporation prepay a franchise tax fee, the tax will be automatically refunded if the Franchise Tax Board grants the corporation nonprofit exemption status retroactive to the date of incorporation.

As with regular corporations, a nonprofit corporation is formed and corporate existence begins on the filing of the articles of incorporation.

As with regular corporations, a nonprofit corporation may be formed by one or more persons executing articles of incorporation.

Information to Include in the Articles of Incorporation

The articles of incorporation must set forth this requisite information:

- The name of the corporation,
- A statement of purpose and governing law, and
- The name and address of the corporation's initial agent for service of process.

Optional provisions are set forth in Sections 5131, 5132, 7131, 7132, 9131, and 9132 of the Nonprofit Corporation Law.

Sample articles of incorporation for nonprofit public benefit corporations, mutual benefit corporations, and religious corporations can be found in forms 11-A, 11-B, and 11-C, respectively, in this book. Sample bylaws for a nonprofit public benefit corporation without members are in Form 11-D. Minutes of the first organizational meeting of the board are provided in Form 11-E.

Finally, as with regular corporations, you will want to check the availability of the corporation's proposed name with the Secretary of State's office before preparing the articles of incorporation. Do not be surprised that many names are unavailable.

After filing the articles, the corporation is required to annually file a Statement by Domestic Nonprofit Corporation with the Secretary of State within ninety (90) days of incorporation. The filing fee is $20. A sample of this form can be found in Form 11-F of this book. A new form must be filed every two years regardless of whether the information remains unchanged. For a domestic stock corporation, not specifically a nonprofit, use SI-100, not the SI-200 attached as Form 11-F.

You will then need to draft corporate bylaws. The contents of the bylaws will depend on the type of nonprofit incorporated and whether the corporation has members. It is strongly recommended that you obtain professional assistance in creating the appropriate bylaws and completing the application for tax-exempt status. Initial directors will also need to be appointed (If not set forth in the articles, use Form 11-G.) The Directors should then execute a waiver of notice and consent to hold the organizational meeting of the Board of Directors (use Form 11-H). Attached as Form 11-I are recommended minutes of the organizational meeting of the Board of Directors. In lieu of a meeting, the Board of Directors can also take action by way of a unanimous written consent of the directors (Form 11-G). The corporation should then apply for an Employer Identification Number even if there are no employees (see SS-

After filing the articles, the corporation is required to annually file a Statement by Domestic Nonprofit Corporation with the Secretary of State within 90 days of incorporation.

4 attached as Form 3-U). The next step is to apply for a federal tax exemption.

Exemption from Taxation

All corporations, including nonprofits, are subject to federal and state income taxes unless specifically exempted.[9] They do not automatically enjoy tax-exempt status upon formation. Rather, applications for exemption must be filed with both the Internal Revenue Service and the California Franchise Tax Board (FTB). Sample application forms may be found in Forms 11-K and 11-L, respectively.

> All corporations, including nonprofits, are subject to federal and state income taxes unless specifically exempted. They do not automatically enjoy tax-exempt status upon formation.

To be recognized as tax-exempt, the corporation must fit into one of the specifically listed categories of exempt organizations. With a few exceptions, the California exemption classifications are identical to the federal exemption classifications. Nevertheless, some differences do exist; therefore, a consultation with an attorney experienced in non-profits or a tax consultant is recommended.

"Charitable" Exemption

While there are several categories of exempt organizations, probably the most popular is the "charitable" exemption.[10] To qualify for special tax status under this exemption, the corporation's stated purpose must be religious, charitable, scientific, literary, or educational and the corporation must demonstrate that it is organized and operated exclusively for that purpose and that it will not be conducted for the private benefit or gain of any individual or member. Under this exemption, the corporation also may not lobby or attempt to influence legislation, without risking its nonprofit status. One famous example of an organization losing its nonprofit status is the Sierra Club.

Provided the corporation can qualify under one of these exemptions, most of the income of the corporation will then be tax-exempt.

Potentially Taxable Income

Please note, however, that some of the corporation's income may still be subject to taxation. Even if a corporation is granted tax-exempt status, its "unrelated" business income is still taxable.

"Unrelated" business income is income that is not substantially related to the corporation's exempt purpose. For example, if a nonprofit owned a building that it used as its headquarters and in which it rented out extra space, any rental income generated would constitute taxable income. Moreover, if a corporation's unrelated business income is too substantial, the corporation may lose its tax-exempt status.

An innocent oversight can defeat a nonprofit group's endeavors, so seek the advice of an attorney, an accountant, or both to help you navigate these complex issues.

Application for Exemption

A new nonprofit corporation must file an IRS Form 1023, Application for Recognition of Exemption (Form 11-K) with the IRS within 15 months of incorporation for the nonprofit status to relate back to the date of formation. The corporation must demonstrate that it is organized and will be operated exclusively for one or more of the following purposes: religious, charitable, scientific, testing for public safety, literary, educational, fostering national or international sports competitions, or preventing cruelty to children or animals. There are also exemptions for cooperative hospital service operations, cooperative service or educational organizations, and childcare operations, subject to specific requirements. The organizational test cannot be met by simple conclusory statements in the bylaws; it must be supported by detailed factual projections. Appropriate statements of corporate purpose must be included in the articles of incorporation and a fully articulated statement of proposed activities must be clearly presented as part of the application for exemption. An organization must be "organized exclusively" for the exempt purposes and the corporation's assets must be "irrevocably dedicated" to an exempt purpose. It is crucial in the application that the corporation clearly establish that it is not being organized or operated for the benefit of "private interests" (e.g., the founder's, the founder's family, the corporation's members) or for persons controlled by special interests. If the exemption is granted, it will then be given retroactive effect to the date of incorporation, subject to the 15-month rule set out above. The equivalent California exemption application is Form 3500, Form 11-L. While it is generally less comprehensive than IRS Form 1023, much of the same information is required.

Detailed information, financial schedules, and other supporting documentation must accompany both applications. It is therefore critical that all information requested be provided, as the applications must be fully completed in order to be processed. A certified copy of the corporation's articles of incorporation and bylaws must also accompany the applications. Any additional information that can be provided will also help expedite the application process.

An innocent oversight can defeat a nonprofit group's endeavors, so seek the advice of an attorney, an accountant, or both to help you navigate these complex issues.

Filing

Once completed, the IRS Application for Recognition of Exemption, Form 1023, should be mailed or hand-delivered with a check for the user fee, payable to the Internal Revenue Service, to the following address:

Internal Revenue Service
EP/EO Division
P.O. Box 2350
Los Angeles, CA 90053-2350

The user fee is based on the actual or anticipated annual gross receipts of the corporation. The user fee is $150 for organizations that have averaged $10,000 or less during the preceding four years and for new corporations anticipating gross receipts of $10,000 or less during each of their first four years. For all other organizations, the user fee is $500.

IRS publications and forms can be ordered through 800 829-3676 or the IRS web site: www.irs.gov/formspubs/index.html.

The granting of a federal exemption from the IRS does not automatically exempt the corporation from California state taxes. The completed California Exemption Application, Form 3500, should be sent to the Franchise Tax Board along with a $25 check, payable to that office, at the following address:

Exempt Organizations Unit
Franchise Tax Board
P.O. Box 942857
Sacramento, CA 94257-4041

FTB general information and forms are available at 800 852-5711 or through the FTB web site: www.ftb.ca.gov/forms/index.html.

It must be noted that California has a special rule that no more than 49 percent of the persons serving on the corporation's board of directors can be "interested persons," i.e., persons who have been compensated by the corporation for services rendered over the previous 12 months (except as a director) and relatives of such persons.[11]

Usually, IRS processing takes about 100 days and the FTB usually takes about 60 days. In the interim, either office may request additional information or clarification before it completes the processing of the application. Once the have processed the applications, the offices send the corporation determination letters either recognizing or denying exempt status.

After the exempt status is granted, the corporation must file informational statements annually with both the IRS and the FTB. Substantial penalties may be imposed for the failure to timely file this information.

Newly formed California public benefit corporations, other charitable organizations, and trustees holding property for charitable purposes are also required to register with the California Attorney General within six months after receipt of assets for charitable purposes. (See Form 11-N.) They must also file an annual report.

Loss of Exemption

A corporation may lose its exempt status if it operates in a manner inconsistent with the rules of its exemption or if it engages in certain prohibited transactions. Under some circumstances, the IRS or the FTB may retroactively revoke the corporation's exempt status, which can create severe tax complications.

To the extent a corporation will have members, it should check with counsel to ensure that membership interests are properly issued in compliance with state and federal securities law exemptions. If a nonprofit corporation intends to solicit charitable contributions in states other than California, it may need to register as a charity in those states, as required by local law. Licenses and permits may also be necessary in those states and foreign jurisdictions in which the nonprofit corporation is engaged in business, professions, or solicitation of funds. The nonprofit may also wish to investigate obtaining a nonprofit mailing permit, which will provide for a preferential mailing rate. (See PS Form 3624, attached as Form 11-M.)

A corporation may lose its exempt status if it operates in a manner inconsistent with the rules of its exemption or if it engages in certain prohibited transactions.

Notes

1. California Corporations Code §§5000-9927.
2. California Corporations Code §5110 et seq.
3. California Corporations Code §9110 et seq.
4. California Corporations Code §7110 et seq.
5. See Internal Revenue Code §501(c)(3); General Counsel Memorandum 38459, 39670; American Campaign Academy (1989) 92TC 1053.
6. California Corporations Code §§5231, 5047.5, 7231, and 9231.
7. See *Security-First National Bank v. Cooper* (1944) 62 CA 2d 653; 69 Opinions of the California Attorney General 218, 222 (1986).
8. Revenue and Taxation Code §23152(f)(i).

9. Internal Revenue Code §11 and Revenue and Taxation Code §23701.

10. Internal Revenue Code §501(c)(3) and Revenue and Taxation Code §23701(d).

11. California Corporations Code §5227.

CHAPTER 12

Intellectual Property

I n addition to capitalizing with cash, real property, or other assets, your company may also have or develop ownership rights in intellectual property. Intellectual property consists of intangible assets stemming from original expressions of concepts or ideas and includes copyrights, patents, trademarks, service marks, trade secrets, and trade dress. Some of these rights protect the integrity of a product itself, such as a patent in a new mechanism of an assembly part or a copyright in the artwork of a painter. Others spring from a business and its economic goodwill, such as a trademark, trade dress, and the name itself. One product may comprise several types of intellectual property rights simultaneously.

Consider computer software as an example. A *patent* may be obtainable for the software application or processes, a *copyright* exists in the text of the software program and the cover design, and a *trademark* will likely be affixed to the packaging of the software or the computer disk itself.

Even if your business will not produce new inventions or create original works of art, it will have a name issued by the Secretary of State that it may use as a trade name. Although that particular name was available and the Secretary of State allowed your company the right to use that name to identify your business, there may be problems in the future with respect to the use of that name. It is very important to realize that the Secretary of State registers businesses names without considering whether a name may infringe upon another's pre-existing trademark or service mark rights.

Vision in a strong business concept can greatly aid in creating or fostering intellectual property rights that can become substantial profit centers during the life of an enterprise. Once an entity owns a patent, copyright, or trademark, selling or licensing the use of that copyright, trademark, or patent material can provide a steady stream of revenue from corporate assets with little capital or inventory requirement.

Perhaps as important as creating and enhancing your business assets, it is imperative early on to become aware of any and all intellectual property rights already in existence that are related to your business activities, in order to avoid inadvertent infringement on another's rights that could force you to rename your business or its products, pay substantial sums to a third party in compensation for damages, and even withdraw products from the market. Setting up a business or a line of products without researching similar names or products is comparable to building a house on real estate without clearing ownership of the title. Likewise, obtaining registrations for trademarks, service marks, or patents will protect your business from others using your concepts and products without your permission. The prevention of potential liability due to infringement can require thorough research and analysis of exclusive intellectual property rights. You should take care to seek counsel in this area of law to develop and fully protect your rights.

Setting up a business or a line of products without researching similar names or products is comparable to building a house on real estate without clearing ownership of the title.

Types of Intellectual Property

Trademarks and Service Marks

A *trademark* is any word, name, image, device, or symbol used or intended to be used in commerce to identify and distinguish the *goods* of one seller from the goods of another. In contrast, a *service mark* is any word, name, image, device, or symbol used or intended to be used in commerce to identify and distinguish the *services* of one provider from services provided by others and to indicate the source of the services.

Trademarks and service marks originally arose from common law, but state and federal statutes now exist, so that individuals and businesses may register and protect their distinguishing marks from unauthorized use.[1] Legal protection exists in large part to protect the public from confusion between different products or services that appear to be similar. The laws also help to protect a business that has established a market for its goods from latecomers that enter the marketplace with a replica to take advantage of an established reputation. Once you have begun to use your mark, you may include the TM or SM symbols after it, indicating to others that you claim rights in the mark. You can use the "®" symbol only you have successfully completed registration. With an amendment in 1998 to the Federal Trademark Act of 1946 (Lanham Act), a person may now also apply to register to protect a mark that he or she intends to use but has not actually done so as of the date of application.[2]

As discussed above, to ensure that others do not have superior rights to a mark, which could result in an infringement claim against your business, it is recommended that you have a comprehensive trademark search done before you introduce a name into the marketplace. This will usually cost between $400 and $700, depending on the depth and scope of the search, and will help identify potential conflicts early in process of business formation. A good search will include the current state and United States Patent and Trademark Office (PTO) applications and registrations, internet information, and general publications such as telephone books and magazines.

Trade dress encompasses a broad concept that includes the total design, shape, exterior characteristics, or overall look and feel of a product, building, or other item. This category extends to architecture and interior design, in addition to packaging details, and its registration is subject to great scrutiny by the PTO, which carefully considers the functionality and distinctiveness of the proposed trade dress.

A *trade name* or a *commercial name* is defined by the Lanham Act as any name used by a person to identify his or her business or vocation.[3] A trade name is not a registered trademark. Trade names may include individual names or surnames for businesses, unions, or other organizations. Again, given the variety of rights with regard to trademarks, service marks, and other interests, competent intellectual property counsel should be consulted, so that any new business or product will not infringe upon pre-existing rights of other individuals and businesses and latecomers will be precluded from profiting on your established reputation and goodwill.

Registering a Trademark or Service Mark
The federal trademark and service mark application process is lengthy

and is not inexpensive. Filing a name reservation, fictitious business name statement, or articles of incorporation with the Secretary of State does not ensure trademark or service mark protection for your business name or the names of any particular products or services. To receive exclusive rights nationwide, you must file an application with the PTO. An applicant describes the mark he or she would like to register, how it is used or intended to be used, and when the first use occurred.

The PTO has created general categories or classes to designate each mark. The application filing fee is currently $335 per class per mark. Thus, to register a trademark that is used on labels on books, computer software, and toys, you would likely have to pay for registration in three classes, or $1005. The application must include a drawing of the mark meeting the specifications of the PTO along with sample specimens.

The review process in the PTO can take 12-18 months or longer and it is not unusual for the PTO examining attorney to find some fault in the application and require some form of amendment. However, once registered, your rights in the mark start at the date of first use of the mark, not the date of issuance, and you may continue indefinitely by filing timely renewals.

The PTO and courts have recognized four classifications for marks: fanciful and arbitrary, suggestive, descriptive, and generic. The strongest marks (and most likely to be registered easily) are *fanciful* words that have no meaning in themselves, such as "Kodak" or "Exxon," and *arbitrary* labels that do not imply a connection between the goods or services and the description, such as "Peanut Butter Books." The next strongest are *suggestive* marks that have some connotation with the goods or services sold, such as "Cheetah Copies" for a quick copy business. The weakest marks are mere *descriptions* of the items, such as "Brass Lamps" or "E-Z Chairs," and *generic* labels, such as "The Dentist's Office." The PTO will not likely register a mark it considers to be "generic" or even too descriptive if there is no additional basis for the mark.

If your business will not expand beyond California, registering for a state trademark may make sense. It is faster and less expensive (currently a $70 filing fee) and it will protect your business name or symbol against commerce entering or existing in the state, provided that a federal registration does not already exist that would preclude your registration.[4] If your business is of a type that will increasingly cross state lines as it grows, however, you should pursue a federal registration.

The review process in the PTO can take 12-18 months or longer and it is not unusual for the PTO examining attorney to find some fault in the application and require some form of amendment.

Benefits of Registration

Why register at a state or federal level when rights exist under common law from mere use of the mark for as long as the use continues? Whereas the common law rights extend only to the geographic region of use, having a federally registered trademark will preclude others from later using or applying to register an identical or similar mark throughout the United States.

As of the date of registration, all others are in effect put on notice that the mark belongs to you; this can have benefits beyond goods and services themselves. For example, the registered trademark owner will generally have a right to use the corresponding domain name for its internet web site address as well. In addition, once your mark is registered, no one else may register that mark, at a state or federal level. Additionally, greater penalties exist for infringement of a registered mark than for one that is unregistered. If another applicant beat you to the PTO and registered the mark you wanted, an experienced trademark attorney may be able to help you register another version of your mark, depending on the benefits of obtaining a registration at that point.

> As of the date of registration, all others are in effect put on notice that the mark belongs to you; this can have benefits beyond goods and services themselves.

Copyright

Copyright protection applies to a broad category of works of art, including music, literature, drama, choreography, photography, sculpture, motion pictures, audiovisual and sound recordings, and artistic works, such as poetry, novels, movies, songs, computer software, and architecture. Unlike the policy behind trademarks to protect the public from deceptive or confusingly similar consumer goods and services, copyright protection arose to encourage the creation and implementation of the original expression of ideas.

In general, copyright prevents unauthorized copying of another's work. Owning a copyright will afford the author five exclusive rights: distribution, publication, reproduction, modification (including derivative products), and performance or display of the original and fixed expression of an idea or work.[5] Copyright interests are born immediately upon creation of a work and its fixation in a tangible medium of expression. The moment the artist puts brush to canvas or the advertising copy is written, a copyright exists, usually owned by the creator or its assignee.

For works created at the present time, no notice or © is required to have the full force of the copyright protection, although it is often beneficial to include such a notice. Use of the notice may be significant, since it informs the public that the work is protected by copyright, identifies the copyright owner, and shows the year of first publication. Further, in the event that a work is infringed, if a proper notice of copyright appears on the published copy to which a defendant in a copyright infringement suit had access, then a defense based on innocent infringement will likely be without merit. Note, however, that it is the specific expression of the idea or fact that warrants the copyright and not the idea itself. Furthermore, another individual having no access or knowledge of the prior work may independently create a similar or even identical work and will not infringe on a pre-existing copyright. Moreover, another creator may see the copyrighted material, use the same idea for a different expression, and not infringe upon the initial copyright interest.

In some instances, the actual creator of the work of art will not hold the copyright interest. For example, if a company hires an independent contractor to create a logo for company use, the copyright owner is the employer, not the individual who designed the artwork, provided that both parties signed a contract to that effect. This would likely be a "work made for hire," so that the hiring company would hold the rights in the finished work product, not the creator himself or herself.

Under copyright law, works made for hire can be of two origins: either employees develop a new work as part of their job description or a work is specially commissioned through a written agreement by the parties, with language creating the relationship and the interests.[6] Thus, if your business contemplates hiring an individual to create copyrightable work, you should first consult counsel to ensure that the rights in the finished product will be the property of the company and not the author. Be aware also that the California Labor Code restricts in certain circumstances an employer's rights to inventions created by employees, even where the employees have signed an agreement transferring all interests in inventions over to the employer.[7]

Also, note that a copyright may also be owned jointly. Where two or more people create a work of art without a contractual agreement to the contrary, the co-creators automatically jointly own undivided and equal rights to the entire work. This means that each may use or manipulate the work without the consent of the other owner. Be forewarned: this scenario may inadvertently occur where a work-for-hire relationship is not properly created and the hiring company ultimately co-creates copyrighted material with an employee or an independent contractor.

Be aware that the California Labor Code restricts in certain circumstances an employer's rights to inventions created by employees.

Registering a Copyright

Over the years, Congress has passed numerous copyright acts, so that the parameters and requirements for copyrights depend, among other things, upon the year of creation of the work. For works created after 1978, the term of a registered copyright for an individual author is the life of the author plus 70 years; for a work made for hire, the term is 95 years from publication or 120 years from creation, whichever is shorter. The current filing fee ranges from $30 to $75 for each application, depending on the type and nature of the work that is being registered. There is no time limit for registering a copyright, but sooner is better to clearly establish the date of your claim to the work.

Benefits of registration include establishing a public record for copyright ownership as of the date of registration, eligibility for statutory damages and attorneys' fees in the event of infringement actions, and added protection with U.S. Customs against the importation of infringing copies. Unlike trademarks and patents examination procedures, the Library of Congress does not review or analyze copyright registrations in light of other registrations, so that it is relatively easy to obtain.

In contrast to the ease of registration, difficulty may arise in enforcing your copyright, given that the law allows third-party use or infringement in limited instances. First, if a person uses copyrighted material without permission and it falls within the elements of "fair use," no infringement will be found. The "fair use" doctrine allows limited copying of all or portions of copyrighted works for certain purposes, such as teaching, research, reporting, comment, and criticism. Second, certain uses are automatically allowed without permission from the copyright holder, so long as fees or royalties are paid for those "compulsory licenses." Third, after what is considered the "first sale" of one of your works, the buyers may transfer that version of the work in a number of ways that will not constitute an infringement. Fourth, an "innocent" infringer may independently create a similar work without access to or knowledge of the copyrighted work. Finally, as previously discussed, because copyright extends only to the fixed expression of an idea or fact, all the underlying facts and ideas of a copyrighted work will not remain in the exclusive control of the copyright holder.

> The "fair use" doctrine allows limited copying of all or portions of copyrighted works for certain purposes, such as teaching, research, reporting, comment, and criticism.

Patents

Similar to copyright's protection of a creative work of art, patents protect an inventor's creation and provide the owner the right to exclude others from commercially profiting from the patented item.[8] Under patent law, an inventor basically gains a limited monopoly over his or her invention for the duration of the patent. Because this is a highly technical area, before attempting to obtain a patent or substantially invest in a new product, it would be wise to consult with an experienced, licensed patent attorney.

There are two major types of patents—*design* and *utility*. A design patent protects a new, ornamental design for a manufactured item, such as a water fountain or a lamp. Utility patents cover new and non-obvious electrical, mechanical, and chemical inventions, processes, and improvements.

Under the U.S. patent statute, an inventor has a one-year time limit to apply for a patent after the first "public use" or "printed publication" anywhere in the world regarding his or her invention. Further, the invention must cross several legal and technical hurdles before the PTO issues the applicant a patent registration. For an invention to be patentable, the invention must be novel or new, that is, not disclosed or generally known to the public. It must also have a useful purpose or be operational or functional. Finally, it must have non-obvious characteristics. That is, it cannot have similar features or consist of an obvious combination of previously patented work. Because the examining attorneys will likely find some basis to reject the application initially, it is advisable to have a patent attorney prepare your application and oversee the process with the PTO.

Once issued, the patent registration provides the owner the exclusive right to use, make, or sell the invention for generally 20 years, subject to timely payment of maintenance fees as provided by law. A maintenance fee is due 3.5, 7.5, and 11.5 years after the original grant for all patent applications filed on and after December 12, 1980. The maintenance fee must be paid at the stipulated times to maintain the patent in force. After the patent has expired, anyone may make, use, offer for sale, sell, or import the invention without permission of the patentee, provided that matter covered by other pre-existing and unexpired patents is not used. The terms may be extended for certain pharmaceuticals and for certain circumstances as provided by law.

Contrary to copyright registration, an independently created prod-

Under the U.S. patent statute, an inventor has a one-year time limit to apply for a patent after the first "public use" of or "printed publication" anywhere in the world regarding his or her invention.

uct identical to a patented one infringes on the rights of the patent holder, regardless of whether the second or simultaneous creator was aware of the first patented object. Although stronger in relation to simultaneous or later inventions, patents are always subject to a later discovery of any "prior art" or patented work created earlier from anywhere in the world. This makes a prior thorough patent search crucial to the process of obtaining protection.

Overall, while the requirements to obtain a patent are tougher and the time period to hold those rights is shorter, patent holders have greater protections against infringement during the patent period than copyright and trademark owners. Be aware, however, that in applying for a patent you will divulge the details of your invention or discovery, with information on file with the PTO and publicly available. As such, competitors may use it when your patent registration expires or if you inadvertently abandon your registration for failure to timely pay the maintenance fees. Consequently, an inventor may wish to bypass patent registration altogether and rely upon trade secret protections if utmost confidentiality of the details of the invention is a priority.

Registering a Patent

Lengthy and costly, the process to register for a patent requires a certified patent attorney, licensed with the federal patent board, and much detailed information along with technical drawings. The patent office may take nine months to one year to respond to an application. The application filing fees range greatly, depending on the type of patent, the size of the applicant's business, and the number of claims asserted in the application. After obtaining a registered patent, the applicant, who is the individual inventor, must also pay an issuance fee, which also ranges depending again on the factors discussed. The filing fees and the legal fees in obtaining a patent may cost from three to ten thousand dollars or more. Unlike trademarks, there is no state equivalent to a federally granted patent.

Trade Secrets

Although not registrable, trade secrets are another example of intellectual property rights. The United States Congress passed the Economic Espionage Act of 1996 to codify the scope of matters considered trade secrets and the remedies for misappropriation of such information. Trade secrets include information that gains its value from not being

The patent application filing fees range greatly, depending on the type of patent, the size of the applicant's business, and the number of claims asserted in the application.

known by competitors or the public and the secrecy of which the owner takes reasonable steps to ensure. A well-known example is the formula for Coca-Cola. By relying upon trade secret protection rather than a patent, Coca-Cola has preserved its exclusive rights over its formula for substantially longer than the 20-year period usually allowed for patents. Because part of the legal definition of "trade secret" demands action by the business to protect its information, in this area it is especially important to have in place a security policy that the company follows. Alternatives for protecting trade secrets involve a variety of contracts and other agreements to police the security of the proprietary information. Confidentiality agreements will provide a contractual obligation between the employer and employee or between the business and any business associates who may receive trade secrets.[9]

Similarly, noncompete clauses and non-solicitation agreements between the company and its service providers, if well crafted to be enforceable, can help structure business relationships during and after the term of employment. In addition, it often makes common sense to limit any disclosure of confidential trade secrets to only those employees who have a legitimate need to know. Many companies rely upon trade secret law to protect their inventions while a patent application is pending. Similarly, if an applicant is denied a patent, trade secret law may fill the gap to afford some level of protection for proprietary information with no time limit restrictions.

If you are going to rely on trade secret protection, it is crucial that you develop a protective, all-encompassing course of action from the start. An attorney can be helpful in this process. All it takes is one or more random acts of disclosure to undermine any claim that your company considered a product or process confidential and eligible for trade secret protection.

> If you are going to rely on trade secret protection, it is crucial that you develop a protective, all-encompassing course of action from the start.

Protect Your Rights

As mentioned previously, it is important to establish clear rights to intellectual property owned by a business, to avoid infringing on others' rights, expand and protect assets of the business, and provide a framework to transfer those assets if desired. Protecting a company's intellectual property rights may entail the use of carefully worded employment agreements and assignments of rights from the service providers to your company as well as work-for-hire contracts.

In addition to recognizing pre-existing intellectual property rights of others and verifying your own, maintaining an ongoing policing and security program will strengthen enforcement and value of your intellectual property rights, whether that includes copyright, trade secrets, trademarks, or service marks. It is advisable to consult with an attorney regarding the practical means by which your company will protect and maximize the benefits from its intellectual property, as well as avoid litigation or other problems from infringing on the rights of others.

Helpful Information

There are several sources of information you can utilize in your search, including:

PTO (for federal patent and trademark registration)
The Assistant Commissioner for Trademarks
U.S. Patent and Trademark Office
2900 Crystal Drive
Arlington, VA 22202-3513
general information: 800 PTO-9199
trademark assistance center: 703 308-9000
web site: www.uspto.gov

Library of Congress (for copyright registration)
Copyright Office
Register of Copyrights
Library of Congress
101 Independence Avenue, S.E.
Washington, DC 20559-6000
202 707-3000
202 707-2600 for selected circulars and announcements via fax
web site: www.loc.gov/copyright

California Secretary of State (for state trademark and service mark registration)
Trademarks/Service Marks
1500 11th Street, Suite 345
Sacramento, CA 95814
P.O. Box 944225
Sacramento, CA 94244-2250
916 653-4984
web site: www.ss.ca.gov/business/ts/ts.htm

Notes

1. Federal Trademark Act of 1946 (Lanham Act), 15 United States Code §1051-1127, California Business and Professions Code §14200 et seq.
2. 15 United States Code §1051(b) (intent to use basis for registration).
3. 15 United States Code §1127.
4. California Business and Professions Code §14200.
5. 17 United States Code §106.
6. 17 United States Code §101 (re work for hire).
7. California Labor Code Section 2870 (West 1979) (amended by Statutes 1991, Chapter 647, Section 5). Also see Chapter 13, "Protecting the Company's Trade Secrets and Confidential Information."
8. 35 United States Code §1 et seq.
9. For further discussion on such agreements, refer to Chapter 13, "Legal Obligations of Employers."

Legal Obligations of Employers

Once your corporation becomes an employer, it becomes subject to many additional legal obligations and requirements, including payroll tax payments and withholding requirements as well as compliance with various California and federal labor laws and regulations.

This chapter will first address an employer's reporting and tax payment obligations, followed by a discussion of key issues affecting most California employers, including topics such as at-will employment, classification of employees and independent contractors, company policies and employment regulations about payroll practices and overtime wages, exempt and non-exempt status, vacation pay, retention of employee records, discrimination in the workplace, immigration law compliance, worker's compensation insurance, protection of the company's trade secrets and confidential information, and dispute resolution policies.

Employer's Reporting and Tax Obligations

The following list of employer's reporting and tax obligations is not intended to be an exhaustive list but should help direct a small business employer to the appropriate sources of information. For compliance and cost purposes, you should consider using a bank payroll service to handle employee payroll matters. Your accountant or attorney may be able to give you a recommendation.

Most employers are required by law to withhold federal income and social security taxes as well as California withholding taxes from taxable wages paid to employees, but not to independent contractors. (For a discussion of general factors in determining an independent contractor as opposed to an employee, see "Employee vs. Independent Contractor" section below.) Failure to comply with withholding obligations can result in personal liability. An officer or other person who is charged with the requirement to withhold taxes on behalf of the corporation may become personally liable for a 100-percent penalty for failure to do so. Based upon the potential general liability, if you are forced to close your business, the tax authorities are the last creditor you want to leave unpaid. You should keep all records of employment taxes for at least four years.

Most employers must withhold federal income, Social Security, and Medicare taxes from taxable wages paid to employees, based on each employee's Form W-4.

Withholding Federal Income and Social Security Taxes (FICA)

As an employer, you must require each new employee to sign a Withholding Allowance Certificate Form W-4 (Form 13-A) when he or she starts work, which will remain effective until the employee gives you a new one. Make the form effective with the first wage payments. If a new employee does not give you a completed Form W-4, you should withhold income taxes as if he or she were single, with no withholding allowances.

Most employers must withhold federal income, Social Security, and Medicare taxes from taxable wages paid to employees, based on each employee's Form W-4. FICA provides for a federal system of old-age, survivors, and disability insurance (OASDI) that is financed by the Social Security tax, whereas hospital insurance is financed by the Medicare tax. Each of these taxes is reported separately. Generally, an employer withholds Social Security and Medicare taxes from its employees' wages and must also pay a matching amount of these taxes.

Federal Unemployment Tax (FUTA)

Generally, an employer is subject to unemployment tax if, during the current or preceding calendar year, it had one or more employees at any time in each of 20 calendar weeks or paid wages of $1,500 or more during any calendar quarter. The employer may receive credit for contributions it has paid into state unemployment funds. If the amount of tax aggregates more than $100, quarterly deposits of tax will be required.

For further information and advice on your federal payroll tax responsibilities, you should contact an attorney or an accountant. For available publications on the issue published by the Internal Revenue Service (e.g., IRS Publication 15 [Circular E]), visit the IRS's web site at www.irs.gov. Call the IRS at (800) 829-4933 for your employment tax questions.

California Withholding Taxes

The California Employment Development Department (EDD) is a significant California governmental agency that administers the following California payroll tax programs: State Disability Insurance (SDI), Unemployment Insurance (UI), California Personal Income Tax (PIT) withholding, and Employment Training Tax (ETT). Most people are familiar with the UI and SDI taxes, which will be discussed at greater length below. You may not be as familiar with the ETT and the PIT.

The ETT is an employer-paid tax that provides funds to train employees in targeted industries to make California businesses more competitive. Employers subject to ETT pay one-tenth percent (.001) on the first $7,000 in wages paid to each employee in a calendar year. The ETT funds are designed to promote a competitive labor market by helping California businesses invest in a skilled and productive workforce and develop the skills of workers who directly produce or deliver goods and services.

The California PIT is a tax levied by the Franchise Tax Board (FTB) on the income of California residents and the income of nonresidents derived within California and is administered by both FTB and EDD for the governor to provide resources needed for California public services such as schools, public parks, roads, and health and human services. California PIT is withheld from employees' pay based on the Employee's Withholding Allowance Certificate (Form W-4 or DE 4) on file with their employer.

State Disability Insurance (SDI)

Most employers will also be required to withhold state income taxes and state disability insurance (SDI) premiums from taxable wages paid to employees. The procedures for such withholdings are similar to those for federal income tax and Social Security taxes. The SDI tax provides temporary benefit payments to workers for disabilities not related to work. Conversely, worker's compensation insurance, which is dis-

Most employers will also be required to withhold state income taxes and state disability insurance (SDI) premiums from taxable wages paid to employees.

cussed later in this chapter, is an insurance obtained by employers to provide mandatory benefit payments to workers for work-related disabilities and injuries. SDI is funded by deductions from employees' wages. Employers are required to withhold a percentage for SDI on the first $79,418 in wages paid to each employee in any given calendar year. The SDI tax rate may change each year. The 2005 tax rate is 1.08 percent (.0108) of SDI taxable wages per employee, per year (which includes the rate for Paid Family Leave).

California Unemployment Insurance (UI)

The UI tax provides temporary payments to individuals who are unemployed through no fault of their own. UI is an employer-paid tax. Tax-rated employers pay a percentage of the first $7,000 in wages paid to each employee in a calendar year. The UI rate schedule and amount of taxable wages are determined annually. New employers pay 3.4 percent (.034) for up to three years. Employers who pay $100 or more in taxable wages in any calendar quarter and employ one or more employees are generally subject to the California Unemployment Insurance Code. The employer must register with the nearest office of the California Employment Tax District Office. Quarterly returns are required and the forms for such return are mailed automatically to all registered employers.

For information and advice on your California payroll tax responsibilities, you should contact an accountant or an attorney, as with federal payroll taxes. There are numerous publications on point available from the California Employment Development Department. You may contact the EDD at 888 745-3886 or visit your local Employment Tax Office by using the EDD's web site (www.edd.ca.gov/taxrep/taxloc.htm) to find the location nearest you.

EDD Reporting Requirements for New Hires

As stated above, if you have paid more than $100 in total wages in a calendar quarter to one or more employees, you are considered an employer under California law and must apply for a California employer account number. In order to obtain your employer account number, you are required to submit a Registration Form for Commercial Employers, Pacific Maritime, and Fishing Boats (DE 1) (Form 13-B) to the EDD, within 15 days after the date you paid in excess of $100 in quarterly wages. Updated forms and further information may be obtained from the EDD.

As stated above, if you have paid more than $100 in total wages in a calendar quarter to one or more employees, you are considered an employer under California law.

Anytime you hire or rehire employees, you become subject to the EDD's reporting requirements. Within 20 days of the employee's start-of-work date, you must submit a Report of New Employee(s) (DE 34) (Form 13-C). If you pay an independent contractor $600 or more or enter into a contract with an independent contractor for $600 or more, you are required to submit a Report of Independent Contractor(s) (DE 542) (Form 13-D) to the EDD, within 20 days of the applicable date of payment or contract date. You may also be required to file information returns with the IRS to report certain types of payments made during the year to independent contractors. For example, you must file Form 1099-MISC, Miscellaneous Income, to report payments of $600 or more to independent contractors for services performed for your business. For more information on reporting requirements, you may visit the IRS's web site at www.irs.gov or call the IRS at 866 455-7438.

Employee Pamphlets and Notice Postings

As an employer, you are also required to provide your employees pamphlets on employee withholdings and Unemployment Insurance (UI) and State Disability Insurance (SDI). In addition, you must post in a prominent location easily seen by your employees an employee notice containing UI and SDI benefits and claims information. The EDD will send you the appropriate notices for posting after you register.

In addition to the UI and SDI notices, an employer is obligated to post a myriad of other mandatory notices, depending in part on the aggregate number of employees in the company's employ at the time. Since the complete list of notices can be rather lengthy and will vary based on the actual number of your employees, the following is a list of the more prominent notices that every employer (regardless of size) must post:

- Federal minimum wage notice, WH Publication 1088;
- California IWC Order No. MW-2001, Minimum Wage;
- California Department of Industrial Relations, Payday Notice, DLSE 8;
- Notice of nondiscrimination under California Labor Code Section 98.7;
- Internal Revenue Service, Notice of Withholding;
- Internal Revenue Service, Advance Earned Income Tax Credit;
- Equal Employment Opportunity Commission poster, "Equal Employment Opportunity is the Law";

In addition to the UI and SDI notices, an employer is obligated to post a myriad of other mandatory notices, depending in part on the aggregate number of employees in the company's employ at the time.

- Immigration and Naturalization Service notice concerning discrimination;
- Department of Labor, Wage and Hour Division, Employee Polygraph Protection Act of 1988, WH Publication 1462;
- Notice with information on California worker's compensation coverage, reporting procedures and employee rights;
- California Division of Occupational Safety and Health poster, "Safety and Health Protection on the Job";
- Department of Industrial Relations, Division of Occupational Safety and Health, emergency telephone numbers (S-500); and
- Proposition 65 smoking notices.

Overview of California Employment Laws

Implementation of Company Policies

Employers will find that an employee handbook becomes helpful when the number of employees approaches a sizeable number, particularly since various federal and California employment laws are triggered when a company employs 15 or more employees. An employee handbook provides a written compilation of the employer's policies, procedures, and other vital information that is disseminated to all employees. Every business will have its own unique needs and policies and, therefore, no one set of enclosures will be adequate for all employee handbooks. A detailed discussion of all subjects potentially to be covered in a handbook is outside the scope of this book; however this chapter will address some key issues that employers should be generally aware of, regardless of whether or not they are included in an employee handbook.

In formulating employment policies and procedures or drafting an employee handbook, all employers should give due consideration to the following topics:

- At-will employment.
- Service provider's status as an employee (exempt or non-exempt) or an independent contractor.
- Equal employment opportunity affirmations and protocols.
- Company policies against harassment; grievance policies and procedures.
- Protecting the company's trade secrets and confidential information.

Be aware that the California Labor Code restricts in certain circumstances an employer's rights to inventions created by employees.

- Pay policies and procedures, including pay periods, payroll deductions, bonuses and commission pay, timekeeping, overtime policies, rest and meal breaks, expense reimbursements, and wage garnishments.
- Employee benefits, including health insurance, pension/profit-sharing plans, education benefits, cafeteria plans, and severance pay.
- Paid and unpaid leave policies for vacation, sick days, personal time off, holidays, leaves of absence, medical leave, family care leave, military service, jury or witness duty, voting time, and bereavement leave.
- Worker's compensation claims and procedures for filing.
- Standards of employee's performance and professional conduct, attendance, punctuality, performance evaluations, discipline, and termination.
- Policies concerning workplace safety and health, violence prevention, OSHA guidelines, and substance abuse.
- Grievance policies and procedures.
- Dispute resolution policies (e.g., mediation and arbitration).

Because employment laws regularly change, you are well advised to develop a relationship with an attorney or other professional who can help keep you informed and in compliance.

At-Will Employment

An employer should explicitly make the employee aware that his or her employment is at will: either the company or the employee may terminate it at any time, with or without cause or notice. In addition, the employer should reserve the right to modify the terms and conditions of employment at its sole discretion. Although most employers do not terminate employees without some reason, you should nevertheless reserve the right to terminate at will in order to insulate your company from lawsuits by former employees claiming that their termination was without good cause.

Notwithstanding an at-will employment status, an employer is prohibited from conduct that constitutes wrongful termination. In other words, you can terminate an employee for no reason, but you cannot terminate an employee for the wrong reasons (e.g., race, gender, disability, whistle-blowing, or on the basis of any other legally protected cate-

An employer should explicitly make the employee aware that his or her employment is at will.

gory). For further discussion, see the "Anti-Discrimination Laws" section below.

Under California law,[1] there is a presumption that employment is at will. Nevertheless, an agreement to terminate employment only for good cause can arise by implication even if the issue was never expressly addressed between the employer and employee. Thus, it is prudent for employers to have a written agreement signed by their employees or to expressly provide in their employee handbooks that the employees' employment is at will, thereby precluding the implication of an agreement (whether express or implied in fact) that termination will occur only for cause. This is often effectuated by an employee offer letter. For a sample employee offer letter establishing an at-will employment, see Form 13-E.

Employee vs. Independent Contractor

An important issue that confronts most employers is whether a service provider is an employee or an independent contractor. In an effort to avoid employment-related withholding taxes, the payment of benefits, and tax return filing obligations, inexperienced employers often try to categorize all or many of their workers as independent contractors rather than employees. Most employers erroneously believe that if the service provider and the company enter into an agreement that explicitly classifies the individual as an independent contractor, that agreement provides conclusive proof of an independent contractor relationship and not an employment relationship. State and federal government agencies have their own guidelines and tests for determining whether a service provider is in fact an independent contractor or an employee disguised as an independent contractor.

Different government agencies use different definitions and terminology in making the final determination regarding an individual's status, some of which are statutory definitions while others are derived from common-law tests that have been refined over the years. Some of the factors readily used under California and federal guidelines are compiled and outlined below, but you should consult an attorney about the varying requirements in the different government agencies. Certain key issues that must be carefully considered include, but are not limited to, the following:

An important issue that confronts most employers is whether a service provider is an employee or an independent contractor.

- The extent and level of control exercised by the company or principal over the service provider's work product, time, and place of work;
- Whether the service provider is engaged in a distinct occupation, profession, or business;
- The skills required in performing the duties and whether the provider is required to hold a license to do the work;
- Whether the alleged employer is representing itself as a business;
- Whether the instrumentalities, tools, and place of work are supplied by the service provider or the company;
- Whether a capital investment is required by the company;
- The level of investment a service provider commits to the facilities that he or she uses in performing the services;
- The length of time that the service provider is retained;
- Whether the work is usually done under the direction of an employer or by a specialist, using the locality as point of reference;
- Whether payment for services is based on time spent or by project;
- Whether the work is an integral part of the company's regular business;
- The intention of the parties and whether they believe their relationship is employer-employee or independent contractor-principal;
- Whether the service provider participates in any benefit plans made available to the company's employees;
- Whether the service provider realizes a profit or suffers a loss as a result of his or her services;
- Whether the service provider is free to perform services for unrelated companies or firms at the same time;
- Whether the service provider has his or her own employees;
- A service provider's ability to terminate the relationship at any time, without incurring any liability.

You should be aware that both the IRS and the state are inclined to apply these tests to determine an employment status rather than an independent contractor status. If an employer misclassifies a service provider as an independent contractor rather than as an employee, there are many financial risks and it may result in payment of back payroll taxes, penalties, interests, and sanctions. Additionally, "the responsible person" of an employer may be subject to personal liability and criminal penalties. In 1991, the EDD and the IRS agreed to share information and resources, which means that an audit by one agency is likely to instigate in an audit by the other. Given the complexity of the classification analysis and the severity of the consequences, it is best to consult your attorney and accountant before classifying a worker as an independent contractor. If it is a close call, it is better to classify a worker as an employee and withhold.

Given the complexity of the classification analysis and the severity of the consequences, it is best to consult your attorney and accountant before classifying a worker as an independent contractor.

Minimum Wage and Payroll Practices

Once you have determined that a service provider is in fact an employee, you must comply with all federal and California laws and regulations regarding payment of wages. The federal Fair Labor Standards Act sets minimum wages that apply to substantially all employees who are engaged in interstate commerce, with exceptions for certain *exempt* employees, such as executive, administrative, professional, and outside salesmen and personnel, and other miscellaneous occupations.

A significant issue for many employers is the regulations and laws concerning overtime wages for *nonexempt* employees. Nonexempt employees must be paid time-and-one-half compensation for all hours worked in excess of eight hours in one day, in excess of 40 hours in one workweek, and for the first eight hours on the seventh day of work in a single workweek. Double time must be paid for hours worked in excess of 12 hours in one day and in excess of eight hours on the seventh day of work in a single workweek. Conversely, exempt employees are expected to work as much of each workday as is necessary to complete their job responsibilities, without overtime or additional compensation.

A related and equally important issue concerning payment of wages is the time period that an employer has to pay an employee's final wages after termination of employment. Generally, if an employer discharges an employee, the wages earned and unpaid as of the time of discharge are due and payable immediately.[2] On the other hand, if an employee who does not have a written contract for a definite period quits his or her employment, without 72 hours' advance notice, then the employee's final wages are due no later than 72 hours after the time of resignation.[3] However, if an employee gives the employer 72 hours' advance notice of his or her intention to quit, then the employee is entitled to receive his or her final wages at the time of quitting.[4] If an employer fails to pay final wages when due, the California Division of Labor Standards Enforcement commissioner can impose substantial fines, equal to one day's worth of wages for every late day of payment.

If a person in charge of hiring and firing employees and negotiating wages fails to make certain that the required minimum wages or overtime wages are paid, that person may become personally liable for twice the amount of the unpaid minimum wages, plus attorneys' fees, in addition to substantial criminal penalties.

Vacation Leave and Pay

An employer is not required by law to provide employees with paid vacation leave. However, an employer who adopts a policy that provides paid vacation, holiday, and sick leave cannot discriminate among employees in applying that policy. Additionally, a formal vacation policy adopted by an employer, although it may be modified, cannot result in an employee's forfeiture of earned vacation pay.

An employer may impose reasonable restrictions on an employee's accrual and use of vacation time, but if the vacation time vests, then an employer is required to pay all accrued and unpaid vacation time upon an employee's termination of employment, regardless of the cause of termination.[5]

A vacation plan cannot be based on a "use it or lose it" policy such that an employee would forfeit earned vacation time if he or she does not use it by a particular time. However, in order to avoid accumulation of substantial vacation time and pay, an employer may place a cap on the accrual of an employee's vacation. For example, an employer may adopt a plan that precludes its employees from accruing any additional vacation time after accumulating a certain specified amount.

If your company intends to adopt a formal vacation policy for its employees, it is recommended that you consult with an attorney or some other professional to ensure that the plan is legally enforceable and implementing and executing it will not violate federal and state employment laws.

Inspection and Retention of Employee Records

An issue that often arises when firing an employee is whether the employer has an obligation to provide, and the employee has legal rights to inspect, the employee's records and files maintained by the

An employer who adopts a policy that provides paid vacation, holiday, and sick leave cannot discriminate among employees in applying that policy.

California law mandates all employers to provide a copy, on request, of any document signed by an employee relating to the obtaining or holding of employment.

employer. California law[6] mandates all employers to provide a copy, on request, of any document signed by an employee relating to the obtaining or holding of employment. California law[7] also requires that all employers maintain and make available for inspection copies of an employee's personnel records relating to the employee's performance or to any grievance concerning the employee.

The requirements for how long an employer is required to retain an employee's personnel files vary depending on the type of records and the federal or California statutes that apply. Destroying personnel records before the expiration of the statutory period will likely lead to a presumption that the records contained information favorable to the employee, in the event that there is a dispute between the former employee and the employer. Therefore, due consideration and care should be given to creating and maintaining a personnel file for each of your employees and it is recommended that you retain such records for at least four years to ensure that you are in compliance with most federal and California statutes.

Anti-Discrimination Laws

California employers should be aware of the following laws that prohibit employment discrimination and may apply to all areas of employment, including recruitment, hiring, training, promotion, compensation, benefits, transfer, social and recreational programs, disciplinary actions, and termination.

- Title VII of the Civil Rights Act of 1964 (Title VII Act), which prohibits discrimination on the basis of race, color religion, sex, or national origin.
- The Americans with Disabilities Act (ADA), which prohibits discrimination against qualified persons with disabilities, compelling employers to provide such persons with reasonable accommodation to perform the essential functions of their jobs.
- The Fair Employment and Housing Act (FEHA), which prohibits discrimination on the basis of race, religion, ancestry, national origin, color, physical disability, medical or mental conditions, pregnancy, martial status, sex, age, or sexual orientation.
- The Age Discrimination in Employment Act of 1967 (ADEA), which prohibits discrimination on the basis of age against persons who are 40 years or older.

- The California Labor Code, Section 1102, which prohibits discrimination on the basis of political belief.

The foregoing list does not purport to cover all relevant legislation and laws that provide employees protection against an employer's unlawful and discriminatory conduct; however, it outlines some of the more prevalent topics. Of those, the Title VII Act (federal) and FEHA (California) are the primary legislation in the anti-discrimination domain and serve as the main source of employee administrative complaints and legal actions against employers.

FEHA applies generally to employers that regularly employ five or more persons,[8] but its prohibitions against harassment cover any employer regularly employing one or more employee and also provides protection to certain independent contractors. The Title VII Act, on the other hand, applies to employers that employ 15 or more employees on each working day in 20 or more calendar weeks of the current or preceding year in an industry affecting commerce.[9]

The state and federal anti-discrimination statutes afford employees administrative remedies and allow private action in courts, assuming there is no arbitration agreement between the parties compelling arbitration.[10] Generally, an employee must exhaust administrative remedies before pursuing a private action in court. The Department of Fair Employment and Housing (DFEH) is principally responsible for administrative enforcement of the FEHA and the Equal Employment Opportunity Commission (EEOC) is responsible for enforcement of the federal statutes, including the Title VII Act, the ADA, and the ADEA.

Since each legislative act has its own distinctive definitions and guidelines, you should review them carefully or contact an attorney to advise you on establishing company policies and procedures that comply with the laws and regulations that apply to your corporation.

Immigration Law Requirements

As an employer in a global economy, your company may seek, from time to time, to hire a foreign national. Obtaining the proper visa often depends upon careful compliance with complex regulations governing immigration. Regardless, all employers must comply with applicable immigration laws, including the Immigration Reform and Control Act of 1986 and the Immigration Act of 1990. Accordingly, all employers are required, prior to the commencement of employment, to obtain, verify, and retain documentary confirmation of a worker's legal authority to work in the United States. You must require all of your service providers, as a condition of employment, to complete the Employment Eligibility Verification Form I-9 (Form 13-F) and provide satisfactory evidence of his or her identity and legal authority to work in the United States. If your company intends to hire foreign nationals, you should seek legal advice *before* hiring and preferably before they apply for entry into the United States. Notwithstanding the foregoing, it is unlawful to discriminate against foreign nationals who are U.S. permanent residents or who have work authorization. Updated forms and further information may be obtained from the U.S. Citizenship and Immigration Services web site at www.uscis.gov or by calling 800 375-5283 or 800 870-3676.

Worker's Compensation Insurance

Most California employees are subject to the state's worker's compensation laws. These laws impose liability upon the employer for employees' injuries in work-related accidents, whether or not the employer was negligent, and provide a schedule of benefits to be paid for such injuries or to the heirs of an employee killed in such an accident. Your company should obtain worker's compensation liability insurance from an authorized insurer in a coverage amount sufficient to satisfy the law or obtain from the Director of Industrial Relations a certificate of consent to self-insure. Insurance coverage may be obtained through the local office of the State Compensation Insurance Fund or may be placed with a licensed worker's compensation private carrier.

> Your company should obtain worker's compensation liability insurance from an authorized insurer in a coverage amount sufficient to satisfy the law.

Protecting the Company's Trade Secrets and Confidential Information

Most of the subjects covered in this chapter have provided you with a general survey of an employee's federal and state rights and your obligations as an employer to ensure that your corporation complies with the applicable laws. Consequently, the content has thus focused on a defensive approach by offering you some suggestions for implementing policies and procedures that are in compliance with the applicable laws in order to minimize your exposure and to insulate your corporation from potential claims that an employee may file against it. This section, on the other hand, provides an offensive approach for employers, by offering you suggestions for protecting your corporation's most valuable assets and properties from temporary or disloyal employees or independent contractors.

Due to the competitive marketplace and greater employee mobility, it is now more important than ever for employers to proactively implement procedures to ensure that their trade secrets, confidential information, and proprietary assets are secured and well protected. A business's most valuable assets may be intangible and more difficult to safeguard and to account for, without a written contract that clearly identifies the company's ownership interest and rights. These assets may include the company's inventions, designs, discoveries, processes, data, business plans and models; workers' inventions and developments; customer lists and data; intellectual property; employees' data and personnel information; vendor information and data; and financial reports and forecasts.

Although an employer may have certain statutory and common law protections, it is best to complement and support such rights by requiring your service providers to enter into confidentiality agreements that protect and preserve your trade secrets and other valuable properties. By requiring an employee or an independent contractor to enter into an invention assignment and confidentiality agreement that clearly set forth the parties' mutual understanding and identify the worker's obligations to the corporation, there will be little room for ambiguity in the future. Such documents will also provide your corporation with direct recourse against the service provider, in the event he or she violates the terms of the agreement. In such an event, the company may seek monetary damages for breach of contract or lost profit damages suffered, injunctive relief if future irreparable harm is threatened, and liquidated damages if the amount of actual damages sustained by a breach would be impractical or difficult to determine.

Since confidentiality and invention assignment agreements have the potential of transferring significant and valuable rights, due care should be given in drafting them so that they can withstand the scrutiny of the courts in applying California laws, which are favorable to competition and free mobility and creativity. Accordingly, such agreements should be as specific as possible without disclosing the trade secrets. Coverage that is overly broad or vague may not be enforceable. You should also carefully consider whether or not to insert a noncompete clause into the confidentiality agreements with employees, given that most noncompetition clauses are generally invalid in California as they stifle

> It is now more important than ever for employers to proactively implement procedures to ensure that their trade secrets, confidential information, and proprietary assets are secured and well protected.

competition and employee mobility. Indeed, a nonsolicitation clause will increase the probability that former employees will refrain from soliciting clients, employees, and vendors for a specific period of time past termination of their employment (12 months to two years) and has a much greater chance of being enforced than a noncompete clause, which more likely than not will be viewed as an illegal restraint of trade.

The law, however, does recognize and provides employers with some protection. Under the work-for-hire doctrine, an employer owns the rights to an employee's inventions if the employee creates and develops the product or concept within the scope of his or her employment. But California law also generally invalidates clauses that try to transfer an employee's invention rights to the employer where the employee made the invention on his or her own time, the invention does not relate to the employer's business, and the employee did not use the employer's equipment or facilities.[11]

To ensure maximum protection, employee agreements should be signed at the time of hire and must comply with the mandatory requirements of Section 2870 of the California Labor Code, which statutory terms must be included or attached to the employee's agreement. Any termination of a pre-existing employee for refusing to sign a confidentiality, nondisclosure, or non-solicitation agreement could provide the basis for a claim for wrongful termination. One approach that can be taken with pre-existing employees is to obtain their signature on such an agreement at the time of promotion.

Agreements with third parties such as independent contractors or business partners should be signed prior to disclosure. It is important to note that, without a written agreement, an independent contractor generally owns the work and the company may only have a license to use it. Using the term "work for hire" in an agreement with the independent contractor or stating that the company is the owner may be insufficient for software-related work; therefore, an assignment clause should be always be used.

Forms 13-G and 13-H are sample confidentiality and invention assignment agreements that you may use for your employees and independent contractors.

California law generally invalidates clauses that try to transfer an employee's invention rights to the employer where the employee made the invention on his or her own time.

Dispute Resolution Policies

As a result of the substantial costs and time involved with litigation and the fear of jury verdicts, many companies are now making mandatory mediation and arbitration a condition of employment. Mediation is a nonbinding process involving a neutral third party who acts as a facilitator in an attempt to resolve the dispute. The mediator does not have any authority to make a ruling or to render a final judgment. Rather, his or her sole role and authority is to persuade, but not compel, the parties to settle the dispute. As part of the terms and conditions of employment, via an agreement or employee handbook, an employer can require an employee to mediate a dispute first before taking further legal action.

However, if mediation is unsuccessful and the parties are unable to reach a settlement, as a backup plan (if properly established in advance) an employer may compel arbitration, rather than litigation, for all employment-related matters and disputes that arise between the company and employees. In deciding whether to compel arbitration, an employer should keep in mind the practical reality that arbitrators are sometimes not trained lawyers and may be unable to correctly apply the rules of law.

In a prominent California case,[12] the California Supreme Court held that an agreement to arbitrate an employee's statutory claims, or an arbitration policy, must meet the following requirements: provide a mechanism for selecting a neutral arbitrator; allow the employee to conduct adequate discovery; not limit the employee's remedies and ability to fully recover all amounts available in a civil trial (e.g., attorneys' fees and punitive damages); limit the employee's share of costs that are unique to arbitration (e.g., employer must be prepared to pay the forum costs, arbitrator's fees, meeting room charges, and other costs not involved if the case were tried in court); require a written decision by the arbitrator that allows limited judicial review; and must be deemed fair and equitable, not one-sided, unconscionable, and onerous. To avoid the appearance of impropriety, it is recommended that an employee expressly and distinctly sign the arbitration agreement upon hire, as a condition of employment, with an explicit and conspicuous statement that the employee waives his or her right to have a jury trial. For a sample mediation and arbitration policy, see Form 13-I.

As a result of the substantial costs and time involved with litigation and the fear of jury verdicts, many companies are now making mandatory mediation and arbitration a condition of employment.

It should be noted, however, that this is one area of the law that is changing constantly. Consequently, you should review the continued appropriateness and enforceability of this form with counsel on a regular basis.

Notwithstanding the foregoing, an arbitration policy or agreement cannot interfere with an employee's rights and abilities to file administrative charges with and to seek assistance from the California Department of Fair Employment and Housing or the Equal Employment Opportunity Commission, which are the California and federal governmental agencies charged with the responsibility of taking and processing an employee's administrative complaint of discrimination or wrongful termination against an employer.

Notes

1. California Labor Code Section 2922.
2. California Labor Code Section 201(a).
3. California Labor Code Section 202(a).
4. California Labor Code Section 202(a).
5. California Labor Code Section 227.3.
6. California Labor Code Section 432.
7. California Labor Code Section 1198.5.
8. Government Code Section 12926(d).
9. 42 United States Code section 2000e(b).
10. For further discussion regarding binding arbitration, see "Dispute Resolution Policies" section in this chapter.
11. California Labor Code Sections 2870-2872.
12. *Armendariz v. Foundation Health Psychcare Services* (2000) 24 Cal. 4th 83.

Forms for Setting up Your California Corporation or LLC

I n this part of the book you will find forms that you can use to set up your California corporation or LLC. These are organized according to chapters in this book:

Chapter 1. Choosing Your Business Entity
No Forms

Chapter 2. Setting up Out of State
Form 2-A   Statement and Designation by Foreign Corporation
Form 2-B   Statement of Information (Foreign Corporation) — SI-350
Form 2-C   Limited Liability Company Application for Registration—LLC-5
Form 2-D   Limited Liability Company Tax Voucher—FTB 3522
Form 2-E   Limited Liability Company Application for Registration, Certificate of Amendment—LLC-6
Form 2-F   Statement of Information (Limited Liability Company)—LLC-12

Chapter 3. Steps to Incorporating
Form 3-A   Name Reservation—Order Form
Form 3-B   Fictitious Business Name Statement

Form 3-C	Statement of Abandonment of Use of Fictitious Business Name
Form 3-D	Articles of Incorporation (General Stock)
Form 3-E	Articles of Incorporation Designating Initial Directors
Form 3-F	Articles of Incorporation Not Designating Initial Directors
Form 3-G	Bylaws
Form 3-H	Sample Document Filing Request
Form 3-I	Certificate of Amendment of Articles of Incorporation (before issuance of shares)
Form 3-J	Certificate of Amendment of Articles of Incorporation (after issuance of shares)
Form 3-K	Sample Document Filing Request for Articles of Incorporation
Form 3-L	Sample Letter for Certificate of Amendment of Articles of Incorporation
Form 3-M	Action of Incorporator
Form 3-N	Resolution of Board of Directors Amending Certain Bylaws
Form 3-O	Waiver of Notice and Consent to Holding of the First Meeting of the Board of Directors
Form 3-P	Waiver of Notice and Consent to Holding of the First Meeting of the Board of Directors (Nonprofit Corporation)
Form 3-Q	Minutes of the First Meeting of the Board of Directors
Form 3-R	Minutes of a Special Meeting of the Board of Directors
Form 3-S	Minutes of a Special Meeting of the Shareholders
Form 3-T	Statement of Information (Domestic Stock Corporation)
Form 3-U	Application for Employer Identification Number (EIN)—SS-4
Form 3-V	Seller's Permit Application—BOE-400-SPA

Chapter 4. Capitalizing the Corporation and Issuing Stock

Form 4-A	Notice of Sale of Securities—Form D
Form 4-B	Notice of Transaction Pursuant to Corporations Code Section 25102(f)
Form 4-C	Investor Questionnaire for Individuals
Form 4-D	Investor Questionnaire for Entities
Form 4-E	Form Transmittal Letter to Department of Corporations
Form 4-F	Notice of Issuance of Shares Pursuant to Subdivision (h) of Section 25102

Chapter 5. Incorporating or Forming an LLC from an Ongoing Business

Form 5-A   Agreement to Transfer Partnership Assets to Corporation
Form 5-B   Transfer of Assets of Sole Proprietorship to Corporation
Form 5-C   Notice to Creditors of Bulk Sale
Form 5-D   Bill of Sale Agreement
Form 5-E   Notice of Dissolution of Partnership

Chapter 6. Maintaining the Corporation or LLC

Form 6-A   Application for Certificate of Revivor
Form 6-B   Minutes of the Annual Meeting of the Shareholders
Form 6-C   Minutes of the Annual Meeting of the Board of Directors
Form 6-D   Minutes of a Special Meeting of the Shareholders
Form 6-E   Minutes of a Special Meeting of the Board of Directors
Form 6-F   Waiver of Notice and Consent to Holding of a Special Meeting of the Shareholders
Form 6-G   Waiver of Notice and Consent to Holding of a Special Meeting of the Board of Directors
Form 6-H   Action by Unanimous Written Consent of Directors Without Meeting
Form 6-I   Affidavit of Mailing of Notice of the Annual Meeting of the Shareholders
Form 6-J   Limited and Revocable Proxy
Form 6-K   Bylaws
Form 6-L   Operating Agreement for a Limited Liability Company
Form 6-M   Buy-Sell Agreement
Form 6-N   Certificate of Amendment of Articles of Incorporation

Chapter 7. Corporate and LLC Variations

Form 7-A   Sample Articles of Incorporation Designating Initial Directors
Form 7-B   Sample Articles of Incorporation Not Designating Initial Directors

Chapter 8. S Corporations

Form 8-A   Election by a Small Business Corporation—IRS Form 2553
Form 8-B   S Corporation's List of Shareholders and Consents—FTB Form 3830

Chapter 9. Limited Liability Companies

Form 9-A Limited Liability Company Articles of Organization—
          LLC-1
Form 9-B Operating Agreement for LLC (Short Form)
Form 9-C Operating Agreement for LLC (Long Form)
Form 9-D Limited Liability Company—Statement of Information—
          LLC-12

Chapter 10. Taxes

Form 10-A Corporation Estimated Tax—FTB Form 100-ES
Form 10-B Registration Form for Commercial Employers—EDD
           Form DE 1
Form 10-C California Seller's Permit Application—BOE-400-SPA
Form 10-D California Resale Exemption Certificate Form
Form 10-E Application for Employer Identification Number—IRS
           Form SS-4
Form 10-F Determination of Worker Status for Purposes of Federal
           Employment Taxes and Income Tax Withholding—IRS
           Form SS-8
Form 10-G Employee's Withholding Allowance Certificate—IRS
           Form W-4
Form 10-H Employer's Quarterly Federal Tax Return—IRS Form 941
Form 10-I Wage and Tax Statement—IRS Form W-2
Form 10-J Transmittal of Wage and Tax Statements—IRS Form W-3
Form 10-K Federal Tax Deposit Coupon—IRS Form 8109-B
Form 10-L Estimated Tax for Corporations—IRS Form 1120-W
Form 10-M Minutes of First Meeting of the Board of Directors
Form 10-N Instructions for Form 1065
Form 10-O Limited Liability Company Tax—FTB Form 568

Chapter 11. Nonprofit Corporations

Form 11-A Articles of Incorporation for Nonprofit Public Benefit
           Corporation
Form 11-B Articles of Incorporation for Nonprofit Mutual Benefit
           Corporation
Form 11-C Articles of Incorporation for Nonprofit Religious
           Corporation
Form 11-D Bylaws for Nonprofit Public Benefit Corporation
Form 11-E Minutes of the First Meeting of the Board of Directors for
           Nonprofit Corporation

Form 11-F Statement of Information (Domestic Stock Corporation)—SI-200 C

Form 11-G Action by Sole Incorporator Appointing Initial Directors and Adopting Bylaws

Form 11-H Waiver of Notice and Consent to the First Meeting of the Board of Directors

Form 11-I Minutes of the Organizational Meeting of the Board of Directors

Form 11-J Charity Registration Form—Form CT-1

Form 11-K Application for Recognition of Exemption—IRS Form 1023

Form 11-L Exemption Application—FTB Form 3500

Form 11-M Application to Mail at Nonprofit Standard Mail Rates—PS Form 3624

Form 11-N Registration/Renewal Fee Report

Chapter 12. Intellectual Property
No Forms

Chapter 13. Legal Obligations of Employers

Form 13-A Employee's Withholding Allowance Certificate—IRS Form W-4

Form 13-B Registration Form for Commercial Employers, Pacific Maritime, and Fishing Boats—EDD Form DE 1

Form 13-C Report of New Employee(s)—EDD Form DE 34

Form 13-D Report of Independent Contractor(s)—EDD Form DE 542

Form 13-E Offer of Employment

Form 13-F Employment Eligibility Verification—Form I-9

Form 13-G Employee Proprietary Information and Inventions Assignment Agreement

Form 13-H Independent Contractor Proprietary Information and Inventions Assignment Agreement

Form 13-I Mediation and Arbitration Policy

Forms for Chapter 2

There are six forms that accompany **Chapter 2, Setting up Out of State**. They include the following:

Form 2-A   Statement and Designation by Foreign Corporation, 4 pages (133 - 136)

Form 2-B   Statement of Information (Foreign Corporation)—SI-350, 2 pages (137 - 138)

Form 2-C   Limited Liability Company Application for Registration—LLC-5, 3 pages (139 - 141)

Form 2-D   Limited Liability Company Tax Voucher—FTB 3522, 1 page (142)

Form 2-E   Limited Liability Company Application for Registration, Certificate of Amendment—LLC-6, 2 pages (143 - 144)

Form 2-F   Statement of Information (Limited Liability Company)—LLC-12, 2 pages (145 - 146)

REQUIREMENTS FOR QUALIFICATION
OF FOREIGN STOCK CORPORATIONS

Foreign stock corporations must file a signed statement consistent with the requirements of California Corporations Code Section 2105 to qualify to transact intrastate business in California. A Statement and Designation by Foreign Corporation form designed for compliance with these requirements is attached.

A certificate by an authorized public official of the state or place of incorporation, to the effect that the corporation is an existing corporation in good standing status in that state or place, must be attached to the Statement and Designation by Foreign Corporation form at the time of filing. A certified copy of the Articles of Incorporation does not meet statutory requirements and cannot be accepted in lieu of the required certificate.

Upon the filing of the Statement and Designation by Foreign Corporation form, a Certificate of Qualification will be issued to the corporation. The certificate is issued only at the time of qualification and will not be reissued if lost or misplaced.

The fee for filing the Statement and Designation by Foreign Corporation for a stock (profit) corporation is $100.00. Check(s) should be made payable to the Secretary of State.

PLEASE NOTE: Corporations qualified to transact intrastate business in California are subject to California corporation franchise tax requirements until such time as they formally surrender their right to transact intrastate business. Information regarding franchise tax requirements can be obtained from the Franchise Tax Board's Internet Web site or by calling the Franchise Tax Board at 1-800-852-5711.

Documents can be mailed or hand delivered for over-the-counter processing to the Sacramento office at:

> Business Programs Division   (916) 657-5448
> 1500 11th Street
> Sacramento, CA 95814
> Attention: Document Filing Support Unit

OR

can be hand delivered for over-the-counter processing to any of the regional offices located in:

- Fresno   (559) 445-6900
  1315 Van Ness Avenue, Suite 203
  Fresno, CA 93721-1729

- Los Angeles   (213) 897-3062
  The Ronald Reagan Building
  12th Floor South Tower, Room 12513
  300 South Spring Street
  Los Angeles, CA 90013-1233

- San Diego   (619) 525-4113
  1350 Front Street, Suite 2060
  San Diego, CA 92101-3609

Secretary of State Information
S&DC-STOCK (*Rev 07/2004*)   (Please see reverse)

- San Francisco   (415) 557-8000
    455 Golden Gate Avenue, Suite 14500
    San Francisco, CA 94102-7007

NOTE: • Cash is accepted **only** in the Sacramento office.

- Duplicate original documents must be submitted when filing in any of the regional offices.

- Regional offices do not process mailed in documents.

A $15.00 special handling fee   is applicable for processing documents delivered in person at the public counter in the Sacramento office or in any of the regional offices located in Fresno, Los Angeles, San Diego and San Francisco. The $15.00 special handling fee must be remitted by separate check for each submittal and will be retained whether the documents are filed or rejected. The special handling fee does not apply to documents submitted by mail.

Preclearance or expedited filing of eligible corporate documents can be requested in a specified time frame, for an additional fee (in lieu of the $15.00 special handling fee), as described in the Preclearance/Expedited Filing Service Information. The preclearance/expedited filing service is not available in the regional offices.

Secretary of State Information
S&DC-STOCK (*Rev 07/2004*)   (Please see reverse)

INSTRUCTIONS:

1. To qualify to transact intrastate business in California the attached Statement and Designation by Foreign Corporation form must be completed with the information called for in the form itself. The information must be typed with letters in dark contrast to the paper. Documents submitted with poor microfilm characteristics will be returned unfiled.

2. There must be annexed to this statement a certificate by an authorized public official of the state or place of incorporation of the corporation to the effect that the corporation making the statements is an existing corporation in good standing in that state or place.

3. No domestic corporation may be designated as agent for service of process unless it has filed with the California Secretary of State a Certificate pursuant to California Corporations Code Section 1505 , and no foreign corporation may be designated unless it has qualified for the transaction of intrastate business in California and has filed with the California Secretary of State a Certificate pursuant to Corporations Code Section 1505. A domestic or foreign corporation must be currently authorized to engage in business in this state and be in good standing status on the records of the California Secretary of State to file a certificate pursuant to this section.

    NOTE: A corporation cannot act as agent for itself for service of process.

4. If a corporation is required to qualify under an assumed name (a name other than the true corporate name) pursuant to Corporations Code Section 2106(b) , the first line of the statement form must be completed with the true corporate name, followed by the words "which will do business in California as _____" and the assumed name. The assumed name should not be included with the corporate name anywhere else in the statement.

NOTE: If the corporation changes its name, the corporation must file an Amended Statement by Foreign Corporation .

The original Statement and Designation form, together with the applicable fee, must be mailed or hand delivered to the Secretary of State's office in Sacramento or hand delivered to one of the regional offices located in Fresno, Los Angeles, San Diego or San Francisco. Regional offices do not process mailed in documents. If documents are submitted to a regional office, a duplicate original is also required.

To facilitate the processing of documents mailed to the Sacramento office, a self-addressed envelope and a letter referencing the corporate name as well as your own name, return address and telephone number should also be submitted.

Secretary of State Instructions
S&DC-STOCK (*Rev 07/2004*)

STATEMENT AND DESIGNATION
BY FOREIGN CORPORATION

_____
(Name of Corporation)

_____ , a corporation organized and existing under the

laws of _____ ,makes the following statements and designation:
(State or Place of Incorporation)

1. The address of its principal executive office is _____

    _____ .

2. The address of its principal office in the State of California is _____

    _____ .

DESIGNATION OF AGENT FOR SERVICE OF PROCESS IN THE STATE OF CALIFORNIA
(Complete either Item 3 or Item 4.)

3. (Use this paragraph if the process **agent is a natural person.**)

    _____ , **a natural person residing in the State of**

    California, whose complete address is _____

    _____ , is designated as agent upon whom process directed to
    this corporation may be served within the State of California, in the manner provided by law.

4. (Use this paragraph if the process **agent is a corporation.**)

    _____ , a corporation organized and existing

    under the laws of _____ , is designated as agent upon whom process directed
    to this corporation may be served within the State of California, in the manner provided by law.

    **NOTE: Corporate agents must have complied with California Corporations Code Section 1505
    prior to designation.**

5. It irrevocably consents to service of process directed to it upon the agent designated above, and to service
    of process on the Secretary of State of the State of California if the agent so designated or the agent's
    successor is no longer authorized to act or cannot be found at the address given.

_____   _____
(Signature of Corporate Officer)   (Typed Name and Title of Officer Signing)

Secretary of State Form
S&DC-STOCK/NONPROFIT (Rev 07/2004)

INSTRUCTIONS FOR COMPLETING FORM SI-350

For faster processing, the required statement for most corporations can be filed online at https://businessfilings.ss.ca.gov. Alternatively, statement forms are available on the Secretary of State's website at http://www.ss.ca.gov/business and can be viewed, filled in and printed from your computer. Completed forms along with the applicable fees can be mailed to Secretary of State, Statement of Information Unit, P.O. Box 944230, Sacramento, CA 94244-2300 or delivered in person to the Sacramento office, 1500 11th Street, 3rd Floor, Sacramento, CA 95814. If you are not completing this form online, please type or legibly print in black or blue ink. This form should not be altered.

Every foreign corporation shall file a Statement of Information with the Secretary of State annually during the applicable filing period. The applicable filing period for a foreign corporation is the calendar month during which its original Statement and Designation by Foreign Corporation was filed and the immediately preceding five calendar months. If the name and/or address of the agent for service of process has changed, a corporation must file a complete Statement of Information. A corporation is required to file this statement even though it may not be actively engaged in business at the time this statement is due.

Statutory filing provisions are found in California Corporations Code **section 2117**, unless otherwise indicated. Failure to file this Statement of Information by the due date will result in the assessment of a $250.00 penalty. (Corporations Code **section 2206**; Revenue and Taxation Code **section 19141**)

FILING FEES: The annual Statement of Information must be accompanied by a $20.00 filing fee and $5.00 disclosure fee. The filing fee and the disclosure fee may be included in a single check made payable to the Secretary of State. All foreign corporations must pay a total of $25.00 at the time of filing the annual statement. If this statement is being filed to amend any information on a previously filed statement and is being filed outside the applicable filing period, as defined above, no fee is required.

PUBLICLY TRADED FOREIGN CORPORATIONS: Every publicly traded foreign corporation must also file a Corporate Disclosure Statement (**Form SI-PT**) annually, within 150 days after the end of its fiscal year. Form SI-PT may be obtained from the Secretary of State's website at http://www.ss.ca.gov/business or by calling the Statement of Information Unit at (916) 657-5448.

A "publicly traded foreign corporation" is a foreign corporation, as defined in Corporations Code **section 171**, that is an issuer as defined in Section 3 of the Securities Exchange Act of 1934, as amended (15 U.S.C. Sec. 78c), and has at least one class of securities listed or admitted for trading on a national securities exchange, on the National or Small-Cap Markets of the NASDAQ Stock Market, on the OTC-Bulletin Board, or on the electronic service operated by Pink Sheets, LLC.

Complete the Statement of Information (Form SI-350) as follows:

Item 1. Please do not alter the preprinted name. If the corporate name is not correct, please attach a statement indicating the correct name and the date the Amended Statement by Foreign Corporation (Corporations Code **section 2107**) was filed with the Secretary of State. If blank, enter the name of the corporation exactly as it is of record with the California Secretary of State.

Item 2. If there has been <u>any</u> change to the last Statement of Information filed with the Secretary of State, including a change to any address, or no Statement of Information has ever been filed, complete this form in its entirety.

       If there has been no change in the information contained in the last Statement of Information filed with the Secretary of State, check the box and proceed to Item 11.

Item 3. Enter the complete street address, city, state and zip code of the principal executive office. Please do not enter a P.O. Box or abbreviate the name of the city. This address will be used for mailing purposes.

Item 4. Enter the complete street address, city and zip code of the corporation's principal office in California, if any. Please do not enter a P.O. Box or abbreviate the name of the city. Complete this item only if the address in Item 3 is outside of California.

Items 5-7. Enter the name and complete business or residential address of the corporation's chief executive officer (i.e., president), secretary and chief financial officer (i.e., treasurer). Please do not abbreviate the name of the city. The corporation must have these three officers. An officer may hold more than one office. A comparable title for the specific officer may be added; however, the preprinted titles on this form must not be altered.

Item 8. Enter the name of the agent for service of process in California. The person named as agent must be a resident of California or a corporation that has filed a certificate pursuant to Corporations Code **section 1505**. If an individual is designated as agent, complete Items 8 and 9. If a corporation is designated as agent, complete Item 8 and proceed to Item 10 (do not complete Item 9).

       An Agent for Service of Process is an individual or another corporation designated by a corporation to accept service of process if the corporation is sued.

       Please note: A corporation cannot name itself as agent for service of process and no domestic or foreign corporation may file pursuant to **section 1505** unless the corporation is currently authorized to engage in business in California and is in good standing on the records of the Secretary of State.

Item 9. If an individual is designated as agent for service of process, enter a business or residential address in California. Please do not enter "in care of" (c/o) or abbreviate the name of the city. Please do not enter an address if a corporation is designated as agent for service of process.

Item 10. Briefly describe the general type of business that constitutes the principal business activity of the corporation.

Item 11. Type or print the name and title of the person completing this form and enter the date this form was completed.

State of California $\boxed{\text{F}}$

Kevin Shelley
Secretary of State

STATEMENT OF INFORMATION
(Foreign Cor poration)

FEES (Filing and Disclosure): $25.00.   If amendment, see instr uctions.

IMPORTANT — READ INSTRUCTIONS BEFORE COMPLETING THIS FORM

1.   CORPORATE NAME (Please do not alter if name is preprinted.)

This Space For Filing Use Only

DUE DATE:

CALIFORNIA CORPORATE DISCLOSURE ACT (Corporations Code **section 2117.1**)

A publicly traded corporation must file with the Secretary of State a Corporate Disclosure Statement (**Form SI-PT**) annually, within 150 days after the end of its fiscal year. Please see reverse for additional information regarding publicly traded corporations.

NO CHANGE STATEMENT

2. ☐   If there has been no change in any of the information contained in the last Statement of Information filed with the Secretary of State, check the box and proceed to Item 11 .

If there have been any changes to the information contained in the last Statement of Information filed with the Secretary of State, or no statement has been previously filed, this form must be completed in its entirety.

COMPLETE ADDRESSES FOR THE FOLLOWING (Do not abbreviate the name of the city. Items 3 and 4 cannot be P.O. Boxes.)

3.   STREET ADDRESS OF PRINCIPAL EXECUTIVE OFFICE | CITY AND STATE | ZIP CODE

4.   STREET ADDRESS OF PRINCIPAL BUSINESS OFFICE IN CALIFORNIA, IF ANY | CITY | STATE CA | ZIP CODE

NAMES AND COMPLETE ADDRESSES OF THE FOLLOWING OFFICERS (The corporation must have these three officers. A comparable title for the specific officer may be added; however, the preprinted titles on this form must not be altered.)

5.   CHIEF EXECUTIVE OFFICER/ | ADDRESS | CITY AND STATE | ZIP CODE

6.   SECRETARY/ | ADDRESS | CITY AND STATE | ZIP CODE

7.   CHIEF FINANCIAL OFFICER/ | ADDRESS | CITY AND STATE | ZIP CODE

AGENT FOR SERVICE OF PROCESS (If the agent is an individual, the agent must reside in California and Item 9 must be completed with a California address. If the agent is another corporation, the agent must have on file with the California Secretary of State a certificate pursuant to Corporations Code **section 1505** and Item 9 must be left blank.)

8.   NAME OF AGENT FOR SERVICE OF PROCESS

9. ADDRESS OF AGENT FOR SERVICE OF PROCESS IN CALIFORNIA, IF AN INDIVIDUAL | CITY | STATE CA | ZIP CODE

TYPE OF BUSINESS

10. DESCRIBE THE TYPE OF BUSINESS OF THE CORPORATION

11. THE INFORMATION CONTAINED HEREIN IS TRUE AND CORRECT.

TYPE OR PRINT NAME OF PERSON COMPLETING THE FORM | SIGNATURE | TITLE | DATE

SI-350 (REV 09/2004) | APPROVED BY SECRETARY OF STATE

ATTENTION: LIMITED LIABILITY COMPANY FILERS

Tax Information

Pursuant to California Revenue and Taxation Code section 17941, every Limited Liability Company (LLC) that is doing business in California or that has Articles of Organization accepted or a Certificate of Registration issued by the Secretary of State's office (pursuant to California Corporations Code section 17050 or 17451) AND is not taxed as a corporation, is subject to the annual LLC minimum tax of $800 (as well as the appropriate fee pursuant to Revenue and Taxation Code section 17942). The tax is paid to the California Franchise Tax Board; is due for the taxable year of organization/registration and must be paid for each taxable year, or part there of, until a Certificate of Cancellation of Registration or Certificate of Cancellation of Articles of Organization (pursuant to Corporations Code section 17356 or 17455) is filed with the Secretary of State's office. For further information regarding the payment of this tax, please contact the Franchise Tax Board at:

From within the United States (toll free) ....(800) 852-5711
From outside the United States (not toll free)...(916) 845-6500
Automated Toll Free Phone Service..(800) 338-0505

Professional Services

Pursuant to California Corporations Code section 17375, a domestic or foreign limited liability company may not render professional services, as defined in Corporations Code sections **13401(a)** and **13401.3**. Professional services are defined as:

> Any type of professional services that may be lawfully rendered only pursuant to a license, certification, or registration authorized by the Business and Professions Code, the Chiropractic Act, the Osteopathic Act or the Yacht and Ship Brokers Act.

If your business is required to be licensed, registered or certified, it is recommended that you contact the appropriate licensing authority before filing with the Secretary of State's office in order to determine whether your services are considered professional.

LLC Info (REV 09/2004)

State of California
Kevin Shelley
Secretary of State

File # _____

LIMITED LIABILITY COMPANY
APPLICATION FOR REGISTRATION

A $70.00 filing fee must accompany this form.

IMPORTANT – Read instructions before completing this form.

This Space For Filing Use Only

---

1. NAME UNDER WHICH THE FOREIGN LIMITED LIABILITY COMPANY PROPOSES TO REGISTER AND TRANSACT BUSINESS IN CALIFORNIA:
(End the name with the words "Limited Liability Company," "Ltd. Liability Co." or the abbreviations "LLC" or "L.L.C.")

2. NAME OF THE FOREIGN LIMITED LIABILITY COMPANY, IF DIFFERENT FROM THAT ENTERED ABOVE:

3. THIS FOREIGN LIMITED LIABILITY COMPANY WAS FORMED ON _____ IN _____

   (MONTH) (DAY) (YEAR)   (STATE OR COUNTRY)

   AND IS AUTHORIZED TO EXERCISE ITS POWERS AND PRIVILEGES IN THAT STATE OR COUNTRY.

4. NAME OF THE AGENT FOR SERVICE OF PROCESS IN THIS STATE, AND CHECK THE APPROPRIATE PROVISION BELOW:

   _____ WHICH IS,

   [ ] AN INDIVIDUAL RESIDING IN CALIFORNIA. PROCEED TO ITEM 5.

   [ ] A CORPORATION WHICH HAS FILED A CERTIFICATE PURSUANT TO SECTION 1505. PROCEED TO ITEM 6.

5. IF AN INDIVIDUAL, CALIFORNIA ADDRESS OF THE AGENT FOR SERVICE OF PROCESS:

   ADDRESS

   CITY   S   TATE CA   ZIP CODE

6. IN THE EVENT THE ABOVE AGENT FOR SERVICE OF PROCESS RESIGNS AND IS NOT REPLACED, OR IF THE AGENT CANNOT BE FOUND OR SERVED WITH THE EXERCISE OF REASONABLE DILIGENCE, THE SECRETARY OF STATE OF THE STATE OF CALIFORNIA IS HEREBY APPOINTED AS THE AGENT FOR SERVICE OF PROCESS OF THIS FOREIGN LIMITED LIABILITY COMPANY.

7. ADDRESS OF THE PRINCIPAL EXECUTIVE OFFICE: CITY   STATE   ZIP CODE

8. ADDRESS OF THE PRINCIPAL OFFICE IN CALIFORNIA, IF ANY: CITY   STATE   ZIP CODE

9. TYPE OF BUSINESS OF THE LIMITED LIABILITY COMPANY: (FOR INFORMATION PURPOSES ONLY.)

10. IT IS HEREBY DECLARED THAT I AM THE PERSON WHO EXECUTED THIS INSTRUMENT, WHICH EXECUTION IS MY ACT AND DEED.

    SIGNATURE OF AUTHORIZED PERSON   D   ATE

    TYPE OR PRINT NAME AND TITLE OF AUTHORIZED PERSON

11. RETURN TO:

    NAME
    FIRM
    ADDRESS
    CITY/STATE
    ZIP CODE

SEC/STATE FORM LLC-5 (Rev. 12/2003) – FILING FEE $70.00

APPROVED BY SECRETARY OF STATE

INSTRUCTIONS FOR COMPLETING THE APPLICATION FOR REGISTRATION (LLC- 5)

For easier completion, this form is available in a "fillable" version online at the Secretary of State's website at http://www.ss.ca.gov/business/business.htm. The form can be filled in on your computer, printed and mailed to the Secretary of State, Document Filing Support Unit, P O Box 944228, Sacramento, CA 94244-2280 or can be delivered in person to the Sacramento office, 1500 11th Street, 3rd Floor, Sacramento, CA 95814. If you are not completing this form online, please type or legibly print in black or blue ink. DO NOT ALTER THIS FORM.

FILING FEE: The filing fee is $70.00. Make the check(s) payable to the Secretary of State and send the executed document and filing fee to the address stated above.

Statutory filing provisions can be found in California Corporations Code section 17451. All statutory references are to the California Corporations Code, unless otherwise stated.

The registration may become effective not more than ninety (90) days after filing the application. If such a future effective date is desired, indicate in a cover letter the month, day, and year upon which the registration is to become effective. (Section 17056(c).)

- Pursuant to California Corporation Code section 17375, nothing in this title shall be construed to permit a domestic or foreign limited liability company to render professional services, as defined in subdivision (a) of Section 13401, in this state.

- Attach an original certificate of good standing from an authorized public official of the jurisdiction under which the foreign limited liability company was formed. If issuance of such a certificate is not permissible in that jurisdiction, then attach a statement by the foreign limited liability company indicating such. (Section 17451(b).)

Complete the Application For Registration (Form LLC- 5) as follows:

Item 1. Enter the name under which the foreign limited liability company is to be registered and transact business in California. The name shall contain the words "Limited Liability Company," or the abbreviations "LLC" or "L.L.C." at the end. The words "Limited" and "Company" may be abbreviated to "Ltd." and "Co." The name of the limited liability company may not contain the words "bank," "trust," "trustee," "incorporated," "inc.," "corporation," or "corp." and shall not contain the words "insurer" or "insurance company" or any other words suggesting that it is in the business of issuing policies of insurance and assuming insurance risks. (Section 17052.)

Item 2. Enter the name of the foreign limited liability company as it appears on its articles of organization, if different from than entered in Item 1.

Item 3. Enter the date and state or country of formation and make the required statement concerning the authority of the limited liability company to exercise its powers and privileges in its state or country of formation.

Item 4. Enter the name of the agent for service of process in this state. Check the appropriate provision indicating whether the agent is an individual residing in California or a corporation which has filed a certificate pursuant to Section 1505 of the California Corporations Code. If an individual is designated as agent, proceed to Item 5. If a corporation is designated, proceed to Item 6.

Item 5. If an individual is designated as the initial agent for service of process, enter an address in California. Do not enter "in care of" (c/o) or abbreviate the name of the city. DO NOT enter an address if a corporation is designated as the agent for service of process.

Item 6. Execution of this document confirms the following statement which has been preprinted on this form and may not be altered. "IN THE EVENT THE ABOVE AGENT FOR SERVICE OF PROCESS RESIGNS AND IS NOT REPLACED, OR IF THE AGENT CANNOT BE FOUND OR SERVED WITH THE EXERCISE OF REASONABLE DILIGENCE, THE SECRETARY OF STATE OF THE STATE OF CALIFORNIA IS HEREBY APPOINTED AS THE AGENT FOR SERVICE OF PROCESS OF THIS LIMITED LIABILITY COMPANY."

Item 7. Enter the complete address, including the zip code, of the principal executive office. DO NOT abbreviate the name of the city.

Item 8. Enter the complete address, including the zip code, of the principal office in California, if any. DO NOT abbreviate the name of the city.

Item 9. Briefly describe the type of business that constitutes the principal business activity of the limited liability company. Note restrictions in the rendering of professional services by limited liability companies. Professional services are defined in California Corporations Code section 13401(a) as: "any type of professional services that may be lawfully rendered only pursuant to a license, certification, or registration authorized by the Business and Professions Code or the Chiropractic Act." For informational purposes only

Item 10. The Application for Registration (LLC-5) shall be executed with an original signature of an authorized person.

Item 11. Enter the name and address of the person or firm to whom a copy of the filing should be returned.

- For further information contact the Business Filings Section at (916) 657-5448.

Instructions for Form FTB 3522
Limited Liability Company Tax Voucher

General Information

Form FTB 3522 is used to pay the annual limited liability company (LLC) tax of $800 for taxable year 2004. An LLC should use this form if it:

- Has articles of organization accepted by the California Secretary of State (SOS);
- Has a certificate of registration issued by the SOS; or
- Is doing business in California.

You can download, view, and print California tax forms and publications from our Website at **www.ftb.ca.gov**

Access other state agencies' websites through the State Agency Index on California's Website at **www.ca.gov**

Who Must Pay the Annual LLC Tax

Every LLC that is doing business in California or that has articles of organization accepted or a certificate of registration issued by the SOS **is subject to the annual LLC tax of $800.** The tax must be paid for each taxable year until a certificate of cancellation of registration or of articles of organization is filed with the SOS.

How to Complete Form FTB 3522

Enter all the information requested on this form. To ensure the timely and proper application of the payment to the LLC's account, enter the SOS file number (assigned upon registration with the SOS), and the federal employer identification number (FEIN).

Note: If the LLC leases a private mailbox (PMB) from a private business rather than a PO box from the United States Postal Service, include the box number in the field labeled "PMB no." in the address area.

Where to Mail

Detach and mail the voucher portion with the payment to:

> FRANCHISE TAX BOARD
> PO BOX 942857
> SACRAMENTO CA   94257-0631

When to Pay the Annual LLC Tax

The annual LLC tax is due and payable **on or before the 15th day of the 4th month** after the **beginning** of the LLC's taxable year (fiscal year) or April 15, 2004 (calendar year).

Note: The first taxable year of an LLC that was not previously in existence begins when the LLC is organized.

If the 15th day of the 4th month of an existing foreign LLC's taxable year has passed before the foreign LLC commences business in California or registers with the SOS, the annual LLC tax should be paid immediately after commencing business or registering with the SOS.

Example: LLC1, a newly-formed calendar year taxpayer, organizes as an LLC in Delaware on June 1, 2004. LLC1 registers with the SOS on August 16, 2004, and begins doing business in California on August 17, 2004. Because LLC1's initial taxable year began on June 1, 2004, the annual LLC tax is due September 15, 2004 (the 15th day of the 4th month of the short period taxable year). LLC1's short period (June 1, 2004-December 31, 2004) tax return is due April 15, 2005. The annual tax payment for tax year 2005, with form FTB 3522 also is due April 15, 2005.

Penalties and Interest

If the LLC fails to pay its annual tax by the 15th day of the 4th month after the beginning of the taxable year, a late payment penalty plus interest will be assessed for failure to pay the annual LLC tax by the return due date. The penalty and interest will be computed from the due date of the tax to the date of payment.

Late Payment of Prior Year Annual LLC Tax

If a prior year LLC tax of $800 was not paid on or before the 15th day of the 4th month after the beginning of the taxable year, the tax should be remitted as soon as possible, using the appropriate taxable year form FTB 3522. **Do not** use any other form for payment of the tax. This will assure proper application of the payment to the LLC's account.

✂— DETACH HERE — — — — — —   **IF NO PAYMENT IS DUE, DO NOT MAIL THIS FORM** — — — — — — — DETACH HERE —✂

DUE 15TH DAY OF 4TH MONTH OF TAXABLE YEAR (fiscal year) OR APRIL 15, 2004 (calendar year).

TAXABLE YEAR	Limited Liability Company	CALIFORNIA FORM
2004	**Tax Voucher**	**3522**

For calendar year 2004 or fiscal year beginning month _____ day _____ year 2004, and ending month _____ day _____ year _____.

Limited liability company name

Secretary of State (SOS) file number

DBA

Federal employer identification number (FEIN)

Address   STE. no.   PMB no.

City   State   ZIP Code

Make your check or money order payable to "Franchise Tax Board." Write the SOS file number, FEIN, and "FTB 3522 2004" on the check or money order. Mail this voucher and the check or money order to:
> FRANCHISE TAX BOARD
> PO BOX 942857
> SACRAMENTO CA   94257-0631

If amount of payment is zero, do not mail form ▶

Amount of payment

352204103

FTB 3522 2003

State of California
Kevin Shelley
Secretary of State

LIMITED LIABILITY COMPANY
APPLICATION FOR REGISTRATION
CERTIFICATE OF AMENDMENT

A $30.00 filing fee must accompany this form
IMPORTANT – Read instructions before completing this form.

This Space For Filing Use Only

1. Secretary of State File Number

2. Name under which this foreign limited liability company is conducting business in California:

3. **COMPLETE ONLY THE SECTIONS WHERE INFORMATION IS BEING CHANGED. ADDITIONAL PAGES MAY BE ATTACHED, IF NECESSARY. CONSULT THE INSTRUCTIONS BEFORE COMPLETING THIS FORM.**

   A. The name under which this foreign limited liability company conducts business in California. (End the name with the words "Limited Liability Company," or "Ltd. Liability Co.," or the abbreviations "LLC" or "L.L.C.")

   B. The name of the foreign limited liability company has been changed as follows and has been recorded in the home state or country:

   C. State or country of formation of the foreign limited liability company, i f false or erroneous at time of registration.

   D. Date on which the foreign limited liability company was formed, if false or erroneous at time of registration.

   E. Address of the principal executive office: City   State   Zip Code

   F. Address of the principal office in California: City   State   **CA**   Zip Code

4. Future effective date, if any: Month   Day   Year

5. Number of pages attached, if any:

6. **Declaration:** It is hereby declared that I am the person who executed this instrument, which execution is my act and deed.

   _____   _____
   Signature of Authorized Person   Type or Print Name and Title of Authorized Person

   _____
   Date

   RETURN TO:
   NAME
   FIRM
   ADDRESS
   CITY/STATE
   ZIP CODE

SEC/STATE (REV. 12/2003)   FORM LLC-6 – FILING FEE: $30.00
                                         Approved by Secretary of State

INSTRUCTIONS FOR COMPLETING THE CERTIFICATE OF AMENDMENT
TO THE APPLICATION FOR REGISTRATION (LLC-6)

- If any statement in the Application of Registration (LLC-5) was false when made or any statements made have become erroneous, the foreign limited liability company shall promptly file with the Secretary of State of California a Certificate of Amendment to the Application for Registration (LLC-6). (Section 17454.)

- The Certificate of Amendment to the Application for Registration (LLC-6) may become effective not more than ninety (90) days after filing the Certificate. If such future effective date is desired, indicate in a cover letter the month, day, and year upon which the Certificate of Amendment of the Application for Registration (LLC-6) is to become effective. (Section 17056(c)).

DO NOT ALTER THIS FORM

Type or legibly print in black ink.

- Attach the fee for filing the Certificate of Amendment to the Application for Registration (LLC-6) with the Secretary of State. The fee is thirty dollars ($30).

- Make check(s) payable to the Secretary of State.

- Send the executed document and filing fee to:

  California Secretary of State
  Document Filing Support Unit
  P.O. Box 944228
  Sacramento, CA 94244-2280

- Fill in the items as follows:

Item 1. Enter the file number issued by the California Secretary of State.

Item 2. Enter the name of the foreign limited liability company as registered with the California Secretary of State.

Item 3. Enter only the information which is being amended. Provide the text of each amendment adopted, using the A-F space provided and/or attaching additional pages.

Item 4. Enter the future effective date of the Certificate of Amendment to the Application for Registration (LLC-6), if any. If none is entered, the amendment shall be effective upon filing with the California Secretary of State.

Item 5. Enter the number of pages attached, if any. All attachments should be 8½ " x 11", one-sided and legible.

Item 6. The Certificate of Amendment to the Application for Registration (LLC-6) shall be executed with an original signature and title.

   If the Certificate of Amendment to the Application for Registration (LLC-6) is signed by an entity, the person who signs for the entity must note the exact entity name, his/her name and his/her position/title.

   If the Certificate of Amendment to the Application for Registration (LLC-6) is signed by a trust, the certificate must be signed by a trustee as follows:
   _____, trustee for _____trust (including the date of the trust, if applicable). Example: Mary Todd, trustee of the Lincoln Family Trust (U/T/A 5/1/94).

Item 7. Enter the name and address of the person or firm to whom a copy of the filing should be mailed.

- Statutory provisions can be found in Section 17454 of the California Corporations Code, unless otherwise indicated.

- For further information contact the Business Filings Section at (916) 657-5448.

INSTRUCTIONS FOR COMPLETING FORM LLC-12

For easier completion, this form is available on the Secretary of State's website at http://www.ss.ca.gov/business and can be viewed, filled in and printed from your computer. Completed forms along with the applicable fees can be mailed to Secretary of State, Statement of Information Unit, P.O. Box 944230, Sacramento, CA 94244-2300 or delivered in person to the Sacramento office, 1500 11th Street, 3rd Floor, Sacramento, CA 95814. If you are not completing this form online, please type or legibly print in black or blue ink. This form should not be altered.

Every domestic and registered foreign limited liability company shall file a Statement of Information with the Secretary of State, within 90 days after filing of its original Articles of Organization or Application for Registration, and biennially thereafter during the applicable filing period. The applicable filing period for a limited liability company is the calendar month during which its original Articles of Organization or Application for Registration were filed and the immediately preceding five calendar months. If the name and/or address of the agent for service of process have changed, a limited liability company must file a complete Statement of Information. A limited liability company is required to file this statement even though it may not be actively engaged in business at the time this statement is due.

Statutory filing provisions are found in California Corporations Code **section 17060**, unless otherwise indicated. Failure to file this Statement of Information by the due date will result in the assessment of a $250.00 penalty. (Corporations Code **sections 17651(b) and 17653**; Revenue and Taxation Code **section 19141**)

FILING FEES: The fee for filing the initial or biennial Statement of Information is $20.00. Checks should be made payable to the Secretary of State. If this statement is being filed to amend any information on a previously filed statement and is being filed outside the applicable filing period, as defined above, no fee is required.

Complete the Statement of Information (Form LLC-12) as follows:

Item 1.   Please do not alter the preprinted name. If the name is not correct, please attach a statement indicating the correct name and the date the name change amendment was filed with the Secretary of State. If blank, enter the name of the limited liability company exactly as it is of record with the California Secretary of State.

Item 2.   Please do not alter the preprinted file number. If blank, enter the file number issued by the California Secretary of State.

Item 3.   Please do not alter the preprinted jurisdiction. If blank, and the limited liability company is a registered foreign limited liability company (organized outside the state of California), enter the state or place under the laws of which the limited liability company is organized.

Item 4.   Enter the complete street address, city and zip code of the limited liability company's principal executive office. Please do not enter a P.O. Box or abbreviate the name of the city. This address will be used for mailing purposes.

Item 5.   If the limited liability company is formed under the laws of the state of California, enter the complete street address, city and zip code of the office required to be maintained pursuant to Corporations Code **section 17057(a)**. Please do not enter a P.O. Box or abbreviate the name of the city.

Item 6.   Enter the name and complete business or residential address of the chief executive officer, if any. Please do not abbreviate the name of the city.

Items 7-9.   Enter the name and complete business or residential address of any manager or managers, appointed or elected in accordance with the Articles of Organization or Operating Agreement, or if no manager has been so elected or appointed, the name and business or residential address of each member. Attach additional pages, if necessary. Please do not abbreviate the name of the city.

Item 10.   Enter the name of the agent for service of process in California. The person named as agent must be a resident of California or a corporation that has filed a certificate pursuant to Corporations Code **section 1505**. If an individual is designated as agent, complete Items 10 and 11. If a corporation is designated as agent, complete Item 10 and proceed to Item 12 (do not complete Item 11).

An Agent for Service of Process is an individual or a corporation designated by the limited liability company to accept service of process if the limited liability company is sued.

Please note: A limited liability company cannot name itself as agent for service of process. Further, no domestic or foreign corporation may file pursuant to **section 1505** unless the corporation is currently authorized to engage in business in California and is in good standing on the records of the Secretary of State.

Item 11.   If an individual is designated as agent for service of process, enter a business or residential address in California. Please do not enter "in care of" (c/o) or abbreviate the name of the city. Please do not enter an address if a corporation is designated as agent for service of process.

Item 12.   Briefly describe the general type of business that constitutes the principal business activity of the limited liability company.

Item 13.   Type or print the name and title of the person completing this form and enter the date this form was completed.

State of California
Kevin Shelley
Secretary of State

STATEMENT OF INFORMATION
(Limited Liabilit y Compan y)

| L |

Filing Fee $2 0.00. If amendment, se e instruc tions.

IMPORTANT — READ INSTRUCTIONS BEFORE COMPLETING THIS FORM

1.   LIMITED LIABILITY COMPANY NAME (Please do not alter if name is preprinted.)

This Space For Filing Use Only

DUE DATE:

FILE NUMBER AND STATE OR PLACE OF ORGANIZATION

2.   SECRETARY OF STATE FILE NUMBER

3. STATE OR PLACE OF ORGANIZATION

COMPLETE ADDRESSES FOR THE FOLLOWING (Do not abbreviate the name of the city. Items 4 and 5 cannot be P.O. Boxes.)

4. STREET ADDRESS OF PRINCIPAL EXECUTIVE OFFICE	CITY AND STATE	ZIP CODE

5. CALIFORNIA OFFICE WHERE RECORDS ARE MAINTAINED (DOMESTIC ONLY)	CITY	STATE	ZIP CODE
		CA	

NAME AND COMPLETE ADDRESS OF THE CHIEF EXECUTIVE OFFICER, IF ANY

6. NAME	ADDRESS	CITY AND STATE	ZIP CODE

NAME AND COMPLETE ADDRESS OF ANY MANAGER OR MANAGERS, OR IF NONE HAVE BEEN APPOINTED OR ELECTED, PROVIDE THE NAME AND ADDRESS OF EACH MEMBER (Attach additional pages, if necessary.)

7. NAME	ADDRESS	CITY AND STATE	ZIP CODE
8. NAME	ADDRESS	CITY AND STATE	ZIP CODE
9. NAME	ADDRESS	CITY AND STATE	ZIP CODE

AGENT FOR SERVICE OF PROCESS (If the agent is an individual, the agent must reside in California and Item 11 must be completed with a California address. If the agent is a corporation, the agent must have on file with the California Secretary of State a certificate pursuant to Corporations Code **section 1505** and Item 11 must be left blank.)

10. NAME OF AGENT FOR SERVICE OF PROCESS

11. ADDRESS OF AGENT FOR SERVICE OF PROCESS IN CALIFORNIA, IF AN INDIVIDUAL	CITY	STATE	ZIP CODE
		CA	

TYPE OF BUSINESS

12. DESCRIBE THE TYPE OF BUSINESS OF THE LIMITED LIABILITY COMPANY

13. THE INFORMATION CONTAINED HEREIN IS TRUE AND CORRECT.

TYPE OR PRINT NAME OF PERSON COMPLETING THE FORM	SIGNATURE	TITLE	DATE

LLC 12 (REV 09/2004)

APPROVED BY SECRETARY OF STATE

Forms for Chapter 3

There are 21 forms that accompany **Chapter 3, Steps to Incorporating**. They include the following:

Form 3-A Name Reservation—Order Form, 2 pages (149 - 150)

Form 3-B Fictitious Business Name Statement, 2 pages (151 - 152)

Form 3-C Example of Statement of Abandonment of Use of Fictitious Business Name, 2 pages (153 - 154)

Form 3-D Articles of Incorporation (General Stock), 2 pages (155 - 156)

Form 3-E Articles of Incorporation Designating Initial Directors, 4 pages (157 - 160)

Form 3-F Articles of Incorporation Not Designating Initial Directors, 2 pages (161 - 162)

Form 3-G Bylaws, For Profit (3-G) 28 pages (163 - 190)

Form 3-H Sample Document Filing Request, 1 page (191)

Form 3-I Certificate of Amendment of Articles of Incorporation (before issuance of shares), 1 page (192)

Form 3-J Certificate of Amendment of Articles of Incorporation (after issuance of shares), 1 page (193)

Form 3-K Sample Document Filing Request for Articles of Incorporation, 2 pages (194 - 195)

Ch 3 Forms

Form 3-L   Sample Letter for Certificate of Amendment of Articles of Incorporation, 1 page (196)

Form 3-M   Action of Incorporator, 1 page (197)

Form 3-N   Resolution of Board of Directors Amending Certain Bylaws, 1 page (198)

Form 3-O   Waiver of Notice and Consent to Holding of the First Meeting of the Board of Directors, 1 page (199)

Form 3-P   Waiver of Notice and Consent to Holding of the First Meeting of the Board of Directors (Nonprofit Corporation), 1 page (200)

Form 3-Q   Minutes of the First Meeting of the Board of Directors, 6 pages (201 - 206)

Form 3-R   Minutes of a Special Meeting of the Board of Directors, 1 page (207)

Form 3-S   Minutes of a Special Meeting of the Shareholders, 1 page (208)

Form 3-T   Statement of Information (Domestic Stock Corporation), 2 pages (209 - 210)

Form 3-U   Application for Employer Identification Number (EIN)—SS-4, 2 pages (211 - 212)

Form 3-V   Seller's Permit Application—BOE-400-SPA, 7 pages (213 - 219)

Name Reservation Request Form
Corporations, Limited Partnerships, and Limited Liability Companies

To request the reservation of a corporation, limited partnership or limited liability company name, complete the order form on the following page and attach a check in the amount of $10.00 (made payable to the Secretary of State). Your request may be submitted:

- **by mail**, along with a self-addressed envelope, to:

    Secretary of State
    Name Availability Unit
    1500 11th Street, 3rd Floor
    Sacramento, CA 95814

- **in person** at the Secretary of State's office in Sacramento. Please note, **corporation** names may also be reserved, in person, at any of the Secretary of State's regional offices. Please refer to Contact Information for office locations and addresses. A special handling fee of $10.00 is applicable for each name reserved in person. The special handling fee must be remitted by separate check (made payable to the Secretary of State), as it will be retained whether the proposed name is accepted or denied for reservation. The special handling fee is not applicable to requests submitted by mail.

Only one reservation will be made per request form. You may list up to three names, in order of preference, and the first available name will be reserved for a period of 60 days. The remaining names will not be researched.

Email and/or online requests for reservations cannot be accepted at this time.

NAME RESERVATION - ORDER FORM

THE PROPOSED NAME IS BEING RESERVED FOR USE BY:

YOUR NAME:	
NAME OF BUSINESS: (if applicable)	
MAILING ADDRESS:	

CITY:	STATE:	ZIP:
TELEPHONE NUMBER:	FAX NUMBER:	

INDICATE TYPE OF ENTITY: (Choose <u>only</u> one) ☐ Corporation ☐ Limited Partnership ☐ Limited Liability Company

NAME TO BE RESERVED (in order of preference)

1st Choice:	
For Office Use Only:	( ) is not available – we have:
2nd Choice:	
For Office Use Only:	( ) is not available – we have:
3rd Choice:	
For Office Use Only:	( ) is not available – we have:

☐ Check here if the proposed name is being reserved for the purposes of reviving a suspended/forfeited entity.   File Number:

☐ Check here if a **counter** reservation is to be mailed back (Please include a self addressed envelope.)

RESERVATION

Reservation Fee (per name request)	$10.00

SPECIAL HANDLING

Special Handling Fee (per name request – applicable to all over-the counter processing)	$10.00 *

* The special handling fee must be remitted by separate check, as it will be retained whether the proposed name is accepted or denied for reservation. Please note, the special handling fee is not applicable to requests submitted by mail.

FOR OFFICE USE ONLY

Date:	R# :	Amt Recd: $	By:

Email and/or online requests for reservations cannot be accepted at this time.

**Ch 3
Forms**

A

Your Return Mailing Address	REGISTRAR - RECORDER / COUNTY CLERK's FILING STAMP
Name:	
Address:	
City: State: Zip Code:	

1   ☐ First Filing   ☐ Renewal Filing
Check one only

FICTITIOUS BUSINESS NAME STATEMENT
THE FOLLOWING PERSON(S) IS (ARE) DOING BUSINESS AS: (Attach additional pages if required)

2
Fictitious Business Name(s)

1.

2.

3.

Articles of Incorporation or Organization Number *(if applicable)*

AI #/ON

3   Street Address, City & State of Principal Place of Business in California (P.O. Box alone not acceptable)

4
Full name of Registrant / Corporation / Limited Liability Company   (if corporation - incorporated in what state)

Residence Street Address (P.O. Box not accepted) City   State   Zip Code

4A
Full name of Registrant / Corporation / Limited Liability Company   (if corporation - incorporated in what state)

Residence Street Address (P.O. Box not accepted) City   State   Zip Code

4B
Full name of Registrant / Corporation / Limited Liability Company   (if corporation - incorporated in what state)

Residence Street Address (P.O. Box not accepted) City   State   Zip Code

5
This Business is
conducted by:
(check one only)

(   ) an individual   (   ) a general partnership   (   ) joint venture   (   ) a business trust
(   ) co-partners   (   ) husband and wife   (   ) a corporation   (   ) a limited partnership
(   ) an unincorporated association other than a partnership   (   ) a limited liability company   (   ) _____ Other

6
(   ) The registrant commenced to transact business under the fictitious business name or names listed on (Date): _____
(   ) Registrant has not yet begun to transact business under the fictitious business name or names listed herein.

7
I declare that all information in this statement is true and correct.
(A registrant who declares as true information which he or she knows to be false is guilty of a crime.)

8   Signature of Registrant(s)

Signature   type/print name

Signature   type/print name

Signature   type/print name

Signature   type/print name

8A   If Registrant is a CORPORATION or LLC, sign below

Corporation Name / Limited Liability Company

Signature

Title

Type or Print Name

This statement was filed with the County Clerk of _____**LOS ANGELES**_____ County on date indicated by file stamp above.

NOTICE - THIS FICTITIOUS NAME STATEMENT EXPIRES FIVE YEARS FROM DATE IT WAS FILED IN THE OFFICE OF THE COUNTY CLERK. A NEW FICTITIOUS BUSINESS NAME STATEMENT MUST BE FILED PRIOR TO THAT DATE. The filing of this statement does not of itself authorize the use in this state of a fictitious business name in violation of the rights of another under federal, state, or common law (See Section 14411 et seq., Business and Professions Code)

REGISTRAR - RECORDER/COUNTY CLERK
BUSINESS FILING AND REGISTRATION
P.O. BOX 53592, LOS ANGELES, CA 90053-0592
PH: (562) 462-2177

FILING FEE: $23.00 for 1 FBN and 2 registrants
plus $4.00 for each additional FBN/registrant
RENEWAL FILING FEE: $18.00
REFER TO THE BACK OF FORM FOR INSTRUCTIONS

FORM # 76F286D-F029 (Rev. 5/04)

INSTRUCTIONS FOR COMPLETION OF STATEMENT
Type or carefully print in ink

Box A. Insert the name and address of the person who should receive this original and certified copy.
Box 1. Check one box only.
Box 2. Insert exact name of business. If you are registering more than one business located at the same address, number each name entered.
Box 3. Insert street address of principle place of business (Post Office Boxes are not acceptable).
Box 4. Registrants: list each owner or partner and his/her residence address separately (Post Office Boxes are not acceptable). If the owner is a corporation insert the name of the corporation and the business address. Do not list stockholders or officers of the corporation. If a business name or a registrant's name includes the words Corporation, Incorporated, or Inc., Limited Liability Company (whether using the complete words or abbreviations LLC and Co.) or LLC or LC, the County Clerk of Los Angeles requires either a certified copy of the Articles of Incorporation or Organization.
Box 5. Check one item which best describes who is conducting business.
Box 6. Have you started doing business? If yes, check the first box and enter the date you started. If not, check the bottom box ONLY.
Box 7. Please read before signing.
Box 8. Signatures are required as follows ( ) Individual - the individual ( ) Partnership or other association of other persons - A general partner ( ) Joint Venture - All parties of the joint venture ( ) Business Trust - A trustee ( ) Co Partners - All partners ( ) Husband and wife - both ( ) Limited partnership - one partner.
Box 8A. Corporation/Limited Liability Co. - An officer must sign, state the title, and attach a copy of the Articles of Incorporation or Organization.

CALIFORNIA BUSINESS AND PROFESSIONS CODE

SECTION 14411, 14412 - TRADE NAME REGISTRATION
The filing of any fictitious business name statement by a person required to file such statement shall establish a rebuttable presumption that the registrant has the exclusive right to use the fictitious business name as a trade name as well as any confusingly similar trade name, in the county in which the statement is filed, if the registrant is the first to file such a statement containing the fictitious business name in the county. The rebuttable presumption shall be applicable until the statement is abandoned or otherwise expires and no new statement has been filed by the registrant.

SECTION 17900 -
    (a) - as used in this chapter, 'fictitious business name' means:
        (1) In the case of an individual, a name that does not include the surname of the individual or a name that suggests the existence of additional owners.
        (2) In the case of a partnership or other association of persons, other than a limited partnership which has filed a certificate of limited partnership with the Secretary of State pursuant to Section 15621 of the Corporations Code, a name that does not include the surname of each general partner or a name that suggests the existence of additional owners.
        (3) In the case of a corporation, any name other than the corporate name stated in its articles of incorporation.
        (4) In the case of a limited partnership which has filed a certificate of limited partnership with the Secretary of State pursuant to Section 15621 of the Corporations Code and in the case of a foreign limited partnership which has filed an application for registration with the Secretary of State pursuant to Section 15621 of the Corporations Code, any name other than the name of the limited partnership as on file with the Secretary of State.
    (b) A name that suggests the existence of additional owners within the meaning of subdivision (a) is one which includes such words as 'Company', '& Company,' 'Son,' '& Associates,' 'Brothers,' and the like, but not words that merely describe the business being conducted.
SECTION 17910 - Every person who regularly transacts business in this state for profit under a fictitious business name shall:
    (a) File a fictitious business name statement in accordance with this chapter not later than 40 days from the time he commences to transact such business; and
    (b) File a new statement in accordance with this chapter on or before the date of expiration of the statement on file.
SECTION 17910.5 -
    (a) No person shall adopt any fictitious business name which includes 'Corporation, 'Corp,' 'Incorporated,' or 'Inc,' unless such person is a corporation organized pursuant to the laws of this state or some other jurisdiction.
    (b) No person shall adopt any Fictitious Business Name which includes "Limited Liability Company" (whether using the complete words or the abbreviations "LTD and Co." or either of them) or "LLC" or "LC" unless such a person is a Limited Company organized pursuant to the laws of this state or some other jurisdiction.
SECTION 17917 -
    (a) Within 30 days after a fictitious business name statement has been filed pursuant to this chapter, the registrant shall cause a statement in the form prescribed by subdivision (a) of Section 17913 to be published pursuant to Government Code Section 6064 in a newspaper of general circulation in the county in which the principal place of business of the registrant is located or, if there is no such newspaper in that county, then in a newspaper of general circulation in an adjoining county. If the registrant does not have a place of business in this state, the notice shall be published in a newspaper of general circulation in Sacramento County.
    (b) Subject to the requirements of subdivision (a), the newspaper selected for the publication of the statement should be one that circulates in the area where the business is to be conducted.
    (c) If a refiling is required because the prior statement has expired, the refiling need not be published unless there has been a change in the information required in the expired statement, provided the refiling is filed within 40 days of the date the statement expires.
    (d) An affidavit showing the publication of the statement shall be filed with the county clerk within 30 days after the completion of the publication.
SECTION 17920. Expiration of statement
    (a) Unless the statement expires earlier under subdivision (b) or (c), a fictitious business name statement expires five years from the date it was filed in the office of the county clerk.
    (b) Except as provided in Section 17923, a fictitious business name statement expires 40 days after any change in the facts set forth in the statement pursuant to Section 17913, except that a change in the residence of an individual, a general partner or trustee does not cause the statement to expire.
    (c) A fictitious business name statement expires when registrant files a statement of abandonment of the fictitious business name described in the statement.
SECTION 17930 - Any person who executes, files, or publishes any statement under this chapter, knowing that such statement is false, in whole or in part, shall be guilty of a misdemeanor and upon conviction thereof shall be punished by a fine not to exceed one thousand dollars ($1,000).

*NOTE: It is your responsibility not to file the same name or one confusingly similar to one already registered on the County FBN Index of Secretary of State Corporate Index. We suggest you search available records before filing.

SUTTER COUNTY CLERK

FILE NO. _____   (Filing Fee - $30.00)

STATEMENT OF ABANDONMENT OF USE OF FICTITIOUS BUSINESS NAME

The following person (persons) have abandoned the use of the fictitious business name

_____

AT _____
                    (Street Address of Principal Place of Business)

The fictitious business name referred to above was filed in Sutter County on

_____

(*)   1. _____   2. _____
          (Full name - type/print)   (Full name - type/print)

          _____   _____
          (Address)   (Address)

          _____   _____
          (City)   (City)

       3. _____   4. _____
          (Full name - type/print)   (Full name - type/print)

          _____   _____
          (Address)   (Address)

          _____   _____
          (City)   (City)

(**)   This business was conducted by _____

          _____

                        Signed: _____

This statement was filed with the County Clerk of Sutter County on date indicated by
file stamp above.

SEE REVERSE SIDE FOR INSTRUCTIONS

**Ch 3
Forms**

THE BELOW INSTRUCTIONS ARE NOT TO BE PUBLISHED (Sec. 17924,B&P)

INSTRUCTIONS FOR COMPLETION OF STATEMENT

Section 17922 Business and Professions Code

(*) In the case of an individual, the full name and address of the individual is to be inserted. In the case of a partnership or other association of persons, the full names and residence addresses of all the general partners are to be inserted. In the case of a corporation, the name of the corporation as set forth in its articles of incorporation and the State of incorporation is to be inserted. In the case of a business trust, the full name and residence address of each of the trustees are to be inserted. (Attach additional sheet of paper if necessary.)

(**) Insert whichever of the following best describes the nature of the business being abandoned: "an individual", "a general partnership", "a limited partnership", "an unincorporated association other than a partnership", "a corporation", "a business".

If the person is an individual, the statement shall be signed by the individual; if a partnership or other association of persons, by a general partner; if a business trust, by a trustee; if a corporation, by an officer. (Section 17914 B&P Code.)

NOTICE TO PERSON - Section 17924/17922 Business & Professions Code

(1) The statement of Abandonment of Use of Fictitious Business Name must be published in a newspaper once a week for four successive weeks and an affidavit of publication filed with the county clerk within 30 days after publication has been accomplished. The statement should be published in a newspaper of general circulation in the county where the principal place of business was located. The statement should be published in such county in a newspaper that circulates in the area where the business was conducted.

(2) Any person who executes, files, or publishes any fictitious business name statement, knowing that such statement is false, in whole or in part, is guilty of a misdemeanor and upon conviction thereof shall be fined not to exceed five hundred dollars ($500). (Section 17930 B&P Code.)

ORGANIZATION OF CALIFORNIA STOCK CORPORATIONS

Business corporations authorized to issue stock, excluding such special organizations as cooperatives, credit unions, etc., are organized under the General Corporation Law, and particularly Title 1, Division 1, Chapter 2, California Corporations Code.

California Corporations Code Sections 200-202 outline the minimum content requirements of Articles of Incorporation for stock corporations. The attached sample has been drafted to meet those **minimum** statutory requirements. The sample may be used as a guide in preparing documents to be filed with the Secretary of State to incorporate. It is, however, suggested that you seek private counsel for advice regarding the proposed corporation's specific business needs, which may require the inclusion of special permissive provisions.

The fee for filing Articles of Incorporation on behalf of a stock corporation is $100.00. Check(s) should be made payable to the Secretary of State.

PLEASE NOTE: Businesses incorporating in California are subject to California corporation franchise tax requirements until such time as they formally dissolve. Information regarding franchise tax requirements can be obtained from the Franchise Tax Board's Internet Web site or by calling the Franchise Tax Board at 1-800-852-5711.

The original and at least two copies of the Articles of Incorporation should be included with your submittal. The Secretary of State will certify two copies of the filed document without charge, **provided that the copies are submitted to the Secretary of State with the original to be filed.** Any additional copies submitted with the original will be certified upon request and payment of the $8.00 per copy certification fee.

Documents can be mailed or hand delivered for over-the-counter processing to the Sacramento office at:

Business Programs Division   (916) 657-5448
1500 11th Street
Sacramento, CA 95814
Attention: Document Filing Support Unit

OR

can be hand delivered for over-the-counter processing to any of the regional offices located in:

♦   Fresno   (559) 445-6900
    1315 Van Ness Avenue, Suite 203
    Fresno, CA 93721-1729

♦   Los Angeles   (213) 897-3062
    The Ronald Reagan Building
    12th Floor South Tower, Room 12513
    300 South Spring Street
    Los Angeles, CA 90013-1233

♦   San Diego   (619) 525-4113
    1350 Front Street, Suite 2060
    San Diego, CA 92101-3609

♦   San Francisco   (415) 557-8000
    455 Golden Gate Avenue, Suite 14500
    San Francisco, CA 94102-7007

NOTE: •   Cash is accepted **only** in the Sacramento office.

•   Duplicate original documents must be submitted when filing in any of the regional offices.

•   Regional offices do not process mailed in documents.

Secretary of State *Information*   *(Please see reverse)*
ARTS-GENERAL (Rev 07/2004)

A $15.00 **special handling fee** is applicable for processing documents delivered in person at the public counter in the Sacramento office or in any of the regional offices located in Fresno, Los Angeles, San Diego and San Francisco. The $15.00 special handling fee must be remitted by separate check for each submittal and will be retained whether the documents are filed or rejected. The special handling fee does not apply to documents submitted by mail.

Preclearance or expedited filing of *eligible corporate documents* can be requested in a specified time frame, for an additional fee (in lieu of the $15.00 special handling fee), as described in the Preclearance/Expedited Filing Service Information. The preclearance/expedited filing service is not available in the regional offices.

When forming a new corporation you may need to contact one or more of the following agencies for additional information:

♦ The Franchise Tax Board -for information regarding **franchise tax** requirements.

♦ The Board of Equalization - for information regarding **sales tax** and/or **use tax** liability.

♦ The Department of Corporations - for information regarding **issuance** and **sale** of securities in California, Franchise Investment Law, Personal Property Brokers Law and/or Escrow Law requirements.

♦ The Department of Insurance - for information regarding **insurer** requirements

♦ The Department of Financial Institutions - for information regarding the organization of **banks** and corporate name style requirements.

♦ The Department of Consumer Affairs - for information regarding **licensing** requirements.

♦ The Employment Development Department - for information regarding **disability unemployment insurance tax**.

♦ The Department of Industrial Relations, Division of Worker's Compensation - for information regarding **workman's compensation** requirements.

♦ The city and/or county clerk and/or recorder where the principal place of business is located - for information regarding business licenses, fictitious business names (if doing business under a name other than the corporate name), and for specific requirements regarding zoning, building permits, etc. based on the business activities of the corporation.

♦ The Internal Revenue Service (IRS) - for information regarding **federal employer identification numbers.**

The Secretary of State does not license corporations or business entities. For licensing requirements, please contact the city and/or county where the principal place of business is located and/or the state agency with jurisdiction over the business, e.g. Contractors' State License Board.

Secretary of State Information
ARTS-GENERAL (Rev 07/2004)   *(Please see reverse)*

INSTRUCTIONS:

Using the attached sample as a guide, Articles of Incorporation must be drafted to include all required provisions and may include other provisions, such as the names and addresses of the initial directors, if those provisions are permitted under California law. The Secretary of State's office, however, does not provide samples that include permissive provisions. The document **must** be typed with letters in dark contrast to the paper. Documents that would produce poor quality microfilm will be returned unfiled.

Article I – The Articles must include a statement of the name of the corporation, which name must be exactly as you want it to appear on the records of the Secretary of State.

Article II – This **exact** statement is required by the California Corporations Code and cannot be modified.

Article III – The Articles must include a statement as to the name and California address of the initial agent for service of process. The designated agent, whether an individual or a corporation, **must** agree to accept service of process on behalf of the corporation prior to designation. A corporation cannot designate itself as its own agent for service of process. When designating another corporation as agent, that other corporation **must have previously filed** a Certificate Pursuant to Section 1505, California Corporations Code, with the Secretary of State. When a corporate agent is used, the address of the designated corporation must be omitted.

Article IV – The Articles must include a statement of the total number of shares that the corporation will be authorized to issue.

NOTE: Before shares of stock are sold or issued the corporation must comply with the Corporate Securities Law administered by the Department of Corporations. For information regarding permits to issue shares please contact that agency.

The Articles of Incorporation must be signed by an incorporator, or by directors, if initial directors have been named in the document. If directors are named, each director must both sign and acknowledge the articles. The names of incorporators or directors must be typed beneath their signatures.

The original and at least two copies of the Articles of Incorporation, together with the applicable fee, must be mailed or hand delivered to the Secretary of State's office in Sacramento or hand delivered to the one of the regional offices located in Fresno, Los Angeles, San Diego or San Francisco. Regional offices do not process mailed in documents. If documents are submitted to a regional office, a duplicate original is also required.

To facilitate the processing of documents mailed to the Sacramento office, a self-addressed envelope and a letter referencing the corporate name as well as your own name, return address and telephone number should also be submitted.

*Secretary of State **Instructions**
ARTS-GENERAL (Rev 07/2004)*

SAMPLE

ARTICLES OF INCORPORATION

I

The name of this corporation is _____ *(NAME OF CORPORATION)* _____.

II

The purpose of the corporation is to engage in any lawful act or activity for which a corporation may be organized under the **GENERAL CORPORATION LAW** of California other than the banking business, the trust company business or the practice of a profession permitted to be incorporated by the California Corporations Code.

III

The name and address in the State of California of this corporation's initial agent for service of process is:

Name _____

Address _____

City _____   State **CALIFORNIA** Zip _____

IV

This corporation is authorized to issue only one class of shares of stock; and the total number of shares which this corporation is authorized to issue is _____.

_____ *(Signature of Incorporator)* _____
(Typed Name of Incorporator), Incorporator

Secretary of State Sample
ARTS-GENERAL (Rev 07/2004)

There is an additional $15 counter fee for Articles of Incorporation filed in person with the Secretary of State.

Ch 3 Forms

ARTICLES OF INCORPORATION DESIGNATING INITIAL DIRECTORS

ARTICLES OF INCORPORATION OF _____

ARTICLE I. Name

The name of the corporation is _____ .

ARTICLE II. Purpose

The purpose of this corporation is to engage in any lawful act or activity for which a corporation may be organized under the General Corporation Law of California other than the banking business, the trust company business or the practice of a profession permitted to be incorporated by the California Corporations Code.

ARTICLE III. Directors

The number of Directors of the corporation is _____. The names and addresses of the persons appointed as initial directors are:

Name   Address

1. _____   _____

2. _____   _____

3. _____   _____

The liability of the directors of the corporation for monetary damages shall be eliminated to the fullest extent permissible under California law.

ARTICLE IV. Agent for Service of Process

The name and address in the state of California of the corporation=s initial agent for service of process is:

_____

_____

_____

ARTICLE V. Indemnification

The corporation is authorized, to the fullest extent permissible under California law, to indemnify its agents (as defined in Section 317 of the California Corporations Code), whether by bylaw, agreement or otherwise, for breach of duty to this corporation and its shareholders in excess of that expressly permitted in Section 317 and to advance defense expenses to its agents in connection with such matters as they are incurred, subject to the limits on such excess indemnification set forth in Section 204 of the California Corporations Code.

ARTICLE VI

The corporation is authorized to issue only one class of shares of stock; and the total number of shares which this corporation is authorized to issue is 100,000.

Dated: _____, 20_____

_____
Typed Name and Signature of Director

_____
Typed Name and Signature of Director

_____
Typed Name and Signature of Director

The undersigned, being all of the persons named above as the initial directors, declare that they are the persons who executed the foregoing Articles of Incorporation, which execution is their act and deed.

_____
Typed Name and Signature of Director

_____
Typed Name and Signature of Director

_____
Typed Name and Signature of Director

Note: This is only an example and not to be used or submitted to the Secretary of State's office. Use the reproduction of this form following this sample as the articles to be submitted to the Secretary of State. It is also advised to type the information on the form.

There is an additional $15 counter fee for Articles of Incorporation filed in person with the Secretary of State.

Sample Articles of Incorporation by Incorporator, Not Designating Initial Directors

SAMPLE ARTICLES OF INCORPORATION OF

_____

ARTICLE I. Name

The name of the corporation is _____.

ARTICLE II. Purpose

The purpose of this corporation is to engage in any lawful act or activity for which a corporation may be organized under the General Corporation Law of California other than the banking business, the trust company business or the practice of a profession permitted to be incorporated by the California Corporations Code.

ARTICLE III. Directors

The number of Directors of the corporation is _____.

The liability of the directors of the corporation for monetary damages shall be eliminated to the fullest extent permissible under California law.

ARTICLE IV. Agent for Service of Process

The name and address in the state of California of the corporation=s initial agent for service of process is:

_____

_____

_____

ARTICLE V. Indemnification

The corporation is authorized, to the fullest extent permissible under California law, to indemnify its agents (as defined in Section 317 of the California Corporations Code), whether by bylaw, agreement or otherwise, for breach of duty to this corporation and its shareholders in excess of that expressly permitted in Section 317 and to advance defense expenses to its agents in connection with such matters as they are incurred, subject to the limits on such excess indemnification set forth in Section 204 of the California Corporations Code.

ARTICLE VI

The corporation is authorized to issue only one class of shares of stock; and the total number of shares which this corporation is authorized to issue is 100,000.

Dated: _____, 20_____

_____
Name and Signature of Incorporator

I declare that I am the person who executed the foregoing Articles of Incorporation, and that this instrument is my act and deed.

_____
Name and Signature of Incorporator

Note: *This is only an example and not to be used or submitted to the Secretary of State's office. Use the reproduction of this form following this sample as the articles to be submitted to the Secretary of State. It is also advised to type the information on the form.*

TABLE OF CONTENTS TO BYLAWS OF

(Name of corporation)

ARTICLES TITLE AND SECTION

I OFFICES
1.01 Principal Office
1.02 Other Offices

II MEETINGS OF SHAREHOLDERS
2.01 Place of Meetings
2.02 Annual Meetings
2.03 Special Meetings
2.04 Notice of Shareholders' Meetings
2.05 Manner of Giving Notice; Affidavit of Notice
2.06 Quorum
2.07 Adjourned Meeting and Notice Thereof
2.08 Voting
2.09 Waiver of Notice or Consent by Absent Shareholders
2.10 Shareholder Action by Written Consent Without a Meeting
2.11 Record Date for Shareholder Notice, Voting, and Giving Consents
2.12 Proxies
2.13 Inspectors of Election

III DIRECTORS
3.01 Powers
3.02 Number and Qualification of Directors
3.03 Election and Term of Office of Directors
3.04 Vacancies
3.05 Place of Meetings and Telephonic Meetings
3.06 Annual Meetings
3.07 Other Regular Meetings
3.08 Special Meetings
3.09 Quorum
3.10 Waiver of Notice
3.11 Adjournment
3.12 Notice of Adjournment
3.13 Action Without Meeting
3.14 Fees and Compensation of Directors
3.15 Standard of Care; Liability

IV COMMITTEES
4.01 Committees of Directors
4.02 Meetings and Action of Committees

V OFFICERS
5.01 Officers
5.02 Election of Officers
5.03 Subordinate Officers, Etc.
5.04 Removal and Resignation of Officers
5.05 Vacancies in Offices
5.06 Chairman of the Board
5.07 President
5.08 Vice Presidents
5.09 Secretary
5.10 Chief Financial Officer

VI INDEMNIFICATION OF DIRECTORS, OFFICERS, EMPLOYEES, AND OTHER AGENTS
6.01 Agents, Proceedings, and Expenses
6.02 Actions Other than by the Corporation
6.03 Actions by the Corporation
6.04 Successful Defense by Agent
6.05 Required Approval
6.06 Advance of Expenses
6.07 Other Contractual Rights
6.08 Limitations
6.09 Insurance
6.10 Fiduciaries of Corporate Employee Benefit Plan
6.11 Amendment to California Law

VII CORPORATE LOANS AND GUARANTEES TO DIRECTORS, OFFICERS, AND EMPLOYEES
7.01 Limitations on Corporate Loans and Guarantees
7.02 Permissible Corporate Loans and Guarantees

VIII GENERAL CORPORATE MATTERS
8.01 Record Date for Purposes Other than Notice and Voting
8.02 Checks, Drafts, Evidences of Indebtedness
8.03 Corporate Contracts and Instruments; How Executed
8.04 Certificates for Shares
8.05 Lost Certificates
8.06 Representation of Shares of Other Corporations
8.07 Construction and Definitions

Ch 3
Forms

8.08 Legend Condition

8.09 Close Corporation Certificates

IX RECORDS AND REPORTS

9.01 Maintenance and Inspection of Share Register

9.02 Maintenance and Inspection of Bylaws

9.03 Maintenance and Inspection of Other Corporate Records

9.04 Inspection by Directors

9.05 Annual Report to Shareholders

9.06 Financial Statements

9.07 Annual Statement of General Information

X OWNERSHIP AND TRANSFER OF SHARES

10.01 Stock

10.02 Price or Consideration for Shares

10.03 Grant of Pre-emptive Rights

10.04 Restriction on Transfer of Shares

XI AMENDMENTS

11.01 Amendment by Shareholders

11.02 Amendment by Directors

BYLAWS OF

_____

A California Corporation

ARTICLE I. Offices

Section 1.01 Principal Offices. The Board of Directors shall fix the location of the principal executive office of the corporation at any place within or outside the State of California. If the principal executive office is located outside this state, and the corporation has one or more business offices in this state, the Board of Directors shall fix and designate a principal business office in the State of California.

Section 1.02 Other Offices. The officers or the Board of Directors may at any time establish branch or subordinate offices at any place or places where the corporation is qualified to do business and may change the location of any office of the corporation.

ARTICLE II. Meetings of Shareholders

Section 2.01 Place of Meetings. Meetings of shareholders shall be held at any place within or outside the State of California designated by the Board of Directors upon proper notice. In the absence of any such designation, shareholders' meetings shall be held at the principal executive office of the corporation. Section 2.02 Annual Meetings. Unless held at a time and date designated each year by the Board of Directors in accordance with applicable law, an annual meeting of shareholders shall be held on the _____ of each year at _____ ; provided, however, that should such day fall upon a legal holiday, then the annual meeting of shareholders shall be held at the same time and place on the next day thereafter which is a full business day. At the annual meeting, Directors shall be elected and any other proper business may be transacted.

Section 2.03 Special Meetings.
(a) A special meeting of the shareholders may be called at any time by the Board of Directors, or by the Chairman of the Board, or by the President, or by one or more shareholders holding shares which, in the aggregate, entitle them to cast not less than ten percent (10%) of the votes at any such meeting.
(b) If a special meeting is called by any person or persons other than the Board of Directors, the request shall be in writing, specifying the time of such meeting and the general nature of the business proposed to be transacted, and shall be delivered personally or sent by registered mail or by telegraphic or other facsimile transmission to the Chairman of the Board, the President, any Vice President, and the Secretary of the corporation. The secretary upon receiving the request shall cause notice to be promptly given to the shareholders entitled to vote, in accordance with the provisions of Sections 2.01, 2.04 and 2.05 of this Article II, that a meeting will be held at the time requested by the person or persons calling the meeting, not less than thirty-five (35) nor more than sixty (60) days after the receipt of the request. If the notice is not given within twenty (20) days after receipt of the request, the person or persons requesting the meeting may give the notice. Nothing contained in this Section 2.03 shall be construed as limiting, fixing, or affecting the time when a meeting of shareholders called by action of the Board of Directors may be held.

Section 2.04 Notice of Shareholders Meetings.
(a) All notices of meetings of shareholders shall be sent or otherwise given in accordance with Section 2.05 not less than ten (10) nor more than sixty (60) days before the date of the meeting being noticed. The notice shall specify the place, date and hour of the meeting and (i) in the case of a special meeting, the general nature of the business to be transacted, or (ii) in the case of the annual meeting, those matters which the Board of Directors, or the other person or persons calling the meeting, at the time of giving the notice, intend to present for action by the shareholders. The notice of any meeting at which Directors are to be elected shall include the names of any nominees which, at the time of the notice, the Board of Directors or management intends to present for election.

(b) If action is proposed to be taken at any meeting for approval of (i) a contract or transaction in which a Director has a direct or indirect financial interest, as contemplated by Section 310 of the Corporations Code of California, (herein the "Code"), (ii) an amendment of the Articles of Incorporation, pursuant to Section 902 of the Code, (iii) a reorganization of the corporation, pursuant to Section 1201 of such Code, (iv) a voluntary dissolution of the corporation, pursuant to Section 2000 of such Code, the notice shall also state the general nature of such proposal, or (v) a distribution in dissolution that requires approval of the outstanding shares under Corporation Code Section 2007.

Section 2.05 Manner of Giving Notice; Affidavit of Notice.
(a) Notice of any meeting of shareholders shall be given either personally or by first class mail or telegraphic or other written communication (including facsimile, telegram, or electronic email message), charges prepaid, addressed to each shareholder at the address of such shareholder appearing on the books of the corporation or more recently given by the shareholder to the corporation for the purpose of notice. If no such address appears on the corporations books or has been so given, notice shall be deemed to have been properly given to such shareholder if sent by first class mail or telegraphic or other written communication to the corporation's principal executive office to the attention of such shareholder, or if published at least once in a newspaper of general circulation in the county where such office is located. Notice shall be deemed to have been given at the time when delivered personally or deposited in the mail or sent by telegram or other means of written communication.

(b) If any notice addressed to a shareholder at the address of such shareholder appearing on the books of the corporation is returned to the corporation by the United States Postal Service marked to indicate that the United States Postal Service is unable to deliver the notice to the shareholder at such address, all future notices or reports shall be deemed to have been duly given without further mailing if the same shall be available to the shareholder upon written demand of the shareholder at the principal executive office of the corporation for a period of one (1) year from the date of the giving of such notice.

(c) An affidavit of the mailing or other means of giving any notice of any shareholders' meeting shall be executed by the Secretary, Assistant Secretary, or any transfer agent of the corporation giving such notice, and shall be filed and maintained in the minute book of the corporation.

Section 2.06 Quorum. The presence, in person or by proxy, of the holders of a majority of the shares entitled to vote at the subject meeting of shareholders shall constitute a quorum for the transaction of business. The shareholders present at a duly called or held meeting at which a quorum is present may continue to trans-

**Ch 3
Forms**

act business until adjournment, notwithstanding the withdrawal of enough share-holders to leave less than a quorum, if any action taken (other than adjournment) is approved by at least a majority of the shares required to constitute a quorum, unless the General Corporation Law requires the vote of a greater number of shareholders or a vote by classes.

Section 2.07 Adjourned Meeting and Notice Thereof.
(a) Any shareholders meeting, annual or special, whether or not a quorum is pres-ent, may be adjourned from time to time by the vote of a majority of the shares represented at such meeting, either in person or by proxy, but in the absence of a quorum, no other business may be transacted at such meeting, except as pro-vided in Section 2.06.

(b) When any meeting of shareholders, either annual or special, is adjourned to another time and place, notice need not be given of the adjourned meeting if the time and place thereof are announced at the meeting at which the adjournment is taken, unless a new record date for the adjourned meeting is fixed, or unless the adjournment is for more than forty-five (45) days from the date set for the original meeting, in which case the Board of Directors shall set a new record date. Notice of any such adjourned meeting, if required, shall be given to each shareholder of record entitled to vote at the adjourned meeting in accordance with the provi-sions of Sections 2.04 and 2.05. At any adjourned meeting the corporation may transact any business which might have been transacted at the original meeting.

Section 2.08 Voting.
(a) The shareholders entitled to vote at any meeting of shareholders shall be determined in accordance with the provisions of Section 2.11, subject to the provi-sions of Sections 702 to 704, inclusive, of the Code (relating to voting shares held by a fiduciary, in the name of a corporation or in joint ownership). Such vote may be by voice vote or by ballot; provided, however, that all elections for Directors must be by ballot upon demand by a shareholder if made before the voting begins. Any shareholder entitled to vote on any matter (other than the election of directors) may vote part of the shares in favor of the proposal and refrain from voting the remaining shares or vote them against the proposal, but if the share-holder fails to specify the number of shares such shareholder is voting affirma-tively, it will be conclusively presumed that the shareholder's approving vote is with respect to all shares such shareholder is entitled to vote. If a quorum is pres-ent, the affirmative vote of a majority of the shares represented at the meeting and entitled to vote on any matter (other than the election of Directors) shall be the act of the shareholders, unless the vote of a greater number or voting by classes is required by the Code or the Articles of Incorporation.

(b) At a shareholders' meeting involving the election of Directors, no shareholder shall be entitled to cumulate votes (i.e., cast for any one or more candidates a number of votes greater than the number of the shareholder's shares) unless the names of such candidates have been placed in nomination prior to commencement of the voting and a shareholder has given notice to the meeting prior to commencement of the voting, of the shareholder's intention to cumulate his votes. If any shareholder has given such notice, then every shareholder entitled to vote may cumulate his votes for candidates in nomination and give any candidate up to a number of votes equal to the number of Directors to be elected multiplied by the number of votes to which such shareholder's shares are entitled, or distribute the total number of his votes as so calculated among any or all of the candidates. The candidates receiving the highest number of votes shall be elected.

Section 2.09 Waiver of Notice or Consent by Absent Shareholders.
(a) The transactions of any meeting of shareholders, either annual or special, however called and noticed, and whenever held, shall be as valid as if it had occurred at a meeting duly held after regular call and notice, if a quorum be present either in person or by proxy, and if, either before or after the meeting, each person entitled to vote but not present in person or by proxy, signs a written waiver of notice, a consent to the holding of the meeting, or any approval of the minutes thereof. The waiver of notice or consent need not specify either the business to be transacted or the purpose of any annual or special meeting of shareholders, except that if action is taken or proposed to be taken for approval of any of those matters specified in Section 2.04(b), the waiver of notice of consent shall state the general nature of such proposal. All such waivers, consents, and approvals shall be filed with the corporate records or made a part of the minutes of the meeting.

(b) Attendance of a person at a meeting shall constitute a waiver of notice of such meeting, unless such person objects at the beginning of the meeting to the transaction of any business because the meeting is not lawfully called or convened, except that attendance at a meeting is not a waiver of any right to object to the consideration of matters not included in the notice of the meeting if such objection is expressly made at the meeting.

Section 2.10 Shareholder Action by Written Consent Without a Meeting.
(a) Any action which may be taken at any annual or special meeting of shareholders, other than the election of Directors, may be taken without a meeting and without prior notice, if a consent or consents in writing, setting forth the action so taken, are signed by the holders of outstanding shares representing not less than the minimum number of votes that would be necessary to authorize or take such action at a meeting at which all shares entitled to vote thereon were present and voted. In the case of election of Directors, such consents shall be effective only if signed by the holders of all outstanding shares entitled to vote for the election of Directors; provided, however, that a Director may be elected at any time to fill a

vacancy not filled by the current Directors by the written consent of the holders of a majority of the outstanding shares entitled to vote for the election of Directors.

(b) All such consents shall be filed with the Secretary of the corporation and shall be maintained in the corporate records. Any shareholder giving a written consent, or the shareholder's proxyholder, or a transferee of the shares or a personal representative of the shareholder or their respective proxyholders, may revoke the consent in writing effective upon receipt by the Secretary of the corporation if occurring prior to the time that written consents respecting the number of shares required to authorize the proposed action have been filed with the Secretary.

(c) If the consents of all shareholders entitled to vote have been solicited in writing, and if the unanimous written consent of all such shareholders has been received, the Secretary shall give prompt notice of the corporate action approved by the shareholders without a meeting. This notice shall be given in the manner specified in Section 2.05 of this Article II. In the case of approval of (i) contracts or transactions in which a director has a direct or indirect financial interest, pursuant to Section 310 of the Code, (ii) indemnification of agents of the corporation, pursuant to Section 317 of the Code, (iii) a reorganization of the corporation, pursuant to Section 1201 of the Code, and (iv) a distribution in dissolution other than in accordance with the rights of outstanding preferred shares, pursuant to Section 2007 of the Code, the notice shall be given at least ten (10) days before the consummation of any action authorized by that approval.

Section 2.11 Record Date for Shareholder Notice, Voting, and Giving Consents.
(a) For purposes of determining the shareholders entitled to notice of any meeting, to vote, or to give consent to corporate action without a meeting, the Board of Directors may fix, in advance, a record date which shall not be more than sixty (60) days nor less than ten (10) days prior to the date of any such meeting nor more than sixty (60) days prior to such action without a meeting, and in such case only shareholders of record on the date so fixed are entitled to notice and to vote or to give consents, as the case may be, notwithstanding any transfer of any shares on the books of the corporation after the record date fixed as aforesaid, except as otherwise provided in the California General Corporation Law.

(b) If the Board of Directors does not so fix a record date:
(i) the record date for determining shareholders entitled to notice of, or to vote at, a meeting of shareholders shall be at the close of business on the business day next preceding the day on which notice is given or, if notice is waived, at the close of business on the business day next preceding the day on which the meeting is held; and
(ii) the record date for determining those shareholders entitled to give consent to corporation action in writing without a meeting, when no prior action by the

Board has been taken, shall be the day on which the first written consent is given. When prior action of the Board has been taken, the record date shall be at the close of business on the day on which the Board adopts the resolution relating thereto, or the sixtieth (60th) day prior to the date of such other action, whichever is later.

(c) A new determination of Shareholders of record entitled to receive notice of a shareholders' meeting will apply to any adjournment of the meeting if the adjournment date is more than forty-five (45) days after the date of the original meeting.

Section 2.12 Proxies. Every person entitled to vote for Directors or on any other matter shall have the right to do so either in person or by one or more agents authorized by a written proxy signed by such person or filed with the Secretary of the corporation. A proxy shall be deemed signed if the shareholder's name is placed on the proxy (whether by manual signature, typewriting, telegraphic transmission, or otherwise) by the shareholder or the shareholder's attorney-in-fact. A validly executed proxy which does not state that it is irrevocable shall continue in full force and effect unless: (i) revoked by the person executing it, prior to the vote pursuant thereto, by a writing delivered to the corporation stating that the proxy is revoked, or by a subsequent proxy executed by the person executing the earlier proxy, or such person's attendance at the meeting and voting in person; or (ii) written notice of the death or incapacity of the maker of such proxy is received by the corporation before the vote pursuant thereto is counted; provided, however, that no such proxy shall be valid after the expiration of eleven (11) months from the date of such proxy, unless otherwise provided in the proxy. The revocability of a proxy that states on its face that it is irrevocable shall be governed by the provisions of Section 705(e) and (f) of the Code.

Section 2.13 Inspectors of Election.

(a) Before any meeting of shareholders, the Board of Directors may appoint any persons other than nominees for office to act as inspectors of election at the meeting or its adjournment. If no inspectors of election are so appointed, the chairman of the meeting may, and on the request of any shareholder or a shareholder's proxy shall, appoint said inspectors at the meeting. The number of inspectors shall be either one (1) or three (3). If inspectors are appointed at a meeting on the request of one or more shareholders or proxies, the holders of a majority of shares, or their proxies present at the meeting, shall determine whether one (1) or three (3) inspectors are to be appointed. If any person appointed as inspector fails to appear or fails or refuses to act, the chairman of the meeting may, and upon the request of any shareholder or shareholder's proxy shall, appoint a person to fill the vacancy.

(b) The inspector shall:

(i) determine the number of shares outstanding and the voting power of each, the shares represented at the meeting, the existence of a quorum, and the authenticity, validity, and effect of proxies;

(ii) receive votes, ballots, or consents;

(iii) hear and determine all challenges and questions in any way arising in connection with the right to vote;

(iv) count and tabulate all votes or consents;

(v) determine when the polls shall close;

(vi) determine the result; and

(vii) do any other acts that may be proper to conduct the election or vote with fairness to all shareholders.

ARTICLE III. Directors

Section 3.0l Powers.

(a) Subject to the provisions of the Code and any limitations in the Articles of Incorporation and these Bylaws relating to action required to be approved by the shareholders or by the outstanding shares, the business and affairs of the corporation shall be managed and all corporate powers shall be exercised by or under the direction of the Board of Directors.

(b) Without prejudice to such general powers, but subject to the same limitations, it is hereby expressly declared that the Directors shall have the power and authority to:

(i) select and remove all officers, agents, and employees of the corporation, prescribe such powers and duties for them as are not inconsistent with the law, the Articles of Incorporation or these Bylaws, fix their compensation, and require from them security for faithful service;

(ii) change the principal executive office or the principal business office in the State of California from one location to another; cause the corporation to be qualified to do business in any other state, territory, dependency, or foreign country and conduct business within or outside the State of California; designate any place within or without the State for the holding of any shareholders' meeting or meetings, including annual meetings; adopt, make, and use a corporate seal, and prescribe the forms of certificates of stock, and alter the form of such seal and of such certificates;

(iii) authorize the issuance of shares of stock of the corporation from time to time, upon such terms as may be lawful, in consideration of money paid, labor done, or services actually rendered, debts or securities cancelled or tangible or intangible property actually received; and

(iv) borrow money and incur indebtedness for the purposes of the corporation, and cause to be executed and delivered therefore, in the corporate name, promissory notes, bonds, debentures, deeds of trust, mortgages, pledges, hypothecations, or other evidences of debt and securities therefore.

Section 3.02 Number and Qualification of Directors. The authorized number of Directors shall be _____ until changed by a duly adopted amendment to the Articles of Incorporation or by an amendment to this bylaw adopted by the vote or written consent of holders of a majority of the outstanding shares entitled to vote; provided, however, in the event there are ever more than five (5) directors in this corporation, that an amendment reducing the number of Directors to a number less than five (5) cannot be adopted if the votes cast against its adoption at a meeting, or the shares not consenting in the case of action by written consent, are equal to more than one sixth (162/3 percent) of the outstanding shares entitled to vote.

Section 3.03 Election and Term of Office of Directors. Directors shall be elected at each annual meeting of the shareholders to hold office until the next annual shareholders' meeting. Each Director, including a Director elected to fill a vacancy, shall hold office until the expiration of the term for which elected and until a successor has been elected and qualified.

Section 3.04 Vacancies.

(a) Vacancies in the Board of Directors may be filled by a majority vote of the remaining Directors, although less than a quorum, or by a sole remaining Director, except that a vacancy created by the removal of a Director by the vote or written consent of the shareholders or by court order may be filled only by the vote of a majority of the shares entitled to vote represented at a duly held meeting at which a quorum is present, or by the written consent of holders of a majority of the outstanding shares entitled to vote. Each Director so elected shall hold office until the next annual meeting of the shareholders and until a successor has been elected and qualified.

(b) A vacancy or vacancies in the Board of Directors shall be deemed to exist in the case of the death, resignation, or removal of any Director, or if the Board of Directors by resolution declares vacant the office of a Director who has been declared of unsound mind by an order of court or convicted of a felony, or if the authorized number of Directors is increased, or if the shareholders fail, at any meeting of shareholders at which any Director or Directors are elected, to elect the full authorized number of Directors to be voted for at that meeting.

(c) The shareholders may elect a Director or Directors at any time to fill any vacancy or vacancies not filled by the Directors, but any such election by written consent shall require the consent of a majority of the outstanding shares entitled to vote.

(d) Any director may resign upon giving written notice to the Chairman of the Board, the President, the Secretary, or the Board of Directors. A resignation shall

Ch 3
Forms

be effective upon the receipt of said notice, unless the notice specifies a later time for its effectiveness. If the resignation of a Director is effective at a future time, the Board of Directors may elect a successor to take office when the resignation becomes effective.

(e) No reduction of the authorized number of Directors shall have the effect of removing any Director prior to the expiration of his term of office.

Section 3.05 Place of Meetings and Telephonic Meetings. Regular meetings of the Board of Directors may be held without notice, at any time and at any place within or outside the State of California that is designated by these Bylaws, or by resolution of the Board. In the absence of the designation of a place, regular meetings shall be held at the principal executive office of the corporation. Special meetings of the Board shall be held at any place that has been designated in the notice of the meeting or, if not stated in the notice, at the principal executive office of the corporation. Any meeting, regular or special, may be held by conference telephone or similar communications equipment, so long as all Directors participating in such meeting can hear one another, and all such Directors shall be deemed to be present in person at such meeting.

Section 3.06 Annual Meetings. Immediately following each annual meeting of shareholders, the Board of Directors shall hold a regular meeting for purposes of organization, the election of officers, and the transaction of other business. Notice of such meeting shall not be required.

Section 3.07 Other Regular Meetings. Other regular meetings of the Board of Directors may be held without call at such time as shall from time to time be fixed by the Board of Directors. Such regular meetings may be held without notice.

Section 3.08 Special Meetings.

(a) Special meetings of the Board of Directors for any purpose or purposes may be called at any time by the Chairman of the Board, the President, any Vice President, the Secretary, or the majority of the Directors.

(b) Notice of the time and place of special meetings shall be delivered personally or by telephone to each Director or sent by first-class mail or telegram, charges pre-paid, addressed to each Director at his or her address as it is shown upon the records of the corporation. In case such notice is mailed, it shall be deposited in the United States mail at least four (4) working days prior to the time of the holding of the meeting. In case such notice is delivered personally, or by telephone or telegram, it shall be delivered personally or by telephone or to the telegraph company at least forty-eight (48) hours prior to the time of the holding of the meeting. Any oral notice given personally or by telephone may be communicated to either the Director or to a person at the office of the Director who the person giving the notice has reason to believe will promptly communicate it to the Director. The notice need not specify the purpose of the meeting nor the place if the meeting is

Ch 3 Forms

to be held at the principal executive office of the corporation.

Section 3.09 Quorum. A majority of the authorized number of Directors shall constitute a quorum for the transaction of business, except to adjourn as hereinafter provided. Every act or decision done or made by a majority of the Directors present at a meeting duly held at which a quorum is present shall be regarded as the act of the Board of Directors, subject to the provisions of Section 310 of the Code (regarding approval of contracts or transactions in which a director has a direct or indirect material financial interest), Section 311 (regarding appointment of committees), and Section 317(e) (regarding indemnification of directors). A meeting at which a quorum is initially present may continue to transact business not withstanding the withdrawal of Directors, if any action taken is approved by at least a majority of the required quorum for such meeting.

Section 3.10 Waiver of Notice. The transactions of any meeting of the Board of Directors, however called and noticed or wherever held, shall be as valid as though had been conducted at a meeting duly held after regular call and notice if a quorum is present and if, either before or after the meeting, each of the Directors not present signs a written waiver of notice, a consent to holding the meeting or an approval of the minutes thereof. The waiver of notice or consent need not specify the purpose of the meeting. All such waivers, consents, and approvals shall be filed with the corporate records or made a part of the minutes of the meeting. Notice of a meeting shall also be deemed given to any Director who attends the meeting without protesting the lack of notice.

Section 3.11 Adjournment. A majority of the Directors present, whether or not constituting a quorum, may adjourn any meeting to another time and place.

Section 3.12 Notice of Adjournment. Notice of the time and place of holding an adjourned meeting need not be given, unless the meeting is adjourned for more than twenty-four (24) hours, in which case notice of such time and place shall be given prior to the time of the adjourned meeting, to the Directors who were not present at the time of the adjournment.

Section 3.13 Action Without Meeting. Any action required or permitted to be taken by the Board of Directors may be taken without a meeting, if all members of the Board shall individually or collectively consent in writing to such action. Such action by written consent shall have the same force and effect as a unanimous vote of the Board of Directors. Such written consent or consents shall be filed with the minutes of the proceedings of the Board.

Section 3.14 Fees and Compensation of Directors. Directors and members of committees may receive such compensation, if any, for their services, and such reimbursement of expenses, as may be fixed or determined by resolution of the Board of Directors. Nothing herein contained shall be construed to preclude any Director from serving the corporation in any other capacity as an officer, agent, employee, or otherwise, and receiving compensation for such services.

Section 3.15 Standard of Care; Liability.

(a) Each Director shall exercise such powers and otherwise perform such duties in good faith, in the matters such Director believes to be in the best interests of the corporation, and with such care including reasonable inquiry, using ordinary prudence, as a person in a like position would use under similar circumstances.

(b) In performing the duties of a Director, a Director shall be entitled to rely on information, opinions, reports, or statements, including financial statements and other financial data, in which case prepared or presented by:

(i) One or more officers or employees of the corporation whom the Director believes to be reliable and competent in the matters presented;

(ii) Counsel, independent accountants, or other persons as to matters which the Director believes to be within such person's professional or expert competence; or

(iii) A Committee of the Board upon which the Director does not serve, as to matters within its designated authority, which Committee the Director believes to merit confidence, so long as in any such case, the Director acts in good faith, after reasonable inquiry when the need therefore is indicated by the circumstances, and without knowledge that would cause such reliance to be unwarranted.

ARTICLE IV. Committees

Section 4.01 Committees of Directors. The Board of Directors may, by resolution adopted by a majority of the authorized number of Directors, designate one or more committees, each consisting of one (1) or more Directors, to serve at the pleasure of the Board. The Board may designate one or more Directors as alternate members of any committee. Any such committee, to the extent provided in the resolution of the Board, shall have all the authority of the Board, except with respect to:

(a) the approval of any action which, under the Code, also requires shareholders' approval or approval of the outstanding shares;

(b) the filling of vacancies on the Board of Directors or in any committee;

(c) the fixing of compensation of the Directors for serving on the Board or on any committee;

(d) the amendment or repeal of bylaws or the adoption of new bylaws;

(e) the amendment or repeal of any resolution of the Board of Directors which by its express terms is not so amendable or repealable;

(f) a distribution to the shareholders of the corporation (as defined in Section 166 of the Code), except at a rate or in a periodic amount or within a price range determined by the Board of Directors; or

(g) the appointment of any other committees of the Board of Directors or the members thereof.

Section 4.02 Meetings and Actions of Committees. Meetings and action of committees shall be governed by, and held and taken in accordance with, the provisions of Article III of these Bylaws, Section 3.05 (place of meetings and telephonic meetings), Section 3.07 (regular meetings), Section 3.08 (special meetings and notice), Section 3.09 (quorum), Section 3.10 (waiver of notice), Section 3.11 (adjournment), Section 3.12 (notice of adjournment), and Section 3.13 (action without meeting), with such changes in the context of those sections as are necessary to substitute the committee and its members for the Board of Directors and its members, except that the time of regular meetings of committees may be determined by resolution of the Board of Directors as well as the committee, special meetings of committees may also be called by resolution of the Board of Directors and notice of special meetings of committees shall also be given to all alternate members, who shall have the right to attend all meetings of the committee. The Board of Directors may adopt rules for the government of any committee consistent with the provisions of these Bylaws.

ARTICLE V. Officers

Section 5.01 Officers. The officers of the corporation shall be a Chairman of the Board or a President, or both, a Secretary, and a Chief Financial Officer. The corporation may also have, at the discretion of the Board of Directors, one or more Vice Presidents, a Treasurer, one or more Assistant Secretaries, one or more Assistant Treasurers, and such other officers as may be appointed in accordance with the provisions of Section 5.03 of this Article V. Any number of offices may be held by the same person, except that the post of Secretary and President shall not be held by the same individual.

Section 5.02 Election of Officers. The officers of the corporation, except such officers as may be appointed in accordance with the provisions of Section 5.03 or Section 5.05 of this Article V, shall be chosen by the Board of Directors, and each shall serve at the pleasure of the Board, subject to the rights, if any, of an officer under any contract of employment.

Section 5.03 Subordinate Officers, Etc. The Board of Directors may appoint, and may empower the President to appoint, such other officers as the business of the corporation may require, each of whom shall hold office for such period, have such authority and perform such duties as are provided in the Bylaws or as the Board of Directors may determine.

Section 5.04 Removal and Resignation of Officers.
(a) Subject to the rights, if any, of an officer under any contract of employment, any officer may be removed, either with or without cause, by the Board of Directors, at any regular or special meeting thereof, or by any officer upon whom

such power of removal may be conferred by the Board of Directors.

(b) Any officer may resign at any time by giving written notice to the corporation. Any such resignation shall take effect upon the receipt of such notice or at any later time specified therein; and, unless otherwise specified therein, the acceptance of such resignation shall not be necessary to make it effective. Any such resignation is without prejudice to the rights, if any, of the corporation under any contract to which the officer is a party.

Section 5.05 Vacancies in Offices. A vacancy in any office because of death, resignation, removal, disqualification, or any other cause shall be filled in the manner prescribed in these Bylaws for regular appointments to such office.

Section 5.06 Chairman of the Board. The Chairman of the Board, if such an officer be elected, shall, if present, preside at all meetings of the Board of Directors and exercise and perform such other powers and duties as may be from time to time assigned to him by the Board of Directors or prescribed by the Bylaws.

Section 5.07 President. Subject to such supervisory powers which may be given by the Board of Directors to the Chairman of the Board, if there be such an officer, the President shall be the general manager and chief executive officer of the corporation and shall, subject to the control of the Board of Directors, have general supervision, direction, and control of the business and the officers of the corporation. He shall preside at all meetings of the shareholders and, in the absence of the Chairman of the Board, or if there be none, at all meetings of the Board of Directors. He shall have the general powers and duties of management usually vested in the office of President of a corporation, and shall have such other powers and duties as may be prescribed by the Board of Directors or the Bylaws.

Section 5.08 Vice President(s). In the absence or disability of the President, the Vice President(s), if any, in order of their rank as fixed by the Board of Directors, or, if not ranked, a Vice President designated by the Board of Directors, shall perform all the duties of the President, and when so acting shall have all the powers of, and be subject to all the restrictions upon, the President. The Vice President(s) shall have such other powers and perform such other duties as from time to time may be prescribed for them respectively by the Board of Directors, the Bylaws, the President, or the Chairman of the Board if there is no President.

Section 5.09 Secretary.

(a) The Secretary shall keep or cause to be kept at the principal executive office, or such other place as the Board of Directors may designate, a book of minutes of all meetings and actions of Directors, committees of Directors, and shareholders, with the time and place of holding, whether regular or special, and, if special, how authorized, the notice thereof given, the names of those present at Directors' and committee meetings, the number of shares present or represented at shareholders' meetings, and the proceedings thereof.

(b) The Secretary shall keep or cause to be kept at the principal executive office or at the office of the corporation's transfer agent or registrar, as determined by resolution of the Board of Directors, a share register, or a duplicate share register, showing the names of all shareholders and their addresses, the number of shares held by each, the number and date of certificates issued for the same, and the number and date of cancellation of every certificate surrendered for cancellation.

(c) The Secretary shall give, or cause to be given, notice of all meetings of the shareholders and of the Board of Directors required by the Bylaws or by law to be given, and he shall keep the seal of the corporation, if one be adopted, in safe custody, and shall have such other powers and perform such other duties as may be prescribed by the Board of Directors or by the Bylaws.

Section 5.10 Chief Financial Officer.

(a) The Chief Financial Officer shall keep and maintain, or cause to be kept and maintained, adequate and correct books and records of accounts of the properties and business transactions of the corporation, including accounts of its assets, liabilities, receipts, disbursements, gains, losses, capital, retained earnings, and shares. The books of account shall be open at all reasonable times to inspection by any Director upon demand.

(b) The Chief Financial Officer shall cause to be deposited all moneys and other valuables in the name and to the credit of the corporation with such depositaries as may be designated by the Board of Directors. He shall cause the funds of the corporation to be disbursed as he may be properly directed from time to time, shall render to the President and Directors an account of all of his transactions as Chief Financial Officer and of the financial condition of the corporation whenever requested, and shall have other such powers and perform such other duties as may be prescribed by the Board of Directors or the Bylaws.

ARTICLE VI. Indemnification of Directors, Officers, Employees, and Other Agents

Section 6.01 Definitions: Agents, Proceedings, and Expenses. For the purposes of this Article, "agent" means any person who is or was a Director, officer, employee, or other agent of this corporation, or is or was serving at the request of this corporation as a Director, officer, employee, or agent of another foreign or domestic corporation, partnership, joint venture, trust, or other enterprise, or was a director, officer, employee, or agent of a foreign or domestic corporation which was a predecessor corporation of this corporation or of another enterprise at the request of such predecessor corporation; "proceeding" means any threatened, pending, or completed action or proceeding, whether civil, criminal, administrative, or investigative; and "expenses" includes, without limitation, attorneys' fees and any expenses of establishing a right to indemnification under Section 6.04 or Section 6.05(c) of this Article VI.

Section 6.02 Actions Other than by the Corporation. This corporation shall indemnify any person who was or is a party, or is threatened to be made a party, to any proceeding (other than an action by or in the right of this corporation) by reason of the fact that such person is or was an agent of this corporation, against expenses, judgments, fines, settlements, and other amounts actually and reasonably incurred in connection with such proceeding, if that person acted in good faith and in a manner that person reasonably believed to be in the best interests of this corporation, and, in the case of a criminal proceeding, had no reasonable cause to believe his or her conduct was unlawful. The termination of any proceeding by judgment, order, settlement, conviction, or upon a plea of nolo contendere or its equivalent shall not, of itself, create a presumption that the person did not act in good faith and in a manner which the person reasonably believed to be in the best interests of this corporation or that the person had reasonable cause to believe that his or her conduct was unlawful.

Section 6.03 Actions by the Corporation. This corporation shall indemnify any person who was or is a party, or is threatened to be made a party, to any threatened, pending, or completed action by or in the right of this corporation to procure a judgment in its favor by reason of the fact that that person is or was an agent of this corporation, against expenses actually and reasonably incurred by that person in connection with the defense or settlement of that action if that person acted in good faith, in a manner that person believed to be in the best interests of this corporation, and with such care, including reasonable inquiry, as an ordinary prudent person in a like position would use under similar circumstances. No indemnification, however, shall be made under this section:
(a) In respect of any claim, issue, or matter as to which that person shall have been adjudged to be liable to this corporation in the performance of that person's duty to this corporation, unless and only to the extent that the court in which that action was brought shall determine upon application that, in view of all the circumstances of the case, that person is fairly and reasonably entitled to indemnity for the expenses which the court shall determine;
(b) of amounts paid in settling or otherwise disposing of a threatened or pending action, with or without court approval; or
(c) of expenses incurred in defending a threatened or pending action which is settled or otherwise disposed of without court approval.

Section 6.04 Successful Defense by Agent. To the extent that an agent of this corporation has been successful on the merits in defense of any proceeding referred to in Section 6.02 or Section 6.03 of this Article VI, or in defense of any claim, issue, or matter therein, the agent shall be indemnified against expenses actually and reasonably incurred by the agent in connection therewith.

Section 6.05 Required Approval. Except as provided in Section 6.04 of this Article, any indemnification under this Article shall be made by this corporation only if authorized upon a determination that indemnification of the agent in the specific case is proper because the agent has met the applicable standard of conduct set forth in Section 6.02 or Section 6.03 of this Article VI, by:

(a) a majority vote of a quorum consisting of Directors who are not parties to the proceeding;

(b) approval by the affirmative vote of the holders of a majority of the shares of this corporation entitled to vote represented at a duly held meeting at which a quorum is present, or by the written consent of holders of a majority of the outstanding shares entitled to vote (for this purpose, the shares owned by the person to be indemnified shall not be considered outstanding or entitled to vote thereon);

(c) the court in which the proceeding is or was pending, upon application made by this corporation or the agent or the attorney or other person rendering services in connection with the defense, whether or not such application by the agent, attorney, or other person is opposed by this corporation; or

(d) a written opinion of independent legal counsel, if a quorum of Directors who are not parties to the proceeding are not available.

Section 6.06 Advance of Expenses. Expenses incurred in defending any proceeding may be advanced by this corporation before the final disposition of the proceeding upon receipt of an undertaking by or on behalf of the agent to repay the amount of the advance unless it shall be determined ultimately that the agent is entitled to be indemnified as authorized in this Article VI.

Section 6.07 Other Contractual Rights. Nothing contained in this Article VI shall affect any right to indemnification to which persons other than Directors and officers of this corporation or any subsidiary hereof may be entitled by contract or otherwise.

Section 6.08 Limitations. No indemnification or advance shall be made under this Article VI, except as provided in Section 6.04 or Section 6.05(c), in any circumstance where it appears:

(a) that it would be inconsistent with a provision of the Articles, the Bylaws, a resolution of the shareholders, or an agreement in effect at the time of the accrual of the alleged cause of action asserted in the proceeding in which the expenses were incurred or other amounts were paid which prohibits or otherwise limits indemnification; or

(b) that it would be inconsistent with any condition expressly imposed by a court in approving a settlement.

Section 6.09 Insurance. The corporation may, upon a determination by the Board of Directors, purchase and maintain insurance on behalf of any agent of the corporation against any liability which might be asserted against or incurred by the agent in such capacity, or which might arise out of the agent's status as such, whether or not this corporation would have the power to indemnify the agent against that liability under the provisions of this Article VI.

Section 6.10 Fiduciaries of Corporate Employee Benefit Plan. This Article VI does not apply to any proceeding against any trustee, investment manager, or other fiduciary of an employee benefit plan in that person's capacity as such, even though that person may also be an agent of this corporation as defined in Section 6.01 of this Article VI. Nothing contained in this Article VI shall limit any right to indemnification to which such a trustee, investment manager, or other fiduciary may be entitled by contract or otherwise, which shall be enforceable to the extent permitted by applicable law.

Section 6.11 Amendment to California Law. In the event that California Law regarding indemnification of directors, officers, employees, and other agents of corporation, as in effect at the time of adoption of these Bylaws, is subsequently amended to in any way increase the scope of permissible indemnification beyond that set forth herein, the indemnification authorized by this Article VI shall be deemed to be coextensive with the maximum afforded by the California Law as so amended.

Section 6.12 No Duplication of Payments. The Corporation will not be liable to make any payment in connection with any claim made under this Article VI to any party entitled to indemnification to the extent said party has otherwise already actually received payment of the amounts otherwise indemnifiable regardless of source.

ARTICLE VII. Corporate Loans and Guarantees to Directors, Officers, and Employees

Section 7.01 Limitation on Corporate Loans and Guarantees. Except as provided in Section 7.02 of this Article VII this corporation shall not make any loan of money or property to, or guarantee any obligations of,

(a) any Director or officer of the corporation or of its parent or any subsidiary, or
(b) any person, upon the security of shares of this corporation or of its parent, unless the loan or guaranty is otherwise adequately secured, except by the vote of the holders of a majority of the shares of all classes, regardless of limitations or restrictions on voting rights, other than shares held by the benefited Director, officer, or person.

Section 7.02 Permissible Corporate Loans and Guarantees. This corporation may lend money to, or guarantee any obligation of, or otherwise assist, any officer or other employee of this corporation or of any subsidiary, including any officer or employee who is also a Director, pursuant to an employee benefit plan (including, without limitation, a stock purchase or stock option plan) available to executives or other employees, whenever the Board determines that such loan or guaranty could benefit the corporation. If such plan includes officers or Directors, it shall be approved or ratified by the affirmative vote of the holders of a majority of the shares of this corporation entitled to vote, by written consent, or represented at a duly held meeting at which a quorum is present, after disclosure of the right under such plan to include officers or Directors is made. Such loan or guaranty or other assistance must be at legal interest and may be unsecured or secured in such manner as the Board shall approve, including, without limitation, a pledge of shares of the corporation. This corporation may advance money to a Director or officer of the corporation or of its parent or any subsidiary for expenses incurred in the performance of the duties of such Director or officer, provided that in the absence of such advance such Director or officer would be entitled to be reimbursed for such expenses by such corporation, its parent or any subsidiary.

ARTICLE VIII. General Corporate Matters

Section 8.01 Record Date for Purposes Other than Notice and Voting.

(a) For purposes of determining the shareholders entitled to receive payment of any dividend or other distribution or allotment of any rights or entitled to exercise any rights in respect of any other lawful action (other than for the purposes prescribed by Section 2.11 of Article II of these Bylaws), the Board of Directors may fix, in advance, a record date, which shall not be more than sixty (60) days prior to any such action. Only shareholders of record on the date so fixed are entitled to receive the dividend, distribution, or allotment of rights or to exercise the rights, as the case may be, notwithstanding any transfer of any shares on the books of the corporation after the record date fixed as aforesaid, except as otherwise provided in the California General Corporation Law.

(b) If the Board of Directors does not so fix a record date, the record date for determining shareholders for any such purpose shall be at the close of business on the day on which the Board adopts the resolution relating thereto, or the sixtieth (60th) day prior to the date of such action, whichever is later.

Section 8.02 Checks, Drafts, Evidences of Indebtedness. All checks, drafts or other orders for payment of money, notes, or other evidences of indebtedness, issued in the name of or payable to the corporation, shall be signed or endorsed by such person or persons and in such manner as, from time to time, shall be determined by resolution of the Board of Directors.

Section 8.03 Corporate Contracts and Instruments; How Executed. The Board of Directors, except as otherwise provided in these Bylaws, may authorize any officer or agent to enter into any contract or execute any instrument in the name of and on behalf of the corporation, and such authority may be general or confined to specific instances. However, unless so authorized or ratified by the Board of Directors or within the agency power of an officer, no officer, agent, or employee shall have any power or authority to bind the corporation by any contract or engagement or to pledge its credit or to render it liable for any purpose or for any amount.

Section 8.04 Certificates for Shares. A certificate or certificates for shares of the capital stock of the corporation shall be issued to each shareholder when any such shares are fully paid, and the Board of Directors may authorize the issuance of certificates for shares as partly paid provided that such certificates shall state the amount of the consideration to be paid therefore and the amount paid thereon. All certificates shall be signed in the name of the corporation by the Chairman of the Board or Vice Chairman of the Board, or the President or a Secretary or any Assistant Secretary, certifying the number of shares and the class or series of shares owned by the shareholder. Any or all of the signatures on the certificate may be facsimile. In case any officer, transfer agent or registrar who has signed or whose facsimile signature has been placed upon a certificate shall have ceased to be such officer, transfer agent, or registrar before such certificate is issued, it may be issued by the corporation with the same effect as if such person were an officer, transfer agent, or registrar at the date of issue.

Section 8.05 Lost Certificates. Except as hereinafter provided in this Section 8.05, no new certificate for shares shall be issued in lieu of an old certificate unless the old certificate is surrendered to the corporation and cancelled at the same time. The Board of Directors may, if any share certificate or certificate for any other security is lost, stolen, or destroyed, authorize issuance of a new certificate in lieu thereof, upon such terms and conditions as the Board may require, including provision for indemnification of the corporation secured by a bond of other adequate security sufficient to protect the corporation against any claim that may be made against it, including, but not limited to, any expense or liability, on account of the alleged loss, theft, or destruction of such certificate or the issuance of such new certificate.

Section 8.06 Representation of Shares of Other Corporations. The Chairman of the Board, the President, or any Vice President, or any other person authorized by resolution of the Board of Directors or by any of the foregoing designated officers, is authorized to vote on behalf of the corporation any and all shares of any other corporation or corporations, foreign or domestic, standing in the name of the corporation. The authority herein granted to said officers to vote or represent on behalf of the corporation any and all shares held by the corporation in any other corporation or corporations may be exercised by any such officer in person or by any person authorized to do so by proxy duly executed by said officer.

Section 8.07 Construction and Definitions. Unless the context requires otherwise, the general provisions, rules of construction, and definitions in the California General Corporation Law shall govern the construction of these Bylaws. Without limiting the generality of the foregoing, the singular number includes the plural, the plural includes the singular, and the term "person" includes both a corporation and a natural person.

Section 8.08 Legend Condition. In the event any shares of the corporation are issued pursuant to a permit or exemption therefrom requiring the imposition of a legend condition, the person or persons issuing or transferring said shares shall make sure said legend appears on the certificate and on the stub relating thereto in the stock record book, and shall not be required to transfer any shares free of such legend unless an amendment to such permit or a new permit be first issued so authorizing said deletion.

Section 8.09 Close Corporation Certificates. All certificates representing shares of this corporation, in the event it should elect to become a statutory close corporation, shall contain the legend required by California Corporations Code section 418(c).

ARTICLE IX. Records and Reports

Section 9.01 Maintenance and Inspection of Share Register.

(a) The corporation shall keep at its principal executive office, or as determined by resolution of the Board of Directors, a record of its shareholders, giving the names and addresses of all shareholders and the number and class of shares held by each shareholder.

(b) A shareholder or shareholders of the corporation holding at least five percent (5%), in the aggregate, of the outstanding voting shares of the corporation may (i) inspect and copy the records of shareholders' names and addresses and shareholdings during usual business hours upon giving the corporation written notice five (5) business days prior to the date of inspection, and/or (ii) obtaining from the transfer agent of the corporation, upon written demand and upon the tender of such transfer agent's usual charges for such list, a list of the names and addresses of the shareholders who are entitled to vote for the election of Directors, and their shareholdings as of the most recent record date for which such list has been compiled, or as of a date specified by the requesting shareholder or shareholders subsequent to the date of demand. Such list shall be made available to such shareholder or shareholders by the transfer agent on or before the later of the fifth (5th) business day after the demand is received or the date specified in the demand as the date as of which the list is to be compiled. The record of shareholders shall also be open to inspection upon the written demand of any shareholder or holder of a voting trust certificate, at any time during usual business hours, for a purpose reasonably related to such holder's interests as a shareholder or as the holder of a voting trust certificate. Any inspection and copying under this section may be made in person or by an agent or attorney of the shareholder or holder of a voting trust certificate making such demand.

Section 9.02 Maintenance and Inspection of Bylaws. The corporation shall keep at its principal executive office, or, if its principal executive office is not in the State of California, at its principal business office in California, the original or a copy of the Bylaws as amended to date, which shall be open to inspection by any shareholder upon the written demand of any such shareholder at all reasonable times during usual business hours. If the principal executive office of the corporation is outside this state and the corporation has no principal business office in this state, the Secretary shall, upon written request of any shareholder, furnish to such shareholder a copy of the Bylaws as amended to date.

Section 9.03 Maintenance and Inspection of Other Corporate Records. The accounting books and records and minutes of proceedings of the shareholders and the Board of Directors and any committee or committees of the Board of Directors shall be kept at such place or places designated by the Board of Directors, or, in the absence of such designation, at the principal executive office of the corporation. The minutes shall be kept in written form and the accounting books and records shall be kept either in written form or in any other form capable of being converted into written form. Such minutes and accounting books and records shall be open to inspection upon the written demand of any shareholder or holder of a voting trust certificate, at any reasonable time during usual business hours, for a purpose reasonably related to such holder's interests as a shareholder or as the holder of a voting trust certificate. Such inspection may be made in person or by an agent or attorney, and shall include the right to copy and make extracts. The foregoing rights of inspection shall extend to the records of each subsidiary corporation of the corporation.

Section 9.04 Inspection by Directors. Every Director shall have the absolute right at any reasonable time to inspect all books, records, and documents of every kind and the physical properties of the corporation and each of its subsidiary corporations. Such inspection by a Director may be made in person or by agent or attorney and the right of inspection includes the right to copy and make extracts.

Section 9.05 Annual Report to Shareholders. Until such time as there are one hundred (100) or more shareholders in this corporation, the annual report to shareholders referred to in Section 1501 of the California General Corporation Law is expressly dispensed with, but nothing herein shall be interpreted as prohibiting the Board of Directors from issuing such annual or other periodic reports to the shareholders of the corporation as they consider appropriate.

Section 9.06 Financial Statements.
(a) A copy of any annual financial statement and any income statement of the corporation for each quarterly period of each fiscal year, and any accompanying balance sheet of the corporation as of the end of each such period, which have been

prepared by the corporation shall be kept on file in the principal executive office of the corporation for twelve (12) months after their respective dates, and each such statement shall be exhibited at all reasonable times to any shareholder requesting an examination. A copy of said statement shall be mailed to any shareholder upon written request.

(b) If a shareholder or shareholders holding at least five percent (5%), in the aggregate, of the outstanding shares of any class of stock of the corporation make a written request to the corporation for an income statement of the corporation for the three (3)-month, six (6)-month, or nine (9)-month period of the current fiscal year having ended more than thirty (30) days prior to the date of the request, and a balance sheet of the corporation as of the end of such period, the Chief Financial Officer shall cause such statement to be prepared, if not already prepared, and shall deliver personally or mail such statement or statements to the person making the request within thirty (30) days after the receipt of such request. If the corporation has not sent to each requesting shareholder or shareholders its annual report for the last fiscal year, this report shall likewise be delivered or mailed within thirty (30) days after such request.

(c) The corporation shall also, upon written request, mail to the shareholder a copy of the last annual, semi-annual, or quarterly income statement which it has prepared and a balance sheet as of the end of such period.

(d) The quarterly income statements and balance sheets referred to in this Section 9.06 shall be accompanied by the report thereon, if any, of any independent accountants engaged by the corporation or the certificate of an authorized officer of the corporation that such financial statements were prepared without audit from the books and records of the corporation.

Section 9.07 Biennial Statement of General Information. The corporation shall at least once every two years, during the calendar month in which its Articles of Incorporation were originally filed with the California Secretary of State, or at any time during the immediately preceding five (5) calendar months, file with the Secretary of State of the State of California, on the prescribed form, a statement setting forth the authorized number of Directors, the names and complete business or residence addresses of all incumbent Directors, the names and complete business or residence addresses of the Chief Executive Officer, Secretary, and Chief Financial Officer, the street address of its principal executive office or principal business office in this state (if any), and the general type of business constituting the principal business activity of the corporation, together with a designation of the agent of the corporation for the purpose of service of process, all in compliance with Section 1502 of the Code. If there has been no change in the information from the Corporation's last statement on file in the Secretary of State's office, the Corporation may simply advise the Secretary of State on the appropriate form that no changes in the required information have taken place since the last filing.

ARTICLE X. Ownership and Transfer of Shares
Section 10.01 Stock. The corporation is authorized to issue only one class of shares (common shares). The total number of shares shall be _____. There shall exist no distinction between the shares of the corporation or the holders thereof.

Section 10.02 Price or Consideration for Shares.
(a) The authorized shares provided for in Section 10.01 shall be issued for such consideration as shall be determined by the Board of Directors. The Board of Directors is empowered to periodically review the set price of the shares and modify said price or consideration subject to the shareholders approval.
(b) The consideration for which shares will issue may consist of money paid, labor performed, services actually rendered to the corporation or for its benefit or in its formation or reorganization, debts or securities cancelled, and tangible and intangible property actually received by either the issuing corporation or by a wholly owned subsidiary, or any one or combination of these. The full agreed upon price or consideration for shares must be paid prior to or concurrently with the issuance of the shares unless the shares are issued in accordance with a stock subscription or purchase agreement in which case the terms of payment delineated in said stock subscription or purchase agreement shall be controlling.
[The Following Sections of ARTICLE X Are Optional]

Section 10.03 Grant of Pre-emptive Rights. Each shareholder of the corporation shall be entitled to full pre-emptive or preferential rights, as such rights are defined by law, to subscribe for or purchase his proportional part of any shares or securities which may be issued by the corporation.

Section 10.04 Restrictions on Transfer of Shares. Before a shareholder can make a valid sale or transfer of any of the shares of this corporation, such shareholder must first offer said shares to the corporation and then to the other shareholders in the following manner:
(a) The offering shareholder shall deliver written notice to the Secretary of the Corporation stating the price, terms, and conditions of such proposed sale or transfer, the number of shares to be sold or transferred, and his or her intention to so sell or transfer such shares. The corporation shall have thirty (30) days after receipt of said notice to purchase said shares pursuant to the price, terms, and conditions stated in the notice, provided, however, that the corporation shall not at any time be permitted to purchase all of its outstanding voting shares. Should the corporation fail to exercise its option to purchase the offered shares within thirty (30) days from receipt of notice, or prior thereto decline to purchase the shares, the Secretary of the Corporation shall mail or deliver to each of the other

shareholders, within five days of the close of the thirty (30) day period or notice of decline to purchase, a copy of the notice given by the selling shareholder to the Secretary. Within thirty (30) days after the mailing or delivering of the copies of the notice to the shareholders, any shareholder or shareholders desiring to acquire all or a part of the offered shares must deliver to the Secretary by mail, or otherwise, a written offer or offers, expressed to be immediately acceptable, to purchase a specified number of said shares at the price and terms stated in the sellers notice.

(b) If the total number of shares specified in the offers to purchase exceeds the number of shares offered to be sold, each offering shareholder shall be entitled to purchase such proportion of the offered shares as the number of shares of the corporation he holds bears to the total number of shares held by all of the shareholders offering to purchase the shares.

(c) If all of the shares offered to be sold or transferred are not disposed of pursuant to the apportionment plan outlined in paragraph (b), each shareholder wishing to purchase shares in a number in excess of his proportionate share, shall be entitled to purchase such proportion of those shares which remain undisposed of, as the total number of shares which he holds bears proportionately to the total number of shares held by all of the shareholders desiring to purchase shares in excess of those to which they are entitled under such apportionment.

(d) If within the above delineated period, offers to purchase all of the offered shares are not presented, the offering shareholder shall be under no obligations to sell any shares to the Corporation and/or the other Shareholders in which event the offering shareholders may transfer its shares to the original offeree, provided, however, that (i) any transfer shall be in compliance with all applicable laws, including state and federal securities filings, and (ii) the offering shareholder must complete the sale within thirty (30) days of the determination that all of the offered shares will not be repurchased by the corporation and/or other shareholders, and the price, terms, and conditions of the sale to the original offerer cannot vary from the original notice. In the event the third party sale does not take place within said thirty (30) day period and/or in the event, the original price, terms, and conditions of the sale change, a new notice must be issued to the corporation in which event the corporation and other shareholders will have the same rights as under the original notice.

ARTICLE XI. Amendments

Section 11.01 Amendments by Shareholders. New Bylaws may be adopted or these Bylaws may be amended or repealed by the vote or written consent of holders of a majority of the outstanding shares entitled to vote; provided, however, that if the Articles of Incorporation of the corporation set forth the number of authorized Directors of the corporation, the authorized number of Directors may

**Ch 3
Forms**

be changed only by an amendment of the Articles of Incorporation.

Section 11.02 Amendment by Directors. Subject to the rights of the shareholders as provided in Section 11.01 of this Article XI, to adopt, amend, or repeal Bylaws, Bylaws may be adopted, amended, or repealed by the Board of Directors.

Certification of Bylaws

THIS IS TO CERTIFY, that I am the duly elected, qualified, and acting Secretary of _____, a California Corporation, and that the foregoing Bylaws were adopted for the Corporation by the Board of Directors on _____, 20 ____.

IN WITNESS WHEREOF, I have hereto set my hand this _____ day of _____, 20 ____.

_____
Secretary

SAMPLE LETTER TO SECRETARY OF STATE
TO FILE ARTICLES OF INCORPORATION

(Name and Address of Corporation)
Secretary of State
Corporate Filing Division
1500 Eleventh Street
Sacramento, CA 95814

Dear Secretary of State:

Please find enclosed an original and three copies of the proposed Articles of Incorporation of _____.

Also enclosed is a check for $100 in payment of the fee for filing the articles and company, certifying, the returning the enclosed copies fees: _____

Please file the enclosed Articles of Incorporation and return all certified copies to the above address. Your assistance in this matter is appreciated.

_____

(Name)

Incorporator of

_____, Inc.

If you want a following date other than the date of receipt you can request a date not more than ninety (90) days in the future.

Note: There is an additional $15 counter fee for Articles of Incorporation filed in person with the Secretary of State.

**Ch 3
Forms**

CERTIFICATE OF AMENDMENT OF
ARTICLES OF INCORPORATION* OF

_____

_____ and _____ certify that:

1. They constitute a majority of the (directors or incorporators) of said corporation.

2. Said corporation has issued no shares.

3. They adopt the following Amendment of the Articles of Incorporation: (Article _____ of the Articles of Incorporation which now reads " ... "is amended to read in full as follows: " ... ")**

_____   _____
Director or Incorporator   Director or Incorporator

Each of the undersigned declares under penalty of perjury that the matters set forth in the foregoing Certificate of Amendment are true and correct of their own knowledge.

Executed this _____ day of _____, 20_____, at _____, California.

_____   _____
Director or Incorporator***   Director or Incorporator

Notes

*This form is to be used if the Articles are amended before the issuance of shares only. Use Form 1-D after the issuance of the corporation=s shares.

**To avoid the return of your certificate unfiled, it is advised that you quote in its entirety the old paragraph that you are amending as well as the new amended paragraph.

***A Certificate of Amendment of Articles of Incorporation can be signed by the incorporator(s) or director(s) before the issuance of stock. If, however, the directors were not named in the Articles, it is best to have the incorporator(s) sign the instrument.

CERTIFICATE OF AMENDMENT OF
ARTICLES OF INCORPORATION* OF

_____

_____ (president's name) and
_____ (secretary's name) certify:

1. They are the respective president and secretary of
_____ (name of corporation), a California
Corporation.

2. The following amendment of the Articles of Incorporation of said corporation
has been approved by the Board of Directors of the corporation:

(Article _____ of the Articles of Incorporation is amended to read in full as follows: . . .)

3. The foregoing amendment of the Articles of Incorporation was duly approved
by the required vote of shareholders in accordance with Section (California
Corporation Code Section 902 is usually the proper section; in cases where the
amendment affects the number of shares, then Section 903. Amendment of close
corporation provisions must be made under Section 158. The code must be examined to be sure the correct provision is cited.) The total number of outstanding
voting shares entitled to vote with respect to the amendment was
_____. A majority of these shares were required to approve
the amendment and numbers of shares voting in favor of the amendment
_____ (exceeded/equaled) such required vote.

Dated: _____

_____   _____
President   Secretary

*This form is to be used if the Articles are amended after the issuance of the cor-
poration's shares. Use Form 1-E if the corporation has not yet issued shares.

Note that some amendments with respect to the "close corporation" provisions
can require more than a majority vote.

SAMPLE DOCUMENT FILING REQUEST

Date: _____

From: _____

_____

_____

_____   Telephone: _____

To: Secretary of State
Corporate Division
1500 11th Street
Sacramento, CA 95814
Attention: Document Filing Support Unit

Re: _____

Enclosed is the originally signed

❏ Articles of Incorporation ($100-stock)

($30-nonprofit)

❏ Certificate of Amendment ($30)

Corporate # _____

❏ Agreement of Merger ($100)

Corporate #_____

Corporate #_____

❏ Certificate of Election to Wind Up and Dissolve (No Charge)

Corporate #_____

❏ Certificate of Dissolution (No Charge)

Corporate #_____

Other_____

together with _____ copies

The original document is to be filed:

❏ date of receipt

❏ on the future date of_____

_____ copies are to be certified (no charge for the first two copies, $8.00 for each additional copy)

_____ copies are to be endorsed (no charge)

Additionally please provide

_____ Certificate(s) of Filing ($6.00 each)

_____ Certificate(s) of Status ($6.00 each)

Enclosed check (s) in the aggregate amount of $_____.

SAMPLE LETTER FOR CERTIFICATE OF AMENDMENT
OF ARTICLES OF INCORPORATION

Corporation's Address

Secretary of State
Corporate Filing Division
1500 11th Street
Sacramento, CA 95814

RE: Certificate of Amendment of Articles of Incorporation of

Dear Sir/Madam:

Please find enclosed an original and one copy of a Certificate of Amendment of
the Articles of Incorporation of _____. Also enclosed is a check
for $30 to cover the filing fee. Please file the original and return an endorsed copy
to this office by way of the enclosed self-addressed stamped envelope.

Your assistance in this matter is appreciated.

Sincerely,

_____

Title

_____

Corporation's Name

ACTION OF INCORPORATOR OF [NAME OF CORPORATION]

The undersigned, being the sole Incorporator of the above-referenced corporation, pursuant to the authority vested in the Incorporator by Section 210 of the California Corporations Code, does hereby approve and adopt the following resolutions:

ADOPTION OF BYLAWS:

RESOLVED, that the Bylaws of this corporation in the form attached hereto are adopted as the Bylaws of this corporation.

ELECTION OF DIRECTORS:

RESOLVED, the following persons are elected as the initial directors of this corporation: _____

_____

[Typed or printed name of Incorporator]

DATED: _____, _____.

Ch 3 Forms

RESOLUTION OF BOARD OF DIRECTORS
AMENDING CERTAIN BYLAWS*

WHEREAS, it is deemed to be in the best interest of the Corporation and its shareholders that the corporate Bylaws be amended; and

WHEREAS, the Articles of Incorporation, Section 11.01 and 11.02 of the current Bylaws** and the California General Corporation Law do not prohibit the current amendments or limit or restrict the Board of Directors to do so,

NOW THEREFORE, BE IT RESOLVED that the following amendments to the Bylaws of the corporation are approved and adopted:

[Insert appropriate amendment in the following form:

Section _____ of Article _____ of the Bylaws of the Corporation is hereby amended to read in its entirety as follows: (Quote new section in full including the section numbers.)]

RESOLVED FURTHER that the Secretary of the corporation is hereby authorized and directed to compile and certify copies of the amended Bylaws and place a copy of same in the corporate Minute Book, keeping another copy at the corporation's principal executive office where it shall be open to inspection by all shareholders at all reasonable times during office hours.

There being no further business to come before the meeting, upon motion duly made, seconded and carried, the meeting is adjourned.

_____

ATTEST:

_____   _____
Chairman   Secretary

Notes

Don't forget that proper notice must be given to conduct a meeting of the Board of Directors (see Bylaws Section 3.01-3.14) and complete minutes should be taken. The above form contains only the proper resolutions and adjournment provisions. The date and location of the meeting, along with the other introductory provisions of a Board of Directors' meeting, should also be set forth. See the first few paragraphs of Form 4-C for examples of the necessary language that must be included as a preamble.

*** Certain amendments of corporate Bylaws require shareholder approval. (See Sections 11.01 and 11.02 of the Bylaws.) It is suggested that you conduct a special meeting of the shareholders if their approval is necessary.*

**WAIVER OF NOTICE AND CONSENT TO HOLDING OF
THE FIRST MEETING OF THE BOARD OF DIRECTORS OF**

_____

We (I), the undersigned, being all the Directors (being the sole Director) of

_____

a California corporation, hereby waive(s) notice of the first meeting of the Board
of Directors of the California on _____, 20_____, at _____
a.m./p.m., and consent to the transaction of any and all business by the
Director(s) at said meeting including, but not limited to, the principal corporate
office, the adoption of a stock certificate, the authorization of payment expenses
of incorporation, the adoption of corporate bank account, and the authorization of
the sale and issuance of corporate stock.

Date: _____

_____
Director

_____
Director

_____
Director

WAIVER OF NOTICE AND CONSENT TO HOLDING OF
THE FIRST MEETING OF THE BOARD OF DIRECTORS OF

_____

A California Nonprofit Corporation

The undersigned, constituting all of the Directors of _____, a California nonprofit corporation, do hereby waive notice and consent to the holding of the First Meeting of Directors of the Corporation, to be held at _____ on the _____, 20_____, at _____ a.m./p.m., for the purpose of adopting the Bylaws of the Corporation and the corporate seal, of electing the Officer of the Corporation, of authorizing the opening of a depository account for the funds of the Corporation and providing for the payment of the expense of incorporation and organization, of determining the principal office of the Corporation, and of transacting such other business as may be brought before said meeting.

The undersigned further request that this Waiver and Consent be filed with the corporate records and made a part of the minutes of said meeting for the purpose of showing that the business transacted at the meeting is valid and of the same force and effect as though regularly called and noticed.

Date: _____

_____
Director

_____
Director

_____
Director

MINUTES OF THE FIRST MEETING OF THE BOARD OF DIRECTORS

DESIGNATION OF PRINCIPAL OFFICE

The Chairman then proposed that the Corporation should designate an office within the City of _____, California, as its principal office. It was the unanimous decision of the Board that the principal office would be located at _____, California.

ADOPTION OF BYLAWS

The original set of Bylaws, adopted by _____, the Incorporator of the Corporation, was then submitted, read, and discussed among the Board. Upon motion duly made, the following resolution was unanimously adopted:

RESOLVED, that the Bylaws submitted to and reviewed by the Board of Directors of this Corporation be, and they hereby are, adopted as the Bylaws for the regulation of the internal affairs of this Corporation.

RESOLVED FURTHER, that the Secretary of this Corporation certify said Bylaws as having been adopted as of the date of this Action, and insert said Bylaws in the Minute Book of this Corporation.

ADOPTION OF CORPORATE SEAL (Optional)

The Chairman then presented to the meeting a proposed corporate seal in the form prescribed by the Bylaws. Upon motion duly made, the following resolution was unanimously adopted:

RESOLVED, that a corporate seal presented to this meeting be adopted as the corporate seal of the Corporation, and the Secretary is instructed to impress such seal on the document recording this resolution opposite the place where this resolution appears.

(SEAL)

SELECTION OF CORPORATE BANK ACCOUNT

The Chairman then discussed the need for the corporation to open up a bank account or accounts for deposit of the Corporation's funds. After some discussion, upon motion duly made, the following resolutions were unanimously adopted:

RESOLVED, that this Corporation establish in its name one or more deposit and checking accounts with _____ (name of bank), on such terms and conditions as may be agreed upon with such bank, and that the officers of this Corporation be, and they hereby are, authorized to establish such account or accounts.

**Ch 3
Forms**

RESOLVED FURTHER, that the bank account authorization card, a copy of which is attached hereto, is by this reference incorporated herein and the resolutions contained therein are hereby adopted.

ELECTION OF OFFICERS

The meeting then proceeded to elect officers for the Corporation, for the coming year. After discussion and upon nominations duly made and seconded, the following persons were elected to the offices indicated next to their names:

Name	Office
_____	President
_____	Chief Financial Officer
_____	Secretary

ADOPTION OF STOCK CERTIFICATE

The Chairman then presented to the meeting a proposed form of stock certificate for the Corporation's capital stock. Upon motion duly made, seconded, and carried, the following resolutions were unanimously adopted:

RESOLVED, that the share certificates representing the common shares of this corporation be, and they hereby are, approved and adopted in substantially the same form as the form of share certificate presented to this Board, and each such certificate shall bear the name of this Corporation, the number of shares represented thereby, the name of the owner of such shares, and the date such shares were issued.

RESOLVED FURTHER, that such share certificates shall be consecutively numbered beginning with No. 1; shall be issued only when the signature of the President and the signature of the Chief Financial Officer or the Secretary are affixed thereto; and shall bear, if appropriate, other wording related to the ownership, issuance, and transferability of the shares represented thereby.

FILING OF STATEMENT BY DOMESTIC STOCK CORPORATION

The Chairman then noted that Section 1502 of the California Corporations Code requires the Filing of a Statement by Domestic Stock Corporation within ninety (90) days of the filing of the Articles of Incorporation. It was the unanimous decision of the Board that the following resolution be adopted:

RESOLVED, that the appropriate officers of this Corporation file with the California Secretary of State, as required by law, a statement of the names of the officers of this Corporation, together with a statement of the location and address of the principal executive office of the Corporation and the name and address of the agent selected for purposes of receiving service of process on this Corporation.

PLAN OF INITIAL CAPITALIZATION

The Chairman then reviewed the proposed plan for the initial issuance of the Corporation's stock. The Chairman explained that the Corporation planned to issue _____ (number) shares of its capital stock to _____, _____, _____, and _____, for a total consideration of $_____. Upon motion duly made, seconded, and carried, the following resolutions were unanimously adopted:

[Where exempt under Section 25102(h)]:

RESOLVED, that the officers of this Corporation be, and they hereby are, authorized and directed to prepare, execute, verify, and timely file, in the name and on behalf of the Corporation, with the Commissioner of Corporations of the State of California a Notice of Issuance of Securities Pursuant to Subdivision (h) of Section 25102 of the California Corporations Code for the sale and issuance of shares of the Corporation's capital stock for an aggregate consideration of $_____, to the following individuals:

Name	Number of Shares	Consideration
_____	_____	_____
_____	_____	_____
_____	_____	_____
_____	_____	_____

RESOLVED, FURTHER, that within ten (10) days of the filing of the Notice of Issuance of Securities Pursuant to Subdivision (h) of Section 25102 with the Commissioner of Corporations and receipt of the consideration paid for such capital stocks, the President and Secretary of the Corporation, be and they hereby are, authorized and directed to issue and sell up to _____ shares to the individuals set forth above, and such shares, when issued and sold as provided in these resolutions, shall be duly authorized, validly issued, fully paid, and nonassessable, and in all respects shall meet the requirements of that exemption.

RESOLVED, FURTHER, that the officers of this Corporation be, and they hereby are, authorized and directed to execute all documents and to take all other actions as they may deem necessary or appropriate in order to effectuate the issuance of the Corporation's capital stock as provided in these resolutions.

[Where exempt under 25102(f)]:

RESOLVED, that the officers of this Corporation be, and they hereby are, authorized and directed to prepare, execute, verify, and timely file, in the name and on behalf of the Corporation, with the Commissioner of Corporations of the State of California a Notice in the form prescribed pursuant to Section 25102(f) of the California Corporate Securities Law of 1968, for the sale and issuance of shares for an aggregate consideration of $_____, to the following individuals:

Name	Number of Shares	Consideration
_____	_____	_____
_____	_____	_____
_____	_____	_____
_____	_____	_____

RESOLVED, FURTHER, that such shares shall be issued to the foregoing individuals within the exemption from qualification afforded by Section 25012(f), and when issued and sold as provided in these resolutions, such shares shall be duly authorized, validly issued, fully paid, and nonassessable, and in all respects shall meet the requirements of that exemption.

RESOLVED, FURTHER, that the officers of this Corporation be, and they hereby are, authorized and directed to execute all documents and to take all other actions as they may deem necessary or appropriate in order to effectuate the foregoing issuance of stock as provided in these resolutions.

SUBCHAPTER S ELECTION (Optional)

The Chairman then initiated a discussion on the advisability of making a Subchapter S election, pursuant to Section 1372(a) of the Internal Revenue Code of 1954, as amended. After some discussion, and upon motion duly made, seconded, and carried, the following resolutions were unanimously adopted:

WHEREAS, the Directors of this corporation deem it appropriate for the Corporation to elect to be a Small Business Corporation pursuant to Section 1372(a) of the Internal Revenue Code and to be an S corporation for tax purposes;

RESOLVED, that the Corporation hereby elects to be a small business corporation and to be taxed as an S corporation pursuant to Section 1372(a) of the Internal Revenue Code; and further, that the Chief Financial Officer of the Corporation be, and he hereby is, authorized to file, or make arrangements to file, with the appropriate office of the Internal Revenue Service, IRS Form 2553 for this Corporation to receive Subchapter S treatment under Section 1372(a) of the Internal Revenue Code, together with the statement of each shareholder consenting to the Subchapter S election, and to execute such other documents and to take such other action as may be deemed necessary or appropriate to effectuate these resolutions.

SECTION 1244 STOCK ELECTION

The Chairman then informed the Board as to the benefits of qualifying the common stock of the Corporation as Section 1244 Stock and organizing and managing the corporation so that it is a Small Business Corporation, as defined in IRC Section 1244 of the Internal Revenue Code, as amended. Compliance with these sections may enable shareholders to treat any loss sustained by a shareholder on the sale or exchange of shares of the Corporation as an ordinary loss on the shareholder's personal income tax return.

With the intent of achieving this result, it was unanimously

RESOLVED, that the proper officers of the Corporation are authorized to sell and issue common shares pursuant to the IRC Section 1244 in an aggregate amount of money and other property (as a contribution to capital and as paid in surplus), which together with the aggregate amount of common stock, does not exceed $1,000,000.00.

RESOLVED FURTHER, that the Corporation shall sell and issue its common shares in such a manner that, in the hands of qualified shareholders, the shares shall receive the benefit of IRC Section 1244, as amended.

RESOLVED FURTHER, that the proper officers of the Corporation are directed to maintain such records as are necessary, and take such further steps as necessary, pursuant to IRC Section 1244, so as to enable the common shares issued hereunder to qualify as Section 1244 Stock, and allow any shareholder who experiences a loss on the transfer of shares of common stock of the Corporation to qualify for "ordinary loss" deduction treatment on his or her individual income tax return.

FISCAL YEAR (Optional)**

The Chairman then informed the Board that the next order of business was the selection of a fiscal year for the Corporation. After some discussion and upon motion duly made, seconded, and carried, the following resolution was unanimously adopted.

RESOLVED, that the fiscal year of this Corporation shall end on the
_____ day of the month of _____ of each year.

EXPENSES OF THE CORPORATION

The Chairman then stated that certain expenses had been incurred in the incorporation and organization of the Corporation. Upon motion duly made, seconded, and carried, the following resolution was unanimously adopted:

RESOLVED, that the Chief Financial Officer be, and he hereby is, authorized to pay the expenses of the incorporation and organization of this Corporation.

SELECTION OF COUNSEL TO THE CORPORATION

The Chairman then commented that the Board should select corporate legal counsel. After some discussion, it was decided that _____ would be retained as counsel to the Corporation, to serve at the pleasure of the Board.

BUSINESS LICENSES AND TAX FILINGS

The Chairman then initiated a discussion concerning all applicable fictitious business name statements, and tax and license filings. Upon motion duly made, seconded, and carried, the following resolution was unanimously adopted:

RESOLVED, that the Secretary be, and he hereby is, authorized and directed to file for and secure all fictitious business name statements, and business and tax licenses or permits required for the Corporation to properly conduct its business.

ADJOURNMENT

There being no further business to come before the meeting, upon motion duly made, seconded, and unanimously carried, the meeting was adjourned.

_____ ATTEST: _____
(Type Name) Secretary   (Type Name) Chairman of the
of the Meeting   Meeting

Note

**A corporation can always have a calendar year. Note that under the 1986 Tax Reform Act, professional service corporations can no longer have a fiscal year.

**MINUTES OF A SPECIAL MEETING OF
THE BOARD OF DIRECTORS OF**

_____

A CALIFORNIA CORPORATION

A special meeting of the Board of Directors of _____,
a California corporation, was held on _____, 19_____, at _____
o'clock _____ a.m./p.m. of said day, at _____,
California, pursuant to Article III, Section 3.08 of the Bylaws. The special meeting
was held pursuant to a written Notice of Waiver and Consent thereto, signed by
all of the Directors, and inserted into the minute book immediately preceding
these minutes.

There were present at the special meeting the following Directors, constituting all
of the Directors of the Corporation elected at the annual shareholders' meeting:

_____

_____

_____

_____

The President and Secretary of the Corporation acted, respectively, as Chairman
and Secretary of the meeting.

The Chairman announced that the meeting was duly convened and that the Board
was ready to transact such business as may lawfully come before it.

The minutes of the last meeting of the Board of Directors were read and
approved.

On motion duly made, seconded, and carried, the following resolutions were
adopted:

(set forth resolutions)

There being no further business to come before the meeting, upon motion duly
made, seconded, and carried, the special meeting was adjourned.

_____   ATTEST: _____
Secretary   Chairman

MINUTES OF A SPECIAL MEETING OF
THE SHAREHOLDERS OF

_____

A California Corporation

A special meeting of the shareholders of _____,
a California corporation, was held at the hour of _____, on the _____ day of
_____, 19_____, at the offices of the Corporation, located at
_____, California. The meeting was held pur-
suant to a written Waiver of Notice and Consent thereto, signed by all of the
shareholders, and inserted into the minute book immediately preceding these
minutes.

The President and Secretary of the Corporation acted, respectively, as Chairman
and Secretary of the meeting.

The Chairman called the meeting to order and the Secretary called the roll of
shareholders entitled to vote.

The minutes of the last meeting of the shareholders were read and approved.

Those present were the following, constituting all of the shareholders of the
Corporation entitled to vote:

Shareholders

_____

_____

_____

There being present at the special meeting all of the shareholders of record holding all of the shares of common stock of the Corporation issued and outstanding
which have voting power, the Chairman declared that a quorum was present and
that the special meeting was duly opened for business.

On motion made, seconded, and carried, the following resolutions were adopted:

(set forth resolutions)

There being no further business to come before the meeting, upon motion duly
made, seconded, and carried, the meeting was adjourned.

_____   ATTEST: _____
Secretary   Chairman

Ch 3 Forms

State of California
Kevin Shelley
Secretary of State

STATEMENT OF INFORMATION
(Domestic Stock Co rporation)

[S]

FEES (Filing and Disclosure): $25.00.   If amendment, see instr uctions.

IMPORTANT — READ INSTRUCTIONS BEFORE COMPLETING THIS FORM

1. CORPORATE NAME (Please do not alter if name is preprinted.)

This Space For Filing Use Only

DUE DATE:

CALIFORNIA CORPORATE DISCLOSURE ACT (Corporations Code **section 1502.1**)

A publicly traded corporation must file with the Secretary of State a Corporate Disclosure Statement (**Form SI-PT**) annually, within 150 days after the end of its fiscal year. Please see reverse for additional information regarding publicly traded corporations.

COMPLETE ADDRESSES FOR THE FOLLOWING (Do not abbreviate the name of the city. Items 2 and 3 cannot be P.O. Boxes.)

		CITY AND STATE	ZIP CODE
2.	STREET ADDRESS OF PRINCIPAL EXECUTIVE OFFICE		

		CITY	STATE	ZIP CODE
3.	STREET ADDRESS OF PRINCIPAL BUSINESS OFFICE IN CALIFORNIA, IF ANY		CA	

NAMES AND COMPLETE ADDRESSES OF THE FOLLOWING OFFICERS (The corporation must have these three officers. A comparable title for the specific officer may be added; however, the preprinted titles on this form must not be altered.)

		ADDRESS	CITY AND STATE	ZIP CODE
4.	CHIEF EXECUTIVE OFFICER/			
5.	SECRETARY/			
6.	CHIEF FINANCIAL OFFICER/			

NAMES AND COMPLETE ADDRESSES OF ALL DIRECTORS, INCLUDING DIRECTORS WHO ARE ALSO OFFICERS (The corporation must have at least one director. Attach additional pages, if necessary.)

	NAME	ADDRESS	CITY AND STATE	ZIP CODE
7.				
8.				
9.				

10. NUMBER OF VACANCIES ON THE BOARD OF DIRECTORS, IF ANY:

AGENT FOR SERVICE OF PROCESS (If the agent is an individual, the agent must reside in California and Item 12 must be completed with a California address. If the agent is another corporation, the agent must have on file with the California Secretary of State a certificate pursuant to Corporations Code **section 1505** and Item 12 must be left blank.)

11. NAME OF AGENT FOR SERVICE OF PROCESS

		CITY	STATE	ZIP CODE
12.	ADDRESS OF AGENT FOR SERVICE OF PROCESS IN CALIFORNIA, IF AN INDIVIDUAL		CA	

TYPE OF BUSINESS

13. DESCRIBE THE TYPE OF BUSINESS OF THE CORPORATION

14. BY SUBMITTING THIS STATEMENT OF INFORMATION TO THE SECRETARY OF STATE, THE CORPORATION CERTIFIES THE INFORMATION CONTAINED HEREIN, INCLUDING ANY ATTACHMENTS, IS TRUE AND CORRECT.

TYPE OR PRINT NAME OF PERSON COMPLETING THE FORM	SIGNATURE	TITLE	DATE

SI-200 C (REV 09/2004)

APPROVED BY SECRETARY OF STATE

INSTRUCTIONS FOR COMPLETING FORM SI-200 C

For faster processing, the required statement for most corporations can be filed online at https://businessfilings.ss.ca.gov. Alternatively, statement forms are available on the Secretary of State's website at http://www.ss.ca.gov/business and can be viewed, filled in and printed from your computer. Completed forms along with the applicable fees can be mailed to Secretary of State, Statement of Information Unit, P.O. Box 944230, Sacramento, CA 94244-2300 or delivered in person to the Sacramento office, 1500 11th Street, 3rd Floor, Sacramento, CA 95814. If you are not completing this form online, please type or legibly print in black or blue ink. This form should not be altered.

Every domestic stock corporation shall file a Statement of Information with the Secretary of State, within 90 days after filing of its original Articles of Incorporation, and annually thereafter during the applicable filing period. The applicable filing period for a corporation is the calendar month during which its original Articles of Incorporation were filed and the immediately preceding five calendar months. If the name and/or address of the agent for service of process have changed, a corporation must file a complete Statement of Information. A corporation is required to file this statement even though it may not be actively engaged in business at the time this statement is due.

Statutory filing provisions are found in California Corporations Code **section 1502**, unless otherwise indicated. Failure to file this Statement of Information by the due date will result in the assessment of a $250.00 penalty. (Corporations Code **section 2204**; Revenue and Taxation Code **section 19141**)

FILING FEES: The initial or annual Statement of Information must be accompanied by a $20.00 filing fee and $5.00 disclosure fee. The filing fee and the disclosure fee may be included in a single check made payable to the Secretary of State. All domestic stock corporations must pay a total of $25.00 at the time of filing the initial or annual statement. If this statement is being filed to amend any information on a previously filed statement and is being filed outside the applicable filing period, as defined above, no fee is required.

PUBLICLY TRADED CORPORATIONS: Every publicly traded corporation must also file a Corporate Disclosure Statement (**Form SI-PT**) annually, within 150 days after the end of its fiscal year. Form SI-PT may be obtained from the Secretary of State's website at http://www.ss.ca.gov/business or by calling the Statement of Information Unit at (916) 657-5448.

A "publicly traded corporation" is a corporation, as defined in Corporations Code **section 162**, that is an issuer as defined in Section 3 of the Securities Exchange Act of 1934, as amended (15 U.S.C. Sec. 78c), and has at least one class of securities listed or admitted for trading on a national securities exchange, on the National or Small-Cap Markets of the NASDAQ Stock Market, on the OTC-Bulletin Board, or on the electronic service operated by Pink Sheets, LLC.

Complete the Statement of Information (Form SI-200 C) as follows:

Item 1. Please do not alter the preprinted name. If the corporate name is not correct, please attach a statement indicating the correct name and the date the name change amendment was filed with the Secretary of State. If blank, enter the name of the corporation exactly as it is of record with the California Secretary of State.

Item 2. Enter the complete street address, city, state and zip code of the principal executive office. Please do not enter a P.O. Box or abbreviate the name of the city. This address will be used for mailing purposes.

Item 3. Enter the complete street address, city and zip code of the corporation's principal office in California, if any. Please do not enter a P.O. Box or abbreviate the name of the city. Complete this item only if the address in Item 2 is outside of California.

Items 4-6. Enter the name and complete business or residential address of the corporation's chief executive officer (i.e., president), secretary and chief financial officer (i.e., treasurer). Please do not abbreviate the name of the city. The corporation must have these three officers (Corporations Code **section 312(a)**). An officer may hold more than one office. A comparable title for the specific officer may be added; however, the preprinted titles on this form must not be altered.

Items 7-9. Enter the name and complete business or residential address of each incumbent director. If there are more than three directors, please attach additional pages. Please do not abbreviate the name of the city. The corporation must have at least one director. (Corporations Code **section 212(a)**).

Item 10. Enter the number of vacancies on the board of directors, if any.

Item 11. Enter the name of the agent for service of process in California. The person named as agent must be a resident of California or a corporation that has filed a certificate pursuant to Corporations Code **section 1505**. If an individual is designated as agent, complete Items 11 and 12. If a corporation is designated as agent, complete Item 11 and proceed to Item 13 (do not complete Item 12).

An Agent for Service of Process is an individual or another corporation designated by a corporation to accept service of process if the corporation is sued.

Please note: A corporation cannot name itself as agent for service of process and no domestic or foreign corporation may file pursuant to **section 1505** unless the corporation is currently authorized to engage in business in California and is in good standing on the records of the Secretary of State.

Item 12. If an individual is designated as agent for service of process, enter a business or residential address in California. Please do not enter "in care of" (c/o) or abbreviate the name of the city. Please do not enter an address if a corporation is designated as agent for service of process.

Item 13. Briefly describe the general type of business that constitutes the principal business activity of the corporation.

Item 14. Type or print the name and title of the person completing this form and enter the date this form was completed. By submitting this Statement of Information to the Secretary of State, the corporation certifies the information contained herein, including any attachments, is true and correct.

Form **SS-4**

(Rev. December 2001)
Department of the Treasury
Internal Revenue Service

Application for Employer Identification Number

(For use by employers, corporations, partnerships, trusts, estates, churches,
government agencies, Indian tribal entities, certain individuals, and others.)

See separate instructions for each line.   Keep a copy for your records.

EIN

OMB No. 1545-0003

Type or print clearly.

1 Legal name of entity (or individual) for whom the EIN is being requested	

2 Trade name of business (if different from name on line 1)	**3** Executor, trustee, "care of" name

4a Mailing address (room, apt., suite no. and street, or P.O. box)	**5a** Street address (if different) (Do not enter a P.O. box.)
4b City, state, and ZIP code	**5b** City, state, and ZIP code

6 County and state where principal business is located

7a Name of principal officer, general partner, grantor, owner, or trustor	**7b** SSN, ITIN, or EIN

8a **Type of entity** (check only one box)

☐ Sole proprietor (SSN) _____
☐ Partnership
☐ Corporation (enter form number to be filed) _____
☐ Personal service corp.
☐ Church or church-controlled organization
☐ Other nonprofit organization (specify) _____
☐ Other (specify)

☐ Estate (SSN of decedent) _____
☐ Plan administrator (SSN) _____
☐ Trust (SSN of grantor) _____
☐ National Guard   ☐ State/local government
☐ Farmers' cooperative   ☐ Federal government/military
☐ REMIC   ☐ Indian tribal governments/enterprises
Group Exemption Number (GEN) _____

8b If a corporation, name the state or foreign country (if applicable) where incorporated

State	Foreign country

9 **Reason for applying** (check only one box)

☐ Started new business (specify type) _____

☐ Hired employees (Check the box and see line 12.)
☐ Compliance with IRS withholding regulations
☐ Other (specify)

☐ Banking purpose (specify purpose) _____
☐ Changed type of organization (specify new type) _____
☐ Purchased going business
☐ Created a trust (specify type) _____
☐ Created a pension plan (specify type) _____

10 Date business started or acquired (month, day, year)	**11** Closing month of accounting year

12 First date wages or annuities were paid or will be paid (month, day, year). **Note:** *If applicant is a withholding agent, enter date income will first be paid to nonresident alien. (month, day, year)* . . . .

13 Highest number of employees expected in the next 12 months. **Note:** *If the applicant does not expect to have any employees during the period, enter "-0-."* . . . .

Agricultural	Household	Other

14 Check **one** box that best describes the principal activity of your business.

☐ Construction ☐ Rental & leasing ☐ Transportation & warehousing   ☐ Health care & social assistance   ☐ Wholesale-agent/broker
☐ Real estate ☐ Manufacturing ☐ Finance & insurance   ☐ Accommodation & food service   ☐ Wholesale-other   ☐ Retail
☐ Other (specify)

15 Indicate principal line of merchandise sold; specific construction work done; products produced; or services provided.

16a Has the applicant ever applied for an employer identification number for this or any other business? . . . . ☐ Yes   ☐ No
Note: *If "Yes," please complete lines 16b and 16c.*

16b If you checked "Yes" on line 16a, give applicant's legal name and trade name shown on prior application if different from line 1 or 2 above.
Legal name _____   Trade name _____

16c Approximate date when, and city and state where, the application was filed. Enter previous employer identification number if known.
Approximate date when filed (mo., day, year) | City and state where filed | Previous EIN

Third Party Designee	Complete this section **only** if you want to authorize the named individual to receive the entity's EIN and answer questions about the completion of this form.	
	Designee's name	Designee's telephone number (include area code) ( )
	Address and ZIP code	Designee's fax number (include area code) ( )

Under penalties of perjury, I declare that I have examined this application, and to the best of my knowledge and belief, it is true, correct, and complete.

Name and title (type or print clearly) _____

Applicant's telephone number (include area code) ( )

Signature _____   Date _____

Applicant's fax number (include area code) ( )

For Privacy Act and Paperwork Reduction Act Notice, see separate instructions.   Cat. No. 16055N   Form **SS-4** (Rev. 12-2001)

Form SS-4 (Rev. 12-2001)   Page **2**

Do I Need an EIN?

File Form SS-4 if the applicant entity does not already have an EIN but is required to show an EIN on any return, statement, or other document.[1] **See also the separate instructions for each line on Form SS-4.**

IF the applicant...	AND...	THEN...
Started a new business	Does not currently have (nor expect to have) employees	Complete lines 1, 2, 4a–6, 8a, and 9–16c.
Hired (or will hire) employees, including household employees	Does not already have an EIN	Complete lines 1, 2, 4a–6, 7a–b (if applicable), 8a, 8b (if applicable), and 9–16c.
Opened a bank account	Needs an EIN for banking purposes only	Complete lines 1–5b, 7a–b (if applicable), 8a, 9, and 16a–c.
Changed type of organization	Either the legal character of the organization or its ownership changed (e.g., you incorporate a sole proprietorship or form a partnership)[2]	Complete lines 1–16c (as applicable).
Purchased a going business[3]	Does not already have an EIN	Complete lines 1–16c (as applicable).
Created a trust	The trust is other than a grantor trust or an IRA trust[4]	Complete lines 1–16c (as applicable).
Created a pension plan as a plan administrator[5]	Needs an EIN for reporting purposes	Complete lines 1, 2, 4a–6, 8a, 9, and 16a–c.
Is a foreign person needing an EIN to comply with IRS withholding regulations	Needs an EIN to complete a Form W-8 (other than Form W-8ECI), avoid withholding on portfolio assets, or claim tax treaty benefits[6]	Complete lines 1–5b, 7a–b (SSN or ITIN optional), 8a–9, and 16a–c.
Is administering an estate	Needs an EIN to report estate income on Form 1041	Complete lines 1, 3, 4a–b, 8a, 9, and 16a–c.
Is a withholding agent for taxes on non-wage income paid to an alien (i.e., individual, corporation, or partnership, etc.)	Is an agent, broker, fiduciary, manager, tenant, or spouse who is required to file **Form 1042,** Annual Withholding Tax Return for U.S. Source Income of Foreign Persons	Complete lines 1, 2, 3 (if applicable), 4a–5b, 7a–b (if applicable), 8a, 9, and 16a–c.
Is a state or local agency	Serves as a tax reporting agent for public assistance recipients under Rev. Proc. 80-4, 1980-1 C.B. 581[7]	Complete lines 1, 2, 4a–5b, 8a, 9, and 16a–c.
Is a single-member LLC	Needs an EIN to file **Form 8832,** Classification Election, for filing employment tax returns, **or** for state reporting purposes[8]	Complete lines 1–16c (as applicable).
Is an S corporation	Needs an EIN to file **Form 2553,** Election by a Small Business Corporation[9]	Complete lines 1–16c (as applicable).

[1] For example, a sole proprietorship or self-employed farmer who establishes a qualified retirement plan, or is required to file excise, employment, alcohol, tobacco, or firearms returns, must have an EIN. **A partnership, corporation, REMIC (real estate mortgage investment conduit), nonprofit organization (church, club, etc.), or farmers' cooperative must use an EIN for any tax-related purpose even if the entity does not have employees.**

[2] However, **do not** apply for a new EIN if the existing entity only **(a)** changed its business name, **(b)** elected on Form 8832 to change the way it is taxed (or is covered by the default rules), or **(c)** terminated its partnership status because at least 50% of the total interests in partnership capital and profits were sold or exchanged within a 12-month period. (The EIN of the terminated partnership should continue to be used. See Regulations section 301.6109-1(d)(2)(iii).)

[3] Do not use the EIN of the prior business unless you became the "owner" of a corporation by acquiring its stock.

[4] However, IRA trusts that are required to file **Form 990-T,** Exempt Organization Business Income Tax Return, must have an EIN.

[5] A plan administrator is the person or group of persons specified as the administrator by the instrument under which the plan is operated.

[6] Entities applying to be a Qualified Intermediary (QI) need a QI-EIN even if they already have an EIN. **See Rev. Proc. 2000-12.**

[7] See also *Household employer* on page 4. (**Note:** State or local agencies may need an EIN for other reasons, e.g., hired employees.)

[8] Most LLCs **do not** need to file Form 8832. See **Limited liability company (LLC)** on page 4 for details on completing Form SS-4 for an LLC.

[9] An existing corporation that is electing or revoking S corporation status should use its previously-assigned EIN.

BOE-400-SPA (4-04)

California Seller's Permit Application
for Individuals/Partnerships/Corporations/Organizations
(Regular or Temporary)
State Board of Equalization

Frequently Asked Questions

Who must have a permit?

You are generally required to obtain a California seller's permit if you sell or lease merchandise, vehicles, or other tangible personal property in California. A seller's permit allows you to sell items at the wholesale or retail level. If your sales are ongoing, you should apply for a "Regular" permit. If your sales are of a temporary nature (90 days or less) apply for a "Temporary" permit. You cannot legally sell taxable items in California until you have been issued a seller's permit.

Do I need more than one permit?

Each location where sales of taxable items are made requires, and must display, a seller's permit. If you have more than one selling location, attach a list that includes the address for each location and we will issue the permits needed. If your application is for a temporary permit, one permit will be enough, but you need to display a copy of that permit at each temporary location.

Is there a charge for a permit?

No. However, we may require a security deposit. Deposits are used to cover any unpaid taxes that may be owed at the time a business closes.

Is information about my account subject to public disclosure?

State laws that protect your privacy generally cover your records. Some records are subject to public disclosure, such as the information on your seller's permit, names of owners or partners, your business address, and your permit status. See the disclosure information on the back page.

Why do you need to verify my driver license number?

When it is required, it is used to ensure the accuracy of the information provided and to protect against fraudulent use of your identification.

Why am I being asked if I sell tires, consumer electronic devices, or tobacco products at retail?

On January 1, 2001 California retailers of new tires began collecting a tire fee (currently $1.00), for each new tire sold to consumers. Starting on July 1, 2004, consumers will begin to pay a recycling fee for every "covered electronic device," purchased from a retailer.

A covered electronic device is a cathode ray tube or device, flat panel screen, or any other similar video display with a screen whose diagonal measurement is four inches or greater, and is classified to be a hazardous waste when disposed of. Effective on June 30,2004, if you sell cigarettes and/or tobacco products, you must obtain a license (separate from a seller's permit) from each location you intend to sell these products. Depending on your response and type of business, the Board will send you information about these license and fee programs.

What are my rights and responsibilities as a seller?

When you obtain a seller's permit, you acquire certain rights and responsibilities.

- **You may buy property for resale without paying tax to your supplier.** By providing the vendor a completed resale certificate, you are not required to pay sales tax on property you are buying for resale. You cannot use a resale certificate to buy property for your own use (even if you plan to sell it after its use).

- **You must keep records** to substantiate your sales, purchases and return deductions, and keep them for four years.

- **You must file returns** according to the Board's instructions for the filing basis that we determine from your application. You must file a return even if you have no tax to report.

- **You must pay the sales tax due** on your retail sales in California. You may be reimbursed by collecting the amount of tax from your customers.

- **You must notify the Board of any business changes.** A permit is issued only to the owner and address listed on the permit. If you change ownership, address, add another location, sell or close your business, add or drop a partner, you must notify the Board by calling or in writing. Your notification will help us close your account and return any security on deposit. If you do not, you could be held liable for continuing business taxes. Note: Notify us immediately if you drop or add a partner in order to protect former partners from tax liabilities incurred by the business after the partnership changes.

Seller's Permit Application ■ Individuals/Partnerships/Corporations/Organizations (Regular or Temporary) (4-04)

INFORMATION CENTER

1-800-400-7115

FOR TDD ASSISTANCE

From TDD phones: 1-800-735-2929

From voice phones: 1-800-735-2922

FIELD OFFICES

CALL FOR ADDRESSES

City	Area Code	Number
Bakersfield	661	395-2880
Culver City	310	342-1000
El Centro	760	352-3431
Eureka	707	445-6500
Fresno	559	248-4219
Kearney Mesa	858	636-3191
Laguna Hills	949	461-5711
Long Beach	562	901-2483
Norwalk	562	466-1694
Oakland	510	622-4100
Rancho Mirage	760	346-8096
Redding	530	224-4729
Riverside	909	680-6400
Sacramento	916	227-6700
Salinas	831	443-3003
San Diego	619	525-4526
San Francisco	415	356-6600
San Jose	408	277-1231
San Marcos	760	510-5850
Santa Ana	714	558-4059
Santa Rosa	707	576-2100
Stockton	209	948-7720
Suisun City	707	428-2041
Torrance	310	516-4300
Van Nuys	818	904-2300
Ventura	805	677-2700
West Covina	626	480-7200

Business Located

Out-of-State

916-227-6600

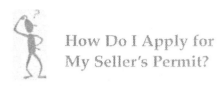

How Do I Apply for My Seller's Permit?

Step 1: Complete Your Application

Complete the application on page 5. If your business is an ongoing operation check permit type "Regular." If your business will operate at the location(s) for 90 days or less, check "Temporary." Please provide **all** the information requested on the application. If you do not this will delay the issuance of your permit. Refer to the "Tips" on page 4. If you need assistance, please call your local Board office or the Information Center, 800-400-7115.

Note: If your business is located outside California, complete form BOE-403-B, *Registration Information for Out-of-State Account.* Visit our website at *www.boe.ca.gov,* call the Out-of-State Office at (916) 227-6600, or the Information Center at 800-400-7115, to request a copy by mail or by fax (select the automated fax-back option).

Step 2: Send Your Application for Processing

Send or take your application to the district office nearest your place of business. If you plan to apply in person, contact the local office to find out when they are open. Note: A permit is required before you begin making sales. Advise the Board if you have an urgent need for a permit.

Step 3: After Your Application Is Approved

If your application is complete you should receive your permit in about two weeks. Based on the information on your application, the Board will provide you with regulations, forms and other publications that may help you with your business. Or, you may choose to view and download information from our website at *www.boe.ca.gov.* You will also be informed of when to file tax returns: monthly, quarterly, fiscal or calendar yearly. You will also start receiving tax returns for reporting and paying the taxes due on your sales and purchases. If you do not receive a return, download one from our website, or call the district office.

Post your permit at your place of business in a location easily seen by your customers.

Seller's Permit Application ▪ Individuals/Partnerships/Corporations/Organizations (Regular or Temporary) (4-04)

Tips for Filling Out Your Application

Item 1: Permit Type

Check whether you are applying for a **regular** or **temporary** permit. You may apply for a temporary permit if you intend to make sales for a period of 90 days or less. Otherwise, you must apply for a regular permit.

Items 2–8: Business Identification Information

Check your type of ownership and provide all of the information requested. Partnerships should provide a copy of their written partnership agreement, if one exists. If it is filed with us at the time you apply for a permit and it specifies that all business assets are held in the name of the partnership, we will attempt to collect any delinquent tax liability from the partnership's assets before we attempt to collect from the partners' personal assets.

Items 9–35: Ownership Information

Indicate whether those listed are owners, partners, etc., and enter their driver license or California Identification Card number and, except in the case of corporate officers, their social security number. Also, provide a reference for each person, who does not live with that person. This information will be kept in strict confidence. If mailing your application, you must provide a photocopy of your driver license or California Identification Card.

Items 36–46, 65: Type of Business and Business Locations

Check whether the business is a retailer, wholesaler, etc., and whether the business is full time or part time. Describe the types of items you will sell. Avoid using broad descriptions, such as "general merchandise." Instead, list specific examples such as sports equipment or garden supplies. Indicate the number of selling locations, the address and telephone number of the business, and the landlord's name, address, and telephone number. If there are multiple selling locations, additional addresses can be listed on the reverse side (Item 65). Tax returns and other materials will be sent to the business address unless a different mailing address is specified (Item 42).

Items 47–48: Projected Monthly Sales

Indicate your projected monthly gross and taxable sales. If unsure, provide an estimate. Your projection helps to determine how often you will need to file a return. If your actual sales vary, we may adjust your filing frequency.

Items 49–54: Related Program Information

Provide your Alcoholic Beverage Control license number, if applicable. Indicate if you will be selling new tires, consumer electronics, or tobacco products. We will contact you to determine if you need to register for any of these other programs.

Items 55–64: Related Party Information

Identify the person maintaining your records, your bank, and if you accept credit cards, your merchant card account. Also, identify major California-based suppliers and the products that you purchase from them.

Items 66–73: Ownership and Organizational Changes

If you are purchasing a business, or changing from one type of business organization to another, provide the previous owner's name and seller's permit number. If you are purchasing a business, you should request a tax clearance in advance to assure that you won't have to pay any taxes owed by the previous owner.

Items 74–78: Temporary Permit Event Information

Applicants for a temporary permit must complete each item in this section.

Certification

Each owner, co-owner, partner, or corporate officer must sign the application.

Seller's Permit Application ■ Individuals/Partnerships/Corporations/Organizations (Regular or Temporary) (4-04)

Ch 3 Forms

BOE-400-SPA (FRONT) (4-04)
APPLICATION FOR SELLER'S PERMIT

STATE OF CALIFORNIA
BOARD OF EQUALIZATION

1. PERMIT TYPE: *(check one)* ☐ Regular ☐ Temporary

FOR BOARD USE ONLY			

2. TYPE OF OWNERSHIP *(check one)*   * Must provide partnership agreement

☐ Sole Owner   ☐ Husband/Wife Co-ownership
☐ Corporation   ☐ Limited Liability Company (LLC)
☐ General Partnership   ☐ Unincorporated Business Trust
☐ Limited Partnership (LP) *   ☐ Limited Liability Partnership (LLP) *
☐ Domestic Partnership *   *(Registered to practice law, accounting or architecture)*
☐ Other *(describe)* _____

TAX	IND	OFFICE	PERMIT NUMBER
S			
NAICS CODE		BUSINESS CODE	AREA CODE
PROCESSED BY		PERMIT ISSUE DATE	REPORTING BASIS
		___ / ___ / ___	VERIFICATION ☐ DL ☐ PA ☐ Other

3. NAME OF SOLE OWNER, CORPORATION, LLC, PARTNERSHIP, OR TRUST

4. STATE OF INCORPORATION OR ORGANIZATION

5. BUSINESS TRADE NAME/"DOING BUSINESS AS" [DBA] *(if any)*

6. DATE YOU WILL BEGIN BUSINESS ACTIVITIES *(month, day and year)*

7. CORPORATE. LLC, LLP OR LP NUMBER FROM CALIFORNIA SECRETARY OF STATE

8. FEDERAL EMPLOYER IDENTIFICATION NUMBER (FEIN)

CHECK ONE ☐ Owner/Co-Owners ☐ Domestic Partners ☐ Corp. Officers ☐ LLC Officers/ Managers/Members ☐ Partners ☐ Trustees/ Beneficiaries

Use additional sheets to include information for more than three individuals.

9. FULL NAME *(first, middle, last)*

10. TITLE

11. SOCIAL SECURITY NUMBER *(corporate officers excluded)*

12. DRIVER LICENSE NUMBER *(attach verification)*

13. HOME ADDRESS *(street, city, state, zip code)*

14. HOME TELEPHONE NUMBER ( )

15. NAME OF A PERSONAL REFERENCE NOT LIVING WITH YOU AND

16. ADDRESS *(street, city, state, zip code)*

17. REFERENCE TELEPHONE NUMBER ( )

18. FULL NAME *(first, middle, last)*

19. TITLE

20. SOCIAL SECURITY NUMBER *(corporate officers excluded)*

21. DRIVER LICENSE NUMBER *(attach verification)*

22. HOME ADDRESS *(street, city, state, zip code)*

23. HOME TELEPHONE NUMBER ( )

24. NAME OF A PERSONAL REFERENCE NOT LIVING WITH YOU AND

25. ADDRESS *(street, city, state, zip code)*

26. REFERENCE TELEPHONE NUMBER ( )

27. FULL NAME *(first, middle, last)*

28. TITLE

29. SOCIAL SECURITY NUMBER *(corporate officers excluded)*

30. DRIVER LICENSE NUMBER *(attach verification)*

31. HOME ADDRESS *(street, city, state, zip code)*

32. HOME TELEPHONE NUMBER ( )

33. NAME OF A PERSONAL REFERENCE NOT LIVING WITH YOU AND

34. ADDRESS *(street, city, state, zip code)*

35. REFERENCE TELEPHONE NUMBER ( )

36. TYPE OF BUSINESS *(check one that best describes your business)*
☐ Retail ☐ Wholesale ☐ Mfg. ☐ Repair ☐ Service ☐ Construction Contractor ☐ Leasing

37. NUMBER OF SELLING LOCATIONS *(if 2 or more, see Item No. 65)*

38. WHAT ITEMS WILL YOU SELL?

39. CHECK ONE ☐ Full Time ☐ Part Time

40. BUSINESS ADDRESS *(street, city, state, zip code) [do not list P.O. Box or mailing service]*

41. BUSINESS TELEPHONE NUMBER ( )

42. MAILING ADDRESS *(street, city, state, zip code) [if different from business address]*

43. BUSINESS FAX NUMBER ( )

44. NAME OF BUSINESS LANDLORD

45. LANDLORD ADDRESS *(street, city, state, zip code)*

46. LANDLORD TELEPHONE NUMBER ( )

47. PROJECTED MONTHLY GROSS SALES $

48. PROJECTED MONTHLY TAXABLE SALES $

49. ALCOHOLIC BEVERAGE CONTROL LICENSE NUMBER *(if applicable)* ___ ___ - ___ ___ ___ ___ ___ ___

50. BUSINESS WEBSITE ADDRESS www.

51. DO YOU MAKE INTERNET SALES? ☐ Yes ☐ No

52. SELLING NEW TIRES? ☐ Yes ☐ No

53. SELLING CONSUMER ELECTRONIC DEVICES? ☐ Yes ☐ No

54. SELLING TOBACCO AT RETAIL? ☐ Yes ☐ No

(continued on reverse)

Ch 3
Forms

BOE-400-SPA (BACK) (4-04)

55. NAME OF PERSON MAINTAINING YOUR RECORDS	56. ADDRESS (street, city, state, zip code)	57. TELEPHONE NUMBER
58. NAME OF BANK OR OTHER FINANCIAL INSTITUTION (note whether business or personal)		59. BANK BRANCH LOCATION
60. NAME OF MERCHANT CREDIT CARD PROCESSOR (if you accept credit cards)		61. MERCHANT CARD ACCOUNT NUMBER
62. NAMES OF MAJOR CALIFORNIA-BASED SUPPLIERS	63. ADDRESSES (street, city, state, zip code)	64. PRODUCTS PURCHASED

ADDITIONAL SELLING LOCATIONS (List All Other Selling Locations)

65. PHYSICAL LOCATION OR STREET ADDRESS (attach separate list, if required)

OWNERSHIP AND ORGANIZATIONAL CHANGES (Do Not Complete for Temporary Permits)

66. Are you buying an existing business?   ☐ Yes ☐ No   If yes, complete items 69 through 73.

67. Are you changing from one type of business organization to another (for example, from a sole owner to a corporation or from a partnership to a limited liability company, etc.)? ☐ Yes ☐ No   If yes, complete items 69 and 70.

68. Other Ownership Changes (please describe): _____

69. FORMER OWNER'S NAME	70. SELLER'S PERMIT NUMBER
71. PURCHASE PRICE $	72. VALUE OF FIXTURES & EQUIPMENT $

73. IF AN ESCROW COMPANY IS REQUESTING A TAX CLEARANCE ON YOUR BEHALF, PLEASE LIST THEIR NAME, ADDRESS, TELEPHONE NUMBER AND THE ESCROW NUMBER

TEMPORARY PERMIT EVENT INFORMATION

74. PERIOD OF SALES FROM: ___ / ___ / ___ THROUGH: ___ / ___ / ___	75. ESTIMATED EVENT SALES $	76. SPACE RENTAL COST (if any) $	77. ADMISSION CHARGED? ☐ Yes ☐ No
78. ORGANIZER OR PROMOTER OF EVENT (if any)	79. ADDRESS (street, city, state, zip code)		80. TELEPHONE NUMBER ( )

81. ADDRESS OF EVENT (If more than one, use line 65, above. Attach separate list, if required.)

CERTIFICATION

All Corporate Officers, LLC Managing Members, Partners, or Owners must sign below.
I am duly authorized to sign the application and certify that the statements made are correct to the best of my knowledge and belief.
I also represent and acknowledge that the applicant will be engaged in or conduct businesses as a seller of tangible personal property.

NAME (typed or printed)	SIGNATURE	DATE
NAME (typed or printed)	SIGNATURE	DATE
NAME (typed or printed)	SIGNATURE	DATE

FOR BOARD USE ONLY

SECURITY REVIEW	FORMS	PUBLICATIONS
☐ BOE-598 ($ _____) or ☐ BOE-1009 REQUIRED BY APPROVED BY	☐ BOE-8 ☐ BOE-400-Y ☐ BOE-162 ☐ BOE-519 ☐ BOE-467 ☐ BOE-1241-D	☐ PUB 73 ☐ PUB DE 44
	REGULATIONS	RETURNS
	☐ REG. 1668 ☐ REG. 1698 ☐ REG. 1700 ☐ _____	

Where Can I Get Help?

No doubt you will have questions about how the Sales and Use Tax Law applies to your business operations. For assistance, you may take advantage of the resources listed below.

INTERNET

www.boe.ca.gov

You can log onto our website for additional information. For example, you can find out what the tax rate is in a particular county, or you can download numerous publications — such as laws, regulations, pamphlets, and policy manuals — that will help you understand how the law applies to your business. You can also verify sellers' permit numbers online, read about upcoming Taxpayers' Bill of Rights hearings, and obtain information on Board field office addresses and telephone numbers.

Another good resource — especially for starting businesses — is the California Tax Information Center at *www.taxes.ca.gov.*

CLASSES

You may enroll in a basic sales and use tax class offered by some local Board offices. You should call ahead to find out when your local office conducts classes for beginning sellers.

WRITTEN TAX ADVICE

It is best to get tax advice from the Board in writing. You may be relieved of tax, penalty, or interest charges if we determine you did not correctly report tax because you reasonably relied on our written advice regarding a transaction.

For this relief to apply, your request for advice must be in writing, identify the taxpayer to whom the advice applies, and fully describe the facts and circumstances of the transaction.

Send your request for written advice to: State Board of Equalization; Audit and Information Section, MIC:44; P.O. Box 942879, Sacramento, CA 94279-0044.

INFORMATION CENTER
1-800-400-7115

FOR TDD ASSISTANCE

From TDD phones: 800-735-2929
From voice phones: 800-735-2922

Customer service representatives are available from 8 a.m. through 5 p.m., Monday-Friday, excluding state holidays.

Fax-Back Service. To order fax copies of selected forms and notices, call 800-400-7115 and choose the fax-back option. You can call at any time for this service.

Translator Services. We can provide bilingual services for persons who need assistance in a language other than English.

TAXPAYERS' RIGHTS
ADVOCATE OFFICE

If you would like to know more about your rights as a taxpayer or if you are unable to resolve an issue with the Board, please contact the Taxpayers' Rights Advocate office for help. Call 916-324-2798 (or toll-free, 888-324-2798). Their fax number is 916-323-3319.

If you prefer, you can write to: State Board of Equalization; Taxpayers' Rights Advocate, MIC:70; P.O. Box 942879; Sacramento, CA 94279-0070.

To request a copy of publication 70, *The California Taxpayers' Bill of Rights*, call the Information Center or visit our Internet site.

FIELD OFFICES

See page 3.

Seller's Permit Application ▪ Individuals/Partnerships/Corporations/Organizations (Regular or Temporary) (4-04)

BOE-324-SUT REV. 1 (2-03)

Sales and Use Tax Privacy Notice
Information Provided to the Board of Equalization

We ask you for information so that we can administer the state's sales and use tax laws (Revenue and Taxation Code sections 6001-7176, 7200-7226, 7251-7279.6, 7285-7288.6). We will use the information to determine whether you are paying the correct amount of tax and to collect any amounts you owe. You must provide all of the information we request, including your social security number (used for identification purposes [see Title 42 U.S. Code sec.405(c)(2)(C)(i)]).

What happens if I don't provide the information?

If your application is incomplete, we may not issue your seller's permit or use tax certificate. If you do not file complete returns, you may have to pay penalties and interest. Penalties may also apply if you don't provide other information we request or that is required by law, or if you give us fraudulent information. In some cases, you may be subject to criminal prosecution.

In addition, if you don't provide information we request to support your exemptions, credits, exclusions, or adjustments, we may not allow them. You may end up owing more tax or receiving a smaller refund.

Can anyone else see my information?

Your records are covered by state laws that protect your privacy. However, we may share information regarding your account with certain government agencies. We may also share certain information with companies authorized to represent local governments.

Under some circumstances we may release to the public the information printed on your permit, account start and closeout dates, and names of business owners or partners. When you sell a business, we can give the buyer or other involved parties information regarding your outstanding tax liability.

With your written permission, we can release information regarding your account to anyone you designate.

We may disclose information to the proper officials of the following agencies, among others:

- United States government agencies: U.S. Attorney's Office; Bureau of Alcohol, Tobacco and Firearms; Depts. of Agriculture, Defense, and Justice; Federal Bureau of Investigation; General Accounting Office; Internal Revenue Service; Interstate Commerce Commission

- State of California government agencies and officials: Air Resources Board; Dept. of Alcoholic Beverage Control; Auctioneer Commission; Dept. of Motor Vehicles, Employment Development Department; Energy Commission; Exposition and Fairs; Dept. of Food and Agriculture; Board of Forestry; Forest Products Commission; Franchise Tax Board; Dept. of Health Services; Highway Patrol; Dept. of Housing and Community Development; California Parent Locator Service

- State agencies outside of California for tax enforcement purposes

- City attorneys and city prosecutors; county district attorneys, police and sheriff departments.

Can I review my records?

Yes. Please contact your closest Board office (see the white pages of your phone book). If you need more information, you may contact our Disclosure Officer in Sacramento by calling 916-445-2918. You may also want to obtain publication 58-A, *How To Inspect and Correct Your Records*. You may order a copy from our Information Center: 800-400-7115 or download it from the Internet: *www.boe.ca.gov* (look under "Forms and Publications").

Who is responsible for maintaining my records?

The deputy director of the Sales and Use Tax Department, whom you may contact by calling 916-445-6464 or writing at the address shown.

Deputy Director, Sales and Use Tax Department MIC:43
450 N Street
Sacramento, CA 95814

Forms for Chapter 4

There are six forms that accompany **Chapter 4, Capitalizing the Corporation and Issuing Stock.** They include the following:

Form 4-A   Notice of Sale of Securities—Form D, 9 pages (221 - 229)

Form 4-B   Notice of Transaction Pursuant to Corporations Code Section 25102(f), 3 pages (230 - 232)

Form 4-C   Investor Questionnaire for Individuals, 4 pages (233 - 236)

Form 4-D   Investor Questionnaire for Entities, 5 pages (237 - 241)

Form 4-E   Form Transmittal Letter to Department of Corporations, 1 page (242)

Form 4-F   Notice of Issuance of Shares Pursuant to Subdivision (h) of Section 25102, 4 pages (243 - 246)

FORM D

UNITED STATES
SECURITIES AND EXCHANGE COMMISSION
Washington, D.C. 20549

OMB APPROVAL	
OMB Number:	3235-0076
Expires:	May 31, 2005
Estimated average burden hours per response......16.00	

FORM D

NOTICE OF SALE OF SECURITIES
PURSUANT TO REGULATION D,
SECTION 4(6), AND/OR
UNIFORM LIMITED OFFERING EXEMPTION

SEC USE ONLY	
Prefix	Serial
DATE RECEIVED	

Name of Offering (☐ check if this is an amendment and name has changed, and indicate change.)

Filing Under (Check box(es) that apply): ☐ Rule 504 ☐ Rule 505 ☐ Rule 506 ☐ Section 4(6) ☐ ULOE
Type of Filing: ☐ New Filing ☐ Amendment

A. BASIC IDENTIFICATION DATA

1. Enter the information requested about the issuer

Name of Issuer (☐ check if this is an amendment and name has changed, and indicate change.)

Address of Executive Offices	(Number and Street, City, State, Zip Code)	Telephone Number (Including Area Code)
Address of Principal Business Operations (if different from Executive Offices)	(Number and Street, City, State, Zip Code)	Telephone Number (Including Area Code)

Brief Description of Business

Type of Business Organization
☐ corporation   ☐ limited partnership, already formed   ☐ other (please specify):
☐ business trust   ☐ limited partnership, to be formed

Month   Year
Actual or Estimated Date of Incorporation or Organization: ☐☐ ☐☐ ☐ Actual ☐ Estimated
Jurisdiction of Incorporation or Organization: (Enter two-letter U.S. Postal Service abbreviation for State;
CN for Canada; FN for other foreign jurisdiction) ☐☐

GENERAL INSTRUCTIONS

Federal:

Who Must File: All issuers making an offering of securities in reliance on an exemption under Regulation D or Section 4(6), 17 CFR 230.501 et seq. or 15 U.S.C. 77d(6).

When To File: A notice must be filed no later than 15 days after the first sale of securities in the offering. A notice is deemed filed with the U.S. Securities and Exchange Commission (SEC) on the earlier of the date it is received by the SEC at the address given below or, if received at that address after the date on which it is due, on the date it was mailed by United States registered or certified mail to that address.

Where To File: U.S. Securities and Exchange Commission, 450 Fifth Street, N.W., Washington, D.C. 20549.

Copies Required: Five (5) copies of this notice must be filed with the SEC, one of which must be manually signed. Any copies not manually signed must be photocopies of the manually signed copy or bear typed or printed signatures.

Information Required: A new filing must contain all information requested. Amendments need only report the name of the issuer and offering, any changes thereto, the information requested in Part C, and any material changes from the information previously supplied in Parts A and B. Part E and the Appendix need not be filed with the SEC.

Filing Fee: There is no federal filing fee.

State:
This notice shall be used to indicate reliance on the Uniform Limited Offering Exemption (ULOE) for sales of securities in those states that have adopted ULOE and that have adopted this form. Issuers relying on ULOE must file a separate notice with the Securities Administrator in each state where sales are to be, or have been made. If a state requires the payment of a fee as a precondition to the claim for the exemption, a fee in the proper amount shall accompany this form. This notice shall be filed in the appropriate states in accordance with state law. The Appendix to the notice constitutes a part of this notice and must be completed.

--- **ATTENTION** ---

Failure to file notice in the appropriate states will not result in a loss of the federal exemption. Conversely, failure to file the appropriate federal notice will not result in a loss of an available state exemption unless such exemption is predicated on the filing of a federal notice.

SEC 1972 (6-02)

Persons who respond to the collection of information contained in this form are not required to respond unless the form displays a currently valid OMB control number.

1 of 9

Ch 4
Forms

A. BASIC IDENTIFICATION DATA

2. Enter the information requested for the following:

- Each promoter of the issuer, if the issuer has been organized within the past five years;
- Each beneficial owner having the power to vote or dispose, or direct the vote or disposition of, 10% or more of a class of equity securities of the issuer.
- Each executive officer and director of corporate issuers and of corporate general and managing partners of partnership issuers; and
- Each general and managing partner of partnership issuers.

Check Box(es) that Apply: ☐ Promoter   ☐ Beneficial Owner   ☐ Executive Officer   ☐ Director   ☐ General and/or Managing Partner

Full Name (Last name first, if individual)

Business or Residence Address   (Number and Street, City, State, Zip Code)

Check Box(es) that Apply: ☐ Promoter   ☐ Beneficial Owner   ☐ Executive Officer   ☐ Director   ☐ General and/or Managing Partner

Full Name (Last name first, if individual)

Business or Residence Address   (Number and Street, City, State, Zip Code)

Check Box(es) that Apply: ☐ Promoter   ☐ Beneficial Owner   ☐ Executive Officer   ☐ Director   ☐ General and/or Managing Partner

Full Name (Last name first, if individual)

Business or Residence Address   (Number and Street, City, State, Zip Code)

Check Box(es) that Apply: ☐ Promoter   ☐ Beneficial Owner   ☐ Executive Officer   ☐ Director   ☐ General and/or Managing Partner

Full Name (Last name first, if individual)

Business or Residence Address   (Number and Street, City, State, Zip Code)

Check Box(es) that Apply: ☐ Promoter   ☐ Beneficial Owner   ☐ Executive Officer   ☐ Director   ☐ General and/or Managing Partner

Full Name (Last name first, if individual)

Business or Residence Address   (Number and Street, City, State, Zip Code)

Check Box(es) that Apply: ☐ Promoter   ☐ Beneficial Owner   ☐ Executive Officer   ☐ Director   ☐ General and/or Managing Partner

Full Name (Last name first, if individual)

Business or Residence Address   (Number and Street, City, State, Zip Code)

Check Box(es) that Apply: ☐ Promoter   ☐ Beneficial Owner   ☐ Executive Officer   ☐ Director   ☐ General and/or Managing Partner

Full Name (Last name first, if individual)

Business or Residence Address   (Number and Street, City, State, Zip Code)

(Use blank sheet, or copy and use additional copies of this sheet, as necessary)

2 of 9

B. INFORMATION ABOUT OFFERING

	Yes	No
1. Has the issuer sold, or does the issuer intend to sell, to non-accredited investors in this offering?	☐	☐

Answer also in Appendix, Column 2, if filing under ULOE.

2. What is the minimum investment that will be accepted from any individual? .... $_____

	Yes	No
3. Does the offering permit joint ownership of a single unit?	☐	☐

4. Enter the information requested for each person who has been or will be paid or given, directly or indirectly, any commission or similar remuneration for solicitation of purchasers in connection with sales of securities in the offering. If a person to be listed is an associated person or agent of a broker or dealer registered with the SEC and/or with a state or states, list the name of the broker or dealer. If more than five (5) persons to be listed are associated persons of such a broker or dealer, you may set forth the information for that broker or dealer only.

Full Name (Last name first, if individual)
_____

Business or Residence Address (Number and Street, City, State, Zip Code)
_____

Name of Associated Broker or Dealer
_____

States in Which Person Listed Has Solicited or Intends to Solicit Purchasers

(Check "All States" or check individual States) .... ☐ All States

AL	AK	AZ	AR	CA	CO	CT	DE	DC	FL	GA	HI	ID
IL	IN	IA	KS	KY	LA	ME	MD	MA	MI	MN	MS	MO
MT	NE	NV	NH	NJ	NM	NY	NC	ND	OH	OK	OR	PA
RI	SC	SD	TN	TX	UT	VT	VA	WA	WV	WI	WY	PR

Full Name (Last name first, if individual)
_____

Business or Residence Address (Number and Street, City, State, Zip Code)
_____

Name of Associated Broker or Dealer
_____

States in Which Person Listed Has Solicited or Intends to Solicit Purchasers

(Check "All States" or check individual States) .... ☐ All States

AL	AK	AZ	AR	CA	CO	CT	DE	DC	FL	GA	HI	ID
IL	IN	IA	KS	KY	LA	ME	MD	MA	MI	MN	MS	MO
MT	NE	NV	NH	NJ	NM	NY	NC	ND	OH	OK	OR	PA
RI	SC	SD	TN	TX	UT	VT	VA	WA	WV	WI	WY	PR

Full Name (Last name first, if individual)
_____

Business or Residence Address (Number and Street, City, State, Zip Code)
_____

Name of Associated Broker or Dealer
_____

States in Which Person Listed Has Solicited or Intends to Solicit Purchasers

(Check "All States" or check individual States) .... ☐ All States

AL	AK	AZ	AR	CA	CO	CT	DE	DC	FL	GA	HI	ID
IL	IN	IA	KS	KY	LA	ME	MD	MA	MI	MN	MS	MO
MT	NE	NV	NH	NJ	NM	NY	NC	ND	OH	OK	OR	PA
RI	SC	SD	TN	TX	UT	VT	VA	WA	WV	WI	WY	PR

(Use blank sheet, or copy and use additional copies of this sheet, as necessary.)

3 of 9

C. OFFERING PRICE, NUMBER OF INVESTORS, EXPENSES AND USE OF PROCEEDS

1. Enter the aggregate offering price of securities included in this offering and the total amount already sold. Enter "0" if the answer is "none" or "zero." If the transaction is an exchange offering, check this box ☐ and indicate in the columns below the amounts of the securities offered for exchange and already exchanged.

Type of Security	Aggregate Offering Price	Amount Already Sold
Debt	$_____	$_____
Equity	$_____	$_____
☐ Common ☐ Preferred		
Convertible Securities (including warrants)	$_____	$_____
Partnership Interests	$_____	$_____
Other (Specify _____)	$_____	$_____
Total	$ 0.00	$ 0.00

Answer also in Appendix, Column 3, if filing under ULOE.

2. Enter the number of accredited and non-accredited investors who have purchased securities in this offering and the aggregate dollar amounts of their purchases. For offerings under Rule 504, indicate the number of persons who have purchased securities and the aggregate dollar amount of their purchases on the total lines. Enter "0" if answer is "none" or "zero."

	Number Investors	Aggregate Dollar Amount of Purchases
Accredited Investors	_____	$_____
Non-accredited Investors	_____	$_____
Total (for filings under Rule 504 only)	0	$ 0.00

Answer also in Appendix, Column 4, if filing under ULOE.

3. If this filing is for an offering under Rule 504 or 505, enter the information requested for all securities sold by the issuer, to date, in offerings of the types indicated, in the twelve (12) months prior to the first sale of securities in this offering. Classify securities by type listed in Part C — Question 1.

Type of Offering	Type of Security	Dollar Amount Sold
Rule 505	_____	$_____
Regulation A	_____	$_____
Rule 504	_____	$_____
Total		$ 0.00

4. a. Furnish a statement of all expenses in connection with the issuance and distribution of the securities in this offering. Exclude amounts relating solely to organization expenses of the insurer. The information may be given as subject to future contingencies. If the amount of an expenditure is not known, furnish an estimate and check the box to the left of the estimate.

Transfer Agent's Fees	☐	$_____
Printing and Engraving Costs	☐	$_____
Legal Fees	☐	$_____
Accounting Fees	☐	$_____
Engineering Fees	☐	$_____
Sales Commissions (specify finders' fees separately)	☐	$_____
Other Expenses (identify) _____	☐	$_____
Total	☐	$ 0.00

4 of 9

C. OFFERING PRICE, NUMBER OF INVESTORS, EXPENSES AND USE OF PROCEEDS

b.　Enter the difference between the aggregate offering price given in response to Part C — Question 1 and total expenses furnished in response to Part C — Question 4.a. This difference is the "adjusted gross proceeds to the issuer." .... $ 0.00

5.　Indicate below the amount of the adjusted gross proceed to the issuer used or proposed to be used for each of the purposes shown. If the amount for any purpose is not known, furnish an estimate and check the box to the left of the estimate. The total of the payments listed must equal the adjusted gross proceeds to the issuer set forth in response to Part C — Question 4.b above.

	Payments to Officers, Directors, & Affiliates	Payments to Others
Salaries and fees	☐ $_____	☐ $_____
Purchase of real estate	☐ $_____	☐ $_____
Purchase, rental or leasing and installation of machinery and equipment	☐ $_____	☐ $_____
Construction or leasing of plant buildings and facilities	☐ $_____	☐ $_____
Acquisition of other businesses (including the value of securities involved in this offering that may be used in exchange for the assets or securities of another issuer pursuant to a merger)	☐ $_____	☐ $_____
Repayment of indebtedness	☐ $_____	☐ $_____
Working capital...	☐ $_____	☐ $_____
Other (specify):_____	☐ $_____	☐ $_____
_____	☐ $_____	☐ $_____
Column Totals	☐ $ 0.00	☐ $ 0.00
Total Payments Listed (column totals added)	☐ $ 0.00	

D. FEDERAL SIGNATURE

The issuer has duly caused this notice to be signed by the undersigned duly authorized person. If this notice is filed under Rule 505, the following signature constitutes an undertaking by the issuer to furnish to the U.S. Securities and Exchange Commission, upon written request of its staff, the information furnished by the issuer to any non-accredited investor pursuant to paragraph (b)(2) of Rule 502.

Issuer (Print or Type)	Signature	Date
Name of Signer (Print or Type)	Title of Signer (Print or Type)	

─── **ATTENTION** ───
Intentional misstatements or omissions of fact constitute federal criminal violations. (See 18 U.S.C. 1001.)

5 of 9

| E. STATE SIGNATURE | | |

1. Is any party described in 17 CFR 230.262 presently subject to any of the disqualification provisions of such rule? ....

Yes   No
☐   ☐

See Appendix, Column 5, for state response.

2. The undersigned issuer hereby undertakes to furnish to any state administrator of any state in which this notice is filed a notice on Form D (17 CFR 239.500) at such times as required by state law.

3. The undersigned issuer hereby undertakes to furnish to the state administrators, upon written request, information furnished by the issuer to offerees.

4. The undersigned issuer represents that the issuer is familiar with the conditions that must be satisfied to be entitled to the Uniform limited Offering Exemption (ULOE) of the state in which this notice is filed and understands that the issuer claiming the availability of this exemption has the burden of establishing that these conditions have been satisfied.

The issuer has read this notification and knows the contents to be true and has duly caused this notice to be signed on its behalf by the undersigned duly authorized person.

Issuer (Print or Type)	Signature	Date
Name (Print or Type)	Title (Print or Type)	

Instruction:
Print the name and title of the signing representative under his signature for the state portion of this form. One copy of every notice on Form D must be manually signed. Any copies not manually signed must be photocopies of the manually signed copy or bear typed or printed signatures.

6 of 9

Ch 4
Forms

1	2		3	4				5	
	Intend to sell to non-accredited investors in State (Part B-Item 1)		Type of security and aggregate offering price offered in state (Part C-Item 1)	Type of investor and amount purchased in State (Part C-Item 2)				Disqualification under State ULOE (if yes, attach explanation of waiver granted) (Part E-Item 1)	
State	Yes	No		Number of Accredited Investors	Amount	Number of Non-Accredited Investors	Amount	Yes	No
AL									
AK									
AZ									
AR									
CA									
CO									
CT									
DE									
DC									
FL									
GA									
HI									
ID									
IL									
IN									
IA									
KS									
KY									
LA									
ME									
MD									
MA									
MI									
MN									
MS									

APPENDIX

7 of 9

Ch 4 Forms

	APPENDIX									
1	2		3	4					5	
	Intend to sell to non-accredited investors in State (Part B-Item 1)		Type of security and aggregate offering price offered in state (Part C-Item 1)	Type of investor and amount purchased in State (Part C-Item 2)					Disqualification under State ULOE (if yes, attach explanation of waiver granted) (Part E-Item 1)	
State	Yes	No		Number of Accredited Investors	Amount	Number of Non-Accredited Investors	Amount		Yes	No
MO										
MT										
NE										
NV										
NH										
NJ										
NM										
NY										
NC										
ND										
OH										
OK										
OR										
PA										
RI										
SC										
SD										
TN										
TX										
UT										
VT										
VA										
WA										
WV										
WI										

8 of 9

	APPENDIX								
1	**2**		**3**	**4**				**5**	
	Intend to sell to non-accredited investors in State (Part B-Item 1)		Type of security and aggregate offering price offered in state (Part C-Item 1)	Type of investor and amount purchased in State (Part C-Item 2)				Disqualification under State ULOE (if yes, attach explanation of waiver granted) (Part E-Item 1)	
State	**Yes**	**No**		**Number of Accredited Investors**	**Amount**	**Number of Non-Accredited Investors**	**Amount**	**Yes**	**No**
WY									
PR									

(Department of Corporations Use Only)   DEPARTMENT OF CORPORATIONS FILE NO., if any:
Fee paid $_____
Receipt No. _____

Insert File number(s) of Previous Filings
Before the Department, if any.

FEE: $25.00 $35.00 $50.00 $150.00 $300.00
(Circle the appropriate amount of fee.
See Corporations Code Section 25608(c))

COMMISSIONER OF CORPORATIONS
STATE OF CALIFORNIA
NOTICE OF TRANSACTION PURSUANT TO CORPORATIONS CODE SECTION 25102(f)

A.   Check one: Transaction under ( ) Section 25102(f) ( ) Rule 260.103.

1.   Name of Issuer: _____

2.   Address of Issuer: _____
                  Street   City   State   ZIP

        Mailing Address: _____
                  Street   City   State   ZIP

3.   Area Code and Telephone Number: _____
4.   Issuer's state (or other jurisdiction) of incorporation or
        organization: _____
5.   Title of class or classes of securities sold in transaction: _____

6.   The value of the securities sold or proposed to be sold in the
transaction, determined in accordance with Corporations Code Sec. 25608(g)
in connection with the fee required upon filing this notice, is (fee based
on amount shown in line (iii) under Total Offering"):

                                     California   Total
Offering
(a) (i)   in money $_____ $_____
      (ii) in consideration other than money $_____ $_____
     (iii) total of (i) and (ii) $_____ $_____

(b) ( ) Change in rights, preferences, privileges or restrictions of or on
          outstanding securities. ($25.00 fee.) (See Rule 260.103.)
7.   Type of filing under Securities Act of 1933, if applicable: _____

8.   Date of Notice: _____   _____
                                       Issuer

( ) Check if issuer already has a   _____
    consent to service of process   **Authorized Signature on behalf of Issuer**
    on file with the Commissioner.

                              _____
                              Print name and title of signatory
Name, Address and Phone number of contact person:

_____

_____

Instruction: Each issuer (other than a California Corporation) filing a notice under Section 25102(f) must file
a consent to service of process (Form 260.165), unless it already has a consent to service on file with the
Commissioner.

COMMISSIONER OF CORPORATIONS
STATE OF CALIFORNIA
NOTICE OF TRANSACTION PURSUANT TO
CORPORATIONS CODE SECTION 25102(f)
INSTRUCTIONS

1. This Notice is to provide information on transactions conducted under the Section 25102(f) exemption from the qualification requirements of Section 25110 of the Corporate Securities Law of 1968 and under the Rule 260.103 exemption from the qualification requirements of Section 25120 of that Law.

The form is not designed to indicate whether or not the transaction complies with the requirements of those exemptions but only to provide notice to the commissioner that the exemption is being relied on.

2. When to File Notice. The Notice must be filed with, or mailed to, the Commissioner within 15 calendar days after the first sale of a security in the transaction in this state, or, if the issuer has failed to file a notice, within 15 business days after demand by the Commissioner. The first sale in this state occurs when the issuer has obtained a contractual commitment in this state to purchase one or more of the securities the issuer intends to sell in connection with the transaction. No notice is required if none of the securities offered are purchased in this state. No subsequent notices are required for sales in connection with the same transaction. The information required by the form is to relate to the entire transaction, not just the first sale or sales in this state.

3. The Notice may be filed in person or by mail at any office of the Department. The Heading. If the issuer has previously qualified securities with the Department, insert the file number of the qualification in the upper right hand corner of the form in the space provided. Circle the appropriate fee for filing this Notice. The fee is based on the value of all securities sold or intended to be sold in the entire transaction as follows (see Item 6 for valuing securities):

Value of Securities	Filing Fee
$ 25,000 or less	$ 25
$ 25,001-$100,000	$ 35
$100,001-$500,000	$ 50
$500,001-$1,000,000	$150
Over $1,000,000	$300

Item A. Check appropriate box for exemption being relied on.

Item 1. Give the issuer's legal name.

Item 2. Give the street address, and the mailing address if different, of the issuer's principal place of business.

Item 3. Give the telephone number of issuer's principal place of business.

Item 4. Give the name of the state or other jurisdiction under whose laws the issuer is incorporated or organized. If the issuer is not incorporated or organized under the laws of any jurisdiction, provide the name of the jurisdiction where issuer is domiciled and include parenthetical "(domicile)."

Item 5. Set forth the name or title of each class or type of security to be sold in the transaction.

Item 6. See Corp. Code Sec. 25608(g). Generally, the value of the securities shall be the price at which the issuer proposes to sell the securities, as alleged in the notice, or the actual value of the consideration (if other than money) to be received in exchange for the securities. See Sec. 25608(g) for valuing voting trust certificates, warrants, rights, and share dividends.

Item 7. If the transaction was registered under the Securities Act of 1933, insert "registered." If conducted pursuant to an exemption from registration under that Act which requires a filing with the Securities and Exchange Commission, indicate the number of the rule pursuant to which such filing was made. If no such filing was required, insert none."

Item 8. Date and Signature. The notice should be signed by an authorized officer, director, general partner or trustee of the issuer (or a person occupying a position with the issuer of equivalent responsibility) or by the authorized attorney of the issuer. If the person the Department is to contact in the event of questions concerning the transaction or the notice is different than the signer, insert the contact person's name, telephone number and correspondence address in the spaces provided. Otherwise, provide this information with respect to the signer.

Filing Fee. Each notice, whether under Section 25102(f) or Rule 260.103, must be accompanied by the filing fee required by Section 25608(c) of the Code. Corporations Code Section 25165 requires each issuer, other than a California corporation, to file a consent to service of process with the notice filed pursuant to Section 25102(f) unless it already has a consent to service on file with the Commissioner. Use Form 260.165 (see Rule 260.165, Title 10, California Code of Regulations).

CONFIDENTIAL

INVESTOR QUESTIONNAIRE FOR INDIVIDUALS

(Rules 505 and 506, Reg. D; §25102(f))

This Questionnaire is to be completed by each INDIVIDUAL purchasing securities of _____, a California corporation (the "Company"). The purpose of this Questionnaire is to assure the Company that each proposed investor will meet certain suitability standards in connection with investment in the Company and the purchase of _____ (the "Shares"), including those imposed by applicable state and federal securities laws and the regulations under those laws.

Individuals investing in the name of a trust should not complete this Questionnaire but should instead complete an "Investor Questionnaire for Entities." If the answer to any question is "None" or "Not Applicable," please so state. If more space is needed for any answer, additional sheets may be attached.

Your answers will be kept confidential at all times. However, by signing this Questionnaire, you agree that the Company may present this Questionnaire to such parties as it deems appropriate to establish the availability of exemptions from registration or qualification requirements under federal and state securities laws.

1. IDENTIFICATION

1.1 Name(s) in which the Shares are to be registered:

_____

_____

1.2 If the Shares are to be registered in the name of two or more individuals or are to be community property, check one of the following:

_____ Joint Tenants with Right of Survivorship*

_____ Tenants in Common*

_____ Community Property*

Each joint tenant and tenant in common other than your spouse must complete a separate Questionnaire. Your spouse, if any, must execute this Questionnaire.

1.3 Social Security Number: _____

1.4 Principal Residence Address: _____

_____

Ch 4
Forms

**Ch 4
Forms**

1.5 Telephone Number: _____

1.6 Principal Occupation (if retired, previous occupation): _____

     Position or Title: _____

1.7. Education: _____

_____

2. ACCREDITATION

2.1 Amount of the proposed investment: $_____

Is your cash flow from all sources sufficient to satisfy your current needs, including possible contingencies, such that you have no need for liquidity in this proposed investment?   Yes_____   No_____

Do you have the ability to bear the economic risk of the investment, i.e., can you afford to lose your entire investment?   Yes_____   No_____

Do you, by reason of your business and financial experience or the business and financial experience of a professional advisor, have the capacity to evaluate the merits and risks of your proposed investment and to protect your own interests in connection with the investment?   Yes_____   No_____

IF YES, please describe your business and financial experience, indicating the factual basis for your conclusion that you have such capacity:

_____

_____

_____

Are you relying on the business or financial experience of an accountant, attorney, or other professional advisor in evaluating the merits and risks of this investment in order to protect your own interest?   Yes_____   No_____

IF YES, please (a) have your advisor complete the Company's form of Advisor's Questionnaire and submit it with this Questionnaire, and (b) identify the advisor.

Name of professional advisor: _____

Is the proposed investment less than 10% of your net worth or joint net worth with your spouse?   Yes_____   No_____

Have you previously invested in private placements of securities of recently formed, non-public companies or of companies without a history of significant earnings or profits?   Never _____   Rarely _____   On Several Occasions _____

2.2 Please initial which, if any, of the following statements are applicable to you:

_____ My individual net worth, or my joint net worth with my spouse, exceeds $1,000,000.

_____ My proposed total investment in the Company is at least $150,000 and does not exceed 10% of my net worth or joint net worth with my spouse.

_____ I personally have had an individual income in excess of $200,000 in each of the two (2) most recent years and I reasonably expect an income in excess of $200,000 in the current year.

_____ My joint income with my spouse has been in excess of $300,000 in each of the two (2) most recent years and I reasonably expect a joint income in excess of $300,000 in the current year.

2.3 If you have not initialed one of the responses in Question 2.2 above, please answer the following questions:

My net worth or joint net worth with my spouse exceeds: $_____.

My estimated gross income together with my spouse for this calendar year is: (check one)

_____ under $75,000   _____ $75,000-$99,999

_____ $100,000-$199,999   _____ $200,000 and over

2.4 Are you related in any way to any other person who also intends to purchase Shares in this offering? If so, please state the name and nature of the relationship of each such person:

_____

_____

2.5 If you have used the services of a securities broker or dealer or a finder in submitting subscription documentation for the Shares, please identify the broker, dealer, or finder:

_____

_____

3. EXECUTION

The information provided in this Questionnaire is true and complete as of the date provided below in all material respects and the undersigned recognizes that the Company is relying on the truth and accuracy of such information. The undersigned agrees to notify the Company promptly of any changes in the foregoing information that may occur prior to the closing of the sale of Shares of the Company.

_____
(Signature of Purchaser)

Name: _____
     (Please Print or Type)

Date: _____

_____
(Signature of Spouse, if any)

Name: _____
     (Please Print or Type)

Date: _____

CONFIDENTIAL
INVESTOR QUESTIONNAIRE FOR ENTITIES

(Rules 505 and 506, Reg. D; §25102(f))

This Questionnaire is to be completed by each **ENTITY** (trust, corporation, partnership, or other organization) purchasing securities of _____, a California corporation (the "Company"). The purpose of this Questionnaire is to assure the Company that each proposed investor will meet certain suitability standards in connection with investment in the Company and the purchase of _____ (the "Shares"), including those imposed by applicable state and federal securities laws and the regulations under those laws.

If the answer to any question is "None" or "Not Applicable," please so state. If more space is needed for any answer, additional sheets may be attached.

Your answers will be kept confidential at all times. However, by signing this Questionnaire, you agree that the Company may present this Questionnaire to such parties as it deems appropriate to establish the availability of exemptions from registration or qualification requirements under federal and state securities laws.

1. IDENTIFICATION

1.1 Name(s) in which the Shares are to be registered:

_____

1.2 Tax Identification Number:

_____

1.3 Address of principal place of business:

_____

_____

1.4 Telephone number: _____

1.5 Jurisdiction of formation or of incorporation (Name the State or Country):

_____

1.6 Form of entity (e.g., corporation, general partnership, limited partnership, trust, etc.):

_____

Ch 4 Forms

1.7 Nature of business (e.g., investment, banking, manufacturing, venture capital investment fund, etc.):

_____

2. ACCREDITATION

2.1 Amount of the proposed investment: $_____

2.2 Is the entity's cash flow from all sources sufficient to satisfy its current needs, including possible contingencies, such that the entity has no need for liquidity in this proposed investment?   Yes_____   No_____

2.3 Was the entity specifically formed for the purpose of investing in the Company?   Yes_____   No_____

2.4 Does the entity have the ability to bear the economic risk of the investment, i.e., can the entity afford to lose its entire investment?   Yes_____   No_____

2.5 Is the entity an employee benefit plan governed by the Employee Retirement Income Security Act of 1974 (a 401(k) Plan, Keogh Plan, pension plan, etc., maintained by an employer for its employees)?   Yes_____   No_____

IF YES, please indicate which, if any, of the following categories accurately describes the entity:

_____The employee benefit plan has total assets in excess of $5,000,000.

_____The plan is a self-directed plan with investment decisions made solely by persons listed in Section 2.6 below or who are individuals, and each such individual has a net worth in excess $1,000,000 or had an individual income in excess of $200,000 in each of the two most recent years and has a rea sonable expectation of reaching the same income level in the current year.

_____Investment decisions are made by a plan fiduciary which is either a bank, savings and loan association, insurance company, or registered investment advisor.

2.6 Please indicate which, if any, of the following categories accurately describes the entity:

_____ A bank.

_____ A savings and loan association.

_____ A broker-dealer registered under Section 15 of the Securities Exchange Act of 1934.

_____ An insurance company.

_____ An investment company registered under the Investment Company Act of 1940 or a business development company as defined in Section 2(a)(48) of that Act.

_____ A Small Business Investment Company licensed by the U.S. Small Business Administration under Section 301(c) or (d) of the Small Business Investment Act of 1958.

_____ A private business development company defined in Section 202(a)(22) of the Investment Advisors Act of 1940.

_____ An organization described in Section 501(c)(3) of the Internal Revenue Code with total assets in excess of $5,000,000, not formed for the purpose of investing in the Company.

_____ A corporation with total assets in excess of $5,000,000, not formed for the purpose of investing in the Company.

_____ A partnership with total assets in excess of $5,000,000, not formed for the purpose of investing in the Company.

_____ A Massachusetts or similar business trust with total assets in excess of $5,000,000, not formed for the purpose of investing in the Company.

_____ Any other trust with total assets in excess of $5,000,000, not formed for the purpose of investing in the Company.

2.7 Please indicate if one of the following describes the equity owners of the entity:

_____ Each equity owner of the entity (i.e., all shareholders, all general and/or limited partners, or all beneficiaries, as applicable) is an individual whose net worth or joint net worth with his or her spouse exceeds $1,000,000.

_____ Each equity owner of the entity is an individual who has had a personal income in excess of $200,000 in each of the two (2) most recent years or joint income with that person's spouse in excess of $300,000 in each of those years and reasonably expects to reach the same income level in the current year.

_____ Each equity owner of the entity is an entity described in at least one category of Question 2.6 above.

_____ Although not all equity owners are described in the same category above in this Question 2.7, each equity owner is described in at least one such category.

2.8 Please indicate which of the following also describes the equity owners of the entity:

_____ Each equity owner of the entity has, by reason of his, her, or its business and financial experience, the capacity to evaluate the merits and risks of the entity's proposed investment and to protect his, her, or its own interests in connection with the investment.

_____ Each of the equity owners of the entity is able to bear the economic risk of the entity's investment, i.e., can afford loss of the entity's entire investment.

_____ The beneficial interest of each equity owner in the entity's proposed investment is less than 10% of such equity owner's net worth, or joint net worth with his or her spouse.

_____ Although not all equity owners are described in the same category above in this Question 2.8, each equity owner is described in at least one such category.

3. ADDITIONAL INFORMATION

3.1 Has your entity previously invested in private placements of securities of newly formed, non-public companies or companies without a history of significant profits or earnings?

Never_____   Rarely _____   On Several Occasions _____

3.2 Does your entity, by reason of its business and financial knowledge and experience, have the capacity to evaluate the merits and risks of the entity's proposed investment and to protect the entity's own interests in connection with its investment in the Company?   Yes _____   No _____

IF YES, please describe the business and financial knowledge and experience, indicating factual basis for your conclusion that the entity has such capacity.

_____

_____

_____

3.3 Do the persons responsible for making the investment decision for the entity, by reason of their business and financial knowledge and experience, have the capacity to evaluate the merits and risks of the entity's proposed investment? Yes _____   No _____

IF YES, please describe the business and financial knowledge and experience, indicating factual basis for your conclusion that those persons have such capacity.

_____

_____

_____

3.4 If you have used the services of a securities broker or dealer or a finder in submitting subscription documentation for the Shares, please identify the broker, dealer, or finder:

_____

_____

3.5 Are you relying on the business or financial experience of an accountant, attorney, or other professional advisor in evaluating the merits and risks of this investment in order to protect your own interest?   Yes_____   No_____

IF YES, please (a) have your advisor complete the Company's form of Advisor's Questionnaire and submit it with this Questionnaire, and (b) identify the advisor.

Name of professional advisor:_____

4. EXECUTION

The information provided in this Questionnaire is true and complete as of the date provided below in all material respects and the undersigned recognizes that the Company is relying on the truth and accuracy of such information. The undersigned agrees to notify the Company promptly of any changes in the foregoing information that may occur prior to the closing of the sale of Shares of the Company.

Name of Entity: _____
                 (Please Print or Type)

By: _____
     (Signature)

Name: _____
        (Please Print or Type)

Title: _____
      (Please Print or Type)

Date: _____

FORM TRANSMITTAL LETTER TO DEPARTMENT
OF CORPORATIONS FOR FILING 25102(f)

_____ [DATE]

Department of Corporations
State of California
1515 K Street, Suite 200
Sacramento, CA 95814-4017

Re: _____ [COMPANY NAME] (the "Corporation")

Ladies and Gentlemen:

You will find enclosed for filing on behalf of the Corporation:

1. An original and one copy of a Notice of Transaction Pursuant to Corporations Code Section 25102(f) (the "Notice"); [and]

2. A check for the filing fee of $ _____[.][; and

3. A Uniform Consent to Service of Process (Form U-2) (or) A California Consent to Service of Process.] [IF A DELAWARE CORPORATION AND EITHER IS NOT ALREADY ON FILE]

[IF A DELAWARE CORPORATION AND A CONSENT IS ALREADY ON FILE, ADD A Consent to Service of Process is on file for the Issuer.] Please file stamp the enclosed copy of the Notice and return it to me in the enclosed self-addressed stamped envelope. If you have any questions or concerns regarding the foregoing, please contact me directly at [PHONE NUMBER].

Very truly yours,

[INSERT NAME AND TITLE]

Enclosures

Ch 4
Forms

(Department of Corporations
 Use Only)
Fee Paid $ _____

Receipt No. _____

DEPARTMENT OF CORPORATIONS
FILE No., if any:
_____
(Insert File Numbers(s) of Previous
Filings Before the Department, If Any)

FEE: $25.00 $35.00 $50.00 $150.00 $300.00
(Circle the appropriate amount of fee.
See Corporations Code Section 25608(c))

TO THE COMMISSIONER OF CORPORATIONS OF THE STATE OF CALIFORNIA
Notice of Issuance of Shares Pursuant to Subdivision (h) of
Section 25102 of the Corporations Code or Rule 260.103,
Title 10, California Code of Regulations.

Check one of the following:
( )   Notice pursuant to Section 25102(h) as to an issuance subject to qualification under
        Corporations Code Section 25110, unless exempted.

( )   Notice pursuant to Rule 260.103 as to an issuance subject to qualification under
        Corporations Code Section 25120, unless exempted.

Name of Issuer

_____

State of Incorporation

_____

Address of Principal Place of Business

_____
     Number and Street   City   State   Zip Code

1.   Is the issuer a "close corporation" as defined in Section 260.001, Title 10, California Code of
      Regulations?   ( ) Yes   ( ) No

      Instruction: Review Corporations Code Section 158 and Rule 260.001, Title 10, California
      Code of Regulations.

2.   Under the exemption provided by Section 25102(h), shares of voting common stock have
      been or are proposed to be issued pursuant to this Notice beneficially to not more than 35
      persons, whose names are set forth below; together with the names of the corresponding
      record shareholders if other than the beneficial shareholders:

      _____   _____
      _____   _____
      _____   _____
      _____   _____
      _____   _____

      If additional space is needed for the names of shareholders, check this box and attach a
      separate sheet of paper to the Notice.   [ ]
260.102.8 (a) (Revised 5/97)

Ch 4
Forms

3.   The value of the securities sold or proposed to be sold in the transaction, determined in accordance with the provisions of Section 25608(g) of the Corporations Code in connection with the fee required upon filing this notice, is:

(a) $_____ in money

          $_____ in consideration other than money.

(b)   ( ) Change in rights, preferences, privileges or restrictions of or on outstanding securities under Rule 260.103. ($25 fee).

4.   Immediately after the issuance and sale of such shares, the above-named issuer had or will have only one class of stock outstanding which was or will be owned beneficially by no more than 35 persons.

Instruction: Review Sections 260.102.4 and 260.102.5, Title 10, California Code of Regulations.

5.   The offer and sale of such shares was not nor will be accompanied by the publication of any advertisement and neither selling expenses nor promotional considerations were or will be given, paid or incurred in connection therewith.

6.   To the best knowledge of the issuer, its shareholders (or proposed shareholders) have not entered into or granted, and presently do not intend entering into or granted, and presently do not intend entering into or granting a shareholders' agreement, voting agreement, irrevocable proxy or other arrangement the effect of which would cause the statements contained herein to be incorrect.

Instruction: Review Sections 260.001 and 260.102.4, Title 10, California Code of Regulations.

The undersigned officer of the issuer hereby declares that the foregoing is true under penalty of perjury. Executed at _____, _____ this _____ day of _____, _____.

_____
Name

_____
Title

NOTE: If the officer signs this form in a jurisdiction which does not permit verifications under penalty of perjury, there must be attached a verification executed and sworn to before a notary public.

**Ch 4
Forms**

OPINION OF COUNSEL

I certify that I am an active member of the State Bar of California. On the basis of the facts stated in the foregoing Notice and other information, including representations as to the type of consideration received or to be received, supplied to me by officials and shareholders of the issuer and by proposed issuees, it is my opinion that the exemption from qualification with the Commissioner of Corporations provided by Subdivision (h) of Section 25102 of the California Corporations Code is available for the offer and sale of the shares referred to in this Notice.

_____   _____
Signature   Firm Name

_____   _____
Name of Member of the State Bar   Address   Tel. No.
of California

(This opinion of counsel must be signed by an active member of the State Bar for California. Type name of attorney, address, phone number and firm name, if any.)

   NOTE: If the issuer is a non-California corporation, a Consent to Service of Process as prescribed in the Commissioner's Rule 102.8(b) must be filed concurrently.

TO THE COMMISSIONER OF CORPORATIONS OF
THE STATE OF CALIFORNIA

CONSENT TO SERVICE OF PROCESS

KNOW ALL MEN BY THESE PRESENTS:

    That the undersigned, _____ (a corporation organized under the laws of the State of _____), hereby irrevocably appoints the Commissioner of Corporations of the State of California, or the Commissioner's successor in office, to be the attorney to receive service of any lawful process in any noncriminal suit, action or proceeding against it, or its successor which arises under the California Corporate Securities Law of 1968 or any rule or order thereunder after this consent has been filed, with the same force and validity as if served personally on the undersigned.

    For the purpose of compliance with the Corporations Code of the State of California, notice of the service and a copy of the process should be sent by registered or certified mail to the undersigned at the following address:

_____
Name

_____
Street Address

_____
City   State   Zip Code

Dated: _____, _____.

                                  _____

                         By _____

                         Title _____

State of California   )
County of _____)

    On _____ before me, (here insert name and title of the officer), personally appeared _____ personally known to me (or proved to me on the basis of satisfactory evidence) to be the person(s) whose name(s) is/are subscribed to the within instrument and acknowledged to me that he/she/they executed the same in his/her/their authorized capacity(ies), and that by his/her/their signature(s) on the instrument the person(s), or the entity upon behalf of which the person(s) acted, executed the instrument.

    WITNESS my hand and official seal.

Signature_____   (Seal)

    Any certificate of acknowledgement taken in another state shall be sufficient in the State of California if it is taken in accordance with the laws of the place where the acknowledgement is made.

Forms for Chapter 5

There are five forms that accompany **Chapter 5, Incorporating or Forming an LLC from an Ongoing Business**. They include the following:

Form 5-A   Agreement to Transfer Partnership Assets to Corporation, 2 pages (248 - 249)

Form 5-B   Transfer of Assets of Sole Proprietorship to Corporation, 2 pages (250 - 251)

Form 5-C   Notice to Creditors of Bulk Sale, 1 page (252)

Form 5-D   Bill of Sale Agreement, 1 page (253)

Form 5-E   Notice of Dissolution of Partnership, 1 page (254)

AGREEMENT TO TRANSFER PARTNERSHIP ASSETS
TO CORPORATION

_____, 20____

To _____ (name of corporation), a California corporation.

The undersigned are the general partners of a partnership doing business under the name _____ (hereinafter called the "Partnership"). The business address of the Partnership is _____ _____. The most current balance sheet of the partnership, dated _____, 20____, is attached to the offer and fairly presents the financial position of the Partnership at said date in accordance with generally accepted accounting principles.

1. The undersigned, on the terms and condition herein set forth, hereby offer to sell and transfer to you at the close of business on _____, 20____, subject to such changes as may occur therein in the ordinary course of business between the date of this offer and the close of business on said closing date, all of the business and assets of the Partnership, including the trade, business, name, goodwill and other intangible assets of said business, subject to all liens, claims, and encumbrances and to charges occurring therein in the ordinary course of business between the date of said balance sheet and the close of business on the date of transfer. (optional C except for the following:)

2. As consideration for said sale and transfer you agree to:

(a) Assume and pay all debts and liabilities of the Partnership referred to on said balance sheet, together with those resulting from charges occurring in the ordinary course of business between the date of said balance sheet and the close of business on the date of transfer; and

(b) Issue and deliver, on the date of transfer, fully paid and nonassessable shares of your common stock to the persons and in the amounts as follows:

Name	Number of Shares
_____	_____
_____	_____
_____	_____

(c) The sale of securities which are the subject of this offer has not been qualified with the Commissioner of Corporations of this state, and the issuance of such securities or the payment or receipt of any part of the consideration therefore prior to such qualification is unlawful, if such qualification is necessary. The rights of all parties to the offer are expressly conditioned upon such qualification being obtained, if such qualification is necessary.*

3. If this offer is accepted by you, we shall, on delivery of a certificate(s) for the shares described above:

(a) Deliver possession of the business assets of the Partnership at the close of business on the date of transfer and further agree to execute and deliver to you such instruments of transfer and other documents as may be reasonably required to fully perform our obligation hereunder or as may be required for the convenient operation of said business thereafter by you.

If the foregoing is acceptable, please execute the acceptance in the space provided below, whereupon it will constitute a binding agreement.

Dated: _____

_____
Signature

_____
Business Partner Name

_____
Signature

_____
Business Partner Name

The above offer was accepted by the Board of Directors on _____,

20____. _____, a California corporation.

_____
By: President

_____
Secretary

*Subparagraph (c) may be omitted where the issuance of securities will not require qualification. [See Corp. C Section 25102(h)(3).]

Ch 5 Forms

Ch 5
Forms

TRANSFER OF ASSETS OF SOLE PROPRIETORSHIP TO CORPORATION

_____, 20_____

To _____ (name of corporation), a California corporation.

The undersigned is doing business as a sole proprietor under the name
_____ _____ (hereinafter called the "Proprietorship").
Business is transacted at _____ _____ (address). A balance sheet of the proprietorship is attached to this offer which fairly represents the financial position of the Proprietorship at said date in accordance with generally accepted accounting principles.

1. On the terms and conditions set forth herein, the undersigned hereby offers to sell and transfer to you at the close of business on _____, 20____, all of the assets of said business, including those reflected on said balance sheet, as well as its name and good will, subject to all liens, claims, and encumbrances, and to changes occurring therein in the ordinary course of business between the date of said balance sheet and the close of business on the date of transfer (optional—except for the following:)

2. As consideration for said sale and transfer you agree to:

(a) assume all debts and liabilities of the Proprietorship as set forth in said balance sheet, together with those resulting from changes occurring in the ordinary course of business from the date of said balance sheet and the close of business on the date of transfer; and

(b) issue and deliver to the undersigned on the date of transfer _____ (number of shares) fully paid and nonassessable shares of your Common Stock.

(c) The sale of securities which is the subject of this offer has not been qualified with the Commissioner of Corporations of the State of California and the issuance of such securities on the payment or receipt of any part of the consideration therefor prior to such qualification is unlawful, if such qualification is necessary. The rights of all parties to this offer are expressly conditioned upon such qualification being obtained, if such qualification is necessary.*3. If this offer is accepted by you, the undersigned will deliver possession of the Proprietorship business and its assets to you upon delivery of stock certificates described in section 2 (b) at the close of business on the date of transfer. The undersigned further agrees to execute and deliver to you such instruments of transfer and other documents as may be required to transfer title to you and in order to fully carry out the obligations of the undersigned as herein set forth. The undersigned hereby agrees to

* Subparagraph (c) may be omitted where the issuance of securities will not require qualification. [See Corp. C. Section 25102 (h)(3).]

indemnify you against liability for any personal taxes of the undersigned based on or measured by income derived by the undersigned from the Proprietorship and from any loss sustained by reason of liens, claims, and encumbrances, fixed or contingent, not reflected on said balance sheet.

If the foregoing terms and conditions are acceptable to you, please execute the acceptance in the space provided below, whereupon it will then constitute a binding agreement between us.

_____

Signature

_____

Name of Sole Proprietor

(The blanks below should be filled out after the first meeting of the board of directors.)

The above offer was accepted by the Board of Directors on _____, 20____. _____ (name of corporation), a California corporation.

By:

_____

President

_____

Secretary

**Ch 5
Forms**

NOTICE TO CREDITORS OF BULK SALE

NOTICE IS HEREBY GIVEN, that _____
(name of business/partnership) of _____ (address)
intends to transfer all trade fixtures, equipment, inventory, and supplies now
located at _____ (address) to _____
(name of corporation), a California corporation, whose business address is

_____ .

This intended transfer shall be consummated on or after _____,
20____, at the office of _____ (name of attorney).

Within the past three years _____ (name of trans-
feror) has conducted business under the following names at the following locations:

Date   Name of Business   Address

_____   _____   _____

_____   _____   _____

_____   _____   _____

This transfer _____ (is/is not) subject to Section 6106 of the California
Commercial Code.*

[If it is subject to Section 6106 add:

Claims for debts of the transferor may be filed with
_____ (name and address of transferor's attorney). The
last date for filing claims for debts of the transferor is _____, 20____
(specify date immediately prior to intended sale date)].

Dated: _____

_____
Name of Transferee

*If consideration for bulk transfer is less than one million dollars and is substan-
tially all cash or an obligation of the transferee to pay cash in the future to the
transferor or a continuation thereof, attention must be paid to Section 6106 and
its related provisions.*

BILL OF SALE AGREEMENT

_____ (name of transferor), (hereinafter the "Transferor"), in consideration of the issuance to him/her of _____ (number) shares of _____ _____ (name of corporation), a California corporation, (hereinafter the "Corporation"), hereby sells, assigns, and transfers to the Corporation all right, title, and interest in the following property: all tangible assets listed on an inventory attached hereto and marked as Exhibit ___ , as well as all stock in trade, goodwill, leasehold interests, trade names, and other intangible assets except accounts receivable, of that business known as _____ (name of business), located at _____ (address).

The Corporation _____ (agrees/does not agree) to issue, pay, and discharge all debts, duties, and obligations that appear on the date of the instrument on the books of said business to any person or persons whatsoever. The Corporation further _____ (agrees/does not agree) to indemnify and hold Transferor free and harmless from any liability for any such debt, duty, or obligation, or from any suits, actions, or legal proceedings which are brought to enforce or collect any such debt, duty, or obligation.

Transferor hereby appoints the Corporation as attorney-in-fact to demand, receive, and collect for its own use and benefit all debts and obligations now owing to said business. Transferor further authorizes the Corporation to perform any and all acts legally permissible which may be necessary to collect and recover such debts and obligations, provided, however, without cost, expense, or charge to Transferor.

Dated: _____

Transferor   **Corporation**

_____   _____

Name, Position   Name

By: _____
    Name, Title

NOTICE OF DISSOLUTION OF PARTNERSHIP

Public notice* is hereby given that _____ and
_____, heretofore doing business under the fictitious
firm name and style of _____, at
_____ (street address), City of
_____, County of _____, State of California,
did on the day of _____, 20____, by mutual consent (optional, by
withdrawal), dissolve the said partnership and terminate their relations as partners therein.

(Note: The following two paragraphs are optional. Either or both may be stricken
if they do not apply. They may be amended if they are not sufficient.)

Said business in the future will be conducted by _____
and _____, who will pay and discharge all liabilities
and debts of the firm and receive all monies payable to the firm.

Further notice is hereby given that the undersigned will not be responsible, from
this day on, for any obligation incurred by the other(s) in (his) (her) (their) own
name(s) or in the name of the firm.

Dated: _____, 20____, at _____, California.

Attorney(s) (Not required)

_____
Signature

_____
Typed or Printed Name

*Section 15035.5 of the Corporations Code requires that whenever a partnership is
dissolved, notice of the dissolution shall be published at least once in a newspaper
of general circulation in the place, or in each place if more than one, at which partnership business was regularly carried on. A printer's affidavit showing such publication date shall be filed with the County of publication. The County Clerk will not
accept for filing the original notice of dissolution. For publication in the proper newspaper and for filing of the affidavit of publication with the appropriate County Clerk,
mail one copy of this notice to California Newspaper Service Bureau, Inc., 915 East
1st Street, Los Angeles, CA 90012. Call 213 229-5500, if you have any questions.

Forms for Chapter 6

There are 14 forms that accompany **Chapter 6, Maintaining the Corporation or LLC**. They include the following:

Form 6-A   Application for Certificate of Revivor, 1 page (257)

Form 6-B   Minutes of the Annual Meeting of the Shareholders, 1 page (258)

Form 6-C   Minutes of the Annual Meeting of the Board of Directors, 2 pages (259 - 260)

Form 6-D   Minutes of a Special Meeting of the Shareholders, 2 pages (261 - 262)

Form 6-E   Minutes of a Special Meeting of the Board of Directors, 1 page (263)

Form 6-F   Waiver of Notice and Consent to Holding of a Special Meeting of the Shareholders, 1 page (264)

Form 6-G   Waiver of Notice and Consent to Holding of a Special Meeting of the Board of Directors, 1 page (265)

Form 6-H   Action by Unanimous Written Consent of Directors Without Meeting, 1 page (266)

Form 6-I   Notice of the Annual Meeting of Shareholders and Affidavit of Mailing of Notice of the Annual Meeting of Shareholders, 1 page (267)

Form 6-J Limited and Revocable Proxy, 1 page (268)

Form 6-K Bylaws (see Form 3-G, starting on page 163)

Form 6-L Operating Agreement for a Limited Liability Company, 59 pages (269 - 327)

Form 6-M Buy-Sell Agreement, 10 pages (328 - 337)

Form 6-N Certificate of Amendment of Articles of Incorporation (see Form 3-J on page 193)

STATE OF CALIFORNIA
FRANCHISE TAX BOARD
PO BOX 942840
SACRAMENTO CA 94240

Notice Date

APPLICATION FOR CERTIFICATE OF REVIVOR

Before the California Franchise Tax Board

In the matter of the application for certificate of revivor of:

Entity Number   :

FEIN/SOS Number   :

Entity Name   :

Address   :

I request relief from suspension or forfeiture for this entity. I previously submitted or I am enclosing all required payments, returns, or documents.

Print Name _____   Title _____

Signature _____   Date _____

Daytime Phone Number _____

Those who can sign this application on behalf of an entity (domestic or foreign) include:

- Any stockholder, creditor, member, general partner, or officer.
- Any person having an interest in relief from suspension or forfeiture.

Domestic entities can also have a majority of the surviving trustees or directors sign on their behalf.

FTB 3557 BC (REV 04-2003)

Ch 6 Forms

MINUTES OF THE ANNUAL MEETING OF
THE SHAREHOLDERS OF

_____

A California Corporation

An annual meeting of the shareholders of _____,
a California corporation, was held at the hour of _____, on the _____ day of
_____, 20_____, at the offices of the corporation, located at
_____, California. The meeting was held pur-
suant to a written Waiver of Notice and Consent thereto, signed by each of the
shareholders of the corporation.

The President and Secretary of the corporation acted, respectively, as Chairman
and Secretary of the meeting. The Chairman called the meeting to order and the
Secretary called the roll of shareholders entitled to vote. Those present were the
following, constituting all of the shareholders of the corporation entitled to vote:

Shareholders

_____   _____

_____   _____

There being present at the meeting of shareholders of record holding all of the
shares of common stock of the corporation issued and outstanding which have
voting power, the Chairman declared that a quorum was present and that the
meeting was duly opened for business.

The Minutes of the previous shareholders' meeting were then read and approved.

After a discussion concerning the election of directors, upon motion duly made,
seconded, and approved, the following directors were nominated and elected:

_____   _____

[If other resolutions were presented to the shareholders, besides the election of
directors, include the following:

On motion duly made, seconded, and carried, the following resolutions were
adopted:

(set forth resolutions)]

There being no further business to come before the meeting, upon motion duly
made, seconded, and carried, the meeting was adjourned.

_____   ATTEST: _____
Secretary   Chairman

MINUTES OF THE ANNUAL MEETING OF
THE BOARD OF DIRECTORS OF

_____

An annual meeting of the Directors of
_____, a California corporation, was
held _____, 20_____ at _____ o'clock _____ a.m./p.m. of said day, at
_____, California, pursuant to Article III, Section 3.06
of the Bylaws. The meeting was held pursuant to a written Waiver of Notice and
Consent thereto, signed by all of the Directors of the corporation and inserted into
the minute book immediately preceding these minutes.

There were present at said meeting the following Directors, being all of the
Directors of the corporation elected at the annual shareholders' meeting:

_____

_____

_____

The President and Secretary of the corporation acted, respectively, as Chairman
and Secretary of the meeting.

The Chairman announced that the meeting was duly convened and that the Board
was ready to transact such business as may lawfully come before it. The minutes
of the last meeting of the Board of Directors were read and approved.

The following nominations for officers of the corporation, to serve for one year or
until their successors are elected and qualified, were made:

President   _____

Chief Financial Officer _____

Secretary   _____

There being no further nominations, the foregoing persons were unanimously
elected to the offices set forth opposite their respective names.

[If other resolutions were presented to the directors, besides the election of officers, include the following:

On motion duly made, seconded, and carried, the following resolutions were
adopted:

(set forth resolutions)]

There being no further business to come before the meeting, upon motion duly

Ch 6 Forms

made, seconded, and carried, the meeting was adjourned.

_____   ATTEST: _____
Secretary   Chairman

MINUTES OF A SPECIAL MEETING OF
THE SHAREHOLDERS OF

_____

A California Corporation

A special meeting of the shareholders of _____,
a California corporation, was held at the hour of _____, on the _____ day of
_____, 20___, at the offices of the corporation, located at
_____, California. The meeting was held pursuant to a written Waiver of Notice and Consent thereto, signed by all of the shareholders, and inserted into the minute book immediately preceding these minutes.*

The President and Secretary of the corporation acted, respectively, as Chairman and Secretary of the meeting.

The Chairman called the meeting to order and the Secretary called the roll of shareholders entitled to vote.

The minutes of the last meeting of the shareholders were read and approved.

Those present were the following, constituting all of the shareholders of the corporation entitled to vote:

Shareholders

_____   _____

_____   _____

_____   _____

_____   _____

_____   _____

There being present at the special meeting all of the shareholders of record holding all of the shares of common stock of the corporation issued and outstanding which have voting power, the Chairman declared that a quorum was present and that the special meeting was duly opened for business.

On motion made, seconded, and carried, the following resolutions were adopted:

(set forth resolutions)

In the absence of a waiver, a general meeting of the Shareholders needs to be noted as set forth in article 2.036 of the Bylaws. Should the special meeting take place by written notice, other than waiver, this form should be modified to so reflect.

Ch 6 Forms

There being no further business to come before the meeting, upon motion duly made, seconded, and carried, the meeting was adjourned.

_____   ATTEST: _____
Secretary   Chairman

MINUTES OF A SPECIAL MEETING OF
THE BOARD OF DIRECTORS OF

_____

A California Corporation

A special meeting of the Board of Directors of _____,
a California corporation, was held on _____, 20____, at _____ o'clock
____ a.m./p.m. of said day, at _____, California, pursuant
to Article III, Section 3.08 of the Bylaws. The special meeting was held pursuant to
a written Notice of Waiver and Consent thereto, signed by all of the Directors, and
inserted into the minute book immediately preceding these minutes.*

There were present at the special meeting the following Directors, constituting all
of the Directors of the corporation elected at the annual shareholders' meeting:

_____

_____

_____

The President and Secretary of the Corporation acted, respectively, as Chairman
and Secretary of the meeting.

The Chairman announced that the meeting was duly convened and that the Board
was ready to transact such business as may lawfully come before it.

The minutes of the last meeting of the Board of Directors were read and
approved.

On motion duly made, seconded, and carried, the following resolutions were
adopted:

(set forth resolutions)

There being no further business to come before the meeting, upon motion duly
made, seconded, and carried, the special meeting was adjourned.

_____   ATTEST: _____
Secretary   Chairman

*In the absence of a waiver, a special meeting of directors needs to be noticed as
set forth in article 3.08 of the Bylaws. Should the special meeting take place present to written notice other than waiver, this form should be amended to so reflect._

WAIVER OF NOTICE AND CONSENT TO HOLDING OF
A SPECIAL MEETING* OF THE SHAREHOLDERS OF

_____

A California Corporation

The undersigned, constituting all of the shareholders of _____,
a California corporation, desiring to hold a special meeting, hereby waive notice
of, and consent to the holding of, such meeting, at _____
(address), on _____, 20____, at _____ o'clock _____ a.m./p.m., for
the purpose of considering and acting upon the following corporate matters:

(insert purpose for special shareholder meeting)**

The undersigned further agree that any business transacted at said special meeting shall be as valid and legal as if it had transpired at a regularly called and
noticed meeting.

Dated: _____

_____
(Print or type name)

Holding _____ shares out of _____ issued.

_____
(Print or type name)

Holding _____ shares out of _____ issued.

_____
(Print or type name)

Holding _____ shares out of _____ issued.

* A waiver of notice and consent can be signed either before or after a special
meeting. It is preferable, however, to have such an agreement executed prior to
the meeting.

**This same waiver form can be used for waiving notice of the annual meeting of
the shareholders, with slight modifications. It is advisable to also include the
names of the Directors nominated for the new Board. This can be done in the
space provided above for discussing the purpose of the meeting.

**WAIVER OF NOTICE AND CONSENT TO HOLDING OF
A SPECIAL MEETING OF THE BOARD OF DIRECTORS OF**

_____

A California Corporation

The undersigned, constituting all of the Directors of the above corporation, hereby waive notice of and consent to the holding of a special meeting of the Board of Directors of said corporation, at _____ on _____, 20____, at _____ o'clock _____ a.m./p.m., and further agree that any business transacted at said meeting shall be as valid and legal, and have the same force and effect as though the meeting had been regularly called and noticed.

Dated: _____

_____
(Print or type name) Director

_____
(Print or type name) Director

_____
(Print or type name) Director

**Ch 6
Forms**

**ACTION BY UNANIMOUS WRITTEN CONSENT OF
DIRECTORS WITHOUT MEETING* OF**

_____

A California Corporation

The undersigned, constituting all of the directors of _____,
a California corporation, hereby adopt the following resolutions pursuant to the
authority of Section 307(b) of the California Corporations Code and the Bylaws of
this corporation:

(insert resolutions adopted)

Dated: _____

_____

(Print or type name) Director

_____

(Print or type name) Director

_____

(Print or type name) Director

*The Board of Directors can take action without a meeting, only if all the members of the Board consent in writing to such action. Written consents must then be filed in the minute book of the corporation.

NOTICE OF THE ANNUAL MEETING OF THE SHAREHOLDERS OF

_____

PLEASE TAKE NOTICE THAT the annual meeting of the shareholders of _____, a California corporation, will be held on the date and at the time and place stated below:

Date of Meeting: _____

Time of Meeting: _____

Place of Meeting: _____

The meeting will consider and act upon the following:

(1) Election of Directors.
(2) Annual report to shareholders.
(3) [General nature of other business to be considered].
(4) Other business as may properly be brought before the meeting.

The stock transfer ledger of the corporation shall remain closed from _____ to _____, 20___.

Dated: _____

_____
Secretary

AFFIDAVIT OF MAILING OF NOTICE OF THE ANNUAL MEETING OF SHAREHOLDERS

_____, being duly sworn according to law, disposes and states:

I am the Secretary of _____, and swear that on _____, 20____, I personally deposited in a post office box in the city of _____, county of _____, State of California, copies of the above Notice of Annual Meeting of Shareholders, each enclosed in a securely sealed postage-paid envelope, one of the notices addressed to each person whose name appears on the annexed list of shareholders and to their respective post office addresses as therein set forth.

_____
Secretary
Sworn to before me this _____ day of _____, 20___.

LIMITED AND REVOCABLE PROXY

1, _____ (name) record owner of _____ (number of shares) shares of _____ (name of corporation), a California corporation (hereinafter the "corporation"), hereby revoke any previous proxies and appoint (name of proxy) as my proxy to attend the shareholders' meeting set for (date of shareholders' meeting) at the Company's office in _____ (city), California, and to vote, execute consents, and otherwise represent my interests as both a shareholder in the same manner and with the same effect as if I were personally present. This proxy is entered into in compliance with Section 2.12 of the Corporation's bylaws.

If not previously revoked, this proxy will terminate once the _____, 20_____ (date of meeting) meeting of the shareholders has been adjourned.

Dated: _____

_____
(Signature of Shareholder)

_____
(Print Name of Shareholder)

OPERATING AGREEMENT FOR

_____, **LLC**

A CALIFORNIA LIMITED LIABILITY COMPANY

This Operating Agreement is made as of _____, _____ ("Effective Date") by and among the parties listed on the signature pages hereof, with reference to the following facts:

A. On _____, _____, Articles of Organization for _____ LLC (the "Company"), a limited liability company organized under the laws of the State of California, were filed with the California Secretary of State.

B. The parties desire to adopt and approve an operating agreement for the Company.

RECITAL:

The Members desire to enter into this Agreement for the Company to delineate their rights and liabilities as members, to provide for the Company's management, and to provide for certain other matters, all as permitted under the Beverly-Killea Limited Liability Company Act.

AGREEMENT:

NOW, THEREFORE, IN CONSIDERATION OF THE MUTUAL PROMISES, COVENANTS, AND UNDERTAKINGS HEREIN SPECIFIED AND FOR OTHER GOOD AND VALUABLE CONSIDERATION, THE RECEIPT AND SUFFICIENCY OF WHICH ARE HEREBY ACKNOWLEDGED, WITH THE INTENT TO BE OBLIGATED LEGALLY AND EQUITABLY, THE PARTIES HERETO AGREE AS FOLLOWS:

ARTICLE I. DEFINITIONS

Capitalized terms used in this Agreement shall have the meanings specified below or elsewhere in this Agreement and when not so defined shall have the meanings specified in California Corporations Code Section 17001 (such terms are equally applicable to both the singular and plural derivations of the terms defined):

1.1 "Act" shall mean the Beverly-Killea Limited Liability Company Act, codified in the California Corporations Code, Section 17000 et seq., as the same may be amended from time to time.

1.2 "Affiliate" of a Member or Manager shall mean any Person, directly or indirectly, through one or more intermediaries, controlling, controlled by, or under common control with a Member or Manager, as applicable. The term "control," as used in the immediately preceding sentence, shall mean with respect to a corpo-

Ch 6
Forms

ration or limited liability company the right to exercise, directly or indirectly, more than fifty percent (50%) of the voting rights attributable to the controlled corporation or limited liability company, and, with respect to any individual, partnership, trust, or other entity or association, the possession, directly or indirectly, of the power to direct or cause the direction of the management or policies of the controlled entity.

1.3 "Agreement" shall mean this Operating Agreement, as originally executed and as amended from time to time.

1.4 "Articles" shall mean the Articles of Organization for the Company originally filed with the California Secretary of State and as amended from time to time.

1.5 "Assignee" shall mean the owner of an Economic Interest who has not been admitted as a substitute Member in accordance with Article VIII.

1.6 "Bankruptcy" shall mean: (a) the filing of an application by a Member for, or his or her consent to, the appointment of a trustee, receiver, or custodian of his or her other assets; (b) the entry of an order for relief with respect to a Member in proceedings under the United States Bankruptcy Code, as amended or superseded from time to time; (c) the making by a Member of a general assignment for the benefit of creditors; (d) the entry of an order, judgment, or decree by any court of competent jurisdiction appointing a trustee, receiver, or custodian of the assets of a Member unless the proceedings and the person appointed are dismissed within ninety (90) days; or (e) the failure by a Member generally to pay his or her debts as the debts become due within the meaning of Section 303(h)(1) of the United States Bankruptcy Code, as determined by the Bankruptcy Court, or the admission in writing of his or her inability to pay his or her debts as they become due.

1.7 "Capital Account" shall mean with respect to any Member the capital account which the Company establishes and maintains for such Member pursuant to Section 3.4.

1.8 "Capital Contribution" shall mean the total amount of cash and fair market value of property contributed and/or services rendered or to be rendered to the Company by Members.

1.9 "Code" shall mean the Internal Revenue Code of 1986, as amended from time to time, the provisions of succeeding law, and to the extent applicable, the Regulations.

1.10 "Company" shall mean _____ LLC, a California limited liability company.

1.11 "Company Minimum Gain" shall have the meaning ascribed to the term

"Partnership Minimum Gain" in the Regulations Section 1.704-2(d).

1.12 "Corporations Code" shall mean the California Corporations Code, as amended from time to time, and the provisions of succeeding law.

1.13 "Dissolution Event" shall have the meaning ascribed to that term in Section 11.1.

1.14 "Distributable Cash" shall mean the amount of cash which the Manager(s) deem available for distribution to the Members, taking into account all debts, liabilities, and obligations of the Company then due, and working capital and other amounts which the Manager(s) deem necessary for the Company's business or to place into reserves for customary and usual claims with respect to such business.

1.15 "Economic Interest" shall mean the right to receive distributions of the Company's assets and allocations of income, gain, loss, deduction, credit, and similar items from the Company pursuant to this Agreement and the Act, but shall not include any other rights of a Member, including, without limitation, the right to vote or participate in the management of the Company, or except as provided in Section 17106 of the Corporations Code, any right to information concerning the business and affairs of the Company.

1.16 "Effective Date" shall have the meaning ascribed to that term in Section 2.1.

1.17 "Family Member" shall mean (a) with respect to any individual, such individual's spouse, domestic partner, parent, sibling, in-law, child, or grandchild (whether natural, adopted, or in the process of adoption), any trust all of the beneficial interests of which are owned by any such individuals or by any such individuals together with any organization described in Code Section 501(c)(3), the estate of any such individual, and any corporation, association, partnership, or limited liability company all of the equity interests of which are owned by those above-described individuals, trust or organizations, and (b) with respect to any trust, the owners of the beneficial interests of such trust.

1.18 "Fiscal Year" shall mean the Company's fiscal year, which shall be the calendar year.

1.19 "Former Member" shall have the meaning ascribed to it in Section 9.2.

1.20 "Former Member's Interest" shall have the meaning ascribed to it in Section 9.2.

1.21 "Majority Interest" shall mean those Members who hold a majority of the Percentage Interests which all Members hold.

1.22 "Manager" shall mean each of _____, _____, and _____, or any other persons that succeed any of them as a manager of the Company. At any time when there is only one Manager of the Company, the term "Manager(s)" shall mean such sole Manager.

1.23 "Member" shall mean each Person who (a) is an initial signatory to this Agreement, has been admitted to the Company as a Member in accordance with the Articles or this Agreement, or is an Assignee who has become a Member in accordance with Article VIII, and (b) has not ceased to be a Member in accordance with Article IX or for any other reason.

1.24 "Member Nonrecourse Debt" shall have the meaning ascribed to the term "Partner Nonrecourse Debt" in Regulations Section 1.704-2(b)(4).

1.25 "Member Nonrecourse Deductions" shall mean items of Company loss, deduction, or Code Section 705(a)(2)(B) expenditures which are attributable to Member Nonrecourse Debt.

1.26 "Membership Interest" shall mean a Member's entire interest in the Company including the Member's Economic Interest, the right to vote on or participate in the management, and the right to receive information concerning the business and affairs, of the Company.

1.27 "Net Profits" and "Net Losses" shall mean the income, gain, loss, and deductions of the Company in the aggregate or separately stated, as appropriate, determined in accordance with the method of accounting at the close of each Fiscal Year on the Company's information tax return filed for federal income tax purposes.

1.28 "Nonrecourse Liability" shall have the meaning set forth in Regulations Section 1.752-1(a)(2).

1.29 "Optional Purchase Event" shall have the meaning set forth in Section 9.1.

1.30 "Percentage Interest" shall mean the percentage of a Member set forth opposite the name of such Member under the column "Member's Percentage Interest" in Exhibit A hereto, as such percentage may be adjusted from time to time pursuant to the terms of this Agreement. Percentage Interests shall be determined annually, unless otherwise provided herein, in accordance with the relative proportions of the aggregate Capital Contributions of the Members.

1.31 "Permitted Transfer" shall have the meaning ascribed to that term in Section 8.4.

1.32 "Person" shall mean an individual, partnership, limited partnership, limited liability company, corporation, trust, estate, association, or any other entity.

1.33 "Prime Rate" as of a particular date shall mean the prime rate of interest as published on that date in *The Wall Street Journal*, and generally defined therein as "the base rate on corporate loans posted by at least 75% of the nation's 30 largest banks." If *The Wall Street Journal* is not published on a date for which the Prime Rate must be determined, the Prime Rate shall be the prime rate published in *The Wall Street Journal* on the nearest preceding date on which *The Wall Street Journal* was published.

1.34 "Purchaser Questionnaire" shall mean that certain Purchaser Questionnaire executed by each Member as a condition precedent to purchasing Membership Interests.

1.35 "Regulations" shall, unless the context clearly indicates otherwise, mean the regulations in force as final or temporary that have been issued by the U.S. Department of Treasury pursuant to its authority under the Code, and any successor regulations.

1.36 "Remaining Members" shall have the meaning ascribed to it in Section 9.2.

1.37 "Secretary of State" shall mean the California Secretary of State.

1.38 "Subscription Agreement" means the contract between the Company and a Member for the Member's purchase of Membership Interests from the Company.

1.39 "Tax Matters Partner" (as defined in Code Section 6231) shall be _____ or his or her successor as designated pursuant to Section 10.8.

1.40 "Transfer" or "Transferred" shall mean any sale, assignment, transfer, conveyance, pledge, hypothecation, or other disposition voluntarily or involuntarily, by operation of law, with or without consideration, or otherwise (including, without limitation, by way of intestacy, will, gift, bankruptcy, receivership, levy, execution, charging order or other similar sale or seizure by legal process) of all or any portion of any Membership Interest.

Without limiting the generality of the foregoing, the sale or exchange of at least fifty percent (50%) of the voting stock of a Member, if a Member is a corporation, or the Transfer of an interest or interests of at least fifty percent (50%) in the capital or profits of a Member (whether accomplished by the sale or exchange of interests or by the admission of new partners or members), if a Member is a partnership or limited liability company, or the cumulative Transfer of such interests in a Member effectively equivalent to the foregoing (including Transfer of interests followed by the incorporation of a Member and subsequent stock Transfers, or Transfers of stock followed by the liquidation of a Member and subsequent Transfers of interests) will be deemed to constitute a Transfer of the Member's entire Membership Interest.

Ch 6 Forms

ARTICLE II. ORGANIZATIONAL MATTERS

2.1 Formation. The Members have formed a California limited liability company by filing the Articles with the Secretary of State and entering into this Agreement. The rights and liabilities of the Members shall be determined pursuant to the Act and this Agreement. To the extent that the rights or obligations of any Member are different because of any provision of this Agreement than those rights or obligations would be in the absence of such provision, this Agreement shall control to the extent permitted by the Act.

2.2 Name. The name of the Company is "_____ LLC." The business of the Company may be conducted under that name or, upon compliance with applicable laws, any other name that the Manager(s) deem appropriate or advisable. The Manager(s) shall file any fictitious name certificates and similar filings, and any amendments thereto, that the Manager(s) consider appropriate or advisable. The Company's name shall be the exclusive property of the Company, and no Member shall have any rights in the name or any derivation thereof.

2.3 Term. The Company's existence commenced on the Effective Date and shall continue until terminated as hereinafter provided.

2.4 Registered Office and Agent. The Company shall continuously maintain a registered office ("Office") and registered agent ("Agent") in the State of California. The Office shall be that of the Agent. The Agent shall be as stated in the Articles or as otherwise determined by the Manager(s). If the Agent ceases to act as such for any reason or the Company changes the Office's location, the Manager(s) shall designate promptly a replacement Agent and/or notify the Secretary of State of the new Office location on the form prescribed by the Secretary of State ("Notification"). If the Manager(s) fail to designate a replacement Agent or notify the Secretary of State of the new Office location, a Majority Interest may file the Notification with the Secretary of State specifying the Agent and/or Office, as the case may be.

2.5 Principal Place of Business. The Company's principal place of business shall be

_____

or as the Manager(s) may determine. The Company may also have such offices, anywhere within and without the State of California, as the Manager(s) may determine from time to time, or the business of the Company may require.

2.6 Member and Manager Information. The name, address, taxpayer identification number, and Percentage Interest of each Member and Manager are set forth in Exhibit A. A Member may change his or her address in the Company's books and records upon notice thereof to the Manager(s).

2.7 Purpose and Business of the Company. The purpose of the Company is to engage in any lawful activity for which a limited liability company may be organized under the Act. Notwithstanding the foregoing, without the consent of a Majority Interest, the Company shall not engage in any business other than the following:

A. The business of _____; and

B. Such other activities directly related to and in furtherance of the foregoing business as may be necessary, advisable, or appropriate, in the reasonable opinion of the Manager(s).

2.8 Tax Classification. The Members acknowledge that pursuant to Regulation Section 301.7701-3, the Company shall be classified as a partnership for federal income tax purposes until the effective date of any election ("Election") to change its classification on IRS Form 8832, Entity Classification Election. The Members agree the Manager(s) shall have the authority to file and make the Election on behalf of the Company and each Member at such time as the Manager(s) determine such a change is in the Company's best interests.

2.9 No State Law Partnership. The Company's classification as a partnership will apply only for federal (and, as appropriate, state, and local) income tax purposes. This characterization does not create or imply a general partnership, limited partnership, or joint venture among the Members for state law or any other purpose. Instead, the Members acknowledge the Company's status as a limited liability company formed under the Act.

ARTICLE III. CAPITAL CONTRIBUTIONS

3.1 Initial Capital Contributions. Each Member shall contribute to the Company, as that Member's initial Capital Contribution, the money, property and/or services specified in Exhibit A to this Agreement. Exhibit A shall be revised to reflect any additional contributions made in accordance with Section 3.2.

3.2 Additional Capital Contributions. No Member shall be required to make any additional Capital Contributions. To the extent approved by the Manager(s), from time to time, the Members may be permitted to make additional Capital Contributions if and to the extent they so desire, and if the Manager(s) determine that such additional Capital Contributions are necessary or appropriate for the conduct of the Company's business, including without limitation, expansion, or diversification. In that event, the Members shall have the opportunity, but not the obligation, to participate in such additional Capital Contributions on a pro rata basis in accordance with their Percentage Interests. Each Member shall receive a credit to his or her Capital Account in the amount of any additional capital which he or she contributes to the Company. Immediately following such Capital Contributions, the Percentage Interests shall be adjusted by the Manager(s) to

**Ch 6
Forms**

reflect the new relative proportions of the Capital Accounts of the Members.

3.3 Failure to Make Contributions. If a Member does not timely contribute capital when required, that Member shall be in default under this Agreement. In such event, the Manager(s) shall send the defaulting Member written notice of such default, giving him or her _____ (___) days from the date such notice is given to contribute the entire amount of his or her required capital contribution. (If the defaulting Member did not make a required contribution of property or services, the Company may instead require the defaulting Member to contribute cash equal to that portion of the fair market value of the contribution that has not been made.) If the defaulting Member does not contribute his or her required capital to the Company within said_____ (___)-day period, a majority of the Manager(s) or those non-defaulting Members who hold a majority of the Percentage Interests held by all non-defaulting Members may elect any one or more of the following remedies:

A. The non-defaulting Members may advance funds to the Company to cover those amounts which the defaulting Member fails to contribute. Amounts which a non-defaulting Member so advances on behalf of the defaulting Member shall become a loan due and owing from the defaulting Member to such non-defaulting Member and bear interest at the rate of _____ percent (___%) per annum, payable monthly. All cash distributions otherwise distributable to the defaulting Member under this Agreement shall instead be paid to the non-defaulting Members making such advances until such advances and interest thereon are paid in full. In any event, any such advances shall be evidenced by a promissory note and be due and payable by the defaulting Member one (1) year from the date that such advance was made. Any amounts repaid shall first be applied to interest and thereafter to principal. Effective upon a Member becoming a defaulting Member, each Member grants to the non-defaulting Members who advance funds under this Section 3.3A a security interest in his or her Economic Interest to secure his or her obligation to repay such advances and agrees to execute and deliver a promissory note as described herein together with a security agreement in such UCC-1 financing statements and assignments of certificates of membership (or other documents of transfer) as such non-defaulting Members may reasonably request.

B. The Percentage Interests shall be adjusted, in which event each Member's Percentage Interest shall be a fraction, the numerator of which represents the aggregate amount of such Member's Capital Contributions and the denominator of which represents the sum of all Members' Capital Contributions.

C. The non-defaulting Members who hold a majority of the Percentage Interests held by all non-defaulting Members may dissolve the Company, in which event the

Company shall be wound up, liquidated, and terminated pursuant to Article XI.

D. The Company or the non-defaulting Members may purchase the defaulting Member's entire Membership Interest in accordance with the same terms and conditions as those set forth in Article IX except that the purchase price shall be an amount equal to _____ percent (___%) of the purchase price determined in accordance with Section 9.3.

E. The defaulting Members shall have no right to receive any distributions from the Company until the non-defaulting Members have first received distributions in an amount equal to the additional capital contributed by each non-defaulting Member to the Company plus a cumulative, non-compounded return thereon at the rate of _____ percent (___%) per annum.

F. The defaulting Member shall lose his or her voting and approval rights under the Act, the Articles and this Agreement until such time as the defaulting Member cures the default.

G. The defaulting Member shall lose his or her ability (whether as a Member or a Manager) to participate in the management and operations of the Company until such time as the defaulting Member cures the default.

Each Member acknowledges and agrees that (i) a default by any Member in making a required capital contribution will result in the Company and the non-defaulting Members incurring certain costs and other damages in an amount that would be extremely difficult or impractical to ascertain and (ii) the remedies described in this Section 3.3 bear a reasonable relationship to the damages which the Members estimate may be suffered by the Company and the non-defaulting Members by reason of the failure of a defaulting Member to make any required Capital Contribution and the election of any or all of the above described remedies is not unreasonable under the circumstances existing as of the date hereof.

The election of the Manager(s) or non-defaulting Members, as applicable, to pursue any remedy provided in this Section 3.3 shall not be a waiver or limitation of the right to pursue an additional or different remedy available hereunder or of law or equity with respect to any subsequent default.

3.4 Capital Accounts.

A. Maintenance. The Company shall maintain a separate Capital Account for each Member. The Capital Account of each Member shall be credited with the Member's Initial Capital Contribution, increased by (i) any other cash contributed after the date hereof by such Member to the Company; (ii) the fair market value, as determined by the Manager(s), of any property contributed after the date hereof by such Member to the Company (net of liabilities that are secured by such contributed property or that the Company or any other Member is considered to assume or take subject to under Code Section 752); (iii) allocations to such Member of Net Profit pursuant to Article VI; and (iv) other additions allocated to such Member in accordance with the Code; and decreased by (i) the amount of cash distributed to such Member by the Company; (ii) allocations to such Member of Net Loss pursuant to Article VI; (iii) the fair market value, as determined by the Manager(s), of property distributed to such Member by the Company (net of liabilities that are secured by such distributed property or that such Member is considered to assume or take subject to under Code Section 752); and (iv) other deductions allocated to such Member in accordance with the Code.

B. Compliance with Treasury Regulations. The foregoing provisions and the other provisions of this Agreement relating to the maintenance of Capital Accounts are intended to comply with Code Section 704(b) and Regulations Section 1.704-1(b)(2)(iv), and shall be interpreted and applied in a manner consistent with such regulations.

C. Assignment. On the Transfer of all or any part of a Member's Membership Interest as permitted by this Agreement, the Capital Account of the transferor, or portion thereof that is attributable to the Transferred interest, shall carry over to the transferee as prescribed in Regulations Section 1.704-1(b)(2)(iv).

D. Revaluation. At such times as may be required or permitted by Code Section 704 and any Regulations thereunder, the Capital Accounts shall be revalued and adjusted to reflect the then fair market value of the Company's property. The Capital Accounts shall be maintained in compliance with Regulation Section 1.704-1(b)(2)(iv)(f). All allocations of gain resulting from such revaluation shall be made consistently with regulation Section 1.704-1(b)(2)(iv)(f) and, to the extent not inconsistent therewith, provisions of Section 6.1 on the allocation of Net Profit.

3.5 Withdrawal and Return of Capital. No Member shall be entitled to withdraw or to demand the return of any or all of that Member's Capital Contribution, except as specifically provided in this Agreement.

3.6 No Interest. No Member shall be entitled to receive interest on that Member's Capital Contributions or the balance of that Member's Capital Account without the Manager(s)' prior written consent.

3.7 No Priority Return. Except as otherwise provided in this Agreement, no Member shall have priority over any other Member regarding the return of a Capital Contribution.

3.8 Member Loans.

A. Any Member or an Affiliate of a Member may lend money to the Company with the Manager(s)' prior written consent. The loan shall not be treated as a Capital Contribution by that Member or entitle the Member to an increase in that Member's Percentage Interest. The loan amount shall be a debt due from the Company, repayable out of the Company's assets, bear interest at the lower of the Prime Rate or the maximum rate permitted by law, and be on such other terms as the Company and the Member agree. Notwithstanding the foregoing, no Member shall be required to make any loans to the Company or guaranty the payment or performance of any Company obligation.

B. The Members acknowledge that any Member, Manager, or Affiliate of a Member or Manager (each, a "Lender") who loans money to the Company pursuant to this Section 3.8 shall have rights, the exercise of which may be in conflict with the Company's best interests. In that regard, the Members hereby authorize, agree, and consent to the Lender's exercise of any of Lender's rights under any promissory note, security agreement, or other loan document, even though the Lender's exercise of those rights may be detrimental to the Company or the Company's business. Further, the Members agree that any Lender's proper exercise of the Lender's rights shall not be deemed a breach of that Lender's fiduciary duties (if any) to the Company.

ARTICLE IV. MEMBERS

4.1 Limited Liability. Except as expressly set forth in this Agreement or required by law, no Member shall be personally liable for any debt, obligation, or liability of the Company, whether that liability or obligation arises in contract, tort, or otherwise.

4.2 Issuance of Additional Membership Interests; Admission of Additional Members. The Manager(s), with the approval of a Majority Interest, may cause the Company to issue Membership Interests to, and to admit any Person as, a Member on such terms as are determined by the Manager(s) and approved a Majority Interest. The Manager(s) shall amend this Agreement, and the Members hereby consent to such amendment, to reflect (a) the sale of additional Membership Interests, (b) the admission of additional Members, and (c) any changes in allocations of Net Profits, Net Losses, distributions, voting rights, and management participation in connection with the admission of such additional Members. Notwithstanding the foregoing, Assignees may only be admitted as substitute Members in accordance with Article VIII.

4.3 Withdrawals or Resignations. No Member may withdraw, resign, or retire from the Company.

4.4 Termination of Membership Interest. Upon (a) the Transfer of a Member's Membership Interest in violation of Article VIII, (b) the occurrence of an Optional Purchase Event as to such Member, or (c) the withdrawal, resignation or retire-

Ch 6 Forms

**Ch 6
Forms**

ment of a Member in violation of Section 4.3, the Membership Interest of a Member shall be terminated by the Manager(s) and thereafter that Member shall be an Assignee only unless such Membership Interest shall be purchased by the Company and/or the remaining Members as provided in Article IX. Each Member acknowledges and agrees that such termination or purchase of a Membership Interest upon the occurrence of any of the foregoing events is not unreasonable under the circumstances existing as of the date hereof.

4.5 Competing Activities. The Members and their officers, directors, shareholders, partners, members, managers, agents, employees, and Affiliates may engage or invest in, independently or with others, any business activity of any type or description, including without limitation those that might be the same as or similar to the Company's business and that might be in direct or indirect competition with the Company. Neither the Company nor any Member shall have any right in or to such other ventures or activities or to the income or proceeds derived therefrom. The Members shall not be obligated to present any investment opportunity or prospective economic advantage to the Company, even if the opportunity is of the character that, if presented to the Company, could be taken by the Company. The Members shall have the right to hold any investment opportunity or prospective economic advantage for their own account or to recommend such opportunity to Persons other than the Company. Each Member acknowledges that the other Members and their Affiliates own and/or manage other businesses, including businesses that may compete with the Company and for the Members' time. Each Member hereby waives any and all rights and claims which they may otherwise have against the other Members and their officers, directors, shareholders, partners, members, managers, agents, employees, and Affiliates as a result of any of such activities.

4.6 Transactions with the Company. Subject to any limitations set forth in this Agreement and with the prior approval of the Manager(s), a Member or an Affiliate of a Member may transact business with the Company so long as the transaction is not expressly prohibited by this Agreement and so long as the terms and conditions of such transaction, on an overall basis, are fair and reasonable to the Company and are at least as favorable to the Company as those terms and conditions that are generally available in similar transactions from Persons operating at arm's length and, in the case of services, from Persons capable of performing similar services. Subject to other applicable laws, such Member has the same rights and obligations with respect thereto as a Person who is not a Member.

4.7 Remuneration to Members. Except as otherwise specifically provided in this Agreement or pursuant to a transaction permitted by Section 4.6, no Member or an Affiliate of a Member is entitled to remuneration for services rendered or goods provided to, or on behalf of, the Company.

4.8 **Members Are Not Agents.** Pursuant to Section 5.1 and the Articles, the management of the Company is vested in the Manager(s). The Members shall have no power to participate in the management of the Company except as expressly authorized by this Agreement or the Articles and except as expressly required by the Act. No Member, acting solely in the capacity of a Member, is an agent of the Company nor does any Member, unless expressly and duly authorized in writing to do so by a Manager or Manager(s), have any power or authority to (a) bind or act on behalf of the Company in any way, (b) pledge its credit, (c) execute any instrument on its behalf, or (d) render it liable for any purpose.

Each Member shall indemnify, defend, and hold harmless the Company and the other Members from and against any and all loss, cost, expense, liability, or damage arising from or relating to any action by such Member in contravention of this Section 4.8.

4.9 **Voting Rights.** Except as expressly provided in this Agreement or the Articles or required by law, Members shall have no voting, approval, or consent rights and, to the extent permitted by applicable law, each Member waives that Member's right to vote on any matters other than those set forth in this Section 4.9.

A. **Super-Majority Approval.** The affirmative vote of Members holding _____ percent (___%) of the Percentage Interests (not including for such purposes the Percentage Interests held by Members who are the subject of an Optional Purchase Event or an assignor of a Membership Interest):

(i) Any amendment of the Articles or, in accordance with Section 14.16, this Agreement; and

(ii) A decision to compromise the obligation of a Member to make a Capital Contribution or return money or property paid or distributed in violation of the Act.

B. **Approval by Members Holding a Majority Interest.** Except as set forth in Section 4.9A or Section 5.3B, in all matters in which a vote, approval, or consent of the Members is required, a vote, consent, or approval of a Majority Interest (or, in instances in which there are defaulting or remaining members, non-defaulting or remaining Members who hold a majority of the Percentage Interests held by all non-defaulting or remaining Members) shall be sufficient to authorize or approve such act.

C. **Approval Standard.** Except as otherwise specifically provided in this Agreement, all votes, approvals or consents of the Members may be given or withheld, conditioned or delayed as the Members may determine in their sole discretion.

Ch 6 Forms

4.10 Member Meetings; Action by Written Consent. No annual or regular meetings of the Members are required. However, if such meetings are held, meeting notices and procedures shall be in accordance with Corporations Code Section 17104 or any applicable successor statue, except that Corporations Code Section 17104(h)(2) shall not apply to any meetings of the Members. Any action that may be taken by Members under this Agreement may be taken by a written consent executed by Members having not less than the aggregate Percentage Interests that would be necessary to take that action at a meeting at which all Members entitled to vote thereon were present and voted. Written consent shall be governed by Corporations Code Section 17104(i), except that notwithstanding anything to the contrary in Corporations Code Section 17104(i), action taken by written consent shall be effective as of the date set forth in the consent.

4.11 Certificate of Membership Interest.

A. Certificate. A Membership Interest may be represented by a certificate of membership. The exact contents of a certificate of membership may be determined by action of the Manager(s) but shall be issued substantially in conformity with the following requirements. The certificates of membership shall be respectively numbered serially, as they are issued, shall be impressed with the Company seal or a facsimile thereof, if any, and shall be signed by the Manager(s) of the Company. Each certificate of membership shall state the name of the Company, the fact that the Company is organized under the laws of the State of California as a limited liability company, the name of the person to whom the certificate is issued, the date of issue, and the Percentage Interest represented thereby. A statement of the designations, preferences, qualifications, limitations, restrictions, and special or relative rights of the Membership Interest, if any, shall be set forth in full or summarized on the face or back of the certificates which the Company shall issue, or in lieu thereof, the certificate may set forth that such a statement or summary will be furnished to any holder of a Membership Interest upon request without charge. Each certificate of membership shall be otherwise in such form as may be determined by the Manager(s).

B. Cancellation of Certificate. Except as herein provided with respect to lost, stolen, or destroyed certificates, no new certificates of membership shall be issued in lieu of previously issued certificates of membership until former certificates for a like number of Membership Interests shall have been surrendered and cancelled. All certificates of membership surrendered to the Company for transfer shall be cancelled.

C. Replacement of Lost, Stolen, or Destroyed Certificate. Any Member claiming that his or her certificate of membership is lost, stolen, or destroyed may make an affidavit or affirmation of that fact and request a new certificate. Upon the giving of a satisfactory indemnity to the Company as reasonably required by the Manager(s), a new certificate may be issued of the same tenor and representing the same Percentage Interest of membership as was represented by the certificate alleged to be lost, stolen, or destroyed.

ARTICLE V. MANAGEMENT AND CONTROL OF THE COMPANY

5.1 Management of the Company by Manager(s).

A. Exclusive Management by Manager(s). The business, property, and affairs of the Company shall be managed exclusively by the Manager(s). Except for situations in which the approval of the Members is expressly required by the Articles or this Agreement, the Manager(s) shall have full, complete, and exclusive authority, power, and discretion to manage and control the business, property and affairs of the Company, to make all decisions regarding those matters and to perform any and all other acts or activities customary or incident to the management of the Company's business, property, and affairs.

B. Agency Authority of Manager(s). Subject to Section 5.3B:

Any Manager, acting alone, is authorized to endorse checks, drafts, and other evidences of indebtedness made payable to the order of the Company, but only for the purpose of deposit into the Company's accounts. All checks, drafts, and other instruments obligating the Company to pay money in an amount of less than $_____ may be signed by any one Manager, acting alone. All checks, drafts, and other instruments obligating the Company to pay money in an amount of $_____ or more must be signed on behalf of the Company by any _____ [number] Manager(s) acting together. Any _____ [number] Manager(s), acting together, shall be authorized to sign contracts and obligations on behalf of the Company.

C. Meetings of Manager(s). Meetings of the Manager(s) may be called by any Manager. All meetings shall be held upon four (4) days notice by mail or forty-eight (48) hours notice (or upon such shorter notice period if necessary under the circumstances) delivered personally or by telephone, electronic mail, telegraph, or facsimile. A notice need not specify the purpose of any meeting. Notice of a meeting need not be given to any Manager who signs a waiver of notice or a consent to holding the meeting (which waiver or consent need not specify the purpose of the meeting) or an approval of the minutes thereof, whether before or after the meeting, or who attends the meeting without protesting, prior to its commencement, the lack of notice to such Manager. All such waivers, consents, and approvals shall be filed with the Company records or made a part of the minutes of the meeting. A majority of the Manager(s) present, whether or not a quorum is present, may adjourn any meeting to another time and place. If the meeting is adjourned for more than twenty-four (24) hours, notice of any adjournment shall be given prior to the time of the adjourned meeting to the Manager(s) who are not present at the time of the adjournment. Meetings of the Manager(s) may be held at any place within or without the State of California which has been designated in the notice of the meeting or at such place as may be approved by the Manager(s). Manager(s) may participate in a meeting through use of conference telephone, or similar communications equipment, so long as all Manager(s) participating in such meeting can hear one another. Participation in a meeting in such manner constitutes a presence in person at such meeting. A majority of the authorized number of Manager(s) constitutes a quorum of the Manager(s) for the transaction of business. Except to the extent that this Agreement expressly requires the approval of all Manager(s), every act or decision done or made by a majority of the Manager(s) present at a meeting duly held at which a quorum is present is the act of the Manager(s). A meeting at which a quorum is initially present may continue to transact business notwithstanding the withdrawal of Manager(s), if any action taken is approved by at least a majority of the required quorum for such meeting.

Any action required or permitted to be taken by the Manager(s) may be taken by the Manager(s) without a meeting, if a majority of the Manager(s) individually or collectively consent in writing to such action, unless the action requires the unanimous vote of the Manager(s), in which case all Manager(s) must consent in writing. Such action by written consent shall have the same force and effect as a majority vote or unanimous vote, as applicable, of such Manager(s).

The provisions of this Section 5.1C govern meetings of the Manager(s) if the Manager(s) elect, in their discretion, to hold meetings. However, nothing in this Section 5.1C or in this Agreement is intended to require that meetings of Manager(s) be held, it being the intent of the Members that meetings of Manager(s) are not required.

5.2 Election of Manager(s).

A. Number, Term, and Qualifications. The Company shall initially have _____ (___) Manager(s). The number of Manager(s) of the Company shall be fixed from time to time by the affirmative vote or written consent of a Majority Interest, provided that in no instance shall there be less than one Manager and provided further that if the number of Manager(s) is increased to more than one, the Articles shall be amended to so state, and if the number of Manager(s) is reduced from more than one to one, the Articles shall be amended to so state. Unless he or she resigns or is removed, each Manager shall hold office until a successor shall have been elected and qualified. Manager(s) shall be elected by the affirmative vote or written consent of Members holding a Majority Interest. A Manager need not be a

Member, an individual, a resident of the State of California, or a citizen of the United States.

B. Resignation. Any Manager may resign at any time by giving written notice to the Members and remaining Manager(s) without prejudice to the rights, if any, of the Company under any contract to which the Manager is a party. The resignation of any Manager shall take effect upon receipt of that notice or at such later time as shall be specified in the notice. Unless otherwise specified in the notice, the acceptance of the resignation shall not be necessary to make it effective. The resignation of a Manager who is also a Member shall not (i) affect the Manager's rights as a Member; (ii) constitute a withdrawal of a Member; or (iii) affect any rights a Manager or a Manager's Affiliate may have under any written agreement with the Company.

C. Removal. Any Manager may be removed at any time, with or without cause, by the affirmative vote of a Majority Interest at a meeting called expressly for that purpose, or by the written consent of a Majority Interest. Any removal shall be without prejudice to the rights, if any, of the Manager under any employment contract and, if the Manager is also a Member, shall not affect the Manager's rights as a Member or constitute a withdrawal of a Member. For purpose of this Section, "cause" shall mean fraud, gross negligence, willful misconduct, embezzlement, or a breach of such Manager's obligations under this Agreement or any employment contract with the Company.

D. Vacancies. Any vacancy occurring for any reason in the number of Manager(s) may be filled by the affirmative vote or written consent of a Majority Interest or by a majority of the remaining Manager(s).

5.3 Powers of Manager(s).

A. Powers of Manager(s). Without limiting the generality of Section 5.1, but subject to Section 5.3B and to the express limitations set forth elsewhere in this Agreement, the Manager(s) shall have all necessary powers to manage and carry out the purposes, business, property, and affairs of the Company, including, without limitation, the power to exercise on behalf and in the name of the Company all of the powers described in Corporations Code Section 17003, including, without limitation, the power to:

(i) Acquire, purchase, renovate, improve, alter, rebuild, demolish, replace, and own real property and any other property or assets that the Manager(s) determine is necessary or appropriate or in and to acquire options for the purchase of any such property;

(ii) Sell, exchange, lease, or otherwise dispose of the real property and other property and assets owned by the Company, or any part thereof, or any interest therein;

(iii) Borrow money from any party including the Manager(s) and their Affiliates, issue evidences of indebtedness in connection therewith, refinance, increase the amount of, modify, amend, or change the terms of, or extend the time for the payment of any indebtedness or obligation of the Company, and secure such indebtedness by mortgage, deed of trust, pledge, security interest, or other lien on Company assets;

(iv) Guarantee the payment of money or the performance of any contract or obligation of any Person;

(v) Sue on, defend, or compromise any and all claims or liabilities in favor of or against the Company; submit any or all such claims or liabilities to arbitration; and confess a judgment against the Company in connection with any litigation in which the Company is involved; and

(vi) Retain legal counsel, auditors, and other professionals in connection with the Company business and to pay therefor such remuneration as the Manager(s) may determine.

B. Limitations on Power of Manager(s). Notwithstanding any other provisions of this Agreement, if the Company has more than one Manager, no debt or liability of more than $_____ may be contracted on behalf of the Company except by the written consent of all Managers. In addition, the Manager(s) shall not have authority hereunder to cause the Company to engage in the following transactions without first obtaining the affirmative vote or written consent of a Majority Interest (or such greater Percentage Interests set forth below) of the Members:

(i) The sale, exchange, or other disposition of all, or substantially all, of the Company's assets occurring as part of a single transaction or plan, or in multiple transactions over a _____ (___) month period, except in the orderly liquidation and winding up of the business of the Company upon its duly authorized dissolution, shall require the affirmative vote or written consent of Members holding at least _____ percent (___%) in Percentage Interests;

(ii) The conversion of the Company into, or the merger of the Company with, another limited liability company or limited partnership shall require the affirmative vote or written consent of Members holding at least _____ percent (___%) in Percentage Interests provided in no event shall a Member be required to become a general partner in a merger with a limited partnership without his express written consent or unless the agreement of merger provides each Member with the dissenter's rights described in the Act;

(iii) The merger of the Company with, or conversion into, a corporation or a general partnership or other Person shall require the affirmative vote or written consent of all Members;

(iv) The establishment of different classes of Members;

(v) An alteration of the primary purpose or business of the Company as set forth in Section 2.7;

(vi) Any act which would make it impossible to carry on the ordinary business of the Company.

(vii) Any other transaction described in this Agreement as requiring the vote, consent, or approval of the Members.

5.4 Devotion of Time. The Manager(s) are not obligated to devote all of their time or business efforts to the affairs of the Company. The Manager(s) shall devote whatever time, effort, and skill they deem appropriate for the operation of the Company.

5.5 Competing Activities. The Manager(s) and their officers, directors, shareholders, partners, members, managers, agents, employees, and Affiliates may engage or invest in, independently or with others, any business activity of any type or description, including without limitation those that might be the same as or similar to the Company's business and that might be in direct or indirect competition with the Company. Neither the Company nor any Member shall have any right in or to such other ventures or activities or to the income or proceeds derived therefrom. The Manager(s) shall not be obligated to present any investment opportunity or prospective economic advantage to the Company, even if the opportunity is of the character that, if presented to the Company, could be taken by the Company. The Manager(s) shall have the right to hold any investment opportunity or prospective economic advantage for their own account or to recommend such opportunity to Persons other than the Company. The Members acknowledge that the Manager(s) and their Affiliates own and/or manage other businesses, including businesses that may compete with the Company and for the Manager(s)' time. The Members hereby waive any and all rights and claims which they may otherwise have against the Manager(s) and their officers, directors, shareholders, partners, members, managers, agents, employees, and Affiliates as a result of any of such activities.

5.6 Transactions Between the Company and the Manager(s). Notwithstanding that it may constitute a conflict of interest, the Manager(s) may, and may cause their Affiliates to, engage in any transaction, including, without limitation, the purchase, sale, lease, or exchange of any property or the rendering of any service, or the establishment of any salary, other compensation, or other terms of employment with the Company so long as such transaction is not expressly prohibited by this Agreement and so long as the terms and conditions of such transaction, on an overall basis, are fair and reasonable to the Company and are at least as

Ch 6 Forms

favorable to the Company as those terms and conditions that are generally available in similar transactions from Persons operating at arm's length and, in the case of services, from Persons capable of performing similar services.

A transaction between the Manager(s) and/or their Affiliates, on the one hand, and the Company, on the other hand, shall be conclusively determined to constitute a transaction on terms and conditions, on an overall basis, fair and reasonable to the Company and at least as favorable to the Company as those generally available in a similar transaction between parties operating at arm's length if a Majority Interest of the Members having no interest in such transaction (other than their interests as Members) affirmatively vote or consent in writing to approve the transaction. Notwithstanding the foregoing, the Manager(s) shall not have any obligation, in connection with any such transaction between the Company and the Manager(s) or an Affiliate of the Manager(s), to seek the consent of the Members.

5.7 Payments to Manager(s). Except as specified in this Agreement, no Manager or Affiliate of a Manager is entitled to remuneration for services rendered or goods provided to the Company. The Manager(s) and their Affiliates shall receive only the following payments:

A. Management Fee. The Company shall pay the Manager(s) a monthly fee for services in connection with the management of the Company in the amount of $_____. Such fee may be changed from time to time only by an affirmative vote of Members holding at least a Majority Interest, and no Manager shall be prevented from receiving any fee because the Manager is also a Member of the Company.

B. Services Performed by Manager(s) or Affiliates. The Company shall pay the Manager(s) or Affiliates of the Manager(s) for services rendered or goods provided to the Company to the extent that the Manager(s) are not required to render such services or goods themselves without charge to the Company, and to the extent that the fees paid to such Manager(s) or Affiliates do not exceed the fees that would be payable to an independent responsible third party that is willing to perform such services or provide such goods.

C. Expenses. The Company shall pay or reimburse the Manager(s) for all reasonable and necessary business expenses incurred or paid by the Manager(s) in connection with the Manager(s)' performance of services on the Company's behalf, upon presentation to the Company of invoices or other acceptable documentation substantiating such expenses. Additionally, the Company shall also pay or reimburse the Manager(s) or their Affiliates for organizational expenses (including, without limitation, legal and accounting fees and costs) incurred to form the Company and prepare and file the Articles and this Agreement.

5.9 Membership Interests of Manager(s). Except as otherwise provided in this Agreement, Membership Interests held by the Manager(s) as Members shall entitle each Manager to all the rights of a Member, including without limitation the economic, voting, information, and inspection rights of a Member.

5.10 Fiduciary Duties. The only fiduciary duties a Manager owes to the Company and the Members are the duty of loyalty and the duty of care set forth in subsections (i) and (ii) below:

(i) A Manager's duty of loyalty to the Company and the Members is limited to accounting to the Company and holding as trustee for the Company any property, profit, or benefit derived by the Manager in the conduct or winding up of the Company's business or derived from any use by the Manager of Company property;

(ii) A Manager's duty of care to the Company and the Members in the conduct and winding up of the Company's business is limited to refraining from engaging in grossly negligent or reckless conduct, intentional misconduct, or a knowing violation of law by the Manager.

5.11 Limitation of Liability.

A. Liability for Company Obligations. No Person who is a Manager or officer or both a Manager and an officer of the Company, shall be personally liable under any judgment of a court, or in any other manner, for any debt, obligation, or liability of the Company, whether that liability or obligation arises in contract, tort, or otherwise, solely by reason of being a Manager or officer, or both a Manager and an officer.

B. Liability of Manager Limited to Manager's Assets. Under no circumstances will any director, officer, shareholder, member, manager, partner, employee, agent, or Affiliate of any Manager have any personal responsibility for any liability or obligation of the Manager (whether on a theory of alter ego, piercing the corporate veil, or otherwise), and any recourse permitted under this Agreement or otherwise of the Members, any former Member or the Company against a Manager will be limited to the assets of the Manager as they may exist from time to time.

ARTICLE VI. ALLOCATIONS OF NET PROFIT AND NET LOSS

6.1 Allocations of Net Profit and Net Loss.

A. Net Loss. Net Loss shall be allocated to the Members in proportion to their Percentage Interests.

B. Net Profit. Net Profit shall be allocated to the Members in proportion to their Percentage Interests.

C. Reallocations. Notwithstanding anything to the contrary in Section 6.1A, Net

Loss allocations to a Member shall be made only to the extent that such loss allocations will not create a deficit Capital Account balance for that Member in excess of an amount, if any, equal to such Member's share of Company Minimum Gain. Any Net Loss not allocated to a Member because of the foregoing provision shall be allocated to the other Members (to the extent the other Members are not limited in respect of the allocation of losses under this Section 6.1C). Any loss reallocated under this Section 6.1C shall be taken into account in computing subsequent allocations of income and losses pursuant to this Article VI, so that the net amount of any item so allocated and the income and losses allocated to each Member pursuant to this Article VI, to the extent possible, shall be equal to the net amount that would have been allocated to each such Member pursuant to this Article VI if no reallocation of losses had occurred under this Section 6.1C.

6.2 Special Allocations. Notwithstanding Section 6.1:

A. Minimum Gain Chargeback. If there is a net decrease in Company Minimum Gain during any Fiscal Year, each Member shall be specially allocated items of Company income and gain for such Fiscal Year (and, if necessary, in subsequent fiscal years) in an amount equal to the portion of such Member's share of the net decrease in Company Minimum Gain that is allocable to the disposition of Company property subject to a Nonrecourse Liability, which share of such net decrease shall be determined in accordance with Regulations Section 1.704-2(g)(2). Allocations pursuant to this Section 6.2A shall be made in proportion to the amounts required to be allocated to each Member under this Section 6.2A. The items to be so allocated shall be determined in accordance with Regulations Section 1.704-2(f). This Section 6.2A is intended to comply with the minimum gain chargeback requirement contained in Regulations Section 1.704-2(f) and shall be interpreted consistently therewith.

B. Chargeback of Minimum Gain Attributable to Member Nonrecourse Debt. If there is a net decrease in Company Minimum Gain attributable to a Member Nonrecourse Debt, during any Fiscal Year, each member who has a share of the Company Minimum Gain attributable to such Member Nonrecourse Debt (which share shall be determined in accordance with Regulations Section 1.704-2(i)(5)) shall be specially allocated items of Company income and gain for such Fiscal Year (and, if necessary, in subsequent Fiscal Years) in an amount equal to that portion of such Member's share of the net decrease in Company Minimum Gain attributable to such Member Nonrecourse Debt that is allocable to the disposition of Company property subject to such Member Nonrecourse Debt (which share of such net decrease shall be determined in accordance with Regulations Section 1.704-2(i)(5)). Allocations pursuant to this Section 6.2B shall be made in proportion to the amounts required to be allocated to each Member under this Section 6.2B. The items to be so allocated shall be determined in accordance with

Regulations Section 1.704-2(i)(4). This Section 6.2B is intended to comply with the minimum gain chargeback requirement contained in Regulations Section 1.704-2(i)(4) and shall be interpreted consistently therewith.

C. Nonrecourse Deductions. Any nonrecourse deductions (as defined in Regulations Section 1.704-2(b)(1)) for any Fiscal Year or other period shall be specially allocated to the Members in proportion to their Percentage Interests.

D. Member Nonrecourse Deductions. Those items of Company loss, deduction, or Code Section 705(a)(2)(B) expenditures which are attributable to Member Nonrecourse Debt for any Fiscal Year or other period shall be specially allocated to the Member who bears the economic risk of loss with respect to the Member Nonrecourse Debt to which such items are attributable in accordance with Regulations Section 1.704-2(i).

E. Qualified Income Offset. If a Member unexpectedly receives any adjustments, allocations, or distributions described in Regulations Section 1.704-1(b)(2)(ii)(d)(4), (5) or (6), or any other event creates a deficit balance in such Member's Capital Account in excess of such Member's share of Company Minimum Gain, items of Company income and gain shall be specially allocated to such Member in an amount and manner sufficient to eliminate such excess deficit balance as quickly as possible. Any special allocations of items of income and gain pursuant to this Section 6.2E shall be taken into account in computing subsequent allocations of income and gain pursuant to this Article VI so that the net amount of any item so allocated and the income, gain, and losses allocated to each Member pursuant to this Article VI to the extent possible, shall be equal to the net amount that would have been allocated to each such Member pursuant to the provisions of this Section 6.2E if such unexpected adjustments, allocations, or distributions had not occurred.

6.3 Section 754 Adjustments. Regulations Section 1.704-1(b)(2)(iv)(m) may require the Company to adjust the Members' Capital Accounts if the Company adjusts the tax bases of its assets pursuant to Code Sections 734(b) or 743(b) following an election pursuant to Code Section 754. Any such adjustment shall be treated as an item of gain (if the adjustment increases the basis of the asset) or loss (if the adjustment decreases such basis). Such gain or loss shall be specially allocated among the Members in a manner consistent with the manner in which their Capital Accounts are required to be adjusted. Such gain or loss shall also be included in any calculation of the aggregate Net Profit or Net Loss allocated to a Member for the purpose of determining the amount of any subsequent allocation that Member is to receive pursuant to this Agreement.

6.4 Member Services; Interest Payments. Notwithstanding any other provision of this Agreement, if a final determination, assessment, or adjudication is made or conceded to on behalf of the Company that any amount paid to a Member or an

Ch 6 Forms

Affiliate of a Member for services authorized to be rendered by such Person, or interest authorized to be paid to such Person, under this Agreement is not deductible for income tax purposes during any Fiscal Year of the Company, the Company shall specially allocate items of income and gain, for that Fiscal Year or subsequent Fiscal Years as necessary, to the Member in the amount of the disallowed payment. Notwithstanding any other provision of this Agreement, such items of income and gain shall not be included in any calculation of the aggregate amount of Net Profit and Net Loss allocated to such Member.

6.5 Curative Allocations. The allocations set forth in this Agreement are intended to comply with certain requirements of Regulation Section 1.704-1(b). Because it is not possible to foresee every possible future event during the term of the Company, the Allocations might not be consistent with the manner in which the Members intend to share Company distributions in all situations. Accordingly, the Manager(s) may allocate income, gain, loss, and deductions among the Members in a manner to prevent the allocations from distorting the manner in which Company distributions are intended to be shared among the Members. The Manager(s) shall have the discretion to accomplish this result in any reasonable manner.

6.6 Other Allocation Rules.

A. Unless otherwise herein expressly provided to the contrary, all allocations to the Members pursuant to this Article VI shall be divided among the Members in proportion to their respective Percentage Interests.

B. For purposes of determining Net Profit, Net Loss, or any other items allocable to any period, Net Profit, Net Loss, and any such other items shall be determined on a daily, monthly, or other basis, as determined by the Tax Matters Partner using any permissible method under Section 706 of the Code and the Treasury Regulations thereunder.

C. Solely for purposes of determining a Member's proportionate share of the "excess nonrecourse liabilities" of the Company within the meaning of Section 1.752-3(a)(3) of the Regulations, the Members' interests in Net Profit shall be in accordance with their respective Percentage Interests.

D. Notwithstanding any other provision in this Article VI, in accordance with Code Section 704(c) and the Regulations promulgated thereunder, income, gain, loss, and deduction with respect to any property contributed to the capital of the Company shall, solely for tax purposes, be allocated among the Members so as to take account of any variation between the adjusted basis of such property to the Company for federal income tax purposes and its fair market value on the date of contribution. Allocations pursuant to this Section 6.6 are solely for purposes of federal, state, and local taxes. As such, they shall not affect or in any way be taken into account in computing a Member's Capital Account or share of profits, losses, or other items of distributions pursuant to any provision of this Agreement.

6.7 Allocation of Net Profits and Losses and Distributions in Respect of a Transferred Interest. If any Economic Interest is transferred, or is increased or decreased by reason of the admission of a new Member or otherwise, during any Fiscal Year of the Company, Net Profit or Net Loss for such Fiscal Year shall be assigned pro rata to each day in the particular period of such Fiscal Year to which such item is attributable (i.e., the day on or during which it is accrued or otherwise incurred) and the amount of each such item so assigned to any such day shall be allocated to the Member or Assignee based upon his or her respective Economic Interest at the close of such day.

However, for the purpose of accounting convenience and simplicity, the Company shall treat a transfer of, or an increase or decrease in, an Economic Interest which occurs at any time during a semi-monthly period (commencing with the semi-monthly period including the date hereof) as having been consummated on the last day of such semi-monthly period, regardless of when during such semi-monthly period such transfer, increase, or decrease actually occurs (i.e., sales and dispositions made during the first fifteen (15) days of any month will be deemed to have been made on the 15th day of the month).

Notwithstanding any provision above to the contrary, gain or loss of the Company realized in connection with a sale or other disposition of any of the assets of the Company shall be allocated solely to the parties owning Economic Interests as of the date such sale or other disposition occurs.

6.8 Obligations of Members to Report Allocations. The Members are aware of the income tax consequences of the allocations made by this Article VI and hereby agree to be bound by the provisions of this Article VI in reporting their shares of Company income and loss for income tax purposes.

ARTICLE VII. INTERIM DISTRIBUTIONS

7.1 Minimum Distribution to Pay Tax Liabilities. The Company shall make minimum annual cash distributions to each Member in an amount of cash equal to at least 40% of the net profit allocated to that Member with respect to each tax year of the Company. The foregoing percentage is based on the current highest marginal income tax rates under federal and California law, after taking into account the deductibility of California income taxes from federal taxable income. Such percentage shall be readjusted to account for any change in the tax laws that would affect such percentage.

Ch 6 Forms

7.2 Discretionary Distributions. Subject to applicable law and any limitations contained elsewhere in this Agreement, the Manager(s) may elect from time to time to distribute Distributable Cash to the Members, which distributions shall be in proportion to their Percentage Interests. All such distributions shall be made only to the Persons who, according to the books and records of the Company, are the holders of record of the Economic Interests on the actual date of distribution. Neither the Company nor any Manager shall incur any liability for making distributions in accordance with this Section 7.2.

7.3 Form of Distribution. A Member, regardless of the nature of the Member's Capital Contribution, has no right to demand and receive any distribution from the Company in any form other than money. Except as provided in Section 11.4, no Member may be compelled to accept from the Company (a) a distribution of any asset in kind in lieu of a proportionate distribution of money being made to other Members, or (b) a distribution of any asset in kind.

7.4 Restriction on Distribution.

A. No distribution shall be made if, after giving effect to the distribution:

(i) The Company would not be able to pay its debts as they become due in the usual course of business; or

(ii) The Company's total assets would be less than the sum of its total liabilities plus, unless this Agreement provides otherwise, the amount that would be needed, if the Company were to be dissolved at the time of the distribution, to satisfy the preferential rights of other Members, if any, upon dissolution that are superior to the rights of the Member receiving the distribution.

B. The Manager(s) may base a determination that a distribution is not prohibited on any of the following:

(i) Financial statements prepared on the basis of accounting practices and principles that are reasonable in the circumstances;

(ii) A fair valuation; or

(iii) Any other method that is reasonable in the circumstances.

Except as provided in Corporations Code Section 17254(e), the effect of a distribution is measured as of the date the distribution is authorized if the payment occurs within 120 days after the date of authorization, or the date payment is made if it occurs more than 120 days of the date of authorization.

C. A Member or Manager who votes for a distribution in violation of this Agreement or the Act is personally liable to the Company for the amount of the distribution that exceeds what could have been distributed without violating this

Agreement or the Act if it is established that the Member or Manager did not act in compliance with Section 7.4 or Section 11.4. Any Member or Manager who is so liable shall be entitled to compel contribution from (i) each other Member or Manager who also is so liable; and (ii) each Member for the amount the Member received with knowledge of facts indicating that the distribution was made in violation of this Agreement or the Act.

7.5 Return of Distributions. Members and Assignees who receive distributions made in violation of the Act or this Agreement shall return such distributions to the Company. Except for those distributions made in violation of the Act or this Agreement, no Member or Assignee shall be obligated to return any distribution to the Company or pay the amount of any distribution for the account of the Company or to any creditor of the Company. The amount of any distribution returned to the Company by a Member or Assignee or paid by a Member or Assignee for the account of the Company or to a creditor of the Company shall be added to the account or accounts from which it was subtracted when it was distributed to the Member or Assignee.

7.6 Tax Withholding. If any federal, foreign, state, or local jurisdiction requires the Company to withhold taxes or other amounts with respect to any Member's allocable share of Net Profits, taxable income or any portion thereof, or with respect to distributions, the Company shall withhold from distributions or other amounts then due to such Member (or shall pay to the relevant taxing authority with respect to amounts allocable to such Member) an amount necessary to satisfy the withholding responsibility. In such a case, the Member for whom the Company has paid the withholding tax shall be deemed to have received the withheld distribution or other amount so paid, and to have paid the withholding tax directly.

If it is anticipated that at the due date of the Company's withholding obligation the Member's share of cash distributions or other amounts due is less than the amount of the withholding obligation, the Member to which the withholding obligation applies shall have the option to pay to the Company the amount of such shortfall. In the event a Member fails to make such payment and the Company nevertheless pays the full amount to be withheld, the amount paid by the Company shall be deemed a nonrecourse loan from the Company to such Member bearing interest at the lower of the Prime Rate or the maximum rate permitted by law, and the Company shall apply all distributions or payments that would otherwise be made to such Member toward payment of the loan and interest, which payments or distributions shall be applied first to interest and then to principal until the loan is repaid in full.

Each Member agrees to cooperate fully with the Company's efforts to comply with the Company's tax withholding and information reporting obligations and agrees to provide the Company with such information as the Company may reasonably request from time to time in connection with such obligations.

ARTICLE VIII. TRANSFER OF INTERESTS

8.1 Restrictions on Transfer. No Member shall Transfer all or any part of that Member's Membership Interest except with the prior written consent of the Manager(s), which consent may be given or withheld, conditioned or delayed (as allowed by this Agreement or the Act), as the Manager(s) may determine in their sole discretion. Transfers of Membership Interests in violation of this Article VIII shall be effective only to the extent set forth in Section 8.7. After the consummation of any Transfer of any part of a Membership Interest, the Membership Interest so Transferred shall continue to be subject to the terms and provisions of this Agreement and any further Transfers shall be required to comply with all the terms and provisions of this Agreement.

8.2 Further Restrictions on Transfer of Interests. In addition to other restrictions found in this Agreement, no Member shall Transfer all or any part of that Member's Membership Interest: (i) without compliance with applicable securities laws; (ii) if the Transfer would cause the Company's tax termination within the meaning of Code Section 708(b)(1)(B); or (iii) if the Transfer would cause the Company to be treated as a corporation pursuant to Code Section 7704 or Regulations Section 1.7704-1.

8.3 Substitution of Members. An Assignee of a Membership Interest shall have the right to become a substitute Member only if (i) the requirements of Sections 8.1 and 8.2 are met; (ii) the Manager(s) have consented to such substitution in its sole and absolute discretion; (iii) the Assignee executes an instrument satisfactory to the Manager(s) accepting and adopting the terms and provisions of this Agreement; and (iv) the Assignee pays any reasonable expenses in connection with such Assignee's admission as a new Member. The admission of an Assignee as a substitute Member shall not result in the release of the Member who assigned the Membership Interest from any liability that such Member may have to the Company.

8.4 Permitted Transfers. Subject to compliance with Section 8.2, a Member may Transfer that Member's Membership Interest as follows (each, a "Permitted Transfer"):

(A) to any Affiliate of the Member so long as that Member remains in voting control of the Affiliate (and at such time as the Member is no longer in voting control of such Affiliate, a Transfer shall be deemed to have occurred); or

(B) by inter vivos gift or by testamentary Transfer to any Family Member; it being agreed that, in executing this Agreement, the Manager(s) have consented to such Transfers.

8.5 Effective Date of Transfers. Any Transfer of all or any portion of an Economic Interest which complies with this Article VIII shall be effective as of the date provided in Section 6.7 following the date upon which the requirements of Sections 8.1, 8.2, and 8.3 (collectively, "Transfer Requirements") have been met. The Company shall provide the Members with written notice of such Transfer as promptly as possible after the Transfer Requirements have been met. Any transferee of a Membership Interest shall take subject to the restrictions on Transfer imposed by this Agreement.

8.6 Rights of Legal Representatives. If a Member who is an individual dies or is adjudged by a court of competent jurisdiction to be incompetent to manage the Member's person or property, the Member's executor, administrator, guardian, conservator, or other legal representative may exercise all of the Member's rights for the purpose of settling the Member's estate or administering the Member's property, including any power the Member has under the Articles or this Agreement to give an assignee the right to become a Member. If a Member is a corporation, trust, or other entity and is dissolved or terminated, the powers of that Member may be exercised by his or her legal representative or successor.

8.7 No Effect to Transfers in Violation of Agreement. Upon any Transfer of a Membership Interest in violation of this Article VIII, the transferee shall have no right to vote or participate in the management of the business, property, and affairs of the Company or to exercise any rights of a Member. Such transferee shall only be entitled to become an Assignee and thereafter shall only receive the share of one or more of the Company's Net Profits, Net Losses, and distributions of the Company's assets to which the transferor of such Economic Interest would otherwise be entitled. Notwithstanding the immediately preceding sentences, if, in the determination of the Company's legal counsel, a Transfer in violation of this Article VIII would cause the Company to (a) be treated as a corporation pursuant to Code Section 7704 or Regulations Section 1.7704-1, or (b) be terminated for tax purposes under IRC Section 708(b)(1)(B), the Transfer shall be null and void and the purported transferee shall not become either a Member or an Assignee.

Except as otherwise provided in Section 8.4, on and contemporaneously with any Transfer of a Member's Economic Interest which does not at the same time Transfer the balance of the rights associated with the Membership Interest Transferred by the Member (including, without limitation, the rights of the Member to vote or participate in the management of the business, property and affairs of the Company), the Company shall purchase from the Member, and the Member shall sell to Company for a purchase price of $100, all remaining rights and interests retained by the Member (including voting and inspection rights) that immediately before the Transfer were associated with the Transferred Economic Interest. Such purchase and sale shall not, however, result in the release of the

Member from any liability to the Company as a Member.

Each Member acknowledges and agrees that the right of the Company to purchase such remaining rights and interests from a Member who Transfers a Membership Interest in violation of this Article VIII is not unreasonable under the circumstances existing as of the date hereof.

8.8 Right of First Negotiation. The Company and the other Members shall have a right of first offer on any Membership Interest that a Member desires to Transfer, other than a Transfer pursuant to Section 8.4. If any Member desires to Transfer all or any part of his or her Membership Interest other than pursuant to Section 8.4, such Member shall notify the Company and the other Members in writing of such desire and, for a period of thirty (30) days thereafter, the Members and the Company shall negotiate with respect to the purchase of such Member's Membership Interest. During such period, the Member desiring to Transfer his or her Membership Interest may not solicit a transferee for such Membership Interest and may not continue any pending negotiations for the sale of the Membership Interest with third parties other than the Company.

8.9 Right of First Refusal. If the period described in Section 8.8 expires without an agreement being reached as to the purchase of the Membership Interest referred to therein, the Member desiring to transfer his or her Membership Interest may solicit transferees. In such event, each time a Member proposes to transfer all or any part of his or her Membership Interest (or as required by operation of law or other involuntary transfer to do so), other than pursuant to Section 8.4, such Member shall first offer such Membership Interest to the Company and the non-transferring Members in accordance with the following provisions:

A. Notice of Proposed Transfer. Such Member shall deliver a written notice ("Option Notice") to the Company and the other Members stating (i) such Member's bona fide intention to transfer such Membership Interest; (ii) the Membership Interest to be transferred; (iii) the purchase price and terms of payment for which the Member proposes to transfer such Membership Interest; (iv) the nature of the proposed transfer (e.g., sale or pledge); and (iv) the name and address of the proposed transferee.

B. Company Option. Within thirty (30) days after receipt of the Option Notice, the Company shall have the right, but not the obligation, to elect to purchase all or any part of the Membership Interest upon the price and terms of payment designated in the Option Notice. If the Option Notice provides for the payment of non-cash consideration, the Company may elect to pay the consideration in cash equal to the good faith estimate of the present fair market value of the non-cash consideration offered as determined by the Manager(s). If the Company exercises such right within such thirty (30)-day period, the Manager(s) shall give written notice of that fact to the transferring and non-transferring Members.

C. Members' Option. If the Company fails to elect to purchase the entire Membership Interest proposed to be transferred within the thirty (30)-day period described in Section 8.9B, the non-transferring Members shall have the right, but not the obligation, to elect to purchase any remaining share of such Membership Interest upon the same the price and terms of payment designated in the Option Notice. If the Option Notice provides for the payment of non-cash consideration, such purchasing Members each may elect to pay the consideration in cash equal to the good faith estimate of the present fair market value of the non-cash consideration offered as determined by the Manager(s). Within sixty (60) days after receipt of the Option Notice, each non-transferring Member shall notify the Manager(s) in writing of his or her desire to purchase a portion of the Membership Interest proposed to be so transferred. The failure of any Member to submit a notice within the applicable period shall constitute an election on the part of that Member not to purchase any of the Membership Interest which may be so transferred. Each Member so electing to purchase shall be entitled to purchase a portion of such Membership Interest in the same proportion that the Percentage Interest of such Member bears to the aggregate of the Percentage Interests of all of the Members electing to so purchase the Membership Interest being transferred. In the event any Member elects to purchase none or less than all of his or her pro rata share of such Membership Interest, then the other Members can elect to purchase more than their pro rata share.

D. Closing. If the Company and the other Members elect to purchase or obtain any or all of the Membership Interest designated in the Option Notice, then the closing of such purchase shall occur within ninety (90) days after the Company's receipt of the Option Notice. The Transferring Member, the Company, and/or the other Members shall execute such documents and instruments and make such deliveries as may be reasonably required to consummate such purchase.

E. Failure to Exercise Options. If the Company and the other Members elect not to purchase or obtain, or default in their obligations following an election to purchase or obtain, all of the Membership Interest designated in the Option Notice, then the transferring Member may transfer the portion of the Membership Interest described in the Option Notice not so purchased, to the proposed transferee providing such transfer (i) is completed within thirty (30) days after the expiration of the Company's and the other Members' right to purchase such Membership Interest; (ii) is made on terms no less favorable to the transferring Member than as designated in the Option Notice; and (iii) complies with Sections 8.1, 8.2, and 8.3; it being acknowledged by the Members that compliance with Sections 8.8 and 8.9A-D does not modify any of the transfer restrictions in this Article VIII or otherwise entitle a Member to transfer his or her Membership

Ch 6 Forms

Interest other than in the manner prescribed by this Article VIII. If such Membership Interest is not so transferred, the transferring Member must give notice in accordance with this Section prior to any other or subsequent transfer of such Membership Interest.

8.10 Transfers and Assignments of Manager(s)' Interests. Notwithstanding Section 8.9, upon the transfer of the Membership Interest of a Manager, the remaining Manager(s) shall have the first right, pro rata as to their Membership Interests as Manager(s), to elect to exercise the right of first refusal set forth in Section 8.9 for a period of ten (10) days after receipt of the Option Notice described in Section 8.9A. Such exercise shall be made in writing to the Company. If any Manager fails to exercise his or her rights under this Section 8.10, the other remaining Manager(s) may elect to purchase the balance pro rata. If the remaining Manager(s) elect to purchase less than all of the transferor's Membership Interest, the portion of such Membership Interest not elected to be purchased shall be subject to purchase and sale in accordance with Section 8.9.

ARTICLE IX. OPTIONAL PURCHASE EVENTS AND TERMINATION OF MEMBERSHIP INTEREST

9.1 Optional Purchase Event Defined. As used in this Article IX, "Optional Purchase Event" means, with respect to any Member, the occurrence of any of the following events:

A. The death, withdrawal, resignation, retirement, insanity, bankruptcy, or dissolution of a Member;

B. The failure of a Member to make the Member's Capital Contribution pursuant to the provisions of Article III of this Agreement;

C. The occurrence of any other event that is, or that would cause, a Transfer in contravention of this Agreement; or

D. The filing by a Member of an action seeking a decree of judicial dissolution pursuant to Code Section 17351.

9.2 Optional Purchase Event. Upon the occurrence of an Optional Purchase Event that is not a Permitted Transfer, the Company and/or the remaining Members ("Remaining Members") shall have the option to purchase, and if such option is exercised, the Member whose actions or conduct resulted in the Optional Purchase Event ("Former Member") or such Former Member's legal representative shall sell, the Former Member's Membership Interest ("Former Member's Interest") as provided in this Article IX. Each Former Member agrees to give prompt notice of the Optional Purchase Event to the Manager(s).

9.3 Purchase Price. The purchase price for the Former Member's Interest shall be the fair market value of the Former Member's Interest as determined by (i) mutual agreement between the Former Member (or the Former Member's legal representative) and the Manager(s), or (ii) in the absence of such agreement, by an independent appraiser jointly selected by the Former Member (or the Former Member's legal representative) and the Manager(s).

If the Former Member (or the Former Member's legal representative) and the Manager(s) are unable to agree on the selection of an appraiser within thirty (30) days after the Optional Purchase Event, each shall select an independent appraiser within twenty (20) days after expiration of the thirty (30)-day period. The two appraisers so selected shall each independently appraise the Former Members' Interest and, if the difference in the two appraisals does not exceed five percent (5%) of the lower of the two appraisals, the fair market value shall be conclusively deemed to equal the average of the two appraisals. The determination of such appraisers shall be binding on the parties. If either party fails to select an independent appraiser within the time required by this Section 9.3, the fair market value of the Former Member's Interest shall be conclusively deemed to equal the appraisal of the independent appraiser timely selected by the other.

If the difference between the two appraisals referred to above exceeds five percent (5%) of the lower of the two appraisals, the two appraisers selected shall select a third appraiser who shall also independently appraise the Former Member's Interest. In such case the fair market value of the Former Member's Interest shall be the average of the two closest appraisals. The determination of such appraisers shall be binding on the parties. The Company and the Former Member shall each pay one half (1/2) of the cost of the third appraisal.

In determining the fair market value, the appraisers appointed under this Agreement shall consider all opinions and relevant evidence submitted to them by the parties, or otherwise obtained by them, and shall set forth their determination in writing together with their opinions and the considerations on which the opinions are based, with a signed counterpart to be delivered to each party, within sixty (60) days after commencing the appraisal.

Notwithstanding the foregoing, if the Optional Purchase Event results from a breach of this Agreement by the Former Member, the purchase price shall be reduced by an amount equal to the damages suffered by the Company or the Remaining Members as a result of such breach.

9.4 Notice of Intent to Purchase. Within fifteen (15) days after the purchase price of the Former Member's Interest determined in accordance with Section 9.3, the Manager shall notify each Remaining Member of such price. Within thirty (30) days after the Manager(s) have notified the Remaining Members as to the purchase price of the Former Member's Interest determined in accordance with

Section 9.3, each Remaining Member shall notify the Manager(s) in writing of his or her desire to purchase a portion of the Former Member's Interest. The failure of any Remaining Member to submit a notice within the applicable period shall constitute an election on the part of the Member not to purchase any of the Former Member's Interest. Each Remaining Member so electing to purchase shall be entitled to purchase a portion of the Former Member's Interest in the same proportion that the Percentage Interest of the Remaining Member bears to the aggregate of the Percentage Interests of all of the Remaining Members electing to purchase the Former Member's Interest.

9.5 Election to Purchase Less than All of the Former Member's Interest. If any Remaining Member elects to purchase none or less than all of his or her pro rata share of the Former Member's Interest, then the Remaining Members may elect to purchase more than their pro rata share. If the Remaining Members fail to purchase the entire Interest of the Former Member, the Company may purchase any remaining share of the Former Member's Interest. If the Remaining Members and the Company do not elect to purchase all of the Former Member's Interest, such unpurchased Interest shall be that of an Economic Interest only.

9.6 Payment of Purchase Price. The purchase price shall be paid by the Company or the Remaining Members, as the case may be, by either of the following methods, each of which may be selected separately by the Company or the Remaining Members:

A. At the Closing, the Company or the Remaining Members shall pay in cash the total purchase price for the Former Member's Interest; or

B. At the Closing, the Company or the Remaining Members shall pay one-fifth (1/5) of the purchase price and the balance of the purchase price shall be paid in four equal annual principal installments, plus accrued interest, and be payable each year on the anniversary date of the closing. The unpaid principal balance shall accrue interest at the current applicable federal rate as provided in the Code for the month in which the initial payment is made, but the Company and the Remaining Members shall have the right to prepay in full or in part at any time without penalty. The obligation of each purchasing Remaining Member, and the Company, as applicable, to pay its portion of the balance due shall be evidenced by a separate promissory note executed by the respective purchasing Remaining Member or the Company, as applicable. Each such promissory note shall be in an original principal amount equal to the portion owed by the respective purchasing Remaining Member or the Company, as applicable. The promissory note executed by each purchasing Remaining Member shall be secured by a pledge of that portion of the Former Member's Interest purchased by such Remaining Member.

9.7 Closing of Purchase of Former Member's Interest. Unless court approval is required, the closing ("Closing") for the sale of a Former Member's Interest pursuant to this Article IX shall be held at 10:00 a.m. at the principal office of Company no later than sixty (60) days after the determination of the purchase price, except that if the Closing date falls on a Saturday, Sunday, or California legal holiday, then the Closing shall be held on the next succeeding business day. If court approval is required, (i) the Closing of the sale of a Former Member's Interest shall occur not later than five (5) business days after entry of the order approving such sale; (ii) the Former Member or such Former Member's legal representative shall file the application seeking court approval within thirty (30) days following the determination of the purchase price; and (iii) the parties to the court proceeding shall make every effort to obtain the court's approval in an expeditious manner. At the Closing, the Former Member or such Former Member's legal representative shall deliver to the Company and/or the Remaining Members an instrument of Transfer (containing warranties of title and no encumbrances) conveying the Former Member's Interest. The Former Member or such Former Member's legal representative, the Company and the Remaining Members shall do all things and execute and deliver all papers as may be necessary to consummate fully such sale and purchase in accordance with the terms and provisions of this Agreement.

9.8 Purchase Terms Varied by Agreement. Nothing contained herein is intended to prohibit Members from agreeing upon other terms and conditions for the purchase by the Company or any Member of the Membership Interest of any Member in the Company desiring to retire, withdraw or resign, in whole or in part, as a Member.

9.9 Noncompetition.

A. Prohibited Activities. If any Member Transfers his or her Membership Interest pursuant to either Article VIII or IX, such Member agrees that, for a period of _____ (__) years from the date of such transfer, he or she shall not:

(i) Enter, directly or indirectly, into the employment of, or render, directly or indirectly, any services (whether as a director, officer, agent, representative, independent contractor, consultant, or advisor or any other similar relationship or capacity) to any Person (such person is referred to as a "Competitor") which provides those services, or which otherwise competes with, or carries on a similar business to any business now carried on by the Company in the following counties (and all cities located therein) in the State of California: _____ (the "Territory"), whether such business is carried on by the Company or by a successor or assign in any of these counties;

(ii) Engage, directly or indirectly, in any such business in the Territory as a Competitor;

Ch 6
Forms

(iii) Become interested, directly or indirectly, in any such Competitor as an individual, proprietor, franchisee, partner, joint venturer, shareholder, principal, member, investor, trustee, or any other similar other relationship or capacity;

(iv) Directly or indirectly, by sole action or in concert with others, solicit, induce, or influence, or seek to solicit, induce, or influence, any Person who is engaged by the Company as an employee, agent, independent contractor, or otherwise, to leave the employ of the Company or any successor or assign;

(v) Directly or indirectly, by sole action or in concert with others, solicit, induce, or influence, or seek to solicit, induce, or influence, any customer or client of the Company during the twelve (12) calendar months immediately preceding the date of transfer of the Membership Interest; and such Member also agrees that, in such event, he or she shall not use, divulge, furnish, or make accessible to any Person (other than at the written request of the Company) any secret, confidential, or proprietary knowledge or information of the Company including, but not limited to, any trade secrets, financial information, customer or client lists, marketing methods, data, properties, specifications, personnel, organization, or internal affairs of the Company.

B. Separate Covenants. The agreements contained in Section 9.9A shall be construed as a series of separate covenants, one for each activity of the Member, capacity in which the Member is prohibited from competing and each part of the Territory in which the Company is carrying on in such activity.

C. Intent; Severability. The Members intend that Section 9.9A satisfy the terms of, and be enforceable in accordance with California Business and Professions Code Section 16602.5, which authorizes any member who sells his or her interest in a limited liability company to enter into an agreement with the buyer of such interest to refrain from carrying on a similar business within the specified geographic area in which a limited liability company carries on a like business therein. Each Member recognizes that the territorial and time restrictions set forth herein are reasonable, not burdensome and are properly required by law for the adequate protection of the Company and its Members. If such territorial or time restrictions or any other provision contained herein shall be deemed to be illegal, unenforceable, or unreasonable by a court of competent jurisdiction, each Member agrees and submits to the reduction of such territorial or time restriction or other provision to such an area or period as such court shall deem reasonable.

D. Injunctive Relief. Each Member acknowledges that (i) the covenants and the restrictions contained in Section 9.9A are a material factor to such Member's execution of this Agreement and are necessary and required for the protection of the Company; (ii) such covenants relate to matters that are of a special, unique and extraordinary character that gives each of such covenants a special, unique and extraordinary value; and (iii) a breach of any of such covenants will result in irreparable harm and damages to the Company in an amount difficult to ascertain and which cannot be adequately compensated by a monetary award. Accordingly, in addition to any of the relief to which the Company may be entitled at law or in equity, the Company shall be entitled to temporary and/or permanent injunctive relief from any breach or threatened breach by a Member of the provisions of Section 9.9A without proof of actual damages that have been or may be caused to the Company by such breach or threatened breach.

ARTICLE X. ACCOUNTING, RECORDS, AND REPORTS

10.1 Books and Records. The accounting records of the Company shall be kept, and the financial position and the results of its operations recorded, in accordance with the accounting methods followed for federal income tax purposes. The books and records of the Company shall reflect all the Company transactions and shall be appropriate and adequate for the Company's business. The Company shall maintain at its principal office in California all of the following:

A. A current list of the full name and last known business or residence address of each Member and Assignee set forth in alphabetical order, together with the Capital Contributions, Capital Account, and Percentage Interest of each Member and Assignee;

B. A current list of the full name and business or residence address of each Manager;

C. A copy of the Articles and any and all amendments thereto together with executed copies of any powers of attorney pursuant to which the Articles or any amendments thereto have been executed;

D. Copies of the Company's federal, state, and local income tax or information returns and reports, if any, for the six (6) most recent taxable years;

E. A copy of this Agreement and any and all amendments thereto together with executed copies of any powers of attorney pursuant to which this Agreement or any amendments thereto have been executed;

F. Copies of the financial statements of the Company, if any, for the six (6) most recent Fiscal Years; and

G. The Company's books and records as they relate to the internal affairs of the Company for at least the current and past four (4) Fiscal Years.

10.2 Delivery to Members and Inspection.

A. Upon the request of any Member or Assignee for purposes reasonably related to the interest of that Person as a Member or Assignee, the Manager(s) shall promptly deliver to the requesting Member or Assignee, at the expense of the Company, a copy of the information required to be maintained under Sections 10.1A, B, and D, and a copy of this Agreement.

B. Each Member, Manager, and Assignee has the right, upon reasonable request for purposes reasonably related to the interest of the Person as Member, Manager, or Assignee, to:

(i) inspect and copy during normal business hours any of the Company records described in Sections 10.1A through G; and

(ii) obtain from the Manager(s), promptly after their becoming available, a copy of the Company's federal, state, and local income tax or information returns for each Fiscal Year.

(iii) Members representing at least five percent (5%) of the Percentage Interests, or three or more Members, may make a written request to the Manager(s) for an income statement of the Company for the initial three-month, six-month, or nine-month period of the current Fiscal Year ended more than thirty (30) days prior to the date of the request, and a balance sheet of the Company as of the end of that period. Such statement shall be accompanied by the report thereon, if any, of the independent accountants engaged by the Company or, if there is no report, the certificate of a Manager that the statement was prepared without audit from the books and records of the Company. If so requested, the statement shall be delivered or mailed to the Members within thirty (30) days thereafter.

C. Any request, inspection, or copying by a Member or Assignee under this Section 10.2 may be made by that Person or that Person's agent or attorney.

D. The Manager(s) shall promptly furnish to a Member a copy of any amendment to the Articles or this Agreement executed by a Manager pursuant to a power of attorney from the Member.

10.3 Annual Statements.

A. If the Company has more than thirty-five (35) Members, the Manager(s) shall cause an annual report to be sent to each of the Members not later than one hundred twenty (120) days after the close of the Fiscal Year. The report shall contain a balance sheet as of the end of the Fiscal Year and an income statement and statement of changes in financial position for the Fiscal Year. Such financial statements shall be accompanied by the report thereon, if any, of the independent accountants engaged by the Company or, if there is no report, the certificate of a Manager that the financial statements were prepared without audit from the books and records of the Company.

B. The Manager(s) shall cause to be prepared at least annually, at Company expense, information necessary for the preparation of the Members' and Assignees' federal and state income tax returns. The Manager(s) shall send or cause to be sent to each Member or Assignee within ninety (90) days after the end of each taxable year such information as is necessary to complete federal and state income tax or information returns, and, if the Company has thirty-five (35) or fewer Members, a copy of the Company's federal, state, and local income tax or information returns for that year.

C. The Manager(s) shall cause to be filed at least annually with the California Secretary of State the statement required under California Corporations Code §17060.

10.4 **Financial and Other Information.** The Manager(s) shall provide such financial and other information relating to the Company or any other Person in which the Company owns, directly or indirectly, an equity interest, as a Member may reasonably request. The Manager(s) shall distribute to the Members, promptly after the preparation or receipt thereof by the Manager(s), any financial or other information relating to any Person in which the Company owns, directly or indirectly, an equity interest, including any filings by such Person under the Securities Exchange Act of 1934, as amended, that is received by the Company with respect to any equity interest of the Company in such Person.

10.5 **Filings.** The Manager(s), at Company expense, shall cause the income tax returns for the Company to be prepared and timely filed with the appropriate authorities. The Manager(s), at Company expense, shall also cause to be prepared and timely filed, with appropriate federal and state regulatory and administrative bodies, amendments to, or restatements of, the Articles and all reports required to be filed by the Company with those entities under the Act or other then current applicable laws, rules, and regulations. If a Manager required by the Act to execute or file any document fails, after demand, to do so within a reasonable period of time or refuses to do so, any other Manager or Member may prepare, execute, and file that document with the California Secretary of State.

10.6 **Bank Accounts.** The Manager(s) shall maintain the funds of the Company in one or more separate bank accounts in the name of the Company, and shall not permit the funds of the Company to be commingled in any fashion with the funds of any other Person.

10.7 **Accounting Decisions and Reliance on Others.** All decisions as to accounting matters, except as otherwise specifically set forth herein, shall be made by the Manager(s). The Manager(s) may rely upon the advice of their accountants as to whether such decisions are in accordance with accounting methods followed for federal income tax purposes.

Ch 6 Forms

10.8 Tax Matters for the Company Handled by Manager(s) and Tax Matters Partner. The Manager(s) shall from time to time cause the Company to make such tax elections as they deem to be in the best interests of the Company and the Members. The Tax Matters Partner shall represent the Company (at the Company's expense) in connection with all examinations of the Company's affairs by tax authorities, including resulting judicial and administrative proceedings, and shall expend the Company funds for professional services and costs associated therewith. The Tax Matters Partner shall oversee the Company tax affairs in the overall best interests of the Company. If for any reason the Tax Matters Partner can no longer serve in that capacity or ceases to be a Member or Manager, as the case may be, a Majority Interest or a majority of the Manager(s) may designate another to be Tax Matters Partner.

ARTICLE XI. DISSOLUTION AND WINDING UP

11.1 Dissolution. The Company shall dissolve, its assets disposed of, and its affairs wound up on the first to occur of the following (each, a "Dissolution Event"):

A. Upon the entry of a decree of judicial dissolution pursuant to Act Section 17351;

B. Upon the vote of Members holding at least _____ percent (__%) of the Membership Interests;

C. The sale of all or substantially all of the assets of Company; or

D. The happening of any event that makes it unlawful or impossible to carry on the business of the Company.

11.2 Certificate of Dissolution. As soon as possible following the occurrence of a Dissolution Event, the Manager(s) who have not wrongfully dissolved the Company or, if none, the Members, shall execute a Certificate of Dissolution in such form as shall be prescribed by the California Secretary of State and file the Certificate as required by the Act.

11.3 Winding Up. Upon the occurrence of a Dissolution Event, the Company shall continue solely for the purpose of winding up its affairs in an orderly manner, liquidating its assets, and satisfying the claims of its creditors. The Manager(s) who have not wrongfully dissolved the Company or, if none, the Members, shall be responsible for overseeing the winding up and liquidation of Company, shall take full account of the liabilities of Company and assets, shall either cause its assets to be sold or distributed, and if sold, shall cause the proceeds therefrom, to the extent sufficient therefore, to be applied and distributed as provided in Section 11.5. The Persons winding up the affairs of the Company shall give written notice of the commencement of winding up by mail to all known creditors and claimants whose addresses appear on the records of the Company. The Manager(s) or Members winding up the affairs of the Company shall be entitled to reasonable compensation for such services.

11.4 Distributions in Kind. Any non-cash asset distributed to one or more Members shall first be valued at its fair market value to determine the Net Profit or Net Loss that would have resulted if such asset were sold for such value, such Net Profit or Net Loss shall then be allocated pursuant to Article VI, and the Members' Capital Accounts shall be adjusted to reflect such allocations. The amount distributed and charged to the Capital Account of each Member receiving an interest in such distributed asset shall be the fair market value of such interest (net of any liability secured by such asset that such Member assumes or takes subject to). The fair market value of such asset shall be determined by the Manager(s) or by the Members or if any Member objects by an independent appraiser (any such appraiser must be recognized as an expert in valuing the type of asset involved) selected by the Manager or liquidating trustee and approved by the Members.

11.5 Order of Payment upon Dissolution.

A. After determining that all known debts and liabilities of the Company, including, without limitation, debts and liabilities to Members who are creditors of the Company, have been paid or adequately provided for, the remaining assets shall be distributed to the Members in accordance with their positive Capital Account balances, after taking into account income and loss allocations for the Company's taxable year during which liquidation occurs. Such liquidating distributions shall be made by the end of the Company's taxable year in which the Company is liquidated, or, if later, within ninety (90) days after the date of such liquidation.

B. The payment of a debt or liability, whether the whereabouts of the creditor is known or unknown, has been adequately provided for if the payment has been provided for by either of the following means:

(i) Payment thereof has been assumed or guaranteed in good faith by one or more financially responsible persons or by the United States government or any agency thereof, and the provision, including the financial responsibility of the Person, was determined in good faith and with reasonable care by the Members or Manager(s) to be adequate at the time of any distribution of the assets pursuant to this Section.

(ii) The amount of the debt or liability has been deposited as provided in Corporations Code Section 2008.

This Section 11.5B shall not prescribe the exclusive means of making adequate provision for debts and liabilities.

Ch 6
Forms

11.6 Limitations on Payments Made in Dissolution. Except as otherwise specifically provided in this Agreement, each Member shall only be entitled to look solely at the assets of the Company for the return of his or her positive Capital Account balance and shall have no recourse for his or her Capital Contribution and/or share of Net Profits (upon dissolution or otherwise) against the Manager(s) or any other Member.

11.7 Certificate of Cancellation. The Manager(s) or Members who filed the Certificate of Dissolution shall cause to be filed in the office of, and on a form prescribed by, the California Secretary of State, a Certificate of Cancellation of the Articles upon the completion of the winding up of the affairs of the Company.

11.8 No Action for Dissolution. Except as expressly permitted in this Agreement, a Member shall not take any voluntary action that directly causes a Dissolution Event. The Members acknowledge that irreparable damage would be done to the goodwill and reputation of the Company if any Member should bring an action in court to dissolve the Company under circumstances where dissolution is not required by Section 11.1. This Agreement has been drawn carefully to provide fair treatment of all parties and equitable payment in liquidation of the Economic Interests. Accordingly, except where the Manager(s) have failed to liquidate the Company as required by this Article XI, each Member hereby waives and renounces his or her right to initiate legal action to seek the appointment of a receiver or trustee to liquidate the Company or to seek a decree of judicial dissolution of the Company on the ground that (a) it is not reasonably practicable to carry on the business of the Company in conformity with the Articles or this Agreement, or (b) dissolution is reasonably necessary for the protection of the rights or interests of the complaining Member. Damages for breach of this Section 11.8 shall be monetary damages only (and not specific performance), and the damages may be offset against distributions by the Company to which such Member would otherwise be entitled.

ARTICLE XII. INDEMNIFICATION AND INSURANCE

12.1 Definitions. For purposes of this Article XII, the following definitions shall apply:

A. "Expenses" shall include, without limitation, attorneys' fees, disbursements and retainers, court costs, transcript costs, fees of accountants, experts and witnesses, travel expenses, duplicating costs, printing and binding costs, telephone charges, postage, delivery service fees, and all other expenses of the types customarily incurred in connection with prosecuting, defending, preparing to prosecute or defend, investigating, or being or preparing to be a witness or other participant in a Proceeding.

B. "Proceeding" includes any action, suit, arbitration, alternative dispute resolution mechanism, investigation, administrative hearing, or other proceeding, whether civil, criminal, administrative, or investigative in nature, except a proceeding initiated by a Person pursuant to Section 12.10B of this Agreement to enforce such Person's rights under this Article XII.

12.2 Indemnification of Manager(s) and Officers.

A. The Company shall indemnify any Manager or officer of the Company who was or is a party or is threatened to be made a party to, or otherwise becomes involved in, any Proceeding (other than a Proceeding by or in the right of the Company) by reason of the fact that such Manager or officer of the Company is or was an agent of the Company against all Expenses, amounts paid in settlement, judgments, fines, penalties, and ERISA excise taxes actually and reasonably incurred by or levied against such Manager or officer in connection with such Proceeding if it is determined as provided in Section 12.4 or by a court of competent jurisdiction that such Manager or officer acted in good faith, in a manner he or she reasonably believed to be in or not opposed to the best interests of the Company, and in a manner not in violation of this Agreement or the Act, and with respect to any criminal Proceeding, had no reasonable cause to believe his or her conduct was unlawful. The termination of any Proceeding, whether by judgment, order, settlement, or conviction, or upon a plea of nolo contendere or its equivalent, shall not, of itself, create a presumption that a Manager or officer of the Company did not act in good faith, and in a manner which he or she reasonably believed to be in or not opposed to the best interests of the Company or, with respect to any criminal Proceeding, that a Manager or officer had reasonable cause to believe that his or her conduct was unlawful.

B. The Company shall indemnify any Manager or officer of the Company who was or is a party or is threatened to be made a party to, or otherwise becomes involved in, any Proceeding by or in the right of the Company to procure a judgment in its favor by reason of the fact that such Manager or officer is or was an agent of the Company only against Expenses actually and reasonably incurred by such Manager or officer in connection with such Proceeding if it is determined as provided in Section 12.4 or by a court of competent jurisdiction that such Manager or officer acted in good faith and in a manner he or she reasonably believed to be in or not opposed to the best interests of the Company, except that no indemnification shall be made with respect to any claim, issue or matter as to which such Manager or officer shall have been adjudged to be in violation of this Agreement or the Act or otherwise liable to the Company unless and only to the extent that the court in which such Proceeding was brought or other court of competent jurisdiction shall determine upon application that, despite the adjudication of liability but in view of all the circumstances of the case, such Manager or officer is fairly and reasonably entitled to indemnification for such Expenses which such court shall deem proper.

12.3 Successful Defense. Notwithstanding any other provision of this Agreement, to the extent that a Manager or officer of the Company has been successful on the merits or otherwise in defense of any Proceeding referred to in Section 12.2, or in defense of any claim, issue, or matter therein, such Manager or officer shall be indemnified against Expenses actually and reasonably incurred in connection therewith.

12.4 Determination of Conduct. Any indemnification under Section 12.2 (unless ordered by a court as referred to in such Section) shall be made by the Company only as authorized in the specific case upon a determination that indemnification of the Manager or officer of the Company is proper in the circumstances because such Manager or officer has met the applicable standard of conduct set forth in Section 12.2. Such determination shall be made (i) by the Manager(s) by a majority vote of a quorum consisting of Manager(s) who were not parties to such Proceeding; or (ii) if such quorum is not obtainable or, even if obtainable, a quorum of such disinterested Manager(s) so directs, by independent legal counsel in a written opinion; or (iii) by the Members by a vote of a majority-in-interest of Members, whether or not constituting a quorum, who were not parties to such Proceeding.

12.5 Payment of Expenses in Advance. Expenses incurred by a Manager or officer of the Company in connection with a Proceeding shall be paid by the Company in advance of the final disposition of such Proceeding upon receipt of a written undertaking by or on behalf of such Manager or officer to repay such amount if it shall ultimately be determined that such Manager or officer is not entitled to be indemnified by the Company as authorized in this Article XII.

12.6 Indemnification of Other Agents. The Company may, but shall not be obligated to, indemnify any Person (other than a Manager or officer of the Company) who was or is a party or is threatened to be made a party to, or otherwise becomes involved in, any Proceeding (including any Proceeding by or in the right of the Company) by reason of the fact that such Person is or was an agent of the Company (including Members who are not Manager(s) or officers of the Company), against all Expenses, amounts paid in settlement, judgments, fines, penalties, and ERISA excise taxes actually and reasonably incurred by such Person in connection with such Proceeding under the same circumstances and to the same extent as is provided for or permitted in this Article XII with respect to a Manager or officer of the Company.

12.7 Indemnity Not Exclusive. The indemnification and advancement of Expenses provided by, or granted pursuant to, the provisions of this Article XII, shall not be

Ch 6 Forms

deemed exclusive of any other rights to which any Person seeking indemnification or advancement of Expenses may be entitled under any agreement, vote of Manager(s) or Members, or otherwise, both as to action in such Person's capacity as an agent of the Company and as to action in another capacity while serving as an agent. All rights to indemnification under this Article XII shall be deemed to be provided by a contract between the Company and each Manager and officer, if any, of the Company who serves in such capacity at any time while this Agreement and relevant provisions of the Act and other applicable law, if any, are in effect. Any repeal or modification hereof or thereof shall not affect any such rights then existing.

12.8 Insurance. The Company shall have the power to purchase and maintain insurance on behalf of any Person who is or was an agent of the Company against any liability asserted against such Person and incurred by such Person in any such capacity, or arising out of such Person's status as an agent, whether or not the Company would have the power to indemnify such Person against such liability under the provisions of this Article XII or of Section 17155 of the Act. In the event a Person shall receive payment from any insurance carrier or from the plaintiff in any action against such Person with respect to indemnified amounts after payment on account of all or part of such indemnified amounts having been made by the Company pursuant to this Article XII, such Person shall reimburse the Company for the amount, if any, by which the sum of such payment by such insurance carrier or such plaintiff and payments by the Company to such Person exceeds such indemnified amounts; provided, however, that such portions, if any, of such insurance proceeds that are required to be reimbursed to the insurance carrier under the terms of its insurance policy shall not be deemed to be payments to such Person hereunder. In addition, upon payment of indemnified amounts under the terms and conditions of this Agreement, the Company shall be subrogated to such Person's rights against any insurance carrier with respect to such indemnified amounts (to the extent permitted under such insurance policies). Such right of subrogation shall be terminated upon receipt by the Company of the amount to be reimbursed by such Person pursuant to the second sentence of this Section 12.8.

12.9 Heirs, Executors, and Administrators. The indemnification and advancement of Expenses provided by, or granted pursuant to, this Article XII shall, unless otherwise provided when authorized or ratified, continue as to a Person who has ceased to be an agent of the Company and shall inure to the benefit of such Person's heirs, executors, and administrators.

12.10 Right to Indemnification upon Application.

A. Any indemnification or advance under Section 12.2 or Section 12.5 shall be

Ch 6 Forms

made promptly, and in no event later than sixty (60) days, after the Company's receipt of the written request of a Manager or officer of the Company therefor, unless, in the case of an indemnification, a determination shall have been made as provided in Section 12.4 that such Manager or officer has not met the relevant standard for indemnification set forth in Section 12.2.

B. The right of a Person to indemnification or an advance of Expenses as provided by this Article XII shall be enforceable in any court of competent jurisdiction. Neither the failure by the Manager(s) or Members of the Company or its independent legal counsel to have made a determination that indemnification or an advance is proper in the circumstances, nor any actual determination by the Manager(s) or Members of the Company or its independent legal counsel that indemnification or an advance is not proper, shall be a defense to the action or create a presumption that the relevant standard of conduct has not been met. The burden of proving that indemnification or an advance is not proper shall be on the Company. In any such action, the Person seeking indemnification or advancement of Expenses shall be entitled to recover from the Company any and all expenses of the types contained in the definition of Expenses in Section 12.1A of this Agreement actually and reasonably incurred by such Person in such action, but only if he or she prevails therein.

12.11 Limitations on Indemnification. No payments pursuant to this Agreement shall be made by the Company:

A. To indemnify or advance funds to any Person with respect to a Proceeding initiated or brought voluntarily by such Person and not by way of defense, except as provided in Section 12.10B with respect to a Proceeding brought to establish or enforce a right to indemnification under this Agreement, otherwise than as required under California law, but indemnification or advancement of Expenses may be provided by the Company in specific cases if a determination is made in the manner provided in Section 12.4 that it is appropriate; or

B. If a court of competent jurisdiction finally determines that any indemnification or advance of Expenses hereunder is unlawful.

12.12 Partial Indemnification. If a Person is entitled under any provision of this Article XII to indemnification by the Company for a portion of Expenses, amounts paid in settlement, judgments, fines, penalties, or ERISA excise taxes incurred by such Person in any Proceeding but not, however, for the total amount thereof, the Company shall nevertheless indemnify such Person for the portion of such Expenses, amounts paid in settlement, judgments, fines, penalties, or ERISA excise taxes to which such Person is entitled.

ARTICLE XIII. INVESTMENT REPRESENTATIONS

Each Member hereby represents and warrants to, and agrees with, the Manager(s), the other Members, and the Company as follows:

13.1 Pre-existing Relationship or Experience. (i) He or she has a pre-existing personal or business relationship with the Company or one or more of its officers, Manager(s), or controlling persons; or (ii) by reason of his or her business or financial experience, or by reason of the business or financial experience of his or her financial advisor who is unaffiliated with and who is not compensated, directly or indirectly, by the Company or any affiliate or selling agent of the Company, he or she is capable of evaluating the risks and merits of an investment in the Membership Interest and of protecting his or her own interests in connection with this investment.

13.2 No Advertising. He or she has not seen, received, been presented with, or been solicited by any leaflet, public promotional meeting, newspaper or magazine article or advertisement, radio or television advertisement, or any other form of advertising or general solicitation with respect to the sale of the Membership Interest.

13.3 Investment Intent. He or she is acquiring the Membership Interest for investment purposes for his or her own account only and not with a view to or for sale in connection with any distribution of all or any part of the Membership Interest. No other person will have any direct or indirect beneficial interest in or right to the Membership Interest.

13.4 Accredited Investor. He or she is an "accredited investor" as defined in Rule 501(a) of Regulation D promulgated by the Securities and Exchange Commission (the "SEC") under the Securities Act of 1933, as amended (the "Securities Act").

13.5 Purpose of Entity. If the Member is a corporation, partnership, limited liability company, trust, or other entity, it was not organized for the specific purpose of acquiring the Membership Interest.

13.6 Residency. He or she is a resident of the state of _____

13.7 Economic Risk. He or she is financially able to bear the economic risk of an investment in the Membership Interest, including the total loss thereof.

13.8 No Registration of Membership Interest. He or she acknowledges that the Membership Interest has not been registered under the Securities Act of 1933, as amended (the "Securities Act"), or qualified under the California Corporate Securities Law of 1968, as amended, or any other applicable state securities laws in reliance, in part, on his or her representations, warranties, and agreements herein.

Ch 6 Forms

13.9 Membership Interest Is Restricted Security. He or she understands that the Membership Interest is a "restricted security" under the Securities Act in that the Membership Interest will be acquired from the Company in a transaction not involving a registered public offering, and that the Membership Interest may not be resold without registration under the Securities Act except in certain limited circumstances and that otherwise the Membership Interest must be held indefinitely. In this connection, he or she understands the resale limitations imposed by the Securities Act and is familiar with SEC Rule 144, as presently in effect, and the conditions which must be met in order for that Rule to be available for resale of "restricted securities," including the requirement that the securities must generally be held for at least two years after purchase thereof from the Company (or an affiliate of the Company) prior to resale pursuant to paragraph (k) of SEC Rule 144. He or she understands that the Company has no present plans to undertake a registered public offering of the Membership Interest or other securities.

13.10 No Obligation to Register. He or she represents, warrants, and agrees that the Company and the Manager(s) are under no obligation to register or qualify the Membership Interest under the Securities Act or under any state securities law, or to assist him or her in complying with any exemption from registration and qualification.

13.11 No Disposition in Violation of Law. Without limiting the representations set forth above, and without limiting Article VIII of this Agreement, he or she will not make any disposition of all or any part of the Membership Interest which will result in the violation by him or her or by the Company of the Securities Act, the California Corporate Securities Law of 1968, or any other applicable securities laws. Without limiting the foregoing, he or she agrees not to make any disposition of all or any part of the Membership Interest unless and until:

A. There is then in effect a registration statement under the Securities Act covering such proposed disposition and such disposition is made in accordance with such registration statement and any applicable requirements of state securities laws; or

B. (i) He or she has notified the Company of the proposed disposition and has furnished the Company with a detailed statement of the circumstances surrounding the proposed disposition; and (ii) if reasonably requested by the Manager(s), he or she has furnished the Company with a written opinion of counsel, reasonably satisfactory to the Company, that such disposition will not require registration of any securities under the Securities Act or the consent of or a permit from appropriate authorities under any applicable state securities law.

13.12 Legends. He or she understands that the certificates (if any) evidencing the Membership Interest may bear one or all of the following legends:

A. "THE SECURITIES REPRESENTED BY THIS CERTIFICATE HAVE NOT BEEN REGISTERED UNDER THE SECURITIES ACT OF 1933 NOR REGISTERED OR QUALIFIED UNDER ANY STATE SECURITIES LAWS. SUCH SECURITIES MAY NOT BE OFFERED FOR SALE, SOLD, DELIVERED AFTER SALE, TRANSFERRED, PLEDGED, OR HYPOTHECATED UNLESS QUALIFIED AND REGISTERED UNDER APPLICABLE STATE AND FEDERAL SECURITIES LAWS OR UNLESS, IN THE OPINION OF COUNSEL SATISFACTORY TO THE COMPANY, SUCH QUALIFICATION AND REGISTRATION IS NOT REQUIRED. ANY TRANSFER OF THE SECURITIES REPRESENTED BY THIS CERTIFICATE IS FURTHER SUBJECT TO OTHER RESTRICTIONS, TERMS, AND CONDITIONS WHICH ARE SET FORTH HEREIN IN THE COMPANY'S OPERATING AGREEMENT, A COPY OF WHICH IS ON FILE AT THE PRINCIPAL OFFICE OF THE COMPANY."

B. Any legend required by applicable state securities laws.

13.13 Investment Risk. He or she acknowledges that the Membership Interest is a speculative investment which involves a substantial degree of risk of loss by him or her of his or her entire investment in the Company (and he or she could bear such a loss), that he or she understands and takes full cognizance of the risk factors related to the purchase of the Membership Interest, and that the Company is newly organized and has no financial or operating history.

13.14 Investment Experience. He or she is an experienced investor in unregistered and restricted securities of speculative and high-risk ventures. This representation shall not be applicable to any Person that provides the Manager(s) with such written information as the Manager(s) deem necessary to substantiate that the Member engaged and designated a Professional Advisor to assist the Member in evaluating the risks and merits of an investment in the Company. As used in this Section 13.14, a "Professional Advisor" shall have the meaning ascribed to that term in Corporations Code Section 25009, 10 California Code of Regulations Section 260.102.12(g)(1), or any successor statutes or regulations.

13.15 Restrictions on Transferability. He or she acknowledges that there are substantial restrictions on the transferability of the Membership Interest pursuant to this Agreement, that there is no public market for the Membership Interest and none is expected to develop, and that, accordingly, it may not be possible for him or her to liquidate his or her investment in the Company.

13.16 Information Reviewed. He or she has received and reviewed all information he or she considers necessary or appropriate for deciding whether to purchase the Membership Interest. He or she has had an opportunity to ask questions and receive answers from the Company and its Manager(s) and employees regarding the terms and conditions of purchase of the Membership Interest and regarding the business, financial affairs, and other aspects of the Company and has further

Ch 6
Forms

had the opportunity to obtain all information (to the extent the Company possesses or can acquire such information without unreasonable effort or expense) which he or she deems necessary to evaluate the investment and to verify the accuracy of information otherwise provided to him or her.

13.17 No Representations by Company. Neither any Manager, any agent or employee of the Company or of any Manager, or any other Person has at any time expressly or implicitly represented, guaranteed, or warranted to him or her that he or she may freely transfer the Membership Interest, that a percentage of profit and/or amount or type of consideration will be realized as a result of an investment in the Membership Interest, that past performance or experience on the part of the Manager(s) or their Affiliates or any other person in any way indicates the predictable results of the ownership of the Membership Interest or of the overall Company business, that any cash distributions from Company operations or otherwise will be made to the Members by any specific date or will be made at all, or that any specific tax benefits will accrue as a result of an investment in the Company.

13.18 Consultation with Attorney. He or she has been advised to consult with his or her own attorney regarding all legal matters concerning an investment in the Company and the tax consequences of participating in the Company, and has done so, to the extent he or she considers necessary.

13.19 Tax Consequences. He or she acknowledges that the tax consequences to his or her of investing in the Company will depend on his or her particular circumstances, and neither the Company, the Manager(s), the Members, nor the partners, shareholders, members, managers, agents, officers, directors, employees, Affiliates, or consultants of any of them will be responsible or liable for the tax consequences to him or her of an investment in the Company. He or she will look solely to, and rely upon, his or her own advisers with respect to the tax consequences of this investment.

13.20 No Assurance of Tax Benefits. He or she acknowledges that there can be no assurance that the Code or the Regulations will not be amended or interpreted in the future in such a manner so as to deprive the Company and the Members of some or all of the tax benefits they might now receive, nor that some of the deductions claimed by the Company or the allocations of items of income, gain, loss, deduction, or credit among the Members may not be challenged by the Internal Revenue Service.

13.21 Indemnity. He or she shall defend, indemnify, and hold harmless the Company, each and every Manager, each and every other Member, and any officers, directors, shareholders, managers, members, employees, partners, agents, attorneys, accountants, registered representatives, and control persons of any such entity who was or is a party or is threatened to be made a party to any threatened, pending, or completed action, suit, or proceeding, whether civil, criminal, administrative, or investigative, by reason of or arising from any misrepresentation or misstatement of facts or omission to represent or state facts made by him or her including, without limitation, the information in this Agreement, against losses, liabilities, and expenses of the Company, each and every Manager, each and every other Member, and any officers, directors, shareholders, managers, members, employees, partners, attorneys, accountants, agents, registered representatives, and control persons of any such Person (including attorneys' fees, judgments, fines, and amounts paid in settlement, payable as incurred) incurred by such Person in connection with such action, suit, proceeding, or the like.

ARTICLE XIV. MISCELLANEOUS

14.1 Counsel to the Company. Counsel to the Company may also be counsel to any Manager or any Affiliate of a Manager. The Manager(s) may execute on behalf of the Company and the Members any consent to the representation of the Company that counsel may request pursuant to the California Rules of Professional Conduct or similar rules in any other jurisdiction ("Rules"). The Company has initially selected _____ ("Company Counsel") as legal counsel to the Company. Each Member acknowledges that Company Counsel does not represent any Member in the absence of a clear and explicit written agreement to such effect between the Member and Company Counsel, and that in the absence of any such agreement Company Counsel shall owe no duties directly to a Member. Notwithstanding any adversity that may develop, in the event any dispute or controversy arises between any Members and the Company, or between any Members or the Company, on the one hand, and a Manager (or Affiliate of a Manager) that Company Counsel represents, on the other hand, then each Member agrees that Company Counsel may represent either the Company or such Manager (or his or her Affiliate), or both, in any such dispute or controversy to the extent permitted by the Rules, and each Member hereby consents to such representation. Each Member further acknowledges that: (a) Company Counsel has represented the interests of _____ in connection with the formation of the Company and the preparation and negotiation of this Agreement and (b) although communications with Company Counsel concerning the formation of the Company, its Members and Manager(s) may be confidential with respect to third parties, no Member has any expectation that such communications are confidential with respect to the Manager(s) and the other Members.

14.2 Complete Agreement. This Agreement and the Articles constitute the complete and exclusive statement of agreement among the Members and Manager(s) with respect to the subject matter herein and therein and replace and supersede all prior written and oral agreements or statements by and among the Members and Manager(s) or any of them. No representation, statement, condition, or warranty not contained in this Agreement or the Articles will be binding on the Members or Manager(s) or have any force or effect whatsoever. To the extent that any provision of the Articles conflict with any provision of this Agreement, the Articles shall control. Notwithstanding the foregoing, the Company may enter into one or more buy-sell agreements ("Buy-Sell Agreement(s)") with one or more Members containing additional provisions relating to the purchase by the Company from a Member, and/or the sale by a Member to the Company, of such Member's Units. In the event of a conflict between the terms of a Buy-Sell Agreement and Article VIII or Article IX of this Agreement, the terms of the Buy-Sell Agreement shall govern.

14.3 Binding Effect. Subject to the provisions of this Agreement relating to transferability, this Agreement will be binding upon and inure to the benefit of the Members, and their respective successors and assigns.

14.4 Parties in Interest. Except as expressly provided in the Act, nothing in this Agreement shall confer any rights or remedies under or by reason of this Agreement on any Persons other than the Members and Manager(s) and their respective successors and assigns nor shall anything in this Agreement relieve or discharge the obligation or liability of any third person to any party to this Agreement, nor shall any provision give any third person any right of subrogation or action over or against any party to this Agreement.

14.5 Pronouns; Statutory References. All pronouns and all variations thereof shall be deemed to refer to the masculine, feminine, or neuter, singular or plural, as the context in which they are used may require. Any reference to the Code, the Regulations, the Act, Corporations Code, or other statutes or laws will include all amendments, modifications, or replacements of the specific sections and provisions concerned.

14.6 Headings. All headings herein are inserted only for convenience and ease of reference and are not to be considered in the construction or interpretation of any provision of this Agreement.

14.7 Interpretation. In the event any claim is made by any Member relating to any conflict, omission, or ambiguity in this Agreement, no presumption or burden of proof or persuasion shall be implied by virtue of the fact that this Agreement was prepared by or at the request of the Company, a particular Member, or its, his, or her counsel.

14.8 References to this Agreement. Numbered or lettered articles, sections, and subsections herein contained refer to articles, sections, and subsections of this

Agreement unless otherwise expressly stated.

14.9 Governing Law; Jurisdiction. This Agreement is governed by and shall be construed in accordance with the law of the State of California, excluding any conflict-of-laws rule or principle that might refer the governance or the construction of this Agreement to the law of another jurisdiction. Each Member hereby consents to the exclusive jurisdiction of the state and federal courts sitting in California in any action on a claim arising out of, under, or in connection with this Agreement or the transactions contemplated by this Agreement, provided such claim is not required to be arbitrated pursuant to Section 14.10. Each Member further agrees that personal jurisdiction over him or her may be effected by service of process by registered or certified mail addressed as provided in Section 14.14 of this Agreement, and that when so made shall be as if served upon him or her personally within the State of California.

14.10 Arbitration. Except as otherwise provided in this Agreement, any dispute, controversy, or claim arising out of or relating to this Agreement, or any breach thereof, including without limitation any claim that this Agreement, or any part hereof, is invalid, illegal, or otherwise voidable or void, shall be submitted, at the request of the Company or any Member, to binding arbitration by a Judicial Arbitration and Mediation Service ("JAMS") arbitrator, or such other arbitrator as may be agreed upon by the parties. Hearings on such arbitration shall be conducted in _____, California. A single arbitrator shall arbitrate any such controversy. The arbitrator shall hear and determine the controversy in accordance with applicable law and the intention of the parties as expressed in this Agreement, upon the evidence produced at an arbitration hearing scheduled at the request of either party. Such pre-arbitration discovery shall be permitted to the fullest extent permitted by California law applicable to arbitration proceedings, including, without limitation, the provisions of Title 9 of Part 3 of the California Code of Civil Procedure, including Section 1283.05, and successor statutes, permitting expanded discovery proceedings. The arbitrator shall decide all discovery disputes. The arbitrator shall issue a written reasoned decision and award within ninety (90) days from the date the arbitration proceedings are initiated. Judgment on the award of the arbitrator may be entered in any court having jurisdiction thereof.

A. Provisional Remedy. Each of the parties reserves the right to file with a court of competent jurisdiction an application for temporary or preliminary injunctive relief, writ of attachment, writ of possession, temporary protective order, and/or appointment of a receiver on the grounds that the arbitration award to which the applicant may be entitled may be rendered ineffectual in the absence of such relief.

Ch 6 Forms

B. Consolidation. Any arbitration hereunder may be consolidated by JAMS with the arbitration of any other dispute arising out of or relating to the same subject matter when the arbitrator determines that there is a common issue of law or fact creating the possibility of conflicting rulings by more than one arbitrator. Any disputes over which arbitrator or panel of arbitrators shall hear any consolidated matter shall be resolved by JAMS.

C. Power and Authority of Arbitrator. The arbitrator shall not have any power to alter, amend, modify, or change any of the terms of this Agreement nor to grant any remedy which is either prohibited by the terms of this Agreement or not available in a court of law.

D. Governing Law. All questions in respect of procedure to be followed in conducting the arbitration as well as the enforceability of this Agreement to arbitrate which may be resolved by state law shall be resolved according to the laws of the State of California.

E. Costs. The costs of the arbitration, including any JAMS administration fee, the arbitrator's fee, and costs for the use of facilities during the hearings, shall be borne equally by the parties to the arbitration.

14.11 Exhibits. All Exhibits attached to this Agreement are incorporated and shall be treated as if set forth herein.

14.12 Severability. If any provision of this Agreement or the application of such provision to any person or circumstance shall be held invalid, the remainder of this Agreement or the application of such provision to persons or circumstances other than those to which it is held invalid shall not be affected thereby.

14.13 Specific Performance. The Members agree that irreparable damage will result if this Agreement is not performed in accordance with its terms, and the Members agree that any damages available at law for a breach of this Agreement would not be an adequate remedy. Therefore, the provisions hereof and the obligations of the Members hereunder shall be enforceable in a court of equity, or other tribunal with jurisdiction, by a decree of specific performance, and appropriate injunctive relief may be applied for and granted in connection therewith. Such remedies and all other remedies provided for in this Agreement shall, however, be cumulative and not exclusive and shall be in addition to any other remedies that a Member may have under this Agreement, at law or in equity.

14.14 Additional Documents and Acts. Each Member agrees to execute and deliver such additional documents and instruments and to perform such additional acts as may be necessary or appropriate to effectuate, carry out, and perform all of the terms, provisions, and conditions of this Agreement and the transactions contemplated hereby.

14.15 Notices. Any notice, demand, consent, election, offer, approval, request, or other communication (collectively, "Notice") given under this Agreement shall be in writing and shall be served personally or delivered by first class, registered or certified, return receipt requested U.S. mail, postage prepaid. Notices may also be given by transmittal over electronic transmitting devices such as electronic mail, facsimile, or telecopy machine, if the party to whom the notice is being sent has such a device in its office, provided a complete copy of any notice so transmitted shall also be mailed in the same manner as required for a mailed notice. Notices shall be deemed received at the earlier of actual receipt or three (3) days following deposit in U.S. mail, postage prepaid. Notices shall be directed to the Company at the Company's principal place of business as specified in Section 2.6 of this Agreement, and to the Members at the addresses shown on Exhibit A provided a Member may change such Member's address for notice by giving written notice to the Company and all other Members in accordance with this Section 14.15.

14.16 Amendments. Except as otherwise expressly provided in this Agreement, all amendments to this Agreement will be in writing and signed by a Majority Interest of the Members.

14.17 Reliance on Authority of Person Signing Agreement. If a Member is not a natural person, neither the Company nor any other Member will (a) be required to determine the authority of the individual signing this Agreement to make any commitment or undertaking on behalf of such entity or to determine any fact or circumstance bearing upon the existence of the authority of such individual; or (b) be responsible for the application or distribution of proceeds paid or credited to individuals signing this Agreement on behalf of such entity.

14.18 No Interest in Company Property; Waiver of Action for Partition. No Member or Assignee has any interest in specific property of the Company. Without limiting the foregoing, each Member and Assignee irrevocably waives during the term of the Company any right that he or she may have to maintain any action for partition with respect to the property of the Company.

14.19 Multiple Counterparts. This Agreement may be executed in two or more counterparts, each of which shall be deemed an original, but all of which shall constitute one and the same instrument.

14.20 Attorney Fees. In the event that any dispute between the Company and the Members or among the Members should result in litigation or arbitration, the prevailing party in such dispute shall be entitled to recover from the other party all reasonable fees, costs, and expenses of enforcing any right of the prevailing party, including without limitation, reasonable attorneys' fees and expenses, all of which shall be deemed to have accrued upon the commencement of such action

Ch 6 Forms

and shall be paid whether or not such action is prosecuted to judgment. Any judgment or order entered in such action shall contain a specific provision providing for the recovery of attorney fees and costs incurred in enforcing such judgment and an award of prejudgment interest from the date of the breach at the maximum rate of interest allowed by law. For the purposes of this Section: (a) "attorneys' fees" shall include, without limitation, fees incurred in the following: (1) post-judgment motions; (2) contempt proceedings; (3) garnishment, levy, and debtor and third-party examinations; (4) discovery; and (5) bankruptcy litigation and (b) "prevailing party" shall mean the party who is determined in the proceeding to have prevailed or who prevails by dismissal, default, or otherwise.

14.21 Time Is of the Essence. All dates and times in this Agreement are of the essence.

14.22 Remedies Cumulative. The remedies under this Agreement are cumulative and shall not exclude any other remedies to which any person may be lawfully entitled.

14.23 Special Power of Attorney.

A. Limited Power. By signing this Agreement, each Member designates and appoints the Manager(s) as that Member's true and lawful attorney-in-fact, in that Member's name and stead, to make, execute, sign, and file such instruments, documents, or certificates which may from time to time be required by the laws of the United States of America, the State of California, and any political subdivisions thereof (or any other state or political subdivision in which the Company shall do business) to carry out the purposes of this Agreement, except where such action requires the express approval of the Members. The Manager(s) are not granted any authority on behalf of the Members to amend this Agreement except that the Manager(s) shall have the authority, as attorney-in-fact for each of the Members, to amend this Agreement and the Certificate as may be necessary or appropriate to give effect to the transactions specified below following any necessary approvals or consents of the Members:

(i) admissions of additional Members;

(ii) transfers of Membership Interests;

(iii) withdrawals or distributions of Capital Contributions or Distributable Cash;

(iv) contributions of additional capital;

(v) changes in the amount of Capital Contribution or Percentage Interest of any Member; or

(vi) admissions of Persons as successor Manager(s).

Each Member authorizes each such attorney-in-fact to take any action necessary or advisable in connection with the foregoing, hereby giving each attorney-in-fact full power and authority to do and perform each and every act or thing whatsoever requisite or advisable to be done in connection with the foregoing as fully as such Member might or could do so personally, and hereby ratifying and confirming all that any such attorney-in-fact shall lawfully do or cause to be done by virtue thereof or hereof.

B. Nature of Power of Attorney. This power of attorney is a special power of attorney coupled with an interest and (a) is irrevocable; (b) may be exercised by any such attorney-in-fact by listing the Member executing any agreement, certificate, instrument, or other document with the single signature of any such attorney-in-fact acting as attorney-in-fact for such Members; (c) shall survive the death, disability, legal incapacity, bankruptcy, insolvency, dissolution, or cessation of existence of a Member; and (d) shall survive the delivery of an assignment by a Member of the whole or a portion of his Membership Interest in the Company, except that where the assignment is of such Member's entire Membership Interest in the Company and the Assignee is admitted as a Member under the terms of this Agreement, the power of attorney shall survive the delivery of such assignment for the sole purpose of enabling any such attorney-in-fact to effect such substitution.

C. Signatures. The Manager(s) may exercise the special power of attorney granted in Section 14.23A by a facsimile signature of the Manager(s) or one of the Manager(s)' officers.

14.24 Estoppel Certificate. Each Member shall, within ten (10) days after written request by any Manager, deliver to the requesting Person a certificate stating, to the Member's knowledge, that: (a) this Agreement is in full force and effect; (b) this Agreement has not been modified except by any instrument or instruments identified in the certificate; and (c) there is no default hereunder by such Member, or if there is a default, the nature or extent thereof.

14.25 Waiver. No waiver by any party to this Agreement of any breach of, or default under, this Agreement by any other party shall be construed or deemed a waiver of any other breach of or default under this Agreement, and shall not preclude any party from exercising or asserting any rights under the Agreement with respect to any other breach or default.

14.26 Confidentiality. Each Member agrees not to disclose the provisions of this Agreement to any Person not a signatory to this Agreement, except as otherwise approved by the Manager(s) in writing. However, nothing herein shall preclude the Parties from (i) complying with any legal or judicial process that compels disclosure of the provisions of this Agreement; (ii) commencing legal action to

Ch 6 Forms

enforce the provisions of this Agreement; (iii) discussing the Agreement with their respective attorneys, accountants, or financial planners, as long as the parties clearly advise and instruct such individual that all information regarding the terms and conditions of the Agreement is disclosed in strict confidence and must not be repeated or disclosed to others; or (iv) complying with the requests of federal, state, or local taxing authorities.

14.27 Consent of Spouse or Domestic Partner. Within ten (10) days after any individual becomes a Member or a Member marries or registers as a domestic partner, such Member shall have his or her spouse or domestic partner execute a consent substantially in the form attached to this Agreement.

IN WITNESS WHEREOF, the parties have signed this Agreement on the date first written above and each of the individuals signing below warrants that he or she has the authority to sign for and on behalf of the respective parties.

MANAGER: _____ Print Name: _____

MEMBER: _____ Print Name: _____

MANAGER: _____ Print Name: _____

MEMBER: _____ Print Name: _____

MANAGER: _____ Print Name: _____

MEMBER: _____ Print Name: _____

MEMBER: _____ Print Name: _____

MEMBER: _____ Print Name: _____

EXHIBIT A
CAPITAL CONTRIBUTION OF MEMBERS AND
ADDRESSES OF MEMBERS AND MANAGERS OF

_____ LLC

Member's Name and Taxpayer I.D.	Member's Address	Member's Capital Contribution	Member's Percentage Interest

The undersigned spouse(s) or domestic partner(s) of the party (parties) to the foregoing Agreement acknowledge(s) on his or her own behalf that: I have read the foregoing Agreement and I know its contents. I am aware that by its provision my spouse or domestic partner grants the Company and/or the other Members an option to purchase all of his or her Membership Interest, including my community interest (if any) in it. I hereby consent to the sale, approve of the provisions of the Agreement, and agree that such Membership Interest and my interest in it are subject to the provisions of the Agreement and that I will take no action at any time to hinder operation of the Agreement on such Membership Interest or my interest in it.

_____
Signature of spouse or domestic partner

_____
Print name

_____
Print name of member

_____
Signature of spouse or domestic partner

_____
Print name

_____
Print name of member

_____
Signature of spouse or domestic partner

_____
Print name

_____
Print name of member

BUY-SELL AGREEMENT

BETWEEN

_____

AND ITS SHAREHOLDERS

THIS BUY-SELL AGREEMENT (hereinafter referred to as the "Agreement") is effective the ___ day of _____, 20 ____ by and between _____, a California corporation (hereinafter referred to as the "Corporation") and _____, _____, and _____ (hereinafter collectively referred to as the "Shareholders") and their current spouses.

ARTICLE I. PARTIES AND PURPOSE

Section 1.01. Identity of Parties. The above-named Shareholders own all of the outstanding shares of the Corporation as follows:

Shareholders	Number of Shares
_____	_____
_____	_____
_____	_____

Section 1.02. Protective Purpose of Agreement. It is the purpose of this Agreement to protect the management and control of the Corporation against intrusion by persons not active in the business of the Corporation or not acceptable to all of the Shareholders as a co-manager or co-owner of the Corporation's business.

Section 1.03. Market Purpose of Agreement. It is also the purpose of this Agreement to provide a ready market for the shares of the Corporation in the event of the death, disability, or retirement of a Shareholder from the Corporation's business and a mechanism for their transfer.

ARTICLE II. ENFORCEMENT PROVISIONS

Section 2.01. Agreement Available for Inspection. A copy of this Agreement, duly executed by the Corporation and the Shareholders, shall be maintained by the Secretary of the Corporation at the principal office of the Corporation in the State of California, available for inspection upon request by any person with a legitimate interest therein.

Section 2.02. Restrictions on Shares. Each certificate representing shares of the Corporation shall have conspicuously printed on it the following statement:

"The transfer, sale, assignment, hypothecation, encumbrance, or alienation of the Shares represented by this certificate is restricted by a Buy-Sell Agreement

Ch 6 Forms

between the Shareholders of this Corporation and the Corporation dated _____, 20__."

Section 2.03. Stamping of Certificate. Upon execution of this Agreement, each of the Shareholders agrees to cause the Secretary of the Corporation to stamp on his certificate(s) in a prominent manner the statement set forth in Section 2.02 hereof.

ARTICLE III. RESTRICTIONS ON TRANSFER

Section 3.01. Restrictions on Transfer and Notice. Except as otherwise provided in this Agreement, no Shareholder may sell, transfer, assign, pledge, hypothecate, or in any way encumber his shares in the Corporation, or any interest therein, whether voluntarily or by operation of law, and any transfer or attempted transfer in contravention of this Agreement shall be null and void and not confer on any transferee or purported transferee any rights whatsoever.

ARTICLE IV. SALE OF SHARES ON OCCURRENCE OF CERTAIN EVENTS

Section 4.01. Death of a Shareholder. Following the death of a Shareholder, and within ten (10) days after the Corporation's receipt of insurance proceeds as set forth under Section 4.03 hereof, the Corporation shall purchase and redeem, and the deceased Shareholder's estate shall sell, all of the deceased Shareholder's shares in the Corporation at the price set forth under Section 4.07 of this Agreement.

Section 4.02. Disability of a Shareholder. Following the disability of a Shareholder, as hereafter defined, and within ten (10) days after the Corporation's receipt of insurance proceeds as set forth under Section 4.03 hereof, the Corporation shall purchase and redeem, and the disabled Shareholder shall sell, all of the disabled Shareholder's shares in the Corporation at the price set forth under Section 4.07 of this Agreement. For purposes of this paragraph, "disability" shall be defined in accordance with the terms of the disability insurance policy on the disabled Shareholder that is owned at the time of the onset of the disability. In the absence of such a disability definition in said insurance policy, "disability" shall mean any Shareholder's inability to perform all or substantially all of his regular duties as contemplated by his employment by the Corporation for a period of twelve (12) consecutive months. If the disabled Shareholder should die after becoming disabled but before the actual sale of his shares, then the purchase and sale of his shares shall be treated and conducted in accordance with Section 4.01 hereof.

Section 4.03. Insurance to Fund Buyout in the Event of Death or Disability. To fund the payment of the purchase price for any Shareholder's shares to be purchased by the Corporation upon a Shareholder's death or disability, the Corporation shall maintain life and disability insurance policies on each of the Shareholders. Said

Ch 6 Forms

policies shall belong exclusively to the Corporation which shall reserve all powers and rights of ownership of said policies. In that event, too, the Corporation shall be named as the beneficiary of said policies and shall pay all premiums as they become due. Any proceeds paid on said policies before maturity or upon any Shareholder's death or disability shall be paid directly to the Corporation. Upon receipt of said proceeds following a Shareholder's death or disability, he consideration to be paid for that Shareholder's shares under this Article IV shall then be paid by the Corporation to the disabled Shareholder or his estate, as the case may be. The Corporation shall file all necessary proofs of death or disability and the deceased or disabled Shareholder's executor or personal representative shall apply for and obtain any necessary court approval or confirmation of the sale of that Shareholder's shares to the Corporation under this Agreement. In the event that the purchase price exceeds the amount of insurance proceeds, the Corporation shall pay the balance due on the purchase price pursuant to Section 4.08 hereof. In the event, however, that the insurance proceeds exceed the purchase price, the excess shall be paid to the disabled Shareholder or his estate, as the case may be.

Section 4.04. Retirement of a Shareholder from Business. For the first three (3) years of this Agreement, no Shareholder shall be permitted to voluntarily retire or resign from his employment by the Corporation without forfeiting his equity investment and interest in the Corporation. Following the third anniversary of this Agreement, any Shareholder who wishes to no longer be employed by the Corporation or be affiliated with the business of the Corporation (hereinafter referred to as the "Retiring Shareholder") shall be obligated to first offer his shares to the remaining Shareholders pursuant to the terms of this Section 4.04. In that event, the remaining Shareholders shall then have the option, but not the obligation, for a period of forty-five (45) days following notice from the Retiring Shareholder to purchase the shares of the Retiring Shareholder for the price and on the terms provided under Section 4.07 and 4.08 hereof. Within said forty-five (45) -day period, each interested remaining Shareholder shall deliver to the Retired Shareholder as well as the Secretary of the Corporation a written election to purchase up to one-third (1/3) of the Retiring Shareholder's shares. Any shares of the Retiring Shareholder not purchased on such a proportionate basis shall then be allocated in one or more successive allocations to those remaining Shareholders interested in purchasing more shares than those to which he has a proportionate right, up to the number of shares remaining. The Secretary of the Corporation shall then promptly give written notice of the foregoing purchases to each of the purchasing remaining Shareholder(s), who shall then pay the purchase price to the Retired Shareholder and otherwise complete the purchase within ten (10) days thereafter in accordance with Sections 4.07 and 4.08 hereof.

In the event that the Remaining Shareholders fail to collectively or individually purchase any or all of the shares of the Retiring Shareholder within said forty-five (45) -day period pursuant to this paragraph, the Corporation shall then have the option, but not the obligation, for an additional ten (10) days, to purchase any or all remaining shares of the Retiring Shareholder for the price and on the terms provided under Section 4.07 and 4.08 hereof. If the Corporation so elects within said ten (10)-day period, the Secretary of the Corporation shall then give written notice to that effect to the Retiring Shareholder and the Corporation shall pay the purchase price and otherwise complete the purchase within ten (10) days thereafter in accordance with Sections 4.07 and 4.08 hereof.

In the event that the remaining Shareholders and the Corporation collectively fail to purchase all of the shares of the Retired Shareholder, the Retired Shareholder may either retain any unpurchased shares or solicit offers from bona fide third parties; provided, however, that any offers thereafter received from such bona fide third parties shall be subject to Section 4.09 hereof and the other terms and conditions of this Agreement.

Section 4.05. Divorce of a Shareholder. Each of the Shareholders of the Corporation, together with his respective spouse, all of which are signatories to this Agreement, agree that, to the extent possible or practicable, the husband Shareholder shall, in any division of property, retain all of the shares in the Corporation upon the divorce or permanent separation of the husband Shareholder from his spouse. In the event, however, that part or all of a husband Shareholder's shares in the Corporation are nonetheless transferred or awarded to his spouse under a decree of divorce or judgment of dissolution or separate maintenance, or under a property settlement or separation agreement, each of the Shareholders of the Corporation, together with his respective spouse, acknowledges and agrees that said transfer or award shall constitute an offer by the spouse to sell to her estranged husband Shareholder, for a period of forty-five (45) days, any or all of those shares transferred or awarded to her (hereinafter referred to as the "Offered Shares"), for the price and on the terms provided under Sections 4.07 and 4.08 hereof. In the event that the estranged husband Shareholder elects not to purchase all of the Offered Shares within said forty-five (45) -day period, the remaining Shareholders shall then have the option, but not the obligation, for a period of forty-five (45) days following notice from the spouse of the estranged husband Shareholder to purchase the Offered Shares for the price and on the terms provided under Section 4.07 and 4.08 hereof. Within said forty-five (45) -day period, each interested remaining Shareholder shall deliver to the spouse of the estranged husband Shareholder as well as the Secretary of the Corporation a written election to purchase up to one-third (1/3) of the Offered Shares. Any Offered Shares not purchased on such a proportionate basis shall then

Ch 6 Forms

be allocated in one or more successive allocations to those remaining Shareholders interested in purchasing more shares than those to which he has a proportionate right, up to the number of Offered Shares remaining. The Secretary of the Corporation shall then promptly give written notice of the foregoing purchases to each of the purchasing remaining Shareholder(s), who shall then pay the purchase price to the spouse and otherwise complete the purchase within ten (10) days thereafter in accordance with Sections 4.07 and 4.08 hereof.

In the event that the Remaining Shareholders fail to collectively or individually purchase any or all of the Offered Shares within said forty-five (45)-day period pursuant to this paragraph, the Corporation shall then have the option, but not the obligation, for an additional ten (10) days, in which to purchase any or all remaining Offered Shares for the price and on the terms provided under Section 4.07 and 4.08 hereof. If the Corporation so elects within said ten (10) -day period, the Secretary of the Corporation shall then give written notice to that effect to the spouse of the estranged husband Shareholder and the Corporation shall pay the purchase price and otherwise complete the purchase within ten (10) days thereafter accordance with Sections 4.07 and 4.08 hereof.

In the event that the remaining Shareholders and the Corporation collectively fail to purchase all of the Offered Shares, the spouse of the estranged husband Shareholder may then either retain any unpurchased Offered Shares or solicit offers from bona fide third parties; provided, however, that any offers thereafter received from such bona fide third parties shall be subject to Section 4.09 hereof and the other terms and conditions of this Agreement.

Section 4.06. Redemption Limitations. In the event it is not legally possible for the Corporation to purchase a deceased or disabled Shareholder's shares under Sections 4.01 and 4.02 hereof because the insurance proceeds are insufficient and the Corporation independently cannot meet the purchase price without violating the requirements of California Corporations Code sections 500-501, the Corporation shall purchase as many of that Shareholder's shares as it is legally permitted to purchase under those sections, and the balance of the shares shall continue to be held by the disabled Shareholder or his estate subject to this Agreement.

Section 4.07. Purchase Price for Shares. Except as otherwise provided for instances arising under Section 4.09, the purchase price to be paid for each share subject to this Article IV shall be equal to the agreed value of the Corporation divided by the number of shares outstanding. The initial agreed value of the Corporation is $45,000.00. Every anniversary hereafter, within ninety (90) days of the close of the Corporation's calendar year, the Shareholders agree to meet and review the Corporation's financial condition as of the end of the preceding calendar year and decide, by mutual agreement, the Corporation's current fair market value, which, if agreed upon, shall be the Corporation's value until a different value is agreed upon or otherwise established under this Agreement. Whenever the Shareholders agree on the Corporation's value, they shall provide evidence of their agreement by placing their written and executed agreement in the Corporation's minute book. If the Shareholders are unable to mutually agree upon the Corporation's fair market value, said value shall be determined by appraisal. An appraiser shall be mutually selected by the parties. If the parties are unable to mutually agree upon an appraiser, each shall have five (5) days in which to appoint a qualified appraiser. If either party fails to appoint an appraiser within said five (5) -day period, the other parties' appraiser(s) shall fix the fair market value of the Corporation. In the event that there are only two (2) appraisers and they cannot agree on an appraised value, they shall together select a third appraiser whose sole appraisal shall establish the value of the Corporation. The cost of the appraisal shall be borne equally among the parties. In the event no agreed value is reached by the Corporation's shareholders for a period of two years or more, the prior agreed to value will not be controlling and the value of the shares will be subject to mutual agreement or approval as set forth herein. In the event a third party appeal is necessary, the appraiser shall factor in appropriate discounts for minority interests and lack of a public market.

Section 4.08. Payment of Purchase Price. In the event that there are insufficient insurance proceeds pursuant to Section 4.03 hereof to fund the purchase price of any shares purchased by the Corporation under Section 4.01 or Section 4.02, or in any buyout instance triggered by Sections 4.04, 4.05, or 4.09 by either the remaining Shareholders or the Corporation, the purchase price may be paid in thirty-six (36) consecutive equal monthly installments, with the unpaid balance of the purchase price evidenced by a promissory note bearing interest at the lesser of the then going prime interest rate last published by the Bank of America, N.T. & S.A. plus five (5) points, or the maximum rate permitted by applicable law. The note shall provide that in the event of default in payment of principal, the note will be accelerated and become immediately due and payable. The note may be prepaid in whole or in part at any time without a prepayment penalty.

Section 4.09. Right of First Refusal. For the first three (3) years of this Agreement, no Shareholder shall be permitted to sell, transfer, or otherwise dispose of his shares in the Corporation to any third party without forfeiting his equity investment and interest in the Corporation. Following the third anniversary of this Agreement, should any Shareholder receive an offer from a bona fide third party (as hereafter defined) to sell, transfer, or otherwise dispose of any of his shares in the Corporation, or any interest therein (hereinafter referred to as the "Offering Shareholder"), the Offering Shareholder shall be obligated to first offer his shares to the remaining Shareholders in the manner prescribed hereunder (hereinafter referred to as the "Offering Notice"). For purposes of Article IV, a "bona fide third party" shall be defined to mean a person, entity, or firm who has offered to purchase the shares and who has tendered no less than ten percent (10%) of the purchase price for the shares as a deposit to the Offering Shareholder. The Offering Notice shall specify: (1) the name and address of the bona fide third party; (2) the number of shares the Offering Shareholder proposes to sell or transfer; (3) the price or amount per share to be paid; and (4) all other terms and conditions of the proposed sale.

Upon receipt of the Offering Notice from the Offering Shareholder, the remaining Shareholders shall then have the option, but not the obligation, for a period of forty-five (45) days thereafter to purchase the shares of the Offering Shareholder at the price and on the terms and conditions stated in the Offering Notice, subject to Section 4.08 hereof. Within said forty-five (45) -day period, each interested remaining Shareholder shall deliver to the Offering Shareholder as well as the Secretary of the Corporation a written election to purchase up to one-third (1/3) of the Offering Shareholder's shares. Any shares of the Offering Shareholder not purchased on such a proportionate basis shall then be allocated in one or more successive allocations to those remaining Shareholders interested in purchasing more shares than those to which he has a proportionate right, up to the number of shares remaining. The Secretary of the Corporation shall then promptly give written notice of the foregoing purchases to each of the purchasing remaining Shareholder(s), who shall then pay the purchase price to the Offering Shareholder and otherwise complete the purchase in accordance with the terms of the sale to the proposed transferee as set forth in the Offering Notice, except, however, that the purchase price to the Offering Shareholder may, at the election of the purchasing remaining Shareholders, be paid pursuant to Section 4.08 hereof.

In the event that the remaining Shareholders fail to collectively or individually purchase any or all of the shares of the Offering Shareholder specified in the Offering Notice within said forty-five (45) -day period pursuant to this paragraph, the Corporation shall then have the option, but not the obligation, for an additional ten (10) days, in which to purchase any or all remaining shares of the Offering Shareholder at the price and on the terms and conditions stated in the Offering Notice, subject to Section 4.08 hereof. If the Corporation so elects within said ten (10) -day period, the Secretary of the Corporation shall then give written notice to that effect to the Offering Shareholder and the Corporation shall pay the purchase price to the Offering Shareholder and otherwise complete the purchase in accordance with the terms of the sale to the proposed transferee as set forth in the Offering Notice, except, however, that the purchase price to the Offering Shareholder may, at the election of the Corporation, be paid pursuant to Section 4.08 hereof.

Should the remaining Shareholders and the Corporation fail to collectively purchase all of the shares of the Offering Shareholder specified in the Offering Notice, the Offering Shareholder may sell any unpurchased shares to the bona fide third party specified in the Offering Notice, at the price and on the terms and conditions specified therein. The Offering Shareholder may not, however, sell any or all of the Offered Shares to any other person, firm, or third party or at any other price or on any other terms or conditions than those specified in the Offering Notice without first giving new written notice of his intention to do so pursuant to this Section 4.09, upon which event, the remaining Shareholders and the Corporation shall then be entitled once again to the rights of first refusal set forth herein.

Section 4.10. Obligations of Transferees. Each permitted transferee of shares of the Corporation, or any interest therein, as a precondition to obtaining any interest in the Corporation's shares, shall (i) hold such shares or interest subject to all of the provisions of this Agreement; (ii) become a signatory to this Agreement upon receipt of the shares; (iii) execute and deliver to the Corporation an appropriate investment representation letter in form and substance satisfactory to the Corporation, its counsel, and the other Shareholders; and (iv) make no further transfers of the shares except as herein provided. Notwithstanding the foregoing, no shares shall hereafter be transferred to any transferee unless the transfer is made pursuant to (i) an effective registration statement under the Securities Act of 1933, as amended, and applicable state securities laws; or (ii) an appropriate exemption therefrom, in which event the transferee shall furnish to the Corporation an opinion of counsel, reasonably satisfactory to the Corporation and its counsel, that the transfer is exempt from such registration requirements. The transferor of the shares also agrees to make it an express condition of any transfer of his shares that the transferee become a signatory to this Agreement upon receipt of the shares and be bound by the provisions hereof.

ARTICLE V. MISCELLANEOUS

Section 5.01. Shareholders' Will. Each of the Shareholders agrees to include in his Will a direction and authorization to his executor to comply with the provisions of this Agreement and to sell and/or transfer his shares only in accordance with the terms hereof; the failure, however, of a Shareholder to do so shall not affect the validity of this Agreement.

Section 5.02. Necessary Acts. Each party to this Agreement agrees to perform such further acts and execute and deliver such additional documents as may be reasonably necessary to carry out the provisions hereof. Section 5.03. Construction. This Agreement shall be construed and enforced in accordance with the laws of the State of California.

Ch 6 Forms

Section 5.04. Notices. All notices, requests, demands, and other communications contemplated hereunder shall be in writing and shall be deemed to have been duly given when personally delivered or when mailed by United States express, certified or registered mail, postage prepaid, to the parties at the addresses set forth below.

Section 5.05. Successors-in-Interest. This Agreement shall be binding upon and shall inure to the benefit of the parties hereto and their respective heirs, legal representatives, successors, and assigns.

Section 5.06. Binding Arbitration in Event of Dispute. In the event of a dispute arising out of or relating to any of the terms or conditions of this Agreement, the parties agree to submit the matter to binding arbitration in accordance with the then current rules of the American Arbitration Association, from which any judgment rendered by the arbitrator may be admitted and enforced in any court having jurisdiction thereof.

Section 5.07. Attorneys' Fees and Litigation Costs. Should any arbitration, proceeding, or other legal action be brought for the enforcement of this Agreement, the successful or prevailing party shall be entitled to recover its reasonable attorneys', accounting, and other professional fees, if any, and any other costs incurred in such arbitration, proceeding, or other action, at trial, on appeal, or in collection thereof, in addition to any other relief to which he or it may be entitled.

Section 5.08. Entire Agreement. This Agreement constitutes the entire agreement between the parties hereto with respect to the subject matter hereof and supersedes any and all prior or contemporaneous agreements, understandings, discussions, negotiations, and/or commitments of any kind. This Agreement may not be amended or supplemented, nor may any right hereunder be waived, except by a written instrument signed by each of the parties affected thereby.

Section 5.09. Section Headings. The section headings in this Agreement are included for convenience only, are not a part of this Agreement, and shall not be used in construing it.

Section 5.10. Severability. In the event that any provision of this Agreement is held to be illegal, invalid, or unenforceable, such illegality, invalidity, or unenforceability shall not affect the validity or enforceability of any other provision or part hereof.

Section 5.11. Counterparts. This Agreement may be executed in one or more counterparts, each of which shall be deemed an original but all of which shall together constitute one and the same instrument.

IN WITNESS WHEREOF, the parties hereto have executed this Agreement effective the date and year first above written.

"Corporation"

_____

a California corporation   Address

By: _____

Title: _____

"Shareholders" and Spouses

_____   _____

Spouse   Address

_____   _____

Spouse   Address

_____   _____

Spouse   Address

We, the above consenting spouses, acknowledge that we have read the foregoing Agreement and know the contents thereof. We are aware that by its provisions our respective spouses agree to sell their shares in the Corporation, including any community interest we may have in them, on the occurrence of certain events. We each nonetheless hereby consent to any sale authorized by this Agreement, approve of the provisions of this Agreement, and agree that those shares and our respective interests therein are subject to the provisions of this Agreement and that we each shall take no action at any time to hinder operation of this Agreement or those shares or our interests, if any, therein.

Ch 6 Forms

Forms for Chapter 7

There are two forms that accompany **Chapter 7, Corporate and LLC Variations**. They include the following:

Form 7-A   Sample Articles of Incorporation Designating Initial Directors, 2 pages (339 - 340)

Form 7-B   Sample Articles of Incorporation Not Designating Initial Directors, 2 pages (341 - 342)

There is an additional $15 counter fee for Articles of Incorporation filed in person with the Secretary of State.

ARTICLES OF INCORPORATION DESIGNATING INITIAL DIRECTORS

ARTICLES OF INCORPORATION OF

_____

ARTICLE I. NAME

The name of the corporation is_____.

ARTICLE II. PURPOSE

The purpose of this corporation is to engage in any lawful act or activity for which a corporation may be organized under the General Corporation Law of California other than the banking business, the trust company business, or the practice of a profession permitted to be incorporated by the California Corporations Code.

ARTICLE III. DIRECTORS

The number of Directors of the corporation is _____. The names and addresses of the persons appointed as initial directors are:

Name   Address

1. _____   _____

2. _____   _____

3. _____   _____

The liability of the directors of the corporation for monetary damages shall be eliminated to the fullest extent permissible under California law.

ARTICLE IV. AGENT FOR SERVICE OF PROCESS

The name and address in the state of California of the corporation's initial agent for service of process is:

_____

_____

_____

ARTICLE V. INDEMNIFICATION

The corporation is authorized, to the fullest extent permissible under California law, to indemnify its agents (as defined in Section 317 of the California

Ch 7 Forms

Corporations Code), whether by bylaw, agreement, or otherwise, for breach of duty to this corporation and its shareholders in excess of that expressly permitted in Section 317 and to advance defense expenses to its agents in connection with such matters as they are incurred, subject to the limits on such excess indemnification set forth in Section 204 of the California Corporations Code.

ARTICLE VI

The corporation is authorized to issue only one class of shares of stock; and the total number of shares which this corporation is authorized to issue is 100,000.

Dated: _____, 20_____

_____
Typed Name and Signature of Director

_____
Typed Name and Signature of Director

_____
Typed Name and Signature of Director

The undersigned, being all of the persons named above as the initial directors, declare that they are the persons who executed the foregoing Articles of Incorporation, which execution is their act and deed.

_____
Typed Name and Signature of Director

_____
Typed Name and Signature of Director

_____
Typed Name and Signature of Director

This is only an example and not to be used or submitted to the Secretary of State's office.

There is an additional $15 counter fee for Articles of Incorporation filed in person with the Secretary of State.

**SAMPLE ARTICLES OF INCORPORATION BY INCORPORATOR,
NOT DESIGNATING INITIAL DIRECTORS**

SAMPLE ARTICLES OF INCORPORATION OF

_____

ARTICLE I. NAME

The name of the corporation is _____.

ARTICLE II. PURPOSE

The purpose of this corporation is to engage in any lawful act or activity for which a corporation may be organized under the General Corporation Law of California other than the banking business, the trust company business, or the practice of a profession permitted to be incorporated by the California Corporations Code.

ARTICLE III. DIRECTORS

The number of Directors of the corporation is _____.*

The liability of the directors of the corporation for monetary damages shall be eliminated to the fullest extent permissible under California law.

ARTICLE IV. AGENT FOR SERVICE OF PROCESS

The name and address in the state of California of the corporation's initial agent for service of process is:**

_____

_____

_____

ARTICLE V. INDEMNIFICATION

The corporation is authorized, to the fullest extent permissible under California law, to indemnify its agents (as defined in Section 317 of the California Corporations Code), whether by bylaw, agreement, or otherwise, for breach of duty to this corporation and its shareholders in excess of that expressly permitted in Section 317 and to advance defense expenses to its agents in connection with such matters as they are incurred, subject to the limits on such excess indemnification set forth in Section 204 of the California Corporations Code.

Ch 7
Forms

ARTICLE VI

The corporation is authorized to issue only one class of shares of stock; and the total number of shares which this corporation is authorized to issue is 100,000.***

Dated: _____, 20_____

_____
Name and Signature of Incorporator

I declare that I am the person who executed the foregoing Articles of Incorporation, and that this instrument is my act and deed.

_____
Name and Signature of Incorporator

This is only an example and not to be used or submitted to the Secretary of State's office.

*It is preferable to have an odd number of directors to avoid the possibility of a tie vote. I suggest either one or three. Please note, however, if there is more than one shareholder, there has be at least an equal number of directors up to three. That is, if there is one shareholder, there must be at least one director; if there are two shareholders, there must be at least two directors. But if there are three or more shareholders, three directors will suffice.

**The agent for process is that person whom you wish to authorize to receive legal documents on the corporation's behalf. Usually, a director or attorney of the corporation is chosen, and the address of the corporation's principal place of business or their attorney's office is given.

***A larger or smaller number of shares can be authorized. For the corporation to be exempt from registration of its shares under Cal. Corp. Code Sec. 25102(h), all of the corporation's issued shares must be held by not more than thirty-five persons.

Forms for Chapter 8

There are two forms that accompany **Chapter 8, S Corporations**. They include the following:

Form 8-A   Election by a Small Business Corporation—IRS Form 2553, 2 pages (344 - 345)

Form 8-B   S Corporation's List of Shareholders and Consents—FTB Form 3830, 1 page (346)

Form **2553**
(Rev. December 2002)
Department of the Treasury
Internal Revenue Service

Election by a Small Business Corporation

(Under section 1362 of the Internal Revenue Code)
See Parts II and III on back and the separate instructions.
The corporation may either send or fax this form to the IRS. See page 2 of the instructions.

OMB No. 1545-0146

Notes:
1. *Do not file Form 1120S*, U.S. Income Tax Return for an S Corporation, for any tax year before the year the election takes effect.
2. This election to be an S corporation can be accepted only if all the tests are met under **Who May Elect** on page 1 of the instructions; all shareholders have signed the consent statement; and the exact name and address of the corporation and other required form information are provided.
3. If the corporation was in existence before the effective date of this election, see **Taxes an S Corporation May Owe** on page 1 of the instructions.

Part I	**Election Information**

Please Type or Print

Name of corporation (see instructions)	**A** Employer identification number
Number, street, and room or suite no. (If a P.O. box, see instructions.)	**B** Date incorporated
City or town, state, and ZIP code	**C** State of incorporation

D Check the applicable box(es) if the corporation, after applying for the EIN shown in **A** above, changed its name ☐ or address ☐

E Election is to be effective for tax year beginning (month, day, year) . . . . / /

F Name and title of officer or legal representative who the IRS may call for more information **G** Telephone number of officer or legal representative
( )

H If this election takes effect for the first tax year the corporation exists, enter month, day, and year of the **earliest** of the following: (1) date the corporation first had shareholders, (2) date the corporation first had assets, or (3) date the corporation began doing business . . . . / /

I Selected tax year: Annual return will be filed for tax year ending (month and day) --------------------------------

If the tax year ends on any date other than December 31, except for a 52-53-week tax year ending with reference to the month of December, you **must** complete Part II on the back. If the date you enter is the ending date of a 52-53-week tax year, write 52-53-week year" to the right of the date.

J Name and address of each shareholder; shareholder's spouse having a community property interest in the corporation's stock; and each tenant in common, joint tenant, and tenant by the entirety. (A husband and wife (and their estates) are counted as one shareholder in determining the number of shareholders without regard to the manner in which the stock is owned.)	**K** Shareholders' Consent Statement. Under penalties of perjury, we declare that we consent to the election of the above-named corporation to be an S corporation under section 1362(a) and that we have examined this consent statement, including accompanying schedules and statements, and to the best of our knowledge and belief, it is true, correct, and complete. We understand our consent is binding and may not be withdrawn after the corporation has made a valid election. (Shareholders sign and date below.)		**L** Stock owned		**M** Social security number or employer identification number (see instructions)	**N** Share-holder's tax year ends (month and day)
	Signature	Date	Number of shares	Dates acquired		

Under penalties of perjury, I declare that I have examined this election, including accompanying schedules and statements, and to the best of my knowledge and belief, it is true, correct, and complete.

Signature of officer   Title   Date

For Paperwork Reduction Act Notice, see page 4 of the instructions.   Cat. No. 18629R   Form **2553** (Rev. 12-2002)

Ch 8
Forms

Form 2553 (Rev. 12-2002)   Page **2**

Part II   Selection of Fiscal Tax Year (All corporations using this part must complete item O and item P, Q, or R.)

O   Check the applicable box to indicate whether the corporation is:

   1. ☐ A new corporation adopting the tax year entered in item I, Part I.

   2. ☐ An existing corporation retaining the tax year entered in item I, Part I.

   3. ☐ An existing corporation changing to the tax year entered in item I, Part I.

P   Complete item P if the corporation is using the automatic approval provisions of Rev. Proc. 2002-38, 2002-22 I.R.B. 1037, to request **(1)** a natural business year (as defined in section 5.05 of Rev. Proc. 2002-38) or **(2)** a year that satisfies the ownership tax year test (as defined in section 5.06 of Rev. Proc. 2002-38). Check the applicable box below to indicate the representation statement the corporation is making.

   1. Natural Business Year ☐ I represent that the corporation is adopting, retaining, or changing to a tax year that qualifies as its natural business year as defined in section 5.05 of Rev. Proc. 2002-38 and has attached a statement verifying that it satisfies the 25% gross receipts test (see instructions for content of statement). I also represent that the corporation is not precluded by section 4.02 of Rev. Proc. 2002-38 from obtaining automatic approval of such adoption, retention, or change in tax year.

   2. Ownership Tax Year ☐ I represent that shareholders (as described in section 5.06 of Rev. Proc. 2002-38) holding more than half of the shares of the stock (as of the first day of the tax year to which the request relates) of the corporation have the same tax year or are concurrently changing to the tax year that the corporation adopts, retains, or changes to per item I, Part I, and that such tax year satisfies the requirement of section 4.01(3) of Rev. Proc. 2002-38. I also represent that the corporation is not precluded by section 4.02 of Rev. Proc. 2002-38 from obtaining automatic approval of such adoption, retention, or change in tax year.

Note: *If you do not use item P and the corporation wants a fiscal tax year, complete either item Q or R below. Item Q is used to request a fiscal tax year based on a business purpose and to make a back-up section 444 election. Item R is used to make a regular section 444 election.*

Q   Business Purpose—To request a fiscal tax year based on a business purpose, you must check box Q1. See instructions for details including payment of a user fee. You may also check box Q2 and/or box Q3.

   1. Check here ☐ if the fiscal year entered in item I, Part I, is requested under the prior approval provisions of Rev. Proc. 2002-39, 2002-22 I.R.B. 1046. Attach to Form 2553 a statement describing the relevant facts and circumstances and, if applicable, the gross receipts from sales and services necessary to establish a business purpose. See the instructions for details regarding the gross receipts from sales and services. If the IRS proposes to disapprove the requested fiscal year, do you want a conference with the IRS National Office?
   ☐ Yes   ☐ No

   2. Check here ☐ to show that the corporation intends to make a back-up section 444 election in the event the corporation's business purpose request is not approved by the IRS. (See instructions for more information.)

   3. Check here ☐ to show that the corporation agrees to adopt or change to a tax year ending December 31 if necessary for the IRS to accept this election for S corporation status in the event (1) the corporation's business purpose request is not approved and the corporation makes a back-up section 444 election, but is ultimately not qualified to make a section 444 election, or (2) the corporation's business purpose request is not approved and the corporation did not make a back-up section 444 election.

R   Section 444 Election—To make a section 444 election, you must check box R1 and you may also check box R2.

   1. Check here ☐ to show the corporation will make, if qualified, a section 444 election to have the fiscal tax year shown in item I, Part I. To make the election, you must complete **Form 8716**, Election To Have a Tax Year Other Than a Required Tax Year, and either attach it to Form 2553 or file it separately.

   2. Check here ☐ to show that the corporation agrees to adopt or change to a tax year ending December 31 if necessary for the IRS to accept this election for S corporation status in the event the corporation is ultimately not qualified to make a section 444 election.

Part III   Qualified Subchapter S Trust (QSST) Election Under Section 1361(d)(2)*

Income beneficiary's name and address	Social security number
Trust's name and address	Employer identification number

Date on which stock of the corporation was transferred to the trust (month, day, year) . . . . ▸   / /

In order for the trust named above to be a QSST and thus a qualifying shareholder of the S corporation for which this Form 2553 is filed, I hereby make the election under section 1361(d)(2). Under penalties of perjury, I certify that the trust meets the definitional requirements of section 1361(d)(3) and that all other information provided in Part III is true, correct, and complete.

_____   _____
Signature of income beneficiary or signature and title of legal representative or other qualified person making the election   Date

*Use Part III to make the QSST election only if stock of the corporation has been transferred to the trust on or before the date on which the corporation makes its election to be an S corporation. The QSST election must be made and filed separately if stock of the corporation is transferred to the trust after the date on which the corporation makes the S election.

                                              ✪   Form **2553** (Rev. 12-2002)

Ch 8 Forms

TAXABLE YEAR

2001   S Corporation's List of Shareholders and Consents

CALIFORNIA FORM
3830

For use by S corporations with one or more nonresident shareholders or trusts with nonresident fiduciaries. Attach to Form 100S and give a copy to each nonresident shareholder or fiduciary. Use additional sheet(s) if necessary.

Corporation name	California corporation number
	Federal employer identification number (FEIN)

Note: Completion of this form does not satisfy the requirements for filing an income tax return for California. See General Information B.

List below the names and identification numbers of shareholders of record at the end of the corporation's taxable year.

Number	Shareholder's name	Only nonresident shareholders and nonresident fiduciaries must sign: I consent to the jurisdiction of the State of California to tax my pro-rata share of the S corporation income attributable to California sources.		Shareholder's Social security no./Federal employer identification no.
		Signature	Date	
1				
2				
3				
4				
5				
6				
7				
8				
9				
10				
11				
12				
13				
14				
15				

List below the names and identification numbers of shareholders who sold or transferred their ownership interests before the end of the corporation's taxable year.

Number	Shareholder's name	Only nonresident shareholders and nonresident fiduciaries must sign: I consent to the jurisdiction of the State of California to tax my pro-rata share of the S corporation income attributable to California sources.		Shareholder's Social security no./Federal employer identification no.
		Signature	Date	
1				
2				
3				
4				
5				

A   Purpose

When an S corporation has one or more shareholders who are nonresidents of California or trusts with nonresident fiduciaries, use form FTB 3830 to:

- List the names and social security numbers or federal employer identification numbers of all shareholders; and
  Obtain the signature of each nonresident shareholder or fiduciary evidencing consent to the jurisdiction of California to tax their pro-rata share of income attributable to California sources. If the nonresident shareholder or nonresident fiduciary has a spouse, the spouse must also sign the form. For ease in gathering proper signatures, multiple copies of the form FTB 3830 may be used.

Caution: Failure to attach this form (with required signatures) to Form 100S is grounds for the Franchise Tax Board to retroactively revoke the S corporation election. Revenue and Taxation Code (R&TC) Section 23801(b).

For Privacy Act Notice, see form FTB 1131.

B   Nonresidents Who Must File a California Tax Return

If you are a nonresident shareholder, in addition to signing form FTB 3830, you may also need to file Form 540NR, California Nonresident or Part-Year Resident Income Tax Return (Long Form). Long Form 540NR must be filed if you had income from California sources and:

You were single or unmarried by the end of 2001 and your gross income from all sources was more than $11,901; or adjusted gross income from all sources was more than $9,521; or

You were married by the end of 2001, and you and your spouse had a combined gross income from all sources of more than $23,803; or adjusted gross income from all sources of more than $19,042; or

You can be claimed as a dependent as provided in Internal Revenue Code (IRC) Section 63(c)(5) when the individual's gross income from all sources exceeds the standard deduction allowed under the IRC; or
If you owe the State of California $1 or more of tax. (R&TC Section 18507).

C   Group Nonresident Shareholder Return

Certain nonresident shareholders of an S corporation doing business in California may elect to file a group nonresident return using Form 540NR (long). For more information, get FTB Pub. 1067, Guidelines for Filing a Group Form 540NR.

383001109

FTB 3830 c1 2001

Forms for
Chapter 9

There are four forms that accompany **Chapter 9, Limited Liability Companies**. They include the following:

Form 9-A   Limited Liability Company Articles of Organization—LLC-1, 3 pages (348 - 350)

Form 9-B   Operating Agreement for LLC (Short Form), 10 pages (351 - 360)

Form 9-C   Operating Agreement for LLC (Long Form) (same as Form 3-G, starting on page 163)

Form 9-D   Limited Liability Company—Statement of Information—LLC-12, 2 pages (361 - 362)

KEVIN SHELLEY
Secretary of State

1500 11th Street, 3rd Floor
Sacramento, CA 95814

Business Entities
(916) 657-5448

ATTENTION: LIMITED LIABILITY COMPANY FILERS

Tax Information

Pursuant to California Revenue and Taxation Code section **17941**, every Limited Liability Company (LLC) that is doing business in California or that has Articles of Organization accepted or a Certificate of Registration issued by the Secretary of State's office (pursuant to California Corporations Code section **17050** or **17451**) AND is not taxed as a corporation, is subject to the annual LLC minimum tax of $800 (as well as the appropriate fee pursuant to Revenue and Taxation Code section **17942**). The tax is paid to the California Franchise Tax Board; is due for the taxable year of organization/registration and must be paid for each taxable year, or part there of, until a Certificate of Cancellation of Registration or Certificate of Cancellation of Articles of Organization (pursuant to Corporations Code section **17356** or **17455**) is filed with the Secretary of State's office. For further information regarding the payment of this tax, please contact the Franchise Tax Board at:

From within the United States (toll free) ....(800) 852-5711
From outside the United States (not toll free) ....(916) 845-6500
Automated Toll Free Phone Service...(800) 338-0505

Professional Services

Pursuant to California Corporations Code section **17375**, a domestic or foreign limited liability company may not render professional services, as defined in Corporations Code sections **13401(a)** and **13401.3**. Professional services are defined as:

> Any type of professional services that may be lawfully rendered only pursuant to a license, certification, or registration authorized by the Business and Professions Code, the Chiropractic Act, the Osteopathic Act or the Yacht and Ship Brokers Act.

If your business is required to be licensed, registered or certified, it is recommended that you contact the appropriate licensing authority before filing with the Secretary of State's office in order to determine whether your services are considered professional.

LLC Info (REV 09/2004)

State of California
Kevin Shelley
Secretary of State

File # _____

**LIMITED LIABILITY COMPANY
ARTICLES OF ORGANIZATION**

NOTE: A limited liability company is not permitted to render professional services.

A $70.00 filing fee must accompany this form.

IMPORTANT – Read instructions before completing this form.

This Space For Filing Use Only

1. **NAME OF THE LIMITED LIABILITY COMPANY** (END THE NAME WITH THE WORDS "LIMITED LIABILITY COMPANY," "LTD. LIABILITY CO.," OR THE ABBREVIATIONS "LLC" OR "L.L.C.")

2. **THE PURPOSE OF THE LIMITED LIABILITY COMPANY IS TO ENGAGE IN ANY LAWFUL ACT OR ACTIVITY FOR WHICH A LIMITED LIABILITY COMPANY MAY BE ORGANIZED UNDER THE BEVERLY-KILLEA LIMITED LIABILITY COMPANY ACT.**

   INITIAL AGENT FOR SERVICE OF PROCESS - If the agent is an individual, the agent must reside in California and both Items 3 and 4 must be completed. If the agent is a corporation, the agent must have on file with the California Secretary of State a certificate pursuant to Corporations Code section 1505 and Item 3 must be completed (leave Item 4 blank).

3. **NAME OF THE INITIAL AGENT FOR SERVICE OF PROCESS** _____

4. **IF AN INDIVIDUAL, THE ADDRESS OF THE INITIAL AGENT FOR SERVICE OF PROCESS IN CALIFORNIA**

   ADDRESS _____

   CITY _____ STATE **CA** ZIP CODE _____

5. **THE LIMITED LIABILITY COMPANY WILL BE MANAGED BY: (CHECK ONLY ONE)**

   ☐ ONE MANAGER

   ☐ MORE THAN ONE MANAGER

   ☐ ALL LIMITED LIABILITY COMPANY MEMBER(S)

6. **ADDITIONAL INFORMATION SET FORTH ON THE ATTACHED PAGES, IF ANY, IS INCORPORATED HEREIN BY THIS REFERENCE AND MADE A PART OF THIS CERTIFICATE.**

7. **TYPE OF BUSINESS OF THE LIMITED LIABILITY COMPANY (FOR INFORMATIONAL PURPOSES ONLY)**

8. **I DECLARE I AM THE PERSON WHO EXECUTED THIS INSTRUMENT, WHICH EXECUTION IS MY ACT AND DEED.**

   _____   _____
   SIGNATURE OF ORGANIZER   DATE

   _____
   TYPE OR PRINT NAME OF ORGANIZER

9. **RETURN TO:**

   NAME

   FIRM

   ADDRESS

   CITY/STATE

   ZIP CODE

LLC-1 (REV 06/2004)   APPROVED BY SECRETARY OF STATE

INSTRUCTIONS FOR COMPLETING THE ARTICLES OF ORGANIZATION (Form LLC-1)

For easier completion, this form is available on the Secretary of State's website at http://www.ss.ca.gov/business and can be viewed, filled in and printed from your computer. The completed form along with the applicable fees can be mailed to Secretary of State, Document Filing Support Unit, P O Box 944228, Sacramento, CA 94244-2280 or delivered in person to the Sacramento office, 1500 11th Street, 3rd Floor, Sacramento, CA 95814. If you are not completing this form online, please type or legibly print in black or blue ink.

Statutory filing requirements can be found in California Corporations Code section 17051 and 17052. All statutory references are to the California Corporations Code, unless otherwise stated.

Pursuant to Section 17375, a business that is required to be licensed, registered, or certified under the Business and Professions Code is not permitted to be a California or foreign qualified limited liability company.

FEES: The fee for filing the Articles of Organization is $70.00. A $15.00 special handling fee is applicable for processing documents delivered in person to the Sacramento office. The $15.00 special handling fee must be remitted by separate check for each submittal and will be retained whether the documents are filed or rejected. The special handling fee does not apply to documents submitted by mail. Check(s) should be made payable to the Secretary of State.

Filing this document shall obligate most limited liability companies to pay an annual minimum tax of $800 to the Franchise Tax Board pursuant to Revenue and Taxation Code section 17941.

Complete the Articles of Organization (Form LLC-1) as follows:

Item 1. Enter the name of the limited liability company. The name must contain the words "Limited Liability Company," "Ltd. Liability Co.," or the abbreviations "LLC" or "L.L.C." The name of the limited liability company may not contain the words "bank," "trust," "trustee," incorporated," "inc.," "corporation," or "corp.," and must not contain the words "insurer" or "insurance company" or any other words suggesting that it is in the business of issuing policies of insurance and assuming insurance risks.

Item 2. This statement is required by statute and must not be altered. Provisions limiting or restricting the business of the limited liability company may be included as an attachment.

Item 3. Enter the name of the agent for service of process in California. The person named as agent must be a resident of California or a corporation that has filed a certificate pursuant to Corporations Code section 1505. If an individual is designated as agent, both Items 3 and 4 must be completed. If a corporation is designated, complete Item 3 and proceed to Item 5 (do not complete Item 4). An Agent for Service of Process is an "individual" or corporation designated by a limited liability company to accept service of process if the limited liability company is sued.

Item 4. If an individual is designated as the initial agent for service of process, enter the agent's address in California. Do not enter "in care of" (c/o) or abbreviate the name of the city. DO NOT enter an address if a corporation is designated as the agent for service of process.

Item 5. Check the appropriate provision indicating whether the limited liability company is to be managed by one manager, more than one manager or all limited liability company members.

Item 6. If additional information is to be included in the Articles of Organization, attach additional pages, as necessary. Additional information may include the latest date on which the limited liability company is to dissolve.

Item 7. Briefly describe the type of business that constitutes the principal business activity of the limited liability company. A limited liability company is not permitted to render professional services pursuant to Section 17375. **Professional services** are defined as: "Any type of professional services that may be lawfully rendered only pursuant to a license, certification, or registration authorized by the Business and Professions Code, the Chiropractic Act, the Osteopathic Act or the Yacht and Ship Brokers Act." (Sections 13401 and 13401.3.)

Item 8. The Articles of Organization must be signed by the organizer. The person signing the Articles of Organization need not be a member or manager of the limited liability company.

If the Articles of Organization are signed by an attorney-in-fact, the signature should be followed by the words "Attorney-in-fact for (name of person)."

If the Articles of Organization are signed by an entity, the person who signs on behalf of the entity should note their name and position/title and the entity name. Example: If a limited liability company ("Smith LLC") is the organizer, the signature of the person signing on behalf of the Smith LLC should be reflected as Joe Smith, Manager of Smith LLC, Organizer.

If the Articles of Organization are signed by a trust, the trustee should sign as follows: _____, trustee for _____ trust (including the date of the trust, if applicable). Example: Mary Todd, trustee of the Lincoln Family Trust (U/T 5-1-94).

Item 9. Enter the name and the address of the person or firm to whom a copy of the filing should be returned.

OPERATING AGREEMENT FOR

_____ **LLC**

A CALIFORNIA LIMITED LIABILITY COMPANY

This Operating Agreement (this "Agreement") is made as of _____, 20___, by and among the parties listed on the signature pages hereof (collectively referred to as the "Members" or individually as a "Member"), with reference to the following facts:

A. The Members have filed Articles of Organization (the "Articles") for _____ LLC (the "Company"), a limited liability company under the laws of the State of California, with the California Secretary of State.

B. The Members desire to adopt and approve an operating agreement for the Company under the Beverly-Killea Limited Liability Company Act (the "Act").

NOW, THEREFORE, the Members by this Agreement set forth the operating agreement for the Company upon the terms and subject to the conditions of this Agreement.

ARTICLE I. ORGANIZATIONAL MATTERS

1.1 Name. The name of the Company shall be "_____ LLC." The Company may conduct business under that name or any other name approved by the Members.

1.2 Term. The Company's existence commenced as of the date of the filing of the Articles and shall continue until dissolved pursuant to the provisions of this Agreement.

1.3 Office and Agent. The Company shall continuously maintain an office and registered agent in the State of California as required by the Act. The principal office of the Company shall be at _____ or such other location as the Members may determine. The registered agent shall be as stated in the Articles or as otherwise determined by the Members.

1.4 Business of the Company. Notwithstanding the Company's purpose described in the Articles, the Company shall not engage in any business other than the following without the consent of all of the Members:

(a) the business of _____; and

(b) such other activities directly related to the foregoing business as may be necessary or advisable in the reasonable opinion of the Members to further such business.

Ch 9
Forms

ARTICLE II. CAPITAL CONTRIBUTIONS

2.1 Capital Contributions. Each Member shall make a cash contribution to the Company's capital in the amount shown opposite the Member's name on Exhibit A to this Agreement. No Member shall be required to make any additional capital contributions to the Company. Additional contributions to the Company's capital shall be made only with the unanimous consent of the Members. Except as provided in this Agreement, no Member may withdraw his or her capital contribution.

2.2 Capital Accounts. The Company shall establish an individual capital account ("Capital Account") for each Member. The Company shall determine and maintain each Capital Account in accordance with Treasury Regulations Section 1.704-1(b)(2)(iv). Upon a valid transfer of a Member's interest in the Company ("Membership Interest") in accordance with Article VI, such Member's Capital Account shall carry over to the new owner.

2.3 No Interest. The Company shall not pay any interest on capital contributions.

ARTICLE III. MEMBERS

3.1 Admission of Additional Members. Additional Members may be admitted with the approval of all Members. Additional Members will participate in the Company's management, Net Profits, Net Losses, and distributions on such terms as the Members determine. The Members shall amend Exhibit A on the admission of an additional Member to set forth such Member's name and capital contribution. "Net Profits" and "Net Losses" shall mean the income, gain, loss, deductions, and credits of the Company in the aggregate or separately stated, as appropriate, determined in accordance with the method of accounting at the close of each fiscal year employed on the Company's information tax return filed for federal income tax purposes.

3.2 Withdrawals or Resignations. No Member may withdraw, retire or resign from the Company.

3.3 Payments to Members. Except as specified in this Agreement or pursuant to a transaction permitted by Section 4.6, no Member or person or entity controlled by, controlling, or under common control with the Member (each such person or entity is defined as an "Affiliate") is entitled to remuneration for services rendered or goods provided to the Company. However, the Company shall reimburse the Members and their Affiliates for organizational expenses (including, without limitation, legal and accounting fees and costs) incurred to form the Company, prepare the Articles and this Agreement and, as approved by the Members, for the actual cost of goods and materials used by the Company.

ARTICLE IV. MANAGEMENT

4.1 Management and Powers. Each Member intends, by entering into this Agreement, to actively engage in the Company's management. Accordingly, unless otherwise limited by the Articles or this Agreement, each Member shall have full, complete, and exclusive authority, power, and discretion to manage and control the Company's business, property, and affairs, to make all decisions regarding those matters, and to perform any and all other acts or activities customary or incident to the management of the Company's business, property, and affairs.

4.2 Member Approval. No annual or regular Member meetings are required. However, if such meetings are held, such meetings shall be noticed, held and conducted pursuant to the Act. In any instance in which the Members' approval is required under this Agreement, such approval may be obtained in any manner permitted by the Act. Unless otherwise provided in this Agreement, Member approval shall mean the approval of Members who hold a majority of the Membership Interests.

4.3 Devotion of Time. Each Member shall devote whatever time or effort as he or she deems appropriate for the furtherance of the Company's business.

4.4 Fiduciary Duties. The only fiduciary duties a Member owes to the Company and the other Members are the duty of loyalty and the duty of care set forth in subsections (i) and (ii) below:

(i) A Member's duty of loyalty to the Company and the other Members is limited to the following:

(a) To account to the Company and hold as trustee for the Company any property, profit, or benefit derived by the Member in the conduct or winding up of the Company's business or derived from any use by the Member of Company property, including the appropriation of a Company opportunity, without the consent of the other Members;

(b) To refrain from dealing with the Company in the conduct or winding up of the Company business as or on behalf of a party having an interest adverse to the Company without the consent of the other Members; and

(c) Except as otherwise provided in this Agreement, to refrain from competing with the Company in the conduct of Company business before the Company's dissolution without the other Members' consent.

(ii) A Member's duty of care to the Company and the other Members in the conduct and winding up of the Company's business is limited to refraining from engaging in grossly negligent or reckless conduct, intentional misconduct, or a knowing violation of law by the Member.

Ch 9
Forms

ARTICLE V. ALLOCATIONS OF NET PROFITS AND NET LOSSES AND DISTRIBUTIONS

5.1 Tax Allocations. All items of Company income, gain, loss, or deduction shall be allocated for federal, state, and local income tax purposes to the Members, pro rata, in accordance with their respective Percentage Interests.

5.2 Qualified Income Offset. If any Member unexpectedly receives an adjustment, allocation, or distribution that results in a deficit balance in that Member's Capital Account, there shall be allocated to that Member items of Company income and gain in an amount and manner sufficient to eliminate such deficit balance as quickly as possible.

5.3 Distribution of Assets by the Company. Subject to applicable law and any limitations contained elsewhere in this Agreement, Members holding a majority of the Membership Interests may elect from time to time to cause the Company to make distributions. Distributions shall be first to the Members in proportion to their unreturned capital contributions until each Member has recovered his or her capital contributions, and then to the Members in proportion to their Membership Interests.

ARTICLE VI. TRANSFER AND ASSIGNMENT OF INTERESTS

6.1 Transfer and Assignment of Interests. No Member shall be entitled to transfer, assign, convey, sell, encumber, or in any way alienate all or any part of his or her Membership Interest (collectively, "transfer") except with the prior approval of all Members, which approval may be given or withheld at the sole discretion of the Members.

6.2 Substitution of Members. A transferee of a Membership Interest shall have the right to become a substitute Member only if (a) Member consent is given in accordance with Section 6.1, (b) such person executes an instrument satisfactory to the Members accepting and adopting the terms and provisions of this Agreement, and (c) such person pays any reasonable expenses in connection with his or her admission as a new Member. The admission of a substitute Member shall not release the Member who assigned the Membership Interest from any liability that such Member may have to the Company.

6.3 Transfers in Violation of This Agreement and Transfers of Partial Membership Interests. Upon a transfer in violation of this Article VI, the transferee shall have no right to vote or participate in the Company's management or to exercise any Member rights. Such transferee shall only be entitled to receive the share of Net Profits, Net Losses, and distributions of the Company's assets to which the transferor would otherwise be entitled. Notwithstanding the immediately preceding sentences, if, in the determination of the remaining Members, a transfer in violation of this Article VI would cause the Company's termination under the Code, in the sole discretion of the remaining Members, the transfer shall be null and void.

ARTICLE VII. ACCOUNTING, RECORDS, REPORTING BY MEMBERS

7.1 Books and Records. The Company's books and records shall be kept in accordance with the accounting methods followed for federal income tax purposes. The Company shall maintain at its principal office in California all records required to be maintained by the Company pursuant to the Act.

7.2 Reports. The Company shall cause to be filed, in accordance with the Act, all reports and documents required to be filed with any governmental agency. The Company shall cause to be prepared at least annually information concerning the Company's operations necessary for the completion of the Members' federal and state income tax returns. The Company shall send or cause to be sent to each Member within ninety (90) days after the end of each taxable year (i) such information as is necessary to complete the Members' federal and state income tax or information returns and (ii) a copy of the Company's federal, state, and local income tax or information returns for the year.

7.3 Bank Accounts. The Members shall maintain the Company's funds in one or more separate bank accounts in the Company's name, and shall not permit the Company's funds to be commingled in any fashion with any other person's funds. Any Member, acting alone, is authorized to endorse checks, drafts, and other evidences of indebtedness made payable to the order of the Company, but only for the purpose of deposit into the Company's accounts. All checks, drafts, and other instruments obligating the Company to pay money in an amount of less than $_____ may be signed by any one Member, acting alone. All checks, drafts, and other instruments obligating the Company to pay money in an amount of $_____ or more must be signed on behalf of the Company by any _____ Members acting together.

ARTICLE VIII. DISSOLUTION AND WINDING UP

8.1 Company Dissolution. The Company shall dissolve, dispose of its assets, and wind up its affairs on the first to occur of the following (each, a "Dissolution Event"):

A. Upon the entry of a decree of judicial dissolution pursuant to Section 17351 of the Corporations Code;

B. Upon the vote of Members holding at least _____ percent (__%) of the Membership Interests;

C. The sale of all or substantially all of the Company's assets; or

D. The happening of any event that makes it unlawful or impossible to carry on the Company's business.

8.2 Winding Up. On the occurrence of a Dissolution Event, the Company shall dispose of its assets and wind up its affairs. The Company shall give written notice of the commencement of the dissolution to all of its known creditors.

8.3 Payment of Liabilities upon Dissolution. After determining that all of the Company's known debts and liabilities have been paid or adequately provided for, the Company shall distribute the remaining assets to the Members in accordance with their positive capital account balances, after taking into account income and loss allocations for the Company's taxable year during which liquidation occurs.

8.4 Limitations on Payments Made in Dissolution. Except as otherwise specifically provided in this Agreement, each Member shall (a) be entitled to look only to the Company's assets for the return of his or her positive Capital Account balance, and (b) have no recourse for his or her Capital Contribution and/or share of Net Profits against any other Member, except as provided in Article X.

8.5 Certificates. The Company shall file a Certificate of Dissolution with the California Secretary of State on the Company's dissolution and a Certificate of Cancellation on the Company's completion of the winding up of its affairs.

ARTICLE IX. INDEMNIFICATION

9.1 Indemnification of Agents. The Company shall indemnify any Member and may indemnify any person who was or is a party or is threatened to be made a party to any threatened, pending, or completed action, suit, or proceeding because he or she is or was a Company Member, officer, employee, or other agent or that, being or having been such a Member, officer, employee, or agent, he or she is or was serving at the Company's request as a manager, director, officer, employee, or other agent of another limited liability company, corporation, partnership, joint venture, trust, or other enterprise (all such persons being referred to hereinafter as an "agent"), to the fullest extent permitted by applicable law in effect on the date hereof and to such greater extent as applicable law may hereafter from time to time permit.

ARTICLE X. INVESTMENT REPRESENTATIONS

Each Member represents and warrants to, and agrees with, the Members and the Company as follows:

10.1 Management Participation. The member will be actively engaged in the management of the Company.

Ch 9 Forms

10.2 Preexisting Relationship or Experience. The Member has a preexisting personal or business relationship with the Company or one or more of its officers or controlling persons, or because of the member's business or financial experience, or because of the business or financial experience of the Member's financial advisor who is unaffiliated with and who is not compensated, directly or indirectly, by the Company or any affiliate or selling agent of the Company, the Member is capable of evaluating the risks and merits of an investment in the Company and of protecting the Member's own interests in connection with this investment.

10.3 No Advertising. The Member has not seen, received, been presented with, or been solicited by any leaflet, public promotional meeting, article, or any other form of advertising or general solicitation with respect to the sale of the Membership Interest.

10.4 Investment Intent. The Member is acquiring the Membership Interest for investment purposes for the Members' own account only and not with a view to or for sale in connection with any distribution of all or any part of the Membership Interest. No other person will have any direct or indirect beneficial interest in or right to the Membership Interest.

10.5 Residency. The Member is a resident of, or incorporated in, the State of California.

ARTICLE XI. MISCELLANEOUS

11.1 Counsel to the Company. Company counsel may also be counsel to any Member or any Affiliate of a Member. The Members may execute on behalf of the Company and the Members any consent to the representation of the Company that counsel may request pursuant to the California Rules of Professional Conduct or similar rules in any other jurisdiction ("Rules"). The Company has initially selected _____ ("Company Counsel") as legal counsel to the Company. Each Member acknowledges that Company Counsel does not represent any Member in the absence of a clear and explicit agreement to such effect between the Member and Company Counsel, and that in the absence of any such written agreement Company Counsel shall owe no duties directly to a Member. Notwithstanding any adversity that may develop, in the event any dispute or controversy arises between any Members and the Company, then each Member agrees that Company Counsel may represent either the Company or such Member in any such dispute or controversy to the extent permitted by the Rules, and each Member hereby consents to such representation. Each Member further acknowledges that Company Counsel has represented the interests of _____ in connection with the formation of the Company and the preparation and negotiation of this Agreement and while communications with Company Counsel concerning the formation of the Company and its Members

Ch 9 Forms

may be confidential with respect to third parties, no Member has any expectation that such communications are confidential with respect to the other Members.

11.2 Complete Agreement. This Agreement and the Articles constitute the complete and exclusive statement of agreement among the Members with respect to the subject matter herein and therein and replace and supersede all prior written and oral agreements among the Members. To the extent that any provision of the Articles conflict with any provision of this Agreement, the Articles shall control.

11.3 Binding Effect. Subject to the provisions of this Agreement relating to transferability, this Agreement will be binding upon and inure to the benefit of the Members and their respective successors and assigns.

11.4 Interpretation. All pronouns shall be deemed to refer to the masculine, feminine, or neuter, singular or plural, as the context in which they are used may require. All headings herein are inserted only for convenience and ease of reference and are not to be considered in the interpretation of any provision of this Agreement. Numbered or lettered articles, sections, and subsections herein contained refer to articles, sections, and subsections of this Agreement unless otherwise expressly stated. In the event any claim is made by any Member relating to any conflict, omission, or ambiguity in this Agreement, no presumption or burden of proof or persuasion shall be implied by virtue of the fact that this Agreement was prepared by or at the request of a particular Member or his or her counsel.

11.5 Governing Law. This Agreement shall be governed by, and construed in accordance with, the laws of the State of California, excluding its conflicts of law principles.

11.6 Severability. If any provision of this Agreement or the application of such provision to any person or circumstance shall be held invalid, the remainder of this Agreement or the application of such provision to persons or circumstances other than those to which it is held invalid shall not be affected thereby.

11.7 Notices. Any notice to be given or to be served upon the Company or any party hereto in connection with this Agreement must be in writing (which may include facsimile) and will be deemed to have been given and received when delivered to the address specified by the party to receive the notice. Such notices will be given to a Member at the address specified in Exhibit A hereto. Any party may, at any time by giving five (5) days' prior written notice to the other Members, designate any other address in substitution of the foregoing address to which such notice will be given.

11.8 Amendments. All amendments to this Agreement will be in writing and signed by all of the Members.

Ch 9 Forms

11.9 Multiple Counterparts. This Agreement may be executed in two or more counterparts, each of which shall be deemed an original, but all of which shall constitute one and the same instrument.

11.10 Remedies Cumulative. The remedies under this Agreement are cumulative and shall not exclude any other remedies to which any person may be lawfully entitled.

11.11 Consent of Spouse or Domestic Partner. Within ten (10) days after any individual becomes a Member or a Member marries or registers as a domestic partner, such Member shall have his or her spouse or domestic partner execute a consent substantially in the form attached to this Agreement.

IN WITNESS WHEREOF, all of the Members have executed this Agreement, effective as of the date first written above.

MEMBER: _____

MEMBER: _____

MEMBER: _____

EXHIBIT A

CAPITAL CONTRIBUTION AND ADDRESSES OF MEMBERS AS OF _____.

Member's Name	Member's Address	Member's Capital Capital Contribution	Member's Membership Interest
_____	_____	_____	_____
_____	_____	_____	_____
_____	_____	_____	_____
_____	_____	_____	_____
_____	_____	_____	_____
		$_____	_____ %

Ch 9 Forms

CONSENT OF SPOUSE

The undersigned spouse(s) of the party (parties) to the foregoing Agreement acknowledge(s) on his or her own behalf that: I have read the foregoing Agreement and I know its contents. I am aware that by its provision my spouse grants the Company and/or the other Members an option to purchase all of his or her Membership Interest, including my community interest (if any) in it. I hereby consent to the sale, approve of the provisions of the Agreement, and agree that such Membership Interest and my interest in it are subject to the provisions of the Agreement and that I will take no action at any time to hinder operation of the Agreement on such Membership Interest or my interest in it.

_____

_____

_____

Ch 9 Forms

State of California
Kevin Shelley
Secretary of State

LIMITED LIABILITY COMPANY – STATEMENT OF INFORMATION

Filing Fee $20.00 – If Amendment, See Instructions

IMPORTANT- Read Instructions Before Completing This Form

1. LIMITED LIABILITY COMPANY NAME: (Do not alter if name is preprinted.)

This Space For Filing Use Only

☐ IF THERE HAS BEEN NO CHANGE IN ANY OF THE INFORMATION CONTAINED IN THE LAST STATEMENT OF INFORMATION ON FILE WITH THE CALIFORNIA SECRETARY OF STATE, CHECK THE BOX AND PROCEED TO ITEM 12.

2. SECRETARY OF STATE FILE NUMBER

3. STATE OR PLACE OF ORGANIZATION

4. PRINCIPAL EXECUTIVE OFFICE
STREET ADDRESS
CITY   STATE   ZIP CODE

5. CALIFORNIA OFFICE WHERE RECORDS ARE MAINTAINED (FOR DOMESTIC ONLY)
STREET ADDRESS
CITY   STATE CA   ZIP CODE

6. CHECK THE APPROPRIATE PROVISION BELOW AND NAME THE AGENT FOR SERVICE OF PROCESS
   [ ] AN INDIVIDUAL RESIDING IN CALIFORNIA.
   [ ] A CORPORATION WHICH HAS FILED A CERTIFICATE PURSUANT TO CALIFORNIA CORPORATIONS CODE SECTION 1505.
   AGENT'S NAME: _____

7. ADDRESS OF THE AGENT FOR SERVICE OF PROCESS IN CALIFORNIA, IF AN INDIVIDUAL
ADDRESS
CITY   STATE CA   ZIP CODE

8. DESCRIBE TYPE OF BUSINESS OF THE LIMITED LIABILITY COMPANY.

9. LIST THE NAME AND COMPLETE ADDRESS OF ANY MANAGER OR MANAGERS, OR IF NONE HAVE BEEN APPOINTED OR ELECTED, PROVIDE THE NAME AND ADDRESS OF EACH MEMBER. ATTACH ADDITIONAL PAGES, IF NECESSARY.
a. NAME
   ADDRESS
   CITY   STATE   ZIP CODE
b. NAME
   ADDRESS
   CITY   STATE   ZIP CODE
c. NAME
   ADDRESS
   CITY   STATE   ZIP CODE

10. CHIEF EXECUTIVE OFFICER (CEO), IF ANY:
    NAME
    ADDRESS
    CITY   STATE   ZIP CODE

11. NUMBER OF PAGES ATTACHED, IF ANY:

12. THIS STATEMENT IS TRUE, CORRECT, AND COMPLETE.

_____   _____   _____   _____
TYPE OR PRINT NAME OF PERSON COMPLETING FORM   SIGNATURE   TITLE   DATE

DUE DATE:

SEC/STATE FORM LLC-12R (REV. 01/03)   APPROVED BY SECRETARY OF STATE

INSTRUCTIONS FOR COMPLETING THE STATEMENT OF INFORMATION

Type or legibly print in black or blue ink.

Statutory filing provisions are found in California Corporations Code Section 17060, unless otherwise indicated.

Every **domestic or foreign limited liability company** shall file a statement with the California Secretary of State, within 90 days after filing of its original Articles of Organization or Application for Registration, and biennially thereafter during the applicable filing period. The applicable filing period for a limited liability company shall be the end of the calendar month during which its original Articles of Organization or Application for Registration were filed and the immediately preceding five calendar months.

A limited liability company is required to file a statement even though it may not be actively engaged in business at the time this statement is due.

FILING FEES: If this statement is the initial 90-day statement or a biennial statement, a **$20.00** filing fee must accompany this statement.
Amendment: If this statement is being filed to amend any information on a previously filed statement, and is not a biennial filing, **no fee** is required.

Failure to file this completed form by its due date will result in the assessment of a penalty. The penalty for limited liability companies is $250 (California Corporations Code Sections 17651(b) and 17653).

For further information, contact the Statement of Information Unit at (916) 657-5448.

> **Make check(s) payable to the Secretary of State.** Send the executed document and filing fee to:
> California Secretary of State, Statement of Information Unit, P.O. Box 944230, Sacramento, CA 94244-2300
>
> The Secretary of State will endorse file one copy of the filed statement at no additional cost, provided that the copy is submitted to the Secretary of State along with the original to be filed.

Fill in the items as follows:

Item 1. Enter the name of the limited liability company.

Item 2. Enter the file number issued by the California Secretary of State.

IF THERE HAS BEEN ANY CHANGE TO THE LAST STATEMENT ON FILE WITH THE CALIFORNIA SECRETARY OF STATE, INCLUDING A CHANGE TO ANY ADDRESS, OR NO STATEMENT HAS EVER BEEN FILED, COMPLETE THIS STATEMENT IN ITS ENTIRETY (ITEMS 2 -12).

IF THERE HAS BEEN NO CHANGE IN THE INFORMATION CONTAINED IN THE LAST STATEMENT ON FILE WITH THE CALIFORNIA SECRETARY OF STATE, CHECK THE BOX AND PROCEED TO ITEM 12.

Item 3. If the limited liability company is organized outside the state of California, enter the state or place under the laws of which the limited liability company is organized.

Item 4. Enter the complete street address, city, state and zip code, of the principal executive office. DO NOT enter a P.O. Box or abbreviate the name of the city.

Item 5. Enter the complete street address, city and zip code of the office required to be maintained, pursuant to California Corporations Code Section 17057(a), if the limited liability company was formed under the laws of the State of California. DO NOT enter a P.O. Box or abbreviate the name of the city.

Item 6. Enter the name of the agent for service of process in California. Check the appropriate provision indicating whether the agent is an individual residing in California or a corporation which has filed a certificate pursuant to California Corporations Code Section 1505. If an individual is designated as agent, proceed to Item 7. If a corporation is designated, proceed to Item 8 (do not complete Item 7).

Item 7. If an individual is designated as the agent for service of process, enter the complete address in California. DO NOT enter "in care of" (c/o) or abbreviate the name of the city. DO NOT enter an address if a corporation is designated as the agent for service of process.

Item 8. Briefly describe the general type of business that constitutes the principal business activity of the limited liability company. (Example: Manufacturer of aircraft, Auto parts distributor, Retail department store).

Item 9. Enter the name and complete business or residential addresses of any manager or managers, appointed or elected in accordance with the Articles of Organization or Operating Agreement, or if no manager has been so elected or appointed. the name and business or residential address of each member. Attach additional pages, if necessary. DO NOT abbreviate the name of the city.

Item 10. Enter the name and complete business or residential address of the Chief Executive Officer (CEO), if any.

Item 11. Enter the number of pages attached, if any. All attachments should be 8 ½ " x 11", white paper, one-sided and legible.

Item 12. Type or print name and title of the person completing the form. Enter the date the form is completed.

Forms for Chapter 10

There are 15 forms that accompany **Chapter 10, Taxes**. They include the following:

Form 10-A Corporation Estimated Tax—FTB Form 100-ES, 2 pages (365 - 366)

Form 10-B Registration Form for Commercial Employers—Pacific Maritime, and Fishing Boats EDD Form DE 1, 2 pages (367 - 368)

Form 10-C California Seller's Permit Application—BOE-400-SPA (See Form 3-V starting on page 213)

Form 10-D California Resale Exemption Certificate Form, 1 page (369)

Form 10-E Application for Employer Identification Number—IRS Form SS-4 (see Form 3-U starting on page 211)

Form 10-F Determination of Worker Status for Purposes of Federal Employment Taxes and Income Tax Withholding—IRS Form SS-8, 5 pages (370 - 374)

Form 10-G Employee's Withholding Allowance Certificate—IRS Form W-4, 2 pages (375 - 376)

Form 10-H Employer's Quarterly Federal Tax Return—IRS Form 941, 4 pages (377 - 380)

Form 10-I   Wage and Tax Statement—IRS Form W-2, 1 page (381)

Form 10-J   Transmittal of Wage and Tax Statements—IRS Form W-3, 1 page (382)

Form 10-K   Federal Tax Deposit Coupon—IRS Form 8109-B, 2 pages (383 - 384)

Form 10-L   Estimated Tax for Corporations—IRS Form 1120-W, 6 pages (385 - 390)

Form 10-M   Minutes of the First Meeting of the Board of Directors, 7 pages (391 - 397)

Form 10-N   Federal Form 1065, Return of Partnership Income (on accompanying CD)

Form 10-O   California From 568, Limited Liability Return of Income (on accompanying CD)

Ch 10
Forms

TAXABLE YEAR

CALIFORNIA FORM

2004   **Corporation Estimated Tax**   **100-ES**

For calendar year 2004 or fiscal year beginning month_____ day_____ year 2004, and ending month_____ day_____ year_____

This entity will file Form: ☐ 100   ☐ 100W   ☐ 100S   ☐ 109   **Installment 1**   Due by the 15th day of 4th month of tax year; for Saturdays, Sundays, or holidays, see instructions.

If no payment is due, do not mail this form.

Return this form with a check or money order payable to:
FRANCHISE TAX BOARD, PO BOX 942857, SACRAMENTO CA 94257-0531

California corporation number   Federal employer identification number (FEIN)

Corporation name

Attention: Owner's or Representative's name

Corporation address   PMB no.

City   State   ZIP Code

Estimated Tax Amount

QSub Tax Amount

Total Installment Amount

EFT TAXPAYER: DO NOT MAIL THIS FORM   100ES04103   Form 100-ES (REV. 2003)

✂— DETACH HERE — — — — — — — — — IF NO PAYMENT IS DUE, DO NOT MAIL THIS FORM — — — — — — — DETACH HERE —✂

TAXABLE YEAR

CALIFORNIA FORM

2004   **Corporation Estimated Tax**   **100-ES**

For calendar year 2004 or fiscal year beginning month_____ day_____ year 2004, and ending month_____ day_____ year_____

This entity will file Form: ☐ 100   ☐ 100W   ☐ 100S   ☐ 109   **Installment 2**   Due by the 15th day of 6th month of tax year; for Saturdays, Sundays, or holidays, see instructions.

If no payment is due, do not mail this form.

Return this form with a check or money order payable to:
FRANCHISE TAX BOARD, PO BOX 942857, SACRAMENTO CA 94257-0531

California corporation number   Federal employer identification number (FEIN)

Corporation name

Attention: Owner's or Representative's name

Corporation address   PMB no.

City   State   ZIP Code

Estimated Tax Amount

QSub Tax Amount

Total Installment Amount

EFT TAXPAYER: DO NOT MAIL THIS FORM   100ES04103   Form 100-ES (REV. 2003)

✂— DETACH HERE — — — — — — — — — IF NO PAYMENT IS DUE, DO NOT MAIL THIS FORM — — — — — — — DETACH HERE —✂

TAXABLE YEAR

CALIFORNIA FORM

2004   **Corporation Estimated Tax**   **100-ES**

For calendar year 2004 or fiscal year beginning month_____ day_____ year 2004, and ending month_____ day_____ year_____

This entity will file Form: ☐ 100   ☐ 100W   ☐ 100S   ☐ 109   **Installment 3**   Due by the 15th day of 9th month of tax year; for Saturdays, Sundays, or holidays, see instructions.

If no payment is due, do not mail this form.

Return this form with a check or money order payable to:
FRANCHISE TAX BOARD, PO BOX 942857, SACRAMENTO CA 94257-0531

California corporation number   Federal employer identification number (FEIN)

Corporation name

Attention: Owner's or Representative's name

Corporation address   PMB no.

City   State   ZIP Code

Estimated Tax Amount

QSub Tax Amount

Total Installment Amount

EFT TAXPAYER: DO NOT MAIL THIS FORM   100ES04103   Form 100-ES (REV. 2003)

Ch 10 Forms

✂← DETACH HERE — — — — — — — IF NO PAYMENT IS DUE, DO NOT MAIL THIS FORM — — — — — — — DETACH HERE →✂

TAXABLE YEAR

CALIFORNIA FORM

2004   Corporation Estimated Tax   100-ES

For calendar year 2004 or fiscal year beginning month_____ day_____ year 2004, and ending month_____ day_____ year_____

This entity will file Form: ☐ 100   ☐ 100W   ☐ 100S   ☐ 109

Installment 4   Due by the 15th day of 12th month of tax year; for Saturdays, Sundays, or holidays, see instructions.

Return this form with a check or money order payable to:
FRANCHISE TAX BOARD, PO BOX 942857, SACRAMENTO CA 94257-0531

If no payment is due, do not mail this form.

California corporation number   Federal employer identification number (FEIN)

Corporation name

Estimated Tax Amount

Attention: Owner's or Representative's name

QSub Tax Amount

Corporation address   PMB no.

City   State   ZIP Code

Total Installment Amount

EFT TAXPAYER: DO NOT MAIL THIS FORM   100ES04103   Form 100-ES (REV. 2003)

Ch 10 Forms

Employment Development Department
State of California

| This form will be the basic record of YOUR ACCOUNT. **DO NOT FILE THIS FORM UNTIL YOU HAVE PAID WAGES THAT EXCEED $100.00.** Please read the **INSTRUCTIONS** on the back before completing this form. **PLEASE PRINT OR TYPE..** Return this form to: ➡ | EMPLOYMENT DEVELOPMENT DEPARTMENT ACCOUNT SERVICES GROUP MIC 13 PO BOX 826880 SACRAMENTO CA 94280-0001 **(916) 654-7041   FAX (916) 654-9211** www.edd.ca.gov |

REGISTRATION FORM FOR COMMERCIAL EMPLOYERS, PACIFIC MARITIME, AND FISHING BOATS

ACCOUNT NUMBER	DEPT. USE	QUARTER	ON-LINE PROCESS DATE	TAS CODE

Industry specific registration forms are required relative to each type of employer. Please use the appropriate form to register.

Commercial/Pacific Maritime/Fishing Boat	DE 1	Household Workers	DE 1HW
Agricultural	DE 1AG	Non-profit	DE 1NP
Government/Public Schools/Indian Tribes	DE 1GS	Personal Income Tax Only	DE 1P

A. THIS IS A:
☐ New business ☐ Hired employees ☐ Change in form - (Individual to corporation; partnership to corporation; merger; corporation to LLC, etc.)
☐ Change of partner(s) ☐ Purchased on-going business ☐ All ☐ Part ☐ Other _____
IF THE BUSINESS WAS PURCHASED, PROVIDE THE FOLLOWING INFORMATION:

Previous Owner   Business Name   Purchase Price   Date of Transfer   EDD Account Number

B. HAVE YOU EVER REGISTERED A BUSINESS WITH THE DEPARTMENT?
☐ No ☐ Yes
IF YES, ENTER THE FOLLOWING:
ACCT NUMBER   BUSINESS NAME   ADDRESS

C. INDICATE FIRST QUARTER AND YEAR IN WHICH WAGES EXCEED $100. ☐ Jan.-Mar. 20__ ☐ Apr.-June 20__ ☐ July-Sept. 20__ ☐ Oct.-Dec. 20

D. BUSINESS NAME (DBA)	OWNERSHIP BEGAN OPERATING MONTH: DAY: YEAR:	FEDERAL I.D. NUMBER
E. INDIVIDUAL OWNER	SOCIAL SECURITY NUMBER	DRIVER'S LICENSE #
F. CORPORATION/LLC/LLP/LP NAME	SECRETARY OF STATE CORP/LLC/LLP/LP I.D. NO.	

G. List all partners*, corporate officers, or LLC/LLP members/managers/officers	**TITLE** (partner, officer title, LLC/LLP member/manager)	SOCIAL SECURITY NUMBER	DRIVER'S LICENSE #

*If entity is a **Limited Partnership**, indicate General Partner with an (*). List additional partners, LLC/LLP members/officers/managers on a separate sheet.

H. MAILING ADDRESS	CITY	STATE	ZIP CODE	PHONE NUMBER ( )
I. BUSINESS ADDRESS (if different from mailing address)	CITY	STATE	ZIP CODE	PHONE NUMBER ( )

J. ORGANIZATION TYPE
☐ (IN) INDIVIDUAL OWNER   ☐ (AS) ASSOCIATION   ☐ (LQ) LIQUIDATION   ☐ (JV) JOINT VENTURE
☐ (HW) HUS/WIFE CO-OWNERSHIP ☐ (LC) LIMITED LIABILITY CO. ☐ (LP) LIMITED PARTNERSHIP   ☐ (RC) RECEIVERSHIP
☐ (GP) GENERAL PARTNERSHIP   ☐ (PL) LIMITED LIABILITY   ☐ (TR) TRUSTEESHIP   ☐ (BK) BANKRUPTCY
☐ (CP) CORPORATION   PARTNERSHIP   ☐ (EA) ESTATE ADMINISTRATION ☐ (OT) OTHER (Specify) _____

K. EMPLOYER TYPE   ☐ (01) COMMERCIAL   ☐ (22) PACIFIC MARITIME   ☐ (25) FISHING BOAT

L. INDUSTRY ACTIVITY: Identify the industry and specific product or service that represents the greatest portion of your sales receipts or revenue. Check one:
☐ SERVICES ☐ RETAIL ☐ WHOLESALE ☐ MANUFACTURING ☐ OTHER _____
Describe specific product and/or service in detail.

Number of CA Employees _____ Are there multiple locations for this business? ☐ No ☐ Yes

M. CONTACT PERSON FOR BUSINESS	TITLE/COMPANY NAME	ADDRESS	PHONE ( )

N. DECLARATION
These statements are hereby declared to be correct to the best knowledge and belief of the undersigned.

Signature _____ Title _____ Date _____
                                        (Owner, Partner, Officer, Member, Manager, etc.)

O. PAYROLL TAX EDUCATION: Attend a payroll tax seminar that will help you understand how, what, and when to report state payroll taxes. Visit our Web site at **www.edd.ca.gov/taxsem** or call us at (888) 745-3886 for more information.

DE 1 Rev. 71 (9-03) **(INTERNET)**   Page 1 of 2   CU

Ch 10 Forms

INSTRUCTIONS FOR REGISTRATION FORM FOR COMMERCIAL/PACIFIC MARITIME/FISHING BOAT EMPLOYERS

An employer is required by law to file a registration form with the Employment Development Department (EDD) within **fifteen (15) calendar days** after paying over $100 in wages for employment in a calendar quarter, or whenever a change in ownership occurs. Please complete all items on the front of this DE 1 and do **one** of the following:

- Mail your completed registration form to EDD, Account Services Group MIC 13, PO Box 826880, Sacramento, CA 94280-0001 **or**
- Fax your completed registration form to EDD at (916) 654-9211 **or**
- Call for telephone registration at (916) 654-8706

There are industry specific registration forms related to each type of employer. Please use the appropriate form to register. A complete list of registration forms is located on the front of this form.

NEED MORE HELP OR INFORMATION?

- Call Account Services Group (ASG) in Sacramento at (916) 654-7041 with questions regarding this form or the registration and account number assignment process.
- Contact the nearest Taxpayer Education and Assistance (TEA) office listed in your local telephone directory under State Government, EDD or call a TEA Customer Service Representative at 1-888-745-3886 with questions about whether your business entity is subject to reporting and paying state payroll taxes. For TTY (nonverbal) access, call 1-800-547-9565.
- Access the EDD Web site at **www.edd.ca.gov**

A. STATUS OF BUSINESS - Check the box that best describes why you are completing this form. If the business was purchased, provide previous owner and business name, purchase price, date ownership was transferred to this ownership and EDD account number.

B. PRIOR REGISTRATION - If any part of the ownership shown in items E, F, or G are operating or have ever operated at another location, check "Yes" and provide account number, business name, and address.

C. WAGES - Check the box for the quarter in which you first paid over $100 in wages.

D. BUSINESS NAME - Enter the name by which your business is known to the public. Enter "None" if no business name is used. Enter the date the new ownership began operating. Enter Federal Employer Identification Number. If not assigned, enter "Applied For".

E. INDIVIDUAL OWNER - Enter the full given name, middle initial, surname, title, social security number, and driver's license number.

F. CORPORATION/LLC/LLP/LP NAME - Enter Corporation/LLC/LLP/LP name exactly as spelled and registered with the Secretary of State. Include the California Corporate/LLC/LLP/LP identification number.

G. LIST ALL PARTNERS, CORPORATE OFFICERS, OR LLC/LLP MEMBERS/MANAGERS/OFFICERS - Enter the name, title, social security number and driver's license of each individual.

H. MAILING ADDRESS - Enter the mailing address where EDD correspondence and forms should be sent. Provide daytime business phone number.

I. BUSINESS ADDRESS - Enter the California address and telephone number where the business is physically conducted. If there is more than one California location, list the business addresses on a separate sheet and attach to this form.

J. ORGANIZATION TYPE - Check the box that best describes the legal form of the ownership shown in items E, F, or G.

K. EMPLOYER TYPE - Check the box that best describes your employer type.

L. INDUSTRY ACTIVITY - Check the box that best describes the industry activity of your business. Describe the particular product or service in detail. This information is used to assign an Industrial Classification Code to your business. If you would like more information on industry coding or the North American Industry Classification System (NAICS), you can visit the Web site:

www.census.gov/epcd/www/naics.html

Enter the number of California employees. Check "Yes" if there are multiple locations under this EDD Account Number.

M. CONTACT PERSON FOR BUSINESS - Enter the name, title/company address, and phone number of the person authorized by the ownership shown in items E, F, or G to provide EDD staff information needed to maintain the accuracy of your employer account.

N. DECLARATION - This declaration should be signed by one of the names shown in item(s) E or G.

O. PAYROLL TAX EDUCATION - EDD provides educational opportunities for taxpayers to learn how to report employees' wages and pay taxes, pointing out the pitfalls that create errors and unnecessary billings. Help is only a telephone call or Web site away.

We will **notify** you of your **EDD Account Number** by mail. To help you understand your tax withholding and filing responsibilities, you will be sent a **California Employer's Guide, DE 44.** Please keep your account status current by notifying ASG of all future changes to the original registration information.

DE 1 Rev. 71 (9-03) **(INTERNET)**　　　　　　　　Page 2 of 2

Ch 10
Forms

CALIFORNIA RESALE EXEMPTION CERTIFICATE FORM

FIRM NAME _____

I HEREBY CERTIFY that I hold valid seller's permit No. _____ issued pursuant to the Sales and Use Tax Law; that I am engaged in the business of selling

_____

_____. that the tangible personal property described herein which I shall purchase from: _____

will be resold by me in the form of tangible personal property; PROVIDED, however, that in the event any of such property is used for any purpose other than retention, demonstration, or display while holding it for sale in the regular course of business, it is understood that I am required by the Sales and Use Tax Law to report and pay for the tax, measured by the purchase price of such property.

Description of property to be purchased:

_____

_____

Dated: _____, 20_____

_____
Signature of Purchaser or Authorized Agent

_____
Title

Form SS-8
(Rev. June 2003)
Department of the Treasury
Internal Revenue Service

**Determination of Worker Status
for Purposes of Federal Employment Taxes
and Income Tax Withholding**

OMB No. 1545-0004

Name of firm (or person) for whom the worker performed services	Worker's name
Firm's address (include street address, apt. or suite no., city, state, and ZIP code)	Worker's address (include street address, apt. or suite no., city, state, and ZIP code)

Trade name	Telephone number (include area code) ( )	Worker's social security number

Telephone number (include area code) ( )	Firm's employer identification number	Worker's employer identification number (if any)

If the worker is paid by a firm other than the one listed on this form for these services, enter the name, address, and employer identification number of the payer.

Important Information Needed To Process Your Request

We must have your permission to disclose your name and the information on this form and any attachments to other parties involved with this request. **Do we have your permission to disclose this information?** . . . . ☐ **Yes** ☐ **No**
If you answered "No" or did not mark a box, we will not process your request and will not issue a determination.

You must answer ALL items OR mark them "Unknown" or "Does not apply." If you need more space, attach another sheet.

A This form is being completed by: ☐ Firm ☐ Worker; for services performed _____ to _____ .
(beginning date)   (ending date)

B Explain your reason(s) for filing this form (e.g., you received a bill from the IRS, you believe you received a Form 1099 or Form W-2 erroneously, you are unable to get worker's compensation benefits, you were audited or are being audited by the IRS). ....
....
....
....

C Total number of workers who performed or are performing the same or similar services _____ .

D How did the worker obtain the job? ☐ Application ☐ Bid ☐ Employment Agency ☐ Other (specify) _____ .

E Attach copies of all supporting documentation (contracts, invoices, memos, Forms W-2, Forms 1099, IRS closing agreements, IRS rulings, etc.). In addition, please inform us of any current or past litigation concerning the worker's status. If no income reporting forms (Form 1099-MISC or W-2) were furnished to the worker, enter the amount of income earned for the year(s) at issue $ _____ .

F Describe the firm's business. ....
....
....
....

G Describe the work done by the worker and provide the worker's job title. ....
....
....
....

H Explain why you believe the worker is an employee or an independent contractor. ....
....
....
....

I Did the worker perform services for the firm before getting this position? . . . . ☐ **Yes** ☐ **No** ☐ **N/A**
If "Yes," what were the dates of the prior service? ....
If "Yes," explain the differences, if any, between the current and prior service. ....
....
....
....

J If the work is done under a written agreement between the firm and the worker, attach a copy (preferably signed by both parties). Describe the terms and conditions of the work arrangement. ....
....

For Privacy Act and Paperwork Reduction Act Notice, see page 5.   Cat. No. 16106T   Form **SS-8** (Rev. 6-2003)

Form SS-8 (Rev. 6-2003)   Page **2**

Part I   Behavioral Control

1   What specific training and/or instruction is the worker given by the firm? ....

....

2   How does the worker receive work assignments? ....

3   Who determines the methods by which the assignments are performed? ....

4   Who is the worker required to contact if problems or complaints arise and who is responsible for their resolution? ....

....

5   What types of reports are required from the worker? Attach examples. ....

....

6   Describe the worker's daily routine (i.e., schedule, hours, etc.). ....

....

7   At what location(s) does the worker perform services (e.g., firm's premises, own shop or office, home, customer's location, etc.)? ....

....

8   Describe any meetings the worker is required to attend and any penalties for not attending (e.g., sales meetings, monthly meetings, staff meetings, etc.). ....

9   Is the worker required to provide the services personally? . . . . □ **Yes** □ **No**

10 If substitutes or helpers are needed, who hires them? ....

11 If the worker hires the substitutes or helpers, is approval required? . . . . □ **Yes** □ **No**
        If "Yes," by whom? ....

12 Who pays the substitutes or helpers? ....

13 Is the worker reimbursed if the worker pays the substitutes or helpers? . . . . □ **Yes** □ **No**
        If "Yes," by whom? ....

Part II   Financial Control

1   List the supplies, equipment, materials, and property provided by each party:
        The firm ....
        The worker ....
        Other party ....

2   Does the worker lease equipment? . . . . □ **Yes** □ **No**
        If "Yes," what are the terms of the lease? (Attach a copy or explanatory statement.) ....

....

3   What expenses are incurred by the worker in the performance of services for the firm? ....

....

4   Specify which, if any, expenses are reimbursed by:
        The firm ....
        Other party ....

5   Type of pay the worker receives: □ Salary   □ Commission   □ Hourly Wage   □ Piece Work
        □ Lump Sum   □ Other (specify) ....
        If type of pay is commission, and the firm guarantees a minimum amount of pay, specify amount $ _____ .

6   Is the worker allowed a drawing account for advances? . . . . □ **Yes** □ **No**
        If "Yes," how often? ....
        Specify any restrictions. ....

7   Whom does the customer pay? . . . . □ Firm   □ Worker
        If worker, does the worker pay the total amount to the firm? □ **Yes** □ **No** If "No," explain. ....

....

8   Does the firm carry worker's compensation insurance on the worker? . . . . □ **Yes** □ **No**

9   What economic loss or financial risk, if any, can the worker incur beyond the normal loss of salary (e.g., loss or damage of equipment, material, etc.)? ....

....

Form **SS-8** (Rev. 6-2003)

Ch 10
Forms

Form SS-8 (Rev. 6-2003)   Page **3**

| **Part III** | **Relationship of the Worker and Firm** |

1 List the benefits available to the worker (e.g., paid vacations, sick pay, pensions, bonuses). ....
....

2 Can the relationship be terminated by either party without incurring liability or penalty? . . . . ☐ **Yes** ☐ **No**
If "No," explain your answer. ....
....

3 Does the worker perform similar services for others? . . . . ☐ **Yes** ☐ **No**
If "Yes," is the worker required to get approval from the firm? . . . . ☐ **Yes** ☐ **No**

4 Describe any agreements prohibiting competition between the worker and the firm while the worker is performing services or during any later
period. Attach any available documentation. ....
....

5 Is the worker a member of a union? . . . . ☐ **Yes** ☐ **No**

6 What type of advertising, if any, does the worker do (e.g., a business listing in a directory, business cards, etc.)? Provide copies, if applicable.
....

7 If the worker assembles or processes a product at home, who provides the materials and instructions or pattern? ....
....

8 What does the worker do with the finished product (e.g., return it to the firm, provide it to another party, or sell it)? ....
....

9 How does the firm represent the worker to its customers (e.g., employee, partner, representative, or contractor)? ....
....

10 If the worker no longer performs services for the firm, how did the relationship end? ....
....

| **Part IV** | **For Service Providers or Salespersons**—Complete this part if the worker provided a service directly to customers or is a salesperson. |

1 What are the worker's responsibilities in soliciting new customers? ....
....

2 Who provides the worker with leads to prospective customers? ....

3 Describe any reporting requirements pertaining to the leads. ....
....

4 What terms and conditions of sale, if any, are required by the firm? ....

5 Are orders submitted to and subject to approval by the firm? . . . . ☐ **Yes** ☐ **No**

6 Who determines the worker's territory? ....

7 Did the worker pay for the privilege of serving customers on the route or in the territory? . . . . ☐ **Yes** ☐ **No**
If "Yes," whom did the worker pay? ....
If "Yes," how much did the worker pay? . . . . $ _____ .

8 Where does the worker sell the product (e.g., in a home, retail establishment, etc.)? ....
....

9 List the product and/or services distributed by the worker (e.g., meat, vegetables, fruit, bakery products, beverages, or laundry or dry cleaning
services). If more than one type of product and/or service is distributed, specify the principal one. ....
....

10 Does the worker sell life insurance full time? . . . . ☐ **Yes** ☐ **No**

11 Does the worker sell other types of insurance for the firm? . . . . ☐ **Yes** ☐ **No**
If "Yes," enter the percentage of the worker's total working time spent in selling other types of insurance. . . . _____ %

12 If the worker solicits orders from wholesalers, retailers, contractors, or operators of hotels, restaurants, or other similar
establishments, enter the percentage of the worker's time spent in the solicitation. . . . . _____ %

13 Is the merchandise purchased by the customers for resale or use in their business operations? . . . . ☐ **Yes** ☐ **No**
Describe the merchandise and state whether it is equipment installed on the customers' premises. ....
....

| **Part V** | **Signature** (see page 4) |

Under penalties of perjury, I declare that I have examined this request, including accompanying documents, and to the best of my knowledge and belief, the facts
presented are true, correct, and complete.

Signature _____ Title _____ Date _____
            (Type or print name below)

Form **SS-8** (Rev. 6-2003)

General Instructions

Section references are to the Internal Revenue Code unless otherwise noted.

Purpose

Firms and workers file Form SS-8 to request a determination of the status of a worker for purposes of Federal employment taxes and income tax withholding.

A Form SS-8 determination may be requested only in order to resolve Federal tax matters. If Form SS-8 is submitted for a tax year for which the statute of limitations on the tax return has expired, a determination letter will not be issued. The statute of limitations expires 3 years from the due date of the tax return or the date filed, whichever is later.

The IRS does not issue a determination letter for proposed transactions or on hypothetical situations. We may, however, issue an information letter when it is considered appropriate.

Definition

Firm. For the purposes of this form, the term "firm" means any individual, business enterprise, organization, state, or other entity for which a worker has performed services. The firm may or may not have paid the worker directly for these services. **If the firm was not responsible for payment for services, be sure to enter the name, address, and employer identification number of the payer on the first page of Form SS-8 below the identifying information for the firm and the worker.**

The SS-8 Determination Process

The IRS will acknowledge the receipt of your Form SS-8. Because there are usually two (or more) parties who could be affected by a determination of employment status, the IRS attempts to get information from all parties involved by sending those parties blank Forms SS-8 for completion. The case will be assigned to a technician who will review the facts, apply the law, and render a decision. The technician may ask for additional information from the requestor, from other involved parties, or from third parties that could help clarify the work relationship before rendering a decision. The IRS will generally issue a formal determination to the firm or payer (if that is a different entity), and will send a copy to the worker. A determination letter applies only to a worker (or a class of workers) requesting it, and the decision is binding on the IRS. In certain cases, a formal determination will not be issued. Instead, an information letter may be issued. Although an information letter is advisory only and is not binding on the IRS, it may be used to assist the worker to fulfill his or her Federal tax obligations.

Neither the SS-8 determination process nor the review of any records in connection with the determination constitutes an examination (audit) of any Federal tax return. If the periods under consideration have previously been examined, the SS-8 determination process will not constitute a reexamination under IRS reopening procedures. Because this is not an examination of any Federal tax return, the appeal rights available in connection with an examination do not apply to an SS-8 determination. However, if you disagree with a determination and you have additional information concerning the work relationship that you believe was not previously considered, you may request that the determining office reconsider the determination.

Completing Form SS-8

Answer all questions as completely as possible. Attach additional sheets if you need more space. Provide information for all years the worker provided services for the firm. Determinations are based on the entire relationship between the firm and the worker.

Additional copies of this form may be obtained by calling 1-800-829-4933 or from the IRS website at **www.irs.gov.**

Fee

There is no fee for requesting an SS-8 determination letter.

Signature

Form SS-8 must be signed and dated by the taxpayer. A stamped signature will not be accepted.

The person who signs for a corporation must be an officer of the corporation who has personal knowledge of the facts. If the corporation is a member of an affiliated group filing a consolidated return, it must be signed by an officer of the common parent of the group.

The person signing for a trust, partnership, or limited liability company must be, respectively, a trustee, general partner, or member-manager who has personal knowledge of the facts.

Where To File

Send the completed Form SS-8 to the address listed below for the firm's location. However, for cases involving Federal agencies, send Form SS-8 to the Internal Revenue Service, Attn: CC:CORP:T:C, Ben Franklin Station, P.O. Box 7604, Washington, DC 20044.

Firm's location:	Send to:
Alaska, Arizona, Arkansas, California, Colorado, Hawaii, Idaho, Illinois, Iowa, Kansas, Minnesota, Missouri, Montana, Nebraska, Nevada, New Mexico, North Dakota, Oklahoma, Oregon, South Dakota, Texas, Utah, Washington, Wisconsin, Wyoming, American Samoa, Guam, Puerto Rico, U.S. Virgin Islands	Internal Revenue Service SS-8 Determinations P.O. Box 630 Stop 631 Holtsville, NY 11742-0630
Alabama, Connecticut, Delaware, District of Columbia, Florida, Georgia, Indiana, Kentucky, Louisiana, Maine, Maryland, Massachusetts, Michigan, Mississippi, New Hampshire, New Jersey, New York, North Carolina, Ohio, Pennsylvania, Rhode Island, South Carolina, Tennessee, Vermont, Virginia, West Virginia, all other locations not listed	Internal Revenue Service SS-8 Determinations 40 Lakemont Road Newport, VT 05855-1555

Instructions for Workers

If you are requesting a determination for more than one firm, complete a separate Form SS-8 for each firm.

 Form SS-8 is not a claim for refund of social security and Medicare taxes or Federal income tax withholding.

If the IRS determines that you are an employee, you are responsible for filing an amended return for any corrections related to this decision. A determination that a worker is an employee does not necessarily reduce any current or prior tax liability. For more information, call 1-800-829-1040.

|

Time for filing a claim for refund. Generally, you must file your claim for a credit or refund within 3 years from the date your original return was filed or within 2 years from the date the tax was paid, whichever is later.

Filing Form SS-8 does not prevent the expiration of the time in which a claim for a refund must be filed. If you are concerned about a refund, and the statute of limitations for filing a claim for refund for the year(s) at issue has not yet expired, you should file **Form 1040X,** Amended U.S. Individual Income Tax Return, to protect your statute of limitations. File a separate Form 1040X for each year.

On the Form 1040X you file, do not complete lines 1 through 24 on the form. Write "Protective Claim" at the top of the form, sign and date it. In addition, you should enter the following statement in Part II, Explanation of Changes to Income, Deductions, and Credits: "Filed Form SS-8 with the Internal Revenue Service Office in (Holtsville, NY; Newport, VT; or Washington, DC; as appropriate). By filing this protective claim, I reserve the right to file a claim for any refund that may be due after a determination of my employment tax status has been completed."

Filing Form SS-8 does not alter the requirement to timely file an income tax return. Do not delay filing your tax return in anticipation of an answer to your SS-8 request. In addition, if applicable, do not delay in responding to a request for payment while waiting for a determination of your worker status.

Instructions for Firms

If a **worker** has requested a determination of his or her status while working for you, you will receive a request from the IRS to complete a Form SS-8. In cases of this type, the IRS usually gives each party an opportunity to present a statement of the facts because any decision will affect the employment tax status of the parties. Failure to respond to this request will not prevent the IRS from issuing a determination letter based on the information he or she has made available so that the worker may fulfill his or her Federal tax obligations. However, the information that you provide is extremely valuable in determining the status of the worker.

If **you** are requesting a determination for a particular class of worker, complete the form for **one** individual who is representative of the class of workers whose status is in question. If you want a written determination for more than one class of workers, complete a separate Form SS-8 for one worker from each class whose status is typical of that class. A written determination for any worker will apply to other workers of the same class if the facts are not materially different for these workers. Please provide a list of names and addresses of all workers potentially affected by this determination.

If you have a reasonable basis for not treating a worker as an employee, you may be relieved from having to pay employment taxes for that worker under section 530 of the 1978 Revenue Act. However, this relief provision cannot be considered in conjunction with a Form SS-8 determination because the determination does not constitute an examination of any tax return. For more information regarding section 530 of the 1978 Revenue Act and to determine if you qualify for relief under this section, you may visit the IRS website at **www.irs.gov.**

Privacy Act and Paperwork Reduction Act Notice. We ask for the information on this form to carry out the Internal Revenue laws of the United States. This information will be used to determine the employment status of the worker(s) described on the form. Subtitle C, Employment Taxes, of the Internal Revenue Code imposes employment taxes on wages. Sections 3121(d), 3306(a), and 3401(c) and (d) and the related regulations define employee and employer for purposes of employment taxes imposed under Subtitle C. Section 6001 authorizes the IRS to request information needed to determine if a worker(s) or firm is subject to these taxes. Section 6109 requires you to provide your taxpayer identification number. Neither workers nor firms are required to request a status determination, but if you choose to do so, you must provide the information requested on this form. Failure to provide the requested information may prevent us from making a status determination. If any worker or the firm has requested a status determination and you are being asked to provide information for use in that determination, you are not required to provide the requested information. However, failure to provide such information will prevent the IRS from considering it in making the status determination. Providing false or fraudulent information may subject you to penalties. Routine uses of this information include providing it to the Department of Justice for use in civil and criminal litigation, to the Social Security Administration for the administration of social security programs, and to cities, states, and the District of Columbia for the administration of their tax laws. We may also disclose this information to Federal and state agencies to enforce Federal nontax criminal laws and to combat terrorism. We may provide this information to the affected worker(s) or the firm as part of the status determination process.

You are not required to provide the information requested on a form that is subject to the Paperwork Reduction Act unless the form displays a valid OMB control number. Books or records relating to a form or its instructions must be retained as long as their contents may become material in the administration of any Internal Revenue law. Generally, tax returns and return information are confidential, as required by section 6103.

The time needed to complete and file this form will vary depending on individual circumstances. The estimated average time is: **Recordkeeping,** 22 hrs.; **Learning about the law or the form,** 47 min.; and **Preparing and sending the form to the IRS,** 1 hr., 11 min. If you have comments concerning the accuracy of these time estimates or suggestions for making this form simpler, we would be happy to hear from you. You can write to the Tax Products Coordinating Committee, Western Area Distribution Center, Rancho Cordova, CA 95743-0001. **Do not** send the tax form to this address. Instead, see **Where To File** on page 4.

Form W-4 (2004)

Purpose. Complete Form W-4 so that your employer can withhold the correct Federal income tax from your pay. Because your tax situation may change, you may want to refigure your withholding each year.

Exemption from withholding. If you are exempt, complete only lines 1, 2, 3, 4, and 7 and sign the form to validate it. Your exemption for 2004 expires February 16, 2005. See **Pub. 505,** Tax Withholding and Estimated Tax.

Note: *You cannot claim exemption from withholding if: **(a)** your income exceeds $800 and includes more than $250 of unearned income (e.g., interest and dividends) and **(b)** another person can claim you as a dependent on their tax return.*

Basic Instructions. If you are not exempt, complete the **Personal Allowances Worksheet** below. The worksheets on page 2 adjust your withholding allowances based on itemized

deductions, certain credits, adjustments to income, or two-earner/two-job situations. Complete all worksheets that apply. **However, you may claim fewer (or zero) allowances.**

Head of household. Generally, you may claim head of household filing status on your tax return only if you are unmarried and pay more than 50% of the costs of keeping up a home for yourself and your dependent(s) or other qualifying individuals. See line **E** below.

Tax credits. You can take projected tax credits into account in figuring your allowable number of withholding allowances. Credits for child or dependent care expenses and the child tax credit may be claimed using the **Personal Allowances Worksheet** below. See **Pub. 919,** How Do I Adjust My Tax Withholding? for information on converting your other credits into withholding allowances.

Nonwage income. If you have a large amount of nonwage income, such as interest or dividends, consider making estimated tax payments using

Form 1040-ES, Estimated Tax for Individuals. Otherwise, you may owe additional tax.

Two earners/two jobs. If you have a working spouse or more than one job, figure the total number of allowances you are entitled to claim on all jobs using worksheets from only one Form W-4. Your withholding usually will be most accurate when all allowances are claimed on the Form W-4 for the highest paying job and zero allowances are claimed on the others.

Nonresident alien. If you are a nonresident alien, see **Instructions for Form 8233** before completing this Form W-4.

Check your withholding. After your Form W-4 takes effect, use Pub. 919 to see how the dollar amount you are having withheld compares to your projected total tax for 2004. See Pub. 919, especially if your earnings exceed $125,000 (Single) or $175,000 (Married).

Recent name change? If your name on line 1 differs from that shown on your social security card, call 1-800-772-1213 to initiate a name change and obtain a social security card showing your correct name.

Personal Allowances Worksheet (Keep for your records.)

A Enter "1" for **yourself** if no one else can claim you as a dependent . . . . **A** _____

B Enter "1" if: You are single and have only one job; or

                 You are married, have only one job, and your spouse does not work; or   . . **B** _____

                 Your wages from a second job or your spouse's wages (or the total of both) are $1,000 or less.

C Enter "1" for your **spouse.** But, you may choose to enter "-0-" if you are married and have either a working spouse or more than one job. (Entering "-0-" may help you avoid having too little tax withheld.) . . . . **C** _____

D Enter number of **dependents** (other than your spouse or yourself) you will claim on your tax return . . . . **D** _____

E Enter "1" if you will file as **head of household** on your tax return (see conditions under **Head of household** above) . **E** _____

F Enter "1" if you have at least $1,500 of **child or dependent care expenses** for which you plan to claim a credit . . **F** _____

   (**Note:** *Do **not** include child support payments. See Pub. **503,** Child and Dependent Care Expenses, for details.*)

G **Child Tax Credit** (including additional child tax credit):

   If your total income will be less than $52,000 ($77,000 if married), enter "2" for each eligible child.

   If your total income will be between $52,000 and $84,000 ($77,000 and $119,000 if married), enter "1" for each eligible child plus "1" **additional** if you have four or more eligible children. . . . . **G** _____

H Add lines A through G and enter total here. **Note:** *This may be different from the number of exemptions you claim on your tax return.* **H** _____

For accuracy, complete all worksheets that apply.	If you plan to **itemize or claim adjustments to income** and want to reduce your withholding, see the **Deductions and Adjustments Worksheet** on page 2.
	If you have **more than one job** or are **married and you and your spouse both work** and the combined earnings from all jobs exceed $35,000 ($25,000 if married) see the **Two-Earner/Two-Job Worksheet** on page 2 to avoid having too little tax withheld.
	If **neither** of the above situations applies, **stop here** and enter the number from line H on line 5 of Form W-4 below.

--------------------   **Cut here and give Form W-4 to your employer. Keep the top part for your records.**   --------------------

Form **W-4** Department of the Treasury Internal Revenue Service	**Employee's Withholding Allowance Certificate** Your employer must send a copy of this form to the IRS if: (a) you claim more than 10 allowances or (b) you claim "Exempt" and your wages are normally more than $200 per week.	OMB No. 1545-0010 **2004**

1 Type or print your first name and middle initial	Last name	**2** Your social security number

Home address (number and street or rural route)	**3** ☐ Single ☐ Married ☐ Married, but withhold at higher Single rate. **Note:** If married, but legally separated, or spouse is a nonresident alien, check the "Single" box.
City or town, state, and ZIP code	**4** If your last name differs from that shown on your social security card, check here. You must call 1-800-772-1213 for a new card. ☐

5 Total number of allowances you are claiming (from line **H** above **or** from the applicable worksheet on page 2)   **5** _____

6 Additional amount, if any, you want withheld from each paycheck . . . . **6** $ _____

7 I claim exemption from withholding for 2004, and I certify that I meet **both** of the following conditions for exemption:

   Last year I had a right to a refund of **all** Federal income tax withheld because I had **no** tax liability **and**

   This year I expect a refund of **all** Federal income tax withheld because I expect to have **no** tax liability.

   If you meet both conditions, write "Exempt" here . . . . **7** _____

Under penalties of perjury, I certify that I am entitled to the number of withholding allowances claimed on this certificate, or I am entitled to claim exempt status.

Employee's signature (Form is not valid unless you sign it.) ▶ _____   **Date** ▶ _____

8 Employer's name and address (Employer: Complete lines 8 and 10 only if sending to the IRS.)	**9** Office code (optional)	**10** Employer identification number (EIN)

For Privacy Act and Paperwork Reduction Act Notice, see page 2.   Cat. No. 10220Q   Form **W-4** (2004)

Ch 10 Forms

Form W-4 (2004)   Page **2**

Deductions and Adjustments Worksheet

Note: *Use this worksheet **only** if you plan to itemize deductions, claim certain credits, or claim adjustments to income on your 2004 tax return.*

1 Enter an estimate of your 2004 itemized deductions. These include qualifying home mortgage interest, charitable contributions, state and local taxes, medical expenses in excess of 7.5% of your income, and miscellaneous deductions. (For 2004, you may have to reduce your itemized deductions if your income is over $142,700 ($71,350 if married filing separately). See **Worksheet 3** in Pub. 919 for details.) . . .   **1** $ _____

2 Enter: $9,700 if married filing jointly or qualifying widow(er)
             $7,150 if head of household
             $4,850 if single
             $4,850 if married filing separately   . . . .   **2** $ _____

3 **Subtract** line 2 from line 1. If line 2 is greater than line 1, enter "-0-". . . . .   **3** $ _____

4 Enter an estimate of your 2004 adjustments to income, including alimony, deductible IRA contributions, and student loan interest   **4** $ _____

5 **Add** lines 3 and 4 and enter the total. (Include any amount for credits from **Worksheet 7** in Pub. 919) .   **5** $ _____

6 Enter an estimate of your 2004 nonwage income (such as dividends or interest) . . . .   **6** $ _____

7 **Subtract** line 6 from line 5. Enter the result, but not less than "-0-" . . . .   **7** $ _____

8 **Divide** the amount on line 7 by $3,000 and enter the result here. Drop any fraction . . . . . .   **8** _____

9 Enter the number from the **Personal Allowances Worksheet,** line H, page 1 . . . .   **9** _____

10 **Add** lines 8 and 9 and enter the total here. If you plan to use the **Two-Earner/Two-Job Worksheet,** also enter this total on line 1 below. Otherwise, **stop here** and enter this total on Form W-4, line 5, page 1 .   **10** _____

Two-Earner/Two-Job Worksheet (See **Two earners/two jobs** on page 1.)

Note: *Use this worksheet **only** if the instructions under line H on page 1 direct you here.*

1 Enter the number from line H, page 1 (or from line 10 above if you used the **Deductions and Adjustments Worksheet**)   **1** _____

2 Find the number in **Table 1** below that applies to the **LOWEST** paying job and enter it here   . . . .   **2** _____

3 If line 1 is **more than or equal to** line 2, subtract line 2 from line 1. Enter the result here (if zero, enter "-0-") and on Form W-4, line 5, page 1. **Do not** use the rest of this worksheet . . . .   **3** _____

Note: *If line 1 is **less than** line 2, enter "-0-" on Form W-4, line 5, page 1. Complete lines 4–9 below to calculate the additional withholding amount necessary to avoid a year-end tax bill.*

4 Enter the number from line 2 of this worksheet . . . .   **4** _____

5 Enter the number from line 1 of this worksheet . . . .   **5** _____

6 **Subtract** line 5 from line 4 . . . .   **6** _____

7 Find the amount in **Table 2** below that applies to the **HIGHEST** paying job and enter it here . . . .   **7** $ _____

8 **Multiply** line 7 by line 6 and enter the result here. This is the additional annual withholding needed . .   **8** $ _____

9 Divide line 8 by the number of pay periods remaining in 2004. For example, divide by 26 if you are paid every two weeks and you complete this form in December 2003. Enter the result here and on Form W-4, line 6, page 1. This is the additional amount to be withheld from each paycheck . . . .   **9** $ _____

Table 1: Two-Earner/Two-Job Worksheet

Married Filing Jointly			Married Filing Jointly			All Others	
If wages from **HIGHEST** paying job are—	AND, wages from **LOWEST** paying job are—	Enter on line 2 above	If wages from **HIGHEST** paying job are—	AND, wages from **LOWEST** paying job are—	Enter on line 2 above	If wages from **LOWEST** paying job are—	Enter on line 2 above
$0 - $40,000	$0 - $4,000	0	$40,001 and over	31,001 - 38,000	6	$0 - $6,000	0
	4,001 - 8,000	1		38,001 - 44,000	7	6,001 - 11,000	1
	8,001 - 17,000	2		44,001 - 50,000	8	11,001 - 18,000	2
	17,001 and over	3		50,001 - 55,000	9	18,001 - 25,000	3
				55,001 - 65,000	10	25,001 - 31,000	4
$40,001 and over	$0 - $4,000	0		65,001 - 75,000	11	31,001 - 44,000	5
	4,001 - 8,000	1		75,001 - 85,000	12	44,001 - 55,000	6
	8,001 - 15,000	2		85,001 - 100,000	13	55,001 - 70,000	7
	15,001 - 22,000	3		100,001 - 115,000	14	70,001 - 80,000	8
	22,001 - 25,000	4		115,001 and over	15	80,001 - 100,000	9
	25,001 - 31,000	5				100,001 and over	10

Table 2: Two-Earner/Two-Job Worksheet

Married Filing Jointly		All Others	
If wages from **HIGHEST** paying job are—	Enter on line 7 above	If wages from **HIGHEST** paying job are—	Enter on line 7 above
$0 - $60,000	$470	$0 - $30,000	$470
60,001 - 110,000	780	30,001 - 70,000	780
110,001 - 150,000	870	70,001 - 140,000	870
150,001 - 270,000	1,020	140,001 - 320,000	1,020
270,001 and over	1,090	320,001 and over	1,090

Privacy Act and Paperwork Reduction Act Notice. We ask for the information on this form to carry out the Internal Revenue laws of the United States. The Internal Revenue Code requires this information under sections 3402(f)(2)(A) and 6109 and their regulations. **Failure to provide a properly completed form will result in your being treated as a single person who claims no withholding allowances; providing fraudulent information may also subject you to penalties.** Routine uses of this information include giving it to the Department of Justice for civil and criminal litigation, to cities, states, and the District of Columbia for use in administering their tax laws, and using it in the National Directory of New Hires. We may also disclose this information to Federal and state agencies to enforce Federal nontax criminal laws and to combat terrorism.

You are not required to provide the information requested on a form that is subject to the Paperwork Reduction Act unless the form displays a valid OMB

control number. Books or records relating to a form or its instructions must be retained as long as their contents may become material in the administration of any Internal Revenue law. Generally, tax returns and return information are confidential, as required by Code section 6103.

The time needed to complete this form will vary depending on individual circumstances. The estimated average time is: **Recordkeeping,** 46 min.; **Learning about the law or the form,** 13 min.; **Preparing the form,** 59 min. If you have comments concerning the accuracy of these time estimates or suggestions for making this form simpler, we would be happy to hear from you. You can write to the Tax Products Coordinating Committee, Western Area Distribution Center, Rancho Cordova, CA 95743-0001. **Do not** send Form W-4 to this address. Instead, give it to your employer.

Ch 10
Forms

Form 941
(Rev. January 2004)
Department of the Treasury
Internal Revenue Service (99)

Employer's Quarterly Federal Tax Return

See separate instructions revised January 2004 for information on completing this return.

Please type or print.

Enter state code for state in which deposits were made **only** if different from state in address to the right (see page 2 of separate instructions).

Name (as distinguished from trade name)	Date quarter ended
Trade name, if any	Employer identification number
Address (number and street)	City, state, and ZIP code

OMB No. 1545-0029

T
FF
FD
FP
I
T

If address is different from prior return, check here

IRS Use

1 1 1 1 1 1 1 1 1 1   2   3 3 3 3 3 3 3   4 4 4   5 5 5

6 7 8 8 8 8 8 8 8   9 9 9   10 10 10 10 10 10 10 10 10 10

A If you **do not have to file** returns in the future, check here ☐ and enter date final wages paid ☐

B If you are a seasonal employer, see **Seasonal employers** on page 1 of the instructions and check here ☐

1	Number of employees in the pay period that includes March 12th . **1**		
2	Total wages and tips, plus other compensation (see separate instructions)	**2**	
3	Total income tax withheld from wages, tips, and sick pay	**3**	
4	Adjustment of withheld income tax for preceding quarters of **this calendar year**	**4**	
5	Adjusted total of income tax withheld (line 3 as adjusted by line 4)	**5**	
6	Taxable social security wages **6a**	· 12.4% (.124) =	**6b**	
	Taxable social security tips **6c**	· 12.4% (.124) =	**6d**	
7	Taxable Medicare wages and tips . . . **7a**	· 2.9% (.029) =	**7b**	
8	Total social security and Medicare taxes (add lines 6b, 6d, and 7b). **Check here if wages are not subject to social security and/or Medicare tax** . . . . ☐		**8**	
9	Adjustment of social security and Medicare taxes (see instructions for required explanation) Sick Pay $ _____ ± Fractions of Cents $ _____ ± Other $ _____ =		**9**	
10	Adjusted total of social security and Medicare taxes (line 8 as adjusted by line 9)	**10**	
11	**Total taxes** (add lines 5 and 10)	**11**	
12	Advance earned income credit (EIC) payments made to employees (see instructions) . . .	**12**	
13	Net taxes (subtract line 12 from line 11). **If $2,500 or more, this must equal line 17, column (d) below (or line D of Schedule B (Form 941))**	**13**	
14	Total deposits for quarter, including overpayment applied from a prior quarter	**14**	
15	**Balance due** (subtract line 14 from line 13). See instructions	**15**	
16	**Overpayment.** If line 14 is more than line 13, enter excess here $ _____ and check if to be: ☐ Applied to next return **or** ☐ Refunded.			

All filers: If line 13 is less than $2,500, **do not** complete line 17 **or** Schedule B (Form 941).

Semiweekly schedule depositors: Complete Schedule B (Form 941) and check here . . . . ☐

Monthly schedule depositors: Complete line 17, columns (a) through (d), and check here. . . . . ☐

17 Monthly Summary of Federal Tax Liability. (Complete **Schedule B (Form 941)** instead, if you were a semiweekly schedule depositor.)

(a) First month liability	**(b)** Second month liability	**(c)** Third month liability	**(d)** Total liability for quarter

Third Party Designee

Do you want to allow another person to discuss this return with the IRS (see separate instructions)? ☐ **Yes.** Complete the following. ☐ **No**

| Designee's name | Phone no. ( ) | Personal identification number (PIN) | ☐☐☐☐☐ |

Sign Here

Under penalties of perjury, I declare that I have examined this return, including accompanying schedules and statements, and to the best of my knowledge and belief, it is true, correct, and complete.

Signature _____ Print Your Name and Title _____ Date _____

For Privacy Act and Paperwork Reduction Act Notice, see back of Payment Voucher.

Cat. No. 17001Z

Form **941** (Rev. 1-2004)

Ch 10 Forms

Form 941 (Rev. 1-2004)

Where to file. In the list below, find the state where your legal residence, principal place of business, office, or agency is located. Send your return to the **Internal Revenue Service** at the address listed for your location. No street address is needed. **Note:** *Where you file depends on whether or not you are including a payment.*

Exception for exempt organizations and government entities. If you are filing Form 941 for an exempt organization or government entity (Federal, state, local, or Indian tribal government), use the following addresses, regardless of your location:

Return without payment: Ogden, UT 84201-0046
Return with payment: P.O. Box 660264, Dallas, TX 75266-0264

YOUR LOCATION	RETURN WITHOUT A PAYMENT	RETURN WITH PAYMENT
Connecticut, Delaware, District of Columbia, Illinois, Indiana, Kentucky, Maine, Maryland, Massachusetts, Michigan, New Hampshire, New Jersey, New York, North Carolina, Ohio, Pennsylvania, Rhode Island, South Carolina, Vermont, Virginia, West Virginia, Wisconsin	Cincinnati, OH 45999-0005	P.O. Box 105703 Atlanta, GA 30348-5703
Alabama, Alaska, Arizona, Arkansas, California, Colorado, Florida, Georgia, Hawaii, Idaho, Iowa, Kansas, Louisiana, Minnesota, Mississippi, Missouri, Montana, Nebraska, Nevada, New Mexico, North Dakota, Oklahoma, Oregon, South Dakota, Tennessee, Texas, Utah, Washington, Wyoming	Ogden, UT 84201-0005	P.O. Box 660264 Dallas, TX 75266-0264
No legal residence or principal place of business in any state	Philadelphia, PA 19255-0005	P.O. Box 80106 Cincinnati, OH 45280-0006

Caution: *Your filing or payment address may have changed from prior years. If you are using an IRS provided envelope, use **only** the labels and envelope provided with this tax package. **Do not** send Form 941 or any payments to the Social Security Administration (SSA).*

Who must sign. Form 941 must be signed as follows:
   Sole proprietorship—The individual owning the business.
   Corporation (including an LLC treated as a corporation)—The president, vice president, or other principal officer.
   Partnership (including an LLC treated as a partnership) **or unincorporated organization**—A responsible and duly authorized member or officer having knowledge of its affairs.
   Single-member limited liability company (LLC) treated as a disregarded entity—The owner of the limited liability company.
   Trust or estate—The fiduciary.

   The return may also be signed by a duly authorized agent of the taxpayer if a valid power of attorney has been filed.

Form 941-V
Payment Voucher

Purpose of Form

Complete Form 941-V if you are making a payment with **Form 941,** Employer's Quarterly Federal Tax Return. We will use the completed voucher to credit your payment more promptly and accurately, and to improve our service to you.

If you have your return prepared by a third party and make a payment with that return, please provide this payment voucher to the return preparer.

Making Payments With Form 941

Make your payment with Form 941 **only if:**

Your net taxes for the quarter (line 13 on Form 941) are less than $2,500 and you are paying in full with a timely filed return or

You are a monthly schedule depositor making a payment in accordance with the **Accuracy of Deposits Rule.** (See section 11 of **Circular E (Pub. 15),** Employer's Tax Guide, for details.) This amount may be $2,500 or more.

Otherwise, you must deposit the amount at an authorized financial institution or by electronic funds transfer. (See section 11 of Circular E (Pub. 15) for deposit instructions.) Do not use the Form 941-V payment voucher to make Federal tax deposits.

Caution: *If you pay amounts with Form 941 that should have been deposited, you may be subject to a penalty. See* **Deposit Penalties** *in section 11 of Circular E (Pub. 15).*

Specific Instructions

Box 1—Employer identification number (EIN). If you do not have an EIN, apply for one on **Form SS-4,** Application for Employer Identification Number, and write "Applied For" and the date you applied in this entry space.

Box 2—Amount paid. Enter the amount paid with Form 941.

Box 3—Tax period. Darken the capsule identifying the quarter for which the payment is made. Darken only one capsule.

Box 4—Name and address. Enter your name and address as shown on Form 941.

Enclose your check or money order made payable to the United States Treasury." Be sure also to enter your EIN, For m 941," and the tax period on your check or money order. Do not send cash. Please do not staple this voucher or your payment to the return (or to each other).

Detach the completed voucher and send it with your payment and Form 941 to the address provided on the back of Form 941.

Note: *You* **must** *also complete the entity information above line A on Form 941.*

Ch 10 Forms

Detach Here and Mail With Your Payment and Tax Return.   Form **941-V** (2004)

Form **941-V**

Department of the Treasury
Internal Revenue Service (99)

Payment Voucher

Do not staple or attach this voucher to your payment.

OMB No. 1545-0029

20**04**

1 Enter your employer identification number (EIN).	2 **Enter the amount of your payment.**		Dollars	Cents

3 Tax period	4 Enter your business name (individual name if sole proprietor).
⃝ 1st Quarter ⃝ 3rd Quarter	Enter your address.
⃝ 2nd Quarter ⃝ 4th Quarter	Enter your city, state, and ZIP code.

Form 941 (Rev. 1-2004)

Electronic filing option. File Form 941 electronically and receive proof of filing acknowledgement. Electronic payment options may also be available. Visit the IRS website at **www.irs.gov** for details.

Privacy Act and Paperwork Reduction Act Notice. We ask for the information on this form to carry out the Internal Revenue laws of the United States. We need it to figure and collect the right amount of tax. Subtitle C, Employment Taxes, of the Internal Revenue Code imposes employment taxes on wages, including income tax withholding. This form is used to determine the amount of the taxes that you owe. Section 6011 requires you to provide the requested information if the tax is applicable to you. Section 6109 requires you to provide your employer identification number (EIN). If you fail to provide this information in a timely manner, you may be subject to penalties and interest.

You are not required to provide the information requested on a form that is subject to the Paperwork Reduction Act unless the form displays a valid OMB control number. Books and records relating to a form or instructions must be retained as long as their contents may become material in the administration of any Internal Revenue law.

Generally, tax returns and return information are confidential, as required by section 6103. However, section 6103 allows or requires the IRS to disclose or give the information shown on your tax return to others as described in the Code. For example, we may disclose your tax information to the Department of Justice for civil and criminal litigation, and to cities, states, and the District of Columbia for use in administering their tax laws. We may also disclose this information to Federal and state agencies to enforce Federal nontax criminal laws and to combat terrorism.

The time needed to complete and file this form will vary depending on individual circumstances. The estimated average time is:

For Form 941:

Recordkeeping	12 hr., 39 min.
Learning about the law or the form	40 min.
Preparing the form	1 hr., 49 min.
Copying, assembling, and sending the form to the IRS	16 min.

For Form 941TeleFile:

Recordkeeping	5 hr., 30 min.
Learning about the law or the Tax Record	18 min.
Preparing the Tax Record	24 min.
TeleFile phone call	11 min.

If you have comments concerning the accuracy of these time estimates or suggestions for making this form simpler, we would be happy to hear from you. You can write to the Tax Products Coordinating Committee, Western Area Distribution Center, Rancho Cordova, CA 95743-0001. **Do not** send Form 941 to this address.

Ch 10 Forms

a Control number	22222	Void ☐	For Official Use Only OMB No. 1545-0008		
b Employer identification number				1 Wages, tips, other compensation	2 Federal income tax withheld
c Employer's name, address, and ZIP code				3 Social security wages	4 Social security tax withheld
				5 Medicare wages and tips	6 Medicare tax withheld
				7 Social security tips	8 Allocated tips
d Employee's social security number				9 Advance EIC payment	10 Dependent care benefits
e Employee's first name and initial	Last name			11 Nonqualified plans	12a See instructions for box 12
			13 Statutory employee ☐ Retirement plan ☐ Third-party sick pay ☐		12b
			14 Other		12c
					12d
f Employee's address and ZIP code					

15 State Employer's state ID number	16 State wages, tips, etc.	17 State income tax	18 Local wages, tips, etc.	19 Local income tax	20 Locality name

Form **W-2** Wage and Tax Statement

2004

Department of the Treasury—Internal Revenue Service

Copy A For Social Security Administration — Send this entire page with Form W-3 to the Social Security Administration; photocopies are **not** acceptable.

For Privacy Act and Paperwork Reduction Act Notice, see back of Copy D.

Cat. No. 10134D

Do Not Cut, Fold, or Staple For ms on This Page — Do Not Cut, Fold, or Staple For ms on This Page

Ch 10 Forms

Note: There are six copies of this form: Copies 1 and 2 for state, city, or local tax departments, Copy B to be filed with Federal Income Tax forms, Copy C for employee's records, Copy D for employer.

DO NOT STAPLE OR FOLD

a Control number	33333	For Official Use Only OMB No. 1545-0008		

b Kind of Payer	941 ☐ Military ☐ 943 ☐ Hshld. emp. ☐ Medicare govt. emp. ☐ Third-party sick pay ☐ CT-1 ☐	1 Wages, tips, other compensation	2 Federal income tax withheld
		3 Social security wages	4 Social security tax withheld
c Total number of Forms W-2 d Establishment number		5 Medicare wages and tips	6 Medicare tax withheld
e Employer identification number		7 Social security tips	8 Allocated tips
f Employer's name		9 Advance EIC payments	10 Dependent care benefits
		11 Nonqualified plans	12 Deferred compensation
		13 For third-party sick pay use only	
		14 Income tax withheld by payer of third-party sick pay	
g Employer's address and ZIP code			
h Other EIN used this year			
15 State Employer's state ID number		16 State wages, tips, etc.	17 State income tax
		18 Local wages, tips, etc.	19 Local income tax
Contact person		Telephone number ( )	For Official Use Only
Email address		Fax number ( )	

Under penalties of perjury, I declare that I have examined this return and accompanying documents, and, to the best of my knowledge and belief, they are true, correct, and complete.

Signature   Title   Date

Form **W-3** Transmittal of Wage and Tax Statements   **2004**   Department of the Treasury Internal Revenue Service

Send this entire page with the entire Copy A page of Form(s) W-2 to the Social Security Administration. Photocopies are not acceptable.

Do not send any payment (cash, checks, money orders, etc.) with Forms W-2 and W-3.

An Item To Note

Separate instructions. See the 2004 Instructions for Forms W-2 and W-3 for information on completing this form.

Purpose of Form

Use this form to transmit Copy A of Form(s) W-2, Wage and Tax Statement. Make a copy of Form W-3, and keep it with Copy D (For Employer) of Form(s) W-2 for your records. Use Form W-3 for the correct year. File Form W-3 even if only one Form W-2 is being filed. If you are filing Form(s) W-2 on magnetic media or electronically, do not file Form W-3.

When To File

File Form W-3 with Copy A of Form(s) W-2 by February 28, 2005.

Where To File

Send this entire page with the entire Copy A page of Form(s) W-2 to:

Social Security Administration
Data Operations Center
Wilkes-Barre, PA 18769-0001

Note: If you use "Certified Mail" to file, change the ZIP code to "18769-0002." If you use an IRS-approved private delivery service, add "ATTN: W-2 Process, 1150 E. Mountain Dr." to the address and change the ZIP code to "18702-7997." See *Circular E (Pub. 15),* Employer's Tax Guide, for a list of IRS approved private delivery services.

Do not send magnetic media to the address shown above.

For Privacy Act and Paperwork Reduction Act Notice, see back of Copy D of Form W-2.

Cat. No. 10159Y

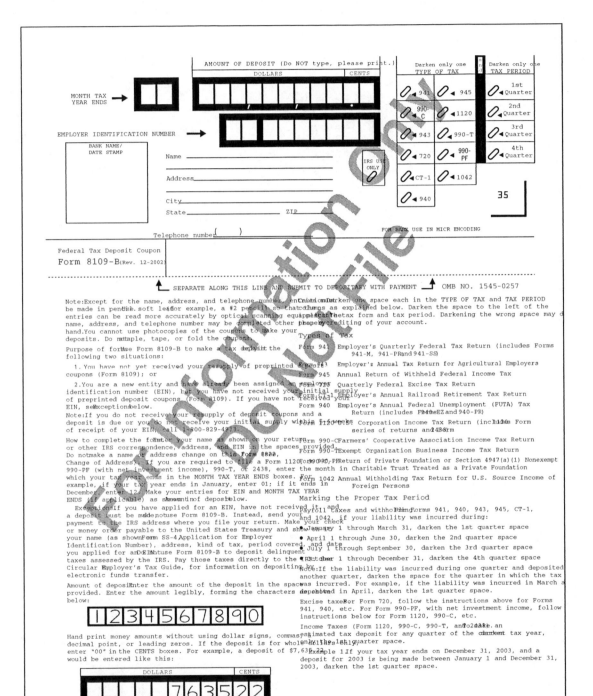

**Ch 10
Forms**

Example 2 If your tax year ends on June 30, 2003, and a deposit for that fiscal year is being made between July 1, 2002, and June 30, 2003, darken the 1st quarter space.

To make a deposit for the prior tax year, darken only the 4th quarter space. This includes:

● Deposits of balance due shown on the return (Forms 1120, 990-T, and 990-PF).

● Deposits of balance due shown on Form 7004 Application for Automatic Extension of Time To File Corporation Income Tax (be sure to darken the 1120 or 990-C space as appropriate).

● Deposits of balance due (Forms 990-T and 990-PF filers) shown on Form 8868 Application for Extension of Time To File an Exempt Organization Return (be sure to darken the 990-T or 990-PF space as appropriate).

● Deposits of balance due (Form 1042) shown on Form 2758, Application for Extension of Time To File Certain Excise, Income, Information, and Other Returns (be sure to darken the 1042 space as appropriate).

● Deposits of tax due shown on Form 2438 Undistributed Capital Gains Tax Return (darken the 1120 space).

Example 1 If your tax year ends on December 31, 2003, and a deposit for 2003 is being made after that date, darken the 4th quarter space.

Example 2 If your tax year ends on June 30, 2003, and a deposit for that fiscal year is being made after this date, darken the 4th quarter space.

How to ensure your deposit is credited to the correct account.

1. Make sure your name and EIN are correct;

2. Prepare only one coupon for each type of tax deposit;

3. Darken only one space for the type of tax you are depositing;

4. Darken only one space for the tax period for which you are making a deposit; and

5. Use separate FTD coupons for each return period.

Telephone number We need your daytime telephone number to call you if we have difficulty processing your deposit.

Miscellaneous We use the "IRS USE ONLY" box to ensure proper crediting to your account. Do not darken this space when making a deposit.

How to make deposits Mail or deliver the completed coupon with the appropriate payment for the amount of the deposit to an authorized depositary (financial institution) for Federal taxes. Make checks or money orders payable to that depositary. To help ensure proper crediting of your account, include your EIN, the type of tax (e.g., Form 941), and the tax period to which the payment applies on your check or money order.

Authorized depositaries must accept cash, postal money orders drawn to the order of the depositary, or checks or drafts drawn on and to the order of the depositary. You can deposit taxes with a check drawn on another financial institution only if the depositary is willing to accept that form of payment.

If you prefer, you may mail your coupon and payment to Financial Agent, Federal Tax Deposit Processing, P.O. Box 970030, St. Louis, MO 63197. Make your check or money order payable to Financial Agent.

Timeliness of deposits. The IRS determines whether deposits are on time by the date they are received by an authorized depositary. However, a deposit received by the authorized depositary after the due date is considered timely if the taxpayer establishes that it was mailed in the United States at least 2 days before the due date.

Note: If you are required to deposit any taxes more than once a month, any deposit of $20,000 or more must be made by its due date to be timely.

When to deposit See the instructions for the applicable return. For deposit rules for employment taxes, see Circular E (Pub. 15). You can get copies of forms and instructions by calling 1-800-TAX-FORM (1-800-829-3676) or by visiting IRS's Web Site at www.irs.gov.

Penalties You may be charged a penalty for not making deposits when due or in sufficient amounts, unless you have reasonable cause. This penalty may also apply if you mail or deliver Federal tax deposits to unauthorized institutions or IRS offices, rather than to authorized depositaries. Additionally, a trust fund recovery penalty may be imposed on all persons who are determined by the IRS to be responsible for collecting, accounting for, and paying over these taxes, and who acted willfully in not doing so. This penalty may apply to you if these unpaid taxes cannot be immediately collected from the employer or business. For more information on penalties, see Circular E (Pub. 15). See the instructions for Form 720 when these penalties apply to excise taxes.

Privacy Act and Paperwork Reduction Act Notice. Internal Revenue Code section 6302 requires certain persons to make periodic deposits of taxes. If you do not deposit electronically, you must provide the information requested on this form. IRC section 6109 requires you to provide your EIN. The information on this form is used to ensure that you are complying with the Internal Revenue laws and to ensure proper crediting of your deposit. Routine uses of this information include providing it to the Department of Justice for civil and criminal litigation, and to cities, states, and the District of Columbia for use in administering their tax laws. We may also disclose this information to Federal agencies to enforce Federal nontax criminal laws and to combat terrorism. We may give this information to other countries pursuant to treaties. Providing incomplete, incorrect, or fraudulent information may subject you to interest and penalties.

You are not required to provide the information requested on a form that is subject to the Paperwork Reduction Act unless the form displays a valid OMB control number. Books or records relating to a form or its instructions must be retained as long as their contents may become material in the administration of any Internal Revenue law. Generally, tax returns and return information are confidential, as required by IRC section 6103.

The time needed to complete and file this form will vary depending on individual circumstances. The estimated average time is 3 minutes. If you have comments concerning the accuracy of this time estimate or suggestions for making this form simpler, we would be happy to hear from you. You can write to the Tax Forms Committee, Western Area Distribution Center, Rancho Cordova, CA 95743-0001. Do not send this form to this address. Instead, see the instructions under How to make deposits on this page.

Form **1120-W**
(WORKSHEET)
Department of the Treasury
Internal Revenue Service

Estimated Tax for Corporations

For calendar year 2004, or tax year beginning .... , 2004, and ending .... , 20 .....

(Keep for the corporation's records—Do *not* send to the Internal Revenue Service.)

OMB No. 1545-0975

2004

1	Taxable income expected for the tax year	**1**
	Qualified personal service corporations (defined in the instructions), skip lines 2 through 13 and go to line 14. Members of a controlled group, see instructions.	
2	Enter the **smaller** of line 1 or $50,000	**2**
3	Multiply line 2 by 15%	**3**
4	Subtract line 2 from line 1	**4**
5	Enter the **smaller** of line 4 or $25,000	**5**
6	Multiply line 5 by 25%	**6**
7	Subtract line 5 from line 4	**7**
8	Enter the **smaller** of line 7 or $9,925,000.	**8**
9	Multiply line 8 by 34%	**9**
10	Subtract line 8 from line 7	**10**
11	Multiply line 10 by 35%.	**11**
12	If line 1 is greater than $100,000, enter the **smaller** of **(a)** 5% of the excess over $100,000 or **(b)** $11,750. Otherwise, enter -0-	**12**
13	If line 1 is greater than $15 million, enter the **smaller** of **(a)** 3% of the excess over $15 million or **(b)** $100,000. Otherwise, enter -0-	**13**
14	Add lines 3, 6, 9, and 11 through 13. (Qualified personal service corporations, multiply line 1 by 35%.).	**14**
15	Alternative minimum tax (see instructions)	**15**
16	**Total.** Add lines 14 and 15	**16**
17	Tax credits (see instructions)	**17**
18	Subtract line 17 from line 16	**18**
19	Other taxes (see instructions)	**19**
20	**Total tax.** Add lines 18 and 19	**20**
21	Credit for Federal tax paid on fuels (see instructions).	**21**
22	Subtract line 21 from line 20. **Note:** *If the result is less than $500, the corporation is not required to make estimated tax payments*	**22**
23a	Enter the tax shown on the corporation's 2003 tax return (see instructions). **Caution:** *If the tax is zero or the tax year was for less than 12 months, skip this line and enter the amount from line 22 on line 23b*	**23a**
b	Enter the **smaller** of line 22 or line 23a. If the corporation is required to skip line 23a, enter the amount from line 22	**23b**

		(a)	(b)	(c)	(d)
24	**Installment due dates** (see instructions)				
25	**Required Installments.** Enter 25% of line 23b in columns **(a)** through **(d)** unless the corporation uses the annualized income installment method or adjusted seasonal installment method or is a "lar ge corporation" (see instructions)				

For Paperwork Reduction Act Notice, see page 6.   Cat. No. 11525G   Form **1120-W** (2004)

Ch 10 Forms

Form 1120-W (WORKSHEET) 2004

Page **2**

Schedule A   Adjusted Seasonal Installment Method and Annualized Income Installment Method. (See pages 5 and 6 of the instructions.)

Part I—Adjusted Seasonal Installment Method
(Use this method only if the base period percentage for any 6 consecutive months is at least 70%.)

		(a)	(b)	(c)	(d)
1	Enter taxable income for the following periods:	First 3 months	First 5 months	First 8 months	First 11 months
a	Tax year beginning in 2001. **1a**				
b	Tax year beginning in 2002. **1b**				
c	Tax year beginning in 2003. **1c**				
2	Enter taxable income for each period for the tax year beginning in 2004. **2**				
3	Enter taxable income for the following periods:	First 4 months	First 6 months	First 9 months	Entire year
a	Tax year beginning in 2001. **3a**				
b	Tax year beginning in 2002. **3b**				
c	Tax year beginning in 2003. **3c**				
4	Divide the amount in each column on line 1a by the amount in column (d) on line 3a. **4**				
5	Divide the amount in each column on line 1b by the amount in column (d) on line 3b. **5**				
6	Divide the amount in each column on line 1c by the amount in column (d) on line 3c. **6**				
7	Add lines 4 through 6. **7**				
8	Divide line 7 by 3. **8**				
9	Divide line 2 by line 8. **9**				
10	Figure the tax on the amount on line 9 by following the same steps used to figure the tax for line 14, page 1, of Form 1120-W. **10**				
11a	Divide the amount in columns (a) through (c) on line 3a by the amount in column (d) on line 3a. **11a**				
b	Divide the amount in columns (a) through (c) on line 3b by the amount in column (d) on line 3b. **11b**				
c	Divide the amount in columns (a) through (c) on line 3c by the amount in column (d) on line 3c. **11c**				
12	Add lines 11a through 11c. **12**				
13	Divide line 12 by 3. **13**				
14	Multiply the amount in columns (a) through (c) of line 10 by the amount in the corresponding column of line 13. In column (d), enter the amount from line 10, column (d). **14**				
15	Enter any alternative minimum tax for each payment period (see instructions). **15**				
16	Enter any other taxes for each payment period (see instructions). **16**				
17	Add lines 14 through 16. **17**				
18	For each period, enter the same type of credits as allowed on lines 17 and 21, page 1, of Form 1120-W (see instructions). **18**				
19	Subtract line 18 from line 17. If zero or less, enter -0-. **19**				

Form **1120-W** (2004)

Form 1120-W (WORKSHEET) 2004

Part II—Annualized Income Installment Method

		(a) First _____ months	(b) First _____ months	(c) First _____ months	(d) First _____ months
20	Annualization periods (see instructions). **20**				
21	Enter taxable income for each annualization period (see instructions). **21**				
22	Annualization amounts (see instructions). **22**				
23	Annualized taxable income. Multiply line 21 by line 22. **23**				
24	Figure the tax on the amount in each column on line 23 by following the same steps used to figure the tax for line 14, page 1, of Form 1120-W. **24**				
25	Enter any alternative minimum tax for each annualization period (see instructions). **25**				
26	Enter any other taxes for each annualization period (see instructions). **26**				
27	Total tax. Add lines 24 through 26. **27**				
28	For each annualization period, enter the same type of credits as allowed on lines 17 and 21, page 1, of Form 1120-W (see instructions). **28**				
29	Total tax after credits. Subtract line 28 from line 27. If zero or less, enter -0-. **29**				
30	Applicable percentage. **30**	25%	50%	75%	100%
31	Multiply line 29 by line 30. **31**				

Part III—Required Installments

Note: *Complete lines 32 through 38 of one column before completing the next column.*

		1st installment	2nd installment	3rd installment	4th installment
32	If only Part I or Part II is completed, enter the amount in each column from line 19 **or** line 31. If both parts are completed, enter the **smaller** of the amounts in each column from line 19 or line 31. **32**				
33	Add the amounts in all preceding columns of line 38 (see instructions). **33**	////////			
34	**Adjusted seasonal or annualized income installments.** Subtract line 33 from line 32. If zero or less, enter -0-. **34**				
35	Enter 25% of line 23b, page 1, in each column. (**Note:** *"Large corporations," see the instructions for line 25 on page 5 for the amount to enter.*) **35**				
36	Subtract line 38 of the preceding column from line 37 of the preceding column. **36**	////////			
37	Add lines 35 and 36. **37**				
38	**Required Installments.** Enter the **smaller** of line 34 or line 37 here and on line 25, page 1. See instructions. **38**				

Form **1120-W** (2004)

Ch 10 Forms

Form 1120-W (WORKSHEET) 2004

Page **4**

General Instructions

Section references are to the Internal Revenue Code unless otherwise noted.

A Change To Note

Twenty percent of any required installment otherwise due in September 2004 is not due until October 1, 2004.

 *At the time these instructions were released, the work opportunity and welfare-to-work credits did not apply for individuals beginning work after December 31, 2003, and the New York Liberty Zone business employee credit did not apply to wages paid for work performed in calendar year 2004. Pending legislation in Congress could extend these credits. It could also provide for a 5-year, rather than a 2-year, carryback period for NOLs arising in tax years ending after 2002. See **Pub. 553,** Highlights of 2003 Tax Changes, or visit **www.irs.gov** to find out if this legislation has become law.*

Who Must Make Estimated Tax Payments

Corporations generally must make estimated tax payments if they expect their estimated tax (income tax less credits) to be $500 or more.

S corporations must also make estimated tax payments for certain taxes. S corporations should see the instructions for **Form 1120S,** U.S. Income Tax Return for an S Corporation, to figure their estimated tax payments.

Tax-exempt organizations subject to the unrelated business income tax and private foundations use **Form 990-W,** Estimated Tax on Unrelated Business Taxable Income for Tax-Exempt Organizations, to figure the amount of their estimated tax payments.

When To Make Estimated Tax Payments

The installments generally are due by the 15th day of the **4th, 6th, 9th, and 12th** months of the tax year. However, 20% of any required installment otherwise due in September 2004 is not due until October 1, 2004. If any due date falls on a Saturday, Sunday, or legal holiday, the installment is due on the next regular business day.

Underpayment of Estimated Tax

A corporation that does not make estimated tax payments when due may be subject to an underpayment penalty for the period of underpayment.

Overpayment of Estimated Tax

A corporation that has overpaid its estimated tax may apply for a quick refund if the overpayment is at least 10% of its expected income tax liability **and** at least $500. To apply, file **Form 4466,** Corporation Application for Quick Refund of Overpayment of Estimated Tax, after the end of the tax year and before the corporation files its income tax return. Form 4466 may not be filed later than the 15th day of the 3rd month after the end of the tax year.

Depository Method of Tax Payment

Some corporations (described below) are required to electronically deposit all depository taxes, including estimated tax payments.

Electronic deposit requirement. The corporation must make electronic deposits of **all** depository taxes (such as employment tax, excise tax, and corporate income tax) using the Electronic Federal Tax Payment System (EFTPS) in 2004 if:

The total deposits of such taxes in 2002 were more than $200,000 or

The corporation was required to use EFTPS in 2003.

If the corporation is required to use EFTPS and fails to do so, it may be subject to a 10% penalty. If the corporation is not required to use EFTPS, it may participate voluntarily. To enroll in or get more information about EFTPS, call 1-800-555-4477 or 1-800-945-8400. To enroll online, visit **www.eftps.gov.**

Depositing on time. For EFTPS deposits to be made timely, the corporation must initiate the transaction at least 1 business day before the date the deposit is due.

Deposits with Form 8109. If the corporation does not use EFTPS, deposit corporation income tax payments (and estimated tax payments) with **Form 8109,** Federal Tax Deposit Coupon. If you do not have a preprinted Form 8109, use Form 8109-B to make deposits. You can get this form **only** by calling 1-800-829-4933. Be sure to have your employer identification number (EIN) ready when you call.

Do not send deposits directly to an IRS office; otherwise, the corporation may have to pay a penalty. Mail or deliver the completed Form 8109 with the payment to an authorized depositary (i.e., a commercial bank or other financial institution authorized to accept Federal tax deposits). Make checks or money orders payable to the depositary.

If the corporation prefers, it may mail the coupon and payment to: Financial Agent, Federal Tax Deposit Processing, P.O. Box 970030, St. Louis, MO 63197. Make the check or money order payable to "Financial Agent."

To help ensure proper crediting, write the corporation's EIN, the tax period to which the deposit applies, and "Form 1120" on the check or money order. Be sure to darken the "1120" box on the coupon. Records of these deposits will be sent to the IRS.

For more information on deposits, see the instructions in the coupon booklet (Form 8109) and **Pub. 583,** Starting a Business and Keeping Records.

Refiguring Estimated Tax

If, after the corporation figures and deposits estimated tax, it finds that its tax liability for the year will be more or less than originally estimated, it may have to refigure its required installments. If earlier installments were underpaid, the corporation may owe a penalty.

An immediate catchup payment should be made to reduce the amount of any penalty resulting from the underpayment of any earlier installments, whether caused by a change in estimate, failure to make a deposit, or a mistake.

Specific Instructions

Line 1—Qualified Personal Service Corporations

A qualified personal service corporation is taxed at a flat rate of 35% of taxable income. A corporation is a qualified personal service corporation if it meets **both** of the following tests.

Substantially all of the corporation's activities involve the performance of services in the fields of health, law, engineering, architecture, accounting, actuarial science, performing arts, or consulting.

At least 95% of the corporation's stock, by value, is owned, directly or indirectly, by employees performing the services, retired employees who had performed the services listed above, any estate of an employee or retiree described above, or any person who acquired the stock of the corporation as a result of the death of an employee or retiree (but only for the 2-year period beginning on the date of the employee's or retiree's death). See Temporary Regulations section 1.448-1T(e) for details.

Lines 2, 5, and 8—Members of a Controlled Group

Members of a controlled group enter on line 2 the **smaller** of **(a)** the amount on line 1 or **(b)** their share of the $50,000 amount. On line 5, enter the **smaller** of **(a)** the amount on line 4 or **(b)** their share of the $25,000 amount. On line 8, enter the **smaller** of **(a)** the amount on line 7 or **(b)** their share of the $9,925,000 amount.

Equal apportionment plan. If no apportionment plan is adopted, members of a controlled group must divide the amount in each taxable income bracket equally among themselves. For example, Controlled Group AB consists of Corporation A and Corporation B. They do not elect an apportionment plan. Therefore, each corporation is entitled to:

$25,000 (one-half of $50,000) on line 2,

$12,500 (one-half of $25,000) on line 5, and

$4,962,500 (one-half of $9,925,000) on line 8.

Unequal apportionment plan. Members of a controlled group may elect an unequal apportionment plan and divide the taxable income brackets as they want. There is no need for consistency among taxable income brackets. Any member may be entitled to all, some, or none of the taxable income bracket. However, the total amount for all members cannot be more than the total amount in each taxable income bracket.

Form 1120-W (WORKSHEET) 2004

Line 12—Additional 5% Tax

Members of a controlled group are treated as one group to figure the applicability of the additional 5% tax and the additional 3% tax. If an additional tax applies, each member will pay that tax based on the part of the amount used in each taxable income bracket to reduce that member's tax. See section 1561(a). Each member of the group must enter on line 12 its share of the **smaller** of (a) 5% of the taxable income in excess of $100,000 or (b) $11,750.

Line 13—Additional 3% Tax

If the additional 3% tax applies, each member of the controlled group must enter on line 13 its share of the **smaller** of (a) 3% of the taxable income in excess of $15 million or (b) $100,000. See the instructions for line 12 above.

Line 15—Alternative Minimum Tax (AMT)

Note. *Skip this line if the corporation is treated as a "small corporation" exempt from the AMT under section 55(e).*

AMT is generally the excess of tentative minimum tax (TMT) for the tax year over the regular tax for the tax year. See section 55 for definitions of TMT and regular tax. A limited amount of the foreign tax credit, as refigured for the AMT, is allowed in computing the TMT.

Line 17—Tax Credits

For information on tax credits the corporation may take, see the instructions for Form 1120, lines 6a through 6f, Schedule J (Form 1120-A, lines 2a and 2b, Part I), or the instructions for the applicable lines and schedule of other income tax returns.

Line 19—Other Taxes

For information on other taxes the corporation may owe, see the instructions for Form 1120, line 10, Schedule J (Form 1120-A, line 5, Part I), or the instructions for the applicable line and schedule of other income tax returns.

Line 21—Credit for Federal Tax Paid on Fuels

See **Form 4136,** Credit for Federal Tax Paid on Fuels, to find out if the corporation qualifies to take this credit. Include on line 21 any credit the corporation is claiming under section 4682(g)(2) for tax on ozone-depleting chemicals.

Line 23a—2003 Tax

Figure the corporation's 2003 tax in the same way that line 22 of this worksheet was figured, using the taxes and credits from the 2003 income tax return. Large corporations, see the instructions for line 25 below.

If a return was not filed for the 2003 tax year showing a liability for at least some amount of tax **or** the 2003 tax year was for less than 12 months, **do not** complete line 23a. Instead, skip line 23a and enter the amount from line 22 on line 23b.

Line 24—Installment Due Dates

Calendar-year taxpayers: Enter 4-15-2004, 6-15-2004, 9-15-2004 (see **Note** below), and 12-15-2004, respectively, in columns (a) through (d).

Fiscal-year taxpayers: Enter the 15th day of the 4th, 6th, 9th, and 12th months of your tax year in columns (a) through (d). If the due date falls on a Saturday, Sunday, or legal holiday, enter the next business day.

Note: *Twenty percent of any required installment otherwise due in September 2004 is not due until October 1, 2004. If the corporation has an installment due in September 2004, make two entries on lines 24 and 25 for the applicable column. Enter 9-15-2004 and 10-1-2004 on line 24, and enter on line 25 80% and 20% of the amount that would otherwise be entered on that line.*

Line 25—Required Installments

Payments of estimated tax should reflect any 2003 overpayment that the corporation chose to credit against its 2004 tax. The overpayment is credited against unpaid required installments in the order in which the installments are required to be paid.

Annualized income installment method and/or adjusted seasonal installment method. If the corporation's income is expected to vary during the year because, for example, it operates its business on a seasonal basis, it may be able to lower the amount of one or more

required installments by using the annualized income installment method and/or the adjusted seasonal installment method. For example, a ski shop, which receives most of its income during the winter months, may be able to benefit from using one or both of these methods in figuring one or more of its required installments.

To use one or both of these methods, complete Schedule A on pages 2 and 3. If Schedule A is used for any payment date, it must be used for **all** payment due dates. To arrive at the amount of each required installment, Schedule A automatically selects the **smallest** of (a) the annualized income installment (if applicable), (b) the adjusted seasonal installment (if applicable), or (c) the regular installment under section 6655(d)(1) (increased by any recapture of a reduction in a required installment under section 6655(e)(1)(B)).

Large corporations. A large corporation is a corporation that had, or whose predecessor had, taxable income of $1 million or more for any of the 3 tax years immediately preceding the 2004 tax year. For this purpose, taxable income is modified to exclude net operating loss and capital loss carrybacks or carryforwards. Members of a controlled group, as defined in section 1563, must divide the $1 million amount among themselves according to rules similar to those in section 1561.

If Schedule A is not used, follow the instructions below to figure the amounts to enter on line 25. If Schedule A is used, follow the instructions below to figure the amounts to enter on line 35 of Schedule A.

If line 22 is smaller than line 23a: Enter 25% of line 22 in columns (a) through (d) of line 25.

If line 23a is smaller than line 22: Enter 25% of line 23a in column (a) of line 25. In column (b), determine the amount to enter as follows:

1. Subtract line 23a from line 22,

2. Add the result to the amount on line 22, and

3. Multiply the result in **2** above by 25% and enter the result in column (b).

Enter 25% of line 22 in columns (c) and (d).

Schedule A

If only the adjusted seasonal installment method (Part I) is used, complete Parts I and III of Schedule A. If only the annualized income installment method (Part II) is used, complete Parts II and III. If both methods are used, complete all three parts. Enter in each column on line 25, page 1, the amounts from the corresponding column of line 38. If Schedule A is used for any payment date, it must be used for **all** payment dates.

 Do not figure any required installment until after the end of the month preceding the due date for that installment.

Part I—Adjusted Seasonal Installment Method

Complete this part only if the corporation's base period percentage for any 6 consecutive months of the tax year equals or exceeds 70%. The base period percentage for any period of 6 consecutive months is the average of the three percentages figured by dividing the taxable income for the corresponding 6-consecutive-month period in each of the 3 preceding tax years by the taxable income for each of their respective tax years.

Example. An amusement park with a calendar year tax year receives the largest part of its taxable income during a 6-month period, May through October. To compute its base period percentage for this 6-month period, the amusement park figures its taxable income for each May–October period in 2001, 2002, and 2003. It then divides the taxable income for each May–October period by the total taxable income for that particular tax year. The resulting percentages are 69% (.69) for May–October 2001, 74% (.74) for May–October 2002, and 67% (.67) for May–October 2003. Because the average of 69%, 74%, and 67% is 70%, the base period percentage for May through October 2004 is 70%. Therefore, the amusement park qualifies for the adjusted seasonal installment method.

Line 15—Alternative Minimum Tax

The corporation may owe AMT unless it will be a "small corporation" exempt from the AMT under section 55(e) for its 2004 tax year. To figure the AMT, use the 2003 Form 4626 and its instructions as a guide. Figure alternative minimum taxable income (AMTI) using

Form 1120-W (WORKSHEET) 2004   Page **6**

income and deductions for the months shown in the column headings above line 1. Divide the AMTI by the amounts on line 8 before subtracting the exemption amount. Multiply that result by 20% and subtract any AMT foreign tax credit plus the amount on line 10 to arrive at the AMT. For columns (a) through (c), multiply the AMT by the amount shown on line 13.

Line 16—Other Taxes

For the same taxes used to figure line 19 of Form 1120-W, figure the amounts for the months shown in the column headings above line 1.

Line 18—Credits

Enter the credits to which the corporation is entitled for the months shown in the column headings above line 1.

Part II—Annualized Income Installment Method

Line 20—Annualization Periods

Enter in the space on line 20, columns (a) through (d), respectively, the annualization periods that the corporation is using, based on the options listed below. For example, if the corporation elects Option 1, enter on line 20 the annualization periods 2, 4, 7, and 10, in columns (a) through (d), respectively.

 *Use Option 1 or Option 2 **only** if the corporation elected to use one of these options by filing **Form 8842,** Election To Use Different Annualization Periods for Corporate Estimated Tax, on or before the due date of the first required installment payment. Once made, the election is irrevocable for the particular tax year.*

	1st Installment	2nd Installment	3rd Installment	4th Installment
Standard option	3	3	6	9
Option 1 . . .	2	4	7	10
Option 2 . . .	3	5	8	11

Line 21—Taxable Income

If a corporation has income includible under section 936(h) (Puerto Rico and possessions tax credits) or section 951(a) (controlled foreign corporation income), special rules apply.

Amounts includible in income under section 936(h) or 951(a) (and allocable credits) generally must be taken into account in figuring the amount of any annualized income installment as the income is earned. The amounts are figured in a manner similar to the way in which partnership income inclusions (and allocable credits) are taken into account in figuring a partner's annualized income installments as provided in Regulations section 1.6654-2(d)(2).

Safe harbor election. Corporations may be able to elect a prior year safe harbor election. Under the election, an eligible corporation is treated as having received ratably during the tax year items of income under sections 936(h) and 951(a) (and allocable credits) equal to a specified percentage of the amounts shown on the corporation's return for the first preceding tax year (the second preceding tax year for the first and second required installments).

For more information, see section 6655(e)(4) and Rev. Proc. 95-23, 1995-1 C.B. 693.

Line 22—Annualization Amounts

Enter the annualization amounts for the option used on line 20. For example, if the corporation elects Option 1, enter on line 22 the annualization amounts 6, 3, 1.71429, and 1.2, in columns (a) through (d), respectively.

	1st Installment	2nd Installment	3rd Installment	4th Installment
Standard option	4	4	2	1.33333
Option 1 . . .	6	3	1.71429	1.2
Option 2 . . .	4	2.4	1.5	1.09091

Line 25—Alternative Minimum Tax

The corporation may owe AMT unless it will be a "small corporation" exempt from the AMT under section 55(e) for its 2004 tax year. To figure the AMT, use the 2003 Form 4626 and its instructions as a guide. Figure AMTI using income and deductions for the annualization period entered in each column on line 20. Multiply the AMTI by the annualization amounts on line 22 before subtracting the exemption amount. Multiply that result by 20% and subtract any AMT foreign tax credit plus the amount on line 24 to arrive at the AMT.

Line 26—Other Taxes

For the same taxes used to figure line 19 of Form 1120-W, figure the amounts for the months shown on line 20.

Line 28—Credits

Enter the credits to which the corporation is entitled for the months shown in each column on line 20. **Do not** annualize any credit. However, when figuring the credits, annualize any item of income or deduction used to figure the credit. For more details, see Rev. Rul. 79-179, 1979-1 C.B. 436.

Part III—Required Installments

Line 33

Before completing line 33 in columns (b) through (d), complete lines 34 through 38 in each of the preceding columns. For example, complete lines 34 through 38 in column (a) before completing line 33 in column (b).

Line 38—Required Installments

For each installment, enter the smaller of line 34 or line 37 on line 38. Also enter the result on line 25, page 1. However, if one of the required installments to be entered on line 25 is for September 2004, see the **Note** in the instructions for line 24 on page 5 before entering an amount on line 25.

Paperwork Reduction Act Notice. Your use of this form is optional. It is provided to aid the corporation in determining its tax liability.

You are not required to provide the information requested on a form that is subject to the Paperwork Reduction Act unless the form displays a valid OMB control number. Books or records relating to a form or its instructions must be retained as long as their contents may become material in the administration of any Internal Revenue law. Generally, tax returns and return information are confidential, as required by section 6103.

The time needed to complete this form will vary depending on individual circumstances. The estimated average time is:

Form	Recordkeeping	Learning about the law or the form	Preparing the form
1120-W	8 hr., 7 min.	1 hr.	1 hr., 10 min.
1120-W, Sch. A (Pt. I)	22 hr., 43 min.	6 min.	28 min.
1120-W, Sch. A (Pt. II)	10 hr., 31 min.	35 min.	48 min.
1120-W, Sch. A (Pt. III)	6 hr., 13 min.	. . . .	6 min.

If you have comments concerning the accuracy of these time estimates or suggestions for making this form simpler, we would be happy to hear from you. You can write to the Tax Products Coordinating Committee, Western Area Distribution Center, Rancho Cordova, CA 95743-0001. **Do not** send the tax form to this office. Instead, keep the form for your records.

MINUTES OF THE FIRST MEETING OF
THE BOARD OF DIRECTORS OF

_____

A California Corporation

The Directors of the above Corporation held their first meeting at
_____ on _____, 20 ____. The meeting was held pursuant to a written Waiver of Notice and Consent thereto signed by each of the Directors, and placed in the Minute Book immediately preceding these Minutes.

The following Directors, constituting a quorum, were present at said meeting:

_____

_____

_____

The following Directors were absent:

_____

_____

_____

Upon motion duly made, seconded, and unanimously carried,
_____ was elected Chairman of the meeting and
_____ was elected Secretary of the meeting.

FILING OF ARTICLES OF INCORPORATION

The Chairman notified the rest of the Board that the Articles of Incorporation were filed in the office of the California Secretary of State on _____, 20 ___. The Chairman presented a certified copy of the Articles of Incorporation for the Board's inspection and the Secretary was directed to insert the copy in the Minute Book of the Corporation.

AGENT FOR SERVICE OF PROCESS

The Chairman pointed out that the Articles of Incorporation had named
_____ the Corporation's initial Agent for Service of Process. Upon motion duly made, the following resolution was unanimously adopted:

RESOLVED, that _____,* named as the initial agent for service of process in the Articles of Incorporation, is hereby confirmed as the Corporation's agent for the purpose of service of process.

*Note: a corporation cannot be named as agent for service of process of itself._

Ch 10 Forms

DESIGNATION OF PRINCIPAL OFFICE

The Chairman then proposed that the Corporation should designate an office within the City of _____, California, as its principal office. It was the unanimous decision of the Board that the principal office would be located at _____, California.

ADOPTION OF BYLAWS

The original set of Bylaws, adopted by _____, the Incorporator of the Corporation, was then submitted, read, and discussed by the Board. Upon motion duly made, the following resolution was unanimously adopted:

RESOLVED, that the Bylaws submitted to and reviewed by the Board of Directors of this Corporation be, and they hereby are, adopted as the Bylaws for the regulation of the internal affairs of this Corporation.

RESOLVED FURTHER, that the Secretary of this Corporation certify said Bylaws as having been adopted as of the date of this Action, and insert said Bylaws in the Minute Book of this Corporation.

ADOPTION OF CORPORATE SEAL (Optional)

The Chairman then presented to the meeting a proposed corporate seal in the form prescribed by the Bylaws. Upon motion duly made, the following resolution was unanimously adopted:

RESOLVED, that a corporate seal presented to this meeting be adopted as the corporate seal of the Corporation, and the Secretary is instructed to impress such seal on the document recording this resolution opposite the place where this resolution appears.

(SEAL)

SELECTION OF CORPORATE BANK ACCOUNT

The Chairman then discussed the need for the Corporation to open a bank account or accounts for deposit of the Corporation's funds. After some discussion, upon motion duly made, the following resolutions were unanimously adopted:

RESOLVED, that this Corporation establish in its name one or more deposit and checking accounts with _____ (name of bank), on such terms and conditions as may be agreed upon with such bank, and that the officers of this Corporation be, and they hereby are, authorized to establish such account or accounts.

RESOLVED FURTHER, that the bank account authorization card, a copy of which is

Ch 10 Forms

attached hereto, is by this reference incorporated herein and the resolutions contained therein are hereby adopted.

ELECTION OF OFFICERS

The meeting then proceeded to elect officers for the Corporation, for the coming year. After discussion and upon nominations duly made and seconded, the following persons were elected to the offices indicated next to their names:

Name   Office

_____   President

_____   Chief Financial Officer

_____   Secretary

ADOPTION OF STOCK CERTIFICATE

The Chairman then presented to the meeting a proposed form of stock certificate for the Corporation's capital stock. Upon motion duly made, seconded, and carried, the following resolutions were unanimously adopted:

RESOLVED, that the share certificates representing the common shares of this Corporation be, and they hereby are, approved and adopted in substantially the same form as the form of share certificate presented to this Board, and each such certificate shall bear the name of this Corporation, the number of shares represented thereby, the name of the owner of such shares, and the date such shares were issued.

RESOLVED FURTHER, that such share certificates shall be consecutively numbered beginning with No. 1; shall be issued only when the signature of the President and the signature of the Chief Financial Officer or the Secretary are affixed thereto; and shall bear, if appropriate, other wording related to the ownership, issuance, and transferability of the shares represented thereby.

FILING OF STATEMENT BY DOMESTIC STOCK CORPORATION

The Chairman then noted that Section 1502 of the California Corporations Code requires the Filing of a Statement by Domestic Stock Corporation within ninety (90) days of the filing of the Articles of Incorporation. It was the unanimous decision of the Board that the following resolution be adopted:

RESOLVED, that the appropriate officers of this Corporation file with the California Secretary of State, as required by law, a statement of the names of the officers of this Corporation, together with a statement of the location and address of the principal executive office of the Corporation and the name and address of the agent selected for purposes of receiving service of process on this Corporation.

Ch 10 Forms

PLAN OF INITIAL CAPITALIZATION

The Chairman then reviewed the proposed plan for the initial issuance of the Corporation's stock. The Chairman explained that the Corporation planned to issue _____ (number) shares of its capital stock to _____, _____, _____, and _____, for a total consideration of $_____. Upon motion duly made, seconded, and carried, the following resolutions were unanimously adopted:

[Where exempt under Section 25102(h)]:

RESOLVED, that the officers of this Corporation be, and they hereby are, authorized and directed to prepare, execute, verify, and timely file, in the name and on behalf of the Corporation, with the Commissioner of Corporations of the State of California a Notice of Issuance of Securities Pursuant to Subdivision (h) of Section 25102 of the California Corporations Code for the sale and issuance of shares of the Corporation's capital stock for an aggregate consideration of $_____, to the following individuals:

Name	Number of Shares	Consideration
_____	_____	_____
_____	_____	_____
_____	_____	_____
_____	_____	_____

RESOLVED, FURTHER, that within ten (10) days of the filing of the Notice of Issuance of Securities Pursuant to Subdivision (h) of Section 25102 with the Commissioner of Corporations and receipt of the consideration paid for such capital stocks, the President and Secretary of the Corporation be, and they hereby are, authorized and directed to issue and sell up to _____ shares to the individuals set forth above, and such shares, when issued and sold as provided in these resolutions shall be duly authorized, validly issued, fully paid, and nonassessable, and in all respects shall meet the requirements of that exemption.

RESOLVED, FURTHER, that the officers of this Corporation be, and they hereby are, authorized and directed to execute all documents and to take all other actions as they may deem necessary or appropriate in order to effectuate the issuance of the Corporation's capital stock as provided in these resolutions.

[Where exempt under 25102(f)]:

RESOLVED, that the officers of this Corporation be, and they hereby are, authorized and directed to prepare, execute, verify, and timely file, in the name and on behalf of the corporation, with the Commissioner of Corporations of the State of California, a Notice in the form prescribed pursuant to Section 25102(f) of the California Corporate Securities Law of 68, for the sale and issuance of shares for an aggregate consideration of $_____, to the following individuals:

Name	Number of Shares	Consideration
_____	_____	_____
_____	_____	_____
_____	_____	_____
_____	_____	_____

RESOLVED, FURTHER, that such shares shall be issued to the foregoing individuals within the exemption from qualification afforded by Section 25012(f), and when issued and sold as provided in these resolutions, such shares shall be duly authorized, validly issued, fully paid, and non-assessable, and in all respects shall meet the requirements of that exemption.

RESOLVED, FURTHER, that the officers of this Corporation be, and they hereby are, authorized and directed to execute all documents and to take all other actions as they may deem necessary or appropriate in order to effectuate the foregoing issuance of stock as provided in these resolutions

SUBCHAPTER ELECTION (Optional)

The Chairman then initiated a discussion on the advisability of making a Subchapter S election, pursuant to Section 1372(a) of the Internal Revenue Code of 54, as amended. After some discussion, and upon motion duly made, seconded, and carried, the following resolutions were unanimously adopted:

WHEREAS, the Directors of this Corporation deem it appropriate for the Corporation to elect to be a "small business corporation" pursuant to Section 1372(a) of the Internal Revenue Code and to be an S corporation for tax purposes;

RESOLVED, that the Corporation hereby elects to be a "small business corporation" and to be taxed as an S corporation pursuant to Section 1372(a) of the Internal Revenue Code; and further, that the Chief Financial Officer of the Corporation be, and he hereby is, authorized to file, or make arrangements to file, with the appropriate office of the Internal Revenue Service, IRS Form 2553 for this Corporation to receive Subchapter S treatment under Section 1372(a) of the Internal Revenue Code, together with the statement of each shareholder consenting to the Subchapter S election, and to execute such other documents and to take such other action as may be deemed necessary or appropriate to effectuate these resolutions.

Ch 10 Forms

SECTION 1244 STOCK ELECTION

The Chairman then informed the Board as to the benefits of qualifying the common stock of the Corporation as "Section 1244 Stock" and organizing and managing the Corporation so that it is a "small business corporation" as defined in Section 1244 of the Internal Revenue Code, as amended. Compliance with these sections may enable shareholders to treat any loss sustained by a shareholder on the sale or exchange of shares of the Corporation as an ordinary loss on the shareholders' personal income tax returns.

With the intent of achieving this result, it was unanimously

RESOLVED, that the proper officers of the Corporation are authorized to sell and issue common shares pursuant to the IRC Section 1244 in an aggregate amount of money and other property (as a contribution to capital and as paid in surplus) that, together with the aggregate amount of common stock, does not exceed $1,000,000.00.

RESOLVED FURTHER, that the Corporation shall sell and issue its common shares in such a manner that, in the hands of qualified shareholders, the shares shall receive the benefit of IRC Section 1244, as amended.

RESOLVED FURTHER, that the proper officers of the Corporation are directed to maintain such records as are necessary, and take such further steps as necessary, pursuant to IRC Section 1244, so as to enable the common shares issued hereunder to qualify as "Section 1244 Stock" and allow any shareholder who experiences a loss on the transfer of shares of common stock of the corporation to qualify for "ordinary loss" deduction treatment on his or her individual income tax return.

FISCAL YEAR (Optional)**

The Chairman then informed the Board that the next order of business was the selection of a fiscal year for the Corporation. After some discussion and upon motion duly made, seconded, and carried, the following resolution was unanimously adopted.

RESOLVED, that the fiscal year of this Corporation shall end on the _____ day of the month of _____ of each year.

EXPENSES OF THE CORPORATION

The Chairman then stated that certain expenses had been incurred in the incorporation and organization of the Corporation. Upon motion duly made, seconded, and carried, the following resolution was unanimously adopted:

RESOLVED, that the Chief Financial Officer be, and he hereby is, authorized to pay the expenses of the incorporation and organization of this Corporation.

SELECTION OF COUNSEL TO THE CORPORATION

The Chairman then commented that the Board should select corporate legal counsel. After some discussion, it was decided that _____ would be retained as counsel to the Corporation, to serve at the pleasure of the Board.

BUSINESS LICENSES AND TAX FILINGS

The Chairman then initiated a discussion concerning all applicable fictitious business name statements and tax and license filings. Upon motion duly made, seconded, and carried, the following resolution was unanimously adopted:

RESOLVED, that the Secretary be, and he hereby is, authorized and directed to file for and secure all fictitious business name statements and business and tax licenses or permits required for the Corporation to properly conduct its business.

ADJOURNMENT

There being no further business to come before the meeting, upon motion duly made, seconded, and unanimously carried, the meeting was adjourned.

Ch 10 Forms

_____
(Type Name), Secretary of the Meeting

ATTEST: _____
(Type Name), Chairman of the Meeting

**A corporation can always have a calendar year. Note that under the 1986 Tax Reform Act, professional service corporations can no longer have a fiscal year.

There are also substantial complications and limitations in obtaining a fiscal year for an S corporation. If you make an S election and would like to have a tax year other than a calendar year, talk with your accountant or attorney to see if this is possible.

Forms for Chapter 11

There are 14 forms that accompany **Chapter 11, Nonprofit Corporations**. They include the following:

Form 11-A Articles of Incorporation for Nonprofit Public Benefit Corporation, 2 pages (400 - 401)

Form 11-B Articles of Incorporation for Nonprofit Mutual Benefit Corporation, 1 page (402)

Form 11-C Articles of Incorporation for Nonprofit Religious Corporation, 2 pages (403 - 404)

Form 11-D Bylaws for Nonprofit Public Benefit Corporation, 17 pages (405 - 421)

Form 11-E Minutes of the First Meeting of the Board of Directors for Nonprofit Corporation, 5 pages (422 - 426)

Form 11-F Statement of Information (Domestic Stock Corporation)—SI-200 C, 1 page (427)

Form 11-G Action by Sole Incorporator Appointing Initial Directors and Adopting Bylaws, 1 page (428)

Form 11-H Waiver of Notice and Consent to the First Meeting of the Board of Directors, 1 page (429)

Form 11-I Minutes of the Organizational Meeting of the Board of Directors, 3 pages (430 - 432)

Form 11-J Charity Registration Form—Form CT-1, 1 page (433)

Form 11-K Application for Recognition of Exemption—IRS Form 1023 (on accompanying CD)

Form 11-L Exemption Application—FTB Form 3500 (on accompanying CD)

Form 11-M Application to Mail at Nonprofit Standard Mail Rates—PS Form 3624, 3 pages (434 - 436)

Form 11-N Registration/Renewal Fee Report, 1 page (437)

**Ch 11
Forms**

ARTICLES OF INCORPORATION OF

_____,

A California Nonprofit Public Benefit Company

ARTICLE I

The name of this corporation is _____.

ARTICLE II

A. This corporation is a nonprofit public benefit corporation and is not organized for the private gain of any person. It is organized under the Nonprofit Public Benefit Corporation Law for charitable purposes.

B. The specific purpose of this corporation is to _____

_____.

ARTICLE III

The name and address in the state of California of the corporation's initial agent for service of process is:

_____

_____

_____

ARTICLE IV

A. This corporation is organized and operated exclusively for charitable purposes within the meaning of Section 501(c)(3) of the Internal Revenue Code.

B. Notwithstanding any other provision of these Articles, the corporation shall not exercise any powers that are not in furtherance of the charitable purposes of this corporation, nor shall it carry on any activities not permitted to be carried on (a) by a corporation exempt from federal income tax under Section 501(c)(3) of the Internal Revenue Code, or (b) by a corporation, contributions to which are deductible under Section 170(c)(2) of the Internal Revenue Code.

C. No substantial part of the activities of this corporation shall consist of carrying on propaganda, or otherwise attempting to influence legislation, and the corporation shall not participate or intervene in any political campaign (including the publishing or distribution of statements) on behalf of any candidate for public office.

ARTICLE V

A. The property of this corporation is irrevocably dedicated to educational pur-

Ch 11
Forms

poses, and no part of the net earnings or assets of this corporation shall ever inure to the benefit of, or be distributed to, any director, officer, member, or other private person. Upon the dissolution or winding up of the corporation, its assets remaining after payment, or provision for the payment, of all debts and liabilities of this corporation, shall be distributed to a nonprofit fund, foundation, or corporation which is organized and operated exclusively for educational purposes and which has established its tax-exempt status under Section 501(c)(3) of the Internal Revenue Code.

B. The corporation shall distribute its income for each tax year at such time and in such manner as not to become subject to the tax on undistributed income imposed by Section 4942 of the Internal Revenue Code.

C. The corporation will not engage in any act of self-dealing as defined in Section 4941(d) of the Internal Revenue Code.

D. The corporation shall not retain any excess business holdings as defined in Section 4943(c) of the Internal Revenue Service.

E. The corporation will not make any investments in such manner as to subject it to tax under Section 4944 of the Internal Revenue Code.

F. The corporation will not make any taxable expenditures as defined in Section 4945(d) of the Internal Revenue Service.

Dated: _____, 20____

_____
Signature of Incorporator

I declare that I am the person who executed the foregoing Articles of Incorporation, and that this instrument is my act and deed.

_____
Signature of Incorporator

**Ch 11
Forms**

ARTICLES OF INCORPORATION OF

_____

ARTICLE I

The name of this corporation is _____.

ARTICLE II

A. This corporation is a nonprofit mutual benefit corporation organized under the Nonprofit Mutual Benefit Corporation Law. The purpose of this corporation is to engage in any lawful act or activity for which a corporation may be organized under such law.

B. The specific purpose of this corporation is to _____

_____.

ARTICLE III

The name and address in the state of California of the corporation's initial agent for service of process are:

_____

_____

_____

ARTICLE IV

Notwithstanding any of the above statements of purposes and powers, this corporation shall not, except to insubstantial degree, engage in any activities or exercise any powers that are not in furtherance of the specific purposes of this corporation.

Dated: _____, 20____

_____

Signature of Incorporator

I declare that I am the person who executed the foregoing Articles of Incorporation, and that this instrument is my act and deed.

_____

Signature of Incorporator

ARTICLES OF INCORPORATION OF

_____

ARTICLE I

The name of this corporation is _____.

ARTICLE II

A. This corporation is a religious corporation and is not organized for the private gain of any person. It is organized under the Nonprofit Religious Corporation Law exclusively for religious purposes.

B. The specific purpose of this corporation is to _____

_____.

ARTICLE III

The name and address in the state of California of the corporation's initial agent for service of process is:

_____

_____

_____

ARTICLE IV

A. This corporation is organized and operated exclusively for religious purposes within the meaning of Section 501(c)(3) of the Internal Revenue Code.

B. No substantial part of the activities of this corporation shall consist of carrying on propaganda, or otherwise attempting to influence legislation, and the corporation shall not participate or intervene in any political campaign (including the publishing or distribution of statements) on behalf of any candidate for public office.

ARTICLE V

The property of this corporation is irrevocably dedicated to religious purposes, and no part of the net earnings or assets of this corporation shall ever inure to the benefit of any director, officer, or member thereof or to the benefit of any private person. Upon the dissolution or winding up of the corporation, its assets remaining after payment, or provision for payment, of all debts and liabilities of this corporation shall be distributed to a nonprofit fund, foundation, or corporation which is organized and operated exclusively for religious purposes and which has established its tax-exempt status under Section 501(c)(3) of the Internal Revenue Code.

Ch 11 Forms

Dated: _____, 20_____

_____
Signature of Incorporator

I declare that I am the person who executed the foregoing Articles of Incorporation, and that this instrument is my act and deed.

_____
Signature of Incorporator

TABLE OF CONTENTS TO BYLAWS OF

A California Nonprofit Public Benefit Corporation

ARTICLES	TITLE AND SECTION
I	**PURPOSE**
1.01	Organization
1.02	Purpose
1.03	Compliance with Internal Revenue Code
II	**OFFICES**
2.01	Principal Office
2.02	Other Offices
III	**MEMBERS**
3.01	Members
IV	**DIRECTORS**
4.01	Number
4.02	Powers
4.03	Duties
4.04	Terms of Office
4.05	Compensation
4.06	Restriction Regarding Interested Directors
4.07	Place of Meetings
4.08	Regular and Annual Meetings
4.09	Special Meetings
4.10	Notice of Meetings
4.11	Contents of Notice
4.12	Waiver of Notice and Consent to Holding Meetings
4.13	Quorum for Meetings
4.14	Majority Action as Board Action
4.15	Conduct of Meetings
4.16	Action by Unanimous Written Consent Without Meeting
4.17	Vacancies
4.18	Non-Liability of Directors
4.19	Indemnification by Corporation of Directors, Officers, Employees, and Other Agents
4.20	Insurance for Corporate Agents
V	**OFFICERS**
5.01	Number of Officers

Ch 11 Forms

5.02	Qualification, Election, and Term of Office
5.03	Subordinate Officers
5.04	Removal and Resignation
5.05	Vacancies
5.06	Duties of President
5.07	Duties of Vice President
5.08	Duties of Secretary
5.09	Duties of Treasurer
5.10	Compensation

VI	**COMMITTEES**
6.01	Executive Committee
6.02	Other Committees
6.03	Meetings and Action of Committees

VII	**EXECUTION OF INSTRUMENTS, DEPOSITS AND FUNDS**
7.01	Execution of Instruments
7.02	Checks and Notes
7.03	Deposits
7.04	Gifts

VIII	**CORPORATE RECORDS, REPORTS, AND SEAL**
8.01	Maintenance of Corporate Records
8.02	Corporate Seal
8.03	Directors' Inspection Rights
8.04	Right to Copy and Make Extracts
8.05	Annual Report
8.06	Annual Statement of Specific Transactions

| **IX** | **FISCAL YEAR** |
| 9.01 | Fiscal Year of the Corporation |

| **X** | **BYLAWS** |
| 10.01 | Amendment |

XI	**AMENDMENTS**
11.01	Amendment of Articles
11.02	Certain Amendments

| **XII** | **PROHIBITION AGAINST SHARING CORPORATE PROFITS AND ASSETS** |
| 12.01 | Prohibition Against Sharing Corporate Profits and Assets |

CERTIFICATION OF BYLAWS

BYLAWS OF _____

A California Nonprofit Public Benefit Corporation

ARTICLE I. Purpose

Section 1.01 Organization. This corporation is a nonprofit public benefit corporation and is not organized for the private gain of any person. It is organized under the California Nonprofit Public Benefit Corporation Law for charitable purposes.

Section 1.02 Purpose. The specific purpose of this corporation is:

_____

_____

Section 1.03 Compliance with Internal Revenue Code. This corporation is organized exclusively for charitable purposes within the meaning of Section 501(c)(3) of the Internal Revenue Code. Notwithstanding any other provision of these Bylaws, this corporation shall not, except to an insubstantial degree, engage in any activities or exercise any powers that are not in furtherance of the purposes of this corporation, and the corporation shall not carry on any other activities not permitted to be carried on (a) by a corporation exempt from federal income tax under Section 501(c)(3) of the Internal Revenue Code of 2054 or the corresponding provision of any future United States internal revenue law, or (b) by a corporation, contributions to which are deductible under Section 170(c)(2) of the Internal Revenue Code of 2054 or the corresponding provision of any future United States internal revenue law.

ARTICLE II. Offices

Section 2.01 Principal Office. The corporation shall maintain its principal office in the City of _____, County of _____, State of California.

Section 2.02 Other Offices. The corporation may also have offices at such other places, within or without the State of California, where it is qualified to do business, as its business may require and as the Board of Directors, may, from time to time, designate.

ARTICLE III. Members

Section 3.01 Members. The corporation shall have no members. Any action which would otherwise, under law or the provisions of the Articles of Incorporation or Bylaws of this corporation, require approval by a majority of all members, or approval by members, shall only require the approval of the Board of Directors.

Ch 11 Forms

ARTICLE IV. Directors

Section 4.01 Members. The corporation shall have _____ (number) Directors. The Directors shall collectively be known as the Board of Directors.

Section 4.02 Powers. Subject to the provisions of the California Nonprofit Public Benefit Corporation Law and any limitations in the Articles of Incorporation and these Bylaws, the activities and affairs of this corporation shall be conducted, and all corporate powers shall be exercised, by or under the direction of the Board of Directors. Directors need not be residents of the State of California.

Section 4.03 Duties.

It shall be the duty of the Directors to:

(a) Perform any and all duties imposed on them, collectively or individually, by law, by the Articles of Incorporation of this corporation, or by these Bylaws.

(b) Appoint and remove, employ and discharge, and except as otherwise provided in these Bylaws, prescribe the duties and fix the compensation, if any, of all officers, agents, and employees of the corporation.

(c) Supervise all officers, agents, and employees of the corporation to assure that their duties are properly performed.

(d) Meet at such times and places as required by these Bylaws.

(e) Register their addresses with the Secretary of the corporation. Notices of meetings mailed or telegraphed to them at such addresses shall be valid notices thereof.

Section 4.04 Terms of Office. Each Director shall hold office until the next annual meeting for election of the Board of Directors, as specified in these Bylaws, and until his or her successor is elected and qualified.

Section 4.05 Compensation. Directors shall serve without compensation except that they shall be allowed and paid their actual and necessary expenses incurred in attending Directors meetings. In addition, they shall be allowed reasonable advancement or reimbursement for expenses incurred in the performance of their regular duties as specified in Section 3 of this Article. Directors may not be compensated for rendering services to the corporation in any capacity other than as Director, unless such other compensation is reasonable and is allowable under the provisions of Section 6 of this Article.

Section 4.06 Restriction Regarding Interested Directors.

Notwithstanding any other provision of these Bylaws, not more than forty-nine percent (49%) of the persons serving on the Board may be interested persons. For purposes of this Section, "interested persons" means either:

Ch 11
Forms

(a) any person currently being compensated by the corporation for services rendered it within the previous twelve (12) months, whether as a full- or part-time officer or other employee, independent contractor, or otherwise, excluding any reasonable compensation paid to a Director as Director; or

(b) any brother, sister, ancestor, descendant, spouse, brother-in-law, sister-in-law, son-in-law, daughter-in-law, mother-in-law, or father-in-law of any such person.

Section 4.07 Place of Meetings.

Meetings shall be held at the principal office of the corporation, unless otherwise provided by the Board, or at such place within or without the State of California which has been designated from time to time by resolution of the Board of Directors.

In the absence of such designation, any meeting not held at the principal office of the corporation shall be valid if held on the written consent of all Directors given either before or after the meeting and filed with the Secretary of the corporation, or after all Board members have been given written notice of the meeting, as hereinafter provided for special meetings of the Board. Any meeting, regular or special, may be held by conference telephone or similar communications equipment, so long as all Directors participating in such meetings can hear one another.

Section 4.08 Regular and Annual Meetings.

Regular meetings of the Board of Directors shall be held on the _____th day of each month at _____ o'clock ____.m., unless such day falls on a legal holiday, in which event the regular meeting shall be held at the same hour and place on the next business day.

The Annual Meeting of the Board of Directors shall be held on the _____th day of _____, at _____ o'clock ____.m., unless such day falls upon a legal holiday, in which event the Annual Meeting shall be held at the same hour and place on the next business day. At the Annual Meeting, Directors shall be elected by the Board of Directors. Cumulative voting for the election of Directors shall not be permitted. The candidates receiving the highest number of votes up to the number of Directors to be elected shall be elected. Each Director shall cast one vote, with voting being by ballot only.

Section 4.09 Special Meetings. Special meetings of the Board of Directors may be called by the Chairman of the Board, the President, the Vice President, the Secretary, or by any two Directors, and such meetings shall be held at the place, within or without the State of California, designated by the person or persons calling the meeting, and in the absence of such designation, at the principal office of the corporation.

Ch 11 Forms

Section 4.10 Notice of Meetings. Regular meetings may be held without notice. Special meetings of the Board shall be held upon four (4) days' notice by first-class mail, or forty-eight (48) hours' notice delivered personally or by telephone or telegraph. If sent by mail or telegram, the notice shall be deemed to be delivered on its deposit in the mails or on its delivery to the telegraph company. Such notices shall be addressed to each Director at his or her address, as shown on the books of the corporation. Notice of the time and place of holding an adjourned meeting need not be given to absent Directors, if the time and place of the adjourned meeting are fixed at the meeting adjourned, and if such adjourned meeting is held no more than twenty-four (24) hours from the time of the original meeting. Notice shall be given of any adjourned regular or special meeting to Directors absent from the original meeting if the adjourned meeting is held more than twenty-four (24) hours from the time of the original meeting.

Section 4.11 Contents of Notice. Notice of meetings not herein dispensed with shall specify the place, day, and hour of the meeting. The purpose of any Board meeting need not be specified in the notice.

Section 4.12 Waiver of Notice and Consent to Holding Meetings. The transactions of any meeting of the Board, however called and notice, or wherever held, are as valid as though the meeting had been duly held after proper call and notice, provided a quorum, as hereinafter defined, is present, and provided that either before or after the meeting, each Director not present signs a Waiver of Notice, a Consent to holding such meeting, or an Approval of the minutes thereof. All such Waivers, Consents, or Approvals shall be filed with the corporate records and made a part of the minutes of the meeting.

Section 4.13 Quorum for Meetings. A majority of the Board of Directors shall constitute a quorum for the transaction of the business at any meeting of the Board; but if less than a majority of the Directors are present at said meeting, a majority of the Directors present may adjourn the meeting from time to time without further notice.

Section 4.14 Majority Action as Board Action. Every act or decision done or made by a majority of the Directors present at a meeting duly held at which a quorum is present is the act of the Board of Directors, unless the Articles of Incorporation or Bylaws of this corporation, or provisions of the California Nonprofit Public Benefit Corporation Law, particularly those provisions relating to appointment of committees (Section 5212), approval of contracts or transactions in which a Director has a material financial interest (Section 5233), and indemnification of Directors (Section 5238e), require a greater percentage or different voting rules for approval of a matter by the Board.

Section 4.15 Conduct of Meetings. Meetings of the Board of Directors shall be presided over by the Chairman of the Board, or, if no such person has been so designated, or in his or her absence, the President of the corporation, or in his or her absence, by the Vice President of the corporation, or in the absence of each of these persons, by a Chairman chosen by a majority of the Directors present at the meeting. The Secretary of the corporation shall act as Secretary of all meetings of the Board, provided that in his or her absence, the presiding Officer shall appoint another person to act as Secretary of the meeting.

Section 4.16 Action by Unanimous Written Consent Without Meeting. An action required or permitted to be taken by the Board of Directors under any provision of law may be taken without a meeting if all members of the Board shall individually or collectively consent in writing to such action. For the purposes of this section only, "all members of the Board" shall not include any "interested Director" as defined in Section 5233 of the California Nonprofit Public Benefit Corporation Law. Such written consent or consents shall be filed with the minutes of the proceedings of the Board. Such action by written consent shall have the same force and effect as the unanimous vote of the Directors. Any certificate or other document filed under any provision of law which related to action so taken shall state that the action was taken by unanimous written consent of the Board of Directors without a meeting, and that the Bylaws of this corporation authorize the Directors to so act. Such statement shall be prima facie evidence of such authority.

Section 4.17 Vacancies. Vacancies on the Board of Directors shall exist (1) on the death, resignation, or removal of any Director, and (2) whenever the number of authorized Directors is increased.

Any vacancy occurring in the Board of Directors may be filed by majority vote of the remaining Directors. A Director elected to fill a vacancy shall be elected for the unexpired term of his predecessor in office.

Directors may be removed without cause by a majority of the Directors then in office.

Any Director may resign effective upon giving written notice to the Chairman of the Board, the President, the Secretary, or the Board of Directors, unless the notice specifies a later time for the effectiveness of such resignation.

Section 4.18 Non-Liability of Directors. The Directors shall not be personally liable for the debts, liabilities, or other obligations of the corporation.

Section 4.20 Indemnification by Corporation of Directors, Officers, Employees, and Other Agents. To the extent that a person, who is, or was, a Director, Officer, employee, or other agent of this corporation, has been successful on the merits in defense of any civil, criminal, administrative, or investigative proceeding brought to procure a judgment against such person by reason of the fact that he or she is,

Ch 11 Forms

or was, an agent of the corporation, or has been successful in defense of any claim, issue, or matter, therein, such person shall be indemnified against expenses actually and reasonably incurred by the person in connection with such proceeding.

If such person either settles any such claim or sustains a judgment against him or her, then indemnification against expenses, judgments, fines, settlements, and other amounts reasonably incurred in connection with such proceedings shall be provided by this corporation, but only to the extent allowed by, and in accordance with, the requirements of Section 5238 of the California Nonprofit Public Benefit Corporation Law.

Section 4.20 Insurance for Corporate Agents. The Board of Directors may adopt a resolution authorizing the purchase and maintenance of insurance on behalf of any agent of the corporation (including a Director, Officer, employee, or other agent of the corporation) against any liability other than for violating provisions of law relating to self-dealing (Section 5233 of the California Nonprofit Public Benefit Corporation Law) asserted against or incurred by the agent in such capacity or arising out of the agent's status as such, whether or not the corporation would have the power to indemnify the agent against such liability under the provisions of Section 5238 of the California Nonprofit Public Benefit Corporation Law.

ARTICLE V. Officers

Section 5.01 Number of Officers. The Officers of this corporation shall be a President, a Secretary, and a Chief Financial Officer who shall be designated the Treasurer. The corporation may also have, as determined by the Board of Directors, a Chairman of the Board, one or more Vice Presidents, Assistant Secretaries, Assistant Treasurers, or other Officers. Any number of offices may be held by the same person, except that neither the Secretary nor the Treasurer may serve as the President or Chairman of the Board.

Section 5.02 Qualification, Election, and Term of Office. Any person may serve as Officer of this corporation. Officers shall be elected by the Board of Directors, at any time, and each officer shall hold office until he or she resigns or is removed or is otherwise disqualified to serve, or until his or her successor shall be elected and qualified, whichever occurs first.

Section 5.03 Subordinate Officers. The Board of Directors may appoint such other Officers or agents as it may deem desirable, and such Officers shall serve such terms, have such authority, and perform such duties as may be prescribed from time to time by the Board of Directors.

Section 5.04 Removal and Resignation. Any Officer may be removed, either with or without cause, by the Board of Directors, at any time. Any officer may resign at any time by giving written notice to the Board of Directors or to the President or Secretary of the corporation. Any such resignation shall take effect at the date of the receipt of such notice or at any later date specified therein, and, unless otherwise specified therein, the acceptance of such resignation shall not be necessary to make it effective. The above provisions of this Section shall be superseded by any conflicting terms of a contract which has been approved or ratified by the Board of Directors relating to the employment of any Officer of the corporation.

Section 5.05 Vacancies. Any vacancy caused by the death, resignation, removal, disqualification, or otherwise, of any Officer shall be filled by a majority vote of the Board of Directors. In the event of a vacancy in any office other than that of President, such vacancy may be as the filled temporarily by appointment by the President until such time as the Board shall fill the vacancy. Vacancies occurring in offices of Officers appointed at the discretion of the Board may or may not be filled as the Board shall determine.

Section 5.06 Duties of President. The President shall be the Chief Executive Officer of the corporation and shall, subject to the control of the Board of Directors, supervise and control the affairs of the corporation and the activities of the Officers. He or she shall perform all duties incident to his or her office and such other duties as may be required by law, by the Articles of Incorporation of this corporation, or by these Bylaws, or which may be prescribed from time to time by the Board of Directors. Unless another person is specifically appointed as Chairman of the Board of Directors, he or she shall preside at all meetings of the Board of Directors. Except as otherwise expressly provided by law, by the Articles of Incorporation, or by these Bylaws, he or she shall, in the name of the corporation, execute such deeds, mortgages, bonds, contracts, checks, or other instruments which may from time to time be authorized by the Board of Directors.

Section 5.07 Duties of the Vice President. In the absence of the President, or in the event of his or her inability or refusal to act, the Vice President shall perform all of the duties of the President, and when so acting shall have all of the powers of, and be subject to all the restrictions on, the President. The Vice President shall have other powers and perform such other duties as may be prescribed by law, by the Articles of Incorporation, or by these Bylaws, or as may be prescribed by the Board of Directors.

Section 5.08 Duties of Secretary. The Secretary shall:

Certify and keep at the principal office of the corporation the original, or a copy, of these Bylaws as amended or otherwise altered to date.

Keep at the principal office of the corporation or at such other place as the Board may determine, a book of minutes of all meetings of the Directors, recording therein the time and place of holding, whether regular or special, how called, how notice thereof was given, the names of those present or represented at the meeting, and the proceedings thereof.

See that all notices are duly given in accordance with the provisions of these Bylaws or as required by law.

Be custodian of the records and of the seal of the corporation and see that the seal is affixed to all duly executed documents, the execution of which on behalf of the corporation under its seal is authorized by law or by these Bylaws.

Exhibit at all reasonable times to any Director of the corporation, or to his or her agent or attorney, on request therefor, the Bylaws and the minutes of the proceedings of the Directors of the corporation.

In general, perform all duties incident to the office of Secretary and such other duties as may be required by law, by the Articles of Incorporation of this corporation, or by these Bylaws, or which may be assigned to him or her from time to time by the Board of Directors.

Section 5.09 Duties of Treasurer. Subject to the provisions of these Bylaws relating to the "Execution of Instruments, Deposits and Funds," the Treasurer shall:

Have charge and custody of, and be responsible for, all funds and securities of the corporation, and deposit all such funds in the name of the corporation in such banks, trust companies, or other depositories as shall be selected by the Board of Directors.

Receive, and give receipt for, monies due and payable to the corporation from any source whatsoever.

Disburse or cause to be disbursed the funds of the corporation as may be directed by the Board of Directors, taking proper vouchers for such disbursements.

Keep and maintain adequate and correct accounts of the corporation's properties and business transactions, including accounts of its assets, liabilities, receipts, disbursements, gains, and losses.

Exhibit at all reasonable times the books of account and financial records to any Director of the corporation, or to his or her agent or attorney, on request therefore.

Render to the President and Directors, whenever requested, an account of any or all of his or her transactions as Treasurer, and of the financial condition of the corporation.

Ch 11 Forms

Prepare, or cause to be prepared, and certify, or cause to be certified, the financial statements, to be included in any required reports.

In general, perform all duties incident to the office of Treasurer and such other duties incident to the office of Treasurer and such other duties as may be required by law, by the Articles of Incorporation of the corporation, or by these Bylaws, or which may be assigned to him or her from time to time by the Board of Directors.

Section 5.10 Compensation. The salaries of the Officers, if any, shall be fixed from time to time by resolution of the Board of Directors, and no Officer shall be prevented from receiving such salary by reason of the fact that he or she is also a Director of the corporation, provided, however, that such compensation paid a Director for serving as an Officer of this corporation shall only be allowed if permitted under the provisions of ARTICLE IV, Section 5, of these Bylaws. In all cases, any salaries received by Officers of this corporation shall be reasonable and given in return for services actually rendered the corporation and which relate to the performance of the charitable purposes of this corporation.

ARTICLE VI. Committees

Section 6.01 Executive Committee. The Board of Directors may, by a majority vote of Directors then in office, designate two (2) or more of its members (who may also be serving as Officers of this corporation) to constitute an Executive Committee, and delegate to such Committee any of the powers and authority of the Board in the management of the business and affairs of the corporation, except with respect to:

(a) The filling of vacancies on the Board or on any committee which has the authority of the Board.

(b) The fixing of compensation of the Directors for serving on the Board or any committee.

(c) The amendment or repeal of Bylaws or the adoption of new Bylaws.

(d) The amendment or repeal of any resolution of the Board which by its express terms is not so amendable or repealable.

(e) The appointment of committees of the Board thereof.

(f) The expenditure of corporate funds to support a nominee for Director after there are more people nominated for Director than can be elected.

(g) The approval of any transaction to which this corporation is a party and in which one or more of the Directors has a material financial interest, except as expressly provided in Section 5233(d)(3) of the California Nonprofit Public Benefit Corporation Law.

Ch 11 Forms

By a majority vote, the Board may at any time revoke or modify any or all of the authority so delegated, increase or decrease but not below two (2) the number of its members, and fill vacancies therein from the members of the Board. The

Committee shall keep regular minutes of its proceedings, cause them to be filed with the corporate records, and report the same to the Board from time to time as the Board may require.

Section 6.02 Other Committees. The corporation shall have such other committees as may from time to time be designated by resolution of the Board of Directors. Such other committees may consist of persons who are not also members of the Board. These additional committees shall act in an advisory capacity only to the Board and shall be clearly titled as "advisory" committees.

Section 6.03 Meetings and Action of Committees. Meetings and action of committees shall be governed by, noticed, held, and taken in accordance with the provisions of these Bylaws concerning meetings of the Board of Directors, with such changes in the context of such Bylaw provisions as are necessary to substitute the committee for the Board of Directors, except that the time for regular meetings or committees may be fixed by resolution of the Board of Directors or by the committee. The time for special meetings of committees may also be fixed by the Board of Directors. The Board of Directors may also adopt rules and regulations pertaining to the conduct of meetings of committees to the extent that such rules and regulations are not inconsistent with the provisions of these Bylaws.

ARTICLE VII. Execution of Instruments, Deposits, and Funds

Section 7.01 Execution of Instruments. The Board of Directors, except as otherwise provided in these Bylaws, may by resolution authorize any Officer or agent of the corporation to enter into any contract, or execute and deliver any instrument, in the name of and on behalf of the corporation, and such authority may be general or confined to specific instances. Unless so authorized, no Officer, agent, or employee shall have any power or authority to bind the corporation by any contract or engagement or to pledge its credit or to render it liable monetarily for any purpose or in any amount.

Section 7.02 Checks and Notes. Except as otherwise specifically determined by resolution of the Board of Directors, or as otherwise required by law, checks, drafts, promissory notes, orders for the payment of money, and other evidence of indebtedness of the corporation shall be signed by the Treasurer and countersigned by the President of the corporation.

Section 7.03 Deposits. All funds of the corporation shall be deposited from time to time to the credit of the corporation in such banks, trust companies, or other depositories as the Board of Directors may select.

Ch 11 Forms

Section 7.04 Gifts. The Board of Directors may accept on behalf of the corporation any contribution, gift, bequest, or devise for the charitable purposes of this corporation.

ARTICLE VIII. Corporate Records, Reports, and Seal

Section 8.01 Maintenance of Corporate Records. The corporation shall keep at its principal office in the State of California:

(a) Minutes of all meetings of Directors and committees of the Board, indicating the time and place of holding such meetings, whether regular or special, how called, the notice given, the names of those present, and the proceedings thereof.

(b) Adequate and correct books and records of account, including accounts of its properties and business transactions and accounts of its assets, liabilities, receipts, disbursements, gains, and losses.

(c) A copy of the corporation's Articles of Incorporation and Bylaws, as amended to-date, which shall be open to inspection by the Board of Directors of the corporation at all reasonable times during office.

Section 8.02 Corporate Seal. The Board of Directors may adopt, use, and at will alter a corporate seal. Such seal shall be kept at the principal office of the corporation. Failure to affix the seal to corporate instruments, however, shall not affect the validity of any such instrument.

Section 8.03 Directors' Inspection Rights. Every Director shall have the absolute right at any reasonable time to inspect and copy all books, records, and documents of every kind, and to inspect the physical properties of the corporation.

Section 8.04 Right to Copy and Make Extracts. Any inspection under the provisions of this Article may be made in person or by agent or attorney and the right to inspection includes the right to copy and make extracts.

Section 8.05 Annual Report. The Board shall cause an annual report to be furnished not later than one hundred and twenty (120) days after the close of the corporation's fiscal year to all Directors of the corporation. The report shall contain the following information in appropriate detail:

(a) The assets and liabilities, including the trust funds, of the corporation as of the end of the fiscal year.

(b) The principal changes in assets and liabilities, including trust funds, during the fiscal year.

(c) The revenue or receipts of the corporation, both unrestricted and restricted to particular purposes, for the fiscal year.

Ch 11 Forms

(d) The expenses or disbursements of the corporation, for both general and restricted purposes, during the fiscal year.

(e) Any information required by Section 6 of this Article.

The annual report shall be accompanied by any report thereon of independent accountants, or, if there is no such report, the certificate of an authorized Officer of the corporation that such statements were prepared without audit from the books and records of the corporation.

Section 8.06 Annual Statement of Specific Transactions. This corporation shall mail or deliver to all directors a statement within one hundred and twenty (120) days after the close of its fiscal year which briefly describes the amount and circumstances of any indemnification or transaction of the following kind:

(a) Any transaction in which the corporation, or its parent or its subsidiary was a party, and in which either of the following had a direct or indirect material financial interest:

(1) any director or officer of the corporation, or its parent or subsidiary (a mere common directorship shall not be considered a material financial interest); or

(2) any holder of more than ten percent (10%) of the voting power of the corporation, its parent, or its subsidiary.

The above statement need only be provided with respect to a transaction during the previous fiscal year involving more than FIFTY THOUSAND DOLLARS ($50,000), or which was one of a number of transactions with the same person involving, in the aggregate, more than FIFTY THOUSAND DOLLARS ($50,000).

Similarly, the statement need only be provided with respect to indemnification or advances aggregating more than TEN THOUSAND DOLLARS ($10,000) paid during the previous fiscal year to any such indemnification was approved by the Directors pursuant to Section 5238(3)(2) of the California Nonprofit Public Benefit Corporation Law.

Any statement required by this Section shall briefly describe the names of the interested persons involved in such transactions, stating each person's relationship to the corporation, the nature of person's interest in the transaction and, where practical, the amount of such interest; provided, that in the case of a transaction with a partnership of which such person is a partner, only the interest of the partnership need be stated.

ARTICLE IX. Fiscal Year

Section 9.01 Fiscal Year of the Corporation. The fiscal year of the corporation shall end on _____ of each year.

ARTICLE X. Bylaws

Section 10.01 Amendment. Subject to any provision of law applicable to the amendment of Bylaws of public benefit nonprofit corporations, these Bylaws, or any of them, may be altered, amended, or repealed, and new Bylaws adopted, by a majority vote of the Board of Directors.

ARTICLE XI. Amendment of Articles

Section 11.01 Amendment of Articles. Amendment of the Articles of Incorporation may be adopted by the approval of a majority of the Board of Directors of this corporation.

Section 11.02 Certain Amendments. Notwithstanding the above Section of this Article, this corporation shall not amend its Articles of Incorporation to alter any statement which appears in the original Articles of Incorporation and any of the names and addresses of the first Directors of this corporation, nor the name and address of its initial agent, except to correct an error in such statement, or to delete either statement after the corporation has filed a "Statement by a Domestic Non-Profit Corporation" pursuant to Section 6210 of the California Nonprofit Corporation Law.

ARTICLE XII. Prohibition Against Sharing Corporate Profits and Assets

Section 12.01 Prohibition Against Sharing Corporate Profits and Assets. No member, Director, Officer, employee, or other person connected with this corporation, or any private individual, shall receive, at any time, any of the net earnings or pecuniary profit from the operations of the corporation; provided, however, that this provision shall not prevent payment to any such person for reasonable compensation for services performed for the corporation in effecting any of its charitable purposes; provided that such compensation is otherwise permitted by these Bylaws and is fixed by resolution of the Board of Directors; and no such person or persons shall be entitled to share in the distribution of, and shall not receive, any of the corporate assets on dissolution of the corporation. Upon dissolution of the corporation, whether voluntarily or involuntarily, the assets of the corporation, after all debts have been satisfied, then remaining in the hands of the Board of Directors, shall be distributed as required by the Articles of Incorporation of this corporation and not otherwise.

CERTIFICATION OF BYLAWS

THIS IS TO CERTIFY, that I am the duly elected, qualified, and acting Secretary of _____ _____, a California nonprofit public benefit corporation, and that the foregoing Bylaws were duly adopted by the Board of Directors of said corporation on _____ _____, _____.

Ch 11 Forms

IN WITNESS WHEREOF, I have hereto set my hand this _____ day of
_____, 20_____.

_____

Secretary

Variations in Bylaws

The form set of Bylaws contained in this book can be varied, within certain limitations. Some regular variations are:

(i) Vote requirements for Board Actions. The Board of Directors can require the effective vote of a majority of the actual directors rather than the majority vote of a quorum of the directors.

(ii) Board Vacancies. The Bylaws can expand or restrict the rules regarding the Board's ability to fill vacancies. Note, however, if a vacancy is created by the removal of a director, said vacancy must be filled by the Shareholders, unless the bylaws which have been adapted by the shareholders expressly provide otherwise. (See California Corporations Code §305.)

(iii) Limitation on Transferability of Shares. Bylaws can restrict a shareholder's right to transfer or encumber their shares, provided, however, any such amendment of the bylaws will not affect previously issued shares. (California Corporations Code §204(b), 212(b)(1).)

(iv) Directors. The Bylaws can set the qualifications, duties and compensation of the directors. The Bylaws can also vary quorum requirements, provided, however, that the required quorum may never be reduced to less than two directors or one-third of the total directors.

(v) Board Committees. The Bylaws may empower committees of the Board to have the same authority as the Board subject to certain limitations. (See California Corporations Code§212(b)(5), 311.)

(vi) Time, Place, and Volume of Meetings. The Bylaws can establish the time, place, manner of calling, notice requirements, and conducting of Board, shareholders', and committee meetings. These rules may not be in conflict with the Articles and by law a Corporation cannot waive the requirement of notice for a special meeting of the Board of Directors. Please note, however, that all of the directors can waive notice. (See Form 6-G.)

(vii) Officers. The Bylaws can provide for more officer positions than required by law. (For example, many corporations have Presidents and Chief Executive Officers). Bylaws can also prescribe the specific duties of the officers and limit the number of officer positions one person may have.

(viii) Shareholder of Record. The Bylaws may vary the mechanism whereby the holders of record are determined

(ix) Shareholders' Meetings. The Bylaws may dictate the location or a procedure for determining a location for the shareholders' meeting, expand the list of who can call a special shareholders' meeting, require within ballots for directors elections, and require that all waivers of notice of a shareholders' meeting be in writing and specify the purpose and business to be transacted at the meeting.

(x) Indemnification. The Bylaws may limit or expand (to the maximum extent permitted by the law) a Corporation's power to indemnify officers, directors, and agents.

(xi) Dividends and Shares Repurchases. The Bylaws may provide restrictions, beyond those already imposed by the law (see, by way of example California Corporations Code §§500, 501), on a corporation's ability to issue dividends or repurchase its own shares.

Statutory Laws That Cannot Be Changed by Bylaws. There are, however, certain rules set forth in the Corporations Code that cannot be varied by the Bylaws. These include:

(i) the prohibitions on any change to the statutory provisions for the appointment by a court of a provisional director;

(ii) The extension of the Corporation's power to indemnify its officers, directors, and agents beyond the California Statutory Limitations; and

(iii) Bylaws cannot limit shareholders' rights to inspect and copy the corporate records or the list of shareholders.

In some circumstances, rules can only be changed by provisions in the articles, as a mere modification of the Bylaws will be insufficient. Examples of this are issuance of shareholders' preferences (see California Corporations Code §204(a)(2)), limiting a corporation's business or powers, and granting voting rights to debt holders.

Ch 11 Forms

MINUTES OF THE FIRST MEETING OF THE BOARD OF DIRECTORS OF

_____

A California Nonprofit Corporation

The first meeting of the Board of Directors of _____,
a California nonprofit corporation, was held at _____
(address), at _____ a.m./p.m. on the _____ day of _____,
20___, pursuant to a written Waiver of Notice and Consent thereto signed by all of
the Directors of the Corporation.

The following Directors were present:

_____

_____

_____

No Directors were absent.

The meeting was called to order by _____, acting as
Temporary Chairman. _____ acted as Temporary
Secretary of the meeting.

The Temporary Chairman reported that the original Articles of Incorporation of the
Corporation had been filed with the Office of the Secretary of State of California
on the _____ day of _____, 20____. A certified copy of said
Articles of Incorporation was presented to the meeting and the Temporary
Secretary was directed to insert said copy into the book of minutes of the
Corporation.

The Temporary Secretary then presented a draft of Bylaws to the meeting, which
were read and discussed among the Board. Upon motion made, seconded, and
unanimously carried, the following resolutions were adopted:

WHEREAS, there has been presented to this meeting a form of Bylaws for the
regulation of the internal affairs of this Corporation; and

WHEREAS, it is deemed to be in the best interest of this Corporation that said
Bylaws be adopted by this Board of Directors as the Bylaws of this Corporation;

NOW, THEREFORE, BE IT RESOLVED, that the Bylaws presented to this meeting
and discussed hereat be, and the same hereby are, adopted as the Bylaws of this
Corporation, and

RESOLVED, that the Secretary of this Corporation be and hereby is authorized and
directed to execute and certify the adoption of said Bylaws by the Board at this

meeting, to insert said Bylaws as so certified into the book of minutes of this Corporation, and to see that a copy of said Bylaws, similarly certified, is kept at the principal office of the Corporation for the transaction of the business of the Corporation, in accordance with section (5160, 7160, or 9160) of the California Corporations Code.

The Temporary Secretary then presented for approval of the Board a proposed seal of the Corporation. On motion made, seconded, and unanimously carried, the following resolution was duly adopted:

RESOLVED, that the corporate seal presented to this Board be and the same is hereby adopted as the seal of this Corporation.

The Temporary Chairman stated that nominations were in order for the election of officers of the Corporation. Thereupon, the following slate of officers was nominated:

_____, President

_____, Chief Financial Officer

_____, Secretary

There being no other nominations, upon motion made, seconded, and unanimously carried, the foregoing individuals were duly elected to hold office until the annual meeting of the Directors, or until their respective successors are duly elected. Each officer so elected, being present, accepted (his/her) office, and the elected President and Secretary acted as Chairman and Secretary, respectively, for the balance of the meeting.

To provide for a depository for the funds of the Corporation, and to authorize certain officers to deal with corporate funds, the following resolutions were duly adopted:

RESOLVED, that this Corporation establish in its name, one or more deposit accounts with the _____ (name of bank), of _____, California, upon such terms and conditions as may be agreed upon with said bank, and that the following named officers of this Corporation be, and they hereby are, authorized to establish such account or accounts; and

RESOLVED, that _____, President, _____, Chief Financial Officer, and _____, Secretary of this Corporation, or any one of them be, and they hereby are, authorized to withdraw funds of this Corporation from said account or accounts upon checks of this Corporation, signed as provided herein with signatures duly certified to said bank by the Secretary of this Corporation, and said bank is hereby authorized to honor

**Ch 11
Forms**

and pay any and all checks so signed, including those drawn to the individual order of any officer or other person authorized to sign the same.

The matter of adoption of a fiscal year was then considered. After discussion, upon motion made, seconded, and unanimously carried, the following resolution was duly adopted:

RESOLVED, that the principal office of this Corporation be and it hereby is fixed as _____ _____, California.

To provide for the payment of the expenses of incorporation and organization of the Corporation, upon motion duly made, seconded, and unanimously carried, the following resolution was duly adopted:

RESOLVED, that _____, President, consult with legal counsel to ascertain the availability of exemptions from taxation under the federal and state tax laws, and if such exemptions are available, execute and file all necessary applications for exemptions from those taxes with the appropriate state and federal authorities, and pay all necessary filing fees.

Upon motion made, seconded, and unanimously carried, the resolution was duly adopted:

RESOLVED, that the President is hereby authorized and directed to execute and file with the Office of the California Secretary of State, at the times required by law, the annual statement required by the California Corporations Code to be filed by domestic nonprofit corporations.

[If the corporation will have members, continue.]

The Secretary then presented a proposed form of membership certificate for use by the Corporation. Upon motion made, seconded, and unanimously carried, the following resolution was duly adopted:

RESOLVED, that the form of membership certificate presented to this Board is approved and adopted as the membership certificate of this Corporation, and the Secretary is hereby directed to insert a copy of the certificate in the book of minutes of the Corporation.

[If the corporation will make public solicitations, continue.]

Upon motion made, seconded, and unanimously carried, the following resolutions were duly adopted:

RESOLVED, that the President be and hereby is directed to consult with legal counsel to ascertain the legal requirements imposed on organizations for the solicitation of funds for charitable purposes; and

RESOLVED, FURTHER, that the President be and hereby is also authorized and directed to make, or cause to be made, all necessary filings, and obtain all necessary permits authorizing and allowing this Corporation to make public solicitations for contributions for charitable purposes.

[If the corporation will engage in or utilize political lobbying, continue.]

Upon motion made, seconded, and unanimously carried, the following resolutions were duly adopted:

RESOLVED, that the President be and hereby is authorized and directed to file, or cause to be filed, the necessary forms registering the Corporation as a (lobbyist/lobbyist employer) with the California Secretary of State, and identify any and all lobbyists presently engaged or employed or to be engaged or employed on behalf of this Corporation; and

RESOLVED, FURTHER, that the President shall make, or cause to be made, all necessary periodic filings required by the Political Reform Act of 74, describing all lobbying and campaign activities and other information required by that Act to be disclosed and reported.

[If the corporation's memberships are exempt from securities registration requirements, continue.]

The Chairman then stated that (he/she) had been advised by legal counsel that the issuance and sale of memberships in the Corporation would be exempt from qualification and registration under state and federal securities laws, and reviewed for the Board the nature and limitations of those exemptions. The following resolutions were then duly adopted on motion made, seconded, and unanimously carried:

RESOLVED, that the consideration for which memberships in this Corporation shall be issued shall be the sum of $_____, payable in full upon initiation or acceptance as a member of this Corporation; and

RESOLVED, that the (annual/monthly) dues to the Corporation shall be $_____, until changed by action of the Board of Directors; and

RESOLVED, FURTHER, that the President and Secretary of the Corporation be, and they hereby are, authorized and directed to issue memberships to those persons who apply for membership, who are found to be qualified by the Board of Directors, and who have tendered the payment of the membership fee as well as the first _____ (year's/month's) dues.

[If the corporation's memberships are not exempt and require qualification or registration, continue.]

Ch 11 Forms

The Chairman then reported that the offer and sale of the Corporation's memberships were subject to state and federal securities law and would therefore have to be qualified and registered with the appropriate regulatory authorities, unless an exemption were available. Upon motion made, seconded, and unanimously carried, the following resolutions were duly adopted:

RESOLVED, that the President of the Corporation consult with legal counsel to ascertain whether an exemption from qualification or registration of the offer and sale of the Corporation's memberships is available under the California Corporate Securities Law or 68 or the Federal Securities Act of 33; and

RESOLVED, FURTHER, that if exemptions are not available, the President be and is hereby authorized and directed to file, or cause to be filed, an application for permit or registration to offer to sell memberships to the public within (or without) California with the California Commissioner of Corporations or the Federal Securities and Exchange Commission, or both, for the public offer and sale of (number) of memberships at $_____ per membership.

The Chairman lastly noted that there was a need for the Corporation to secure a federal employer identification number for use on corporate tax returns and statements. Upon motion made, seconded, and unanimously carried, the following resolution was duly adopted:

RESOLVED, that the proper officers of this Corporation, and each of them, be and they are hereby authorized and directed to make such filings and applications as are necessary to secure for the Corporation a federal employer identification number.

There being no further business, upon motion duly made, seconded, and unanimously carried, the meeting was then adjourned.

_____

Secretary

_____

Chairman

Ch 11 Forms

State of California
Secretary of State

STATEMENT OF INFORMATION
(Domestic Nonprofi t Corporation)

Filing Fee $2 0.00. If amendment, se e instruc tions.

IMPORTANT — READ INSTRUCTIONS BEFORE COMPLETING THIS FORM

1.   CORPORATE NAME (Please do not alter if name is preprinted.)

     "   "

N

This Space For Filing Use Only

DUE DATE:

COMPLETE PRINCIPAL OFFICE ADDRESS (Do not abbreviate the name of the city. Item 2 cannot be a P.O. Box.)

2. STREET ADDRESS OF PRINCIPAL OFFICE IN CALIFORNIA, IF ANY.	CITY	STATE	ZIP CODE
		CA	

NAMES AND COMPLETE ADDRESSES OF THE FOLLOWING OFFICERS (The corporation must have these three officers. A comparable title for the specific officer may be added; however, the preprinted titles on this form must not be altered.)

3. CHIEF EXECUTIVE OFFICER/	ADDRESS	CITY AND STATE	ZIP CODE
4. SECRETARY/	ADDRESS	CITY AND STATE	ZIP CODE
5. CHIEF FINANCIAL OFFICER/	ADDRESS	CITY AND STATE	ZIP CODE

AGENT FOR SERVICE OF PROCESS (If the agent is an individual, the agent must reside in California and Item 7 must be completed with a California address. If the agent is another corporation, the agent must have on file with the California Secretary of State a certificate pursuant to Corporations Code section 1505 and Item 7 must be left blank.)

6.   NAME OF AGENT FOR SERVICE OF PROCESS

7. ADDRESS OF AGENT FOR SERVICE OF PROCESS IN CALIFORNIA, IF AN INDIVIDUAL	CITY	STATE	ZIP CODE
		CA	

DAVIS-STIRLING COMMON INTEREST DEVELOPMENT ACT (California Civil Code section 1350, et seq.)

8.   ☐   Check here if the corporation is an association formed to manage a common interest development under the Davis-Stirling Common Interest Development Act and proceed to Items 9, 10 and 11.

NOTE: Corporations formed to manage a common interest development must also file a Statement by Common Interest Development Association (Form SI-CID) as required by California Civil Code section 1363.6. Please see instructions on the reverse side of this form.

9. ADDRESS OF BUSINESS OR CORPORATE OFFICE OF THE ASSOCIATION, IF ANY	CITY	STATE	ZIP CODE

10. FRONT STREET AND NEAREST CROSS STREET FOR THE PHYSICAL LOCATION OF THE COMMON INTEREST DEVELOPMENT (Complete if the business or corporate office is not on the site of the common interest development.)	9-DIGIT ZIP CODE

11. NAME AND ADDRESS OF ASSOCIATION'S MANAGING AGENT, IF ANY	CITY	STATE	ZIP CODE

12.   THE INFORMATION CONTAINED HEREIN IS TRUE AND CORRECT.

TYPE OR PRINT NAME OF PERSON COMPLETING THE FORM	SIGNATURE	TITLE	DATE

SI-100 (REV 03/2005)

APPROVED BY SECRETARY OF STATE

Ch 11 Forms

ACTION BY SOLE INCORPORATOR APPOINTING INITIAL DIRECTORS

AND ADOPTING BYLAWS OF _____

The undersigned, as sole incorporator of _____, a California nonprofit [public benefit/mutual benefit/religious] corporation (the "Corporation"), adopts the following resolutions on behalf of the Corporation:

WHEREAS, no bylaws have been adopted for the regulation of the affairs of the Corporation;

WHEREAS, it is deemed to be in the best interests of the Corporation and its prospective shareholders that the bylaws, attached to this document as Exhibit A, be adopted as the bylaws of the Corporation; and

WHEREAS, under California Corporations Code section [5134 (public benefit)/7134 (mutual benefit)/9134 (religious)], the sole incorporator is authorized to adopt the bylaws:

IT IS RESOLVED THAT the bylaws attached to these resolutions as Exhibit A are adopted as the Corporation's bylaws; and

IT IS FURTHER RESOLVED THAT the secretary of the Corporation is authorized and directed to execute a certificate of the adoption of these bylaws, to insert the bylaws as so certified in the minute book of the Corporation, and to see that a copy of the bylaws, similarly certified, is kept at the principal office of the Corporation.

WHEREAS, the bylaws of the Corporation provide that the initial authorized number of directors of the Corporation shall be [___]; and

WHEREAS, under California Corporations Code section [5134 (public benefit)/7134 (mutual benefit)/9134 (religious)], the sole incorporator is authorized to elect the initial directors of the Corporation:

IT IS RESOLVED THAT the persons listed below are hereby elected as the initial directors of the Corporation, to serve until they resign or are removed or until their successors are duly elected and qualified.

_____

_____

_____

Dated: _____

_____, Sole Incorporator

Ch 11 Forms

WAIVER OF NOTICE AND CONSENT

TO THE FIRST MEETING OF THE BOARD OF DIRECTORS

OF _____

The following directors of _____, a California nonprofit [public benefit/mutual benefit/religious] corporation (the "Corporation"), hereby waive notice of and consent to the holding of the first meeting of the board of directors of the Corporation on _____, at _____, California, and consent to the transaction of any and all business that may be properly brought before that meeting.

Date: _____

_____
[type name], Director

Date: _____

_____
[type name], Director

Date: _____

_____
[type name], Director

**Ch 11
Forms**

MINUTES OF THE ORGANIZATIONAL MEETING
OF THE BOARD OF DIRECTORS
OF _____

The undersigned, as the initial directors of the Corporation, held their first meeting at _____ [a.m./p.m.], on _____, 20___ at _____, California.

The following directors, constituting a quorum of the board, were present at the meeting:

_____

_____

_____

Waiver of Notice

The meeting of the board of directors was held pursuant to a written waiver of notice and consent to the holding of the meeting, signed by all directors of the Corporation, who were named as directors [by the sole incorporator/in the articles of incorporation]. The waiver and consent was presented and, on motion duly made, seconded, and carried, was made a part of the minutes of the meeting.

Filing of Articles

The board of directors were informed that the Corporation's articles of incorporation were filed with the California Secretary of State on _____, and that _____ was designated as initial agent for service of process.

A certified copy of the articles of the incorporation was presented to the directors. The secretary was directed to insert the certified copy of the articles in the minute book of the Corporation and to keep a copy at the Corporation's principal office. On motion duly made, seconded, and carried, it was resolved that _____ be confirmed as the Corporation's agent for service of process.

Adoption of Bylaws

WHEREAS, the directors of the Corporation have not yet adopted bylaws for the Corporation; and

WHEREAS, it is in the Corporation's best interest to adopt the bylaws:

RESOLVED that the bylaws attached hereto as Exhibit A and presented and discussed at this meeting are adopted as bylaws of the Corporation; and

Ch 11 Forms

IT IS FURTHER RESOLVED that the secretary of the Corporation is authorized and directed to execute a certificate of the adoption of those bylaws, to insert them as so certified in the minute book of the Corporation, and to ensure that a certified copy of the bylaws is kept at the Corporation's principal office.

Election of Officers

RESOLVED that the following persons were duly nominated and elected to the offices indicated after their names to serve for one year or until their respective successors are duly elected and qualified, whichever occurs later:

_____ - President

_____ - Vice President

_____ - Chief Financial Officer

_____ - Secretary

Accounting Year

RESOLVED that the Corporation adopt an accounting year ending on the last day of _____ of each year.

Principal Office Location

RESOLVED that _____ in the County of _____, California is hereby designated and fixed as the principal office of the Corporation, unless changed by resolution of the board of directors.

Bank Account

RESOLVED that the president and secretary of the Corporation, acting jointly on the Corporation's behalf, are authorized to open such bank accounts as may be necessary or appropriate to conduct the Corporation's business; such bank account shall require the signature of [one/two] officer(s) of the Corporation on all checks drawn on such accounts, that all resolutions required by the depository banks with respect to such accounts are hereby adopted, and that the secretary of the Corporation is authorized to certify to any bank the adoption of the resolution in the form used by that bank.

Exemption from Federal and State Taxes

RESOLVED that the president consult with legal counsel to ascertain the availability of exemptions from taxation under state and federal tax laws and, if such exemptions are available, the president is authorized and directed to execute and file all necessary applications for such exemption with the appropriate federal and

Ch 11
Forms

state tax authorities and to pay filing fees.

Statement by Domestic Corporation

RESOLVED that the president is authorized to execute and file with the office of the California Secretary of State, at the times required by law, the annual statement required by the Corporations Code to be filed by domestic nonprofit corporations.

[If the corporation will make public solicitations:]

Compliance with Local Solicitation Ordinances

RESOLVED that the president is authorized and directed to execute and file with the office of the California Secretary of State, at the time required by law, the annual statement required by the Corporations Code to be filed by domestic nonprofit corporations.

IT IS FURTHER RESOVLED that the president is authorized and directed to make all necessary filings and obtain all necessary permits authorizing and allowing the Corporation to make public solicitations for contributions for charitable purposes in the jurisdictions named above.]

Employer Identification Number

RESOLVED that the officers of the Corporation and each of them are authorized and directed to make such filings and applications as are necessary to secure for the Corporation a federal employer identification number.

Nonprofit Mailing Permit

RESOLVED that the officers of the Corporation and each of them are authorized and directed to make such filings and applications as are necessary to secure for the Corporation a nonprofit mailing permit.

There being no further business, on motion duly made, seconded, and carried, the meeting was adjourned.

Date: _____   _____
                                 [type name], Secretary

Ch 11 Forms

MAIL TO:
Registry of Charitable Trusts
P.O. Box 903447
Sacramento, CA 94203-4470
Telephone: (916) 445-2021

WEB SITE ADDRESS:
http://ag.ca.gov/charities/

CHARITY
REGISTRATION FORM
STATE OF CALIFORNIA
OFFICE OF THE ATTORNEY GENERAL
REGISTRY OF CHARITABLE TRUSTS
(Government Code Sections 12580-12599.7)

Official name and mailing address of organization:	Federal Employer Identification Number:
Name of Organization	
Address (Number and Street)	Corporate or Organization Number:
City or Town, State and ZIP Code	

1. Names and addresses of ALL trustees or directors and officers (attach a list if necessary):

2. Attach a statement fully describing the primary activity of the organization. (A copy of the material submitted with the application for federal or state tax exemption will normally provide this information.)

3. If the organization is based outside California, comment fully on the extent of activities in California and how the California activities relate to total activities. In addition, list all funds, property, and other assets held or expected to be held in California. Indicate whether you are monitored in your home state, and if so, by whom.

4. If assets (funds, property, etc.) have been received, enter the date first received: _____

5. Annual accounting period adopted:
   ☐ Fiscal Year Ending _____
   ☐ Calendar Year

6. Attach your founding documents as follows:

   A) <u>Corporations</u> - Furnish a copy of the articles of incorporation and all amendments and current bylaws. If incorporated outside California, enter the date the corporation qualified through the California Secretary of State's Office to conduct activities in California: _____

   B) <u>Associations</u> - Furnish a copy of the instrument creating the organization (bylaws, constitution, and/or articles of association).

   C) <u>Trusts</u> - Furnish a copy of the trust instrument or will and decree of final distribution.

7. Has the organization applied for or been granted IRS tax exempt status Yes ☐ No ☐
   Date of of application _____ OR date of determination letter _____ .
   If granted, exempt under 501(c) _____ .
   Are contributions to the organization tax deductible Yes ☐ No ☐ Attach a copy of the Federal exemption determination letter, if available.

Signature _____ Title _____ Date _____

Address _____

Organization's telephone number _____ E-Mail Address _____

Organization's fax number _____ Web site _____

CT-1 CHARITY REGISTRATION FORM (12/2004)

Ch 11 Forms

United States Postal Service
Application to Mail
at Nonprofit Standard Mail Rates

Section A—Application *(Please read section B on page 2 before completion.)*

Part 1 *(For completion by applicant)*

- All information entered below must be legible so that our records will show the correct information about your organization.

- The complete name of the organization must be shown in item 1. The name shown must agree with the name that appears on all documents submitted to support this application.

- A complete address representing a physical location for the organization must be shown in item 2. If you receive mail through a post office box, show your street address first and then the box number.

- The applicant named in item 5 must be the individual submitting the application for the organization and must be an officer of the organization. Printers and mailing agents may not sign for the organization.

- No additional organization categories may be added in item 6. To be eligible for the Nonprofit Standard Mail rates, the organization must qualify as one of the types listed.

- The applicant must sign the application in item 12.

- The date shown in item 14 must be the date that the application is submitted to the post office.

No application fee is required. All information must be complete and typewritten or printed legibly.

1. Complete Name of Organization *(If voting registration official, include title)*

2. Street Address of Organization *(Include apartment or suite number)*

3. City, State, ZIP+4 Code

4. Telephone *(Include area code)*

5. Name of Applicant *(Must represent applying organization)*

6. Type of Organization *(Check only one)*

☐ (01) Religious   ☐ (03) Scientific   ☐ (05) Agricultural   ☐ (07) Veterans'   ☐ (09) Qualified political committee *(Go to item 9)*

☐ (02) Educational   ☐ (04) Philanthropic   ☐ (06) Labor   ☐ (08) Fraternal   ☐ (10) Voting registration official *(Go to item 9)*

7. Is this a for-profit organization or does any of the net income inure to the benefit of any private stockholder or individual?   ☐ Yes   ☐ No

8. Is this organization exempt from federal income tax? *(If 'Yes,' attach a copy of the exemption issued by the Internal Revenue Service (IRS) that shows the section of the IRS code under which the organization is exempt.)*   ☐ Yes   ☐ No

Is an application for exempt status pending with the IRS? *(If 'Yes,' attach a copy of the application to this Form 3624.)*   ☐ Yes   ☐ No

9. Has this organization previously mailed at the Nonprofit Standard Mail rates? *(If 'Yes,' list the post offices where mailings were most recently deposited at these rates.)*   ☐ Yes   ☐ No

Has the IRS denied or revoked the organization's federal tax exempt status? *(If 'Yes,' attach a copy of the IRS ruling to this Form 3624.)*   ☐ Yes   ☐ No

10. Has your organization had Nonprofit Standard Mail rate mailing privileges denied or revoked? *(If 'Yes,' list the post office (city and state) where the application was denied or authorization was revoked.)*   ☐ Yes   ☐ No

11. Post office (not a station or branch) where authorization requested and bulk mailings will be made *(City, state, ZIP Code)*

*I certify that the statements made by me are true and complete. I understand that anyone who furnishes false or misleading information on this form or who omits material information requested on the form may be subject to criminal sanctions (including fines and imprisonment) and/or civil sanctions (including multiple damages **and** civil penalties). I further understand that, if this application is approved, a postage refund* *for the difference between the regular Standard Mail (A) and Nonprofit Standard Mail rates may be made for only mailings entered at regular Standard Mail (A) rates at the post office identified above while this application is pending, provided that the conditions set forth in Domestic Mail Manual E670.5.0 and E670.9.0 are met.*

12. Signature of Applicant

13. Title

14. Date

Part 2 *(For completion by postmaster at originating office when application filed)*

1. Signature of Postmaster *(Or designated representative)*

2. Date Application Filed With Post Office *(Round stamp)*

PS Form **3624,** October 1996 *(Page 1 of 3)*

Section B—General Information

Organization Eligibility

The Nonprofit Standard Mail rates may be granted only to:

1. The eight categories (01 through 08) of nonprofit organizations specified on page 1 in section A, item 6.

2. Qualified political committees (category 09), including the national and state committees of political parties as well as certain named congressional committees.

3. Voting registration officials (category 10), including local, state, and District of Columbia voting registration officials.

These organizations are defined in *Domestic Mail Manual* (DMM) E670, available for review at any post office.

To qualify, a nonprofit organization must be both **organized** and **operated** for a **primary** purpose that is consistent with one of the types of organizations in DMM E670. Organizations that **incidentally** engage in qualifying activities do not qualify for the Nonprofit Standard Mail rates.

Not all nonprofit organizations are eligible for the Nonprofit Standard Mail rates. DMM E670 lists certain organizations (such as business leagues, chambers of commerce, civic improvement associations, social and hobby clubs, governmental bodies, and others) that, although nonprofit, do not qualify for the Nonprofit Standard Mail rates.

Application Procedures

1. Only organizations may apply. Individuals may not apply (except voting registration officials).

2. Only the **one** category in item 6 that best describes the **primary purpose** of the organization may be checked.

3. The application must be **signed** by someone in authority in the organization, such as the president or treasurer. It must not be signed by a printer or mailing agent.

4. The completed Form 3624 must be submitted to the post office where bulk mailings will be deposited. If the application is approved, the authorization will apply only at that post office.

Supporting Documentation

The documents listed in 1 and 2 below must be submitted with the completed applications for nonprofit organizations. The documents listed in 3 must be submitted for qualified political committees and, in 4, for voting registration officials.

1. Evidence that the organization is **nonprofit** and that none of its net income inures to the benefit of any private stockholder or individual. Acceptable evidence includes:

   - An Internal Revenue Service (IRS) letter of exemption from payment of federal income tax.

   - If an IRS exemption letter is not available, a complete financial statement from an independent auditor (such as a certified public accountant) substantiating that the organization is nonprofit. A statement from a member of the organization is not sufficient.

2. Documents describing the organization's **primary purpose,** such as:

   - Organizing instruments that state the purpose for which the group is organized, such as the constitution, articles of incorporation, articles of association, or trust indenture. The organizing instrument, including all amendments to the original, should bear the seal, certification, or signature of the Secretary of State or other appropriate state official. If one or more of these documents are not sealed, certified, or signed by state officials, an officer or other person authorized to sign for the applicant should submit a written declaration certifying that the documents are complete and accurate copies of the originals.

   - Materials showing how the organization actually **operated** during the previous 6 to 12 months and how it will operate in the future. Bulletins, financial statements, membership forms, publications produced by the organization, minutes of meetings, or a list of its activities may be used.

3. For qualified political committees (category 09), organizational or other documents substantiating that the applicant is the state or national committee of the political party.

4. For voting registration officials (category 10), a copy of the statute, ordinance, or other authority establishing responsibility for voter registration.

Mail Eligibility

An organization authorized to mail at the Nonprofit Standard Mail rates may mail only **its own matter** at those rates. It may not delegate or lend the use of its Nonprofit Standard Mail authorization to any other person or organization. Cooperative mailings may be made at the Nonprofit Standard Mail rates **only** if **each** of the cooperating organizations is individually authorized to mail at those rates at the office where mailings are deposited.

DMM E670 discusses the specific restrictions against the mailing of certain advertising materials and products.

PS Form **3624,** October 1996 *(Page 2 of 3)*

Ch 11 Forms

Postal Service Checklist for Form 3624,
Application to Mail at Nonprofit Standard Mail Rates

Name of Organization

The organization above provided the following evidence of eligibility for Nonprofit Standard Mail rates.

1. Nonprofit Status *(Check one)*

☐ IRS letter of exemption from payment of federal income tax

☐ Financial statement prepared by an independent auditor substantiating organization's nonprofit status (statement must include balance sheets, notes, etc.)

2. Organization *(One complete copy; check one)*

☐ Articles of Incorporation ☐ Constitution ☐ Charter ☐ Articles of Association

☐ Other *(Explain):*

3. Operation *(Several samples of each; check types of information included with application)*

☐ Bulletins ☐ Brochures ☐ Financial statements ☐ Listing of activities for past 6 to 12 months

☐ Membership applications ☐ Minutes of meetings ☐ Newsletters

☐ Other *(Explain):*

The name on all the documentation presented as evidence must match the name on the application. If they do not match, please explain.

I certify that the applicant has completed all the items on the application and that each item is legible.

Signature of Postmaster *(Or designated representative)*	Date
Telephone *(Include area code)*	Post Office *(City, state, ZIP Code)*
Date Application Returned to Organization for Correction	Date Application and Documentation Sent to Nonprofit Service Center

PS Form **3624,** October 1996 *(Page 3 of 3)*

Ch 11 Forms

REGISTRATION/RENEWAL FEE REPORT
TO ATTORNEY GENERAL OF CALIFORNIA
Sections 12586 and 12587, California Government Code
11 CCR Sections 311 and 312

Failure to submit this report annually no later than four months and fifteen days after the end of the organization's accounting period may result in the loss of tax exemption and the assessment of a minimum tax of $800, plus interest, and/or fines or filing penalties as defined in Government Code Section 12586.1.

IRS FORM 990 EXTENSIONS WILL BE HONORED. PLEASE SUBMIT WITH RRF-1 ALL IRS EXTENSION REQUESTS AND, WHERE APPLICABLE, IRS EXTENSION APPROVALS.

MAIL TO:
Registry of Charitable Trusts
P.O. Box 903447
Sacramento, CA 94203-4470
Telephone: (916) 445-2021

WEB SITE ADDRESS:

http://ag.ca.gov/charities/

State Charity Registration Number _____

Name of Organization

Address (Number and Street)

City or Town, State and ZIP Code

Check if:

☐ Change of address

☐ Amended report

Corporate or Organization No. _____

Federal Employer I.D. No. _____

PART A - ACTIVITIES	Yes	No
1. During your most recent full accounting period did your gross receipts or total assets equal $100,000 or more?		

Note: If the answer is yes, you are required by Title 11 of the California Code of Regulations, §§311 and 312, to attach a check in the amount of $25.00 to this report. Make check payable to Department of Justice.

2. For your most recent full accounting period (beginning _____/_____/_____ ending _____/_____/_____) list:

Gross receipts $ _____ Total assets $ _____

PART B - STATEMENTS REGARDING ORGANIZATION DURING THE PERIOD OF THIS REPORT

Note: If you answer "yes" to any of the questions below, you must attach a separate sheet providing an explanation and details for each "yes" response. Please review RRF-1 instructions for information required.

	Yes	No
1. During this reporting period, were there any contracts, loans, leases or other financial transactions between the organization and any officer, director or trustee thereof either directly or with an entity in which any such officer, director or trustee had any financial interest?		
2. During this reporting period, was there any theft, embezzlement, diversion or misuse of the organization's charitable property or funds?		
3. During this reporting period, did non-program expenditures exceed 50% of gross revenues?		
4. During this reporting period, were any organization funds used to pay any penalty, fine or judgment? If you filed a Form 4720 with the Internal Revenue Service, attach a copy.		
5. During this reporting period, were the services of a professional fundraiser or fundraising counsel used? If "yes," provide an attachment listing the name, address, and telephone number of the service provider.		
6. During this reporting period, did the organization receive any governmental funding? If so, provide an attachment listing the name of the agency, mailing address, contact person, and telephone number.		
7. During this reporting period, did the organization hold a raffle for charitable purposes? If "yes," provide an attachment indicating the number of raffles and the date(s) they occurred.		
8. Does the organization conduct a vehicle donation program? If "yes," provide an attachment indicating whether the program is operated by the charity or whether the organization contracts with a commercial fundraiser.		

Organization's area code and telephone number (_____) _____-_____

Organization's e-mail address _____

I declare under penalty of perjury that I have examined this report, including accompanying documents, and to the best of my knowledge and belief, it is true, correct and complete.

_____ _____ _____ _____
Signature of authorized officer   Printed Name   Title   Date

RRF-1 (5-2004)

Forms for Chapter 13

There are nine forms that accompany **Chapter 13, Legal Obligations of Employers**. They include the following:

Form 13-A Employee's Withholding Allowance Certificate—IRS Form W-4, 2 pages (439 - 440)

Form 13-B Registration Form for Commercial Employers, Pacific Maritime, and Fishing Boats—EDD Form DE 1, 2 pages (441 - 442)

Form 13-C Report of New Employee(s)—EDD Form DE 34, 2 pages (443 - 444)

Form 13-D Report of Independent Contractor(s)—EDD Form DE 542, 2 pages (445 - 446)

Form 13-E Offer of Employment, 3 pages (447 - 449)

Form 13-F Employment Eligibility Verification—Form I-9, 3 pages (450 - 452)

Form 13-G Employee Proprietary Information and Inventions Assignment Agreement, 9 pages (453 - 461)

Form 13-H Independent Contractor Proprietary Information and Inventions Assignment Agreement, 9 pages (462 - 470)

Form 13-I Mediation and Arbitration Policy, 2 pages (471 - 472)

Form W-4 (2004)

Purpose. Complete Form W-4 so that your employer can withhold the correct Federal income tax from your pay. Because your tax situation may change, you may want to refigure your withholding each year.

Exemption from withholding. If you are exempt, complete only lines 1, 2, 3, 4, and 7 and sign the form to validate it. Your exemption for 2004 expires February 16, 2005. See **Pub. 505,** Tax Withholding and Estimated Tax.

Note: *You cannot claim exemption from withholding if: (a) your income exceeds $800 and includes more than $250 of unearned income (e.g., interest and dividends) and (b) another person can claim you as a dependent on their tax return.*

Basic Instructions. If you are not exempt, complete the **Personal Allowances Worksheet** below. The worksheets on page 2 adjust your withholding allowances based on itemized deductions, certain credits, adjustments to income, or two-earner/two-job situations. Complete all worksheets that apply. **However, you may claim fewer (or zero) allowances.**

Head of household. Generally, you may claim head of household filing status on your tax return only if you are unmarried and pay more than 50% of the costs of keeping up a home for yourself and your dependent(s) or other qualifying individuals. See line E below.

Tax credits. You can take projected tax credits into account in figuring your allowable number of withholding allowances. Credits for child or dependent care expenses and the child tax credit may be claimed using the **Personal Allowances Worksheet** below. See **Pub. 919,** How Do I Adjust My Tax Withholding? for information on converting your other credits into withholding allowances.

Nonwage income. If you have a large amount of nonwage income, such as interest or dividends, consider making estimated tax payments using **Form 1040-ES,** Estimated Tax for Individuals. Otherwise, you may owe additional tax.

Two earners/two jobs. If you have a working spouse or more than one job, figure the total number of allowances you are entitled to claim on all jobs using worksheets from only one Form W-4. Your withholding usually will be most accurate when all allowances are claimed on the Form W-4 for the highest paying job and zero allowances are claimed on the others.

Nonresident alien. If you are a nonresident alien, see the **Instructions for Form 8233** before completing this Form W-4.

Check your withholding. After your Form W-4 takes effect, use Pub. 919 to see how the dollar amount you are having withheld compares to your projected total tax for 2004. See Pub. 919, especially if your earnings exceed $125,000 (Single) or $175,000 (Married).

Recent name change? If your name on line 1 differs from that shown on your social security card, call 1-800-772-1213 to initiate a name change and obtain a social security card showing your correct name.

Personal Allowances Worksheet (Keep for your records.)

A Enter "1" for **yourself** if no one else can claim you as a dependent . . . . **A** ____

You are single and have only one job; or

B Enter "1" if: You are married, have only one job, and your spouse does not work; or . . **B** ____

Your wages from a second job or your spouse's wages (or the total of both) are $1,000 or less.

C Enter "1" for your **spouse.** But, you may choose to enter "-0-" if you are married and have either a working spouse or more than one job. (Entering "-0-" may help you avoid having too little tax withheld.) . . . . **C** ____

D Enter number of **dependents** (other than your spouse or yourself) you will claim on your tax return . . . . **D** ____

E Enter "1" if you will file as **head of household** on your tax return (see conditions under **Head of household** above) . **E** ____

F Enter "1" if you have at least $1,500 of **child or dependent care expenses** for which you plan to claim a credit . . **F** ____

(**Note:** *Do not* include child support payments. See **Pub. 503,** Child and Dependent Care Expenses, for details.)

G Child Tax Credit (including additional child tax credit):

If your total income will be less than $52,000 ($77,000 if married), enter "2" for each eligible child.

If your total income will be between $52,000 and $84,000 ($77,000 and $119,000 if married), enter "1" for each eligible child plus "1" **additional** if you have four or more eligible children. **G** ____

H Add lines A through G and enter total here. **Note:** *This may be different from the number of exemptions you claim on your tax return.* **H** ____

For accuracy, complete all worksheets that apply.

- If you plan to **itemize or claim adjustments to income** and want to reduce your withholding, see the **Deductions and Adjustments Worksheet** on page 2.
- If you have **more than one job** or are **married and you and your spouse both work** and the combined earnings from all jobs exceed $35,000 ($25,000 if married) see the **Two-Earner/Two-Job Worksheet** on page 2 to avoid having too little tax withheld.
- If **neither** of the above situations applies, **stop here** and enter the number from line H on line 5 of Form W-4 below.

Ch 13 Forms

- - - - - - - - - - - - - - - **Cut here and give Form W-4 to your employer. Keep the top part for your records.** - - - - - - - - - - - - - -

Form **W-4**
Department of the Treasury
Internal Revenue Service

Employee's Withholding Allowance Certificate

Your employer must send a copy of this form to the IRS if: (a) you claim more than 10 allowances or (b) you claim "Exempt" and your wages are normally more than $200 per week.

OMB No. 1545-0010

2004

1 Type or print your first name and middle initial	Last name	**2** Your social security number

Home address (number and street or rural route)	**3** ☐ Single ☐ Married ☐ Married, but withhold at higher Single rate. **Note:** *If married, but legally separated, or spouse is a nonresident alien, check the "Single" box.*

City or town, state, and ZIP code	**4** **If your last name differs from that shown on your social security card, check here. You must call 1-800-772-1213 for a new card.** ☐

5 Total number of allowances you are claiming (from line **H** above **or** from the applicable worksheet on page 2) **5** _____

6 Additional amount, if any, you want withheld from each paycheck . . . . **6** $ _____

7 I claim exemption from withholding for 2004, and I certify that I meet **both** of the following conditions for exemption:

Last year I had a right to a refund of **all** Federal income tax withheld because I had **no** tax liability **and**

This year I expect a refund of **all** Federal income tax withheld because I expect to have **no** tax liability.

If you meet both conditions, write "Exempt" here . . . . **7** _____

Under penalties of perjury, I certify that I am entitled to the number of withholding allowances claimed on this certificate, or I am entitled to claim exempt status.

Employee's signature
(Form is not valid
unless you sign it.) ▶ _____ **Date** ▶ _____

8 Employer's name and address (Employer: Complete lines 8 and 10 only if sending to the IRS.)	**9** Office code (optional)	**10** Employer identification number (EIN)

For Privacy Act and Paperwork Reduction Act Notice, see page 2.   Cat. No. 10220Q   Form **W-4** (2004)

Form W-4 (2004)   Page **2**

Deductions and Adjustments Worksheet

Note: *Use this worksheet **only** if you plan to itemize deductions, claim certain credits, or claim adjustments to income on your 2004 tax return.*

1   Enter an estimate of your 2004 itemized deductions. These include qualifying home mortgage interest, charitable contributions, state and local taxes, medical expenses in excess of 7.5% of your income, and miscellaneous deductions. (For 2004, you may have to reduce your itemized deductions if your income is over $142,700 ($71,350 if married filing separately). See **Worksheet 3** in Pub. 919 for details.) . . .   **1** $ _____

2   Enter: $9,700 if married filing jointly or qualifying widow(er)
      $7,150 if head of household   . . . .   **2** $ _____
      $4,850 if single
      $4,850 if married filing separately

3   **Subtract** line 2 from line 1. If line 2 is greater than line 1, enter "-0-". . . . .   **3** $ _____

4   Enter an estimate of your 2004 adjustments to income, including alimony, deductible IRA contributions, and student loan interest   **4** $ _____

5   **Add** lines 3 and 4 and enter the total. (Include any amount for credits from **Worksheet 7** in Pub. 919) .   **5** $ _____

6   Enter an estimate of your 2004 nonwage income (such as dividends or interest) . . . .   **6** $ _____

7   **Subtract** line 6 from line 5. Enter the result, but not less than "-0-". . . . .   **7** $ _____

8   **Divide** the amount on line 7 by $3,000 and enter the result here. Drop any fraction . . . . . .   **8**   _____

9   Enter the number from the **Personal Allowances Worksheet,** line H, page 1 . . . .   **9**   _____

10   **Add** lines 8 and 9 and enter the total here. If you plan to use the **Two-Earner/Two-Job Worksheet,** also enter this total on line 1 below. Otherwise, **stop here** and enter this total on Form W-4, line 5, page 1 .   **10**   _____

Two-Earner/Two-Job Worksheet (See **Two earners/two jobs** on page 1.)

Note: *Use this worksheet **only** if the instructions under line H on page 1 direct you here.*

1   Enter the number from line H, page 1 (or from line 10 above if you used the **Deductions and Adjustments Worksheet**)   **1**   _____

2   Find the number in **Table 1** below that applies to the **LOWEST** paying job and enter it here . . . .   **2**   _____

3   If line 1 is **more than or equal to** line 2, subtract line 2 from line 1. Enter the result here (if zero, enter "-0-") and on Form W-4, line 5, page 1. **Do not** use the rest of this worksheet . . . .   **3**   _____

Note: *If line 1 is **less than** line 2, enter "-0-" on Form W-4, line 5, page 1. Complete lines 4–9 below to calculate the additional withholding amount necessary to avoid a year-end tax bill.*

4   Enter the number from line 2 of this worksheet . . . .   **4**   _____

5   Enter the number from line 1 of this worksheet . . . .   **5**   _____

6   **Subtract** line 5 from line 4 . . . .   **6**   _____

7   Find the amount in **Table 2** below that applies to the **HIGHEST** paying job and enter it here . . . .   **7** $ _____

8   **Multiply** line 7 by line 6 and enter the result here. This is the additional annual withholding needed . .   **8** $ _____

9   Divide line 8 by the number of pay periods remaining in 2004. For example, divide by 26 if you are paid every two weeks and you complete this form in December 2003. Enter the result here and on Form W-4, line 6, page 1. This is the additional amount to be withheld from each paycheck . . . .   **9** $ _____

Table 1: Two-Earner/Two-Job Worksheet

Married Filing Jointly			Married Filing Jointly			All Others	
If wages from **HIGHEST** paying job are—	AND, wages from **LOWEST** paying job are—	Enter on line 2 above	If wages from **HIGHEST** paying job are—	AND, wages from **LOWEST** paying job are—	Enter on line 2 above	If wages from **LOWEST** paying job are—	Enter on line 2 above
$0 - $40,000	$0 - $4,000	0	$40,001 and over	31,001 - 38,000	6	$0 - $6,000	0
	4,001 - 8,000	1		38,001 - 44,000	7	6,001 - 11,000	1
	8,001 - 17,000	2		44,001 - 50,000	8	11,001 - 18,000	2
	17,001 and over	3		50,001 - 55,000	9	18,001 - 25,000	3
				55,001 - 65,000	10	25,001 - 31,000	4
$40,001 and over	$0 - $4,000	0		65,001 - 75,000	11	31,001 - 44,000	5
	4,001 - 8,000	1		75,001 - 85,000	12	44,001 - 55,000	6
	8,001 - 15,000	2		85,001 - 100,000	13	55,001 - 70,000	7
	15,001 - 22,000	3		100,001 - 115,000	14	70,001 - 80,000	8
	22,001 - 25,000	4		115,001 and over	15	80,001 - 100,000	9
	25,001 - 31,000	5				100,001 and over	10

Table 2: Two-Earner/Two-Job Worksheet

Married Filing Jointly		All Others	
If wages from **HIGHEST** paying job are—	Enter on line 7 above	If wages from **HIGHEST** paying job are—	Enter on line 7 above
$0 - $60,000	$470	$0 - $30,000	$470
60,001 - 110,000	780	30,001 - 70,000	780
110,001 - 150,000	870	70,001 - 140,000	870
150,001 - 270,000	1,020	140,001 - 320,000	1,020
270,001 and over	1,090	320,001 and over	1,090

EDD Employment
Development
Department
State of California

This form will be the basic record of YOUR ACCOUNT. **DO NOT FILE THIS FORM UNTIL YOU HAVE PAID WAGES THAT EXCEED $100.00.** Please read the **INSTRUCTIONS** on the back before completing this form. **PLEASE PRINT OR TYPE..** Return this form to: ➤	EMPLOYMENT DEVELOPMENT DEPARTMENT ACCOUNT SERVICES GROUP MIC 13 PO BOX 826880 SACRAMENTO CA 94280-0001 **(916) 654-7041 FAX (916) 654-9211** www.edd.ca.gov

REGISTRATION FORM FOR COMMERCIAL EMPLOYERS, PACIFIC MARITIME, AND FISHING BOATS

ACCOUNT NUMBER	DEPT. USE	QUARTER	ON-LINE PROCESS DATE	TAS CODE

Industry specific registration forms are required relative to each type of employer. Please use the appropriate form to register.

Commercial/Pacific Maritime/Fishing Boat	DE 1	Household Workers	DE 1HW
Agricultural	DE 1AG	Non-profit	DE 1NP
Government/Public Schools/Indian Tribes	DE 1GS	Personal Income Tax Only	DE 1P

A. THIS IS A:
☐ New business ☐ Hired employees ☐ Change in form - (Individual to corporation; partnership to corporation; merger; corporation to LLC, etc.)
☐ Change of partner(s) ☐ Purchased on-going business ☐ All ☐ Part ☐ Other _____
IF THE BUSINESS WAS PURCHASED, PROVIDE THE FOLLOWING INFORMATION:

Previous Owner   Business Name   Purchase Price   Date of Transfer   EDD Account Number

B. HAVE YOU EVER REGISTERED A BUSINESS WITH THE DEPARTMENT?
☐ No ☐ Yes
IF YES, ENTER THE FOLLOWING:
ACCT NUMBER   BUSINESS NAME   ADDRESS

C. INDICATE FIRST QUARTER AND YEAR IN WHICH WAGES EXCEED $100. ☐ Jan.-Mar. 20__ ☐ Apr.-June 20__ ☐ July-Sept. 20__ ☐ Oct.-Dec. 20

D. BUSINESS NAME (DBA)	OWNERSHIP BEGAN OPERATING	FEDERAL I.D. NUMBER
	MONTH: DAY: YEAR:	
E. INDIVIDUAL OWNER	SOCIAL SECURITY NUMBER	DRIVER'S LICENSE #
F. CORPORATION/LLC/LLP/LP NAME	SECRETARY OF STATE CORP/LLC/LLP/LP I.D. NO.	

G. List all partners*, corporate officers, or LLC/LLP members/managers/officers	**TITLE** (partner, officer title, LLC/LLP member/manager)	SOCIAL SECURITY NUMBER	DRIVER'S LICENSE #

*If entity is a **Limited Partnership**, indicate General Partner with an (*). List additional partners, LLC/LLP members/officers/managers on a separate sheet.

H. MAILING ADDRESS	CITY	STATE	ZIP CODE	PHONE NUMBER ( )
I. BUSINESS ADDRESS (if different from mailing address)	CITY	STATE	ZIP CODE	PHONE NUMBER ( )

J. ORGANIZATION TYPE
☐ (IN) INDIVIDUAL OWNER ☐ (AS) ASSOCIATION ☐ (LQ) LIQUIDATION ☐ (JV) JOINT VENTURE
☐ (HW) HUS/WIFE CO-OWNERSHIP ☐ (LC) LIMITED LIABILITY CO. ☐ (LP) LIMITED PARTNERSHIP ☐ (RC) RECEIVERSHIP
☐ (GP) GENERAL PARTNERSHIP ☐ (PL) LIMITED LIABILITY PARTNERSHIP ☐ (TR) TRUSTEESHIP ☐ (BK) BANKRUPTCY
☐ (CP) CORPORATION ☐ (EA) ESTATE ADMINISTRATION ☐ (OT) OTHER (Specify) _____

K. EMPLOYER TYPE ☐ (01) COMMERCIAL ☐ (22) PACIFIC MARITIME ☐ (25) FISHING BOAT

L. INDUSTRY ACTIVITY: Identify the industry and specific product or service that represents the greatest portion of your sales receipts or revenue. Check one:
☐ SERVICES ☐ RETAIL ☐ WHOLESALE ☐ MANUFACTURING ☐ OTHER_____
Describe specific product and/or service in detail.

Number of CA Employees _____ Are there multiple locations for this business? ☐ No ☐ Yes

M. CONTACT PERSON FOR BUSINESS	TITLE/COMPANY NAME	ADDRESS	PHONE ( )

N. DECLARATION
These statements are hereby declared to be correct to the best knowledge and belief of the undersigned.

Signature _____ Title _____ Date _____
(Owner, Partner, Officer, Member, Manager, etc.)

O. PAYROLL TAX EDUCATION: Attend a payroll tax seminar that will help you understand how, what, and when to report state payroll taxes. Visit our Web site at **www.edd.ca.gov/taxsem** or call us at (888) 745-3886 for more information.

DE 1 Rev. 71 (9-03) **(INTERNET)**   Page 1 of 2   CU

INSTRUCTIONS FOR REGISTRATION FORM FOR COMMERCIAL/PACIFIC MARITIME/FISHING BOAT EMPLOYERS

An employer is required by law to file a registration form with the Employment Development Department (EDD) within **fifteen (15) calendar days** after paying over $100 in wages for employment in a calendar quarter, or whenever a change in ownership occurs. Please complete all items on the front of this DE 1 and do **one** of the following:

- Mail your completed registration form to EDD, Account Services Group MIC 13, PO Box 826880, Sacramento, CA 94280-0001 **or**
- Fax your completed registration form to EDD at (916) 654-9211 **or**
- Call for telephone registration at (916) 654-8706

There are industry specific registration forms related to each type of employer. Please use the appropriate form to register. A complete list of registration forms is located on the front of this form.

NEED MORE HELP OR INFORMATION?

- Call Account Services Group (ASG) in Sacramento at (916) 654-7041 with questions regarding this form or the registration and account number assignment process.
- Contact the nearest Taxpayer Education and Assistance (TEA) office listed in your local telephone directory under State Government, EDD or call a TEA Customer Service Representative at 1-888-745-3886 with questions about whether your business entity is subject to reporting and paying state payroll taxes. For TTY (nonverbal) access, call 1-800-547-9565.
- Access the EDD Web site at **www.edd.ca.gov**

A. STATUS OF BUSINESS - Check the box that best describes why you are completing this form. If the business was purchased, provide previous owner and business name, purchase price, date ownership was transferred to this ownership and EDD account number.

B. PRIOR REGISTRATION - If any part of the ownership shown in items E, F, or G are operating or have ever operated at another location, check "Yes" and provide account number, business name, and address.

C. WAGES - Check the box for the quarter in which you first paid over $100 in wages.

D. BUSINESS NAME - Enter the name by which your business is known to the public. Enter "None" if no business name is used. Enter the date the new ownership began operating. Enter Federal Employer Identification Number. If not assigned, enter "Applied For".

E. INDIVIDUAL OWNER - Enter the full given name, middle initial, surname, title, social security number, and driver's license number.

F. CORPORATION/LLC/LLP/LP NAME - Enter Corporation/LLC/LLP/LP name exactly as spelled and registered with the Secretary of State. Include the California Corporate/LLC/LLP/LP identification number.

G. LIST ALL PARTNERS, CORPORATE OFFICERS, OR LLC/LLP MEMBERS/MANAGERS/OFFICERS - Enter the name, title, social security number and driver's license of each individual.

H. MAILING ADDRESS - Enter the mailing address where EDD correspondence and forms should be sent. Provide daytime business phone number.

I. BUSINESS ADDRESS - Enter the California address and telephone number where the business is physically conducted. If there is more than one California location, list the business addresses on a separate sheet and attach to this form.

J. ORGANIZATION TYPE - Check the box that best describes the legal form of the ownership shown in items E, F, or G.

K. EMPLOYER TYPE - Check the box that best describes your employer type.

L. INDUSTRY ACTIVITY - Check the box that best describes the industry activity of your business. Describe the particular product or service in detail. This information is used to assign an Industrial Classification Code to your business. If you would like more information on industry coding or the North American Industry Classification System (NAICS), you can visit the Web site:

www.census.gov/epcd/www/naics.html

Enter the number of California employees. Check "Yes" if there are multiple locations under this EDD Account Number.

M. CONTACT PERSON FOR BUSINESS - Enter the name, title/company address, and phone number of the person authorized by the ownership shown in items E, F, or G to provide EDD staff information needed to maintain the accuracy of your employer account.

N. DECLARATION - This declaration should be signed by one of the names shown in item(s) E or G.

O. PAYROLL TAX EDUCATION - EDD provides educational opportunities for taxpayers to learn how to report employees' wages and pay taxes, pointing out the pitfalls that create errors and unnecessary billings. Help is only a telephone call or Web site away.

We will **notify** you of your **EDD Account Number** by mail. To help you understand your tax withholding and filing responsibilities, you will be sent a **California Employer's Guide, DE 44.** Please keep your account status current by notifying ASG of all future changes to the original registration information.

DE 1 Rev. 71 (9-03) **(INTERNET)**   Page 2 of 2

EDD Employment Development Department
State of California

REPORT OF NEW EMPLOYEE(S)
See detailed instructions on page 2. Please type or print.
NOTE: Report new employees within 20 days of start of work.

00340600

DATE
M M D D Y Y

CA EMPLOYER ACCOUNT NO.

BRANCH CODE

FEDERAL ID NO.

NO. OF FORMS NEEDED

BUSINESS NAME

CONTACT PERSON

TELEPHONE NO.

ADDRESS   STREET   CITY   STATE   ZIP

EMPLOYEE FIRST NAME   MI   EMPLOYEE LAST NAME
SOCIAL SECURITY NO.   STREET NO.   STREET NAME   UNIT/APT
CITY   STATE   ZIP   START-OF-WORK DATE
M M D D Y Y

EMPLOYEE FIRST NAME   MI   EMPLOYEE LAST NAME
SOCIAL SECURITY NO.   STREET NO.   STREET NAME   UNIT/APT
CITY   STATE   ZIP   START-OF-WORK DATE
M M D D Y Y

EMPLOYEE FIRST NAME   MI   EMPLOYEE LAST NAME
SOCIAL SECURITY NO.   STREET NO.   STREET NAME   UNIT/APT
CITY   STATE   ZIP   START-OF-WORK DATE
M M D D Y Y

EMPLOYEE FIRST NAME   MI   EMPLOYEE LAST NAME
SOCIAL SECURITY NO.   STREET NO.   STREET NAME   UNIT/APT
CITY   STATE   ZIP   START-OF-WORK DATE
M M D D Y Y

EMPLOYEE FIRST NAME   MI   EMPLOYEE LAST NAME
SOCIAL SECURITY NO.   STREET NO.   STREET NAME   UNIT/APT
CITY   STATE   ZIP   START-OF-WORK DATE
M M D D Y Y

EMPLOYEE FIRST NAME   MI   EMPLOYEE LAST NAME
SOCIAL SECURITY NO.   STREET NO.   STREET NAME   UNIT/APT
CITY   STATE   ZIP   START-OF-WORK DATE
M M D D Y Y

DE 34 Rev. 4 (6-00) **(INTERNET)**   MAIL TO: Employment Development Department / P.O. Box 997016, MIC 23 / West Sacramento, CA 95799-7016
or Fax to (916) 255-0951
Page 1 of 2

Ch 13 Forms

INSTRUCTIONS FOR COMPLETING THE REPORT OF NEW EMPLOYEE(S),

WHO MUST BE REPORTED:

Federal law requires all employers to report to EDD within 20 days of start of work all employees who are newly hired or rehired. This information is used to assist state and county agencies in locating parents who are delinquent in their child support obligations.

An individual is considered a **new hire** on the first day in which he/she performs services for wages. An individual is considered a **rehire** if the employer/employee relationship has ended and the returning individual is required to submit a W-4 form to the employer.

WHAT MUST BE REPORTED ON THIS FORM:

Employer's:
- California Employer Account Number
  on each form completed
- Branch Code - Complete only if employer was assigned a Branch Code number
- Federal Employer Identification Number
- Business name and address

Employee's
- First name, middle initial, and last name
- Social security number
- Home Address
- Start of work date (hire date)

HOW TO COMPLETE THIS FORM:

Please record information in the spaces provided. If you use a typewriter or printer, ignore the boxes and type in UPPER CASE as shown. Do not use dashes or slashes

EMPLOYEE FIRST NAME	MI	EMPLOYEE LAST NAME	
IMOGENE	A	SAMPLE	
SOCIAL SECURITY NO.	STREET NO.	STREET NAME	UNIT/APT
123456789	1234	ANY STREET	312

If you **must hand print this form**, write each letter or number in a separate box as shown. Do not use commas or periods.

EMPLOYEE FIRST NAME							MI	EMPLOYEE LAST NAME						
I	M	O	G	E	N	E								A
SOCIAL SECURITY NO.					STREET NO.		STREET NAME						UNIT/APT	
1	2	3	4	5	6	7	8	9	1	2	2	3	A	N

ADDITIONAL INFORMATION:

To obtain information for submitting Reports of New Employee(s) on magnetic media, call (916) 654-6845.

If you have any questions concerning this reporting requirement, please contact your local Employment Tax Customer Service Office (ETCSO) listed in your local telephone directory in the State Government section under "Employment Development Department".

TO OBTAIN ADDITIONAL DE 34s:
- Enter number of forms needed in spaces provided next to Federal ID Number (**on the first page only**);
- Visit EDD's Home Page at www.edd.ca.gov
- Contact your local ETCSO or for 25 or more forms Telephone (916) 322-2835.

An inquiry line (916) 657-0529 has been established to provide information about this reporting requirement. A customer service representative will be available to assist you during normal business hours.

HOW TO REPORT:

Please record the information in the spaces provided and mail to the following address or FAX to (916) 255-0951.

EMPLOYMENT DEVELOPMENT DEPARTMENT
P. O. Box 997016, MIC 23
West Sacramento, CA 95799-7016

DE 34 Rev. 4 (6-00) **(INTERNET)**   Page 2 of 2

Ch 13
Forms

EDD Employment Development Department
State of California

REPORT OF
INDEPENDENT CONTRACTOR(S)

05420101

See detailed instructions on page 2. Please type or print.

SERVICE- RECIPIENT (BUSINESS OR GOVERNMENT ENTITY):

DATE | FEDERAL ID NO. | CA EMPLOYER ACCOUNT NO. | SOCIAL SECURITY NO. | NO. OF FORMS NEEDED

SERVICE-RECIPIENT NAME / BUSINESS NAME | CONTACT PERSON

ADDRESS | TELEPHONE NO.

CITY | STATE | ZIP

SERVICE- PROVIDER (INDEPENDENT CONTRACTOR):

FIRST NAME | MI | LAST NAME

SOCIAL SECURITY NO. | STREET NO. | STREET NAME | UNIT/APT.

CITY | STATE | ZIP

START DATE OF CONTRACT | AMOUNT OF CONTRACT | CONTRACT EXPIRATION DATE | CHECK HERE IF CONTRACT IS ONGOING
M M D D Y Y | | M M D D Y Y

FIRST NAME | MI | LAST NAME

SOCIAL SECURITY NO. | STREET NO. | STREET NAME | UNIT/APT.

CITY | STATE | ZIP

START DATE OF CONTRACT | AMOUNT OF CONTRACT | CONTRACT EXPIRATION DATE | CHECK HERE IF CONTRACT IS ONGOING
M M D D Y Y | | M M D D Y Y

FIRST NAME | MI | LAST NAME

SOCIAL SECURITY NO. | STREET NO. | STREET NAME | UNIT/APT.

CITY | STATE | ZIP

START DATE OF CONTRACT | AMOUNT OF CONTRACT | CONTRACT EXPIRATION DATE | CHECK HERE IF CONTRACT IS ONGOING
M M D D Y Y | | M M D D Y Y

DE 542 Rev. 2 (2-04) **(INTERNET)**   MAIL TO: Employment Development Department • P.O. Box 997350, MIC 96 • Sacramento, CA 95899-7350
or Fax to (916) 319-4410
Page 1 of 2

CU

Ch 13 Forms

INSTRUCTIONS FOR COMPLETING THE REPORT OF INDEPENDENT CONTRACTOR(S)

WHO MUST REPORT:

Any business or government entity (defined as a "Service-Recipient") that is required to file a Federal Form 1099-MISC for service performed by an independent contractor (defined as a "Service-Provider") must report. You must report to the Employment Development Department within twenty (20) days of EITHER making payments of $600 or more OR entering into a contract for $600 or more with an independent contractor in any calendar year, whichever is earlier. This information is used to assist state and county agencies in locating parents who are delinquent in their child support obligations.

An independent contractor is further defined as an individual who is not an employee of the business or government entity for California purposes and who receives compensation or executes a contract for services performed for that business or government entity either in or outside of California. For further clarification, request *Information Sheet: Employment Work Status Determination* (DE 231ES). See below for additional information on how to obtain forms.

YOU ARE REQUIRED TO PROVIDE THE FOLLOWING INFORMATION THAT APPLIES:

Service-Recipient (Business or Government Entity):
- Federal employer identification number
- California employer account number
- Social security number
- Service-recipient name/business name, address, and telephone number

Service-Provider (Independent Contractor):
- First name, middle initial, and last name
- Social security number
- Address
- Start date of contract (if no contract, date payments equal $600 or more)
- Amount of contract including cents (if applicable)
- Contract expiration date (if applicable)
- Ongoing contract (check box if applicable)

HOW TO COMPLETE THIS FORM:

If you use a typewriter or printer, ignore the boxes and type in UPPER CASE as shown. Do not use commas or periods.

FIRST NAME	MI	LAST NAME			
IMOGENE	A	SAMPLE			
SOCIAL SECURITY NO.	STREET NO.	STREET NAME			UNIT / APT.
123456789	12345	MAIN STREET			301

If you **handwrite this form**, print each letter or number in a separate box as shown. Do not use commas or periods.

FIRST NAME	MI	LAST NAME			
IMOGENE	A	SAMPLE			
SOCIAL SECURITY NO.	STREET NO.	STREET NAME			UNIT / APT.
123456789	12345	MAIN STREET			301

GENERAL INFORMATION:

If you have any questions concerning this reporting requirement, please call (916) 657-0529. You may also contact your local Employment Tax Customer Service Office listed in your telephone directory in the State Government section under "Employment Development Department," Or you may access our Internet site at www.edd.ca.gov.

To obtain additional DE 542 forms:
- Enter number of forms needed in upper right hand corner on front of form; or
- Visit our Internet site at www.edd.ca.gov; or
- For 25 or more forms, telephone (916) 322-2835
- For less than 25 forms, telephone (916) 657-0529

To obtain information for submitting *Report of Independent Contractors* on magnetic media, call (916) 651-6945.

HOW TO REPORT:

Please record the information in the spaces provided and mail to the following address or fax to (916) 319-4410.

EMPLOYMENT DEVELOPMENT DEPARTMENT
P. O. Box 997350, Document Management Group, MIC 96
Sacramento, CA 95899-7350

DE 542 Rev. 2 (2-04) **(INTERNET)**   Page 2 of 2   CU

Ch 13 Forms

[COMPANY LETTERHEAD]

_____ [DATE]

Name of Prospective Employee
Home Address
City, State, ZIP Code
Re: Offer of Employment by NAME OF COMPANY

Dear [EMPLOYEE]:

I am very pleased to confirm our offer to you of employment with
_____ (the "Company"). You will initially report to
_____ [INSERT IMMEDIATE SUPERVISOR'S NAME] in the position
of _____ [INSERT JOB TITLE]. The terms of our offer and the benefits currently provided by the Company are as follows:

[CONTACT AN EMPLOYMENT ATTORNEY REGARDING PROPER CLASSIFICATION
OF EMPLOYEES AS EXEMPT OR NONEXEMPT.]

[OPTION A: FOR EXEMPT EMPLOYEES ONLY

1. Starting Salary. Your starting salary will be _____ dollars ($_____)
per [CHOOSE APPLICABLE PERIOD: year/month] and will be subject to [CHOOSE
APPLICABLE PERIOD: annual/quarterly/other review period] review.

[OPTION B: FOR NONEXEMPT EMPLOYEES

1. Starting Rate of Pay. Your starting rate of pay will be _____ dollars
($_____) per hour and will be subject to [CHOOSE APPLICABLE PERIOD:
annual/quarterly/other review period] review. You will be paid overtime as
required by state and federal law.

2. Benefits. In addition, you will be eligible to participate in regular health insurance, bonus, and other employee benefit plans established by the Company for
its employees from time to time. [OPTIONAL: A brief summary of the benefits currently offered is attached to this letter as Appendix A.]

The Company reserves the right to change or otherwise modify, in its sole discretion, the preceding terms of employment, as well as any of the terms set forth
herein, at any time in the future.

3. Confidentiality. As an employee of the Company, you will have access to certain
confidential information of the Company and you may, during the course of your
employment, develop certain information or inventions that will be the property
of the Company. To protect the interests of the Company, you will need to sign the
Company's standard "Employee Invention Assignment and Confidentiality

**Ch 13
Forms**

Agreement" as a condition of your employment. We wish to impress upon you that we do not want you to, and we hereby direct you not to, bring with you any confidential or proprietary material of any former employer or to violate any other obligations you may have to any former employer. During the period that you render services to the Company, you agree to not engage in any employment, business or activity that is in any way competitive with the business or proposed business of the Company. You will disclose to the Company in writing any other gainful employment, business, or activity that you are currently associated with or participate in that competes with the Company. You will not assist any other person or organization in competing with the Company or in preparing to engage in competition with the business or proposed business of the Company. You represent that your signing of this offer letter, agreement(s) concerning stock options granted to you, if any, under the Plan (as defined below), and the Company's Employee Invention Assignment and Confidentiality Agreement and your commencement of employment with the Company will not violate any agreement currently in place between yourself and current or past employers.

4. At-Will Employment. While we look forward to a long and profitable relationship, should you decide to accept our offer, you will be an at-will employee of the Company, which means the employment relationship can be terminated by either of us for any reason, at any time, with or without notice, and with our without cause. Any statements or representations to the contrary (and, indeed, any statements contradicting any provision in this letter) should be regarded by you as ineffective. Further, your participation in any stock option or benefit program is not to be regarded as assuring you of continuing employment for any particular period of time.

5. Authorization to Work. Please note that because of employer regulations adopted in the Immigration Reform and Control Act of 1986, within three (3) business days of starting your new position you will need to present documentation demonstrating that you have authorization to work in the United States. If you have questions about this requirement, which applies to U.S. citizens and non-U.S. citizens alike, you may contact our personnel office.

6. Acceptance. This offer will remain open until _____, _____. If you decide to accept our offer, and I hope you will, please sign the enclosed copy of this letter in the space indicated and return it to me. Your signature will acknowledge that you have read and understood and agreed to the terms and conditions of this offer letter and the attached documents, if any. Should you have anything else that you wish to discuss, please do not hesitate to call me.

We look forward to the opportunity to welcome you to the Company.

Very truly yours,

Ch 13 Forms

[OFFICER NAME AND TITLE UNDER LINE]

Attachments

I have read and understood this offer letter and hereby acknowledge, accept, and agree to the terms as set forth above and further acknowledge that no other commitments were made to me as part of my employment offer except as specifically set forth herein.

Date signed: _____

_____

[NAME OF EMPLOYEE UNDER LINE]

U.S. Department of Justice
Immigration and Naturalization Service

OMB No. 1115-0136

Employment Eligibility Verification

INSTRUCTIONS
PLEASE READ ALL INSTRUCTIONS CAREFULLY BEFORE COMPLETING THIS FORM.

Anti-Discrimination Notice It is illegal to discriminate against any individual (other than an alien not authorized to work in the U.S.) in hiring, discharging, or recruiting or referring for a fee because of that individual's national origin or citizenship status. It is illegal to discriminate against work eligible individuals. Employers **CANNOT** specify which document(s) they will accept from an employee. The refusal to hire an individual because of a future expiration date may also constitute illegal discrimination.

Section 1 - Employee. All employees, citizens and noncitizens, hired after November 6, 1986, must complete Section 1 of this form at the time of hire, which is the actual beginning of employment. **The employer is responsible for ensuring that Section 1 is timely and properly completed.**

Preparer/Translator Certification The Preparer/Translator Certification must be completed if Section 1 is prepared by a person other than the employee. A preparer/translator may be used only when the employee is unable to complete Section 1 on his/her own. However, the employee must still sign Section 1.

Section 2 - Employer. For the purpose of completing this form, the term "employer" includes those recruiters and referrers for a fee who are agricultural associations, agricultural employers or farm labor contractors.

Employers must complete Section 2 by examining evidence of identity and employment eligibility within three (3) business days of the date employment begins. If employees are authorized to work, but are unable to present the required document(s) within three business days, they must present a receipt for the application of the document(s) within three business days and the actual document(s) within ninety (90) days. However, if employers hire individuals for a duration of less than three business days, Section 2 must be completed at the time employment begins. **Employers must record: 1)** document title; **2)** issuing authority; **3)** document number, **4)** expiration date, if any; and **5)** the date employment begins. Employers must sign and date the certification. Employees must present original documents. Employers may, but are not required to, photocopy the document(s) presented. These photocopies may only be used for the verification process and must be retained with the I-9. **However, employers are still responsible for completing the I-9.**

Section 3 - Updating and Reverification Employers must complete Section 3 when updating and/or reverifying the I-9. Employers must reverify employment eligibility of their employees on or before the expiration date recorded in Section 1. Employers **CANNOT** specify which document(s) they will accept from an employee.

- If an employee's name has changed at the time this form is being updated/ reverified, complete Block A.

- If an employee is rehired within three (3) years of the date this form was originally completed and the employee is still eligible to be employed on the same basis as previously indicated on this form (updating), complete Block B and the signature block.

- If an employee is rehired within three (3) years of the date this form was originally completed and the employee's work authorization has expired **or** if a current employee's work authorization is about to expire (reverification), complete Block B and:
  - examine any document that reflects that the employee is authorized to work in the U.S. (see List A **or** C).
  - record the document title, document number and expiration date (if any) in Block C, and complete the signature block.

Photocopying and Retaining Form I-9 A blank I-9 may be reproduced, provided both sides are copied. The Instructions must be available to all employees completing this form. Employers must retain completed I-9s for three (3) years after the date of hire or one (1) year after the date employment ends, whichever is later.

For more detailed information, you may refer to the INS Handbook for Employers, (Form M-274). You may obtain the handbook at your local INS office.

Privacy Act Notice. The authority for collecting this information is the Immigration Reform and Control Act of 1986, Pub. L. 99-603 (8 USC 1324a).

This information is for employers to verify the eligibility of individuals for employment to preclude the unlawful hiring, or recruiting or referring for a fee, of aliens who are not authorized to work in the United States.

This information will be used by employers as a record of their basis for determining eligibility of an employee to work in the United States. The form will be kept by the employer and made available for inspection by officials of the U.S. Immigration and Naturalization Service, the Department of Labor and the Office of Special Counsel for Immigration Related Unfair Employment Practices.

Submission of the information required in this form is voluntary. However, an individual may not begin employment unless this form is completed, since employers are subject to civil or criminal penalties if they do not comply with the Immigration Reform and Control Act of 1986.

Reporting Burden. We try to create forms and instructions that are accurate, can be easily understood and which impose the least possible burden on you to provide us with information. Often this is difficult because some immigration laws are very complex. Accordingly, the reporting burden for this collection of information is computed as follows: **1)** learning about this form, 5 minutes; **2)** completing the form, 5 minutes; and **3)** assembling and filing (recordkeeping) the form, 5 minutes, for an average of 15 minutes per response. If you have comments regarding the accuracy of this burden estimate, or suggestions for making this form simpler, you can write to the Immigration and Naturalization Service, HQPDI, 425 I Street, N.W., Room 4034, Washington, DC 20536. OMB No. 1115-0136.

EMPLOYERS MUST RETAIN COMPLETED FORM I-9
PLEASE DO NOT MAIL COMPLETED FORM I-9 TO INS

Form I-9 (Rev. 11-21-91)N

Ch 13
Forms

U.S. Department of Justice
Immigration and Naturalization Service

OMB No. 1115-0136

Employment Eligibility Verification

Please read instructions carefully before completing this form. The instructions must be available during completion of this form. ANTI-DISCRIMINATION NOTICE: It is illegal to discriminate against work eligible individuals. Employers CANNOT specify which document(s) they will accept from an employee. The refusal to hire an individual because of a future expiration date may also constitute illegal discrimination.

Section 1. Employee Information and Verification To be completed and signed by employee at the time employment begins.

Print Name: Last	First	Middle Initial	Maiden Name

Address (Street Name and Number)		Apt. #	Date of Birth (month/day/year)

City	State	Zip Code	Social Security #

I am aware that federal law provides for imprisonment and/or fines for false statements or use of false documents in connection with the completion of this form.	I attest, under penalty of perjury, that I am (check one of the following): ☐ A citizen or national of the United States ☐ A Lawful Permanent Resident (Alien # A _____) ☐ An alien authorized to work until ___/___/___ (Alien # or Admission #) _____

Employee's Signature	Date (month/day/year)

Preparer and/or Translator Certification. (To be completed and signed if Section 1 is prepared by a person other than the employee.) I attest, under penalty of perjury, that I have assisted in the completion of this form and that to the best of my knowledge the information is true and correct.

Preparer's/Translator's Signature	Print Name

Address (Street Name and Number, City, State, Zip Code)	Date (month/day/year)

Section 2. Employer Review and Verification. To be completed and signed by employer. Examine one document from List A OR examine one document from List B and one from List C, as listed on the reverse of this form, and record the title, number and expiration date, if any, of the document(s)

List A	OR	List B	AND	List C
Document title: _____		_____		_____
Issuing authority: _____		_____		_____
Document #: _____		_____		_____
Expiration Date (if any): ___/___/___		___/___/___		___/___/___
Document #: _____				
Expiration Date (if any): ___/___/___				

CERTIFICATION - I attest, under penalty of perjury, that I have examined the document(s) presented by the above-named employee, that the above-listed document(s) appear to be genuine and to relate to the employee named, that the employee began employment on (month/day/year) ___/___/___ **and that to the best of my knowledge the employee is eligible to work in the United States. (State employment agencies may omit the date the employee began employment.)**

Signature of Employer or Authorized Representative	Print Name	Title

Business or Organization Name	Address (Street Name and Number, City, State, Zip Code)	Date (month/day/year)

Section 3. Updating and Reverification To be completed and signed by employer.

A. New Name (if applicable)	B. Date of rehire (month/day/year) (if applicable)

C. If employee's previous grant of work authorization has expired, provide the information below for the document that establishes current employment eligibility.

Document Title: _____ Document #: _____ Expiration Date (if any): ___/___/___

I attest, under penalty of perjury, that to the best of my knowledge, this employee is eligible to work in the United States, and if the employee presented document(s), the document(s) I have examined appear to be genuine and to relate to the individual.

Signature of Employer or Authorized Representative	Date (month/day/year)

Form I-9 (Rev. 11-21-91)N Page 2

Ch 13
Forms

LISTS OF ACCEPTABLE DOCUMENTS

LIST A		LIST B		LIST C
Documents that Establish Both Identity and Employment Eligibility	**OR**	**Documents that Establish Identity**	**AND**	**Documents that Establish Employment Eligibility**

LIST A — Documents that Establish Both Identity and Employment Eligibility

1. U.S. Passport (unexpired or expired)

2. Certificate of U.S. Citizenship (INS Form N-560 or N-561)

3. Certificate of Naturalization (INS Form N-550 or N-570)

4. Unexpired foreign passport, with I-551 stamp or attached INS Form I-94 indicating unexpired employment authorization

5. Permanent Resident Card or Alien Registration Receipt Card with photograph (INS Form I-151 or I-551)

6. Unexpired Temporary Resident Card (INS Form I-688)

7. Unexpired Employment Authorization Card (INS Form I-688A)

8. Unexpired Reentry Permit (INS Form I-327)

9. Unexpired Refugee Travel Document (INS Form I-571)

10. Unexpired Employment Authorization Document issued by the INS which contains a photograph (INS Form I-688B)

LIST B — Documents that Establish Identity

1. Driver's license or ID card issued by a state or outlying possession of the United States provided it contains a photograph or information such as name, date of birth, gender, height, eye color and address

2. ID card issued by federal, state or local government agencies or entities, provided it contains a photograph or information such as name, date of birth, gender, height, eye color and address

3. School ID card with a photograph

4. Voter's registration card

5. U.S. Military card or draft record

6. Military dependent's ID card

7. U.S. Coast Guard Merchant Mariner Card

8. Native American tribal document

9. Driver's license issued by a Canadian government authority

For persons under age 18 who are unable to present a document listed above:

10. School record or report card

11. Clinic, doctor or hospital record

12. Day-care or nursery school record

LIST C — Documents that Establish Employment Eligibility

1. U.S. social security card issued by the Social Security Administration (other than a card stating it is not valid for employment)

2. Certification of Birth Abroad issued by the Department of State (Form FS-545 or Form DS-1350)

3. Original or certified copy of a birth certificate issued by a state, county, municipal authority or outlying possession of the United States bearing an official seal

4. Native American tribal document

5. U.S. Citizen ID Card (INS Form I-197)

6. ID Card for use of Resident Citizen in the United States (INS Form I-179)

7. Unexpired employment authorization document issued by the INS (other than those listed under List A)

Illustrations of many of these documents appear in Part 8 of the Handbook for Employers (M-274)

Form I-9 (Rev. 10/4/00)Y Page 3

Ch 13 Forms

NOTE: This form should be used only for employees

[COMPANY'S NAME]
EMPLOYEE PROPRIETARY INFORMATION
AND INVENTIONS ASSIGNMENT AGREEMENT

In consideration of my employment or continued employment by [COMPANY'S NAME], a California corporation (the "Company"), and the compensation now and hereafter paid to me, I hereby agree as follows:

1. NONDISCLOSURE

1.1 Recognition of Company's Rights; Nondisclosure. At all times during my employment and thereafter, I will hold in strictest confidence and will not disclose, use, lecture upon, or publish any of the Company's Proprietary Information (defined below), except as such disclosure, use, or publication may be required in connection with my work for the Company, or unless an officer of the Company expressly authorizes such in writing. I will obtain Company's written approval before publishing or submitting for publication any material (written, verbal, or otherwise) that relates to my work at Company and/or incorporates any Proprietary Information. I hereby assign to the Company any rights I may have or acquire in such Proprietary Information and recognize that all Proprietary Information shall be the sole property of the Company and its assigns. I have been informed and acknowledge that the unauthorized taking of the Company's trade secrets could result in a civil liability under California Civil Code Section 3426, and that, if willful, could result in an award for double the amount of the Company's damages and attorneys' fees; and is a crime under California Penal Code Section 444(c), punishable by imprisonment for a time not exceeding one (1) year, or by a fine not exceeding five thousand dollars ($5,000), or by both.

1.2 Proprietary Information. The term "Proprietary Information" shall mean any and all confidential and/or proprietary knowledge, data, or information of the Company. By way of illustration but not limitation, "Proprietary Information" includes (a) trade secrets, inventions, mask works, ideas, processes, formulas, source and object codes, data, programs, other works of authorship, know-how, improvements, discoveries, developments, designs, and techniques (hereinafter collectively referred to as "Inventions"); and (b) information regarding plans for research, development, new products, marketing and selling, business plans, budgets and unpublished financial statements or forecasts, licenses, prices and costs, suppliers and customers; and (c) customer lists and data; and (d) information regarding the skills and compensation of other employees of the Company. Notwithstanding the foregoing, it is understood that, at all such times, I am free to use information which is generally and publicly known in the trade or industry and which is not gained as result of a breach of this Agreement.

**Ch 13
Forms**

1.3 Third Party Information. I understand, in addition, that the Company has received and in the future will receive from third parties confidential or proprietary information ("Third Party Information") subject to a duty on the Company's part to maintain the confidentiality of such information and to use it only for certain limited purposes. During the term of my employment and thereafter, I will hold Third Party Information in the strictest confidence and will not disclose to anyone (other than Company personnel who need to know such information in connection with their work for the Company) or use, except in connection with my work for the Company, Third Party Information unless expressly authorized by an officer of the Company in writing.

1.4 No Improper Use of Information of Prior Employers and Others. During my employment by the Company I will not improperly use or disclose any confidential information or trade secrets, if any, of any former employer or any other person to whom I have an obligation of confidentiality, and I will not bring onto the premises of the Company any unpublished documents or any property belonging to any former employer or any other person to whom I have an obligation of confidentiality unless consented to in writing by that former employer or person. I will use in the performance of my duties only information which is generally known and used by persons with training and experience comparable to my own, which is common knowledge in the industry or otherwise legally in the public domain, or which is otherwise provided or developed by the Company.

2. ASSIGNMENT OF INVENTIONS

2.1 Proprietary Rights and Moral Rights. The term "Proprietary Rights" shall mean all trade secrets, trademarks, and service marks, patent, copyright, mask work, and other intellectual property rights throughout the world. The term "Moral Rights" shall mean any rights to claim authorship of or credit on the Inventions, to object to or prevent the modification or destruction of any Inventions, or to withdraw from circulation or control the publication or distribution of any Inventions, and any similar right, existing under judicial or statutory law of any country or subdivision thereof in the world, or under any treaty, regardless of whether or not such right is denominated or generally referred to as a "moral right."

2.2 Prior Inventions. Inventions, if any, patented or unpatented, which I made prior to the commencement of my employment with the Company are excluded from the scope of this Agreement. To preclude any possible uncertainty, I have set forth on Exhibit B (Previous Inventions) attached hereto a complete list of all Inventions that I have, alone or jointly with others, conceived, developed, or reduced to practice or caused to be conceived, developed, or reduced to practice prior to the commencement of my employment with the Company, that I consider to be my property or the property of third parties and that I wish to have excluded from the scope of this

Ch 13
Forms

Agreement (collectively referred to as "Prior Inventions"). If disclosure of any such Prior Invention would cause me to violate any prior confidentiality agreement, I understand that I am not to list such Prior Inventions in Exhibit B but am only to disclose a cursory name for each such invention, a listing of the party(ies) to whom it belongs, and the fact that full disclosure as to such inventions has not been made for that reason. A space is provided on Exhibit B for such purpose. If no such disclosure is attached, I represent that there are no Prior Inventions. If, in the course of my employment with the Company, I incorporate a Prior Invention into a Company product, process, or machine, the Company is hereby granted and shall have a nonexclusive, royalty-free, irrevocable, perpetual, worldwide license (with rights to sublicense through multiple tiers of sublicensees) to make, have made, modify, use, and sell such Prior Invention. Notwithstanding the foregoing, I agree that I will not incorporate, or permit to be incorporated, Prior Inventions in any Company Inventions without the Company's prior written consent.

2.3 Assignment of Inventions. Subject to Section 2.4 hereof, I hereby assign and agree to assign in the future (when any such Inventions or Proprietary Rights are first reduced to practice or first fixed in a tangible medium, as applicable) to the Company all my right, title, and interest in and to any and all Inventions (and all Proprietary Rights with respect thereto) whether or not patentable or registrable under copyright or similar statutes, made or conceived or reduced to practice or learned by me, either alone or jointly with others, during the period of my employment with the Company, as well as any and all Moral Rights that I may have in or with respect to any Inventions (and all Proprietary Rights with respect thereto). Inventions assigned to the Company pursuant to this Section 2, are hereinafter referred to as "Company Inventions."

2.4 Nonassignable Inventions. This Agreement does not apply to an Invention that qualifies fully as a nonassignable Invention under Section 2870 of the California Labor Code (hereinafter "Section 2870"). I have reviewed the notification on Exhibit A (Limited Exclusion Notification) and agree that my signature acknowledges receipt of the notification.

2.5 Obligation to Keep Company Informed. During the period of my employment and for six (6) months after termination of my employment with the Company, I will promptly disclose to the Company fully and in writing all Inventions authored, conceived, or reduced to practice by me, either alone or jointly with others. In addition, I will promptly disclose to the Company all patent applications filed by me or on my behalf within a year after termination of employment. At the time of each such disclosure, I will advise the Company in writing of any Inventions that I believe fully qualify for protection under Section 2870; and I will at that time provide to the Company in writing all evidence necessary to substantiate that belief. The Company will keep in confidence and will not use for any pur-

Ch 13 Forms

pose or disclose to third parties without my consent any confidential information disclosed in writing to the Company pursuant to this Agreement relating to Inventions that qualify fully for protection under the provisions of Section 2870. I will preserve the confidentiality of any Invention that does not fully qualify for protection under Section 2870.

2.6 Works for Hire. I acknowledge that all original works of authorship that are made by me (solely or jointly with others) within the scope of my employment and that are protectable by copyright are "works made for hire," pursuant to United States Copyright Act (17 U.S.C., Section 101).

2.7 Enforcement of Proprietary Rights. I will assist the Company in every proper way to obtain, and from time to time enforce, United States and foreign Proprietary Rights relating to Company Inventions in any and all countries. To that end I will execute, verify, and deliver such documents and perform such other acts (including appearances as a witness) as the Company may reasonably request for use in applying for, obtaining, perfecting, evidencing, sustaining, and enforcing such Proprietary Rights and the assignment thereof. In addition, I will execute, verify, and deliver assignments of such Proprietary Rights to the Company or its designee. My obligation to assist the Company with respect to Proprietary Rights relating to such Company Inventions in any and all countries shall continue beyond the termination of my employment, but the Company shall compensate me at a reasonable rate after my termination for the time actually spent by me at the Company's request on such assistance.

In the event the Company is unable for any reason, after reasonable effort, to secure my signature on any document needed in connection with the actions specified in the preceding paragraph, I hereby irrevocably designate and appoint the Company and its duly authorized officers and agents as my agent and attorney in fact, which appointment is coupled with an interest, to act for and in my behalf to execute, verify, and file any such documents and to do all other lawfully permitted acts to further the purposes of the preceding paragraph with the same legal force and effect as if executed by me. I hereby waive and quitclaim to the Company any and all claims, of any nature whatsoever, which I now or may hereafter have for infringement of any Proprietary Rights assigned hereunder to the Company.

3. RECORDS

I agree to keep and maintain adequate and current records (in the form of notes, sketches, drawings, and in any other form that may be required by the Company) of all Proprietary Information developed by me and all Inventions made by me during the period of my employment at the Company, which records shall be available to and remain the sole property of the Company at all times.

Ch 13 Forms

4. ADDITIONAL ACTIVITIES

I agree that during the period of my employment by the Company I will not, without the Company's express written consent, engage in any employment or business activity other than for the Company. I agree further that for the period of my employment by the Company and for one (l) year after the date of termination of my employment by the Company I will not, either directly or through others, solicit or attempt to solicit (i) any of the Company's customers or clients that I was directly working with during the last 12 months of my employment with the Company or (ii) any employee, independent contractor, or consultant of the company to terminate his or her relationship with the Company in order to become an employee, consultant, or independent contractor to or for any other person or entity.

5. NO CONFLICTING OBLIGATION

I represent that my performance of all the terms of this Agreement and as an employee of the Company does not and will not breach any agreement to keep in confidence information acquired by me in confidence or in trust prior to my employment by the Company. I have not entered into, and I agree I will not enter into, any agreement either written or oral in conflict herewith.

6. RETURN OF COMPANY DOCUMENTS

When I leave the employ of the Company, I will deliver to the Company any and all drawings, notes, memoranda, specifications, devices, formulas, and documents, together with all copies thereof, and any other material containing or disclosing any Company Inventions, Third Party Information or Proprietary Information of the Company. I further agree that any property situated on the Company's premises and owned by the Company, including disks and other storage media, filing cabinets, or other work areas, is subject to inspection by Company personnel at any time with or without notice. Prior to leaving, I will cooperate with the Company in completing and signing the Company's termination statement.

7. LEGAL AND EQUITABLE REMEDIES

Because my services are personal and unique and because I may have access to and become acquainted with the Proprietary Information of the Company, the Company shall have the right to enforce this Agreement and any of its provisions by injunction, specific performance, or other equitable relief, without bond and without prejudice to any other rights and remedies that the Company may have for a breach of this Agreement.

8. NOTICES

Any notices required or permitted hereunder shall be given to the appropriate

Ch 13 Forms

party at the address specified below or at such other address as the party shall specify in writing. Such notice shall be deemed given upon personal delivery to the appropriate address or if sent by certified or registered mail, three (3) days after the date of mailing.

9. NOTIFICATION OF NEW EMPLOYER

In the event that I leave the employ of the Company, I hereby consent to the notification of my new employer of my rights and obligations under this Agreement.

10. NAME AND LIKENESS RIGHTS

I hereby authorize the Company to use, reuse, and grant others the right to use and reuse, my name, photograph, likeness, voice, and biographical information, and any reproduction or simulation thereof, in any form of media or technology now known or hereafter developed (including, but not limited to, film, video, and digital or other electronic media), both during and after my employment, for any purposes related to the Company's business, such as marketing, advertising, credits, and presentations.

11. GENERAL PROVISIONS.

11.1 Governing Law; Consent to Personal Jurisdiction. This Agreement will be governed by and construed according to the laws of the State of California, as such laws are applied to agreements entered into and to be performed entirely within California between California residents. I hereby expressly consent to the personal jurisdiction of the state and federal courts located in Santa Clara County, California for any lawsuit filed there against me by Company arising from or related to this Agreement.

11.2 Severability. In case any one or more of the provisions contained in this Agreement shall, for any reason, be held to be invalid, illegal, or unenforceable in any respect, such invalidity, illegality, or unenforceability shall not affect the other provisions of this Agreement, and this Agreement shall be construed as if such invalid, illegal, or unenforceable provision had never been contained herein. If moreover, any one or more of the provisions contained in this Agreement shall for any reason be held to be excessively broad as to duration, geographical scope, activity, or subject, it shall be construed by limiting and reducing it, so as to be enforceable to the extent compatible with the applicable law as it shall then appear.

11.3 Successors and Assigns. This Agreement will be binding upon my heirs, executors, administrators, and other legal representatives and will be for the benefit of the Company, its successors, and its assigns.

11.4 Survival. The provisions of this Agreement shall survive the termination of my

Ch 13 Forms

employment and the assignment of this Agreement by the Company to any successor in interest or other assignee.

11.5 Employment. I agree and understand that nothing in this Agreement shall modify the status of my employment as an at-will employment, or confer any right with respect to continuation of employment by the Company, nor shall it interfere in any way with my right or the Company's right to terminate my employment at any time, with or without cause.

11.6 Waiver. No waiver by the Company of any breach of this Agreement shall be a waiver of any preceding or succeeding breach. No waiver by the Company of any right under this Agreement shall be construed as a waiver of any other right. The Company shall not be required to give notice to enforce strict adherence to all terms of this Agreement.

11.7 Advice of Counsel. I ACKNOWLEDGE THAT, IN EXECUTING THIS AGREEMENT, I HAVE HAD THE OPPORTUNITY TO SEEK THE ADVICE OF INDEPENDENT LEGAL COUNSEL, AND I HAVE READ AND UNDERSTOOD ALL OF THE TERMS AND PROVISIONS OF THIS AGREEMENT. THIS AGREEMENT SHALL NOT BE CONSTRUED AGAINST ANY PARTY BY REASON OF THE DRAFTING OR PREPARATION HEREOF.

11.8 Entire Agreement. The obligations pursuant to Sections 1 and 2 of this Agreement shall apply to any time during which I was previously employed, or am in the future employed, by the Company as a consultant if no other agreement governs nondisclosure and assignment of inventions during such period. This Agreement is the final, complete, and exclusive agreement of the parties with respect to the subject matter hereof and supersedes and merges all prior discussions between us. No modification of or amendment to this Agreement, nor any waiver of any rights under this Agreement, will be effective unless in writing and signed by the party to be charged. Any subsequent change or changes in my duties, salary, or compensation will not affect the validity or scope of this Agreement.

This Agreement shall be effective as of the first day of my employment with the Company, namely: _____, _____.

I HAVE READ THIS EMPLOYEE PROPRIETARY INFORMATION AND INVENTIONS ASSIGNMENT AGREEMENT CAREFULLY AND UNDERSTAND ITS TERMS. I HAVE COMPLETELY FILLED OUT EXHIBIT B TO THIS AGREEMENT.

Dated: _____

_____
(Signature)

Ch 13 Forms

_____
(Printed Name of Employee)

ACCEPTED AND AGREED TO:

_____
[COMPANY'S NAME]

By: _____
Name:

_____
Title

Dated: _____

EXHIBIT A
LIMITED EXCLUSION NOTIFICATION

THIS IS TO NOTIFY you in accordance with Section 2872 of the California Labor Code that the foregoing Agreement between you and the Company does not require you to assign or offer to assign to the Company any invention that you developed entirely on your own time without using the Company's equipment, supplies, facilities, or trade secret information except for those inventions that either:

1. Relate at the time of conception or reduction to practice of the invention to the Company's business, or actual or demonstrably anticipated research or development of the Company;

2. Result from any work performed by you for the Company.

To the extent a provision in the foregoing Agreement purports to require you to assign an invention otherwise excluded from the preceding paragraph, the provision is against the public policy of this state and is unenforceable.

This limited exclusion does not apply to any patent or invention covered by a contract between the Company and the United States or any of its agencies requiring full title to such patent or invention to be in the United States.

I ACKNOWLEDGE RECEIPT of a copy of this notification.

By: _____

**Ch 13
Forms**

Date: _____

WITNESSED BY:

_____

EXHIBIT B

TO: [COMPANY'S NAME]

FROM:

DATE:

SUBJECT: PREVIOUS INVENTIONS

1. Except as listed in Section 2 below, the following is a complete list of all inventions or improvements relevant to the subject matter of my employment by [Company's Name] (the "Company") that have been made or conceived or first reduced to practice by me alone or jointly with others prior to my engagement by the Company:

❏ No inventions or improvements.

❏ See below:

_____

_____

❏ Additional sheets attached.

2. Due to a prior confidentiality agreement, I cannot complete the disclosure under Section 1 above with respect to inventions or improvements generally listed below, the proprietary rights and duty of confidentiality with respect to which I owe to the following party(ies):

	Invention or Improvement	Party(ies)	Relationship
1.	_____	_____	_____
2.	_____	_____	_____
3.	_____	_____	_____

❏ Additional sheets attached.

NOTE: This form should be used only for independent contractors

[COMPANY'S NAME]
IDEPENDENT CONTRACTOR PROPRIETARY INFORMATION
AND INVENTIONS ASSIGNMENT AGREEMENT

In consideration of my engagement as an independent contractor to provide services to [COMPANY'S NAME] (the "Company"), a California corporation, and the compensation now and hereafter paid to me, I hereby represent to the Company and agree as follows:

1. NONDISCLOSURE

1.1 Recognition of Company's Rights; Nondisclosure. At all times during my engagement and thereafter, I will hold in strictest confidence and will not disclose, use, lecture upon, or publish any of the Company's Proprietary Information (defined below), except as such disclosure, use, or publication may be required in connection with my work for the Company, or unless an officer of the Company expressly authorizes such in writing. I will obtain Company's written approval before publishing or submitting for publication any material (written, verbal, or otherwise) that relates to my services while with the Company and/or incorporates any Proprietary Information. I hereby assign to the Company any rights I may have or acquire in such Proprietary Information and recognize that all Proprietary Information shall be the sole property of the Company and its assigns. I have been informed and acknowledge that the unauthorized taking of the Company's trade secrets could result in a civil liability under California Civil Code Section 3426, and that, if willful, could result in an award for double the amount of the Company's damages and attorneys' fees; and is a crime under California Penal Code Section 444(c), punishable by imprisonment for a time not exceeding one (1) year, or by a fine not exceeding five thousand dollars ($5,000), or by both.

1.2 Proprietary Information. The term "Proprietary Information" shall mean any and all confidential and/or proprietary knowledge, data, or information of the Company. By way of illustration but not limitation, "Proprietary Information" includes (a) trade secrets, inventions, mask works, ideas, processes, formulas, source and object codes, data, programs, other works of authorship, know-how, improvements, discoveries, developments, designs, and techniques (hereinafter collectively referred to as "Inventions"); and (b) information regarding plans for research, development, new products, marketing and selling, business plans, budgets and unpublished financial statements or forecasts, licenses, prices and costs, suppliers and customers; and (c) customer lists and data; and (d) information regarding the skills and compensation of other employees of the Company. Notwithstanding the foregoing, it is understood that, at all such times, I am free to use information which is generally and publicly known in the trade or industry

Ch 13 Forms

and which is not gained as result of a breach of this Agreement.

1.3 Third Party Information. I understand, in addition, that the Company has received and in the future will receive from third parties confidential or proprietary information ("Third Party Information") subject to a duty on the Company's part to maintain the confidentiality of such information and to use it only for certain limited purposes. During the term of my engagement and thereafter, I will hold Third Party Information in the strictest confidence and will not disclose to anyone (other than Company personnel who need to know such information in connection with their work for the Company) or use, except in connection with performing services for the Company, unless expressly authorized by an officer of the Company in writing.

1.4 No Improper Use of Information of Others. During my engagement by the Company, I will not improperly use or disclose any confidential information or trade secrets, if any, of any former employer or client or any other person to whom I have an obligation of confidentiality, and I will not bring onto the premises of the Company any unpublished documents or any property belonging to any such person or entity to whom I have an obligation of confidentiality unless consented to in writing by that person or entity. I will use in the performance of my services only information which is generally known and used by persons with training and experience comparable to my own, which is common knowledge in the industry or otherwise legally in the public domain, or which is otherwise provided or developed by the Company.

2. ASSIGNMENT OF INVENTIONS

2.1 Proprietary Rights and Moral Rights. The term "Proprietary Rights" shall mean all trade secrets, trademarks and service marks, patent, copyright, mask work, and other intellectual property rights throughout the world. The term "Moral Rights" shall mean any rights to claim authorship of or credit on the Inventions, to object to or prevent the modification or destruction of any Inventions, or to withdraw from circulation or control the publication or distribution of any Inventions, and any similar right, existing under judicial or statutory law of any country or subdivision thereof in the world, or under any treaty, regardless of whether or not such right is denominated or generally referred to as a "moral right."

2.2 Prior Inventions. Inventions, if any, patented or unpatented, which I made prior to the commencement of my services for the Company are excluded from the scope of this Agreement. To preclude any possible uncertainty, I have set forth on Exhibit A (Previous Inventions) attached hereto a complete list of all Inventions that I have, alone or jointly with others, conceived, developed, or reduced to practice or caused to be conceived, developed, or reduced to practice prior to the commencement of my services for the Company, that I consider to be my prop-

Ch 13 Forms

erty or the property of third parties, and that I wish to have excluded from the scope of this Agreement (collectively referred to as "Prior Inventions"). If disclosure of any such Prior Invention would cause me to violate any prior confidentiality agreement, I understand that I am not to list such Prior Inventions in Exhibit A but am only to disclose a cursory name for each such invention, a listing of the party(ies) to whom it belongs, and the fact that full disclosure as to such inventions has not been made for that reason. A space is provided on Exhibit A for such purpose. If no such disclosure is attached, I represent that there are no Prior Inventions. If, in the course of providing services to the Company, I incorporate a Prior Invention into a Company product, process, or machine, the Company is hereby granted and shall have a nonexclusive, royalty-free, irrevocable, perpetual, worldwide license (with rights to sublicense through multiple tiers of sublicensees) to make, have made, modify, use, and sell such Prior Invention. Notwithstanding the foregoing, I agree that I will not incorporate, or permit to be incorporated, Prior Inventions in any Company Inventions without the Company's prior written consent.

2.3 Assignment of Inventions. I hereby assign and agree to assign in the future (when any such Inventions or Proprietary Rights are first reduced to practice or first fixed in a tangible medium, as applicable) to the Company all my right, title, and interest in and to any and all Inventions (and all Proprietary Rights with respect thereto) whether or not patentable or registrable under copyright or similar statutes, made or conceived or reduced to practice or learned by me, either alone or jointly with others, during the period of my engagement with the Company, as well as any and all Moral Rights that I may have in or with respect to any Inventions (and all Proprietary Rights with respect thereto). Inventions assigned to the Company pursuant to this Section 2, are hereinafter referred to as "Company Inventions."

2.4 Obligation to Keep Company Informed. During the period of my engagement and for six (6) months after termination of my engagement with the Company, I will promptly disclose to the Company fully and in writing all Inventions authored, conceived, or reduced to practice by me, either alone or jointly with others. In addition, I will promptly disclose to the Company all patent applications filed by me or on my behalf within a year after termination of engagement. At the time of each such disclosure, I will advise the Company in writing of any Inventions that I believe are outside the scope of the services I performed for the Company during my engagement; and I will at that time provide to the Company in writing all evidence necessary to substantiate that belief. The Company will keep in confidence and will not use for any purpose or disclose to third parties without my consent any confidential information disclosed in writing to the Company pursuant to this Agreement relating to Inventions that fall outside the scope of this Agreement. I will preserve the confidentiality of any Invention that does fall within the protections afforded to the Company under this Agreement.

2.5 Works for Hire. I expressly acknowledge and agree that all original works of authorship that are made by me (solely or jointly with others) within the scope of the services I perform for the Company and that are protectable by copyright are "works made for hire," pursuant to United States Copyright Act (17 U.S.C., Section 101), and that the Company will be considered the author and owner of such copyrightable works.

2.6 Enforcement of Proprietary Rights. I will assist the Company in every proper way to obtain, and from time to time enforce, United States and foreign Proprietary Rights relating to Company Inventions in any and all countries. To that end I will execute, verify, and deliver such documents and perform such other acts (including appearances as a witness) as the Company may reasonably request for use in applying for, obtaining, perfecting, evidencing, sustaining, and enforcing such Proprietary Rights and the assignment thereof. In addition, I will execute, verify, and deliver assignments of such Proprietary Rights to the Company or its designee. My obligation to assist the Company with respect to Proprietary Rights relating to such Company Inventions in any and all countries shall continue beyond the termination of my engagement, but the Company shall compensate me at a reasonable rate after my termination for the time actually spent by me at the Company's request on such assistance.

In the event the Company is unable for any reason, after reasonable effort, to secure my signature on any document needed in connection with the actions specified in the preceding paragraph, I hereby irrevocably designate and appoint the Company and its duly authorized officers and agents as my agent and attorney in fact, which appointment is coupled with an interest, to act for and in my behalf to execute, verify, and file any such documents and to do all other lawfully permitted acts to further the purposes of the preceding paragraph with the same legal force and effect as if executed by me. I hereby waive and quitclaim to the Company any and all claims, of any nature whatsoever, which I now or may hereafter have for infringement of any Proprietary Rights assigned hereunder to the Company.

3. RECORDS

I agree to keep and maintain adequate and current records (in the form of notes, sketches, drawings, and in any other form that may be required by the Company) of all Proprietary Information developed by me and all Inventions made by me during the period of my engagement at the Company, which records shall be available to and remain the sole property of the Company at all times.

Ch 13 Forms

4. ADDITIONAL ACTIVITIES

I agree that during the period of my engagement by the Company I will not, without the Company's express written consent, engage in any other business activities that are competitive with the Company, unless the I first obtain the Company's written consent. I agree further that for the period of my engagement by the Company and for one (I) year after the date of termination of my engagement by the Company I will not, either directly or through others, solicit or attempt to solicit (i) any of the Company's customers or clients that I was directly working with during the last 12 months of my engagement with the Company or (ii) any employee, independent contractor, or consultant of the company to terminate his or her relationship with the Company in order to become an employee, consultant, or independent contractor to or for any other person or entity.

5. NO CONFLICTING OBLIGATION

I represent that my performance of all the terms of this Agreement and as an independent contractor of the Company does not and will not breach any agreement to keep in confidence information acquired by me in confidence or in trust prior to my engagement by the Company. I have not entered into, and I agree I will not enter into, any agreement either written or oral in conflict herewith.

6. RETURN OF COMPANY DOCUMENTS

Upon termination of my services for the Company whatever the reason, I will deliver to the Company any and all drawings, notes, memoranda, specifications, devices, formulas, and documents, together with all copies thereof, and any other material containing or disclosing any Company Inventions, Third Party Information, or Proprietary Information of the Company. I further agree that any property situated on the Company's premises and owned by the Company, including disks and other storage media, filing cabinets, or other work areas, is subject to inspection by Company personnel at any time with or without notice. Prior to leaving, I will cooperate with the Company in completing and signing the Company's termination statement.

7. LEGAL AND EQUITABLE REMEDIES

Because my services are personal and unique and because I may have access to and become acquainted with the Proprietary Information of the Company, the Company shall have the right to enforce this Agreement and any of its provisions by injunction, specific performance, or other equitable relief, without bond and without prejudice to any other rights and remedies that the Company may have for a breach of this Agreement.

8. NOTICES

Any notices required or permitted hereunder shall be given to the appropriate party at the address specified below or at such other address as the party shall specify in writing. Such notice shall be deemed given upon personal delivery to the appropriate address or if sent by certified or registered mail, three (3) days after the date of mailing.

9. Name and Likeness Rights. I hereby authorize the Company to use, reuse, and grant others the right to use and reuse, my name, photograph, likeness, voice, and biographical information, and any reproduction or simulation thereof, in any form of media or technology now known or hereafter developed (including, but not limited to, film, video, and digital or other electronic media), both during and after my engagement, for any purposes related to the Company's business, such as marketing, advertising, credits, and presentations.

10. GENERAL PROVISIONS

10.1 Governing Law; Consent to Personal Jurisdiction. This Agreement will be governed by and construed according to the laws of the State of California, as such laws are applied to agreements entered into and to be performed entirely within California between California residents. I hereby expressly consent to the personal jurisdiction of the state and federal courts located in Santa Clara County, California for any lawsuit filed there against me by Company arising from or related to this Agreement.

10.2 Severability. In case any one or more of the provisions contained in this Agreement shall, for any reason, be held to be invalid, illegal, or unenforceable in any respect, such invalidity, illegality, or unenforceability shall not affect the other provisions of this Agreement, and this Agreement shall be construed as if such invalid, illegal, or unenforceable provision had never been contained herein. If moreover, any one or more of the provisions contained in this Agreement shall for any reason be held to be excessively broad as to duration, geographical scope, activity, or subject, it shall be construed by limiting and reducing it, so as to be enforceable to the extent compatible with the applicable law as it shall then appear.

10.3 Successors and Assigns. This Agreement will be binding upon my heirs, executors, administrators, and other legal representatives and will be for the benefit of the Company, its successors, and its assigns.

10.4 Survival. The provisions of this Agreement shall survive the termination of my engagement and the assignment of this Agreement by the Company to any successor in interest or other assignee.

Ch 13 Forms

10.5 Relationship. I agree and understand that nothing in this Agreement shall be construed as creating or implying an employer-employee relationship, or conferring any right with respect to continuation of my services for the Company, nor shall it interfere in any way with the Company's right to terminate my engagement at any time, with or without cause.

10.6 Waiver. No waiver by the Company of any breach of this Agreement shall be a waiver of any preceding or succeeding breach. No waiver by the Company of any right under this Agreement shall be construed as a waiver of any other right. The Company shall not be required to give notice to enforce strict adherence to all terms of this Agreement.

10.7 Advice of Counsel. I ACKNOWLEDGE THAT, IN EXECUTING THIS AGREEMENT, I HAVE HAD THE OPPORTUNITY TO SEEK THE ADVICE OF INDEPENDENT LEGAL COUNSEL, AND I HAVE READ AND UNDERSTOOD ALL OF THE TERMS AND PROVISIONS OF THIS AGREEMENT. THIS AGREEMENT SHALL NOT BE CONSTRUED AGAINST ANY PARTY BY REASON OF THE DRAFTING OR PREPARATION HEREOF.

10.8 Entire Agreement. The obligations pursuant to Sections 1 and 2 of this Agreement shall apply to any time during which I was previously engaged, or am in the future engaged, by the Company as a consultant if no other agreement governs nondisclosure and assignment of inventions during such period. This Agreement is the final, complete, and exclusive agreement of the parties with respect to the subject matter hereof and supersedes and merges all prior discussions between us. No modification of or amendment to this Agreement, nor any waiver of any rights under this Agreement, will be effective unless in writing and signed by the party to be charged. Any subsequent change or changes in my duties, salary, or compensation will not affect the validity or scope of this Agreement.

This Agreement shall be effective as of the first day of my engagement with the Company, namely: _____, _____.

I HAVE READ THIS INDEPENDENT CONTRACTOR PROPRIETARY INFORMATION AND INVENTIONS ASSIGNMENT AGREEMENT CAREFULLY AND UNDERSTAND ITS TERMS. I HAVE COMPLETELY FILLED OUT EXHIBIT A TO THIS AGREEMENT.

Dated: _____

_____
(Signature)

_____
(Printed Name of Independent Contractor)

Ch 13 Forms

ACCEPTED AND AGREED TO:

[COMPANY'S NAME]

By: _____

Name: _____

Title: _____

Dated: _____

EXHIBIT A

TO: [COMPANY'S NAME]

FROM:

DATE:

SUBJECT: PREVIOUS INVENTIONS

1. Except as listed in Section 2 below, the following is a complete list of all inventions or improvements relevant to the subject matter of engagement of my services by [Company's Name] (the "Company") that have been made or conceived or first reduced to practice by me alone or jointly with others prior to my engagement by the Company:

❑ No inventions or improvements.

❑ See below:

_____

_____

❑ Additional sheets attached.

2. Due to a prior confidentiality agreement, I cannot complete the disclosure under Section 1 above with respect to inventions or improvements generally listed below, the proprietary rights and duty of confidentiality with respect to which I owe to the following party(ies):

	Invention or Improvement	Party(ies)	Relationship
1.	_____	_____	_____
2.	_____	_____	_____
3.	_____	_____	_____

❏ Additional sheets attached.

Ch 13 Forms

MEDIATION AND ARBITRATION POLICY

In the event that an Employee and the Company are unable to amicably resolve their differences, all disputes, claims, causes of action, and controversies (including a controversy as to the arbitrability of any dispute) concerning or relating to the terms, conditions, and/or benefits of Employee's employment with the Company (including any and all discrimination and/or harassment claims) or arising out of or any way related to Employee's employment relationship with the Company (collectively, "disputes"), which disputes in the aggregate are less than $25,000, shall be resolved by way of final and binding arbitration conducted by the Judicial Arbitration and Mediation Services ("JAMS") or the American Arbitration Association ("AAA"), as selected by the Company at such time.

In the event of a dispute, whichever party seeks to initiate this dispute resolution process must submit to the other party a written request for arbitration, which request must state the basis of the dispute and must be submitted within the same time limitation periods that would be applicable if one were to dispute the matter in court. If an Employee or the Company fails to submit and serve a written request for arbitration to the other within the applicable statute of limitations, that party agrees that it will have waived any right to raise this claim or dispute in any forum. When an arbitration hearing is held, each party shall pay its own attorneys' fees. However, the Company shall pay the arbitrator's fee, the hearing room fee, and the administrative fees associated with the arbitration.

The Company and Employee agree that the arbitration hearing shall be held in [NAME COUNTY IN WHICH COMPANY IS LOCATED], California and in a manner consistent with the then applicable rules of JAMS or AAA, as applicable, or their successors. The Company and Employee shall select by mutual agreement a neutral arbitrator. The arbitrator shall have the authority and be empowered to: (1) resolve any issues relating to the arbitrability of the dispute, the interpretation of this arbitration policy, or any other issues arising from said Employee's employment with the Company; (2) compel adequate discovery for the resolution of the dispute and/or to permit post-hearing briefs; and (3) award any remedy at law or in equity to which the prevailing party would otherwise be entitled had the matter been litigated in court. The arbitrator shall issue a written arbitration decision that includes its essential findings and conclusions and a statement of the award. Any judgment upon an award rendered in such arbitration may be entered in any court having proper jurisdiction.

Should any part of this arbitration policy be declared by a court of competent jurisdiction to be invalid, unlawful, or otherwise unenforceable, the remaining parts shall not be affected and the parties shall arbitrate their dispute without reference to the unenforceable part of this policy.

Ch 13 Forms

THIS ARBITRATION POLICY IS EXPRESSLY IN LIEU OF BOTH THE COMPANY'S AND ANY EMPLOYEE'S RIGHT TO HAVE A JURY TRIAL OF ANY DISPUTE ARISING OUT OF OR ANY WAY RELATED TO AN EMPLOYEE'S EMPLOYMENT WITH THE COMPANY.

Note: This arbitration policy does not interfere with either party's ability to seek appropriate interim injunctive relief before, or pending, arbitration proceedings. This policy also does not restrict an employee from exercising his or her statutory rights to seek assistance from the California Department of Fair Employment and Housing or the Equal Employment Opportunity Commission. However, if a right-to-sue letter or notice is issued by either of these agencies, binding arbitration pursuant to this policy shall be the exclusive remedy. This policy does not apply to workers' compensation benefit claims or unemployment insurance benefit claims.

Index

A

Accredited investors, 30, 36–38

Accrual of vacation time, 119

Action by Sole Incorporator Appointing Initial Directors and Adopting Bylaws, 428

Action by Unanimous Written Consent of Directors Without Meeting, 266

Action of Incorporator, 22, 197

Actions by unanimous written consent, 48

Administrative remedies, 121

Advertisement of securities offerings, 32

Affidavit of Mailing of Notice of the Annual Meeting of Shareholders, 267

Age Discrimination in Employment Act of 1967, 120

Agreement to Transfer Partnership Assets to Corporation, 248–249

Amending articles of incorporation, 22, 23–24

Amending bylaws, 24

Americans with Disabilities Act, 120

Annual meetings of shareholders, 45–46

Anti-discrimination laws, 120–121

Application for Certificate of Revivor, 257

Application for Employer Identification Number—IRS Form SS-4, 211–212

Application for Recognition of Exemption, 93, 94

Application to Mail at Nonprofit Standard Mail Rates—PS Form 3624, 434–436

Arbitrary trademarks, 100

Arbitration, mandatory, 125–126

Articles of incorporation
amending, 22, 23–24
filing, 19–22
nonprofit corporations, 91–92

Articles of Incorporation Designating Initial Directors, 157–160

Articles of Incorporation for Nonprofit Mutual Benefit Corporation, 418

Articles of Incorporation for Nonprofit Public Benefit Corporation, 400–401

Articles of Incorporation for Nonprofit Religious Corporation, 403–404

Articles of Incorporation (General Stock), 155–156

Articles of Incorporation Not Designating Initial Directors, 161–162

Articles of organization, 72

Assignment of real property interests, 40

Associations, personal liability in, 90

At-will employment, 115–116

Attorneys, professional corporations for, 58

B

Benefits, 119

Beverly-Killea Limited Liability Company Act of 1994, 84

Bill of Sale Agreement, 41, 253

Binding actions of partners, 3

Board of directors. *See also* Directors
 actions without meetings, 48
 annual and special meetings, 47
 initial meetings, 23

Board of Equalization, 79, 80

Budgets, initial, 28

Bulk transfers, 40

Business assets
 personal use of, 43
 purchase of stock with, 34–35
 transferring into corporation or LLC, 39–40

Business entities compared, 1–9

Business judgment rule, 90

Buy-Sell Agreement, 50–52, 328–337

Bylaws
 amending, 24
 basic purposes, 22–23
 nonprofit corporations, 91
 sample documents, 163–206
 special meeting requirements, 46

Bylaws for Nonprofit Public Benefit Corporation, 405–421

C

C corporations. *See* Corporations

Calendar years, 63, 67

California Employer's Guide, 79

California Employment Development Department, 78, 111, 112–113

California Exemption Application, 94

California incorporation, vs. other states, 10–11

California Labor Code, Section 1102, 121

California Newspaper Service Bureau, 19

California Nonprofit Corporation Act, 87

The California Permit Handbook, 25

The California Professional and Business License Handbook, 25

California Resale Exemption Certificate Form, 369

California securities laws, 31–36

California Seller's Permit Application— BOE-400-SPA, 213–219

California Unemployment Insurance tax, 112

Cancellations of indebtedness, 28

Capitalization, importance of, 27–28

Certificate of Amendment of Articles of Incorporation, 24

Certificate of Amendment of Articles of Incorporation (before issuance of shares), 192

Certificate of Amendment of Articles of Incorporation (after issuance of shares), 209192Certificate of Good Standing, 11, 12

Certificates of limited partnership, 4

Certificates of revivor, 49

"Charitable" exemption, 92

Charity Registration Form—Form CT-1, 433

Close corporations, 54–57

Closely held corporations, 55, 83–84

Coca-Cola, 106

Commercial names, 99

Commissioner of Corporations (California), 33

Common law trademark rights, 101

Common stock, Section 25102(h) exemptions, 34. *See also* Stock

Community property, 2

Compulsory licenses, 103

Computer software, 97

Confidentiality agreements, 106, 123–124

Continuity of corporations, 8

Contracts, 43, 48–49
Conversions to LLCs, 39–41, 75–76
Copyrights, 97, 101–103
Corporate Estimated Tax Form, Form 100-ES, 77
Corporate indemnification, 20–21
Corporation Estimated Tax—FTB Form 100-ES, 365–366
Corporations. *See also* Nonprofit corporations; S corporations
  advantages and disadvantages, 7–9
  in other states, 10–13
  selecting and filing business name, 15–19
  special types, 54–59
  suspension of powers, 48–50
  taxation, 77–84
Courts, piercing the corporate veil, 43–44
Credibility of sole proprietorships, 2
Cross-purchases, 50–51
Cumulative voting, 46–47

D

Delaware corporations, 10–11
Delayed filing dates, 22
Department of Fair Employment and Housing, 121
Descriptive trademarks, 100
Design patents, 104
Determination of Worker Status for Purposes of Federal Employment Taxes and Income Tax Withholding—IRS Form SS-8, 80–81, 370–374
Directors. *See also* Board of directors
  electing, 45, 46–47
  indemnification, 20–21
  initial, 19
  liability in nonprofits, 89–90
  minimum number required, 19–20
Directors' and officers' liability insurance, 20–21, 90
Disability insurance. *See* State disability insurance
Discrimination, laws against, 120–121
Disproportionate distributions of profit, 55, 56
Dispute resolution policies, 125–126

Dissolution of corporations or LLCs, 5, 49, 56
Dissolution of partnerships, 3, 41
Double taxation, 63
Double time compensation, 118
Draws, 85

E

Economic Espionage Act of 1996, 105
Election by a Small Business Corporation—IRS Form 2553, 64, 344–345
Employee handbooks, 114–115
Employee offer letters, 116
Employee pamphlets, 113–114
Employee Proprietary Information and Inventions Assignment Agreement, 453–461
Employee's Withholding Allowance Certificate—IRS Form W-4, 81, 375–376, 439–440
Employer Identification Number, 25, 80, 92
Employers
  anti-discrimination and immigration laws, 120–122
  confidentiality protections, 122–124
  dispute resolution policies, 125–126
  nature of relationships with employees and contractors, 115–118
  personnel records requirements, 119–120
  recommended employment policies, 114–115
  reporting and tax obligations, 78–79, 80–84, 109–114
  wages and benefits issues, 118–119
  worker's compensation laws, 122
Employer's Quarterly Federal Tax Return—IRS Form 941, 377–380
Employer's Tax Guide, 80, 81
Employment Development Department (EDD), 111, 112–113
Employment discrimination laws, 120–121
Employment Eligibility Verification Form I-9, 122, 450–452
Employment taxes
  on corporations, 78–79, 80–82
  on LLCs, 85–86

Employment Training Tax (ETT), 111
Equal Employment Opportunity
    Commission, 121
Estimated Tax for Corporations—IRS Form
    1120-W, 401–406
Estimated tax payments
    for corporations, 77–78, 82–83
    for LLC owners, 7
Exempt employees, 118
Exemptions from qualification, 31–36
Exemptions from taxation, 92–95

F

Fair Employment and Housing Act, 120, 121
Fair use doctrine, 103
Fanciful trademarks, 100
Federal securities laws, 29–30
Federal Tax Deposit Coupon—IRS Form
    8109-B, 81, 82–83, 399–400
Federal taxes on corporations, 80–84
Federal unemployment tax, 82, 110
Fees. *See also* Minimum franchise tax fee
    copyright application, 103
    foreign corporations and LLCs, 11–12
    LLC filings, 72
    name reservation, 16, 72
    patent, 104
    securities filing, 32–33
    Statement by Domestic Nonprofit
        Corporation, 91
    Statement of Information, 73
    for tax-exempt status filings, 94
    trademark registration, 100
FICA taxes, 81–82, 110
Fictitious Business Name Statement, 2,
    18–19, 151–152
Filing dates for articles of incorporation, 22
Fiscal years for S corporations, 67–68
Foreign corporations, 10–13
Foreign workers, employing, 121–122
Form 1099-MISC, Miscellaneous Income,
    113
Form Transmittal Letter to Department of
    Corporations, 241
Formalities of corporations
    close corporation exemptions, 55, 56

maintaining, 43–52
Forms of business, 1–9
Franchise Tax Board
    filing for tax-exempt status with, 94
    PIT levy, 111
    reinstatement applications to, 49
    S corporation filings with, 68
    web site, 79, 94
Franchise taxes
    corporate rates, 78
    as factor in LLC versus S corporation
        election, 68, 71, 85
    failure to file, 49
    LLC rates, 84–85
    minimum required, 9, 12, 21, 60
    nonprofit exemption, 90
Fraud, 30
Fringe benefits, 9, 119

G

General partnerships, 2–3
General Utilities rule, 67
Generic trademarks, 100
Guaranteed payments, 85

I

Immigration laws, 121–122
Inadvertent termination of S corporation
    eligibility, 66
Income taxes
    corporate, 82–83
    on limited liability companies, 84–85
    withholding requirements, 78–79, 80–81,
        110, 111
Incorporation
    advantages and disadvantages, 7–9
    alternate types, 54–59
    bylaw preparation, 22–23
    filing articles, 19–22
    initial meetings, amendments, and fil-
        ings, 23–26
    for licensed professionals, 57–59
    name selection, 15–19
    from ongoing business, 39–41
    in other states, 10–13
Indemnification of directors, 20–21

Independent Contractor Proprietary Information and Inventions Assignment Agreement, 462–470
Independent contractors
employees vs., 116–118
intellectual property rights, 102, 124
reporting requirements concerning, 113
sole proprietors as, 2
treating workers as, 80
Initial directors, 19
Inspection and retention of employee records, 119–120
Intellectual property
copyrights, 101–103
establishing rights, 106–107
overview, 97–98
patents, 104–105
trade secrets, 105–106, 122–124
trademarks and service marks, 98–101
Interested persons, 94
Internal Revenue Service
filing for tax-exempt status with, 93–94
obtaining EIN from, 80
piercing the corporate veil, 43
termination of S corporation status, 66
Invention assignment agreements, 123–124
Investor Questionnaire for Entities, 236–240
Investor Questionnaire for Individuals, 249–252
Investors, accredited, 36–38

J
Joint copyright ownership, 102

L
Law practices, incorporation of, 58
Liability. *See* Personal liability
Library of Congress, 107
Licensed professionals
business forms for, 5, 6–7, 57–60
LLCs prohibited, 70–71
Licensing requirements, 25, 95
Limited and Revocable Proxy, 268
Limited liability companies
advantages and disadvantages, 5–7, 9, 44, 70

basic operations, 74–75
foreign, 10, 12, 13
forming, 39–41, 71, 72, 75–76
management structures, 73
profit and loss distributions, 63
securities law considerations, 75
selecting and filing business name, 15–19, 72–73
single-member, 60–61
Statement of Information, 73
suspension of powers, 48–50
taxation, 6, 7, 61, 68, 71, 84–86
Limited Liability Company Application for Registration—LLC-5, 139–141
Limited Liability Company Application for Registration, Certificate of Amendment—LLC-6, 143–144
Limited Liability Company Articles of Organization—LLC-1, 348–350
Limited Liability Company Tax Voucher—FTB 3522, 142
Limited Liability Company—Statement of Information—LLC-12, 361–362
Limited liability partnerships, 5, 59–60
Limited Offering Exemption Notice, 28, 32, 33
Limited partnerships, 4–5
Liquidation gains, 67
Local licensing requirements, 25
Local payroll taxes, 86
Loss of exempt status, 95

M
Mailing permits, nonprofit, 95
Maintenance fees for patents, 104
Malpractice protections, 60
Managers of LLCs, 73
Mediation and arbitration, mandatory, 125–126
Mediation and Arbitration Policy, 471–472
Medicare tax, 81, 110
Membership interests as securities, 75
Mergers into LLCs, 75–76
Minimum franchise tax fee
on corporations, 21
on LLCs, 9, 12, 71

Minimum franchise tax fee (*continued*)
    on LLPs, 60
    on S corporations, 71
Minimum wages, 118–119
Minutes of a Special Meeting of the Board
    of Directors, 207, 263
Minutes of a Special Meeting of the
    Shareholders, 208, 261–262
Minutes of First Meeting of the Board of
    Directors, 407–413
Minutes of the Annual Meeting of the
    Board of Directors, 259–260
Minutes of the Annual Meeting of the
    Shareholders, 45, 274
Minutes of the First Meeting of the Board of
    Directors, 201–206
Minutes of the First Meeting of the Board of
    Directors for Nonprofit Corporation,
    422–426
Minutes of the Organizational Meeting of
    the Board of Directors, 430–432
Minutes, recommended contents, 44–45
Moscone-Knox Professional Corporation
    Act, 58

N
Name Reservation—Order Form, 16, 149–150
Name reservations, 16, 72–73
Names of businesses
    intellectual property protections, 98–101
    professional corporations, 59
    selecting and filing for corporations and
        LLCs, 15–19, 72–73
    sole proprietorships, 2
Net worth requirements for accredited
    investors, 37–38
New hires, reporting, 113
Newspaper publication
    fictitious business name notice, 18–19
    partnership dissolutions, 41
Noncompete clauses, 106, 123–124
Nonexempt employees, 118
Nonobvious features, for patent eligibility,
    104
Nonprofit corporations
    for-profit types vs., 88–89

formation, 90–92
    selecting status, 87–88
    tax exemptions, 92–95
Nonprofit mailing permits, 95
Nonpublic securities offerings, 31–36
Nonqualification of foreign corporations,
    12–13
Nonsolicitation agreements, 106, 124
Notice of Dissolution of Partnership, 41, 254
Notice of Issuance of Shares Pursuant to
    Subdivision (h) of Section 25102, 35,
    242–245
Notice of Sale of Securities—Form D,
    220–228
Notice of the Annual Meeting of
    Shareholders, 267
Notice of Transaction Pursuant to
    Corporations Code Section 25102(f), 32,
    229–231
Notice postings, employer requirements,
    113–114
Notice requirements for meetings, 45, 46
Notice to Creditors of Bulk Sale, 40, 252
Novelty, for patent eligibility, 104

O
Offer of Employment, 447–449
Officer liability in nonprofits, 89–90
Operating Agreement for a Limited
    Liability Company, 269–327
Operating Agreement for LLC (Short Form),
    351–360
Operating agreements, 74–75
Overtime compensation, 118

P
Paid vacation, 119
Pamphlets, employee, 113–114
Partnership agreements, 3, 4
Partnerships, 2–5, 59–60
Patent and Trademark Office (PTO), 99–100,
    107
Patents, 97, 104–105
Payroll practices, 118–119
Payroll tax withholding
    federal requirements, 80–82, 110
    piercing the corporate veil for, 43

Payroll tax withholding (*continued*)
  as risk for sole proprietorships, 2
  state requirements, 78–79, 111–112
Penalties
  nonregistered foreign corporations and
    LLCs, 12–13
  securities laws noncompliance, 36
  suspension of powers, 48–50
Perpetuity of corporations, 8
Personal income tax (PIT), 111. *See also*
  Income taxes
Personal liability
  in corporations, 7, 20–21, 42
  in general partnerships, 3
  impact of capitalization on, 27, 28
  in limited liability companies, 5, 42
  in limited liability partnerships, 5, 60
  in limited partnerships, 4
  in nonprofit corporations, 89–90
  piercing the corporate veil, 42–44
  in sole proprietorships, 2
  for wage law violations, 119
Personal names as business names, 15
Personal property statements, 25–26
Personnel records, 119–120
Piercing the corporate veil, 42–44, 55
Private filing services, 72
Private letter ruling requests, 66
Professional corporations, 57–59
Profits, distributing, 55, 56, 85
Promotional consideration prohibitions, 34
Property statements, 25–26
Proxies, 45–46
Pseudo foreign rule, 11

Q
Qualification of securities, 31–36
Quorums, 45–46

R
Real property, assigning to corporation or
  LLC, 40
Record dates, 47
Records inspection and retention, 119–120
Redemptions, 50–51
Registration
  copyrights, 103

foreign corporations, 11–12
  patent, 105
  securities, 29–30
  trademarks and service marks, 99–101
Registration Form for Commercial
  Employers, Pacific Maritime, and Fishing
  Boats—EDD Form DE 1, 112, 367–368,
  441–442
Registration/Renewal Fee Report, 437
Reinstating S corporation status, 66–67
Report of Independent Contractor(s)—EDD
  Form DE 542, 113, 445–446
Report of New Employee(s)—EDD Form
  DE 34, 113, 443–444
Resignation of employees, 118
Resolution of Board of Directors Amending
  Certain Bylaws, 198

S
S corporations
  advantages and disadvantages, 62–63
  election deadline, 25, 64–65
  eligibility for status, 63–64
  taxation, 62–63, 67–68, 78
  termination, 66–67
S Corporation's List of Shareholders and
  Consents—FTB Form 3830, 346
Sales and use tax permit, 26, 79–80
Sample Articles of Incorporation
  Designating Initial Directors, 339–340
Sample Articles of Incorporation Not
  Designating Initial Directors, 341–342
Sample Document Filing Request, 191
Sample Document Filing Request for
  Articles of Incorporation, 194–195
Sample Letter for Certificate of Amendment
  of Articles of Incorporation, 196
Secretary of State (California)
  filing articles with, 21–22
  trademark and service mark protection,
    107
  web site, 17
Section 1244 stock, 83–84
Section 25102(f) exemptions, 31–33
Section 25102(h) exemptions, 33–36

Securities and Exchange Commission (SEC), 29–30
Securities laws
    California, 31–36
    federal, 29–30
    LLCs and, 75
    other states, 36
Security requirements, malpractice, 60
Seller's Permit Application—BOE-400-SPA, 229–235
Seller's permits, 79
Service marks, 98–101
Shareholder agreements, 50–52
Shareholder control, 7
Shareholders
    actions without meetings, 48
    annual meetings, 45–46
    close corporation restrictions, 54–55
    prohibited for nonprofits, 89
    in S corporations, 64
    special meetings, 46–47
Shareholders' agreements, 54, 55, 56–57
Sierra Club, 92
Single-member LLCs, 60–61
Small offering exemption, 33–36
Social Security taxes, 81–82, 110
Software, 97
Sole proprietorships, 1–2
Special board meetings, 47
Special meetings of shareholders, 46–47
Spouses' consent to S corporation election, 65
State Board of Equalization, 79, 80
State corporate laws, 10–13
State disability insurance, 78, 111–112, 113
State taxes on corporations, 77–80
Statement and Designation by Foreign Corporation, 11, 133–136
Statement by Domestic Nonprofit Corporation, 91
Statement of Abandonment of Use of Fictitious Business Name, 19, 153–154
Statement of Information
    failure to file, 49
    filing deadline, 24, 73

Statement of Information (Domestic Stock Corporation), 209–210
Statement of Information (Domestic Stock Corporation)—SI-200 C, 427
Statement of Information (Foreign Corporation) — SI-350, 137–138
Statement of Information (Limited Liability Company)—LLC-12, 145–146
Statutory close corporations, 54–57
Stock
    accredited investors, 36–38
    adequate capitalization from, 27–28
    buy-sell agreements, 50–52
    procedures for issuing, 28–29
    Section 1244, 83–84
    securities law requirements, 29–36
Stock certificates, 28–29, 55
Suggestive trademarks, 100
Suspended corporations or LLCs, 17, 48–50

T

Taxes
    on corporations, 8–9, 77–84
    employer withholding requirements, 78–79, 80–82, 110–112
    on general partnerships, 3
    on limited liability companies, 6, 7, 61, 68, 71, 84–86
    on limited partnerships, 4
    nonprofit corporation exemptions, 92–95
    piercing the corporate veil for, 43
    on S corporations, 62–63, 67–68, 78
    on sole proprietorships, 2
Telephone orders for business names, 17
Termination of employees
    at-will, 115–116
    payment of accrued wages upon, 118
    records inspection and retention, 119–120
    for refusing confidentiality agreements, 124
Time-and-one-half compensation, 118
Title VII of the Civil Rights Act of 1964, 120, 121
Trade dress, 99
Trade names, 99
Trade secrets, 105–106, 122–124
Trademarks, 97, 98–101

Transfer of Assets of Sole Proprietorship to Corporation, 250–251
Transmittal of Wage and Tax Statements—IRS Form W-3, 398

U

Undercapitalization, 28
Unemployment insurance
    employee notice requirements, 113
    federal taxes for, 82, 110
    required registration for, 78–79
    state taxes for, 112
Unintentional termination of S corporation eligibility, 66
United States Patent and Trademark Office (PTO), 99–100
"Unrelated" business income, 92–93
U.S. Citizenship and Immigration Services, 122
Utility patents, 104

V

Vacation leave policies, 119
Value of securities, 33, 51

W

W-2 forms, 81, 401
W-4 forms, 81, 110, 395–396, 459–460
Wage and Tax Statement—IRS Form W-2, 81, 401
Wage practices, 118–119
Waiver of Notice and Consent to Holding of a Special Meeting of the Shareholders, 264

Waiver of Notice and Consent to Holding of a Special Meeting of the Board of Directors, 265
Waiver of Notice and Consent to Holding of the First Meeting of the Board of Directors, 23, 199
Waiver of Notice and Consent to Holding of the First Meeting of the Board of Directors (Nonprofit Corporation), 200
Waiver of Notice and Consent to the First Meeting of the Board of Directors, 429
Web sites
    California Employment Development Department, 112
    Commissioner of Corporations (California), 33
    Franchise Tax Board, 79, 94
    Internal Revenue Service, 80
    Library of Congress, 107
    Patent and Trademark Office (PTO), 107
    Secretary of State (California), 17, 170
    State Board of Equalization, 80
    U.S. Citizenship and Immigration Services, 122
Withholding Allowance Certificate Form W-4, 110
Withholding taxes. See Payroll tax withholding
Worker's compensation insurance, 122
Works made for hire, 102, 124
Wrongful termination, 115–116, 124

The Only Start-Up Book You'll Ever Need!

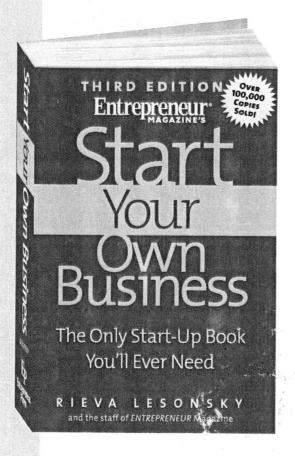

Each month, millions of established and aspiring entrepreneurs turn to Rieva Lesonsky and the staff of *Entrepreneur* magazine to learn how to start a business. So what are you waiting for? Pick up a copy today.

The third edition of *Start Your Own Business* walks you through every step of the start-up process and is packed with advice and information on new topics, such as:

- How to Get New Business Ideas
- Secrets to Getting Government Grants
- How the Internet Can Boost Your Business
- Tips for Starting a Nonprofit Organization
- Updated "Hot Links" to Relevant Web Sites

"*Entrepreneur has created a superb resource for successfully getting your business off the ground.*"
– Fred DeLuca, Founder, Subway Restaurants

PHOTO DAVIS BARBER

A nationally recognized speaker and expert on small business and entrepreneurship with more than 20 years of experience in journalism, bestselling author Rieva Lesonsky and her staff have helped hundreds of thousands of entrepreneurs achieve their dreams.

Pick up your copy today!

AVAILABLE AT ALL FINE BOOKSTORES AND ONLINE BOOKSELLERS | WWW.ENTREPRENEURPRESS.COM

EP
Entrepreneur.
Press